CW01465795

# 1 MONTH OF
# FREE
# READING

## at

## www.ForgottenBooks.com

By purchasing this book you are
eligible for one month membership to
ForgottenBooks.com, giving you
unlimited access to our entire
collection of over 1,000,000 titles via
our web site and mobile apps.

To claim your free month visit:
www.forgottenbooks.com/free848801

\* Offer is valid for 45 days from date of purchase. Terms and conditions apply.

ISBN 978-0-331-81852-9
PIBN 10848801

This book is a reproduction of an important historical work. Forgotten Books uses
state-of-the-art technology to digitally reconstruct the work, preserving the original format
whilst repairing imperfections present in the aged copy. In rare cases, an imperfection in
the original, such as a blemish or missing page, may be replicated in our edition. We do,
however, repair the vast majority of imperfections successfully; any imperfections that
remain are intentionally left to preserve the state of such historical works.

Forgotten Books is a registered trademark of FB &c Ltd.
Copyright © 2018 FB &c Ltd.
FB &c Ltd, Dalton House, 60 Windsor Avenue, London, SW19 2RR.
Company number 08720141. Registered in England and Wales.

For support please visit www.forgottenbooks.com

# HE FOUR BOOKS

### NFUCIAN ANALECTS, THE GREAT LEARNING,
### THE DOCTRINE OF THE MEAN, AND
### THE WORKS OF MENCIUS

WITH

ENGLISH TRANSLATION AND NOTES

BY

## JAMES LEGGE, D.D., LL.D.

THE COMMERCIAL PRESS, LTD.

C. INA

# CONFUCIAN ANALECTS

## BOOK I. HSIO R

乎。不　遠　有　亦　習　學　　第　學
亦　方　朋　說　之、而　子　一　而
樂　來、自　乎。不　時　曰、一　而

CHAPTER I. 1. The Master said, "Is it not pleasant to learn with a constant perseverance and application?

2. "Is it not delightful to have friends coming from distant quarters?

TITLE OF THE WORK.— 論語, "Discourses and Dialogues"; that is, the discourses or discussions of Confucius with his disciples and others on various topics, and his replies to their inquiries. Many chapters, however, and one whole book, are the sayings, hot of the sage himself, but of some of his disciples. The characters may also be rendered "Digested Conversations," and this appears to be the more ancient signification attached to them, the account being that, after the death of Confucius, his disciples collected together and compared the memoranda of his conversations which they had severally preserved, digesting them into the twenty books which compose the work. Hence the title— 論語, "Discussed Sayings," or "Digested Conversations." See 論語註疏解經序. I have styled the work "Confucian Analects," as being more descriptive of its character than any other name I could think of.

HEADING OF THIS BOOK.— 學而第一. The two first characters in the book, after the introductory—"The Master said," are adopted as its heading. This is similar to the custom of the Jews, who name many books in the Bible from the first word in them 第一, "The first"; that is, of the twenty books composing the whole work. In some of the books we find a unity or analogy of subjects, which evidently guided the compilers in grouping the chapters together. Others seem devoid of any such principle of combination. The sixteen chapters of this book are occupied, it is said, with the fundamental subjects which ought to engage the attention of the learner, and the great matters of human practice. The word 學, "learn," rightly occupies the forefront in the studies of a nation, of which its educational system has so long been the distinction and glory.

1. THE WHOLE WORK AND ACHIEVEMENT OF THE LEARNER, FIRST PERFECTING HIS KNOWLEDGE, THEN ATTRACTING BY HIS FAME LIKE-MINDED INDIVIDUALS, AND FINALLY COMPLETE IN HIMSELF. 1. 子, at the commencement, indicates Confucius. 子, "a son," is also the common designation of males—especially of virtuous men. We find it, in conversations, used in the same way as our "Sir." When it follows the surname, it is equivalent to our "Mr.," or may be rendered "the philosopher," "the scholar," "the officer," etc. Often, however, it is better to leave it untranslated. When it precedes the surname, it

2054973

鮮　犯　弟、人　曰、🗌　子　不　而　人三章
矣、上　而　也　其　🗌　有　乎。亦　不　不
不　者　好　孝　爲　子　　　君　愠、知

3. "Is he not a man of complete virtue, who feels no discomposure though men may take no note of him?"

CHAPTER II. 1. The philosopher Yû said, "They are few who, being filial and fraternal, are fond of offending against their superiors. There have been none,

indicates that the person spoken of was the master of the writer, as 子 沈子, "my master, the philosopher 沈." Standing single and alone, as in the text, it denotes Confucius, *the philosopher*, or, rather, *the master*. If we render the term by Confucius, as all preceding translators have done, we miss the indication which it gives of the handiwork of his disciples, and the reverence which it bespeaks for him. 學, in the old commentators, is explained by 誦, "to read chantingly," "to discuss." Chû Hsî interprets it by 效, "to imitate," and makes its results to be 明善而復初, "the understanding of all excellence, and the bringing back original goodness." Subsequent scholars profess, for the most part, great admiration of this explanation. It is an illustration, to my mind, of the way in which Chû Hsî and his followers are continually being wise above what is written in the classical books. 習 is the rapid and frequent motion of the wings of a bird in flying, used for "to repeat," "to practice." 之 is the obj. of the third pers. pronoun, and its antecedent is to be found in the pregnant meaning of 學. 不亦 ... 乎 is explained by 豈不, "is it not?" See 四書補註備旨. To bring out the force of "also" in 亦, some say thus:—"The occasions for pleasure are many, *is this not also one?*" But

it is better to consider 亦 as merely redundant;—see Wang Yin-chih's masterly Treatise on the particles, chap. iii; it forms chaps. 1208 to 1217 of the 皇清經解. 說, read *yuě*, as always when it has the entering tone marked, stands for 悅. What is learned becomes by practice and application one's own, and hence arises complacent pleasure in the mastering mind. 悅, as distinguished from 樂 *(lóh)*, in the next paragraph, is the internal, individual feeling of pleasure, and the other, its external manifestation, implying also companionship. 2. 朋, properly "fellow students"; but, generally, individuals of the same class and character, like-minded. 3. 君子, I translate here—"a man of complete virtue." Literally, it is—"a princely man." See on 子, above. It is a technical term in Chinese moral writers, for which there is no exact correspondency in English, and which cannot be rendered always in the same way. See Morrison's Dictionary, character 子. Its opposite is 小人, "a small, mean man." 人不知, "Man do not know him," but anciently some explained—"man do not know," that is, are stupid under his teaching. The interpretation in the text is, doubtless, the correct one.

2. FILIAL PIETY AND FRATERNAL SUBMISSION ARE THE FOUNDATION OF ALL VIRTUOUS PRACTICE. 1. Yû,

之本與。 者、其爲仁 生、孝弟也 本立、而道 君子務本、 未之有也。 好作亂者、 姤犯上、而

who, not liking to offend against their superiors, have been fond of stirring up confusion.

2. "The superior man bends his attention to what is radical. That being established, all practical courses naturally grow up. Filial piety and fraternal submission!—are they not the root of all benevolent actions?"

named 若, and styled 子有, and 子若, a native of 魯, was famed among the other disciples of Confucius for his strong memory, and love for the doctrines of antiquity. In something about him he resembled the sage. See Mencius, III, Pt. I, iv, 13. 有子 is "Yû, the philosopher," and he and Tsăng Shăn are the only two of Confucius's disciples who are mentioned in this style in the *Lun Yu*. This has led to an opinion on the part of some, that the work was compiled by their disciples. This may not be sufficiently supported, but I have not found the peculiarity pointed out satisfactorily explained. The tablet of Yû's spirit is now in the same apartment of the sage's temples as that of the sage himself, occupying the sixth place in the eastern range of "the wise ones." To this position it was promoted in the third year of Ch'ien Lung of the Manchu dynasty. A degree of activity enters into the meaning of 爲 in 爲人, = "playing the man," "as man, showing themselves filial." etc. 弟 here = 悌, "to be submissive as a younger brother," is in the fourth tone With its proper signification, it was anciently in the third tone. 而 =

"and yet," different from its simple conjunctive use = "and," in the preceding chapter. 好, a verb, "to love," in the fourth tone, differs from the same character in the third tone, an adjective, = "good." 鮮, third tone, = "few." On the idiom 未之有, see Prémare's Grammar, p. 156. 2. 君子 has a less intense signification here than in the last chapter. I translate—"The superior man," for want of a better term. 本, "the root," "what is radical," is here said of filial and fraternal duties, and 道, "ways" or "courses," of all that is intended by 爲 (=行) 仁, below. The particles 也 者 resume the discourse about 孝弟, and introduce some further description of them. See Prémare, p. 158. 與, in the second tone, is half interrogative, an answer in the affirmative being implied. 仁 is explained here as "the principle of love," "the virtue of the heart." Mencius says 一仁也者人也, "仁 is man," in accordance with which, Julien translates it by *humanitas*. Benevolence often comes near it, but, as has been said before of 君子, we cannot give a uniform rendering of the term.

乎。　乎、交、乎、謀、吾　吾日　【seal】　言　【seal】
　　傳而與而身、日　曾　矣。令　子
　　不不朋不爲三　子　　色、曰、
　　習信友忠人省　曰、仁。鮮　巧

CHAPTER III. The Master said, "Fine words and an insinuating appearance are seldom associated with true virtue."

CHAPTER IV. The philosopher Tsăng said, "I daily examine myself on three points:—whether, in transacting business for others, I may have been not faithful;—whether, in intercourse with friends, I may have been not sincere;—whether I may have not mastered and practiced the instructions of my teacher."

'3· FAIR APPEARANCES ARE SUSPICIOUS. 巧言令色.—see Shŭ-ching, II, iii, 2. 巧, "skill in workmanship"; then, "skill," "cleverness," generally, and sometimes with a bad meaning, as here, = "artful," "hypocritical." 令, "a law," "an order," also "good," and here like 巧; with a bad meaning, = "pretending to be good." 色, "the manifestation of the feelings made in the color of the countenance," is here used for the appearance generally.

4. HOW THE PHILOSOPHER TSĂNG DAILY EXAMINED HIMSELF, TO GUARD AGAINST HIS BEING GUILTY OF ANY IMPOSITION Tsăng, whose name was 參 (shăn), and his designation 子輿, was one of the principal disciples of Confucius. A follower of the sage from his sixteenth year, though inferior in natural ability to some others, by his filial piety and other moral qualities, he entirely won the Master's esteem, and by persevering attention mastered his doctrines. Confucius, it is said, employed him in the composition of the 孝經, or "Classic of Filial Piety." The authorship of the 大學, "The Great Learning," is also ascribed to him, though incorrectly, as we shall see. Portions, moreover, of his composition are preserved in the Li Chî. His spirit tablet among the sage's four assessors, occupying the first place on the west, has precedence of that of Mencius. 省, read hsing, "to examine." 三者 is naturally understood of "three times," but the context and consent of commentators make us assent to the interpretation—"on three points." 身, "the body," "one's personality"; 吾身 = myself. 爲 is in the fourth tone. = "for." So, frequently, below. 忠 from 中, "middle," "the center," and 心, "the heart," = loyalty, faithfulness, action with and from the heart. 朋, see chap. i. 友, "two hands joined," denoting union. 朋友, = when together, "friends." 傳不習 is very enigmatical. The translation follows Chû Hsî. 何晏 explained quite differently: "whether I have given instruction in what I had not studied and practiced?" It does seem more correct to take 傳 actively, "to give instruction," rather then passively, "to receive instruction." See Mao Hsî-ho's 四書改錯, XV, article 17.

子曰、道千乘
之國、敬事而信、
節用而愛人使
民以時。
子曰弟子、入
則孝、出則弟、謹
而信、汎愛衆、而
親仁、行有餘力、
則以學文。

CHAPTER V. The Master said, "To rule a country of a thousand chariots, there must be reverent attention to business, and sincerity; economy in expenditure, and love for men; and the employment of the people at the proper seasons."

CHAPTER VI. The Master said, "A youth, when at home, should be filial, and, abroad, respectful to his elders. He should be earnest and truthful. He should overflow in love to all, and cultivate the friendship of the good. When he has time and opportunity, after the performance of these things, he should employ them in polite studies."

5. FUNDAMENTAL PRINCIPLES FOR THE GOVERNMENT OF A LARGE STATE. 道 is used for 導, "to rule," "to lead," and is marked in the fourth tone, to distinguish it from 道, the noun, which was anciently read with the third tone. It is different from 治; which refers to the actual business of government, while 導 is the duty and purpose thereof, apprehended by the prince. The standpoint of the principles is the prince's mind. 乘, in fourth tone, "a chariot," different from its meaning in the second tone, "to ride." A country of one thousand chariots was one of the largest fiefs of the empire, which could bring such an armament into the field. The last principle,— 使 民 以 時. means that the people should not be called from their husbandry at improper seasons, to do service on military expeditions and public works.

6. RULES FOR THE TRAINING OF THE YOUNG:—DUTY FIRST AND THEN ACCOMPLISHMENTS. 弟 子, "younger brothers and sons," taken together, = youths, a youth. The second 弟 is for 悌, as in chap. ii. 入 出, "coming in, going out,"=at home, abroad. 汎 is explained by Chû Hsî by 廣, "wide," "widely"; its proper meaning is "the rush or overflow of water." 力, "strength," here embracing the idea of leisure. 學 文, not literary studies merely, but all the accomplishments of a gentleman also:—ceremonies, music, archery, horsemanship, writing, and numbers.

子夏曰、賢賢易
色、事父母、能竭其
力、事君、能致其身、
與朋友交言而有
信、雖曰未學吾必
謂之學矣。

CHAPTER VII. Tsze-hsiâ said, "If a man withdraws his mind from the love of beauty, and applies it as sincerely to the love of the virtuous; if, in serving his parents, he can exert his utmost strength; if, in serving his prince, he can devote his life; if, in his intercourse with his friends, his words are sincere:— although men say that he has not learned, I will certainly say that he has."

7. TSZE-HSIA'S VIEWS OF THE SUBSTANCE OF LEARNING. Tsze-hsiâ was the designation of 卜 商, another of the sage's distinguished disciples, and now placed fifth in the eastern range of "the wise ones." He was greatly famed for his learning, and his views on the *Shih-ching* and the *Ch'un Ch'iu* are said to be preserved in the commentaries of 毛, and of 公 羊 高 and 穀 梁 赤. He wept himself blind on the death of his son, but lived to a great age, and was much esteemed by the people and princes of the time. With regard to the scope of this chapter, there is some truth in what the commentator Wû, 吳, says,—that Tsze-hsiâ's words may be wrested to depreciate learning, while those of the Master in the preceding chapter hit exactly the due medium. The second 賢 is a concrete noun. Written in full, it is composed of the characters for a *minister*, *loyal*, and a *precious shell*. It conveys the ideas of *talents* and *worth* in the concrete, but it is not easy to render it uniformly by any one term of another language. The first 賢 is a verb, ="to treat as a *hsien*." 色 has a different meaning from that in the third chapter. Here it means "sensual pleasure." Literally rendered, the first sentence would be, "esteeming properly the virtuous, and changing the love of woman," and great fault is found by some, as in 四 書 改 錯, XIII, i, with Chû Hsî's interpretation which I have followed; but there is force in what his adherents say, that the passage is not to be understood as if the individual spoken of had ever been given to pleasure, but simply signifies the sincerity of his love for the virtuous. 致 here=委, "to give to," "to devote."

子貢曰、夫子
歸厚矣。
終追遠、民德
曾子曰、慎
勿憚改。
如己者、過則
忠信、無友不
學則不固、
不重、則不威、
子曰君子

CHAPTER VIII. 1. The Master said, "If the scholar be not grave, he will not call forth any veneration, and his learning will not be solid.

2. "Hold faithfulness and sincerity as first principles.

.3. "Have no friends not equal to yourself.

4. "When you have faults, do not fear to abandon them."

CHAPTER IX. The philosopher Tsăng said, "Let there be a careful attention *to perform the funeral rites* to parents, and let them be followed when long gone *with the ceremonies of sacrifice;*—then the virtue of the people will resume its proper excellence."

CHAPTER X. 1. Tsze-ch'in asked Tsze-kung, saying,

8. PRINCIPLES OF SELF-CULTIVACTION. 1. 君子 has here its lightest meaning, =*a student*, one who wishes to be a *Chün-tsze*. 孔安國, of the Han dynasty, in the second century before Christ, took 固, in the sense of "obscured," "dulled," and interprets —"Let him learn, and he will not fall into error." The received interpretation, as in the transl., is better. 2. 主, as a verb, "to hold to be chief." It is often used thus. 3. The object of friendship, with Chinese moralists, is to improve one's knowledge and virtue;—hence, this seemingly, but not really, selfish maxim. .9. THE GOOD EFFECT OF ATTENTION ON THE PART OF SUPERIORS TO THE OFFICES TO THE DEAD:—AN ADMONITION OF TSĂNG SHĂN. 終, "the end,"=death, and 遠, "distant," have both the force of adjectives,="the dead," and "the departed," or "the long gone." 慎 and 追 mean, "to be careful of," "to follow," but their application is as in the translation. 厚, "thick," in opposition to 薄, "thin"; metaphorically, =*good, excellent*. The force of 歸, "to return," is to show that this virtue is naturally proper to the people.
10. CHARACTERISTICS OF CONFUCIUS, AND THEIR INFLUENCE ON THE PRINCES OF THE TIME. 1. Tsze-ch'in and Tsze-k'ang (亢) are designations

志父沒觀其行、三

子曰、父在觀其

之與。

其諸異乎人之求

之、夫子之求之也、

溫、良、恭、儉、讓、以得

之與子貢曰、夫子

其政、求之與抑與

至於是邦也、必聞

"When our master comes to any country, he does not fail to learn all about its government. Does he ask his information? or is it given to him?"

2. Tsze-kung said, "Our master is benign, upright, courteous, temperate, and complaisant, and thus he gets his information. The master's mode of asking information!—is it not different from that of other men?"

CHAPTER XI. The Master said, "While a man's father is alive, look at the bent of his will; when his father is dead, look at his conduct. If for three years

of 陳亢, one of the minor disciples of Confucius. His tablet occupies the twenty-eighth place, on the west, in the outer part of the temples. On the death of his brother, his wife and major-domo wished to bury some living persons with him, to serve him in the regions below. Tsze-ch'in proposed that the wife and steward should themselves submit to the immolation, which made them stop the matter. Tsze-kung, with the double surname 端木, and named 賜, occupies a higher place in the Confucian ranks. He is conspicuous in this work for his steadiness and smartness in reply, and displayed on several occasions practical and political ability. 夫, "a general designation for males," =a man. 夫

子.—a common designation for a teacher or master. 是邦, "this country," =any country. 必, "must," = does not fail to. The antecedent to both the 之 is the whole clause 聞其政. 與, with no tone marked = "to give to," "with," "to"; 與, as in chap. ii. 2. The force of 其諸 is well enough expressed by the dash in English, the previous 也 indicating a pause in the discourse, which the 其, "it," resumes. See Wang Yin-chub's Treatise, chap. ix.

11. ON FILIAL DUTY. 行, is, in the fourth tone, explained by 行迹, "traces of walking," =conduct. It is to be understood that the way of the father had not been very bad. An old interpretation, that the three years are to be understood of the

義、言可復也、恭近
　　有子曰、信近於
不可行也。
和、不以禮節之、亦
有所不行、知和而
斯爲美、小大由之。
和爲貴先王之道、
　　有子曰、禮之用、
可謂孝矣。
年無改於父之道、

he does not alter from the way of his father, he may be called filial."

CHAPTER XII. 1. The philosopher Yû said, "In practicing the rules of propriety, a natural ease is, to be prized. In the ways prescribed by the ancient kings, this is the excellent quality, and in things small and great we follow them.

2. "Yet it is not to be observed in all cases. If one, knowing *how* such ease *should be prized*, manifests it, without regulating it by the rules of propriety, this likewise is not to be done."

CHAPTER XIII. The philosopher Yû said, "When agreements are made according to what is right, what is spoken can be made good. When respect is shown

three years of mourning for the father. is now rightly rejected. The meaning should not be confined to that period.

12. IN CEREMONIES A NATURAL EASE IS TO BE PRIZED, AND YET TO BE SUBORDINATE TO THE END OF CEREMONIES,—THE REVERENTIAL OBSERVANCE OF PROPRIETY. 1. 禮 is not easily rendered in another language. There underlies it the idea of *what is proper*. It is 事 之 宜, "the fitness of things," what reason calls for in the performance of duties towards superior beings, and between man and man

Our term "ceremonies" comes near its meaning here. 道 is here a name for 禮, as indicating the *courses or ways* to be trodden by men. In 小 大 由 之, the antecedent to 之 is not 利, but 禮 or 道. 2 Observe the force of the 亦, "also," in the last clause, and how it affirms the general principle enunciated in the first paragraph.

13. TO SAVE FROM FUTURE REPENTANCE, WE MUST BE CAREFUL IN OUR FIRST STEPS. A different view of the scope of this chapter is taken by Ho Yen. It illustrates, according to him, the difference

於禮遠恥辱也、因
不失其親亦可宗
也。
曾子曰、君子食無
求飽居無求安敏
於事而愼於言就
有道而正焉可謂
好學也已、
子貢曰、貧而無
諂富而無驕、何
如。

according to what is proper, one keeps far from shame and disgrace. When the parties upon whom a man leans are proper persons to be intimate with, he can make them his guides and masters."

CHAPTER XIV. The Master said, "He who aims to be a man of complete virtue in his food does not seek to gratify his appetite, nor in his dwelling place does he seek the appliances of ease; he is earnest in what he is doing, and careful in his speech he frequents the company of men of principle that he may be rectified:—such a person may be said indeed to love to learn."

CHAPTER XV. I. Tsze-kung said, "What do you pronounce concerning the poor man who yet does not flatter, and the rich man who is not proud?" The

between being sincere and righteousness, between being respectful and propriety, and how a man's conduct may be venerated The later view commends itself, the only difficulty being with 近 於, "near to," which we must accept as a *meiosis* for 合 乎, "agreeing with" 信=信 約, "a covenant," "agreement." 遠, fourth tone, "to keep away from." The force of the 亦="he can *go on* to make them his masters," 宗 being taken as an active verb.

14. WITH WHAT MIND ONE AIMING TO BE A CHÜN-TSZE PURSUES HIS LEARNING. He may be well,

even luxuriously, fed and lodged, but, with his higher aim, these things are not his seeking,—無 求. A nominative to 可 謂 must be supposed,—*all this*, or *such a person*. The closing particles, 也 已, give emphasis to the preceding sentence, =*yes, indeed*.

15. AN ILLUSTRATION OF THE SUCCESSIVE STEPS IN SELF-CULTIVATION. 1. Tsze-kung had been poor, and then did not cringe. He became rich and was not proud. He asked Confucius about the style of character to which he had attained, Confucius allowed its worth, but sent

子曰可也未若貧
而樂富而好禮者
也。子貢曰詩云、如
切如磋如琢如磨、
其斯之謂與。子曰
賜也始可與言詩
已矣、告諸往而知
來者。

Master replied, "They will do; but they are not equal to him, who, though poor, is yet cheerful, and to him, who, though rich, loves the rules of propriety."

2. Tsze-kung replied, "It is said in the Book of Poetry, 'As you cut and then file, as you carve and then polish.'—The meaning is the same, I apprehend, as that which you have just expressed."

3. The Master said, "With one like Ts'ze, I can begin to talk about the odes. I told him one point, and he knew its proper sequence."

him to higher attainments. 而, here, ="and yet." 何 如, "what as?"="what do you say—what is to be thought—of this?" Observe the force of the 未, "not yet." 2. The ode quoted is the first of the songs of Wei (衞), praising the prince Wû, who had dealt with himself as an ivory worker who first cuts the bone, and then files it smooth, or a lapidary whose hammer and chisel are followed by all the appliances for smoothing and polishing. See the Shih-ching, I, v, Ode I, st. 2. In 其 斯 之 謂, the antecedent to 其 is the passage of the ode, and that to 斯 is the reply of Confucius. 之 謂, see Prémare, p. 156 The clause might be translated—"is not that passage the saying of this?" Or, "Does not that mean this?" 3. Intercetta and his coadjutors translate here as if

賜 were in the 2nd pers. But the Chinese comm. put it in the 3rd, and correctly. Prémare, on the character 也, says, "Fere semper adjungitur nominibus propriis. Sic in libro Lun Yu, Confucius loquens de suis discipulis, Yeou, Keou, Hoei, velipsos alloquens, dicit 由 也, 求 也, 同 也." It is not to be denied that the name before 也 is sometimes in the 2nd pers., but generally it is in the 3rd, and the force of the 也= quoad. 賜 也, quoad Ts'ze. 已 矣, nearly=也 已 (or 已 without marking the tone), in chap. xiv. The last clause may be given—"Tell him the past, and he knows the future;" but the connection determines the meaning as in the translation. 諸, as in chap. x, is a particle, a mere 語 助, as it is called, "a helping or supporting word."

也。知 患 己 之 患 曰、🀆
人 不 知、不 人 不 子

**CHAPTER XVI.** The Master said, "I will not be afflicted at men's not knowing me; I will be afflicted that I do not know men."

16. PERSONAL ATTAINMENT SHOULD BE OUR CHIEF AIM. Comp. chap. i, 3. After the negative 不, as in chap. ii, 1, observe the transposition in 己 知, which is more elegant than 知 己 would be. 己,

"self," the person depending on the context. We cannot translate "do not be afflicted," because 不 is not used imperatively, like 勿. A nominative to 患 has to be assumed,—我, "I," or 君子, "the superior man."

## BOOK II.  WEI CHĂNG

之。星 而 其 辰、如 德、政 曰、🀆 第 爲
共 衆 所、居 北 譬 以 爲 子 二 政

**CHAPTER I.** The Master said, "He who exercises government by means of his virtue may be compared to the north polar star, which keeps its place and all the stars turn towards it."

HEADING OF THIS BOOK.—爲 政 第 二. This second Book contains twenty-four chapters, and is named 爲 政, "The practice of government." That is the object to which learning, treated of in the last Book, should lead, and here we have the qualities which constitute, and the character of the men who administer, good government.

1. THE INFLUENCE OF VIRTUE IN A RULER. 德 is explained by 得, and the old commentators say 物 得 以 生 謂 之 德, "what creatures get at their birth is called their virtue"; but this is a mere play on the common sound of different words. Chû Hsî makes it = 行 道 而 有 得 於 心, "the practice of truth and

acquisition thereof in the heart." His view of the comparison is that it sets forth the illimitable influence which virtue in a ruler exercises without his using any effort. This is extravagant. His opponents say that virtue is the polar star, and the various departments of government the other stars. This is far-fetched. We must be content to accept the vague utterance without minutely determining its meaning. 北 辰 is, no doubt, "the north polar star," anciently believed to coincide exactly with the place of the real pole. 共 in the third tone, used for 拱, "to fold the hands in saluting," here = "to turn respectfully towards."

有五、而志于
子曰、吾十
恥且格。
齊之以禮、有
恥。道之以德、
刑、民免而無
以政、齊之以
子曰、道之
之、曰、思無邪。
百、一言以蔽
子曰、詩三

CHAPTER II. The Master said, "In the Book of Poetry are three hundred pieces, but the design of them all may be embraced in one sentence—'Having no depraved thoughts.'"

CHAPTER III. 1. The Master said, "If the people be led by laws, and uniformity sought to be given them by punishments, they will try to avoid *the punishment,* but have no sense of shame.

2. "If they be led by virtue, and uniformity sought to be given them by the rules of propriety, they will have the sense of shame, and moreover will become good."

CHAPTER IV. 1. The Master said, "At fifteen, I had my mind bent on learning.

2. THE PURE DESIGN OF THE BOOK OF POETRY. The number of compositions in the Shih-ching is rather more than the round number here given. 一言＝一句, "one sentence." 蔽＝著, "to cover," "to embrace." 思無邪, see Shih-ching, IV, ii, 1, st. 4. The sentence there is indicative, and in praise of the duke Hsî, who had no depraved thoughts. The sage would seem to have been intending the design in compiling the *Shih.* A few individual pieces are calculated to have a different effect.

3. HOW RULERS SHOULD PREFER MORAL APPLIANCES. 1. 道, as in I, v. 之, "them," refers to 民, below. 政, as opposed to 德,＝laws and prohibitions. 齊＝"corn earing evenly"; hence, what is level, equal, adjusted, and here with the corresponding verbal force. 民免, "The people will avoid," that is, avoid breaking the laws through fear of the punishment. 2. 格 has the signification of "to come to," and "to correct," from either of which the text may be explained,—"will come to good," or "will correct themselves." Observe the different application of 且 and 而 in pars. 1 and 2, i. 而＝"but", 且＝"moreover."

4. CONFUCIUS'S OWN ACCOUNT OF HIS GRADUAL PROGRESS AND ATTAINMENTS. Commentators are perplexed with this chapter. Holding of Confucius that 生而知之, 安而行之, "he was born with knowledge, and did what was right with

學三十而立。
四十而不惑。
五十而知天
命六十而耳
順七十而從
心所欲、不踰
矩。
孟懿子問
孝、子曰、無違。
樊遲御、子告
之曰、孟孫問

2. "At thirty, I stood firm.

3. "At forty, I had no doubts.

4. "At fifty, I knew the decrees of Heaven.

5. "At sixty, my ear was an obedient organ *for the reception of truth.*

6. "At seventy, I could follow what my heart desired, without transgressing what was right."

CHAPTER V. 1. Măng I asked what filial piety was. The Master said, "It is not being disobedient."

2. *Soon after,* as Fan Ch'ih' was driving him, the Master told him, saying, "Măng-sun asked me what

entire ease," they say that he here conceals his sagehood, and puts himself on the level of common men, to set before them a stimulating example. We may believe that the compilers of the Analects, the sage's immediate disciples, did not think of him so extravagantly as later men have done. It is to be wished, however, that he had been more definite and diffuse in his account of himself. 1. 有, in fourth tone,= "and." The "learning," to which, at 15, Confucius gave himself, is to be understood of the subjects of the "Superior Learning." See Chû Hsi's preliminary essay to the Tâ Hsio. 2. The "standing firm" probably indicates that he no more needed to bend his will. 3. The "no doubts" may have been concerning what was proper in all circumstances and events. 4. "The decrees of Heaven,"=the things decreed by Heaven, the constitution of things making what was proper to be so 5. "The ear obedient" is the mind receiving as by intuition the truth from the ear. 6 矩, "an instrument for determining the square." 不踰 矩, "without transgressing the square." The expressions describing the progress of Confucius at the different periods of his age are often employed as numerical designations of age.

5. FILIAL PIETY MUST BE SHOWN, ACCORDING TO THE RULES OF PROPRIETY. 1. Măng I was a great officer of the State of Lû, by name Ho-chi (何忌), and the chief of one of the three great families by which in the time of Confucius the authority of that State was grasped. Those families were descended from three brothers, the sons by a concubine of the duke Hwan (711-694 B.C.), who were distinguished at first by the prænomens of 仲, 叔, and 季. To these was subsequently added

孝於我、我對曰、
無違。樊遲曰、何
謂也、子曰、生事
之以禮、死葬之
以禮、祭之以禮。
孟武伯問孝、
子曰、父母唯其
疾之憂。

filial piety was, and I answered him,—'not being disobedient.'"

3. Fan Ch'ih said, "What did you mean?" The Master replied, "That parents, when alive, should be served according to propriety; that, when dead, they should be buried according to propriety; and that they should be sacrificed to according to propriety."

CHAPTER VI. Măng Wû asked what filial piety was. The Master said, "Parents are anxious lest their children should be sick."

the character 孫, "grandson," to indicate their princely descent, and 仲孫, 叔孫, and 季孫 became the respective surnames of the families. 仲孫 was changed into 孟孫 by the father of Măng Î, on a principle of humility, as he thereby only claimed to be the eldest of the inferior sons or their representatives, and avoided the presumption of seeming to be a younger full brother of the reigning duke. 懿, "mild and virtuous," was the posthumous honorary title given to Ho-chî. On 子, see I, i, 1. 2. Fan, by name 須, and designated 子遲, was a minor disciple of the sage. Confucius repeated his remark to Fan, that he might report the explanation of it to his friend Măng Î, or Măng-sun Î, and thus prevent him from supposing that all the sage intended was disobedience to parents. Comp. the whole of Confucius's explanation with I, ix.

6. THE ANXIETY OF PARENTS ABOUT THEIR CHILDREN—AN ARGUMENT FOR FILIAL PIETY. This enigmatical sentence has been interpreted in two ways. Chû Hsî takes 唯 (=惟) not in the sense of "only," but of "thinking anxiously."— "Parents have the sorrow of thinking anxiously about their—i. e., their children's—being unwell. Therefore children should take care of their persons." The old commentators again take 唯 in the sense of "only" —"Let parents have only the sorrow of their children's illness. Let them have no other occasion for sorrow. This will be filial piety" Măng Wû (the honorary epithet,= "Bold and of straightforward principle") was the son of Măng Î, and by name 彘 (Chih). 伯 merely indicates that he was the eldest son.

子游問孝、子
曰、今之孝者、是
謂能養、至於犬
馬皆能有養、不
敬、何以別乎。
子夏問孝、子
曰、色難、有事弟
子服其勞、有酒
食先生饌、曾是
以爲孝乎。

CHAPTER VII. Tsze-yû asked what filial piety was. The Master said, "The filial piety of nowadays means the support of one's parents. But dogs and horses likewise are able to do something in the way of sûpport;—without reverence, what is there to distinguish the one support given from the other?"

CHAPTER VIII. Tsze-hsiâ asked what filial piety was. The Master said, "The difficulty is with the countenance. If, when *their elders* have any *troublesome* affairs, the young take the toil of them, and if, when *the young* have wine and food, they set them before their elders, is THIS to be considered filial piety?"

7. How THERE MUST BE REVERENCE IN FILIAL DUTY. Tsze-yû was the designation of 言偃, a native of 吳, and distinguished among the disciples of Confucius for his learning. He is now 4th on the west among "the wise ones." 養 is in the 4th tone, = "to minister support to," the act of an inferior to a superior. Chû Hsî gives a different turn to the sentiment.—"But dogs and horses likewise manage to get their support." The other and older interprotation is better. 至於, "Coming to,"='as to, *quoad*. 別="to discriminate," "distinguish."

8. THE DUTIES OF FILIAL PIETY MUST BE PERFORMED WITH A CHEERFUL COUNTENANCE. 事 followed by 勞=the "*troublesome affairs*" in the translation. The use of 弟子 in the phrase here extends filial duty to elders generally,—to the 父兄 as well as to the 父母. We have in translating to supply their respective nominatives to the two 有. 食, read *tsze*, "rice," and then, food generally. 先生饌=與先生饌之="They give them to their elders to eat." 先生=elders. The phrase, here meaning parents, uncles, and elders generally, is applied by foreign students to their teachers. 曾, aspirated,=則, "then," a transition particle. To these different interrogatories, the sage, we are told, made answer according to the character of the questioner, as each one needed instruction.

子曰、吾與囘言
終日不違、如愚退。
而省其私、亦足以
發囘也不愚。
子曰視其所以。
觀其所由察其所
安人焉廋哉人焉
廋哉。

CHAPTER IX.　The Master said, "I have talked with Hûi for a whole day, and he has not made any objection *to anything I said;*—as if he were stupid.　He has retired, and I have examined his conduct when away from me, and found him able to illustrate *my teachings.*　Hûi!—He is not stupid."

CHAPTER X.　1. The Master said, "See what a man does.

2. "Mark his motives.

3. "Examine in what things he rests.

4. "How can a man conceal his character?　How can a man conceal his character?"

9. THE QUIET RECEPTIVITY OF THE DISCIPLE HÛI. Yen Hûi (顏囘), styled 子淵, was Confucius's favorite disciple, and is now honored with the first place east among his four assessors in his temples, and with the title of 復聖顏子, "The second sage, the philosopher Yen." At twenty-nine his hair was entirely white, and at thirty-three he died, to the excessive grief of the sage. The subject of 退 is 囘, and that of 省 (as in I, iv) is 吾. 其私, "his privacy," meaning only his way when not with the master. · 亦, "also," takes up 如愚,—He was so, and also thus. 囘也, see I, xv, 3.

10. HOW TO DETERMINE THE CHARACTERS OF MEN. '1 以 is explained as＝行, or 行用, "does." The same, though not its common meaning, is the first given to it in the dict. For the noun to which the three 其 refer, we must go down to 人 in the 4th par. There is a climax in 所以, 所由 ("what from"), and 所安, and a corresponding one in the verbs 視, 觀, and 察. 4. 焉, generally a final particle, in 2nd tone, is here in the 1st, an interrogative,＝how? Its interrogative force blends with the exclamatory of 哉 at the end.

子曰、溫故而知新、可以爲師矣。

子曰、君子不器。

子貢問君子、子曰先行其言、而後從之。

子曰、君子周而不比、小人比而不周。

CHAPTER XI. The Master said, "If a man keeps cherishing his old knowledge, so as continually to be acquiring new, he may be a teacher of others."

CHAPTER XII. The Master said, "The accomplished scholar is not a utensil."

CHAPTER XIII. Tsze-kung asked what constituted the superior man. The Master said, "He acts before he speaks, and afterwards speaks according to his actions."

CHAPTER XIV. The Master said, "The superior man is catholic and no partisan. The mean man is a partisan and not catholic."

11. TO BE ABLE TO TEACH OTHERS ONE MUST FROM HIS OLD STORES BE CONTINUALLY DEVELOPING THINGS NEW. 溫 is expressed in the dictionary by 燖, and, with reference to this very passage, it is said, "one's old learning being thoroughly mastered, again constantly to practice it, is called 溫." Modern commentators say that the "new learning is in the old." The idea probably is that of assimilating old acquisitions and new. Compare 中庸, XXVII, vi.

12. THE GENERAL APTITUDE OF THE CHUN-TSZE. This is not like our English saying, that "such a man is a machine,"—a blind instrument. A utensil has its particular use. It answers for that and no other. Not so with the superior man, who is ad omnia paratus.

13. HOW WITH THE SUPERIOR MAN WORDS FOLLOW ACTIONS. The reply is literally—"He first acts his words and afterwards follows them." A translator's difficulty is with the latter clause. What is the antecedent to 之? It would seem to be 其 言, but in that case there is no room for words at all. Nor is there according to the old commentators. In the interpretation I have given, Chú Hsî follows the famous Cháu Lien-ch i (周 濂溪).

14. THE DIFFERENCE BETWEEN THE CHÚN-TSZE AND THE SMALL MAN. 比, here in 4th tone, = "partial," "partisanly." The sentiment is this:—"With the Chun-tsze, it is principles not men; with the small man, the reverse."

子曰、學而不
思則罔、思而不
學則殆。

子曰、攻乎異
端、斯害也已。

子曰、由誨女
知之乎、知之為
知之、不知為不
知、是知也。

CHAPTER XV. The Master said, "Learning without thought is labor lost; thought without learning is perilous."

CHAPTER XVI. The Master said, "The study of strange doctrines is injurious indeed!"

CHAPTER XVII. The Master said, "Yû, shall I teach you what knowledge is? When you know a thing, to hold that you know it; and when you do not know a thing, to allow that you do not know it;—this is knowledge."

15. IN LEARNING, READING AND THOUGHT MUST BE COMBINED. 罔, "a net," used also in the sense of "not," as an adverb, and here as an adjective. The old commentators make 殆, "perilous," simply = "wearisome to the body."

16. STRANGE DOCTRINES ARE NOT TO BE STUDIED. 攻, often "to attack," as an enemy, here = "to apply one's self to," "to study." 端, "correct"; then, "beginnings," "first principles"; here = "doctrines." 也已, as in I, xiv. In Confucius's time Buddhism was not in China, and we can hardly suppose him to intend Tâoism. Indeed, we are ignorant to what doctrines he referred, but his maxim is of general application.

17. THERE SHOULD BE NO PRETENSE IN THE PROFESSION OF KNOWLEDGE, OR THE DENIAL OF IGNORANCE. 由, by surname 仲, and generally known by his designation of *Tsze-lû* (子路), was one of the most famous disciples of Confucius, and now occupies in the temples the 4th place east in the sage's own hall. He was noted for his courage and forwardness, a man of impulse rather than reflection. Confucius foretold that he would come to an untimely end. He was killed through his own rashness in a revolution in the State of Wei. The tassel of his cap being cut off when he received his death wound, he quoted a saying—"The superior man must not die without his cap," tied on the tassel, adjusted the cap, and expired. This action—結纓禮全—is much lauded. Of the six 知, the 1st and 6th are knowledge subjective, the other four are knowledge objective. 為 = 以為, "to take to be," "to consider," "to allow." 女, thus marked with a tone, is used for 汝, "you"

為則民服。孔子
哀公問曰、何
祿在其中矣。
言寡尤、行寡悔、
行其餘、則寡悔、
尤、多見闕殆、愼
愼言其餘、則寡
子曰、多聞闕疑、
子張學干祿。

CHAPTER XVIII. 1. Tsze-chang was learning with a view to official emolument.

2. The Master said, "Hear much and put aside the points of which you stand in doubt, while you speak cautiously at the same time of the others:—then you will afford few occasions for blame. See much and put aside the things which seem perilous, while you are cautious at the same time in carrying the others into practice:—then you will have few occasions for repentance. When one gives few occasions for blame in his words, and few occasions for repentance in his conduct, he is in the way to get emolument."

CHAPTER XIX. The duke Âi asked, saying, "What should be done in order to secure the submission of the people?" Confucius replied, "Advance the

18. THE END IN LEARNING SHOULD BF ONE'S OWN IMPROVEMENT, AND NOT EMOLUMENT. 1. Tsze-chang, named 師, with the double surname 顓 孫, a native of Ch'än (陳), was not undistinguished in the Confucian school. Tsze-kung praised him as a man of merit without boasting, humble in a high position, and not arrogant to the helpless. From this chapter, however, it would appear that inferior motives sometimes ruled him. 學 = "was learning," i e., at some particular time. 干 = 求, "to seek for" 2. 闕 is explained by 姑 舍 置, but this meaning of it is not given clearly in the dictionary.

Compare its use in XIII, iii, 4. 祿 在 其 中, "Emolument is herein," i. e., it will come without seeking, the individual is on the way to it. The lesson is that we are to do what is right, and not be anxious about temporal concerns.

19. HOW A PRINCE BY THE RIGHT EMPLOYMENT OF HIS OFFICERS MAY SECURE THE REAL SUBMISSION OF HIS SUBJECTS. Âi was the honorary epithet of 蔣, duke of Lû (494–468 B. C.);—Confucius died in his 16th year. According to the laws for posthumous titles, 哀 denotes "the respectful and benevolent, early cut off." 哀 公 = "The to-be-lamented

對曰、舉直錯諸枉、
則民服舉枉錯諸
直、則民不服。
⬚季康子問使民
敬忠以勸、如之何。
子曰、臨之以莊、則
敬孝慈則忠舉善
而教不能、則勸。
⬚或謂孔子曰、子

upright and set aside the crooked, then the people
will submit. Advance the crooked and set aside the
upright, then the people will not submit."

CHAPTER XX. Chî K'ang asked how to cause the
people to reverence *their ruler,* to be faithful to him,
and to go on to nerve themselves to virtue. The
Master said, "Let him preside over them with gravity;
—then they will reverence him. Let him be filial and
kind to all;—then they will be faithful to him. Let
him advance the good and teach the incompetent;—
then they will eagerly seek to be virtuous."

CHAPTER XXI. 1. Some one addressed Confucius,

duke." 錯, 4th tone=置, "to set
aside." 諸 is partly euphonious,
but also indicates the plural. 孔 子
對 曰, "The philosopher K'ung replied." Here, for the first time, the
sage is called by his surname, and 對
is used, as indicating the reply of an
inferior to a superior.

20. EXAMPLE IN SUPERIORS IS
MORE POWERFUL THAN FORCE. K'ang,
"easy and pleasant, people-soother,"
was the honorary epithet of Chi-sun
Fei (肥), the head of one of the three
great families of Lû; see chap. v.
His idea is seen in 使, "to cause,"
the power of force; that of Confucius
appears in 則, "then," the power of
influence. In 以 勸, 以 is said to=

與, "together with," "mutually."
勸, "to advise," "to teach," has also
in the dictionary the meaning—"to
rejoice to follow," which is its force
here, 爲 善, "the practice of goodness," being understood. Wang Yin-
chih (on the Particles) says that in
this (and similar passages) 以 unites
the meanings of 與 and 而; and this
is the view which I have myself long
held.

21. CONFUCIUS'S EXPLANATION OF
HIS NOT BEING IN ANY OFFICE. I.
或謂孔子,—the surname indicates
that the questioner was not a disciple. Confucius had his reason for
not being in office at the time but it
was not expedient to tell it. He

奚不爲政子曰書云孝

乎、惟孝友于兄弟、施於

有政、是亦爲政奚其爲

爲政。

鼉子曰人而無信、不知

其可也大車無輗小車

無軏、其何以行之哉。

saying, "Sir, why·are you not engaged in the government?"

2.   The Master said, "What does the Shû-ching say
of filial piety?—'You are filial, you discharge your
brotherly duties.  These qualities are displayed in
government.'  This then also constitutes the exercise
of government.  Why must there be THAT—making
one be in the government?"

CHAPTER XXII.   The Master said, "I do not know
how a man without truthfulness is to get on.  How
can a large carriage be made to go without the crossbar for yoking the oxen to, or a small carriage without
the arrangement for yoking the horses?"

replied therefore, as in par. 2.  2.
See the Shû-ching, V, xxi, 1.  But
the text is neither correctly applied
nor exactly quoted.  The old interpreters read in one sentence 孝乎惟
孝, "O filial piety! nothing but filial
piety!"  Chû Hsî, however, pauses
at 乎. and commences the quotation
with 惟孝. 奚其爲爲政, the 1st
爲=以 爲, and 其 refers to the
thought in the question, that *office*

was necessary to one's being in
government.
   22.   THE NECESSITY TO A MAN OF
BEING TRUTHFUL AND SINCERE.  輗
and 軏 are explained in the dictionary in the same way—"the crossbar
at the end of the carriage pole."
Chû Hsî says, "In the light carriage
the end of the pole curved upwards,
and the crossbar was suspended from
a hook."  This would give it more
elasticity.

義　而　鼉　知　周　可　於　益　因　可　鼉
不　祭　子　也　者　知　殷　可　於　知　子
爲　之　曰　。　雖　也　禮　知　夏　也　張
無　諂　非　　　百　、　所　也　禮　、　問
勇　也　其　　　世　其　損　、　所　子　十
也　。　鬼　　　、　或　益　周　損　曰　世
。　見　　　　　可　繼　、　因　、　、　、

CHAPTER XXIII. 1. Tsze-chang asked whether *the affairs of* ten ages *after* could be known.

2. Confucius said, "The Yin dynasty followed the regulations of the Hsiâ: wherein it took from or added to them may be known. The Châu dynasty has followed the regulations of the Yin: wherein it took from or added to them may be known. Some other may follow the Châu, but though it should be at the distance of a hundred ages, its affairs may be known."

CHAPTER XXIV 1. The Master said, "For a man to sacrifice to a spirit which does not belong to him is flattery.

2. "To see what is right and not to do it is want of courage."

23. THE GREAT PRINCIPLES GOVERNING SOCIETY ARE UNCHANGEABLE. 1 世 may be taken as an age=our "century," or as a generation= thirty years, which is its radical meaning, being formed from *three tens* and *one* (卅 and 一). Confucius made no pretension to supernatural powers, and all commentators are agreed that the things here asked about were not what we call contingent or indifferent events. He merely says that the great principles of morality and relations of society had continued the same and would ever do so. 也=乎. 2. The Hsiâ, Yin, and Châu are now spoken of as the 三 代, "The three changes," i. e., the three great dynasties. The first sovereign of the Hsiâ was "The great Yu," 2205 B. C.; of the Yin, T'ang, 1766 B. C.; and of Châu, Wû, 1122 B. C.

24. NEITHER IN SACRIFICE NOR IN ANY OTHER PRACTICE MAY A MAN DO ANYTHING BUT WHAT IS RIGHT. 1. 人神曰鬼. "The spirit of man (i. e., of the dead) is called 鬼." The 鬼 of which a man may say that they are his, are those only of his ancestors, and to them only he may sacrifice. The ritual of China provides for sacrifices to three classes of objects 一天 神, 地 示, 人 鬼, "spirits of heaven, of the earth, of men." This chapter is not to be extended to all the three. It has reference only to the manes of departed men.

## BOOK III. PÁ YIH

八佾第三

孔子謂季氏、

八佾舞於庭、是

可忍也、孰不可

忍也。

三家者、以雍

CHAPTER I. Confucius said of the head of the Chî family, who had eight rows of pantomimes in his area, "If he can bear to do this, what may he not bear to do?"

CHAPTER II. The three families used the YUNG

HEADING OF THIS BOOK.—八佾第三. The last Book treated of the practice of government, and therein no things, according to Chinese ideas, are more important than ceremonial rites and music. With those topics, therefore, the twenty-six chapters of this Book are occupied, and "eight rows," the principal words in the first chapter, are adopted as its heading.

1. CONFUCIUS'S INDIGNATION AT THE USURPATION OF ROYAL RITES. 季氏, by contraction for 季孫氏; see on II, v. 氏 and 姓 are now used without distinction, meaning "surname," only that the 氏 of a woman is always spoken of, and not her 姓. Originally the 氏 appears to have been used to denote the branch families of one surname. 季氏, "The Chî family," with special reference to its head, "The Chî," as we should say. 佾, a row of dancers," or pantomimes rather, who kept time in the temple services, in the 庭, the front space before the raised portion in the principal hall,

moving or brandishing feathers, flags, or other articles. In his ancestral temple, the king had eight rows, each row consisting of eight men, a duke or prince had six, and a great officer only four. For the Chî, therefore, to use eight rows was a usurpation, for though it may be argued, that to the ducal family of Lû royal rites were conceded, and that the offshoots of it (II, v) might use the same, still great officers were confined to the ordinances proper to their rank. 謂 is used here, as frequently, in the sense—"to speak of." Confucius's remark may also be translated, "If this be endured, what may not be endured?" For there is force in the observations of the author of the 四書異註, that this par. and the following must be assigned to the sage during the short time that he held high office in Lû.

2. AGAIN AGAINST USURPED RIGHTS. 三家者, "Those belonging to the three families." They assembled together, as being the descendants of Duke Hwan (II, v), in

徹。子曰、相維辟
公、天子穆穆、
取於三家之堂。
子曰人而不
仁、如禮何人而
不仁、如樂何。
林放問禮之
本。子曰、大哉問。

ode, while the vessels were being removed, *at the conclusion of the sacrifice.* The Master said, "'Assisting are the princes;—the son of heaven looks profound and grave';—what application can these words have in the hall of the three families?"

CHAPTER III. The Master said, "If a man be without the virtues proper to humanity, what has he to do with the rites of propriety? If a man be without the virtues proper to humanity, what has he to do with music?"

CHAPTER IV. 1. Lin Fang asked what was the first thing to be attended to in ceremonies.

2. The Master said, "A great question indeed!

one temple. To this belonged the 庭 in the last chapter, which is called 季 氏 庭, circumstances having concurred to make the Chî the chief of the three families: see 四書改錯, VIII, vii. For the Yung ode, see Shih-ching, IV. i. sec. ii, Ode vii. It was, properly, sung in the royal temples of the Châu dynasty, at the 徹, "the clearing away," of the sacrificial apparatus, and contains the lines quoted by Confucius, quite inappropriate to the circumstances of the three families 辟.—without an aspirate. 相 —4th tone "assistant." "assisting

3. CEREMONIES AND MUSIC VAIN WITHOUT VIRTUE. 仁, see 1. ii. I don't know how to render it here, otherwise than in the translation. Commentators define it—心 之 全 德, "the entire virtue of the heart." As referred to 禮, it indicates the feeling of reverence; as referred to 樂 (yŏ), it indicates harmoniousness.

4. THE OBJECT OF CEREMONIES SHOULD REGULATE THEM:—AGAINST FORMALISM. 1. Lin Fang, styled 子 邱, was a man of Lû, whose tablet is now placed first, on the west, in the outer court of the temples. He is known only by the question in this chapter. According to Chû Hsî, 本 here is not 根 本 "the radical idea," "the essence"; but＝初, "the beginning" (opposed to 末), "the first

禮、與其奢也、寧

儉、喪、與其易也、

寧戚。

子曰、夷狄之

有君不如諸夏

之亡也。

季氏旅於泰

山。子謂冉有曰、

女弗能救與。對

3. "In *festive* ceremonies, it is better to be sparing than extravagant. In the ceremonies of mourning, it is better that there be deep sorrow than a minute attention to observances."

CHAPTER V. The Master said, "The rude tribes of the east and north have their princes, and are not like the States of our great land which are without them."

CHAPTER VI. The chief of the Chî family was about to sacrifice to the T'âi mountain. The Master said to Zan Yû, "Can you not save him from this?" He

thing to be attended to." 3. 禮, as opposed to 喪 (1st tone), must indicate the festive or fortunate (吉) ceremonies,—capping, marriage, and sacrifices. 易, read 1, 4th tone. Chû Hsî explains it by 治, as in Mencius —易其田疇, "to cleanse and dress the fields," and interprets as in the translation. The old commentators take the meaning—和易, "harmony and ease," i. e., not being overmuch troubled.

5. THE ANARCHY OF CONFUCIUS'S TIME. The 夷 were the barbarous tribes on the east of China, and 狄, those on the north. See 禮記, 王制, III, xiv. The two are here used for the barbarous tribes about China generally. 諸夏 is a name for China because of the *multitude* of its regions (諸) and its *greatness* (夏). 華夏, "The Flowery and Great," is still a common designation of it.

Chû Hsî takes 如 as simply = 似, and hence the sentiment in the translation. Ho Yen's commentary is to this effect:—"The rude tribes with their princes are still not equal to China with its anarchy." 亡, read as, and = 無.

6. ON THE FOLLY OF USURPED SACRIFICES. 旅 is said to be the name appropriate to sacrifices to mountains, but we find it applied also to sacrifices to God. The T'âi mountain is the first of the "five mountains" (五嶽), which are celebrated in Chinese literature, and have always received religious honors. It was in Lû, or rather on the borders between Lû and Ch'î, about two miles north of the present department city of T'âi-an (泰安), in Shantung. According to the ritual of China, sacrifice could only be offered to those mountains by the

子夏問曰、巧

飲、其爭也君子。

揖讓而升、下而

所爭、必也射乎、

子曰君子無

如林放乎。

呼、曾謂泰山、不

曰、不能子曰、嗚

answered, "I cannot." Confucius said, "Alas! will you say that the T'âi mountain is not so discerning as Lin Fang?"

CHAPTER VII. The Master said, "The student of virtue has no contentions. If it be said he cannot avoid them, shall this be in archery? *But* he bows complaisantly *to his competitors;* thus he ascends *the hall*, descends, and exacts the forfeit of drinking. In his contention, he is still the Chün-tsze."

CHAPTER VIII. 1. Tsze-hsiâ asked, saying, "What

sovereign, and by the princes in whose States any of them happened to be. For the chief of the Chi family, therefore, to sacrifice to the T'âi mountain was a great usurpation. 女 as in II, vii＝汝, and 曾 as in II, viii＝則, or we may take it as＝經, "Have you said, etc.?" 泰 山＝泰 山 之 神, "The spirit of the T'âi mountain." Lin Fang,—see chap. iv, from which the reason of this reference to him may be understood. Zan Yû, named 求, and by designation 子 有, was one of the disciples of Confucius, and is now third, in the hall, on the west. He entered the service of the Chi family, and was a man of ability and resource.

7. THE SUPERIOR MAN AVOIDS ALL CONTENTIOUS STRIVING. Here 君 子 ＝尙 德 之 人, "the man who prefers virtue"; 必 也 射 乎, literally, "if he must, shall it be in archery?"

揖 讓, according to Chû Hsi, extend over all the verbs, 升, 下, 飲. 下 is marked in the 4th tone, anciently appropriate to it as a verb. 飲, 4th tone, "to give to drink," here＝to exact from the vanquished the forfeit cup. In Confucius's time there were three principal exercises of archery: —the great archery, under the eye of the sovereign; the guests' archery, which might be at the royal court or at the visits of the princes among themselves; and the festive archery, for amusement. The regulations for the archers were substantially the same in them all, and served to prove their virtue. instead of giving occasion to quarreling There is no end to the controversies among commentators on minor points.

8 CEREMONIES ARE SECONDARY AND MERELY ORNAMENTAL 1. The sentences quoted by Tsze-hsiâ are, it is supposed, from a 逸 詩, one of tho

殷禮吾能言之、宋　言之、杞不足徵也、　子曰、夏禮吾能　言詩已矣。　予者商也、始可與　曰、禮後乎子曰、起　也。子曰、繪事後素。　素以爲絢兮何謂　笑倩兮、美目盼兮、

is the meaning of the passage—'The pretty dimples of her artful smile! The well-defined black and white of her eye! The plain ground for the colors?'"

2. The Master said, "The business of laying on the colors follows (the preparation of) the plain ground."

3. "Ceremonies then are a subsequent thing?" The Master said, "It is Shang who can bring out my meaning. Now I can begin to talk about the odes with him."

CHAPTER IX. The Master said, "I could describe the ceremonies of the Hsiâ dynasty, but Chî cannot sufficiently attest my words. I could describe the ceremonies of the Yin dynasty, but Sung cannot

poems which Confucius did not admit into the Shih-ching. The two first lines, however, are found in it, I, v; III, ii. The disciple's inquiry turns on the meaning of 以 爲 in the last line, which he took to mean—"The plain ground is to be regarded as the coloring." 2. Confucius, in his reply, makes 後 a verb, governing 素,="comes after the plain ground." 3. 禮 後 乎;—Tsze-hsiâ's remark is an exclamation rather than a question. 起 予 者, "He who stirs me up,"="He who brings out my meaning." On the last sentence, see I, xv.—The above interpretation, especially as to the meaning of 繪事 後 素, after Chû Hsî, is quite the

opposite of that of the old interpreters. Their view is of course strongly supported by the author of 四書改錯, VIII, iii.

9. THE DECAY OF THE MONUMENTS OF ANTIQUITY. Of Haiâ and Yin, see II, xxiii. In the small State of Chî (originally what is now the district of the same name in Kaifeng department in Honan, but in Confucius's time a part of Shantung), the sacrifices to the emperors of the Hsiâ dynasty were maintained by their descendants. So with the Yin dynasty and Sung, a part also of Honan. But the 文, "literary monuments," of those countries, and their 獻 (=賢, so in

子曰、不知也、知

或問禘之說、

欲觀之矣。

灌而往者、吾不

子曰、禘、自既

吾能徵之矣。

不足故也、足、則

不足徵也、文獻

sufficiently attest my words. (*They cannot do so*) because of the insufficiency of their records and wise men. If those were sufficient, I could adduce them in support of my words."

CHAPTER X. The Master said, "At the great sacrifice, after the pouring out of the libation, I have no wish to look on."

CHAPTER XI. Some one asked the meaning of the great sacrifice. The Master said, "I do not know.

the Shû-ching, V, vii, 5, *et al*), "wise men," had become few. Had Confucius therefore delivered all his knowledge about the two dynasties, he would have exposed his truthfulness to suspicion. 徵, in the sense of 證, "to witness," and, at the end, "to appeal to for evidence." The old commentators, however, interpret the whole differently.—Already in the time of Confucius many of tho records of antiquity had perished.

10. THE SAGE'S DISSATISFACTION AT THE WANT OF PROPRIETY IN CEREMONIES. 禘 is the name belonging to different sacrifices, but here indicates the 大祭, "great sacrifice," which cquld properly be celebrated only by the sovereign The individual sacrificed to in it was the remotest ancestor from whom the founder of the reigning dynasty traced his descent ？ As to who were

his assessors in the sacrifice and how often it was offered;—these are disputed points. See K'ang hsi's dict , char. 禘. Compare also 四書改錯, VII, viii, and 四書拓餘說, 1, xiii. A royal rite, its use in Lû was wrong (see next chap.), but there was something in the service after the early act of libation inviting the descent of the spirits, which more particularly moved the anger of Confucius 而往＝以後, different from 往 in 1. xv.

11. THE PROFOUND MEANING OF THE GREAT SACRIFICE. This chapter is akin to II, xxi. Confucius evades replying to his questioner, it being contrary to Chinese propriety to speak in a country of the faults of its government or rulers 說, "explanation,"＝*meaning*. The anteced. ent to the second 其 is the whole of the preceding clause:—"The relation

其說者、之於
天下也、其如
示諸斯乎。指
其掌。
祭如在、祭
神如神在。子
曰吾不與祭、
如不祭。
王孫賈問
曰與其媚於
奧、寧媚於竈、

He who knew its meaning would find it as easy to govern the kingdom as to look on this;"—pointing to his palm.

CHAPTER XII. 1. He sacrificed *to the dead*, as if they were present. He sacrificed to the spirits, as if the spirits were present.

2. The Master said, "I consider my not being present at the sacrifice, as if I did not sacrifice."

CHAPTER XIII. 1. Wang-sun Chiâ asked, saying, "What is the meaning of the saying, 'It is better to pay court to the furnace than to the southwest corner?'"

to the kingdom of him who knew its meaning;—*that* would be as to look on this." 乎, interjective, more than interrogative. 示=視, "to see." 天下, "under heaven," an ambitious designation for the Chinese Empire, as ἡ οἰκουμένη and *orbis terræ* were used by the Greeks and Romans.

12. CONFUCIUS'S OWN SINCERITY IN SACRIFICING. 1. 祭 here is historical and not to be translated in the imperative. We have to supply an objective to the first 祭, viz., 先祖, *the dead*, his forefathers, as contrasted with 神 in the next clause, =all the "spirits" to which in his official capacity he would have to sacrifice. 2. Observe 與 in the 4th tone, "to be present at," "to take part in."

13 THAT THERE IS NO RESOURCE AGAINST THE CONSEQUENCES OF VIOLATING THE RIGHT. 1. Chiâ was a great officer of Wei (衛), and having the power of the State in his hands insinuated to Confucius that it would be for his advantage to pay court to him. The 奧, or southwest corner, was from the structure of ancient houses the coziest nook, and the place of honor. Chû Hsî explains the proverb by reference to the customs of sacrifice. The furnace was comparatively a mean place, but when the spirit of the furnace was sacrificed to, then the rank of the two places was changed for the time, and the proverb quoted was in vogue. But there does not seem much force in this explanation The *door*, or *well*, or any other of the five things in the regular sacrifices, might take the place of the *furnace*. The old explanation which makes no reference to sacrifice is simpler *Ao* might be the more retired and honorable place, but the *tsâo* was the more important for the support

每　　　　　　　　　　何
事　　　　於　　　不　　謂
問　　　　二　　　然　　也
。　　　　　　　　、　　。
　　　　　　代　　獲　　子
或　　　子　　　罪　　曰
　　子　入　、　於　　、
曰　入　大　　　　　　　二
、　大　廟　二　周　　　而
　　廟　、　代　監　天
周　　　　郁　　、
。　　乎　郁　　無
　　　文　　　　所
　　　哉　吾　　禱
　　　、　從　　也
　　　　　　　　。

2. The Master said, "Not so. He who offends against Heaven has none to whom he can pray."

CHAPTER XIV. The Master said, "Châu had the advantage of viewing the two past dynasties. How complete and elegant are its regulations! I follow Chân."

CHAPTER XV. The Master, when he entered the grand temple, asked about everything. Some one

and comfort of the household. The prince and his immediate attendants might be more honorable than such a minister as Chiâ, but more benefit might be got from him. 媚, from *woman* and *eyebrows*, = "to ogle," "to flatter." 2. Confucius's reply was in a high tone. Chû Hsî says, 天 卽 理 也, "Heaven means principle." But why should Heaven mean principle, if there were not in such a use of the term an instinctive recognition of a supreme government of intelligence and righteousness? We find 天 explained in the 四 書 拓 餘 說 by 高 高 在 上 者, "The lofty One who is on high." A scholar of great ability and research has written to me contending that we ought to find in this chapter a reference to fire worship as having been by the time of Confucius introduced from Persia into China; but I have not found sufficient reference to such an introduction at so early a period. The ordinary explanation seems to me more satisfactory;—simple and sufficient. Ho Yen quotes the words of K'ung An-kwo of our second century on the passage:—"Chiâ held in his hands the government of the State. Wishing to make Confucius pay court to him, he stirred him up in a gentle way by quoting to him a saying common among the people."

14. THE COMPLETENESS AND ELEGANCE OF THE INSTITUTIONS OF THE CHÂU DYNASTY. By the 周 we are specially to understand the founders of the power and polity of the dynasty—the kings Wăn and Wû, and the duke of Châu. The two past dynasties are the Hsiâ and the Shang or Yin. 文 = "elegant regulations."

15. CONFUCIUS IN THE GRAND TEMPLE. 大 (= 太) 廟 was the temple dedicated to the duke of Châu (周 公), and where he was sacrificed to with royal rites. The thing is supposed to have taken place at the beginning of Confucius's official service in Lû, when he went into the temple with other officers to assist at the sacrifice. He had studied all about ceremonies, but he thought it a mark of sincerity

告朔之餼羊。
臺子貢欲去
也。
同科、古之道
主皮爲力不
臺子曰射不
禮也。
子聞之曰、是
大廟、每事問。
子知禮乎、入
孰謂鄹人之

said, "Who will say that the son of the man of Tsâu knows the rules of propriety! He has entered the grand temple and asks about everything." The Master heard the remark, and said, "This is a rule of propriety."

CHAPTER XVI. The Master said, "In archery it is not *going throuyh* the leather which is the principal thing;—because people's strength is not equal. This was the old way."

CHAPTER XVII. 1. Tsze-kung wished to do away with the offering of a sheep connected with the inauguration of the first day of each month.

and earnestness to make minute inquiries about them on the occasion spoken of. 鄹 was the name of the town of which Confucius's father had been governor, who was known therefore as "the man of Tsâu." Confucius would be styled as in the text, only in his early life, or by very ordinary people.—See on page 78.

16. HOW THE ANCIENTS MADE ARCHERY A DISCIPLINE OF VIRTUE. We are not to understand 射不主皮 of all archery among the ancients. The characters are found in the 儀禮, 鄉射, par. 315 of the Chû Sû edition. In the edition of the present dynasty, V, iii, par. 81. There were trials of archery where the strength was tested. Probably Confucius was speaking of some archery of his times, when the strength which could go through the 皮, "skin," or leather, in the middle of the target, was esteemed more than the skill which could hit it.

17. HOW CONFUCIUS CLEAVED TO ANCIENT RITES. 1. The king in the last month of the year gave out to the princes a calendar for the first days of the months of the year ensuing. This was kept in their ancestral temples, and on the 1st of every month they offered a sheep and announced the day, requesting sanction for the duties of the month. This idea of requesting sanction is indicated by 告, read *kŭh*. The dukes of Lû now neglected their part of this ceremony, but the sheep was still offered:—a meaningless formality, it seemed to Tsze-kung. Confucius, however, thought that while any part of the ceremony was retained, there was a better chance of restoring the whole. 去, in the 3rd tone, an active verb, "to put away." It is disputed whether 餼,

子曰、賜也、爾愛其羊、
我愛其禮。

臺子曰事君盡禮、人
以爲諂也。

臺定公問君使臣、臣
事君、如之何。孔子對
曰、君使臣以禮、臣事
君以忠。

臺子曰關雎樂而不
淫、哀而不傷。

臺哀公問社於宰
我。

2. The Master said, "Ts'ze, you love the sheep; I love the ceremony."

CHAPTER XVIII. The Master said, "The full observance of the rules of propriety in serving one's prince is accounted by people to be flattery."

CHAPTER XIX. The duke Ting asked how a prince should employ his ministers, and how ministers should serve their prince. Confucius replied, "A prince should employ his minister according to the rules of propriety; ministers should serve their prince with faithfulness."

CHAPTER XX. The Master said, "The Kwan Tsü is expressive of enjoyment without being licentious, and of grief without being hurtfully excessive."

CHAPTER XXI. 1. The duke Âi asked Tsâi Wo about the altars of the spirits of the land. Tsâi Wo

in the text, mean a *living* sheep, or a sheep killed but not roasted. 2. 愛, in the sense of 愛惜, "to grudge," it is said. But this is hardly necessary.

18. HOW PRINCES SHOULD BE SERVED:—AGAINST THE SPIRIT OF THE TIMES.

19. THE GUIDING PRINCIPLES IN THE RELATION OF PRINCE AND MINISTER. 定, "Greatly anxious, tranquilizer of the people," was the posthumous epithet of 宋, prince of

Lû, 509-495 B. C. 如之何, "As it what?" 之 referring to the two points inquired about.

20. THE PRAISE OF THE FIRST OF THE ODES. 關雎 is the name of the first ode in the Shih-chɪng, and may be translated—"The murmuring of the *ts'ü.*" See Shih-ching, I, i, 1.

21. A RASH REPLY OF TSÂI WO ABOUT THE ALTARS TO THE SPIRITS OF THE LAND, AND LAMENT OF CONFUCIUS THEREON. 1. 哀公, see II, xix. Tsâi Wo, by name 予, and

之器小哉。或
罍子曰管仲
往不咎。
遂事不諫、既
曰、成事不說、
戰栗。子聞之
以栗、曰使民
人以柏、周人
后氏以松、殷
宰我對曰、夏

replied, "The Hsiâ sovereign planted the pine tree about them; the men of the Yin planted the cypress; and the men of the Châu planted the chestnut tree, meaning thereby to cause the people to be in awe."

2. When the Master heard it, he said, "Things that are done, it is needless to speak about; things that have had their course, it is needless to remonstrate about; things that are past, it is needless to blame."

CHAPTER XXII. 1. The Master said, "Small indeed was the capacity of Kwan Chung!"

styled 予 我, was an eloquent disciple of the sage, a native of Lû. His place is the second west among "the wise ones." 社, from 示 (Ch'i), "spirit or spirits of the earth," and 土, "the soil," means 土 地 神 主, "the resting place or altars of the spirits of the land or ground. Wo simply tells the duke that the founders of the several dynasties planted such and such trees about those altars. The reason was that the soil suited such trees; but as 栗, "the chestnut tree," the tree of the existing dynasty, is used in the sense of 慄, "to be afraid," he suggested a reason for its planting which might lead the duke to severe measures against his people to be carried into effect at the altars. Comp. the Shû-ching, IV, ii, 5, "I will put you to death before the 社." 夏 后 氏 is the Great Yu, called 后, to distinguish him from his predecessors, the 帝, and 夏 氏, to distinguish him from 舜. who was 虞 氏, while they

were descended from the same ancestor. See chap. i, on 氏. 殷 人 and 周 人, in parallelism with 夏 后 氏, must mean the founders of these dynasties; why they are simply styled 人, "man," or "men," I have not found clearly explained, though commentators feel it necessary to say something on the point. 2. This is all directed against Wo's reply. He had spoken, and his words could not be recalled.

22. CONFUCIUS'S OPINION OF KWAN CHUNG:—AGAINST HIM. 1. Kwan Chung, by name 夷 吾, is one of the most famous names in Chinese history. He was chief minister to the duke 桓 of 齊 (683–642 B. C.), the first and greatest of the five pa (伯 or 霸), leaders of the princes of the nation under the Châu dynasty. In the times of Confucius and Mencius, people thought more of Kwan than those sages, no hero worshipers, would allow. 器, see II, xii, but its significance here is different,

知禮。

有反坫、管氏而知禮、孰不

兩君之好、有反坫、管氏亦

門、管氏亦樹塞門、邦君爲

管仲知禮乎。曰邦君樹塞

歸官事不攝、焉得儉然則

曰、管仲儉乎。曰管氏有三

2. Some one said, "Was Kwan Chung parsimonious?" "Kwan," was the reply, "had the *San Kwei*, and his officers performed no double duties; how can he be considered parsimonious?"

3. "Then, did Kwan Chung know the rules of propriety?" The Master said, "The princes of States have a screen intercepting the view at their gates. Kwan had likewise a screen at his gate. The princes of States on any friendly meeting between two of them, had a stand on which to place their inverted cups. Kwan had also such a stand. If Kwan knew the rules of propriety, who does not know them?"

and = our *measure* or *capacity*. 2. 三歸, in the dictionary, and the commentary of Chû Hsî, was the name of an extravagant tower built by Kwan. There are other views of the phrase, the oldest and the best supported apparently being that it means "three wives." (A woman's marriage is called 歸.) The *San Kwei* and having no pluralists among his officers proved that he could not be parsimonious. 焉, the 1st tone, "how." 3. 樹, "a tree," here in the sense of 屏, "a screen," the screen of a prince, usurped by Kwan, who was only entitled to the 簾 of a great officer. 好, the 4th tone, = "a friendly meeting." The 坫, from 土 and 占, was a stand, made originally of earth and turf. Kwan usurped the use of it, as he did of the screen; being as regardless of prescribed forms, as in par. 2 of expense, and he came far short therefore of the Confucian idea of the *Chün-tsze*.

之、出曰二三子、何患

嘗不得見也從者見

子之至於斯也、吾未

儀封人請見曰、君

如也、繹如也、以成。

如也、從之、純如也、皦

樂其可知也、始作、翕

子語魯大師樂曰、

CHAPTER XXIII. The Master instructing the Grand music master of Lü said, "How to play music may be known. At the commencement of the piece, all the parts should sound together. As it proceeds, they should be in harmony *while* severally distinct and flowing without break, and thus on to the conclusion."

CHAPTER XXIV. The border warden at Î requested to be introduced to the Master, saying, "When men of superior virtue have come to this, I have never been denied the privilege of seeing them." The followers *of the sage* introduced him, and when he came out from the interview, he said, "My friends, why are you

23. ON THE PLAYING OF MUSIC. 語, the 4th tone, = 告, "to tell," "to instruct." 大 (=太) 師 樂 was the title of the Grand music master. 樂 其 可 知 也, "music, it may be known," but the subject is not of the principles, but the performance of music. Observe the 如. Prémare says, "*adjectivis addita sensum auget et exprimit modum.*" It is our *ly* or *like*,—翕 如, "blended like." 從, the 4th tone, the same as 縱=放, "let go," i. e., proceeding, swelling on.

24. A STRANGER'S VIEW OF THE VOCATION OF CONFUCIUS. Î was a small town on the borders of Wei, referred to a place in the present department of Kaifeng, Honan province. Confucius at the beginning of his wanderings after leaving Lü was retiring from Wei, the prince of which could not employ him. This was the 喪=失位. The 1st and 3rd 見 are read *hsien*, 4th tone, = 通 使 得 見, "to introduce," or "to be introduced." 之 in 君 子 之 至 於 斯 也 has its proper possessive power, —"In the case of a Chun-tsze's coming to this." *Tsung*, the 4th tone, "to attend upon." 二 三 子, "Two or three sons," or "gentlemen," ="my friends." The same idiom occurs elsewhere. The 木 鐸 was a metal bell with a wooden tongue, shaken in making announcements,

臨喪不哀、吾何以觀之哉。

子曰、居上不寬爲禮不敬、

謂武盡美矣、未盡善也。

子謂詔盡美矣、又盡善也、

天將以夫子爲木鐸。

於喪乎、天下之無道也久矣、

distressed by your master's loss of office? The kingdom has long been without the principles *of truth and
right;* Heaven is going to use your master as a bell
with its wooden tongue."

CHAPTER XXV. The Master said of the Shâo that
it was perfectly beautiful and also perfectly good. He
said of the Wû that it was perfectly beautiful but not
.perfectly good.

CHAPTER XXVI. The Master said, "High station
filled without indulgent generosity; ceremonies performed without reverence; mourning conducted without sorrow;—wherewith should I contemplate such
ways?"

or to call people together. Heaven
would employ Confucius to proclaim
the truth and right.

25. THE COMPARATIVE MERITS OF
THE MUSIC OF SHUN AND WÛ. 韶
was the name of the music made by
Shun, perfect in melody and sentiment. 武 was the music of king
Wû, also perfect in melody, but
breathing the martial air, indicative
of its author.

26. THE DISREGARD OF WHAT IS
ESSENTIAL VITIATES ALL SERVICES.
The meaning of the chapter turns
upon 何 以＝何 有, or 以 何 者,
"wherewith." 寬 is essential to
rulers, 敬 to ceremonies, and 哀 to
mourning.

## BOOK IV. LE JIN

利
仁。

仁
者
安
仁、
知
者

不
可
以
長
處
樂、

不
可
以
久
處
約、

畫
子
曰、
不
仁
者、

得
知。

美、
擇
不
處
仁、
焉

畫
子
曰、
里
仁
爲

里
仁
第
四

CHAPTER I. The Master said, "It is virtuous manners which constitute the excellence of a neighborhood. If a man in selecting a residence, do not fix on one where such prevail, how can he be wise?"

CHAPTER II. The Master said, "Those who are without virtue cannot abide long either in a condition of poverty and hardship, or in a condition of enjoyment. The virtuous rest in virtue; the wise desire virtue."

HEADING OF THIS BOOK.—里 仁 第 四, "Virtue in a neighborhood, No. 4."—Such is the title of this fourth Book, which is mostly occupied with the subject of 仁. To render that term invariably by *benevolence*, would by no means suit many of the chapters. See II, i, 2. *Virtue*, as a general term, would answer better. The embodiment of virtue demands an acquaintance with ceremonies and music, treated of in the last Book; and this, it is said, is the eason why the one subject immediately follows the other.

1. RULE FOR THE SELECTION OF A RESIDENCE. According to the 周 禮, five families made a 鄰, and five 鄰 a 里, which we might style, therefore, *a hamlet* or *village*. There are other estimates of the number of its component households. 處, 3rd tone, a verb, "to dwell in." 知, 4th tone,

is the same as 智, "wise," "wisdom." So, not unfrequently, below. Friendship, we have seen, is for the aid of virtue (I, viii, 3), and the same should be the object desired in selecting a residence.

2. ONLY TRUE VIRTUE ADAPTS A MAN FOR THE VARIED CONDITIONS OF LIFE. 約, "to bind," is used for what binds, as an oath, a covenant; and here, the metaphor being otherwise directed, it denotes a condition of poverty and distress. 利, "gain," "profit," used as a verb, = 貪, "to desire," "to covet." 安 仁, "to rest in virtue," being virtuous without effort. 利 仁, "to desire virtue," being virtuous because it is the best policy. Observe how 者 following 仁 and 知 makes those terms adjectives or participles. 不 可, "may not," = 不 能, "cannot." The inability is moral. See 可 in Index VII.

子曰、惟仁者、能好人、能
惡人。

子曰、苟志於仁矣、無惡
也。

子曰、富與貴、是人之所
欲也、不以其道得之不處
也。貧與賤、是人之所惡也、
不以其道得之不去也。君

CHAPTER III. The Master said, "It is only the (*truly*) virtuous man, who can love, or who can hate, others."

CHAPTER IV. The Master said, "If the will be set on virtue, there will be no practice of wickedness."

CHAPTER V. 1. The Master said, "Riches and honors are what men desire. If it cannot be obtained in the proper way, they should not be held. Poverty and meanness are what man dislike. If it cannot be obtained in the proper way, they should not be avoided.

3. ONLY IN THE GOOD MAN ARE EMOTIONS OF LOVE AND HATRED RIGHT, AND TO BE DEPENDED ON. This chapter is incorporated with the 大學傳, X, xv. 好 and 惡 (read *wû*) are both verbs in the 4th tone.

4. THE VIRTUOUS WILL PRESERVES FROM ALL WICKEDNESS. 苟=誠, not merely—"if," but "if really." Comp. the statement, I John iii, 9, "Whosoever is born of God doth not commit sin."

5. THE DEVOTION OF THE CHÜN-TSZE TO VIRTUE. 1. For the antecedent to 之 in the recurring 得之, we are to look to the following verbs, 處 and 去. We might translate the first 不以道得之, "if *they* cannot be obtained, etc.,". but this would not suit the second case. 其道, "*the* way," i. e., the proper way. If we supply a nom. to 處 and 去, it must be 君子;—he will not "abide in," nor "go away from," riches and honors. 2. 惡, read *wû*, the 1st

矣、不使不仁者、加乎其　尙之惡不仁者其爲仁　惡不仁者好仁者無以　子曰、我未見好仁者、　必於是、顛沛必於是。　無終食之閒違仁、造次　子去仁、惡乎成名君子

2.　"If a superior man abandon virtue, how can he fulfill the requirements of that name?

3.　"The superior man does not, even for the space of a single meal, act contrary to virtue.　In moments of haste, he cleaves to it.　In seasons of danger, he cleaves to it."

CHAPTER VI.　1. The Master said, "I have not seen a person who loved virtue, or one who hated what was not virtuous.　He who loved virtue, would esteem nothing above it.　He who hated what is not virtuous, would practice virtue in such a way that he would not allow anything that is not virtuous to approach his person.

tone, "how."　名, "name," not reputation, but the name of a *chüntsze*, which he bears.　3. 終食之間, "The space in which a meal can be *finished*;" meaning a short time.　造次 (interchangeable with 草次) and 顚沛 are well-known expressions, the former for haste and confusion, the latter for change and danger; but it is not easy to trace the attaching of those meanings to the characters.　顚, "to fall down," and 沛, the same, but the former with the face up, the other with the face down.　必於是,—comp. Horace's "*Omnis in hoc sum.*"

6. A LAMENT BECAUSE OF THE RARITY OF THE LOVE OF VIRTUE; AND ENCOURAGEMENT TO PRACTICE VIRTUE.　1. The first four 者 belong to the verbs 好 and 惡, and give them the force of participles.　In 使 不 仁 者, 者 belongs to 不 仁, and 不 仁 者 ＝不 仁 之 事.　Commonly, 者＝"he or those who," but sometimes also＝ "that or those things which."　倘＝ 加, "to add to."　Morrison, character 倘, translates the sentence wrongly—

夕死可矣。　子曰朝聞道、　過斯知仁矣。　也、各於其黨、觀　子曰人之過　未之見也。　者。蓋有之矣、我　我未見力不足　其力於仁矣乎、　身。有能一日用

2. "Is any one able for one day to apply his strength to virtue? I have not seen the case in which his strength would be insufficient.

3. "Should there possibly be any such case, I have not seen it."

CHAPTER VII. The Master said, "The faults of men are characteristic of the class to which they belong. By observing a man's faults, it may be known that he is virtuous."

CHAPTER VIII. The Master said, "If a man in the morning hear the right way, he may die in the evening without regret."

"He who loves virtue and benevolence can have nothing more said in his praise." 3. 蓋 here is 疑 辭, "a particle of doubt:" as often. 未 之 有, a transposition, as in I, ii, 1.

7. A MAN IS NOT TO BE UTTERLY CONDEMNED BECAUSE HE HAS FAULTS. Such is the sentiment found in this chapter, in which we may say, however, that Confucius is liable to the charge brought against Tsze-hsiâ, I, vii. 人 之 過 也 stands absolutely,— "As to the faults of men." 各＝各 人, and 於＝從,—"Each man follows his class." Observe the force of 過, "what goes beyond." The faults are the excesses of the general tendencies. Compare Goldsmith's line, "And even his failings leant to virtue's side."

8. THE IMPORTANCE OF KNOWING THE RIGHT WAY. One is perplexed to translate 道 here. Chú defines it—事 物 當 然 之 理, "the principles of what is right in events and things." Better is the explanation in 四 書 翼 註,—道 即 率 性 之 道, "道 is the path"—i. e., of action— "which is in accordance with our nature." Man is formed for this, and if he die without coming to the knowledge of it, his death is no better than that of a beast. One would fain recognize in such sentences a vague apprehension of some higher truth than Chinese sages have been able to propound.—Ho Yen takes a different view, and makes the whole chapter a lament of Confucius that he was likely to die without hearing of right principles prevailing in the world.—"Could I once hear of the prevalence of right principles, I could die the same evening!" Other views of the meaning have been proposed.

子曰、士志於道、而恥惡衣

惡食者、未足與議也。

子曰君子之於天下也、無

適也、無莫也義之與比。

子曰君子懷德小人懷土、

君子懷刑、小人懷惠。

CHAPTER IX. The Master said, "A scholar, whose mind is set on truth, and who is ashamed of bad clothes and bad food, is not fit to be discoursed with."

CHAPTER X. The Master said, "The superior man, in the world, does not set his mind either for anything, or against anything; what is right he will follow."

CHAPTER XI. The Master said, "The superior man thinks of virtue; the small man thinks of comfort. The superior man thinks of the sanctions of law; the small man thinks of favors *which he may receive*."

9. THE PURSUIT OF TRUTH SHOULD RAISE A MAN ABOVE BEING ASHAMED OF POVERTY. 與 議,—to be discoursed with, i. e., about 道, or "truth," which perhaps is the best translation of the term in places like this.

10. RIGHTEOUSNESS IS THE RULE OF THE CHÚN-TSZE'S PRACTICE. 君子之云云, "The relation of the *Chün-tsze* to the world," i. e., to all things presenting themselves to him. 適, read *ti*, is explained by 專主, "to set the mind exclusively on." We may take the last clause thus—

"his is the according with, and keeping near to (比, the 4th tone,= 從 or 親) righteousness." This gives each character its signification, the 與 blending its meaning with 比.

11. THE DIFFERENT MINDINGS OF THE SUPERIOR AND THE SMALL MAN. *Hwâi* is here emphatic, =*"cherishes* and plans about." 土, "earth," "the ground," is here defined—所 處 之 安, "the rest or comforts one dwells amidst." May it not be used somewhat in our sense of earthly? —"thinks of what is earthly."

子曰、放於利而行、多怨。

子曰、能以禮讓爲國乎、

何有、不能以禮讓爲國如

禮何。

子曰不患無位、患所以

立不患莫己知、求爲可知

也。

CHAPTER XII. The Master said: "He who acts with a constant view to his own advantage will be much murmured against."

CHAPTER XIII. The Master said, "Is *a prince* able to govern his kingdom with the complaisance proper to the rules of propriety, what difficulty will he have? If he cannot govern it with that complaisance, what has he to do with the rules of propriety?"

CHAPTER XIV. The Master said, "*A man should say*, I am not concerned that I have no place, I am concerned how I may fit myself for one. I am not concerned that I am not known, I seek to be worthy to be known."

12. THE CONSEQUENCE OF SELFISH CONDUCT. 放, the 3rd tone, = 依, "to accord with," "to keep along."— "He who acts along the line of gain.'

13. THE INFLUENCE IN GOVERN-MENT OF CEREMONIES OBSERVED IN THEIR PROPER SPIRIT. 禮讓字是二 是一, i. e., they are a hendiadys. 讓 =禮之實, "the sincerity and sub- stance of ceremony," the *spirit* of it. Comp. 和 in I, xii. 爲=治, "to govern." This meaning is found in the dictionary.

14. ADVISING TO SELF-CULTIVA-TION. Comp. I, xvi. Here, as there, 不 not being imperative, we must supply a nominative. 位, "place," i. e., an official situation. 所以立 is to be completed 所以立乎其位.

44 CONFUCIAN ANALECTS 語 論

利。　於義、小人喩於　子曰、君子喩　道忠恕而已矣。　曾子曰、夫子之　人問曰、何謂也。　子曰、唯子出門　道一以貫之。曾　子曰、參乎、吾

CHAPTER XV. 1. The Master said, "Shăn, my doctrine is that of an all-pervading unity." The disciple Tsăng replied, "Yes."

2. The Master went out, and the *other* disciples asked, saying, "What do his words mean?" Tsăng said, "The doctrine of our master is to be true to the principles of our nature and the benevolent exercise of them to others,—this and nothing more."

CHAPTER XVI. The Master said, "The mind of the superior man is conversant with righteousness; the mind of the mean man is conversant with gain."

15. CONFUCIUS'S DOCTRINE THAT OF A PERVADING UNITY. This chapter is said to be the most profound in the *Lun Yü*. 1. 吾道一以貫之;—to myself it occurs to translate, "my doctrines have one thing which goes through them," but such an exposition has not been approved by any Chinese writer. 一以貫之 are made to contain the copula and predicate of 吾道, and 之, it is said, "refers to all affairs and all things." The one thing or unity intended by Confucius was the heart, man's nature, of which all the relations and duties of life are only the development and outgoings. 2. 忠 and 恕, which seem to be two things, are both formed from 心, "the heart," 忠 being compounded of 中, "middle," "center," and 心, and 恕 of 如 "as," and 心. The "center heart"＝I, the *ego;* and the "as heart"＝the I in sympathy with others. 忠 is duty-doing, on a consideration, or from the impulse, of one's own self; 恕 is duty-doing, on the principle of reciprocity. The chapter shows that Confucius only claimed to enforce duties indicated by man's mental constitution. He was simply a moral philosopher. Observe 唯 is the 3rd tone,＝"yes." Some say that 門人 must mean Tsăng's own disciples, and that, had they been those of Confucius, we should have read 弟子. The criticism cannot be depended on. 而已矣 is a very emphatic "and nothing more."

16. HOW RIGHTEOUSNESS AND SELFISHNESS DISTINGUISH THE SUPERIOR MAN AND THE SMALL MAN. 喻=曉, "to understand." 於 is here to be dwelt on, and may be compared with the Hebrew *eth.*

子曰、見賢思齊
焉、見不賢而內自
省也。

子曰、事父母幾
諫、見志不從又敬、
不違、勞而不怨。

子曰、父母在、不
遠遊、遊必有方。

CHAPTER XVII. The Master said, "When we see men of worth, we should think of equaling them; when we see men of a contrary character, we should turn inwards and examine ourselves."

CHAPTER XVIII. The Master said, "In serving his parents, *a son* may remonstrate with them, but gently; when he sees that they do not incline to follow *his advice*, he shows an increased degree of reverence, but does not abandon *his purpose;* and should they punish him, he does not allow himself to murmur."

CHAPTER XIX. The Master said, "While his parents are alive, *the son* may not go abroad to a distance. If he does go abroad, he must have a fixed place to which he goes."

17. THE LESSONS TO BE LEARNED FROM OBSERVING MEN OF DIFFERENT CHARACTERS. Of the final particles 焉 and 也, it is said, 二字顏有抑揚警醒意, "the two characters have something of a repressive, expansive, warning force." Ho Yen's text has a 者 after the second 賢, which is not necessary.

18. HOW A SON MAY REMONSTRATE WITH HIS PARENTS ON THEIR FAULTS. See the 禮記, XI, i, 15. 幾, the 1st tone, "mildly,"=the 下氣, 怡色, 柔聲 of the 內則. 志 is the will of the parents. 又敬=更加孝敬, "again increasing his filial reverence," the 起敬起孝 of the 內則. 不違 is not abandoning his purpose of remonstrance, and not as 包咸 says in the comment given by Ho Yen, 不敢違父母意, "not daring to go against the mind of his parents." 勞= "toiled and pained," what the 內則 says, 撻之流血, "should they beat him till the blood flows."

19. A SON OUGHT NOT TO GO TO A DISTANCE WHERE HE WILL NOT BE ABLE TO PAY THE DUE SERVICES TO HIS PARENTS. 方=一定向, "a fixed direction or quarter," whence he may be recalled, if necessary.

曾子曰以約失之者鮮矣。

躬之不逮也。

曾子曰古者言之不出恥

知也、一則以喜、一則以懼。

曾子曰父母之年、不可不

道、可謂孝矣。

曾子曰、三年無改於父之

CHAPTER XX. The Master said, "If the son for three years does not alter from the way of his father, he may be called filial."

CHAPTER XXI. The Master said, "The years of parents may by no means not be kept in the memory, as an occasion at once for joy and for fear."

CHAPTER XXII. The Master said, "The reason why the ancients did not readily give utterance to their words, was that they feared lest their actions should not come up to them."

CHAPTER XXIII. The Master said, "The cautious seldom err."

20. A REPETITION OF PART OF I, xi.

21. WHAT EFFECT THE AGE OF PARENTS SHOULD HAVE ON THEIR CHILDREN. 知, it is said, conveys here 念 念 不 忘 意, "the meaning of unforgetting thoughtfulness."

22. THE VIRTUE OF THE ANCIENTS SEEN IN THEIR SLOWNESS TO SPEAK. Observe the force of the two 之.— "The not coming forth of the words of the ancients was shame about the not coming up to them of their actions."

23. ADVANTAGE OF CAUTION. Collie's version, which I have adopted, is here happy. 約. see chap. ii. The "binding" here is of one's self, self-restraint, = "caution." 失 之, "loses *it*," 之 referring to whatever business the cautious may be engaged in. 之, after an active verb, often makes it neuter; at least, a neuter verb renders the expression best in English.

數、斯疏矣。

子游曰、事君數斯辱矣、朋友

子曰、德不孤、必有鄰。

行。

子曰、君子欲訥於言、而敏於

CHAPTER XXIV. The Master said, "The superior man wishes to be slow in his speech and earnest in his conduct."

CHAPTER XXV. The Master said, "Virtue is not left to stand alone. *He who practices it* will have neighbors."

CHAPTER XXVI. Tsze-yû said, "In serving a prince, frequent remonstrances lead to disgrace. Between friends, frequent reproofs make the friendship distant."

24. RULE OF THE CHÜN-TSZE ABOUT HIS WORDS AND ACTIONS.

25. THE VIRTUÓUS ARE NOT LEFT ALONE:—AN ENCOURAGEMENT TO VIRTUE. 孤 "fatherless;" here = solitary, friendless. 德不孤＝德無孤立之理, "it is not the nature of virtue to be left to stand alone." 鄰,

see chap. i; here, generally used for friends, associates of like mind.

26. A LESSON TO COUNSELORS AND FRIENDS. 數, the 4th tone, read *sho*, "frequently," understood here in reference to remonstrating or reproving. 斯＝"this," "this leads to," or "thereon is."

## BOOK V.　KUNG-YÊ CH‘ANG

公冶長第五

子謂公冶
長、🈳可妻也、雖
在縲絏之中、
非其罪也。以
其子妻之。
謂南容、邦有
道不廢、邦無
道免於刑戮。
以其兄之子
妻之。

CHAPTER I. 1. The Master said of Kung-yê Ch‘ang that he might be wived; although he was put in bonds, he had not been guilty of any crime. *Accordingly*, he gave him his own daughter to wife.

2. Of Nan Yung he said that if the country were well governed he would not be out of office, and if it were ill governed, he would escape punishment and disgrace. He gave him the daughter of his own elder brother to wife.

HEADING OF THIS BOOK.—一公冶長第五. Kung-yê Ch‘ang, the surname and name of the first individual spoken of in it, heads this Book, which is chiefly occupied with the judgment of the sage on the character of several of his disciples and others. As the decision frequently turns on their being possessed of that zăn, or perfect virtue, which is so conspicuous in the last Book, this is the reason, it is said, why the one immediately follows the other. As Tsze-kung appears in the Book several times, some have fancied that it was compiled by his disciples.

1. CONFUCIUS IN MARRIAGE-MAKING WAS GUIDED BY CHARACTER AND NOT BY FORTUNE. 1. Of Kung-yê Ch‘ang, though the son-in-law of Confucius, nothing certain is known, and his tablet is only 3rd on the west, among the οἱ πολλοί. Silly legends are told of his being put in prison from his bringing suspicion on himself by his knowledge of the language of birds. Chû Hsî approves the interpretation of 縲 as meaning "a black rope," with which criminals were anciently bound (絏) in prison. 妻, and in par. 2, the 3rd tone, "to give a wife to one." 子, in both paragraphs, = "a daughter." Confucius's brother would be the cripple Măng-p‘î;—see p. 78. 2. Nan Yung, another of the disciples, is now 4th, east, in the outer hall. The discussions about who he was, and whether he is to be identified with 南宮适, and several other *aliases*, are very perplexing. 廢, "to lay or be laid aside," *from office*. 戮, "to put to death," has also the lighter meaning of "disgrace." We cannot tell whether Confucius is giving his impression of Yung's character, or referring to events that had taken place.

子謂子賤、君子

哉若人魯無君子

者、斯焉取斯。

子貢問曰、賜也

何如子曰、女器也。

曰、何器也。曰、瑚璉

也。

或曰、雍也仁、而

CHAPTER II. The Master said of Tsze-chien, "Of superior virtue indeed is such a men! If there were not virtuous men in Lû, how could this man have acquired this character?"

CHAPTER III. Tsze-kung asked, "What do you say of me, Ts'ze?" The Master said, "You are a utensil." "What utensil?" "A gemmed sacrificial utensil."

CHAPTER IV. 1. Some one said, "Yung is truly virtuous, but he is not ready with his tongue."

2. THE CHÜN-TSZE FORMED BY INTERCOURSE WITH OTHER CHÜN-TSZE. Tsze-chien, by surname 宓 (=宓, and said to be i. q. 伏), and named 不齊, appears to have been of some note among the disciples of Confucius as an administrator, though his tablet is now only 2nd, west, in the outer hall. See the Narratives of the School, chap. xxxviii. What chiefly distinguished him, as appears here, was his cultivation of the friendship of men of ability and virtue. 若人=若此人, "a man such as this." See the 註疏 in loc. The first 斯 is "this man"; the second, "this virtue." The paraphrasts complete the last clause thus:—斯將何所取以成斯德乎, "what friends must this man have chosen to complete this virtue!"

3. WHERETO TSZE-KUNG HAD ATTAINED. See I, x; II, xiii. The 瑚

璉 were vessels richly adorned, used to contain grain offerings in the royal ancestral temples. Under the Hsiâ dynasty they were called 璉, and 瑚 under the Yin. See the Lî Chî, XII, ii. While the sage did not grant to Ts'ze that he was a Chün-tsze (II, xii), he made him "a vessel of honor," valuable and fit for use on high occasions.

4. OF ZAN YUNG:—READINESS WITH THE TONGUE NO PART OF VIRTUE. 1. 冉雍, styled 仲弓, has his tablet the 2nd, on the east, among the wise ones. His father was a worthless character (see VI, iv) but he himself was the opposite. 佞 means "ability," generally; then, "ability of speech," often, though not here, with the bad sense of artfulness and flattery. 2. Confucius would not grant that Yung was 仁, but his not being 佞 was in his favor rather

梓浮于海從我者、
饗子曰道不行乘
信子説。
對曰吾斯之未能
子使漆雕開仕。
用佞。
於人不知其仁焉
饗人以口給屢憎
不佞子曰、焉用佞、

2. The Master said, "What is the good of being ready with the tongue? They who encounter men with smartnesses of speech for the most part procure themselves hatred. I know not whether he be truly virtuous, but why should he show readiness of the tongue?"

CHAPTER V. The Master was wishing Ch'î-tiâo K'âi to enter on official employment. He replied, "I am not yet able to rest in the assurance of THIS." The Master was pleased.

CHAPTER VI. The Master said, "My doctrines make no way. I will get upon a raft, and float about on the sea. He that will accompany me will be Yû,

than otherwise: 口 給 (read *chieh*: see dict.), "smartnesses of speech." 焉 is here "why," rather than "how." The first 焉 用 仁 is a general statement, not having special reference to Zan Yung. In the 註 疏, 不知其仁焉用佞 is read as one sentence —"I do not know how the virtuous should also use readiness of speech."

5. CH'Î-TIÂᴏ K'ÂI's OPINION OF THE QUALIFICATIONS NECESSARY TO TAKING OFFICE. Ch'î-tiâo, now 6th, on the east, in the outer hall, was styled 子 若. His name originally was 啓, changed into 開 on the accession of the emperor 孝 景, 156 B.C., whose name was also 啓.

The difficulty is with 斯 — what does it refer to? and with 信 — what is its force? In the chapter about the disciples in the 家 語, it is said that K'ai was reading in the Shú-ching, when Confucius spoke to him about taking office, and he pointed to the book, or some particular passage in it, saying, "I am not yet able to rest in the assurance of (信＝眞 知 確 見) *this.*" It may have been so. Obs. the force of the 之.

6. CONFUCIUS ·PROPOSING TO WITHDRAW FROM THE WORLD:—A LESSON TO TSZE-LÙ. Tsze-lù supposed his master really meant to leave the world, and the idea of floating along the coasts pleased his

其由與子路聞之喜子
曰、由也好勇過我、無所
取材。
孟武伯問子路仁乎。
子曰不知也又問子曰、
由也千乘之國可使治
其賦也不知其仁也。
也何如子曰、求也千室

I dare to say." Tsze-lû hearing this was glad, upon
which the Master said, "Yû is fonder of daring than I
am. He does not exercise his judgment upon matters."

CHAPTER VII. 1. Măng Wû asked about Tsze-lû,
whether he was perfectly virtuous. The Master said,
"I do not know."

2. He asked again, when the Master replied, "In
a kingdom of a thousand chariots, Yû might be
employed to manage the military levies, but I do not
know whether he be perfectly virtuous."

3. "And what do you say of Ch'iû?" The Master
replied, "In a city of a thousand families, or a clan of

ardent temper. But Confucius only
expressed in this way his regret at
the backwardness of men to receive
his doctrines. 無所取材 is difficult
of interpretation. Chû Hsî takes 材
as being for 裁, "to cut out clothes,"
"to estimate, discriminate," and
hence the meaning in the translation.
鄭 玄, keeping the meaning of 材,
explains—無 所 取 於 桴 材,= "my
meaning is not to be found in the
*raft*." Another old writer makes
材=哉, and putting a stop at 勇

explains—"Yû is fond of daring;
he cannot go beyond himself to find
my meaning."

7. OF TSZE-LÛ, TSZE-YÛ, AND
TSZE-HWÂ. 1. 孟 武 伯, see II, vi.
2. 千 乘 之 國, see I, v. 賦, properly "revenues," "taxes," but the
quota of soldiers contributed being
regulated by the amount of the
revenue, the term is used here for
the forces, or *military levies*. 3. 求,
see III, vi. 百 乘 之 家, in opposition
to 千 乘 之 國, was the seconÿary

以知十賜也、聞一以

何敢望回、回也、聞一

回也、孰愈對曰、賜也、

子謂子貢曰、女與

仁也。

與賓客言也、不知其

也、束帶立於朝、可使

也。赤也何如子曰、赤

爲之宰也、不知其仁

之邑、百乘之家、可使

a hundred chariots, Ch'iû might be employed as governor, but I do not know whether he is perfectly virtuous."

4. "What do you say of Ch'ih?" The Master replied, "With his sash girt and standing in a court, Ch'ih might be employed to converse with the visitors and guests, but I do not know whether he is perfectly virtuous."

CHAPTER VIII. 1. The Master said to Tsze-kung, "Which do you consider superior, yourself or Hûi?"

2. Tsze-kung replied, "How dare I compare myself with Hûi? Hûi hears one point and knows all about a subject; I hear one point and know a second."

fief, the territory appropriated to the highest nobles or officers in a 國 or state, supposed also to comprehend 1,000 families. 爲 之 宰, "to be its governor." This is a peculiar idiom, something like the double object in Latin. 4. Ch'ih, surnamed 公 西, and styled 子 華, having now the 14th place, west, in the outer hall, was famous among the disciples for his knowledge of rules of ceremony, and those especially relating to dress and intercourse. 朝, in 2nd tone. 賓 and 客 may be distinguished, the former indicating neighboring princes visiting the court; the latter, ministe s and officers of the state present as guests.

8. SUPERIORITY OF YEN HÛI TO TSZE-KUNG.. 2. 望, "to look to," "to look up to," here＝比, "to compare with." "One" is the beginning of numbers, and "ten" the completion; hence the meaning of 聞 一 以

知二子曰、弗如也、吾與女、弗

如也。

鑿宰予晝寢子曰、朽木不可

雕也、糞土之牆、不可杇也、於

予與何誅子曰、始吾於人也、

聽其言而信其行、今吾於人

也、聽其言而觀其行、於予與

改是。

3. The Master said, "You are not equal to him. I grant you, you are not equal to him."

CHAPTER IX. 1. Tsâi Yü being asleep during the daytime, the Master said, "Rotten wood cannot be carved; a wall of dirty earth will not receive the trowel. This Yü!—what is the use of my reproving him?"

2. The Master said, "At first, my way with men was to hear their words, and give them credit for their conduct. Now my way is to hear their words, and look at their conduct. It is from Yü that I have learned to make this change."

知 十, as in the translation. 3. 與＝ 許, "to allow," "to grant to." Ho Yen gives here the comm. of 包 咸 (about A.D. 50), who interprets strangely,—"I and you are both not equal to him," saying that Confucius thus comforted Tsze-kung.

9. THE IDLENESS OF TSÂI YÜ AND ITS REPROOF. 1. 於 子 與, "In the case of Yü!" 與 has here the force of an exclamation; so below. 誅, a strong term, to mark the severity of the reproof. 2. 子 曰 is superfluous. The characters were probably added by a transcriber. If not, they should head another chapter. Tsâi Yü,— the same as Tsâi Wo in III, xxi.

子曰、吾未見剛者。或對

曰、申棖。子曰、棖也慾、焉得

剛。

子貢曰、我不欲人之加

諸我也、吾亦欲無加諸人。

子曰、賜也。非爾所及也。

CHAPTER X. The Master said, "I have not seen a firm and unbending man." Some one replied, "There is Shăn Ch'ang." "Ch'ang," said the Master, "is under the influence of his passions; how can he be pronounced firm and unbending?"

CHAPTER XI. Tsze-kung said, "What I do not wish men to do to me, I also wish not to do to men." The Master said, "Ts'ze, you have not attained to that."

10. UNBENDING VIRTUE CANNOT COEXIST WITH INDULGENCE OF THE PASSIONS. Shăn Ch'ang (there are several *aliases*, but they are disputed) was one of the minor disciples, of whom little or nothing is known. He was styled 子周, and his place is 31st, east, in the outer ranges. 剛 is to be understood with reference to virtue. 慾 is 情所好, "what the passions love," "lusts." 焉 得 are said to＝不 是, and not 不 能. I have translated accordingly.

11. THE DIFFICULTY OF ATTAINING TO THE NOT WISHING TO DO TO OTHERS AS WE WISH THEM NOT TO DO TO US. It is said—此 章 見 無 我 之 不 易 及, "this chapter shows that the *no I* (freedom from selfishness) is not easily reached." In the 中 庸, XIII, iii, it is said—施 諸 己 而 不 願 亦 勿 施 諸 人, "what you do not like when done to yourself, do not do to others." The difference between it and the sentence here is said to be that of 恕, "reciprocity"; and 仁, "benevolence," or the highest virtue, apparent in the adverbs 勿 and 無, the one prohibitive, and the other a simple, unconstrained negation. The golden rule of the Gospel is higher than both,—"Do ye unto others as ye would that others should do unto you." 諸＝於; 加 諸, or 加 於, "to add upon," "to do to."

何　子　行　子　得　之　章　子
以　貢　、　路　而　言　、　貢
謂　問　唯　有　聞　性　可　曰
之　曰　恐　聞　也　與　得　、
文　、　有　、　。　天　而　夫
也　孔　聞　未　　　道　聞　子
子　文　。　之　　　、　也　之
曰　子　　　能　　　不　、　文
、　、　　　　　　　可　夫
　　　　　　　　　　　　子

CHAPTER XII. Tsze-kung said, "The Master's *personal* displays *of his principles* and *ordinary* descriptions of them may be heard. His discourses about *man's* nature, and the way of Heaven, cannot be heard."

CHAPTER XIII. When Tsze-lû heard anything, if he had not yet succeeded in carrying it into practice, he was only afraid lest he should hear *something else*.

CHAPTER XIV. Tsze-kung asked, saying, "On what ground did Kung-wăn get that title of WĂN?" The

12. THE GRADUAL WAY IN WHICH CONFUCIUS COMMUNICATED HIS DOCTRINES. So the lesson of this chapter is summed up but there is hardly another more perplexing to a translator. 文 章 is the common name for essays, elegant literary compositions. Of course that meaning is out of the question. Whatever is *figured* and *brilliant* is 文; whatever is *orderly* and *defined* is 章. The comm., accordingly, make 文 to be the deportment and manners of the sage, and 章 his ordinary discourses, but 聞 is an inappropriate term with reference to the former. These things, however, were level to the capacities of the disciples generally, and they had the benefit of them. As to his views about man's nature, as the gift of Heaven, and the way of Heaven generally; these he only communicated to those who were prepared to receive them, and Tsze-kung is supposed to have expressed himself thus, after being on some occasion so privileged.

13. THE ARDOR OF TSZE-LÛ IN PRACTICING THE MASTER'S INSTRUCTIONS. The concluding 唯 恐 有 聞 is to be completed 唯 恐 復 有 所 聞 as in the translation.

14. AN EXAMPLE OF THE PRINCIPLE ON WHICH HONORARY POSTHUMOUS TITLES WERE CONFERRED. 文, corresponding nearly to our "accomplished," was the posthumous title given to 子 圉, an officer

敏而好學、不恥
下問、是以謂之
文也。

子謂子產、有
君子之道四焉、
其行己也恭、其
事上也敬、其養
民也惠、其使民
也義。

子曰、晏平仲、
善與人交、久而
敬之。

Master said, "He was of an active nature and yet fond of learning, and he was not ashamed to ask *and learn of* his inferiors!—On these grounds he has been styled WĂN."

CHAPTER XV. The Master said of Tsze-ch'an that he had four of the characteristics of a superior man— in his conduct of himself, he was humble; in serving his superior, he ·was respectful; in nourishing the people, he was kind; in ordering the people, he was just."

CHAPTER XVI. The Master said, "Yen P'ing knew well how to maintain friendly intercourse. The acquaintance might be long, but he showed the· *same* respect *as at first*."

of the same surname of the State of Wei, and a contemporary of Confucius. Many of his actions had been of a doubtful character, which made Tszo-kung stumble at the application to him of so honorable an epithet. But Confucius shows that, whatever he might otherwise have been, he *had* those qualities which justified his being so denominated. The rule for posthumous titles in China has been, and is, very much—"*De mortuis nit nisi bonum.*"

15. THE EXCELLENT QUALITIES OF TSZE-CH'AN. Tsze-ch'an, named 公 孫 僑, was the chief minister of the State of Chăng (鄭), the ablest, perhaps, and most upright of all the statesmen among Confucius's contemporaries. The sage wept when he heard of his death. The old interpreters take 使 in the sense of "employing," but it seems to express more, and="ordering," "regulating."

16. HOW TO MAINTAIN FRIENDSHIP. "Familiarity breeds contempt," and with contempt friendship ends. It' was not so with Yen P'ing, another of the worthies of Confucius's time. He was a principal minister of Ch'i (齊) by name 嬰. P'ing (="Ruling and averting calamity") was his posthumous title. If we were to render 仲, the name would be "Yen P'ing, *secundus.*" The antecedent to 之 is 人.

子曰、臧文仲、居蔡、

山節藻梲、何如其知

也。

子張問曰令尹子

文三仕爲令尹、無喜

色、三已之無愠色、舊

令尹之政、必以告新

令尹、何如。子曰、忠

矣。

CHAPTER XVII. The Master said, "Tsang Wăn kept a large tortoise in a house on the capitals of the pillars of which he had hills made, with representations of duckweed on the small pillars *above the beams supporting the rafters.*—Of what sort was his wisdom?"

CHAPTER XVIII. 1. Tsze-chang asked, saying, "The minister Tsze-wăn thrice took office, and manifested no joy in his countenance. Thrice he retired from office, and manifested no displeasure. He made it a point to inform the new minister of the way in which he had conducted the government;—what do you say of him?" The Master replied, "He was

17. THE SUPERSTITION OF TSANG WĂN. Tsang Wăn (Wăn is the honorary epithet, and 仲 see last chapter) had been a great officer in Lû, and left a reputation for wisdom, which Confucius did not think was deserved. His full name was 臧孫辰. He was descended from the duke 孝 (794–767 B.C.), whose son was styled 子臧. This Tsang was taken by his descendants as their surname. Such was one of the ways in which surnames were formed among the Chinese. 蔡, "a large tortoise," so called, because the State of Ts'âi was famous for its tortoises. 居 is used as an active

verb, = 藏. The 節 = 柱頭斗棋, "the capitals of the pillars." The 梲 may be seen in any Chinese house where the whole structure of the roof is displayed and these small pillars are very conspicuous. The old critics make the keeping such a tortoise an act of usurpation on the part of Tsang Wăn. Chû Hsî finds the point of Confucius's words in the keeping it in such a style.

18. THE PRAISE OF PERFECT VIRTUE IS NOT TO BE LIGHTLY ACCORDED. 1. Ling-yin, lit., "good corrector," was the name given to the chief minister of Ch'û (楚). 尹 is still applied to officers: e. g., the prefect

曰、仁矣乎。曰、未知、焉得
仁。崔子弒齊君陳文子
有馬十乘、棄而違之、至
於他邦、則曰、猶吾大夫
崔子也違之之一邦、則
又曰猶吾大夫崔子也、
違之、何如。子曰、清矣。曰、
仁矣乎。曰、未知、焉得仁。
🐛季文子三思而後行。
子聞之曰、再、斯可矣。

loyal." "Was he perfectly virtuous?" "I do not know. How can he be pronounced perfectly virtuous?"

2. *Tsze-chang* proceeded, "When the officer Ch'ûi killed the prince of Ch'î, Ch'ăn Wăn, though he was the owner of forty horses, abandoned them and left the country. Coming to another state, he said, 'They are here like our great officer, Ch'ûi,' and left it. He came to a second state, and with the same observation left it also;—what do you say of him?" The Master replied, "He was pure." "Was he perfectly virtuous?" "I do not know. How can he be pronounced perfectly virtuous?"

CHAPTER XIX. Chî Wăn thought thrice, and then acted. When the Master was informed of it, he said, "Twice may do."

of a department is called 府 尹. Tsze-wăn, surnamed 鬭, and named 穀 於 菟 ("suckled by a tiger"), had been noted for the things mentioned by Tsze-chang, but the sage would not concede that he was therefore 仁. 2. 崔 was a great officer of Ch'î. Yen P'ing (chap. xvi) distinguished himself on the occasion of the murder (547 B.C) here referred to. Ch'ăn Wăn was likewise an officer of Ch'î. 之 一 邦, 之 is a verb,＝往. 乘, 4th tone, as in I, vi, but with a different meaning,＝"a team of four horses."

19. PROMPT DECISION GOOD. Wăn was the posthumous title of 季 行 父, a faithful and disinterested officer of Lû. 三, 4th tone, "three times," but some say it＝二 三, "again and again." Comp. Robert Hall's remark—"In matters of conscience first thoughts are best."

子曰、甯武子、邦

有道、則知、邦無道、

則愚、其知可及也、

其愚不可及也。

子在陳曰、歸與

歸與、吾黨之小子、

狂簡、斐然成章、不

知所以裁之。

CHAPTER XX. The Master said, "When good order prevailed in his country, Ning Wû acted the part of a wise man. When his country was in disorder, he acted the part of a stupid man. Others may equal his wisdom, but they cannot equal his stupidity."

CHAPTER XXI. When the Master was in Ch'ǎn, he said, "Let me return! Let me return! The little children of my school are ambitious and too hasty. They are accomplished and complete so far, but they do not know how to restrict and shape themselves."

20. THE UNCOMMON BUT ADMIRABLE STUPIDITY OF NING WÛ. Ning Wû (武, honorary epithet; see II, vi) was an officer of Wei in the time of Wǎn (660–635 B.C.). In the first part of his official life the State was quiet and prosperous, and he "wisely" acquitted himself of his duties. Afterwards came confusion. The prince was driven from the throne, and Ning Yü (兪 was his name) might, like other wise men, have retired from the danger. But he "foolishly," as it seemed, chose to follow the fortunes of his prince, and yet adroitry brought it about in the end, that the prince was reinstated and order restored.

21. THE ANXIETY OF CONFUCIUS ABOUT THE TRAINING OF HIS DISCIPLES. Confucius was thrice in Ch'ǎn. It must have been the third time, when he thus expressed himself. He was then over sixty years, and being convinced that he was not to see for himself the triumph of his principles, he became the more anxious about their transmission, and the training of the disciples in order to do that. Such is the common view of the chapter. Some say, however, that it is not to be understood of all the disciples. Compare Mencius, VII, ii, ch. 37. 吾黨之小子, an affectionate way of speaking of the disciples. 狂, "mad," also "extravagant," "high-minded." The 狂 are naturally 簡, hasty and careless of minutiæ. 斐然, "accomplished-like," 章, see chap. xii. 成章, "something complete." 裁, see chap. vi, but its application here is somewhat different. The antecedent to 之 is all the preceding description.

子曰、伯夷
叔齊、不念舊
惡、怨是用希。
子曰、孰謂
微生高直、或
乞醯焉、乞諸
其鄰而與之。
子曰巧言
令色、足恭、左

CHAPTER XXII. The Master said, "Po-î and Shû-ch'i did not keep the former wickednesses of men in mind, and hence the resentments directed towards them were few."

CHAPTER XXIII. The Master said, "Who says of Wei-shang Kâo that he is upright? One begged some vinegar of him, and he begged it of a neighbor and gave it to the man."

CHAPTER XXIV. The Master said, "Fine words, an insinuating appearance, and excessive respect;—

22. THE GENEROSITY OF PO-î AND SHÛ-CH'Î AND ITS EFFECTS. These were ancient worthies of the closing period of the Shang dynasty. Compare Mencius, II, i, ch. 2, *et al.* They were brothers, sons of the king of Kû-chû (孤 竹), named respectively 允 and 致. Î and Ch'î are their honorary epithets, and 伯 and 叔 only indicate their relation to each other as elder and younger. Po-î and Shû-ch'î, however, are in effect their names in the mouths and writings of the Chinese. Kû-chû was a small state, included in the present department of 永 平, in Peichili. Their father left his kingdom to Shû-ch'î, who refused to take the place of his elder brother. Po-î in turn declined the throne; so they both abandoned it, and retired into obscurity. When King Wû was taking his measures against the tyrant Châu, they made their appearance, and remonstrated against his course. Finally, they died of hunger, rather than live under the new dynasty. They were celebrated for their purity, and aversion to men whom they considered bad, but Confucius here brings out their generosity. 怨 是 用 希＝怨 是 以 希, "Resentments thereby were few."

23. SMALL MEANNESSES INCONSISTENT WITH UPRIGHTNESS. It is implied that Kâo gave the vinegar as from himself. He was a native of Lû, with a reputation better than he deserved to have.

24. PRAISE OF SINCERITY, AND OF TSO CH'IÛ-MING. 巧言令色, see I, iii. 足 恭, "excessive respect," 足 being in the 4th tone read *tsŭ.* Some of the old commentators, keeping the usual tone and meaning of 足, interpret the phrase of movements of the "feet" to indicate respect. The discussions about Tso Ch'iû-ming are endless. See 拓 餘 説. I,

而無憾。顏淵曰、願
裘、與朋友共、敝之
路曰、願車馬、衣輕
曰、盍各言爾志子
顏淵季路侍子
恥之。
左丘明恥之、丘亦
之、匿怨而友其人、
丘明恥之、丘亦恥

Tso Ch'iû-ming was ashamed of them. I also am ashamed of them. To conceal resentment against a person, and appear friendly with him;—Tso Ch'iû-ming was ashamed of such conduct. I also am ashamed of it."

CHAPTER XXV. 1. Yen Yüan and Chî Lû being by his side, the Master said to them; "Come, let each of you tell his wishes."

2. Tsze-lû said, "I should like, having chariots and horses, and light fur dresses, to share them with my friends, and though they should spoil them, I would not be displeased."

3. Yen Yüan said, "I should like not to boast of

xxx. It is sufficient for us to rest in the judgment of the commentator 程, that "he was an ancient of reputation." It is not to be received that he was a disciple of Confucius, the same whose supplement to the Ch'un Ch'iû chronicles the death of the sage, and carries on the history for many subsequent years. 丘 was the name of Confucius. The Chinese decline pronouncing it, always substituting Mâu (某), "such an one," for it.

25. THE DIFFERENT WISHES OF YEN- YÜAN, TSZE-LÛ, AND CONFUCIUS. 1. 盍各言爾志, "why not each tell your will?" 2. A student is apt to translate—"I should like to have chariots and horses, etc.," but 共 is the important word in the paragraph, and under the regimen of 願. 衣, the 4th tone, "to wear." Several writers carry the regimen of 願 on to 之 and removing the comma at 共, read 共敝 together, but this construction is not so good. 3. In Ho Yen's compilation 施勞 is interpreted, not to impose troublesome affairs ou others. Chû Hsî's

無伐善、無施勞。子
路曰願聞子之志。
子曰老者安之、朋
友信之少者懷之。
子曰已矣乎、吾
未見能見其過、而
內自訟者也。
子曰十室之邑、
必有忠信如丘者
焉不如丘之好學
也。

my excellence, nor to make a display of my meritorious deeds."

4. Tsze-lû then said, "I should like, sir, to hear your wishes." The Master said, "*They are*, in regard to the aged, to give them rest; in regard to friends, to show them sincerity; in regard to the young, to treat them tenderly."

CHAPTER XXVI. The Master said, "It is all over. I have not yet seen one who could perceive his faults, and inwardly accuse himself."

CHAPTER XXVII. The Master said, "In a hamlet of ten families, there may be found one honorable and sincere as I am, but not so fond of learning."

view is better. 4. 信 之＝與 之 以 信, "To be with them with sincerity."—The Master and the disciples, it is said, agreed in being devoid of selfishness. Hûi's, however, was seen in a higher style of mind and object than Yú's. In the sage there was an unconsciousness of self, and without any effort he proposed acting in regard to his classification of men just as they ought severally to be acted to.

26. A LAMENT OVER MEN'S PERSISTENCE IN ERROR. The 乎 has an exclamatory force. 訟, "to litigate." 內 自 訟 者, "one who brings himself before the bar of his conscience." The remark affirms a fact, inexplicable on Confucius's view of the nature of man. But perhaps such an exclamation should not be pressed too closely.

27. THE HUMBLE CLAIM OF CONFUCIUS FOR HIMSELF. 邑 (人 聚 會 之 稱 也) is "the designation of the place where men are collected together," and may be applied from a hamlet upwards to a city. 忠＝忠 厚, "honorable," "substantial." Confucius thus did not claim higher natural and moral qualities than others, but sought to perfect himself by learning.

## BOOK VI.　YUNG YEY

臨其民、不亦可
居敬而行簡以
可也、簡仲弓曰、
子桑伯子。
使南面。仲弓問
子曰雍也、可
雍也第六

CHAPTER I.　1. The Master said, "There is Yung!— He might occupy the place of a prince."

2. Chung-kung asked about Tsze-sang Po-tsze. The Master said, "He may pass. He does not mind small matters."

3. Chung-kung said, "If a man cherish in himself a reverential feeling *of the necessity of attention to business*, though he may be easy in small matters in his government of the people, that may be allowed.　But

HEADING OF THIS BOOK.—雍也第 六. "There is Yung.　Commences the first chapter, and stands as the title of the Book.　Its subjects are in such akin to those of the preceding Book, and therefore, it is said, they are in juxtaposition.

1. THE CHARACTERS OF NAN YUNG AND TSZE-SANG PO-TSZE AS REGARDS THEIR APTITUDE FOR GOVERNMENT.　1. Yung, V, iv, 可 使 南 面, "might be employed with his face to the south."　In China the sovereign sits facing the south.　So did the princes of the states in their several courts in Confucius's time. An explanation of the practice is attempted in the Yi-ching.　説 卦, chap. ix, 離 也 者 明 也, 萬 物 皆 相 見. 南 方 之 卦 也, 聖 人 南 面 而 聽 天 下. 向 明 而 治 蓋 取 此 也. "The

diagram Lî conveys the idea of brightness, when all things are exhibited to one another.　It is the diagram of the south.　The custom of the sage (i. e., monarchs), to sit with their faces to the south, *and listen to the representations* of all in the kingdom, governing towards the bright region, was taken from this." 2. Chung-kung was the designation of Zan Yung, see V, iv.　簡 has here substantially the same meaning as in V, xxi, = 不 煩, "not troubling," i. e., one's self about small matters. With reference to that place, however, the dict., after the old comm., explains it by 大, "great."　Of Tsze-sang Po-tsze we know nothing certain but what is here stated. Chû Hsî seems to be wrong in approving the identification of him

者
也。

死
矣、
今
也
則
亡、
未
聞
好
學

不
遷
怒、
不
貳
過
不
幸
短
命

孔
子
對
曰
有
顏
回
者
好
學、

二
十
八
哀
公
問
弟
子
孰
爲
好
學。

乎
子
曰、
雍
之
言
然。

乎、
居
簡
而
行
簡、
無
乃
大
簡

if he cherish in himself that easy feeling, and also
carry it out in his practice, is not such an easy mode
of procedure excessive?"

4. The Master said, "Yung's words are right."

CHAPTER II. 1. The duke Âi asked which of the
disciples loved to learn. 2. Confucius replied to him,
"There was Yen Hûi; HE loved to learn. He did not
transfer his anger; he did not repeat a fault. Unfortunately, his appointed time was short and he died;
and now there is not *such another*. I have not yet
heard of any one who loves to learn *as he did*." .

with the Tsze-sang Hû of Chwang-
tsze, VI, par. 11. 3. 居敬, "to
dwell in respect," to have the mind
imbued with it. 敬＝敬事 as in
I, v.

2. THE RARITY OF A TRUE LOVE TO
LEARN. HÛI'S SUPERIORITY TO THE
OTHER DISCIPLES. In 有顏回者,
者＝"that."—"There was that Yen
Hûi." "He did not transfer his

anger," i. e., his anger was no tumul-
tuary passion in the mind, but was
excited by some specific cause, to
which alone it was directed. 短命
死矣＝"he died an early death,"
but 命 conveys also the idea in the
translation. The two last clauses
are completed thus:—今也, 則亡
(read as, and＝無) 是人, 未聞如是
之好學者也.

子華使於齊、冉子
爲其母請粟子曰。與
之釜。請益。曰與
冉子與之粟五秉。
曰、赤之適齊也乘肥
馬、衣輕裘、吾聞之也、
君子周急不繼富原
思爲之宰、與之粟九

CHAPTER III. 1. Tsze-hwâ being employed on a mission to 'Ch'î, the disciple Zan requested grain for his mother. The Master said, "Give her a *fû*." *Yen* requested more. "Give her a *yü*," said the Master. Yen gave her five *ping*.

2. The Master said, "When Ch'ih was proceeding to Ch'î, he had fat horses to his carriage, and wore light furs. I have heard that a superior man helps the distressed, but does not add to the wealth of the rich."

3. Yüan Sze being made governor *of his town by the Master*, he gave him nine hundred measures of grain, but Sze declined them.

3. DISCRIMINATION OF CONFUCIUS IN REWARDING OR SALARYING OFFICERS. Kung-hsî Ch'ih, styled Tsze-hwâ;—see V, vii, 3. 1. 使, in the 4th tone, "to commission," or "to be commissioned." Chû Hsî says the commission was a private one from Confucius, but this is not likely. The old interpretation makes it a public one from the court of Lû; see 四 書 改 錯, III, ix. 冉 子, "the disciple Zan;" see III, vi. Zan is here styled 子, like 有 子, in I, ii, but only in narrative, not as introducing any wise utterance. A *fû* contained 6 *tâu* (斗) and 4 *shăng* (升), or 64 *shăng*. The *yü* contained 160 *shăng*, and the *ping* 16 *hŏ* (斛), or 1600 *shăng*. A *shăng* of the present day is about one fourth less than an English pint. 2. The 之 in 吾 聞 之 refers to what follows. 3. In Ho Yen's edition, another chapter commences here. Yüan Sze, named 憲, is now the 3rd, east, in the outer hall of the temples. He was noted for his pursuit of truth, and carelessness of worldly advantages. After the death of Confucius, he withdrew into retirement in Wei. It is related by

川其舍諸。

子、騂且角、雖欲勿用、山

子謂仲弓曰、犁牛之

里鄉黨乎。

百、辭。子曰毋、以與爾鄰

4. The Master said, "Do not decline them. May you not give them away in the neighborhoods, hamlets, towns, and villages?"

CHAPTER IV. The Master, speaking of Chung-kung, said, "If the calf of a brindled cow be red and horned, although men may not wish to use it, would *the spirits of* the mountains and rivers put it aside?"

Chwang-tsze that Tsze-kung, high in official station, came one day in great style to visit him. Sze received him in a tattered coat, and Tsze-kung asking him if he were ill, he replied, "I have heard that to have no money is to be poor, and that to study truth and not be able to find it is to be ill." This answer sent Tsze-kung away in confusion. The 900 measures (whatever they were) was the proper allowance for an officer in Sze's station. 爲之宰, see V, vii, though it is not easy to give the 之 the same reference here as in that passage. 4. According to ancient statutes a *lin*, a *li*, a *hsiang*, and a *tang*, had each their specific number of component families, but the meaning is no more than—"the poor about you." 乎 makes the remark = "may you not, etc."

4. THE VICES OF A FATHER SHOULD NOT DISCREDIT A VIRTUOUS SON. The father of Chung-kung (see V, ii) was a man of bad character, and some would have visited this upon his son, which drew forth Confucius's remark. The rules of the Châu dynasty required that sacrificial victims should be red, and have good horns. An animal with those qualities, though it might spring from one not possessing them, would certainly not be unacceptable on that account to the spirits sacrificed to. I translate 子 by "calf," but it is not implied that the victim was young. 舍, the 3rd tone, = 捨, "to lay aside," "to put away." 其舍諸 = 其舍之乎.

於從政乎何有。
從政也與。曰求也藝、
乎何有曰、求也、可使
與。曰賜也達、於從政
曰、賜也可使從政也
也果、於從政乎何有。
使從政也與。　子
■季康子問、仲由、可
月至焉而已矣。
月不違仁、其餘、則日
■子曰、回也其心三

CHAPTER V.　The Master said, "Such was Hûi that for three months there would be nothing in his mind contrary to perfect virtue. The others may attain to this on some days or in some months, but nothing more."

CHAPTER VI.　Chî K'ang asked about Chung-yû, whether he was fit to be employed as an officer of government. The Master said, "Yû is a man of decision; what difficulty would he find in being an officer of government?" K'ang asked, "Is Ts'ze fit to be employed as an officer of government?" and was answered, "Ts'ze is a man of intelligence; what difficulty would he find in being an officer of government?" And to the same question about Ch'iû the Master gave the same reply, saying, "Ch'iû is a man of various ability."

5. THE SUPERIORITY OF HÛI TO THE OTHER DISCIPLES. It is impossible to say whether we should translate here about Hûi in the past or present tense. 違 is not 違 背, "to oppose," but 違 去, "to depart from." 日 月 至, "come to it," i. e., the line of perfect virtue, "in the course of a day, or a month." 日 月 may also be, "for a day or a month." So in the 註 疏.

-6.- THE QUALITIES OF TSZE-LÛ, TSZE-KUNG, AND TSZE-YÛ, AND THEIR COMPETENCY TO ASSIST IN GOVERNMENT. The prince is called 爲 政 者, "the *doer* of government": his ministers and officers are styled 從 政 者, "the *followers* of government. 也 與 and 何 有 are set, the one expression against the other, the former indicating a doubt of the competency of the disciples, the latter affirming their more than competency.

亡之命矣夫斯人　之自牖執其手曰　🈞伯牛有疾子問　汶上矣。　復我者、則吾必在　善爲我辭焉、如有　爲費宰、閔子騫曰、　🈞季氏使閔子騫

CHAPTER VII. The chief of the Chî family sent to ask Min Tsze-ch'ien to be governor of Pî. Min Tsze-ch'ien said, "Decline the offer for me politely. If any one come again to me with a second invitation, I shall be *obliged to go and live* on the banks of the Wăn."

CHAPTER VIII. Po-niû being ill, the Master went to ask for him. He took hold of his hand through the window, and said, "It is killing him. It is the appointment *of Heaven*, alas! That such a man should

7. MIN TSZE-CH'IEN REFUSES TO SERVE THE CHÎ FAMILY. The tablet of Tsze-ch'ien (his name was 損) is now the first on the east among "the wise ones" of the temple. He was among the foremost of the disciples. Confucius praises his filial piety, and we see here, how he could stand firm in his virtue, and refuse the proffers of the powerful but unprincipled families of his time. 使＝使 人 來 召, in the translation, and in 復 (*fôh*, 4th tone) 我 者, we must similarly understand 復 來 召 我 者. 我, read Pî, was a place belonging to the Chî family. Its name is still preserved in 費 縣 in the department of 沂 州, in Shantung. The Wăn stream divided Ch'î and Lû. Tsze-ch'ien threatens, if he should be troubled again, to retreat to Ch'î, where the Chî family could not reach him.

8. LAMENT OF CONFUCIUS OVER THE MORTAL SICKNESS OF PO-NIÛ. Po-niû, "elder or uncle Niû,", was the denomination of 冉 耕, one of the disciples of the sage. In the old interpretation, his sickness is said to have been 惡 疾, "an evil disease," by which name leprosy, called 癩, is intended, though that character is now employed for "itch." Suffering from such a disease, Po-niû would not see people, and Confucius took his hand through the window. A different explanation is given by Chû Hsî. He says that sick persons were usually placed on the north side of the apartment; but when the prince visited them, in order that he

今女畫。
力不足者中道而廢、
之道、力不足也子曰、
冉求曰、非不說子
改其樂賢哉囘也。
人不堪其憂、囘也不
簞食、一瓢飲、在陋巷、一
子曰賢哉囘也、一
也、而有斯疾也。
也、而有斯疾也、斯人

have such a sickness!   That such a man should have such a sickness!"

CHAPTER IX.  The Master said, "Admirable indeed was the virtue of Hûi!  With a single bamboo dish of rice, a single gourd dish of drink, and living in his mean narrow lane, while others could not have endured the distress, he did not allow his joy to be affected by it.   Admirable indeed was the virtue of Hûi!"

CHAPTER X.  Yen Ch'iû said, "It is not that I do not delight in your doctrines, but my strength is insufficient."  The Master said, "Those whose strength is insufficient give over in the middle of the way but now you limit yourself."

might appear to them with his face to the south (see chap. i), they were moved to the south.  On this occasion, Po-niû's friends wanted to receive Confucius after this royal fashion, which he avoided by not entering the house.  亡 之="It is killing him."  夫, the 2nd tone, generally an initial particle="now." It is here final, and="alas'"

9.  THE HAPPINESS OF HUÎ INDEPENDENT OF HIS POVERTY.  The 簞 was simply a piece of the stem of a bamboo, and the 瓢 half of a gourd cut into two.  食, see II, viii.  The eulogy turns much on 其 in 其 樂, as opposed to 其 憂, "his joy," the delight which he had in the doctrines of his master, contrasted with the grief others would have felt under such poverty.

10.  A HIGH AIM AND PERSEVERANCE PROPER TO A STUDENT.  Confucius would not admit Ch'iû's apology for not attempting more than he did.  "Give over in the middle of the way," i. e., they go as long and as far as they can, and are pursuing when they stop.

也。

公事、未嘗至於偃之室

臺滅明者、行不由徑、非

女得人焉耳乎曰、有澹

臺子游爲武城宰子曰、

子儒、無爲小人儒。

臺子謂子夏曰、女爲君

CHAPTER XI. The Master said to Tsze-hsiâ, "Do you be a scholar after the style of the superior man, and not after that of the mean man."

CHAPTER XII. Tsze-yû being governor of Wû-ch'ăng, the Master said to him, "Have you got *good* men *there?*" He answered, "There is Tan-t'âi Mieh-ming, who never in walking takes a short cut, and never comes to my office, excepting on public business."

11. How LEARNING SHOULD BE PURSUED. 君子 and 小人 here = adjectives, qualifying 儒. The 君子, it is said, learns 爲己 for his own real improvement and from duty; the 小人, 爲人, "for men," with a view to their opinion, and for his own material benefit. We should hardly have judged such a counsel necessary for Tsze-hsiâ.

12. THE CHARACTER OF TAN-T'ÂI MIEH-MING. The chapter shows, according to Chinese commentators, the advantage to people in authority of their having good men about them. In this way after their usual fashion, they seek for a profound meaning in the remark of Confucius. Tan-t'âi Mieh-ming, who was styled 子羽, has his tablet the 2ud, east, outside the hall. The accounts of him are conflicting. According to one, he was very good-looking, while another says he was so bad-looking that Confucius at first formed an unfavorable opinion of him, `an error which he afterwards confessed on Mieh-ming's becoming eminent. He traveled southwards with not a few followers, and places near Sû-châu and elsewhere retain names indicative of his presence. 爲爾乎, three particles coming together, are said to indicate the slow and deliberate manner in which the sage spoke. 滅明者, compare 顏回者 in chap. ii. 室 is said to = 公堂.

子曰、孟之反不伐、
奔而殿將入門、策其
馬曰、非敢後也、馬不
進也。
子曰不有祝鮀之
佞、而有宋朝之美、難
乎免於今之世矣。

CHAPTER XIII. The Master said, "Măng Chih-fan does not boast of his merit. Being in the rear on an occasion of flight, when they were about to enter the gate, he whipped up his horse, saying, "It is not that I dare to be last. My horse would not advance."

CHAPTER XIV. The Master said, "Without the specious speech of the litanist T'o and the beauty of *the prince* Châo of Sung, it is difficult to escape in the present age."

13. THE VIRTUE OF MĂNG CHIH-FAN IN CONCEALING HIS MERIT. But where was his virtue in deviating from the truth? And how could Confucius commend him for doing so? These questions have never troubled the commentators, nor is it wise to bring a railing accusation against the sage for his words here. Măng Chih-fan, named 側, was an officer of Lû. The defeat referred to was in the eleventh year of Duke Âi. To lead the van of an army is called 啟, to bring up the rear is 殿. In retreat, the rear is of course the place of honor.

14. THE DEGENERACY OF THE AGE ESTEEMING GLIBNESS OF TONGUE AND BEAUTY OF PERSON. 祝, "to pray," "prayers;" here, in the concrete, the officer charged with the prayers in the ancestral temple. I have coined the word *litanist* to come as near to the meaning as possible. This T'o was an officer of the State of Wei, styled 子魚. Prince Châo had been guilty of incest with his half sister Nan-tsze (see chap. xxvi), and afterwards, when she was married to Duke Ling of Wei, he served as an officer there, carrying on his wickedness. He was celebrated for his beauty of person. 而 is a simple connective, = 與, and the 不 is made to belong to both clauses. The old commentators construe differently: —"If a man have not the speech of T'o, though he may have the beauty of Châo, etc., making the degeneracy of the age all turn on its fondness for specious talk. This cannot be right.

免。　直罔之生也幸而　臺子曰、人之生也　質彬彬、然後君子。　野、文勝質則史、文　臺子曰、質勝文則　也。　由戶、何莫由斯道　臺子曰、誰能出不

CHAPTER XV. The Master said, "Who can go out but by the door? How is it that men will not walk according to these ways?"

CHAPTER XVI. The Master said, "Where the solid qualities are in excess of accomplishments, we have rusticity; where the accomplishments are in excess of the solid qualities, we have the manners of a clerk. When the accomplishments and solid qualities are equally blended, we then have the man of virtue."

CHAPTER XVII. The Master said, "Man is born for uprightness. If a man lose his uprightness, and yet live, his escape *from death* is the effect of mere good fortune."

15. A LAMENT OVER THE WAYWARDNESS OF MEN'S CONDUCT. 斯道, "these ways," in a moral sense;—not deep doctrines, but rules of life.

16. THE EQUAL BLENDING OF SOLID EXCELLENCE AND ORNAMENTAL ACCOMPLISHMENTS, IN A COMPLETE CHARACTER. 史, "a historian," an officer of importance in China. The term, however, is to be understood here of "a clerk," one that is of a class sharp and well informed, but insincere.

17. LIFE WITHOUT UPRIGHTNESS IS NOT TRUE LIFE, AND CANNOT BE CALCULATED ON. "No more serious warning than this," says one commentator, "was ever addressed to men by Confucius." A distinction is made by Chû Hsî and others between the two 生;—the 1st is 始生, "birth," or "the beginning of life," and the 2nd is 生存, "preservation in life." 人之生也直, "The being born of man is upright," which may mean either that man at his birth is upright, or that he is born for uprightness. I prefer the latter view. 罔之生也, "The living without it," if we take 罔=無, or "to defame it," if 罔=誣. We long here as elsewhere for more perspicuity and fuller development of view. Without uprightness the end of man's existence is not fulfilled, but his preservation in such case is not merely a fortunate accident.

子曰知之者、不如
好之者、好之者不如
樂之者。
子曰中人以上、可
以語上也、中人以下、
不可以語上也。
樊遲問知子曰務
民之義敬鬼神而遠

CHAPTER XVIII. The Master said, "They who know *the truth* are not equal to those who love it, and they who love it are not equal to those who delight in it."

CHAPTER XIX. The Master said, "To those whose talents are above mediocrity, the highest subjects may be announced. To those who are below mediocrity, the highest subjects may not be announced."

CHAPTER XX. Fan Ch'ih asked what constituted wisdom. The Master said, "To give one's self earnestly to the duties due to men, and, while respecting spiritual beings, to keep aloof from them,

18. DIFFERENT STAGES OF ATTAINMENT. The four 之 have all one reference, which must be 道 or 理, the subject spoken of.

19. TEACHERS MUST BE GUIDED IN COMMUNICATING KNOWLEDGE BY THE SUSCEPTIVITY OF THE LEARNERS. In 以 上, 上 is read 2nd tone, a verbal word, and not the prep. "upon," so the 下 in 以 下 is also verbal, as in III, vii. The 中人, "or mediocre people," may have all classes of subjects announced to them, I suppose. 語 is in the 4th tone, "to tell to."

20. CHIEF ELEMENTS IN WISDOM AND VIRTUE. Fan Ch'ih, II, v. The modern comm. take 民 here as=人, and 民 之 義 as=人 道 之 宜, "what is right according to the principles of humanity." With some hesitation I have assented to this view, though 民 properly means "the multitude," "the people," and the old interpreters explain—"Strive to perfect the righteousness of the people." We may suppose from the second clause that Fan Ch'ih was striving after what was uncommon and superhuman. For a full exhibition of the

子曰、齊一變、　者樂、仁者壽。　者動、仁者靜、知　水仁者樂山、知　子曰、知者樂　矣。　而後獲可謂仁　仁曰、仁者先難　之、可謂知矣。問

may be called wisdom." He asked about perfect virtue. The Master said, "The man of virtue makes the difficulty *to be overcome* his first business, and success only a subsequent consideration;—this may be called perfect virtue."

CHAPTER XXI. The Master said, "The wise find pleasure in water; the virtuous find pleasure in hills. The wise are active; the virtuous are tranquil. The wise are joyful; the virtuous are long-lived."

CHAPTER XXII. The Master said, "Ch'î, by one

phrase 鬼 神, see 中 庸, XVI. Here it="spiritual beings," *manes* and others. 遠, the 4th tone; 遠 之, "keep at a distance from them," not "keep them at a distance." The sage's advice therefore is—"attend to what are plainly human duties, and do not be superstitious." 先 and 後 are, as frequently verbs, "put first," "put last." The old interpreters take them differently, but not so well.

21. CONTRASTS OF THE WISE AND THE VIRTUOUS. The two first 樂 are read *âo*, 4th tone,=喜 好, "to find pleasure in." The wise or knowing are active and restless, like the waters of a stream, ceaselessly flowing and advancing. The virtuous are tranquil and firm, like the stable mountains. The pursuit of knowledge brings joy. The life of the virtuous may be expected to glide calmly on and long. After all, the saying is not very comprehensible.

22. THE CONDITION OF THE STATES CH'Î AND LÛ. Ch'î and Lû were both within the present Shantung. Ch'î lay along the coast on the north, embracing the present department of 青 州 and other territory. Lû was on the south, the larger portion of it being formed by the present department of 兖 州. At the rise of the Châu dynasty, King Wû invested Lu-shang, a counselor of King Wû and the commander of his army, with the principality of Ch'î. King

罔也。可欺也、不可陷也、不可逝也、君子可也、何爲其然其從之也。曰、井有仁焉、仁者雖告之曰、鬺宰我問之曰、觚觚哉觚鬺子曰、觚觚、不變、至於道。至於魯、魯一

change, would come to the State of Lû. Lû, by one change, would come to a state where true principles predominated."

CHAPTER XXIII. The Master said, "A cornered vessel without corners.—A strange cornered vessel! A strange cornered vessel!"

CHAPTER XXIV. Tsâi Wo asked, saying, "A benevolent man, though it be told him,—'There is a man in the well,' will go in after him, I suppose." Confucius said, "Why should he do so?" A superior man may be made to go *to the well*, but he cannot be made to go down into it. He may be imposed upon, but he cannot be befooled."

Wû at his first interview with Lü-shang addressed him as Thâi-kung Wang, "Grandfather Hope," the man long looked for in his family. This successor, King Ch'ang, constituted the son of his uncle, the famous duke of Châu, prince of Lû. In Confucius's time, Ch'î had degenerated more than Lû. 道 is 先王盡善盡美之道, "the entirely good and admirable ways of the former kings."

23. THE NAME WITHOUT THE REALITY IS FOLLY. This was spoken (see the 註 疏) with reference to the governments of the time, retaining ancient names without ancient principles. The 觚 was a drinking vessel; others say a wooden tablet. The latter was a later use of the term. It was made with corners as appears from the composition of the character, which is formed from 角, "a

horn," "a sharp corner." In Confucius's time the form was changed, while the name was kept.—See the translation in Williams's Syllabic Dictionary, under syllable *kû*.

24. THE BENEVOLENT EXERCISE THEIR BENEVOLENCE WITH PRUDENCE. Tsâi Wo could see no limitation to acting on the impulses of benevolence. We are not to suppose with modern scholars that he wished to show that benevolence was impracticable. 雖 belongs to the whole following clause, especially to the mention of a well. The 仁 of 仁 褖 should be 人. This happy correction of the text is due to a contemporary and teacher of Chû Hsî whom he calls Lîú P'ing-chûn. 其 ... 也 indicate some doubt in Wo's mind. Observe the *hophal* force of 逝 and 陷.

子曰、君子博
學於文約之以
禮、亦可以弗畔
矣夫。

子見南子子
路不說夫子矢
之曰予所否者、
天厭之天厭之。

子曰中庸之
爲德也其至矣
乎、民鮮久矣。

CHAPTER XXV. The Master said, "The superior man, extensively studying all learning, and keeping himself under the restraint of the rules of propriety, may thus likewise not overstep what is right."

CHAPTER XXVI. The Master having visited Nan-tsze, Tsze-lû was displeased, on which the Master swore, saying, "Wherein I have done improperly, may Heaven reject me! may Heaven reject me!"

CHAPTER XXVII. The Master said, "Perfect is the virtue which is according to the Constant Mean! · Rare for a long time has been its practice among the people."

25. THE HAPPY EFFECT OF LEARN-ING AND PROPRIETY COMBINED. 君子 has here its lighter meaning, = "the student of what is right and true." The 之 in 約 之 we naturally refer to 文, but comparing IX, x, 2—約 我 以 禮—we may assent to the observation that 我 指 已 身, "*me* refers to the learner's own person." See note on IV, xxiii. 畔, "the boundary of a field," also, "to overstep a boundary." 矣 夫, as in V, xxvi, but the force here is more "ah!" than "alas'"

26. CONFUCIUS VINDICATES HIM-SELF FOR VISITING THE UNWORTHY NAN-TSZE. Nan tsze was the wife of the duke of Wei, and half sister of Prince Châo, mentioned in chap. xiv. Her lewd character was well known, and hence Tsze-lû was dis-pleased, thinking an interview with her was disgraceful to the Master. Great pains are taken to explain the incident. "Nan-tsze," says one, "sought the interview from the stirrings of her natural conscience." "It was a rule," says another, "that stranger officers in a state should visit the prince's wife." "Nan-tsze," argues a third, "had all influence with her husband, and Confucius wished to get currency by her means for his doctrine." Whether 矢 is to be understood in the sense of "to swear," = 誓, or "to make a declaration," = 陳, is much debated. Evidently the thing is an oath, or solemn protestation against the suspicions of Tsze-lû. 訊, as in I, i, 1.

27. THE DEFECTIVE PRACTICE OF THE PEOPLE IN CONFUCIUS'S TIME. See the *Chung Yung*.

謂仁之方也已。

達人能近取譬、可

而立人己欲達而

諸夫仁者己欲立

聖乎堯舜其猶病

曰、何事於仁必也

何如、可謂仁乎。

施於民、而能濟衆、

子貢曰、如有博

CHAPTER XXVIII. 1. Tsze-kung said, "Suppose the case of a man extensively conferring benefits on the people, and able to assist all, what would you say of him? Might he be called perfectly virtuous?" The Master said, "Why speak only of virtue in connection with him? Must he not have the qualities of a sage? Even Yâo and Shun were still solicitous about this.

2. "Now the man of perfect virtue, wishing to be established himself, seeks also to establish others; wishing to be enlarged himself, he seeks also to enlarge others.

3. "To be able to judge *of others* by what is nigh *in ourselves;*—this may be called the art of virtue."

28. THE TRUE NATURE AND ART OF VIRTUE. There are no higher sayings in the Analects than we have here. 1. 施, the 4th tone, "to confer benefits." 聖 乎,—乎 is said to be "a particle of doubt and uncertainty," but it is rather the interrogative affirmation of opinion. Tsze-kung appears to have thought that great doings were necessary to virtue, and propounds a case which would transcend the achievements of the ancient model sovereigns Yâo and Shun. From such extravagant views the Master recalls him. 2. This is the description of 仁 者 之 心 體, "the mind of the perfectly virtuous man," as void of all selfishness. 3. It is to be wished that the idea intended by 能 近 取 譬 had been more clearly expressed. Still we seem to have here a near approach to a positive enunciation of "the golden rule."

## BOOK VII. SHÛ R

何有於我哉。 厭誨人不倦、 識之學而不 蕎子曰、默而 老彭。 古、竊比於我 不作、信而好 蕎子曰、述而 述而第七

CHAPTER I. The Master said, "A transmitter and not a maker, believing in and loving the ancients, I venture to compare myself with our old P'ăng."

CHAPTER II. The Master said, "The silent treasuring up of knowledge; learning without satiety; and instructing others without being wearied:—which one of these things belongs to me?"

HEADING OF THIS BOOK.—述 而 第 七, "A transmitter, and—Book VII." We have in this Book much information of a personal character about Confucius, both from his own lips, and from the descriptions of his disciples. The two preceding Books treat of the disciples and other worthies, and here, in contrast with them, we have the sage himself exhibited.

1. CONFUCIUS DISCLAIMS BEING AN ORIGINATOR OR MAKER. 述=傳舊而 已, "simply to hand down the old." Commentators say the Master's language here is from his extreme humility. But we must hold that it expresses his true sense of his position and work. Who the individual called endearingly "our old P'ăng" was, can hardly be ascertained. Some make 老彭 to be Lâo-tsze, the founder of the Tâo sect, and others again make two individuals, one Lâo-tsze, and the other that 彭祖, of whom we read much in Chwangtsze. A P'ăng Hsien appears in the Lî Sâo, st. 21, where Chû Hsî describes him as a worthy of the Yin (or Shang) dynasty, and he supposes him to be the Lâo P'ăng here.

2. CONFUCIUS'S HUMBLE ESTIMATE OF HIMSELF. 識, here by most scholars read chih, 4th tone, "to remember." 之 refers, it is said, to 理, "principles," the subjects of the silent observation and reflection. 何 有 於 我 哉, cannot be,—"what difficulty do these occasion me?" but= 何者能有於我, as in the translation. "The language," says Chû Hsî, "is that of humility upon humility." Some insert, in their explanation, 此 外 before 何—"Besides these, what is there in me?" But this is quite arbitrary. The profession may be inconsistent with what we find in other passages, but the inconsistency must stand rather than violence be done to the language. Ho Yen gives the singular exposition of 鄭 康 成 (about A. D. 150–200)—"Other men have not these things, I only have them."

子曰、德之不脩、學
之不講、聞義不能徙、
不善不能改、是吾憂
也。
子之燕居、申申如
也、夭夭如也。
子曰、甚矣吾衰也、

CHAPTER III. The Master said, "The leaving virtue without proper cultivation; the not thoroughly discussing what is learned; not being able to move towards righteousness of which a knowledge is gained; and not being able to change what is not good:—: these are the things which occasion me solicitude."

CHAPTER IV. When the Master was unoccupied with business, his manner was easy, and he looked pleased.

CHAPTER V. The Master said, "Extreme is my

3. CONFUCIUS'S ANXIETY ABOUT HIS SELF-CULTIVATION:—ANOTHER HUMBLE ESTIMATE OF HIMSELF. Here again commentators find only the expressions of humility, but there can be no reason why we should not admit that Confucius was anxious lest these things, which are only put forth as possibilities, should become in his case actual facts. 講 is in the sense explained in the dictionary by the terms 習 and 究, "practicing," "examining."

4. THE MANNER OF CONFUCIUS WHEN UNOCCUPIED. The first clause, which is the subject of the other two, is literally—"The Master's dwelling at ease." Observe 燕, in

the 4th tone; 夭, in the 1st; 如 as in III, xxiii.

5. HOW THE DISAPPOINTMENT OF CONFUCIUS'S HOPES AFFECTED EVEN HIS DREAMS. 周 公 is now to all intents a proper name, but the characters mean "the duke of Châu." Châu was the name of the seat of the family from which the dynasty so called sprang, and, on the enlargement of this territory, King Wăn divided the original seat between his son 旦 (Tan) and the minister 奭 (Shih). Tan was Châu-kung, in wisdom and politics, what his elder brother, the first sovereign, Wû, was in arms. Confucius had longed to bring the principles and institutions

久矣、吾不
復夢見周
公。
子曰、志
於道、據於
德依於仁。
游於藝。
子曰、自
行束脩以

decay. ·For a long time, I have not dreamed, as I was
wont to do, that I saw the duke of Châu."

CHAPTER VI. 1. The Master said, "Let the will be
set on the path of duty.

2. "Let every attainment in what is good be firmly
grasped.

3. "Let perfect virtue be accorded with.

4. "Let relaxation and enjoyment be found in the
polite arts."·

CHAPTER VII. The Master said, "From the man
bringing his bundle of dried flesh *for my teaching*

of Châu-kung into practice, and in
his earlier years, while hope animated
him, had often dreamed of the former
sage. The original territory of Châu
was what is now the district of
Ch'î-shan (岐 山), department of
Fung-hsiang in Shensi.

6. RULES FOR THE FULL MATUR-
ING OF CHARACTER. 2. 德 might be
translated virtue, but 仁="perfect
virtue" following, we require another
term. 4. 游, "to ramble for amusement," here="to seek recreation."
藝, see note on 文, in I, vi. A full
enumeration makes "six arts," viz.,
ceremonies, music, archery, charioteering, the study of characters or
language, and figures or arithmetic.
The ceremonies were ranged in five
classes: lucky or sacrifices; unlucky
or those of mourning; military; those
of host and guest; and festive.
Music required the study of the

music of Hwang-tî, of Yâo, of Shun,
of Yü, of T'ang, and of Wû.
Archery had a fivefold classification.
Charioteering had the same. The
study of the characters required the
examination of them to determine
whether there predominated in their
formation resemblance to the object,
combination of ideas, indication of
properties, a phonetic principle, a
principle of contrariety, or meta-
phorical accommodation. Figures
were managed according to nine
rules, as the object was the meas-
urement of land, capacity, etc.
These six subjects were the business
of the highest and most liberal
education, but we need not suppose
that Confucius had them all in view
here.

7. THE READINESS OF CONFUCIUS
TO IMPART INSTRUCTION. It was the
rule anciently that when one party

於是日哭、則不歌。
之側、未嘗飽也。子
子食於有喪者
復也。
不以三隅反則不
不悱不發、舉一隅、
子曰、不憤不啓、
上、吾未嘗無誨焉。

upwards, I have never refused instruction to any one."

CHAPTER VIII. The Master said, "I do not open up the truth to one who is not eager *to get knowledge*, nor help out any one who is not anxious to explain himself. When I have presented one corner of a subject to any one, and he cannot from it learn the other three, I do not repeat my lesson."

CHAPTER IX. 1. When the Master was eating by the side of a mourner, he never ate to the full.

2. He did not sing on the same day in which he had been weeping.

waited on another, he should carry some present or offering with him. Pupils did so when they first waited on their teacher. Of such offerings, one of the lowest was a bundle of strips of 脩, "dried flesh." The wages of a teacher are now called 脩金, "the money of the dried flesh." However small the offering brought to the sage, let him only see the indication of a wish to learn, and he imparted his instructions. 以 上 may be translated "upwards," i. e., "to such a man and others with larger gifts," 上 being in the 3rd tone; or the character may be understood in the sense of "coming to my instructions." I prefer the former interpretation.

8. CONFUCIUS REQUIRED A REAL DESIRE AND ABILITY IN HIS DISCIPLES. The last chapter tells of the sage's readiness to teach; this shows that he did not teach where his teaching was likely to prove of no avail. 悱, in the comm. and dict. is explained 口 欲 言 而 未 能 之 貌, "the appearance of one with mouth wishing to speak and yet not able to do so." This being the meaning, we might have expected the character to be 誹. 反, "to turn," is explained 還 以 相 證 之 義, "going round for mutual testimony." 不 復＝不 復 有 所 告, "I tell him nothing more."

9. CONFUCIUS'S SYMPATHY WITH MOURNERS. The weeping is understood to be on the occasion of offering his condolences to a mourner, which was "a rule of propriety."

而成者也。
也、必也臨事而懼、好謀
河、死而無悔者、吾不與
軍則誰與子曰暴虎馮
有是夫子路曰子行三
行、舍之則藏惟我與爾
子謂顏淵曰、用之則

CHAPTER X. 1. The Master said to Yen Yüan, "When called to office, to undertake its duties; when not so called, to lie retired;—it is only I and you who have attained to this."

2. Tsze-lû said, "If you had the conduct of the armies of a great state, whom would you have to act with you?"

3. The Master said, "I would not have him to act with me, who will unarmed attack a tiger, or cross a river without a boat, dying without any regret. My associate must be the man who proceeds to action full of solicitude, who is fond of adjusting his plans, and then carries them into execution."

10. THE ATTAINMENTS OF HÛI LIKE THOSE OF CONFUCIUS. THE EXCESSIVE BOLDNESS OF TSZE-LÛ. 1. In 用 之, 舍 之, 之 is explained by 我, but we have seen that 之 following active verbs imparts to them a sort of neuter signification. 用 之 = "used." 舍 之 = "neglected." 2. A *Chun*, according to the 周 禮, consisted of 12,500 men. The royal forces consisted of six such bodies, and those of a great state of three. 3. 暴 虎 馮 河, see Shih-ching, II, v, 1, st. 6. 懼 does not indicate *timidity*, but *solicitude.*—Tsze-lû, it would appear, was jealous of the praise conferred on Hûi, and, pluming himself on his bravery, put in for a share of the Master's approbation. But he only brought on himself this rebuke.

韶　臺　齊　臺　求　爲　鞭　可　臺
三　子　戰　子　從　之　之　求　子
月　在　疾　之　吾　如　士　也　曰
不　齊　。　所　所　不　吾　雖　富
知　聞　　　愼　好　可　亦　執　而
　　　　　　　、　。　　　・　　

CHAPTER XI. The Master said, "If the search for riches is sure to be successful, though I should become a groom with whip in hand to get them, I will do so. As the search may not be successful, I will follow after that which I love."

CHAPTER XII. The things in reference to which the Master exercised the greatest caution were—fasting, war, and sickness.

CHAPTER XIII. When the Master was in Ch'î, he heard the Shâo, and for three months did not know

11. THE UNCERTAINTY AND FOLLY OF THE PURSUIT OF RICHES. It occurs to a student to understand the first clause—"If it be *proper* to search for riches," and the third—"I will do it." But the translation is according to the modern commentaries, and the conclusion agrees better with it. In explaining 執 鞭 之 士, some refer us to the attendants who cleared the street with their whips when the prince went abroad, but we need not seek any particular allusion of the kind. Observe 而 = 若, "if," and then 如 = "since." Still we may bring out the meaning from 而 taken in its usual significance of "*and*." In this construction the previous 富 = "given riches," and 而 可 求 = "and such as can surely be found."—An objection to the pursuit of wealth may be made on the ground of righteousness, or on that of its uncertainty. It is the latter on which Confucius here rests.

12. WHAT THINGS CONFUCIUS WAS PARTICULARLY CAREFUL ABOUT. 齊, read *châi*, and = 齋, "to fast," or, rather, denoting the whole religious adjustment, enjoined before the offering of sacrifice, and extending over the ten days previous to the great sacrificial seasons. 齊 means "to equalize" (see II, iii), and the effect of those previous exercises was 齊 不 齊 以 致 齊, "to adjust what was not adjusted, so as to produce a perfect adjustment." Sacrifices presented in such a state of·mind were sure to be acceptable. Other people, it is said, might be heedless in reference to sacrifices, to war, and to sickness, but not so the sage.

13. THE EFFECT OF MUSIC ON CONFUCIUS. The *shâo*, see III, xxv. This incident must have happened in the thirty-sixth year of Confucius, when he followed Duke Châo in his flight from Lû to Ch'î. As related in the 史 記, "Historical Records," before the characters 三 月, we have 學 之, "he learned it three

肉味、曰、不圖爲樂
之至於斯也。
畫冉有曰夫子爲
衞君乎子貢曰諾、
吾將問之入曰、伯
夷叔齊何人也曰、
古之賢人也曰、怨
乎曰求仁而得仁、
又何怨出曰、夫子
不爲也。

the taste of flesh. "I did not think," he said, "that music could have been made so excellent as this."

CHAPTER XIV. 1. Yen Yû said, "Is our Master for the ruler of Wei?" Tsze-kung said, "Oh! I will ask him."

2. He went in *accordingly*, and said, "What sort of men were Po-î and Shû-ch'î?" "They were ancient worthies," said the Master. "Did they have any repinings *because of their course?*" The Master again replied, "They sought to act virtuously, and they did so; what was there for them to repine about?" On this, *Tsze-kung* went out and said, "Our Master is not for him."

months," which may relieve us from the necessity of extending the three months over all the time in which he did not know the taste of his food. In Ho Yen's compilation, the 不知 is explained by 忽玉, "he was careless about and forgot." The last clause is also explained there—"I did not think that this music had reached this country of Ch'i."

14. CONFUCIUS DID NOT APPROVE OF A SON OPPOSING HIS FATHER. 1. The eldest son of Duke Ling of Wei had planned to kill his mother (? stepmother), the notorious Nan-tsze (VI, xxvi). For this he had to flee the country, and his son, on the death of Ling, became duke (出 公), and subsequently opposed his father's attempts to wrest the state from him. This was the matter argued among the disciples.—Was Confucius for (爲, 4th tone) the son, the ruling duke? 2. In Wei it would not have been according to *propriety* to speak by name of its ruler, and therefore Tsze-kung put the case of Po-î and Shû-ch'î, see V, xxii. They having given up a throne, and finally their lives, rather than do what they thought wrong, and Confucius fully approving of their conduct, it was plain he could not approve of a son's holding by force what was the rightful inheritance of the father. 求 仁 而 得 仁, "They sought for virtue, and they got virtue;" i. e., such was the character of their conduct.

子曰、飯疏食
飲水、曲肱而枕
之、樂亦在其中
矣、不義而富且
貴、於我如浮雲。
子曰、加我數
年、五十以學易、
可以無大過矣。

CHAPTER XV. The Master said, "With coarse rice to eat, with water to drink, and my bended arm for a pillow;—I have still joy in the midst of these things. Riches and honors acquired by unrighteousness are to me as a floating cloud."

CHAPTER XVI. The Master said, "If some years were added to my life, I would give fifty to the study of the Yî, and then I might come to be without great faults."

15. THE JOY OF CONFUCIUS INDEPENDENT OF OUTWARD CIRCUMSTANCES. 飯, in 3rd tone, "a meal"; also, as here, a verb, "to eat." 枕, 4th tone, "to pillow," "to use as a pillow." Critics call attention to 亦, making the sentiment = "My joy is everywhere.·· It is amid other circumstances. It is *also* here." 不義 云云, = "By unrighteousness I might get riches and honors, but such riches and honors are to me as a floating cloud. It is vain to grasp at them, so uncertain and unsubstantial."

16. THE VALUE WHICH CONFUCIUS SET UPON THE STUDY OF THE Yî. Chû Hsî supposes that this was spoken when Confucius was about seventy, as he was in his sixty-eighth year when he ceased his wanderings, and settled in Lû to the adjustment and compilation of the Yî and other *Ching*. If the remark be referred to that time, an error may well be found in 五 十, for he would hardly be speaking at seventy of having fifty years added to his life. Chû also mentions the report of Liû P'ing-chûn, referred to by him under V, xxiv, that he had been told of a copy of the Lun Yu, which read 假 for 加, and 卒 for 平. Amended thus, the meaning would be—"If I had some *more* years to finish the study of the Yî, etc." Ho Yen interprets the chapter quite differently. Referring to the saying, II, iv, 4, "At fifty, I knew the decrees of Heaven," he supposes this to have been spoken when Confucius was forty-seven, and explains—"In a few years more I will be fifty, and have finished the Yî, when I may be without great faults."—One thing remains upon both views:—Confucius never claimed, what his followers do for him, to be a perfect man.

將至云爾。
以忘憂不知老之
人也發憤忘食樂
曰、女奚不曰其爲
子路。子路不對子
〔二卷〕葉公問孔子於
執禮、皆雅言也。
〔一卷〕子所雅言、詩書、

CHAPTER XVII. The Master's frequent themes of discourse were—the Odes, the History, and the maintenance of the Rules of Propriety. On all these he frequently discoursed.

CHAPTER XVIII. 1. The duke of Sheh asked Tsze-lû about Confucius, and Tsze-lû did not answer him.

2. The Master said, "Why did you not say to him,—He is simply a man, who in his eager pursuit (of knowledge) forgets his food, who in the joy *of its* *attainment* forgets his sorrows, and who does not perceive that old age is coming on?"

17. CONFUCIUS'S MOST COMMON TOPICS. 書, "The History," i. e., the historical documents which were compiled into the Shû-ching that has come down to us in a mutilated condition. 詩 also, and much more 禮, must not be understood of the now existing Shih-ching and Lî Chî. Chû Hsî explains 雅 (3rd tone) by 常, "constantly." The old interpreter Chăng explains it by 正 "correctly," —"Confucius would speak of the Odes, etc., with attention to the correct enunciation of the characters." This does not seem so good.

18. CONFUCIUS'S DESCRIPTION OF HIS OWN CHARACTER, AS BEING

SIMPLY A CHEERFUL, EARNEST LEARNER. 1. 葉 (read *sheh*) was a district of Ch'û (楚), the governor or prefect of which was styled *kung*, after the usurping fashion of Ch'û. Its name is still preserved in a district of the department of 南陽, in the south of Honan. 2. 云 sometimes finishes a sentence (Prémare, "*claudit orationem*"), as here. The 爾 after it = 耳, imparting to all the preceding description a meaning indicated by our *simply* or *only*. Wang Yin-chih, in his treatise on the particles, gives instances of 云 used as a particle, now initial, now medial, and again final.

子曰、我非生
而知之者、好古、
敏以求之者也。
子不語、怪、力、
亂、神。
子曰、三人行、
必有我師焉、擇
其善者而從之、
其不善者而改
之。

CHAPTER XIX. The Master said, "I am not one who was born in the possession of knowledge; I am one who is fond of antiquity, and earnest in seeking it *there*."

CHAPTER XX. The subjects on which the Master did not talk, were—extraordinary things, feats of strength, disorder, and spiritual beings.

CHAPTER XXI. The Master said, "When I walk along with two others, they may serve me as my teachers. I will select their good qualities and follow them, their bad qualities and avoid them."

19. CONFUCIUS'S KNOWLEDGE NOT CONNATE, BUT THE RESULT OF HIS STUDY OF ANTIQUITY. Here again, according to the commentators, is a wonderful instance of the sage's humility disclaiming what he really had. The comment of a Mr. Yin, subjoined to Chû Hsî's own, is to the effect that the knowledge born with a man is only 義 and 理, while ceremonies, music, names of things, history, etc., must be learned. This would make what we may call connate or innate knowledge the moral sense, and those intuitive principles of reason, on and by which all knowledge is built up. But Confucius could not mean to deny his being possessed of these. "I love antiquity;" i. e., the ancients and all their works.

20. SUBJECTS AVOIDED BY CONFUCIUS IN HIS CONVERSATION. 亂, "confusion," meaning rebellious disorder, parricide, regicide, and such crimes. Chû Hsî makes 神 here = 鬼神造化之迹, "the mysterious, or spiritual operations apparent in the course of nature." 王肅 (died A. D. 266) as given by Ho Yen, simply says—鬼神之事, "the affairs of spiritual beings." For an instance of Confucius avoiding such a subject, see XI, xi.

21. HOW A MAN MAY FIND INSTRUCTORS FOR HIMSELF. 三人行, "three men walking"; but it is implied that the speaker is himself one of them. The commentators all take 擇 in the sense of "to distinguish," "to determine."—"I will determine the one who is good, and follow him, etc." I prefer to understand as in the translation. 改之, "change them," i. e., correct them in myself, avoid them.

子曰天生德
於予、桓魋其如
予何。
子曰二三子、
以我爲隱乎、吾
無隱乎爾、吾無
行而不與二三
子者、是丘也。
子以四教、文、
行、忠、信。

CHAPTER XXII. The Master said, "Heaven produced the virtue that is in me. Hwan T'ûi—what can he do to me?"

CHAPTER XXIII. The Master said, "Do you think, my disciples, that I have any concealments? I conceal nothing from you. There is nothing which I do that is not shown to you, my disciples;—that is my way."

CHAPTER XXIV. There were four things which the Master taught,—letters, ethics, devotion of soul, and truthfulness.

22. CONFUCIUS CALM IN DANGER, THROUGH THE ASSURANCE OF HAVING A DIVINE MISSION. According to the historical accounts, Confucius was passing through Sung in his way from Wei to Ch'ăn, and was practicing ceremonies with his disciples under a large tree, when they were set upon by emissaries of Hwan (or Hsiang) T'ûi, a high officer of Sung. These pulled down the tree, and wanted to kill the sage. His disciples urged him to make haste and escape, when he calmed their fears by these words. At the same time, he disguised himself till he had got past Sung. This story may be apocryphal, but the saying remains, —a remarkable one.

23. CONFUCIUS PRACTICED NO CONCEALMENT WITH HIS DISCIPLES. 二三子, see III, xxiv. 與 is explained by Chû Hsî by 示, "to show," as if the meaning were, "There is not one of my doings in which I am not showing my doctrines to you." But the common signification of 與 may be retained, as in Ho Yen,—"which is not given to, shared with, you." To what the concealment has reference we cannot tell. Observe the force of 者 followed by 也 at the end;—"To have none of my actions not shared with you,— that is I, Ch'iû."

24. THE SUBJECTS OF CONFUCIUS'S TEACHING. 以 四 教, "took four things and taught." There were four things which—not four ways in which—Confucius taught. 文 here =our use of letters. 行=人倫日用, "what is daily used in the relations of life." 忠=無一念之不盡, "not a single thought not exhausted." 信=無一事之不實, "not a single thing without its reality." These are the explanations in the 四書備旨. I confess to apprehend but vaguely the two latter subjects as distinguished from the second.

射。
宿。

蠢子釣而不綱弋不

而爲泰難乎有恆矣。

而爲有虛而爲盈、約

見有恆者斯可矣。亡

吾不得而見之矣、得

者、斯可矣。子曰、善人

而見之矣得見君子

蠢子曰、聖人吾不得

CHAPTER XXV. 1. The Master said, "A sage it is not mine to see; could I see a man of real talent and virtue, that would satisfy me."

2. The Master said, "A good man it is not mine to see; could I see a man possessed of constancy, that would satisfy me.

3. "Having not and yet affecting to have, empty and yet affecting to be full, straitened and yet affecting to be at ease:—it is difficult with such characteristics to have constancy."

CHAPTER XXVI. The Master angled,—but did not use a net. He shot,—but not at birds perching.

25. THE PAUCITY OF TRUE MEN IN, AND THE PRETENTIOUSNESS OF, CONFUCIUS'S TIME. 子 曰, par. 2, is supposed by some to be an addition to the text. That being so, we have in the chapter a climax of character —the man of constancy, or the single-hearted, steadfast man; the good man, who on his single-hearted-ness has built up his virtue; the *Chün-tsze*, the man of virtue in large proportions, and intellectually able besides; and the sage, or highest style of man. 聖, from 耳, 口, and 壬, "ear, mouth, and good,"=intuitively apprehensive of truth, and correct in utterance and action. Comp. Mencius, VII, Pt. ii, ch. xxv.

26. THE HUMANITY OF CONFUCIUS: 綱 is properly the large rope attached to a net, by means of which it may be drawn so as to sweep a stream. 弋, "to shoot with a string tied to the arrow, by which it may be drawn back again." 射, applied to such shooting, in the 4th tone, is read *shih.* Confucius would only destroy what life was necessary for his use, and in taking that he would not take advantage of the inferior creatures This chapter is said to be descriptive of him in his early life.

子曰、蓋有不知而作
之者、我無是也。多聞擇
其善者而從之、多見而
識之知之次也。
互鄉難與言、童子見、
門人惑子曰、與其進也、
不與其退也唯何甚人
潔己以進與其潔也、不
保其往也。

CHAPTER XXVII. The Master said, "There may be those who act without knowing why. I do not do so. Hearing much and selecting what is good and following it; seeing much and keeping it in memory:— this is the second style of knowledge."

CHAPTER XXVIII. 1. It was difficult to talk (profitably and reputably) with the people of Hû-hsiang, and a lad of that place having had an interview with the Master, the disciples doubted.

2. The Master said, "I admit people's approach to me without committing myself *as to what they may do* when they have retired. Why must one be so severe? If a man purify himself to wait upon me, I receive him so purified, without guaranteeing his past conduct."

27. AGAINST ACTING HEEDLESSLY. Pâo Hsien, in Ho Yen, says that this was spoken with reference to heedless compilers of records. Chû Hsî makes 作 之 simply = 作 事, "to do things," "to act." The paraphrasts make the latter part descriptive of Confucius—"I hear much, etc." This is not necessary, and the translation had better be as indefinite as the original.

28. THE READINESS OF CONFUCIUS TO MEET APPROACHES TO HIM THOUGH MADE BY THE UNLIKELY. 1. In 互 鄉, the 鄉 appears to be like our local termination *ham*.—"The people of Hû-ham." Its site is now sought in three different places. 2. Chû Hsî would here transpose the order of the text, and read 人 潔 己 云 云 immediately after 子 曰. He also supposes some characters lost in the sentence 唯 何 甚. This is hardly necessary. 與, as in V, vii, 3, = 許, "to allow," "to concede to."

同姓、謂之吳孟子、
黨乎、君取於吳爲
君子不黨君子亦
期而進之曰吾聞
禮。孔子退揖巫馬
知禮乎孔子曰、知
圖陳司敗問昭公
我欲仁斯仁至矣。
醫子曰、仁遠乎哉、

CHAPTER XXIX. The Master said, "Is virtue a thing remote? I wish to be virtuous, and lo! virtue is at hand."

CHAPTER XXX. 1. The minister of crime of Ch'ăn asked whether the duke Châo knew propriety, and Confucius said, "He knew propriety."

2. Confucius having retired, the minister bowed to Wû-mâ Ch'î to come forward, and said, "I have heard that the superior man is not a partisan. May the superior man be a partisan also? The prince married a daughter of *the house of* Wû, of the same surname with himself, and called her,—'The elder *Tsze* of

29. VIRTUE IS NOT FAR TO SEEK. 哉, after 乎, implies the negative answer to be given

30. HOW CONFUCIUS ACKNOWLEDGED HIS ERROR. 1. Ch'ăn, one of the states of China in Confucius's time, is to be referred probably to the present department of Ch'ănchâu in Honan province. 司敗 was the name given in Ch'ăn and Ch'û to the minister elsewhere called 司寇, which terms Morrison and Medhurst translate—"criminal judge" But *judge* does not come up to his functions, which were legislative as well as executive. He was the adviser of his sovereign on all matters relating to crime. See the 周禮, 秋官司寇. Châo was the honorary epithet of Châu (稠), duke of Lû, 541-509 B. C.

He had a reputation for the knowledge and observance of ceremonies, and Confucius answered the minister's question accordingly, the more readily that he was speaking to the officer of another state, and was bound, therefore, to hide any failings that his own sovereign might have had. 2. With all his knowledge of proprieties, the duke Châo had violated an important rule,—that which forbids the intermarriage of parties of the same surname. The ruling houses of Lû and Wû were branches of the imperial house of Châu, and consequently had the same surname—Chî (姬). To conceal his violation of the rule, Châo called his wife by the surname *Tsze* (子), as if she had belonged to the

君而知禮、孰不知禮。

巫馬期以告子曰、丘

也幸苟有過人必知

之。

子與人歌、而善必

使反之、而後和之。

子曰文莫吾猶人

也、躬行君子、則吾未

之有得。

Wû.' If the prince knew propriety, who does not know it?"

3. Wû-mâ Ch'î reported these remarks, and the Master said, "I am fortunate! If I have any errors, people are sure to know them."

CHAPTER XXXI. When the Master was in company with a person who was singing, if he sang well, he would make him repeat the song, while he accompanied it with his own voice.

CHAPTER XXXII. The Master said, "In letters I am perhaps equal to other men, but *the character of* the superior man, carrying out in his conduct what he professes, is what I have not yet attained to."

ducal house of Sung. 取, the 4th tone = 娶. 3. Confucius takes the criticism of his questioner very lightly.

31. THE GOOD FELLOWSHIP OF CONFUCIUS. On this chapter, see the 四書合講, which states very distinctly the interpretation which I have followed, making only two singings and not three. 和, 4th tone, here = "to sing in unison with."

32. ACKNOWLEDGMENT OF CONFUCIUS IN ESTIMATING HIMSELF. 莫 here occasions some difficulty. Ho Yen takes it, as it often is, = 無, and explains, "I am not better than others in letters." In the dictionary, with reference to this passage, it is explained by 強, so that the meaning would be—"By effort, I can equal other men in letters." Chû Hsî makes it 疑辭, a "particle of doubt," = "perhaps." But this is formed for the occasion. 躬行君子, "an in-person-acting *chün-tsze*."

子曰、若聖與仁、則吾
豈敢抑爲之不厭、誨人
不倦、則可謂云爾已矣。
公西華曰正唯弟子不
能學也。
子疾病。子路請禱子
曰、有諸子路對曰、有之、
誄曰、禱爾于上下神祇。

CHAPTER XXXIII. The Master said, "The sage and the man of perfect virtue;—how dare I *rank myself with them?* It may simply be said of me, that I strive to become such without satiety, and teach others without weariness." Kung-hsî Hwâ said, "This is just what we, the disciples, cannot imitate you in."

CHAPTER XXXIV. The Master being very sick, Tsze-lû asked leave to pray for him. He said, "May such a thing be done?" Tsze-lû replied, "It may. In the Eulogies it is said, 'Prayer has been made for thee to the spirits of the upper and lower

33. WHAT CONFUCIUS DECLINED TO BE CONSIDERED, AND WHAT HE CLAIMED. 若 and 抑 are said to be correlatives, in which case they=our "although" and "yet." More naturally, we may join 若 directly with 聖與仁, and take 抑 as=our "but." 云 爾, see chap. xviii. 2. 已 矣, added to 云 爾, increases its emphasis,="just this and nothing more." Kung-hsî Hwâ, see V, vii, 4.

34. CONFUCIUS DECLINES TO BE PRAYED FOR. 疾 病 together mean "very sick." 有 諸;—諸 is interrogative, as we find it frequently in Mencius. 誄, "to write a eulogy,

and confer the posthumous honorary title"; also, "to eulogize in prayer," i. e., to recite one's excellences as the ground of supplication. Lêi is a special form of composition corresponding to the French *éloge*, specimens of which are to be found in the Wăn Hsüan (文 選), of prince Hsiâo T'ung. Wylie, "Notes on Chinese Literature," p. 192, calls them "obituaries." Tsze-lû must have been referring to some well-known collection of such compositions. In 禱爾, 爾 may be taken as the pronoun. 上 下=heaven and earth, 神 being the appropriate designation of

不猛、恭而安。

子溫而厲、威而

蕩、小人長戚戚。

子曰、君子坦蕩

也、寧固。

儉、則固、與其不孫

子曰、奢、則不孫、

子曰、丘之禱久矣。

worlds.'" The Master said, "My praying has been for a long time."

CHAPTER XXXV. The Master said, "Extravagance leads to insubordination, and parsimony to meanness. It is better to be mean than to be insubordinate."

CHAPTER XXXVI. The Master said, "The superior man is satisfied and composed; the mean man is always full of distress."

CHAPTER XXXVII. The Master was mild, and yet dignified; majestic, and yet not fierce; respectful, and yet easy.

the spirits of the former, and 祇 of the latter.—Chû Hsî says, "Prayer is the expression of repentance and promise of amendment, to supplicate the help of the spirits. If there be not those things, then there is no need for praying. In the case of the sage, he had committed no errors, and admitted of no amendment. In all his conduct he had been in harmony with the spiritual intelligences, and therefore he said,—*my praying has been for a long time.*" We must demur to some of these expressions; but the declining to be prayed for, and the concluding remark, seem to indicate the satisfaction of Confucius with himself. We wish that our information about him were not so stinted and fragmentary.

35. MEANNESS NOT SO BAD AS INSUBORDINATION. 孫, read *sun*, like 遜, and with the same meaning.

36. CONTRAST IN THEIR FEELINGS BETWEEN THE CHÜN-TSZE AND THE MEAN MAN. 坦, "a level plain," used adverbially with 然.="lightsomely." This is its force here. 長=常 時, "constantly."

37. HOW VARIOUS ELEMENTS MODIFIED ONE ANOTHER IN THE CHARACTER OF CONFUCIUS.

## BOOK VIII.　T‘ÂI-PO

得而稱焉。 天下讓、民無 也已矣、三以 其可謂至德 子曰、泰伯 泰伯第八

CHAPTER I.　The Master said, "T‘âi-po may be said to have reached the highest point of virtuous action. Thrice he declined the kingdom, and the people *in ignorance of his motives* could not express their approbation of his conduct."

THE HEADING OF THIS BOOK.—泰 伯 第 八. "T‘âi-po, Book VIII." As in other cases, the first words of the Book give the name to it. The subjects of the chapter are miscellaneous, but it begins and ends with the character and deeds of ancient sages and worthies, and on this account it follows the seventh chapter, where we have Confucius himself described.

1. THE EXCEEDING VIRTUE OF T‘ÂI-PO. T‘âi-po was the eldest son of king T‘âi (大), the grandfather of Wăn, the founder of the Châu dynasty. T‘âi had formed the intention of upsetting the Yin dynasty, of which T‘âi-po disapproved. T‘âi, moreover, because of the sage virtues of his grandson Ch‘ang (昌), who afterwards became King Wăn, wished to hand down his principality to his third son, Ch‘ang's father. T‘âi-po observing this, and to escape opposing his father's purpose, retired with his second brother among the barbarous tribes of the south, and left their youngest brother in possession of the state. The motives of his conduct T‘âi-po kept to himself, so that the people 不 得 而 稱 之, "could not find how to praise him." There is a difficulty in making out the refusal of the empire *three* times, there being different accounts of the times and ways in which he did so. Chû Hsî cuts the knot, by making "thrice"="firmly," in which solution we may acquiesce. There is as great difficulty to find out a declining of the kingdom in T‘âi-po's withdrawing from the petty State of Châu. It may be added that King Wû, the first sovereign of the Châu dynasty, subsequently conferred on T‘âi-po the posthumous title of Chief of Wû (吳), the country to which he had withdrawn, and whose rude inhabitants gathered round him. His second brother succeeded him in the government of them, and hence the ruling house of Wû had the same surname as the royal house of Châu, that namely of Chî (姬);—see VII, xxx. 也 已 矣 give emphasis to the preceding declaration;—compare I xiv.

民不偷。

於仁、故舊不遺、則

子篤於親、則民興

直而無禮則絞君

蒽、勇而無禮則亂、

則勞、愼而無禮則

子曰、恭而無禮

CHAPTER II. 1. The Master said, "Respectfulness, without the rules of propriety, becomes laborious bustle; carefulness, without the rules of propriety, becomes timidity; boldness, without the rules of propriety, becomes insubordination; straightforwardness, without the rules of propriety, becomes rudeness.

2. "When those who are in high stations perform well all their duties to their relations, the people are aroused to virtue. When old friends are not neglected by them, the people are preserved from meanness."

2. THE VALUE OF THE RULES OF PROPRIETY; AND OF EXAMPLE IN THOSE IN HIGH STATIONS. 1. We must bear in mind that the ceremonies, or rules of propriety, spoken of in these Books, are not mere conventionalities, but the ordinations of man's moral and intelligent nature in the line of what is *proper*. 絞, "to strangle," is here explained by Chû Hsî by 急切. Ho Yen, after Mâ Yung, early part of 2nd century, makes it=絞剌 "sarcasm." 2.

There does not seem any connection between the former paragraph and this, and hence this is by many considered to be a new chapter, and assigned to the philosopher Tsăng. 君子 differs here from its previous usage, having reference more to the 位 or station of the individuals indicated, than to their 德 or virtue. 故舊=舊臣舊交, "old ministers and old intimacies." 偷, often a verb, "to steal"; here an adjective, "mean."

哀、人之將死、其言
鳥之將死其鳴也
子問之曾子言曰、
曾子有疾、孟敬
知免夫小子。
薄冰、而今而後、吾
予手、詩云、戰戰兢
弟子曰啟予足、啟
曾子有疾、召門

CHAPTER III. The philosopher Tsăng being ill, he called to him the disciples of his school, and said, "Uncover my feet, uncover my hands. It is said in the Book of Poetry, 'We should be apprehensive and cautious, as if on the brink of a deep gulf, as if treading on thin ice,' *and so have I been.* Now and hereafter, I know my escape *from all injury to my person.* O ye, my little children."

CHAPTER IV. 1. The philosopher Tsăng being ill, Măng Chăng went to ask how he was.

2. Tsăng said to him, "When a bird is about to die, its notes are mournful; when a man is about to die, his words are good.

3. THE PHILOSOPHER TSĂNG'S FILIAL PIETY SEEN IN HIS CARE OF HIS PERSON. We get our bodies perfect from our parents, and should so preserve them to the last. This is a great branch of filial piety with the Chinese, and this chapter is said to illustrate how Tsăng-tsze (I, iv) had made this his life-long study. He made the disciples uncover his hands and feet to show them in what preservation those members were. 詩 云,—see the Shih-ching, II, v, I, st. 6. In 而 今, we must take 而＝自. Wang Yin-chih, however, takes the first 而 as ＝乃, and adduces other instances of 乃＝而. Still the usage is remarkable.

4. THE PHILOSOPHER TSĂNG'S DYING COUNSELS TO A MAN OF HIGH RANK. 1. 敬 was the honorary epithet of 仲孫捷, a great officer of Lû, and son of Măng-wû, II, vi. From the conclusion of this chapter, we may suppose that he descended to small matters below his rank. 之 refers to 疾. 2. 言, in 曾子言曰, intimates that Tsăng commenced the conversation. 3. 動, 正, and 出 are all＝ verbs governing the nouns following.

也善君子所貴乎道者三、
動容貌、斯遠暴慢矣、正顏
色、斯近信矣、出辭氣斯遠
鄙倍矣、籩豆之事、則有司
存。
曾子曰以能問於不能、
以多問於寡、有若無、實若

·3. "There are three principles of conduct which the man of high rank should consider specially important:—that in his deportment and manner he keep from violence and heedlessness; that in regulating his countenance he keep near to sincerity; and that in his words and tones he keep far from lowness and impropriety. As to such matters as attending to the sacrificial vessels, there are the proper officers for them."

CHAPTER V. The philosopher Tsăng said, "Gifted with ability, and yet putting questions to those who were not so; possessed of much, and yet putting questions to those possessed of little; having, as though he had not; full, and yet counting himself as empty;

倍 is read like 背, and with the same meaning, "to rebel against," "to be contrary to," that here opposed being 違, "the truth and right." 籩 was a bamboo dish with a stand, made to hold fruits and seeds at sacrifice; 豆 was like it, and of the same size, only made of wood, and used to contain pickled vegetables and sauces 君 子 is used as in chap. ii —In Ho Yen's compilation,

the three clauses, beginning 斯 遠, are taken not so well, and = "thus he will not suffer from men's being violent and insulting, etc. etc."

5. THE ADMIRABLE SIMPLICITY AND FREEDOM FROM EGOTISM OF A FRIEND OF THE PHILOSOPHER TSĂNG This friend is supposed to have been Yen Yûan. 校, "imprisonment by means of wood," "stocks." The dictionary, after the old writers,

虛、犯而不校、昔者吾友嘗

從事於斯矣。

曾子曰可以託六尺之

孤、可以寄百里之命、臨大

節、而不可奪也君子人與、

君子人也。

曾子曰、士、不可以不弘

offended against, and yet entering into no altercation; formerly I had a friend who pursued this style of conduct."

CHAPTER VI. The philosopher Tsăng said, "Suppose that there is an individual who can be intrusted with the charge of a young orphan *prince*, and can be commissioned with authority over *a state of* a hundred *li*, and whom no emergency however great can drive from his principles:—is such a man a superior man? He is a superior man indeed."

CHAPTER VII. 1. The philosopher Tsăng said, "The officer may not be without breadth of mind and

explains it with reference to this passage, by 角 也, 報 也, "altercation," "retorting." 從 事 於 斯, literally, "followed things in this *way.*"

6. A COMBINATION OF TALENTS AND VIRTUE CONSTITUTING A CHÜN-TSZE. 六 尺 之 孤, "an orphan of six cubits." By a comparison of a passage in the Châu Lî and other references, it is established that "of six cubits" is equivalent to "of fifteen years or less," and that for every cubit more or less we should add or deduct five years. See the

經 註 集 證, where it is also said that the ancient cubit was shorter than the modern, and only=7.4 in., so that six cubits=4.44 cubits of the present day. But this estimate of the ancient cubit is probably still too high. King Wăn, it is said, was ten cubits high. 百 里 之 命, see Mencius, V, Pt. ii, ch. ii, 6. 與 amounts nearly to a question, and is answered by 也,—"Yes, indeed."

7. THE NECESSITY TO THE OFFICER OF COMPASS AND VIGOR OF MIND. 1. 士, a learned man, "a scholar"; but in all ages learning has been the

之。由之不可使知　子曰、民可使　立於禮成於樂。　子曰、興於詩。　已、不亦遠乎。　仁以爲己任、不亦重乎、死而後　毅、任重而道遠。

vigorous endurance. His burden is heavy and his course is long.

2. "Perfect virtue is the burden which he considers it is his to sustain;—is it not heavy? Only with death does his course stop;—is it not long?"

CHAPTER VIII. 1. The Master said, "It is by the Odes that the mind is aroused.

2. "It is by the Rules of Propriety that the character is established.

3. "It is from Music that the finish is received."

CHAPTER IX. The Master said, "The people may be made to follow a path of action, but they may not be made to understand it."

qualification for, and passport to, official employment in China, hence it is also a general designation for "an officer." 任, 4th tone, a noun, = "an office," "a burden borne"; with the 2nd tone, it is the verb "to bear."

8. THE EFFECTS OF POETRY, PROPRIETIES, AND MUSIC. These three short sentences are in form like the four, 志 於 道, etc., in VII, vi, but must be interpreted differently. There the first term in each sentence is a verb in the imperative mood, here it is rather in the indicative. There the 於 is to be joined closely to the 1st character and here to the 3rd. There it = our preposition *to;* here it = *by.* The terms 詩, 禮, 樂

have all specific reference to the Books so called.

9. WHAT MAY, AND WHAT MAY NOT, BE ATTAINED TO WITH THE PEOPLE. According to Chû Hsî, the first 之 is 理 之 所 當 然,—*duty,* what principles require, and the second is 理 之 所 以 然, "the *principle* of duty." He also takes 可 and 不 可 as = 能 and 不 能. If the meaning were so, then the sentiment would be much too broadly expressed. See 四 書 改 錯, XVI, xv. As often in other places, the 翼 註 gives the meaning here happily; viz., that a knowledge of the reasons and principles of what they are called to do need not be required from the people,—不 可 責 之 民.

子曰、好勇疾貧、亂也、

人而不仁、疾之已甚、亂

也。

子曰、如有周公之才

之美、使驕且吝、其餘不

足觀也已。

子曰三年學、不至於

穀、不易得也。

CHAPTER X. The Master said, "The man who is fond of daring and is dissatisfied with poverty, will proceed to insubordination. So will the man who is not virtuous, when you carry your dislike of him to an extreme."

CHAPTER XI. The Master said, "Though a man have abilities as admirable as those of the duke of Châu, yet if he be proud and niggardly, those other things are really not worth being looked at."

CHAPTER XII. The Master said, "It is not easy to find a man who has learned for three years without coming to be good."

10. DIFFERENT CAUSES OF INSUBORDINATION:—A LESSON TO RULERS.

11. THE WORTHLESSNESS OF TALENT WITHOUT VIRTUE. "The duke of Châu;"—see VII, v. 其餘, "the overplus," "the superfluity," referring to the "talents," and indicating that ability is not the 本, or root of character, not what is essential. 也 已, as in chap. i.

12. HOW QUICKLY LEARNING MAKES MEN GOOD. This is the interpretation of K'ung Ân-kwo, who takes 穀 in the sense of 善. Chû Hsî takes the term in the sense of 祿, "emolument," and would change 至 into 志, making the whole a lamentation over the rarity of the disinterested pursuit of learning. But we are not at liberty to admit alterations of the text, unless, as received, it is absolutely unintelligible.

其政。子曰不在其位不謀恥也。恥也邦無道富且貴焉則隱邦有道貧且賤焉居天下有道則見無道善道危邦不入亂邦不子曰篤信好學守死

CHAPTER XIII. 1. The Master said, "With sincere faith he unites the love of learning; holding firm to death, he is perfecting the excellence of his course.

2. "*Such a one* will not enter a tottering state, nor dwell in a disorganized one. When right principles of government prevail in the kingdom, he will show himself; when they are prostrated, he will keep concealed.

3. "When a country is well governed, poverty and a mean condition are things to be ashamed of. When a country is ill governed, riches and honor are things to be ashamed of."

CHAPTER XIV. The Master said, "He who is not in any particular office has nothing to do with plans for the administration of its duties."

13. THE QUALIFICATIONS OF AN OFFICER, WHO WILL ALWAYS ACT RIGHT IN ACCEPTING AND DECLINING OFFICE. 1. This paragraph is taken as descriptive of character, the effects of whose presence we have in the next, and of its absence in the last. 2. 見 in opposition to 隱, read *hsien*, in 4th tone. The whole chapter seems to want the warmth of generous principle and feeling. In fact, I doubt whether its parts bear the relation and connection which they are supposed to have.

14 EVERY MAN SHOULD MIND HIS OWN BUSINESS. So the sentiment of this chapter is generalized by the paraphrasts, and perhaps correctly. Its letter, however, has doubtless operated to prevent the spread of right notions about political liberty in China.

子曰學如不及猶恐

子曰師摯之始關雎

之亂洋洋乎、盈耳哉。

子曰狂而不直侗而

不願悾悾而不信吾不

知之矣。

失之。

CHAPTER XV. The Master said, "When the music master Chih first entered on his office, the finish of the Kwan Tsü was magnificent;—how it filled the ears!"

CHAPTER XVI. The Master said, "Ardent and yet not upright, stupid and yet not attentive; simple and yet not sincere:—such persons I do not understand."

CHAPTER XVII. The Master said, "Learn as if you could not reach your object, and were *always* fearing also lest you should lose it."

15. THE PRAISE OF THE MUSIC MASTER CHIH. Neither Morrison nor Medhurst gives what appears to be the meaning of 亂 in this chapter. The K'ang-hsî dictionary has it—樂 之卒章曰亂, "The last part in the musical services is called *lwan*." The program on those occasions consisted of four parts, in the last of which a number of pieces from the *Fäng* or songs of the states was sung, commencing with the *Kwan Tsü*. The name *lwan* was also given to a sort of refrain, at the end of each song —The old interpreters explain differently,—"when the music master Chih 'first corrected the confusion of the Kwan Tsü," etc.

16. A LAMENTATION OVER MORAL ERROR ADDED TO NATURAL DEFECT. 吾不知之, "I do not know them"; that is, say commentators, natural defects of endowment are generally associated with certain redeeming qualities, as hastiness with straight-forwardness, etc., but in the parties Confucius had in view, those redeeming qualities were absent. He did not understand them, and could do nothing for them.

17. WITH WHAT EARNESTNESS AND CONTINUOUSNESS LEARNING SHOULD BE PURSUED.

其有成功也焕乎、其
民無能名焉巍巍乎、
大唯堯則之蕩蕩乎、
君也巍巍乎唯天爲
子曰、大哉堯之爲
爲。
之有天下也、而不與
子曰、巍巍乎、舜禹
有文章。

CHAPTER XVIII. The Master said, "How majestic was the manner in which Shun and Yü held possession of the empire, as if it were nothing to them!"

CHAPTER XIX. 1. The Master said, "Great indeed was Yâo as a sovereign! How majestic was he! It is only Heaven that is grand, and only Yâo corresponded to it. How vast *was his virtue!* The people could find no name for it.

2. "How majestic was he in the works which he accomplished! How glorious in the elegant regulations which he instituted!"

18. THE LOFTY CHARACTER OF SHUN AND YU. Shun received the empire from Yâo, 2255 B. C., and Yu received it from Shun, 2205 B. C. The throne came to them not by inheritance. They were called to it through their talents and virtue. And yet the possession of it did not affect them at all. 不 與,—"it did not concern them," was as if nothing to them. Ho Yen takes 與=求,—"they had the empire without seeking for it." This is not according to usage.

19. THE PRAISE OF YÂO. 1. No doubt, Yâo, as he appears in Chinese annals, is a fit object of admiration, but if Confucius had had a right knowledge of, and reverence for, Heaven, he could not have spoken as he does here. Grant that it is only the visible heaven overspreading all, to which he compares Yâo, even that is sufficiently absurd. 則 之, not simply=法 之, "imitated it," but 能 與 之 準, "could equalize with it." 2. 其 有 成 功=其 所 有 之 成 功, the great achievements of his government. 文 章 (see V, xii)=the music, ceremonies, etc., of which he was the author.

而已。三分天下

有婦人焉、九人

之際、於斯爲盛、

不其然乎、唐虞

人孔子曰才難、

曰予有亂臣十

而天下治武王

舜有臣五人、

CHAPTER XX. 1. Shun had five ministers, and the empire was well governed.

2. King Wû said, "I have ten able ministers."

3. Confucius said, "Is not *the saying* that talents are difficult to find, true? *Only* when the dynasties of T'ang and Yü met, were they more abundant than in this *of Châu, yet* there was a woman among them. *The able ministers* were no more than nine men.

4. · "*King Wăn* possessed two of the three parts of

20. THE SCARCITY OF MEN OF TALENT, AND PRAISE OF THE HOUSE OF CHÂU. 1. Shun's five ministers were 禹, Superintendent of Works; 稷, Superintendent of Agriculture; 契 (hsieh), Minister of Instruction; 皋陶, Minister of Justice; and 伯益, Warden of Woods and Marshes. Those five, as being eminent above all their compeers, are mentioned. 2. See the Shû-ching, V, i, sect. ii, 6. 亂臣, "governing, i. e., able ministers." In the dictionary, the first meaning given of 亂 is "to regulate," and the second is just the opposite, —"to confound," "confusion." Of the ten ministers, the most distinguished of course was the duke of Châu. One of them, it is said, next paragraph, was a woman, but whether she was the mother of King Wăn, or his wife, is much disputed. The ten men were:—the duke of Châu, the duke of Shâo, Grandfather Hope, the duke of Pî, the duke of

Yung, T'âi-tien, Hung-yâo, San-î Shăng, Nan-kung Kwo, and the wife or mother of King Wăn. 3. Instead of the usual "The Master said," we have here 孔子曰 "The philosopher K'ung said." This is accounted for on the ground that the words of *King* Wû having been quoted immediately before, it would not have been right to crown the sage with 'his usual title of "the *Master*." The style of the whole chapter, however, is different from that of any previous one, and we may suspect that it is corrupt. 才難 is a sort of proverb, or common saying, which Confucius quotes and illustrates. 唐虞之際 (Yâo is called T'ang, having ascended the throne from the marquisate of that name, and Yu became a sort of accepted surname or style of Shun) 於斯爲盛 is understood by Chû Hsî as in the translation, while the old writers take exactly the opposite

有其二以服事殷、周
之德其可謂至德也
已矣。
曾子曰、禹吾無間然
矣、菲飲食、而致孝乎
鬼神、惡衣服、而致美
乎黻冕卑宮室而盡
力乎溝洫、禹吾無間
然矣。

the empire, and with those he served the dynasty of Yin. The virtue of the house of Châu may be said to have reached the highest point indeed."

CHAPTER XXI. The Master said, "I can find no flaw in the character of Yü: He used himself coarse food and drink, but displayed the utmost filial piety towards the spirits. His ordinary garments were poor, but he displayed the utmost elegance in his sacrificial cap and apron. He lived in a low, mean house, but expended all his strength on the ditches and water channels. I can find nothing like a flaw in Yü."

view. The whole is obscure. 4. This paragraph must be spoken of King Wăn.

21. THE PRAISE OF YÜ. 間, read *chien*, 4th tone, "a crevice," "a crack." The form 閒 in the text is not so correct. 禹吾無間然矣. "*In Yu, I find* no crevice so," i. e., I find nothing in him to which I can point as a flaw. 鬼神 is interpreted of the spirits of heaven and earth, as well as those sacrificed to in the ancestral temple, but the saying that the rich offerings were filial (孝) would seem to restrict the phrase to the latter. The 黻 was an apron made of leather, and coming down over the knees, and the 冕 was a sort of cap or crown, flat on the top, and projecting before and behind, with a long fringe on which gems and pearls were strung, exactly like the Christ-Church cap of Oxford. They were both used in sacrificing. 溝洫, generally the water channels by which the boundaries of the fields were determined, and provision made for their irrigation, and to carry off the water of floods. The 溝 were four cubits wide and deep, and arranged so as to flow into the 洫, which were double the size.

## BOOK IX. TSZE HAN

而無所成　孔子、博學　人曰、大哉　達巷黨　仁。　利、與命與　子罕言、　子罕第九

CHAPTER I. The subjects of which the Master seldom spoke were—profitableness, and also the appointments *of Heaven*, and perfect virtue.

CHAPTER II. 1. A man of the village of Tâ-hsiang said, "Great indeed is the philosopher K'ung! His learning is extensive, and yet he does not render his name famous by any *particular* thing."

HEADING OF THIS BOOK.—子罕第 九, "The Master seldom, No. 9." The thirty chapters of this Book are much akin to those of the seventh. They are mostly occupied with the doctrine, character, and ways of Confucius himself.

1. SUBJECTS SELDOM SPOKEN OF BY CONFUCIUS. 利 is mostly taken here in a good sense, not as selfish gain, but as it is defined under the first of the diagrams in the Yî-ching, 一義之和, "the harmoniousness of all that is righteous"; that is, how what is right is really what is truly profitable. Compare Mencius, I, i, 1. Yet even in this sense Confucius seldom spoke of it, as he would not have the consideration of the profitable introduced into conduct at all. With his not speaking of 仁 there is a difficulty which I know not how to solve. The fourth Book is nearly all occupied with it, and no doubt it was a prominent topic in Confucius's teachings. 命 is not=our *fate*, unless in the primary meaning of that term,—"*Fatum est quod dii fantur.*" Nor is it *decree*, or antecedent purpose and determination, but the decree embodied and realized in its object.

2. AMUSEMENT OF CONFUCIUS AT THE REMARK OF AN IGNORANT MAN ABOUT HIM. Commentators, old and new, say that the chapter shows the exceeding humility of the sage, educed by his being praised, but his observation on the man's remark was evidently ironical. 1. For want of another word, I render 黨 by "village." According to the statutes of Châu, "five families made a 比, four *pî* a 閭, and five *lü* or 500 families a *tang*." Who the villager was is not recorded, though some would have him to be the same with 項橐, the boy of whom it is said in the 三字經, 昔仲尼師項橐, "of old Confucius was a scholar of Hsiang T'o." The man was able to see that Confucius was very extensively learned, but his idea of fame, common to the age, was that it must be.

名子聞之謂門弟子曰、

吾何執執御乎、執射乎、

吾執御矣。

子曰、麻冕禮也、今也

純、儉、吾從衆拜下、禮也

今拜乎上、泰也雖違衆、

吾從下。

2. The Master heard the observation, and said to his disciples, "What shall I practice? Shall I practice charioteering, or shall I practice archery? I will practice charioteering."

CHAPTER III. 1. The Master said, "The linen cap is that prescribed by the rules of ceremony, but now a silk one is worn. It is economical, and I follow the common practice.

2. "The rules of ceremony prescribe the bowing below *the hall*, but now the practice is to bow *only* after ascending it. That is arrogant. I *continue to* bow below the hall, though I oppose the common practice."

acquired by excellence in some one particular art. In his lips, 孔子 was not more than our "Mr. K'ung."

3. SOME COMMON PRACTICES INDIFFERENT AND OTHERS NOT. 1. The cap here spoken of was that prescribed to be worn in the ancestral temple, and made of very fine linen dyed of a deep dark color. It had fallen into disuse, and was superseded by a simpler one of silk Rather than be singular, Confucius gave in to a practice, which involved no principle of right, and was economical. 2. Chú Hsi explains the 拜 下, 拜 乎 上, thus: "In the ceremonial intercourse between ministers and their prince, it was proper for them to bow below the raised hall. This the prince declined, on which they ascended and completed the homage." See this illustrated in the 經 註 集 證, *in loc.* The prevailing disregard of the first part of the ceremony Confucius considered inconsistent with the proper distance to be observed between prince and minister, and therefore he would be singular in adhering to the rule.

子絕四、毋
意、毋必、毋固、
毋我。

子畏於匡。
曰、文王既沒、
文不在茲乎。
天之將喪斯

CHAPTER IV. There were four things from which the Master was entirely free. He had no foregone conclusions, no arbitrary predeterminations, no obstinacy, and no egoism.

CHAPTER V. 1. The Master was put in fear in K'wang.

2. He said, "After the death of King Wăn, was not the cause of truth lodged here *in me?*

3. "If Heaven had wished to let this cause of truth perish, then I, a future mortal, should not have got

4. FRAILTIES FROM WHICH CONFUCIUS WAS FREE. 毋, it is said, is not prohibitive here, but simply negative;—to make it appear that it was not by any effort, as 絕 and 毋 more naturally suggest that Confucius attained to these things.

5. CONFUCIUS ASSURED IN A TIME OF DANGER BY HIS CONVICTION OF A DIVINE MISSION. Compare VII, xxii, but the adventure to which this chapter refers is placed in the sage's history before the other, not long after he had resigned office, and left Lû. 1. There are different opinions as to what state K'wang belonged to. The most likely is that it was a border town of Chăng, and its site is now to be found in the department of Kaifeng in Honan. It is said that K'wang had suffered from 陽 虎, an officer of Lû, to whom Confucius bore a resemblance. As he passed by the place, moreover, a disciple,

顏 刻, who had been associated with Yang Hu in his measures against K'wang, was driving him. These circumstances made the people think that Confucius was their old enemy, so they attacked him, and kept him prisoner for five days. The accounts of his escape vary, some of them being evidently fabulous. The disciples were in fear. 畏 would indicate that Confucius himself was so, but this is denied 2. The *wăn* I render by "the cause of truth." More exactly, it is the truth embodied in literature, ceremonies, etc., and its use instead of *tâo*, "truth in its principles," is attributed to Confucius's modesty. 在 茲, "in this," referring to himself. 3. There may be modesty in his use of *wăn*, but he here identifies himself with the line of the great sages, to whom Heaven has intrusted the instruction of men. In all the six centuries between

宰知我乎、吾少也賤、故
又多能也子聞之曰、大
子貢曰固天縱之將聖、
子聖者與、何其多能也。
鼇大宰問於子貢曰、夫
也匡人其如予何。
斯文也、天之未喪斯文
文也、後死者不得與於

such a relation to that cause.　While Heaven does not
let the cause of truth perish, what can the people of
K'wang do to me?"

CHAPTER VI.　1. A high officer asked Tsze-kung,
saying, "May we not say that your Master is a sage?
How various is his ability!"

2.　Tsze-kung said, "Certainly Heaven has endowed
him unlimitedly.　He is about a sage.　And, moreover, his ability is various."

3.　The Master heard of the conversation and said,
"Does the high officer know me?　When I was young,
my condition was low, and therefore I acquired my

himself and King Wǎn, he does not
admit of such another.　後 死 者,
"he who dies afterwards,"＝a future
mortal.

6. ON THE VARIOUS ABILITY OF
CONFUCIUS:—HIS SAGEHOOD NOT
THEREIN. 1. According to the 周 禮,
the 大 宰 was the chief of the six
great officers of state, but the use of
the designation in Confucius's time
was confined to the states of Wû
and Sung, and hence the officer in the
text must have belonged to one of
them. See the 註 疏, in loc. The

force of 與 is as appears in the
translation.　2. 與 is responded to
by Tsze-kung with 固, "certainly,"
while yet by the use of 將 he gives
his answer an air of hesitancy. 縱
之, "lets him go," i. e., does not
restrict him at all.　The officer had
found the sagehood of Confucius in
his various ability;—by the yû,
"moreover," Tsze-kung makes that
ability only an additional circumstance.　3. Confucius explains his
possession of various ability, and
repudiates its being essential to the

子曰、鳳鳥不至、

焉。

我叩其兩端而竭

問於我空空如也、

哉、無知也、有鄙夫

子曰吾有知乎

乎哉、不多也。牢曰、

多能鄙事、君子多

子云吾不試故藝。

ability in many things, but they were mean matters. Must the superior man have such variety of ability? He does not need variety of ability."

4. Lâo said, "The Master said, 'Having no official employment, I acquired many arts.'"

CHAPTER VII. The Master said, "Am I indeed possessed of knowledge? I am not knowing. But if a mean person, who appears quite emptylike, ask anything of me, I set it forth from one end to the other, and exhaust it."

CHAPTER VIII. The Master said, "The FĂNG bird

sage, or even to the *chun-tsze*. 4. Lâo was a disciple, by surname Ch'in (琴), and styled Tsze-k'ai (子 開), or Tsze-chang (子 張). It is supposed that when these conversations were being digested into their present form, some one remembered that Lâo had been in the habit of mentioning the remark given, and accordingly it was appended to the chapter. 子 云 indicates that it was a frequent saying of Confucius.

7. CONFUCIUS DISCLAIMS THE KNOWLEDGE ATTRIBUTED TO HIM, AND DECLARES HIS EARNESTNESS IN TEACHING. The first sentence here was probably an exclamation with

reference to some remark upon himself as having extraordinary knowledge. 叩其兩端, "exhibit (叩＝發 動, 'to agitate') its two ends," i. e., discuss it from beginning to end.

8. FOR WANT OF AUSPICIOUS OMENS. CONFUCIUS GIVES UP THE HOPE OF THE TRIUMPH OF HIS DOCTRINES. The *făng* is the male of a fabulous bird, which has been called the Chinese phœnix, said to appear when a sage ascends the throne or when right principles are going to triumph in the world. The female is called 凰. In the days of Shun, they gamboled in his hall, and were heard singing on Mount Ch'i in the

河不出圖、吾已矣
夫。
子見齊衰者、冕
衣裳者、與瞽者見
之、雖少必作、過之
必趨。
顏淵喟然歎曰、
仰之彌高鑽之彌
堅瞻之在前、忽焉

does not come; the river sends forth no map:—it is all over with me!"

CHAPTER IX. When the Master saw a person in a mourning dress, or any one with the cap and upper and lower garments of full dress, or a blind person, on observing them *approaching*, though they were younger than himself, he would rise up, and if he had to pass by them, he would do so hastily.

CHAPTER X. 1. Yen Yüan, *in admiration of the Master's doctrines*, sighed and said, "I looked up to them, and they *seemed to become* more high; I tried to penetrate them, and they *seemed to become* more firm; I looked at them before me, and suddenly they *seemed to be* behind.

time of King Wăn. The river and the map carry us farther back still, —to the time of Fú-hsî, to whom a monster with the head of a dragon, and the body of a horse, rose from the water, being marked on the back so as to give that first of the sages the idea of his diagrams. Confucius indorses these fables. 吾已矣夫, —see V, xxvi, and observe how 乎 and 夫 are interchanged.

9. CONFUCIUS'S SYMPATHY WITH SORROW, RESPECT FOR RANK, AND PITY FOR MISFORTUNE. 齊, read *tsze*, is "the lower edge of a garment," and joined with 衰, read *ts'ui*,

"mourning garments," the two characters indicate the mourning of the second degree of intensity, where the edge is unhemmed, but cut *even*, instead of being ragged, the terms for which are 斬 衰. The phrase, however, seems to be for "in mourning" generally. 少, in 4th tone, "young."

10. YEN YÜAN'S ADMIRATION OF HIS MASTER'S DOCTRINES; AND HIS OWN PROGRESS IN THEM. 1. 喟然歎, "sighingly sighed." 仰 and the other verbs here are to be translated in the past tense, as the chapter seems to give an account of the

而爲有臣、吾誰欺、欺

哉、由之行詐也、無臣

人爲臣病間曰久矣

子疾病、子路使門

雖欲從之末由也已。

吾才、如有所立卓爾、

以禮。欲罷不能、既竭

誘人、博我以文約我

在後。夫子循循然善

2. "The Master, by orderly method, skillfully leads men on. He enlarged my mind with learning, and taught me the restraints of propriety.

3. "When I wish to give over *the study of his doctrines*, I cannot do so, and having exerted all my ability, there seems something to stand right up before me; but though I wish to follow *and lay hold of it*, I really find no way to do so."

CHAPTER XI. 1. The Master being very ill, Tsze-lû wished the disciples to act as ministers to him.

2. During a remission of his illness, he said, "Long has the conduct of Yû been deceitful! By pretending to have ministers when I have them not, whom should I impose upon? Should I impose upon Heaven?

progress of Hûi's mind. 忽 焉＝忽 然, "suddenly." 2. 誘＝引 進, "to lead forward." 博 我 云 云,—comp. VI, x, v. 3. 卓 爾＝卓 然, an adverb, "uprightly," "loftily." 末, in the sense of 無, 末 由＝無 所 由 以 用 其 力, "I find myself unable to use my strength." 也 已, "yea, indeed"—It was this which made him sigh.

11. CONFUCIUS'S DISLIKE OF PRETENSION, AND CONTENTMENT WITH HIS CONDITION. 1. 使, "was causing," or wanted to cause. Confucius had been a great officer, and enjoyed the services of ministers, as in a petty court. Tsze-lû would have surrounded him in his great sickness with the illusions of his former state, and brought on himself this rebuke.

天乎且予與其死於
臣之手也、無寧死於
二三子之手乎、且予
縱不得大葬予死於
道路乎。
子貢曰、有美玉於
斯、韞匵而藏諸求善
賈而沽諸子曰沽之
哉、沽之哉、我待賈者
也。子欲居九夷、或曰、
陋、如之何子曰君子
居之、何陋之有。

3. "Moreover, than that I should die in the hands of ministers, is it not better that I should die in the hands of you, my disciples? And though I may not get a great burial, shall I die upon the road?"

CHAPTER XII. Tsze-kung said, "There is a beautiful gem here. Should I lay it up in a case and keep it? or should I seek for a good price and sell it?" The Master said, "Sell it! Sell it! But I would wait for one to offer the price."

CHAPTER XIII. 1. The Master was wishing to go and live among the nine wild tribes of the east.

2. Some one said, "They are rude. How can you do such a thing?" The Master said, "If a superior man dwelt among them, what rudeness would there be?"

3. 縱 = 縱然, as a conjunction, "letting it be that," = although.

12. HOW THE DESIRE FOR OFFICE SHOULD BE QUALIFIED BY SELF-RESPECT. 諸 is interrogative here, as in VII, xxxiv. There being no nominative to 韞, like the "I" in the translation, we might render, "should it be put," etc. 賈, read *chiâ*, 4th tone = 價, "price," "value." The disciple wanted to elicit from Confucius why he declined office so much, and insinuated his question in this way. It seems better to translate *yü* here by "a gem," or a "precious stone," than by "a piece of jade."

13. HOW BARBARIANS CAN BE CIVILIZED. This chapter is to be understood, it is said, like V, vi, not as if Confucius really wished to go among the Î, but that he thus expressed his regret that his doctrine did not find acceptance in China. 1. The Î,—see III, v. There were nine tribes or varieties (種) of them, the yellow, white, red, etc. 2. 如之何,—the 之 refers to his purpose, to go among the Î.

臺子曰吾自衞

反魯、然後樂正、

雅頌各得其所。

臺子曰、出則事

公卿、入則事父

兄、喪事不敢不

勉、不爲酒困、何

有於我哉。

臺子在川上曰、

CHAPTER XIV. The Master said, "I returned from Wei to Lû, and then the music was reformed, and the pieces in the Royal songs and Praise songs all found their proper places."

CHAPTER XV. The Master said, "Abroad, to serve the high ministers and nobles; at home, to serve one's father and elder brothers; in all duties to the dead, not to dare not to exert one's self; and not to be overcome of wine:—which one of these things do I attain to?"

CHAPTER XVI. The Master standing by a stream,

14. CONFUCIUS'S SERVICES IN CORRECTING THE MUSIC OF HIS NATIVE STATE AND ADJUSTING THE BOOK OF POETRY. Confucius returned from Wei to Lû in his 69th year, and died five years after. The 雅 (read yâ, 3rd tone) and the 頌 are the names of two, or rather three, of the divisions of the Shih-ching, the former being the "elegant" or "correct" odes, to be used with music at royal festivals, and the latter the praise songs, celebrating principally the virtues of the founders of different dynasties, to be used in the services of the ancestral temple.

15. CONFUCIUS'S VERY HUMBLE ESTIMATE OF HIMSELF. Comp. VII, ii, but the things which Confucius

here disclaims are of a still lower character than those there mentioned. Very remarkable is the last, as from the sage. The old interpreters treat 何 有 於 我 哉. as they do in VII, ii;—compare VII, xxv, xxvii, xxxiii, et al. 公 卿 stand together, indicating men of superior rank. If we distinguish between them, the 公 may express the princes, high officers in the royal court, and the 卿, the high officers in the princes' courts.

16. HOW CONFUCIUS WAS AFFECTED BY A RUNNING STREAM. What does the it in the translation refer to? 者 and 如 indicate something in the sage's mind, suggested by the ceaseless movement of the water.

逝者如斯夫、不舍晝
夜。

子曰、吾未見好德、

如好色者也。

子曰、譬如爲山、未

成一簣止吾止也、譬

如平地雖覆一簣、進、

吾往也。

said, "It passes on just like this, not ceasing day or night!"

CHAPTER XVII. The Master said, "I have not seen one who loves virtue as he loves beauty."

CHAPTER XVIII. The Master said, *"The prosecution of learning* may be compared to what may happen in raising a mound. If there want but one basket *of earth* to complete the work, and I stop, the stopping is my own work. It may be compared to *throwing down the earth* on the level ground. Though *but* one basketful is thrown *at a time,* the advancing with it is my own going forward."

Chû Hsî makes it 天地之化,=our "course of nature." In the 註疏 we find for it 時事, "events," "the things of time." Probably Chû Hsî is correct. Comp. Mencius, IV, Pt. ii, ch. xviii.

17. THE RARITY OF A SINCERE LOVE OF VIRTUE. 色, as in I, vii.

18. THAT LEARNERS SHOULD NOT CEASE NOR INTERMIT THEIR LABORS. This is a fragment, like many other chapters, of some conversation, and the subject thus illustrated must be supplied, after the modern com-mentator, as in the translation, or, after the old, by "the following of virtue." See the Shû-ching, V, v, 9, where the subject is virtuous con-sistency. We might expect 平 in 平地 to be a verb, like 爲 in 爲山, but a good sense cannot be made out by taking it so. 雖,="though *only,*" as many take it in VI, xxiv. The lesson of the chapter is—that re-peated acquisitions individually small will ultimately amount to much, and that the learner is never to give over.

子曰後生可畏、焉知來

夫、秀而不實者有矣夫。

子曰、苗而不秀者有矣

其進也、未見其止也。

子謂顏淵曰、惜乎、吾見

回也與。

子曰、語之而不惰者、其

CHAPTER XIX. The Master said, "Never flagging when I set forth anything to him;—ah! that is Hûi."

CHAPTER XX. The Master said of Yen Yüan, "Alas! I saw his constant advance. I never saw him stop in his progress."

CHAPTER XXI. The Master said, "There are cases in which the blade springs, but the plant does not go on to flower! There are cases where it flowers but no fruit is subsequently produced!"

CHAPTER XXII. The Master said, "A youth is to be regarded with respect. How do we know that

19. Hûi THE EARNEST STUDENT.

20. CONFUCIUS'S FOND RECOLLEC- TION OF Hûi AS A MODEL STUDENT. This is said to have been spoken after Hûi's death. 惜乎 looks as if it were so. The 未, "not yet," would rather make us think dif- ferently.

21. IT IS THE END WHICH CROWNS THE WORK.

22. HOW AND WHY A YOUTH SHOULD BE REGARDED WITH RESPECT.

The same person is spoken of throughout the chapter, as is shown by the 亦 in the last sentence. This is not very conclusive, but it brings out a good enough meaning. With Confucius's remark compare that of John Trebonius, Luther's school- master at Eisenach, who used to raise his cap to his pupils on enter- ing the schoolroom, and gave as the reason—"There are among these boys men of whom God will one day

末如之何也已矣。
說而不繹從而不改、吾
言能無說乎繹之爲貴、
從乎、改之爲貴巽與之
子曰法語之言、能無
畏也已。
十而無聞焉、斯亦不足
者之不如今也、四十五

his future will not be equal to our present? If he reach the age of forty or fifty, and has not made himself heard of, then indeed he will not be worth being regarded with respect."

CHAPTER XXIII. The Master said, "Can men refuse to assent to the words of strict admonition? But it is reforming the conduct because of them which is valuable. Can men refuse to be pleased with words of gentle advice? But it is unfolding their aim which is valuable. If a man be pleased with these words, but does not unfold their aim, and assents to those, but does not reform his conduct, I can really do nothing with him."

make burgomasters, chancellors, doctors, and magistrates. Although you do not yet see them with the badges of their dignity, it is right that you should treat them with respect." 後生, "after born," a youth. See 先生, II, viii.

23. THE HOPELESSNESS OF THE CASE OF THOSE WHO ASSENT AND APPROVED WITHOUT REFORMATION OR SERIOUS THOUGHT. 法 語 之 言, "words of lawlike admonition." 巽 is the name of the 5th trigram, to which the element of "wind" is

attached. Wind enters everywhere, hence the character is interpreted by "entering," and also by "mildness," "yielding." 巽 與 之 言, "words of gentle insinuation." In 繹 之 爲 貴, an antecedent to 之 is readily found in the preceding 言, but in 改 之 爲 貴, such an antecedent can only be found in a roundabout way. This is one of the cases which shows the inapplicability to Chinese composition of our strict syntactical apparatus. 末 as in chap. x.

不忮不求、何用不
不恥者其由也與。
與衣狐貉者立、而
子曰、衣敝縕袍。
志也。
帥也、匹夫不可奪
子曰三軍可奪
勿憚改。
友不如己者過則
子曰主忠信毋

CHAPTER XXIV. The Master said, "Hold faithfulness and sincerity as first principles. Have no friends not equal to yourself. When you have faults, do not fear to abandon them."

CHAPTER XXV. The Master said, "The commander of the forces of a large state may be carried off, but the will of even a common man cannot be taken from him."

CHAPTER XXVI. 1. The Master said, "Dressed himself in a tattered robe quilted with hemp, yet standing by the side of men dressed in furs, and not ashamed;—ah! it is Yû who is equal to this!

2. "'He dislikes none, he covets nothing;—what can he do but what is good!'"

24. This is a repetition of part of I, viii.

25. THE WILL UNSUBDUABLE. 三軍, see VII, x. 帥, read *shwâi*, 4th tone, = 將 帥, "a general." 匹, "mate." We find in the dictionary —"Husband and wife of the common people are a pair (相 匹)," and the application of the term being thus fixed, an individual man is called 匹 夫; an individual woman, 匹 婦.

26. TSZE-LÛ'S BRAVE CONTENTMENT IN POVERTY, BUT FAILURE TO SEEK THE HIGHEST AIMS. 1. On the construction of this paragraph, compare chap. xviii. The 狐 is the fox. The 貉, read *heh*, is probably the badger. It is described as nocturnal in its habits, having a soft, warm fur. It sleeps much, and is carnivorous. This last characteristic is not altogether inapplicable to the badger. See the 本 草 獸 部. 2. See

臧。○三册 子路終身誦之子曰、是

道也何足以臧。

㙤子曰、歲寒、然後知松柏

之後彫也。

㙤子曰知者不惑仁者不

憂勇者不懼。

㙤子曰可與共學、未可與

3. Tsze-lû kept continually repeating these *words of the ode,* when the Master said, "Those things are by no means sufficient to constitute *(perfect)* excellence."

CHAPTER XXVII. The Master said, "When the year becomes cold, then we know how the pine and the cypress are the last to lose their leaves."

CHAPTER XXVIII. The Master said, "The wise are free from perplexities; the virtuous from anxiety; and the bold from fear."

CHAPTER XXIX. The Master said, "There are some with whom we may study in common, but we

the Shih-ching, I, iii, Ode VIII, 4. 3. 終身, not "all his life," as frequently, but "continually." Tsze-lû was a man of impulse, with many fine points, but not sufficiently reflective.

27. MEN ARE KNOWN IN TIMES OF ADVERSITY. 後彫, "the after-withering," a meiosis for their being evergreens.

28. THE SEQUENCES OF WISDOM, VIRTUE, AND BRAVERY. 仁者不憂, —this is one of the sayings about virtue, which is only true when it is combined with trust in God.

29. HOW DIFFERENT INDIVIDUALS STOP AT DIFFERENTS TAGES OF PROGRESS. More literally rendered, this chapter would be—"It may be possible with *some parties* together to study, *but* it may not yet be possible with them to go on to principles, etc." 權, the weight of a steelyard, then "to weigh." It is used here with reference to occurring events,—to weigh them and determine the application of principles to them. In the old commentaries, 權 is used here in opposition to 經, the latter being

何遠之有。

而子曰未之思也夫

而豈不爾思室是遠

唐棣之華偏其反

權。

與立可與立未可與

適道可與適道未可

shall find them unable to go along with us to principles. *Perhaps* we may go on with them to principles,
but we shall find them unable to get established
in those along with us. Or if we may get so established along with them, we shall find them unable to
weigh *occurring events* along with us."

CHAPTER XXX. 1. How the flowers of the aspen-
plum flutter and turn! Do I not think of you? But
your house is distant.

2. The Master said, "It is the want of thought
about it. How is it distant?"

that which is always, and everywhere right, the former a deviation
from that in particular circumstances, to bring things right. This
meaning of the term here is denied.
The ancients adopted it probably
from their interpretation of the
second clause in the next chapter,
which they made one with this.

30. THE NECESSITY OF REFLEC-
TION, 1. This is understood to be
from one of the pieces of poetry,
which were not admitted into the
collection of the Shih, and no more
of it being preserved than what we
have here, it is not altogether intelligible. There are long disputes
about the 唐棣. Chû Hsî makes it
a kind of small plum or cherry tree,
whose leaves are constantly quiver-
ing, even when there is no wind; and

adopting a reading, in a book of the
Tsin (晉) dynasty, of 翩 for 偏, and
changing 翻 into 反, he makes out
the meaning in the translation. The
old commentators keep the text, and
interpret,—"How perversely contrary are the flowers of the T'ang-
tâi!" saying that those flowers are
first open and then shut. This view
made them take 權 in the last chapter, as we have noticed. Who or
what is meant by 爾 in 爾思, we
cannot tell. The two 而 are mere
expletives, completing the rhythm.
2. With this paragraph Chû Hsî
compares VII, xxix.—The whole
piece is like the 20th of the last
Book, and suggests the thought of
its being an addition by another
hand to the original compilation.

## BOOK X. HEANG TANG

謹爾。　廷便便言、唯　其在宗廟朝　似不能言者。　黨、恂恂如也、　孔子於鄉　鄉黨第十

CHAPTER. I. 1. ·Confucius, in his village, looked simple and sincere, and as if he were not able to speak.

2. When he was in the *prince's* ancestorial temple, or in the court, he spoke minutely on every point, but cautiously.

HEADING OF THIS BOOK.—一 鄉 黨 第 十, "The village, No. 10." This Book is different in its character from all the others in the work. It contains hardly any sayings of Confucius, but is descriptive of his ways and demeanor in a variety of places and circumstances. It is not uninteresting, but, as a whole, it hardly heightens our veneration for the sage. We seem to know him better from it, and perhaps to Western minds, after being viewed in his bedchamber, his undress, and at his meals, he becomes divested of a good deal of his dignity and reputation. There is something remarkable about the style. Only in one passage is its subject styled 子, "*The Master.*" He appears either as 孔 子, "The philosopher Kung," or as 君 子, "The superior man." A suspicion is thus raised that the chronicler had not the same relation to him as the compilers of the other Books Anciently the Book formed only one chapter, but it is now arranged under seventeen divisions.

These divisions, for convenience in the translation, I continue to denominate chapters, which is done also in some native editions.

1. DEMEANOR OF CONFUCIUS IN HIS VILLAGE, IN THE ANCESTRAL TEMPLE, AND IN THE COURT. 1. According to the dictionary, quoting from a record of "the former Han dynasty, the 鄉 contained 2,500 families, and the 黨 only 500"; but the two terms are to be taken here together, indicating the residence of the sage's relatives. His native place in Lû is doubtless intended, rather than the original seat of his family in Sung. 恂恂如 is explained by Wang Sù "mild-like," and by Chû Hsî, is in the translation, thinking probably that, with that meaning, it suited the next clause better. 2. 便, read *p'ien*, the 2nd tone=辯, "to debate," "to discriminate accurately." 爾=耳. In those two places of high ceremony and of government, it became the sage, it is said, to be precise and particular. Compare III, xv.

也、擯、▨ 如 如 君﹁ 誾﹁ 上 侃 大夫 ▨﹁
足 色 君﹁ 也。 也、 誾 大 如 夫言、與 朝、
躩 勃 召 在 與 誾 夫 也、 侃 與
如 如 使 與 踧 如 言、 與 下
　 　 　 踖 也。

CHAPTER II. 1. When he was waiting at court, in speaking with the great officers of the lower grade, he spoke freely, but in a straightforward manner; in speaking with those of the higher grade, he did so blandly, but precisely.

2. When the ruler was present, his manner displayed respectful uneasiness; it was grave, but self-possessed.

CHAPTER III. 1. When the prince called him to employ him in the reception of a visitor, his countenance appeared to change, and his legs to move forward with difficulty.

2. DEMEANOR OF CONFUCIUS AT COURT WITH OTHER GREAT OFFICERS, AND BEFORE THE PRINCE. 1. 朝 may be taken here as a verb, literally = "courting." It was the custom for all the officers to repair at daybreak to the court, and wait for the ruler to give them audience. 大 夫, "Great officer," was a general name, applicable to all the higher officers in a court. At the royal court they were divided into three classes,— "highest," "middle," and "lowest," 上, 中, 下, but the various princes had only the first and third. Of the first order there were properly three, the 卿, or nobles of the state, who were in Lû the chiefs of the "three families." Confucius belonged himself to the lower grade. 2. 踧 踖 = "the feet moving uneasily," indicating the respectful anxiety of the mind. 與, 2nd tone,

here appears in the phrase 與 與 如 也, in a new sense.
3. DEMEANOR OF CONFUCIUS AT THE OFFICIAL RECEPTION OF A VISITOR. 1. The visitor is supposed to be the ruler of another state. On the occasion of two princes meeting there was much ceremony. The visitor having arrived, he remained outside the front gate, and the host inside his reception room, which was in the ancestral temple. Messages passed between them by means of a number of officers called 介, on the side of the visitor, and 擯, on the side of the host, who formed a zigzag line of communication from the one to the other, and passed their questions and answers along, till an understanding about the visit was thus officially effected. 足 躩 如 probably has the meaning which I have given in the translation. 2.

也、揖所與
立、左右手、
衣前後襜
如也。趨進、
翼如也。賓
退、必復命
曰、賓不顧
矣。

入公門、

2. He inclined himself to the *other officers* among whom he stood, moving his left or right arm, *as their position required*, but keeping the skirts of his robe before and behind evenly adjusted.

3. He hastened forward, *with his arms* like the wings of a bird.

4. When the guest had retired, he would report to the prince, "The visitor is not turning round any more."

CHAPTER IV. 1. When he entered the palace gate,

This shows Confucius's manner when engaged in the transmission of the messages between the prince and his visitor. The prince's nuncio, in immediate communication with him. self, was the 上 擯, the next was the 承 擯, and below were one or more 紹 擯. Confucius must have been the *ch'ang pin*, bowing to the right as he transmitted a message to the *shang pin*, who was an officer of the higher grade, and to the left as he communicated one from him to the *shao pin*. 3. The host having come out to receive his visitor, proceeded in with him, it is said, followed by all their internuncios in a line, and to his manner in this movement this paragraph is generally referred. But the duty of seeing the guest off, the subject of the next paragraph, belonged to the *shang pin*, and could not be performed by Confucius as merely a *ch'ang p,n.* Hence arises a difficulty. Either it is true that Confucius was

at one time raised to the rank of the highest dignitaries of the state, or he was temporarily employed, from his knowledge of ceremonies, after the first act in the reception of visitors, to discharge the duties of one. Assuming this, the 趨 進 is to be explained of some of his movements in the reception room. How could he hurry forward when walking in file with the other internuncios? See the 拓 餘 說, II, xxiii. 4. 必 復 命, "would return the commission," i. e., he had seen the guest off, according to his duty, and reported it. The ways of China, it appears, were much the same anciently as now. A guest turns round and bows repeatedly in leaving, and the host cannot return to his place till these salutations are ended.

4. DEMEANOR OF CONFUCIUS IN THE COURT AT AN AUDIENCE. 1. The royal court consisted of five divisions, each having its peculiar gate. That

不息者。出、降一等、

鞠躬如也、屏氣似

不足者。攝齊升堂、

足躧如也、其言似

閾。過位、色勃如也、

立不中門、行不履

鞠躬如也、如不容。

he seemed to bend his body, as if it were not sufficient to admit him.

2. When he was standing, he did not occupy the middle of the gateway; when he passed in or out, he did not tread upon the threshold.

3. When he was passing the *vacant* place *of the prince*, his countenance appeared to change, and his legs to bend under him, and his words came as if he hardly had breath to utter them.

4. He ascended the reception hall, holding up his robe with both his hands, and his body bent; holding in his breath also, as if he dared not breathe.

5. When he came out *from the audience*, as soon as he had descended one step, he began to relax his

of a prince of a state consisted only of three, whose gates were named 庫, 雉, and 路. The 公門 is the *k'û*, or first of these. The bending his body when passing through, high as the gate was, is supposed to indicate the great reverence which Confucius felt. 2. 不中門＝不中於門, "He did not stand opposite the middle of the gateway." Each gate had a post in the center, called 闑, by which it was divided into two halves, appropriated to ingress and egress. The prince only could stand in the center of either of them, and *he* only could tread on the threshold or sill. 3. At the early formal audience at daybreak, when the prince came out of the inner apartment, and received the homage of the officers, he occupied a particular spot called 宁. This is the 位, now empty, which Confucius passes in his way to the audience in the inner apartment. 4. 齊, see IX, ix. He is now ascending the steps to the 堂, "the dais," or raised platform in the inner apartment, where the prince held his council, or gave entertainments, and from which the family rooms of the

勃如戰色足蹜蹜如

不勝、上如揖下如授、

執圭、鞠躬如也、如

位、踧踖如也。

階、趨進、翼如也復其

逞顏色、怡怡如也、沒

countenance, and had a satisfied look.    When he had
got to the bottom of the steps, he advanced rapidly to
his place, *with his arms* like wings, and on occupying
it, his manner *still* showed respectful uneasiness.

CHAPTER V.    1. When he was carrying the scepter
*of his ruler,* he seemed to bend his body, as if he were
not able to bear its weight.    He did not hold it higher
than the position of the hands in making a bow, nor
lower than their position in giving anything to
another.    His countenance seemed to change, and look
apprehensive, and he dragged his feet along as if they
were held by something to the ground.

palace branched off.  5. The audience is now over, and Confucius is
returning to his usual place at the
formal audience.  K‘ung Ân-kwo
makes the 位 to be the 宁 in par. 3,
but improperly. 進 after 趨 is an
addition that has somehow crept into
the ordinary text.

5.  DEMEANOR OF CONFUCIUS
WHEN EMPLOYED ON A FRIENDLY
EMBASSY.  1. 圭 may be translated
"scepter," in the sense simply of "a
badge of authority."  It was a piece
of jade, conferred by the sovereign
on the princes, and differed in size
and shape, according to their rank.
They took it with them when they
attended the king's court, and, according to Chû Hsî and the old
interpreters, it was carried also
by their representatives, as their
voucher, on occasions of embassies
among themselves.  In the 拓 餘 說,
II, xxxiii, however, it is contended,
apparently on sufficient grounds,
that the scepter then employed was
different from the other. 勝, 1st
tone, "to be equal to," "able for."

必表而出
暑袗絺綌、
爲褻服。當
紅紫不以
以紺緅飾。
■君子不
也。
覿、愉愉如
有容色。私
有循享禮、

2. In presenting the presents *with which he was charged,* he wore a placid appearance.

3. At his private audience, he looked highly pleased.

CHAPTER VI. 1. The superior man did not use a deep purple, or a puce color, in the ornaments of his dress.

2. Even in his undress, he did not wear anything of a red or reddish color.

3. In warm weather, he had a single garment either of coarse or fine texture, but he wore it displayed over an inner garment.

2. The preceding paragraph describes Confucius's manner in the friendly court, at his first interview, showing his credentials and delivering his message. That done, he had to deliver the various presents with which he was charged. This was called 享,＝獻. 3. After all the public presents were delivered, the ambassador had others of his own to give, and his interview for that purpose was called 私 覿.—Chù Hsî remarks that there is no record of Confucius ever having been employed on such a mission, and supposes that this chapter and the preceding are simply summaries of the manner in which he used to say duties referred to in them ought to be discharged.

6. RULES OF CONFUCIUS IN REGARD TO HIS DRESS. The discussions about the colors here mentioned are lengthy and tedious. I am not confident that I have given them all correctly in the translation. 1. 君子, used here to denote Confucius, can hardly have come from the hand of a disciple. 紺＝深青揚赤 色, "a deep azure flushed with carnation." 緅＝絳色, "a deep red"; it was dipped thrice in a red dye, and then twice in a black. 飾, "for ornament," i. e., for the edgings of the collar and sleeves. The *kan,* it is said, by Chù Hsî, after K'ung Ân-kwo, was worn in fasting, and the *tsâu .* in mourning, on which account Confucius would not use them. See this and the account of the colors denied in the 拓餘說, *in loc.* 2. There are five colors which go by the name of 正, "correct," viz., 青, 黃, 赤, 白, 黑, "azure, yellow, carnation, white, and black"; others, among which are 紅 and 紫, go by the name of 間, or "intermediate." See the 集證, *in loc.* Confucius

之緇衣羔裘、
素衣麑裘黃
衣狐裘素裘
長、短右袂必
有寢衣、長一
身有半狐貉
之厚以居去
喪、無所不佩。
非帷裳必殺

4. Over lamb's fur he wore a garment of black; over fawn's fur one of white; and over fox's fur one of yellow.

5. The fur robe of his undress was long, with the right sleeve short.

6. He required his sleeping dress to be half as long again as his body.

7. When staying at home, he used thick furs of the fox or the badger.

8. When he put off mourning, he wore all the appendages of the girdle.

9. His undergarment, except when it was required to be of the curtain shape, was made of silk cut narrow above and wide below.

would use only the correct colors, and moreover, Chû Hsî adds, red and reddish-blue are liked by women and girls. 褻服, his dress, when in private. 3. 絺 and 綌 were made from the fibers of a creeping plant, the 葛. See the Shih-ching, I, i, Ode ii. 必表而出之, "he must display and have it outwards." The interpretation of this, as in the translation, after Chû Hsî, though differing from the old commentators, seems to be correct. 4. The lamb's fur belonged to the court dress, the fawn's was worn on embassies, the fox's on occasions of sacrifice, etc. 5. Confucius knew how to blend comfort and convenience. 6. This paragraph, it is supposed, belongs to the next chapter, in which case it is not the usual sleeping garment of Confucius that is spoken of, but the one he used in fasting. 長, 2nd tone, "over," "overplus." 7. These are the 褻裘 of paragraph 5. 8. The appendages of the girdle were, the handkerchief, a small knife, a spike for opening knots, etc. 去, 3rd tone, "to put away." 9. The 裳 was the lower garment, reaching below the knees like a kilt or petticoat. For court and sacrificial dress, it was made curtainlike, as wide at the top as at the bottom. In that worn on

齋<br>食不厭精膾不

坐。

齋必變食居必遷

齋<br>齊必有明衣布。

朝。

弔吉月必朝服而

之羔裘玄冠不以

10.　He did not wear lamb's fur or a black cap, on a visit of condolence.

11.　On the first day of the month he put on his court robes, and presented himself at court.

CHAPTER VII.　1.　When fasting, he thought it necessary to have his clothes brightly clean and made of linen cloth.

2.　When fasting, he thought it necessary to change his food, and also to change the place where he commouly sat in the apartment.

CHAPTER VIII.　1.　He did not dislike to have his rice finely cleaned, nor to have his minced meat cut quite small.

other occasions, Confucius saved the cloth in the way described.　So, at least, says K'ung Ân-kwo.　殺, read *shâi*, 4th tone.　10. Lamb's fur was worn with black (par. 4), but white is the color of mourning in China, and Confucius would not visit mourners, but in a sympathizing color.　11. 吉月, "the fortunate day of the moon," i. e., the first of the month. This was Confucius's practice after he had ceased to be in office.

7.　RULES OBSERVED BY CONFUCIUS WHEN FASTING.　1. 齊, read *châi*, 1st tone; see VII, xii.　The 6th paragraph of the last chapter should come in as the 2nd here.　2. The fasting was not from all food, but only from wine or spirits, and from pot herbs.　Observe the difference between 變 and 遷, the former "to change," the latter "to change from," "to remove."—The whole chapter may be compared with Matt. 6 : 16-18.

8.　RULES OF CONFUCIUS ABOUT HIS FOOD.　1. 膾, "minced meat," the commentators say, was made of beef, mutton, or fish, *uncooked*.　100 *shing* of paddy were reduced to 30, to bring it to the state of 精 rice.　2. 餲 in the dictionary is "overdone,"

無量不及亂沽酒市脯不

肉雖多不使勝食氣惟酒

不正不食不得其醬不食。

食失飪不食不時不食割。

敗不食色惡不食臭惡不

厭細食饐而餲魚餒而肉

2. He did not eat rice which had been injured by heat or damp and turned sour, nor fish or flesh which was gone. He did not eat what was discolored, or what was of a bad flavor, nor anything which was ill-cooked, or was not in season.

3. He did not eat meat which was not cut properly, nor what was served without its proper sauce.

4. Though there might be a large quantity of meat, he would not allow what he took to exceed the due proportion for the rice. It was only in wine that he laid down no limit for himself, but he did not allow himself to be confused by it.

5. He did not partake of wine and dried meat bought in the market.

hence 失 飪 = "wrong in being over-done." Some, however, make the phrase to mean "badly cooked," either underdone or overdone. 4. 食 (*tsze*) 氣, "the breath of the rice," or perhaps, "the life-sustaining power of it," but 氣 can hardly be translated here. 唯 = 惟, "only," showing, it is said, that in other things he had a limit, but the use of wine being to make glad, he could not beforehand set a limit to the quantity

如　榮　寢　食　三　宿　多　食<sub>。六節</sub>
也<sub>。</sub>　羹　不　之　日　肉　食　不
　　瓜　言<sub>。十節</sub>　矣<sub>。九節</sub>　出　祭　祭　撤
　　祭　雖　食　三　肉　於　薑
　　必　疏　不　日　不　公　食
　　齊　食　語<sub>、</sub>　不　出<sub>。</sub>　不　不<sub>。七節</sub>

6. He was never without ginger when he ate.

7. He did not eat much.

8. When he had been *assisting* at the prince's sacrifice, he did not keep the flesh *which he received* overnight. The flesh of his *family* sacrifice he did not keep over three days. If kept over three days, people could not eat it.

9. When eating, he did not converse. When in bed, he did not speak.

10. Although his food might be coarse rice and vegetable soup, he would offer *a little of it* in sacrifice with a grave, respectful air.

of it. See, however, the singular note in IX, xv. 6. Literally, "He did not take away ginger in eating." 8. The prince, anciently (and it is still a custom), distributed among the assisting ministers the flesh of his sacrifice. Each would only get a little, and so it could be used at once. 10. 瓜 should be changed into 必 according to Chû Hsî. Ho Yen, however, retains it, and putting a comma after it, joins it with the two preceding specimens of spare diet. The "sacrificing" refers to a custom something like our saying grace. The master took a few grains of rice or part of the other provisions, and placed them on the ground, among the sacrificial vessels, a tribute to the worthy or worthies who first taught the art of cooking. The Buddhist priests in their monasteries have a custom of this kind, and on public occasions, as when Ch'î-ying gave an entertainment in Hongkong in 1845, something like it is sometimes observed, but any such ceremony is unknown among the common habits of the people. However poor might be his fare, Confucius always observed it. 齊 (*chài*) = 齋, the grave demeanor appropriate to fasting.

敢
嘗
。

子
饋
藥
拜
而
受
之
曰
丘
未
達
不

再
拜
而
送
之
康
二
問
人
於
他
邦

臺
問
人
於
他
邦

於
阼
階
。

人
儺
朝
服
而
立

者
出
斯
出
矣
。
鄉

二
鄉
人
飲
酒
杖

席
不
正
不
坐
。

CHAPTER IX.  If his mat was not straight, he did
not sit on it.

CHAPTER X.  1. When the villagers were drinking
together, on those who carried staffs going out, he
went out immediately after.

2.  When the villagers were going through their
ceremonies to drive away pestilential influences, he put
on his court robes and stood on the eastern steps.

CHAPTER XI.  1. When he was sending complimentary inquiries to any one in another state, he
bowed twice as he escorted the messenger away.

2.  Chî K'ang having sent him a present of physic,
he bowed and received it, saying, "I do not know it.
I dare not taste it."

9.  RULE OF CONFUCIUS ABOUT HIS
MAT.

10.  OTHER WAYS OF CONFUCIUS
IN HIS VILLAGE.  1. At sixty, people
carried a staff.  Confucius here
showed his respect for age.  斯 has
here an adverbial force, = 卽.  2.
There were three 儺 ceremonies every
year, but that in the text was called
"the great 儺," being observed in
the winter season, when the officers
led all the people of a village about
searching every house to expel de-
mons, and drive away pestilence.
It was conducted with great uproar,
and little better than a play, but
Confucius saw a good old idea in it,
and when the mob was in his house,
he stood on the eastern steps, the
place of a host receiving guests in
full dress.  Some make the steps
those of his ancestral temple, and his
standing there to be to assure the
spirits of his shrine.

11.  TRAITS OF CONFUCIUS'S IN-
TERCOURSE WITH OTHERS.  1. The
two bows were not to the messenger,
but intended for the distant friend
to whom he was being sent.  2. 康
was the 季康子 of II, xx et al.  Confucius accepted the gift, but thought
it necessary to let the donor know he
could not, for the present at least,
avail himself of it.

廄焚子退朝曰傷

人乎不問馬。

君賜食必正席先

嘗之君賜腥必熟而

薦之君賜生必畜之。

侍食於君君祭先飯。

CHAPTER XII. The stable being burned down, when he was at court, on his return he said, "Has any man been hurt?" He did not ask about the horses.

CHAPTER XIII. 1. When the prince sent him a gift of *cooked* meat, he would adjust his mat, *first* taste it, *and then give it away to others.* When the prince sent him a gift of undressed meat, he would have it cooked, and offer it *to the spirits of his ancestors.* When the prince sent him a gift of a living animal, he would keep it alive.

2. When he was in attendance on the prince and joining in the entertainment, the prince only sacrificed. He first tasted everything.

12. HOW CONFUCIUS VALUED HUMAN LIFE. A ruler's 廄 was fitted to accommodate 216 horses. See the 集 證, *in loc.* It may be used indeed for a private stable, but it is more natural to take it here for the 國 or state *chiû.* This is the view in the 家 語.

13. DEMEANOR OF CONFUCIUS IN RELATION TO HIS PRINCE. 1. He would not offer the cooked meat to the spirits of ·his ancestors, not knowing but it might previously have been offered by the prince to the spirits of his. But he reverently tasted it, as if he had been in the prince's presence. He "honored" the gift of cooked food, "glorified" the undressed, and "was kind" to the living animal. 2. The 祭 here is that in chapter viii, 10. Among parties of equal rank, all performed the ceremony, but Confucius, with his prince, held that the prince sacrificed for all. He tasted everything, as if he had been a *cook*, it being the cook's duty to taste every dish, before the prince partook of it.

不　饋　曰　臺　臺　不　朝　疾
拜　雖　於　朋　入　俟　服　君
。　車　我　友　太　駕　拖　視
　　馬　殯　死　廟　行　紳　之
　　非　朋　無　每　矣　君　東
　　祭　友　所　事　。　命　首
　　肉　之　歸　問　　　召　加
　　　　　　　　。　　　、

3. When he was ill and the prince came to visit him, he had his head to the east, made his court robes be spread over him, and drew his girdle across them.

4. When the prince's order called him, without waiting for his carriage to be yoked, he went at once.

CHAPTER XIV. When he entered the ancestral temple of the state, he asked about everything.

CHAPTER XV. 1. When any of his friends died, if he had no relations who could be depended on for the necessary offices, he would say, "I will bury him."

2. When a friend sent him a present, though it might be a carriage and horses, he did nct bow.

3. The only present for which he bowed was that of the flesh of sacrifice.

3. 首, in the 4th tone, 頭 向, "the direction of the head." The head to the east was the proper position for a person in bed; a sick man might for comfort be lying differently, but Confucius would not see the prince but in the correct position, and also in the court dress, so far as he could accomplish it. 4. He would not wait a moment, but let his carriage follow him.

14. A repetition of III, xv. Compare also chap. ii. These two passages make the explanation, given at III, xv, of the questioning being on his first entrance on office very doubtful.

15. TRAITS OF CONFUCIUS IN THE RELATION OF A FRIEND. 1. 殯 properly, "the closing up of the coffin," is here used for all the expenses and services necessary to interment. 2, 3. Between friends there should be a community of goods. "The flesh of sacrifice," however, was that which had been offered by his friend to the spirits of his parents or ancestors. They demanded acknowledgment.

變。　色而作迅雷風烈必　負版者有盛饌必變　以貌凶服者式之式　冕者與瞽者雖褻必　齊衰者雖狎必變見　寢不尸居不容見

CHAPTER XVI. 1. In bed, he did not lie like a corpse. At home, he did not put on any formal deportment.

2. When he saw any one in a mourning dress, though it might be an acquaintance, he would change countenance; when he saw any one wearing the cap of full dress, or a blind person, though he might be in his undress, he would salute them in a ceremonious manner.

3. To any person in mourning he bowed forward to the crossbar of his carriage; he bowed in the same way to any one bearing the tables of population.

4. When he was at an entertainment where there was an abundance of provisions set before him, he would change countenance and rise up.

5. On a sudden clap of thunder, or a violent wind, he would change countenance.

16. CONFUCIUS IN BED, AT HOME, HEARING THUNDER, etc. 2. Compare IX, ix, which is here repeated, with heightening circumstances. 3. 式 is the front bar of a cart or carriage. In fact, the carriage of Confucius's time was only what we call a cart. In saluting, when riding, parties bowed forward to this bar. 4. He showed these signs, with reference to the generosity of the provider.

子路共之三嗅而作。

曰山梁雌雉時哉時哉。

色斯舉矣翔而後集。

指。

中、不內顧、不疾言、不親

升車、必正立執綏。車

CHAPTER XVII.   1. When he was about to mount his carriage, he would stand straight, holding the cord.

2. When he was in the carriage, he did not turn his head quite round, he did not talk hastily, he did not point with his hands.

CHAPTER XVIII.   1. *Seeing* the countenance, it instantly rises. It flies round, and by and by settles.

2. *The Master* said, "There is the hen-pheasant on the hill bridge. At its season! At its season!" Tsze-lû made a motion to it. Thrice it smelled him and then rose.

17. CONFUCIUS AT AND IN HIS CARRIAGE. 1. The 綏 was a strap or cord, attached to the carriage to assist in mounting it. 2. 不內顧, "He did not look round within," i. e., turn his head quite round. See the Lî Chî, I, i, Pt. v, 43

. 18. A fragment, which seemingly has no connection with the rest of the Book. Various alterations of characters are proposed, and various views to the meaning given. Ho Yen's view of the conclusion is this: "Tsze-lû took it and served it up. The Master thrice smelled it and rose." 共, in 3rd tone, = 向.

## BOOK XI.　HSIEN TSIN

從先進。

也。如用之、則吾

進於禮樂、君子

禮樂、野人也、後

子曰先進於

先進第十一

CHAPTER I.　1. The Master said, "The men of former times in the matters of ceremonies and music were rustics, *it is said*, while the men of *these* latter times, in ceremonies and music, are accomplished gentlemen.

2.　"If I have occasion to use those things, I follow the men of former times."

HEADING OF THIS BOOK.—先 進 第 十 一. "The former men, No. 11." With this Book there commences the second part of the Analects, commonly called the *Hsai Lun* (下 論). There is, however, no important authority for this division. It contains 25 chapters, treating mostly of various disciples of the Master, and deciding the point of their worthiness. Min Tsze-ch'ien appears in it four times, and on this account some attribute the compilation of it to his disciples. There are indications in the style of a peculiar hand.

1. CONFUCIUS'S PREFERENCE OF THE SIMPLER WAYS OF FORMER TIMES. 1. 先進, 後進 are said by Chû Hsî to=先 輩, 後 輩. Literally, the expressions are,—"those who first advanced," "those who afterwards advanced," i. e., on the stage of the world. In Ho Yen, the chapter is said to speak of the disciples who had first advanced to office, and those who had advanced subsequently,—評 其 弟 子 之 中 仕 進 先 後 之 輩. But the 2nd paragraph is decidedly against this interpretation. 進 is not to be joined to the succeeding 於 禮 樂, but 於=*quoad*. It is supposed that the characterizing the 先 進 as rustics, and their successors as *chun-tsze*, was a style of his times, which Confucius quotes ironically. We have in it a new instance of the various application of the name *chun-tsze*. In the 備 旨, it is said, "Of the words and actions of men in their mutual intercourse and in the business of government, whatever indicates *respect* is here included in *ceremonies*, and whatever is expressive of *harmony* is here included in *music*."

言無所不說。
助我者也於吾
■子曰回也、非
子夏。
季路文學子游、
子貢。政事冉有、
仲弓言語宰我、
閔子騫冉伯牛、
門也。德行顏淵、
陳蔡者皆不及
■子曰、從我於

CHAPTER II. 1. The Master said, "Of those who were with me in Ch'ăn and Ts'âi, there are none to be found to enter my door."

2. Distinguished for their virtuous principles and practice, there were Yen Yûan, Min Tsze-ch'ien, Zan Po-niû, and Chung-kung; for their ability in speech, Tsai Wo and Tsze-kung; for their administrative talents, Zan Yû and Chî Lû; for their literary acquirements, Tsze-yû and Tsze-hsiâ.

CHAPTER III. The Master said, "Hûi gives me no assistance. There is nothing that I say in which he does not delight."

2. CONFUCIUS'S REGRETFUL MEMORY OF HIS DISCIPLES' FIDELITY:— CHARACTERISTICS OF TEN OF THE DISCIPLES. 1. This utterance must have been made towards the close of Confucius's life, when many of his disciples had been removed by death, or separated from him by other causes. In his 62nd year or thereabouts, as the accounts go, he was passing, in his wanderings from Ch'ăn to Ts'âi, when the officers of Ch'ăn, afraid that he would go on into Ch'ù, endeavored to stop his course, and for several days he and the disciples with him were cut off f om food. Both Ch'ăn and Ts'âi were in the present province of Honan, and are referred to the departments of 陳 州 and 汝 寧. 2. This paragraph is to be taken as a note by the compilers of the Book, enumerating the principal followers of Confucius on the occasion referred to, with their distinguishing qualities. They are arranged in four classes (四 科), and, amounting to ten, are known as the 十 哲. The "four classes" and "ten wise ones" are often mentioned in connection with the sage's school. The ten disciples have all appeared in the previous Books.

3. HÛI'S SILENT RECEPTION OF THE MASTER'S TEACHINGS. A teacher is sometimes helped by the doubts and questions of learners, which lead him to explain himself more fully. Compare III, viii, 3. 說 for 悅 as in I, i, 1, but K'ung An-kwo takes it in its usual pronunciation＝解, "to explain."

子曰孝哉閔子騫、人不間於其父母昆弟之言。

南容三復白圭、孔子以其兄之子妻之。

季康子問弟子孰爲好學孔子對曰、有顏回者好學、不幸短命死矣、今也則亡。

CHAPTER IV. The Master said, "Filial indeed is Min Tsze-ch'ien! Other people say nothing of him different from the report of his parents and brothers."

CHAPTER V. Nan Yung was frequently repeating the *lines about a* white scepter stone. Confucius gave him the daughter of his elder brother to wife.

CHAPTER VI. Chî K'ang asked which of the disciples loved to learn. Confucius replied to him, "There was Yen Hûi; he loved to learn. Unfortunately his appointed time was short, and he died. Now there is no one *who loves to learn, as he did.*"

4. THE FILIAL PIETY OF MIN TSZE-CH'IEN. 閒, as in VIII, xxi, "could pick out no crevice or flaw in the words, etc." 陳羣 (about A. D. 200–250, as given in Ho Yen, explains—"Men had no words of disparagement for his conduct in reference to his parents and brothers." This is the only instance where Confucius calls a disciple by his designation. The use of 子 騫 is supposed, in the 合 講, to be a mistake of the compilers. "Brothers" includes cousins, indeed = kindred.

5. CONFUCIUS'S APPROBATION OF NAN YUNG. Nan Yung, see V, i. 三, as in V, xix. I have translated it by "frequently"; but, in the "Family Sayings," it is related that Yung repeated the lines thrice in one day. 白 圭, see the Shih-ching, III, iii, Ode 11, 5. The lines there are—"A flaw in a white scepter stone may be ground away; but for a flaw in speech, nothing can be done." In his repeating of these lines, we have, perhaps, the ground virtue of the character for which Yung is commended in V, i. Observe 孔 子, where we might expect 子.

6. HOW HÔI LOVED TO LEARN. See VI, ii, where the same question is put by the duke Âi, and the same answer is returned, only in a more extended form.

顏淵死、子曰噫、
天喪予、天喪予。

顏淵死、顏路請
子之車、以爲之椁。
子曰才不才、亦各
言其子也鯉也死、
有棺而無椁、吾不
徒行以爲之椁以
吾從大夫之後、不
可徒行也。

CHAPTER VII. 1. When Yen Yüan died, Yen Lû begged the carriage of the Master to *sell* and get an outer shell for his *son's* coffin.

2. The Master said, "Every one calls his son his son, whether he has talents or has not talents. There was Lî; when he died, he had a coffin but no outer shell. I would not walk on foot to get a shell for him, because, having followed in the rear of the great officers, it was not proper that I should walk on foot."

CHAPTER VIII. When Yen Yüan died, the Master said, "Alas! Heaven is destroying me! Heaven is destroying me!"

7. HOW CONFUCIUS WOULD NOT SELL HIS CARRIAGE TO BUY A SHELL FOR YEN YÜAN. 1. There is a chronological difficulty here. Hûi, according to the "Family Sayings," and the "Historical Records," must have died several years before Confucius's son, Lî. Either the dates in them are incorrect, or this chapter is spurious.—Yen Lù, the father of Hûi, had himself been a disciple of the sage in former years. 爲之椁 (i. q. char. in text),—this is the idiom noticed in V, vii, 3. 爲 would almost seem to be an active verb followed by a double objective. In burying, they used a coffin, called 棺, and an outer shell without a bottom, which was called 椁. 2. 吾 從 大 夫 之 後, literally, "I follow in rear of the great officers." This is said to be an expression of humility. Confucius, retired from office, might still present himself at court, in the robes of his former dignity, and would still be consulted on emergencies. He would no doubt have a foremost place on such occasions.

8. CONFUCIUS FELT HUI'S DEATH AS IF IT HAD BEEN HIS OWN. The old interpreters make this simply the exclamation of bitter sorrow. The modern, perhaps correctly, make the chief ingredient to be grief that the man was gone to whom he looked most for the transmission of his doctrines.

也。非予回門厚鑿顏曰慟鑿
　我不也人葬顏淵二有從顏
　也得視人之淵死曰慟
　夫視予厚子死門子乎。者淵
　二猶猶葬曰門人慟非曰死
　三子父之不人欲矣夫子
　子也也子可。欲爲人慟哭
　　　　曰、　　慟而矣之
　　　　　　　　誰爲

CHAPTER IX. 1. When Yen Yüan died, the Master bewailed him exceedingly, and the disciples who were with him said, "Master, your grief is excessive!"

2. "Is it excessive?" said he.

3. "If I am not to mourn bitterly for this man, for whom should I mourn?"

CHAPTER X. 1. When Yen Yüan died, the disciples wished to give him a great funeral, and the Master said, "You may not do so."

2. The disciples did bury him in great style.

3. The Master said, "Hûi behaved towards me as his father. I have not been able to treat him as my son. The fault is not mine; it belongs to you, O disciples."

9. CONFUCIUS VINDICATES HIS GREAT GRIEF FOR THE DEATH OF HÛI. 1. 哭 is the loud wail of grief. Moaning with tears is called 泣. 3. 夫人 ＝斯人, "this man." The third definition of 夫 in the dictionary is 有所指之辭; "a term of definite indication."

10. CONFUCIUS'S DISSATISFACTION WITH THE GRAND WAY IN WHICH HÛI WAS BURIED. 1. The old interpreters take 門人 as being the disciples of Yen Yuan. This is not natural, and yet we can hardly understand how the disciples of Confucius would act so directly contrary to his express wishes. Confucius objected to a grand funeral as inconsistent with the poverty of the family (see chap. vii). 3. 視, literally, "regarded me," but that term would hardly suit the next clause. 夫, as in the last chapter. This passage, indeed, is cited in the dictionary, in illustration of that use of the term. 二三子, see III, xxiv.

子
曰
未
能
事
人
焉

未
知
生
焉
知
死

閔
子
侍
側
誾
誾

如
也
子
路
行
行
如

也
冉
有
子
貢
侃
侃

能
事
鬼
敢
問
死
曰

季
路
問
事
鬼
神

CHAPTER XI.    Chî Lû asked about serving the spirits *of the dead*.    The Master said, "While you are not able to serve men, how can yon serve *their* spirits?"    *Chî Lû added*, "I venture to ask about death?"    He was answered, "While you do not know life, how can you know about death?"

CHAPTER XII.    1. The disciple Min was standing by his side, looking bland and precise; Tsze-lû, looking bold and soldierly; Zan Yû and Tsze-kung, with a free and straightforward manner.    The Master was pleased.

11. CONFUCIUS AVOIDS ANSWER-ING QUESTIONS ABOUT SERVING SPIRITS, AND ABOUT DEATH.    鬼 神 are here to be taken together, and understood of the spirits of the dead. This appears from Confucius using only 鬼 in his reply, and from the opposition between 人 and 鬼.    人 is man alive, while 鬼 is man dead—a ghost, a spirit.    Two views of the replies are found in commentators. The older ones say—"Confucius put off Chî Lû, and gave him no answer, because spirits and death are ob-scure and unprofitable subjects to talk about."    With this some modern writers agree, as the author of the 翼 註; but others, and the majority,

say—"Confucius answered the dis-ciple profoundly, and showed him how he should prosecute his inquiries in the proper order.    The service of the dead must be in the same spirit as the service of the living.    Obe-dience and sacrifice are equally the expression of the filial heart.    Death is only the natural termination of life.    We are born with certain gifts and principles, which carry us on to the end of our course."    This is ingenious refining, but, after all, Confucius avoids answering the im-portant questions proposed to him.

12. CONFUCIUS HAPPY WITH HIS DISCIPLES ABOUT HIM.    HE WARNS TSZE-LÛ.    1. 閔 子, like 冉 子, VI,

不言言必有中。

何必改作子曰、夫人

騫曰、仍舊貫、如之何、

盍魯人爲長府閔子

得其死然。

如也。子樂若由也、不

2. (He said), "Yû there!—he will not die a natural death."

CHAPTER XIII. 1. Some parties in Lû were going to take down and rebuild the Long Treasury.

2. Min Tsze·chi'en said, "Suppose it were to be repaired after its old style;—why must it be altered and made anew?"

3. The Master said, "This man seldom speaks; when he does, he is sure to hit the point."

iii, 1. 行, read *hang*, 4th tone. 2. There being wanting here 子 曰 at the commencement, some, unwisely, would change the 樂 at the end of the first paragraph into 曰, to supply the blank. 若 由 也,—若 is used with reference to the appearance and manner of Tsze-lû. 然, in the 註 疏 is taken as=the final 焉. Some say that it indicates some uncertainty as to the prediction. But it was verified;—see on II, xvii.

13. WISE ADVICE OF MIN SUN AGAINST USELESS EXPENDITURE. 1. 魯 人, not "the people of Lû," but as in the translation—certain officers, disapprobation of whom is indicated by simply calling them 人. The full meaning of 爲 is collected from the rest of the chapter. 府 is "a treasury," as distinguished from 倉, "a granary," and from 庫, "an arsenal." "The Long Treasury" was the name of the one in question. We read of it in the Tso Chwan under the 25th year of Duke Châo (par. 5), as being then the duke's residence. 2. The use of 貫 is perplexing. Chû Hsî adopts the explanation of it by the old commentators as= 事, "affair," but with what propriety I do not see. The character means "a string of cowries, or cash," then "to thread together," "to connect." May not its force be here,—"suppose it were to be carried on—continued—as before?" 3. 夫 as in chapter ix. 中, 4th tone, a verb, "to hit the mark," as in shooting.

十四子曰、由之瑟、奚爲於丘之門。門人不敬子路。子曰、由也、升堂矣、未入於室也。

十五子貢問師與商也孰賢。子曰、師也過、商也不及。曰、然則師愈與。子曰、過猶不及。

CHAPTER XIV. 1. The Master said, "What has the lute of Yû to do in my door?"

2. The other disciples *began* not to respect Tsze-lû. The Master said, "Yû has ascended to the hall, though he has not yet passed into the inner apartments."

CHAPTER XV. 1. Tsze-kung asked which of the two, Shih or Shang, was the superior. The Master said, "Shih goes beyond *the due mean*, and Shang does not come up to it."

2. "Then," said Tsze-kung, "the superiority is with Shih, I suppose."

3. The Master said, "To go beyond is as wrong as to fall short."

14. CONFUCIUS'S ADMONITION AND DEFENSE OF TSZE-LÛ. 1. The form of the harpsichord or lute seems to come nearer to that of the *shih* than any other of our instruments. The 瑟 is a kindred instrument with the 琴, commonly called "the scholar's lute." See the Chinese Repository, vol. viii, p. 38. The music made by Yû was more martial in its air than befitted the peace-inculcating school of the sage. 2. This contains a defense of Yû, and an illustration of his real attainments.

15. COMPARISON OF SHIH AND SHANG. EXCESS AND DEFECT EQUALLY WRONG. Shang was the name of Tsze-hsiâ, I, vii, and Shih, that of Twan-sun, styled Tsze-chang. 1. 賢, here=勝, "to overcome," "be superior to," being interchanged with 愈 in par. 2. We find this meaning of the term also in the dictionary.

季氏富於周

公、而求也爲之

聚斂而附益之。

子曰、非吾徒也、

小子鳴鼓而攻

之、可也。

柴也愚、參也

魯、師也辟、由也

喭。

CHAPTER XVI. 1. The head of the Chî family was richer than the duke of Châu. had been, and yet Ch'iû collected his imposts for him, and increased his wealth.

2. The Master said, "He is no disciple of mine. My little children, beat the drum and assail him."

CHAPTER XVII. 1. Ch'âi is simple.

2. Shăn is dull.

3. Shih is specious.

4. Yû is coarse.

16. CONFUCIUS'S INDIGNATION AT THE SUPPORT OF USURPATION AND EXTORTION BY ONE OF HIS DISCIPLES. 1. 季 氏, see III, 1. Many illustrations might be collected of the encroachments of the Chî family and its great wealth. 爲 之 聚 歛, "for him collected and ingathered," i. e., all his imposts. This clause and the next imply that Ch'iû was aiding in the matter of laying imposts on the people. 2. "Beat the drum and assail him,"—this refers to the practice of executing criminals in the market place, and by beat of drum collecting the people to hear their crimes. We must, however, say that the Master only required the disciples here to tell Ch'iû of his faults and recover him.

17. CHARACTERS OF THE FOUR DISCIPLES—CH'ÂI, SHĂN, SHIH, AND YÛ. It is supposed a 子曰 is missing from the beginning of this chapter. Admitting this, the sentences are to be translated in the present tense, and not in the past, which would be required if the chapter were simply the record of the compilers. 1. Ch'âi, by surname 高, and styled 子 羔 (of 羔 there are several *aliases*), has his tablet now the 5th west, in the outer court of the temples. He was small and ugly, but distinguished for his sincerity, filial piety, and justice. Such was the conviction of his impartial justice, that in a time of peril he was saved by a man, whom he had formerly punished with cutting off his feet. All the other names have already occurred and been explained. 3. 辟, read *p'î*, is defined in the dictionary,—"practicing airs with little sincerity."—Confucius certainly does not here flatter his followers.

不　　臺　　中　　乎　　而　　臺
入　　子　　。　　屢　　貨　　子
於　　張　　　　空　　殖　　曰
室　　問　　　　賜　　焉　　囘
。　　善　　　　不　　億　　也
　　　人　　　　受　　則　　其
道　　之　　　　命　　屢　　庶
子　　　　　　　　、　　　　乎
曰　　　　　　　　　　　　、
不
踐
迹
亦

CHAPTER XVIII. 1. The Master said, "There is
Hûi! He has nearly attained *to perfect virtue*. He is
often in want."

2. "Ts'ze does not acquiesce in the appointments
*of Heaven*, and his goods are increased by him. Yet
his judgments are often correct."

CHAPTER XIX. Tsze-chang asked what were the
characteristics of the GOOD man. The Master said,
"He does not tread in the footsteps of others, but,
moreover, he does not enter the chamber *of the sage*."

18. HÛI AND TS'ZE CONTRASTED.
In Ho Yen's compilation, this chapter is joined with the preceding as
one. 1. 庶, here=近, "nearly,"
"near to." It is often found with 乎
following, both terms together being
=our "nearly." To make out a
meaning, the old commentators supply 聖道, "the way or doctrines of
the sages," and the modern supply
道, "the truth and right." 空, 4th
tone, "emptied," i. e , brought to
extremity, poor, distressed. Hûi's
being brought often to this state is
mentioned merely as an additional
circumstance about him, intended to
show that he was happy in his deep
poverty. Ho Yen preserves the
comment of some one, which is
worth giving here, and according to
which, 空=虛 中, "empty-hearted,"
free from all vanities and ambitions.
Then 屢=每, "always." In this
sense 屢 空 was the formative element of Hûi's character. 2. 受, "to
receive," here="to acquiesce in."
億=度, "to form a judgment."
Ts'ze, of course, is Tsze-kung.
19. THE GOOD MAN. Compare
VII, xxv. By 善 人 Chû Hsî understands—質 美 而 未 學 者, "one of
fine natural capacity, but who has
not learned." Such a man will in
many things be a law to himself, and
needs not to follow in the wake of
others, but after all his progress will
be limited. The text is rather enigmatical. 入 室, compare chap. xiv.
2. Tsze-chang was the Shih of chap.
xv.

聞斯行諸、子曰、有
公西華曰、由也問
諸。子曰聞斯行之。
之。冉有問聞斯行
如之何其聞斯行
諸。子曰有父兄在、
子路問聞斯行
乎。
君子者乎、色莊者
子曰論篤是與、

CHAPTER XX. The Master said, "If, because a man's discourse appears solid and sincere, we allow him *to be a good man,* is he *really* a superior man? or is his gravity only in appearance?"

CHAPTER XXI. Tsze-lû asked whether he should immediately carry into practice what he heard. The Master said, "There are your father and elder brothers *to be consulted;*—why should you act on that principle of immediately carrying into practice what you hear?" Zan Yû asked the same, whether he should immediately carry into practice what he heard, and the Master answered, "Immediately carry into practice what you hear." Kung-hsî Hwâ said, "Yû asked whether he should carry immediately into practice what he heard, and you said, "There are your father

20. WE MAY NOT HASTILY JUDGE A MAN TO BE GOOD FROM HIS DISCOURSE. 論 is here "speech," "conversation." In Ho Yen this chapter is joined to the preceding one, and is said to give additional characteristics of "the good man," mentioned on a different occasion.—The construction, however, on that view is all but inextricable.

21. AN INSTANCE IN TSZE-LÛ AND ZAN YÛ OF HOW CONFUCIUS DEALT WITH HIS DISCIPLES ACCORDING TO THEIR CHARACTERS. On Tsze-lû's question, compare V, 13. 聞斯行 諸, "Hearing *this* = anything, should I do it *at once* or not?" 行 諸＝行 之 乎, like 舍 諸, in VI, iv. 兼 人,—兼 is explained by Chû Hsî with 勝, "to overcome," "to be superior to."

父兄在、求也問聞斯
行諸子曰、聞斯行之、
赤也惑、敢問子曰、求
也退、故進之、由也兼
人、故退之。
子畏於匡顏淵後、
子曰吾以女爲死矣。
曰、子在囘何敢死。

and elder brothers *to be consulted.*" Ch'iû asked
whether he should immediately carry into practice
what he heard, and you said, "Carry it immediately
into practice." "I, Ch'ih, am perplexed, and venture
to ask you for an explanation." The Master said,
"Ch'iû is retiring and slow; therefore I urged him
forward. Yû has more than his own share of energy;
therefore I kept him back."

CHAPTER XXII. The Master was put in fear in
K'wang and Yen Yüan fell behind. The Master, *on
his rejoining him,* said, "I thought you had died."
*Hûi* replied, "While you were alive, how should I
presume to die?"

But we can well take it in its radical signification of "to unite," as a hand grasps two sheaves of corn. The phrase is equivalent to our English one in the translation. Similarly, the best pure gold is called 兼 金.

22. YEN YÜAN'S ATTACHMENT TO CONFUCIUS, AND CONFIDENCE IN HIS MISSION. See IX, v. If Hûi's answer was anything more than pleasantry, we must pronounce it foolish. The commentators, however, expand it thus:—"I knew that you would not perish in this danger, and therefore I would not rashly expose my own life, but preserved it rather, that I might continue to enjoy the benefit of your instructions." If we inquire how Hûi knew that Confucius would not perish, we are informed that he shared his master's assurance that he had a divine mission.—See VII, xii; IX, v.

君、亦不從也。

之者與子曰、弒父與

謂具臣矣。曰、然則從

則止。今由與求也、可

臣者、以道事君、不可

由與求之問、所謂大

吾以子爲異之問、曾

求、可謂大臣與。子曰、

季子然問仲由冉

CHAPTER XXIII. 1. Chî Tsze-zan asked whether Chung Yû and Zan Ch'iû could be called great ministers.

2. The Master said, "I thought you would ask about some extraordinary individuals, and you only ask about Yû and Ch'iû!

3. "What is called a great minister, is one who serves his prince according to what is right, and when he finds he cannot do so, retires.

4. "Now, as to Yû and Ch'iû, they may be called ordinary ministers."

5. Tsze-zan said, "Then they will always follow their chief;—will they?"

6. The Master said, "In an act of parricide or regicide, they would not follow him."

23. A GREAT MINISTER. CHUNG-YÛ AND ZAN CH'IÛ ONLY ORDINARY MINISTERS. The paraphrasts sum up the contents thus: "Confucius represses the boasting of Chî Tsze-zan, and indicates an acquaintance with his traitorous purposes." 1. Chî Tsze-zan was a younger brother of Chî Hwan, who was the 季氏 of III, i. Having an ambitious purpose on the rulership of Lû, he was increasing his officers, and having got the two disciples to enter his service, he boastingly speaks to Confucius about them. 2. 吾以云云, literally "I supposed you were making a question of (=about) extraordinary men, and lo! it is a question about Yû and Ch'iû." 曾=乃; its force is rather different from what it has in II, viii, but is much akin to that in III, vi. 4. 具臣 is explained 備臣數而已, "simply fitted to rank among the number of officers." 具 often means what is merely "official." 具文, "an official paper." 具臣, "mere officials." 5. 之 supposes an antecedent, such as 主, "their master."

〔廿四章〕子路使子羔爲費宰。子曰、賊夫人之子。子路曰、有民人焉、有社稷焉、何必讀書、然後爲學。子曰、是故惡夫佞者。

〔廿五章〕子路、曾皙、冉有、公西華、侍坐。

CHAPTER XXIV. 1. Tsze-lû got Tsze-kâo appointed governor of Pî.

2. The Master said, "You are injuring a man's son."

3. Tsze-lû said, "There are (there) common people and officers; there are the altars of the spirits of the land and grain. Why must one read books before he can be considered to have learned?"

4. The Master said, "It is on this account that I hate your glib-tongued people."

CHAPTER XXV. 1. Tsze-lû, Tsăng Hsî, Zan Yû, and Kung-hsî Hwâ were sitting by *the Master*.

24. HOW PRELIMINARY STUDY IS NECESSARY TO THE EXERCISE OF GOVERNMENT:—A REPROOF OF TSZE-LÛ. 1. 費,—see VI, vii. Tsze-lû had entered into the service of the Chî family (see last chapter), and recommended (使) Tsze-kâo (see chap. xvii) as likely to keep the turbulent Pî in order, thereby withdrawing him from his studies. 2. 賊, in the sense of 害, "to injure." 夫 as in chap. ix. 3. It qualifies the whole phrase 人之子, and not only the Zăn. By denominating Tsze-kâo—"a man's son," Confucius intimates, I suppose, that the father was injured as well. His son ought not to be so dealt with. 3. The absurd defense of Tsze-lû. It is to this effect: "The whole duty of man is in treating other men right, and rendering what is due to spiritual beings, and it may be learned practically without the study you require." 4. 是故, "on this account," with reference to Tsze-lû's reply.

25. THE AIMS OF TSZE-LÛ, TSĂNG HSÎ, ZAN YÛ, AND KUNG-HSI HWÂ, AND CONFUCIUS'S REMARKS ABOUT THEM. Compare V, vii and xxv. 1. The disciples mentioned here are all familiar to us excepting Tsăng Hsî. He was the father of Tsăng Shăn. and himself by name Tien (點). The four are mentioned in the order of their age, and Tien would have answered immediately after Tsze-lû, but that Confucius passed him by,

子曰、以吾一日長乎
爾、毋吾以也居則曰、
不吾知也、如或知爾、
則何以哉。子路率爾
而對曰千乘之國攝
乎大國之閒、加之以
師旅因之以饑饉、由
也爲之比及三年可
使有勇、且知方也夫

2. He said to them, "Though I am a day or so older than you, do not think of that.

3. "From day to day you are saying, 'We are not known.' If some *ruler* were to know you, what would you like to do?"

4. Tsze-lû hastily and lightly replied, "Suppose the case of a state of ten thousand chariots; let it be straitened between *other* large states; let it be suffering from invading armies; and to this let there be added a famine in corn and in all vegetables:—if I were intrusted with the government of it, in three years' time I could make the people to be bold, and to recognize the rules of righteous conduct." The Master smiled at him.

as he was occupied with his harpsichord. 2. 長, 3rd tone, "senior." Many understand 爾輩, "ye," as nominative to the first 以, but it is better to take 以＝雖, "although." 一 日, "one day," would seem to indicate the importance which the disciples attached to the seniority of their Master, and his wish that they should attach no importance to it. In 勿吾以也 we have a not uncommon inversion;—"do not consider me to be your senior." 3. 居＝平居之時, "the level, ordinary course of your lives." 何以哉＝何以爲用哉, "what would you consider to be your use?" i. e., what course of action would you pursue? 4. 率爾, an adverb, ＝"hastily." 攝, according to Chû Hsî, ＝管束; according to Pâo Hsien, ＝迫, "straitened," "urged." In the Châu Lî, 500 men make a 旅, and 5 旅, or 2,500 men, make a 師. The two terms together have here the meaning given in the translation. 爲之, "managed it." 比, 3rd tone, blends its force with the following 及. 方＝向,, "towards." 知方, "know the quarter to which to turn, the way in

子哂之。求、爾何如。對
曰、方六七十、如五六
十、求也爲之、比及三
年、可使足民、如其禮
樂、以俟君子。赤、爾何
如。對曰非曰能之、願
學焉、宗廟之事、如會
同、端章甫、願爲小相

5. *Turning to Yen Yû, he said,* "Ch'iû, what are your wishes?" Ch'iû replied, "Suppose a state of sixty or seventy *lî* square, or one of fifty or sixty, and let me have the government of it;—in three years' time, I could make plenty to abound among the people. As to *teaching them* the principles of propriety, and music, I must wait for the rise of a superior man *to do that.*"

6. "What are your wishes, Ch'ih," *said the Master next to Kung-hsî Hwâ. Ch'ih* replied, "I do not say that my ability extends to these things, but I should wish to learn them. At the services of the ancestral temple, and at the audiences of the princes with the sovereign, I should like, dressed in the dark square-made robe and the black linen cap, to act as a small assistant."

which to go." 5. At the beginning of this paragraph and the two following, we must supply 子曰. 如＝或, "or." 6. 能之、—之 refers to the 禮樂, in par. 5. 會 is the name for occasional or incidental interviews of the princes with the sovereign, what are called 時見. 同 belongs to occasions when they all presented themselves together at court. The 端 (and from its color called 玄端) was a robe of ceremony, so called from its *straight* make, its component parts having no gathers nor slanting cuttings. 章甫 was the name of a cap of ceremony. It had different names under different dynasties. 甫 means a MAN.

子喟然歎曰、吾與點也。
沂、風乎舞雩、詠而歸夫
六人、童子六七人浴乎
春者、春服既成、冠者五
乎、亦各言其志也曰、莫
三子者之撰子曰、何傷
爾、舍瑟而作、對曰異乎
焉。點、爾何如。鼓瑟希鏗

7. *Last of all, the Master asked Tsăng Hsî,* "Tien, what are your wishes?" *Tien,* pausing as he was playing on his lute, while it was yet twanging, laid the instrument aside, and rose. "My wishes," he said, "are different from the cherished purposes of these three gentlemen." "What harm is there in that?" said the Master; "do you also, as well as they, speak out your wishes." *Tien* then said, "In *this,* the last month of spring, with the dress of the season all complete, along with five or six young men who have assumed the cap, and six or seven boys, I would wash in the Î, enjoy the breeze among the rain altars, and return home singing." The Master heaved a sigh and said, "I give my approval to Tien."

The cap was so named, as "displaying the MAN." 7. 希＝止 "pausing," "stopping." 鏗, an adverb, expressing the twanging sound of the instrument. 莫, read *mû,* 4th tone, the same as 暮, "sunset," "the close of a period of time." 冠 (4th tone) 者, "capped men." Capping was in China a custom similar to the assuming the *toga virilis* among the Romans. It took place at 20. 浴 is not "to bathe," but is used with reference to a custom of washing the hands and clothes at some stream in the 3rd month, to put away evil influences. 雩 was the name of the summer sacrifice for rain, Lî Chî, IV,

三子者出曾晳後曾晳曰、

夫三子者之言何如子曰、

亦各言其志也已矣曰、夫

子何哂由也曰爲國以禮、

其言不讓是故哂之唯求

則非邦也與安見方六七

十、如五六十、而非邦也者。

8. The three others having gone out, Tsăng Hsî remained behind, and said, "What do you think of the words of these three friends?" The Master replied, "They simply told each one his wishes."

9. Hsî pursued, "Master, why did you smile at Yû?"

10. He was answered, "The management of a state demands the rules of propriety. His words were not humble; therefore I smiled at him."

11. Hsî again said, "But was it not a state which Ch'iû proposed for himself?" The reply was, "Yes; did you ever see a territory of sixty or seventy lî or one of fifty or sixty, which was not a state?"

11, Pt. ii, 8. Dancing movements were employed at it, hence the name 一舞 雩. 11. 曾晳 曰 is to be supplied before 唯, and 子 曰 before 安. Similar supplements must be made in the next paragraph.—It does not appear whether Hsî, even at the last, understood why Confucius had laughed at Tsze-lû, and not at the others. "It was not," say the commentators, "because Tsze-lû was extravagant in his aims.

之大。　孰能爲小、　爲之也、　何、赤、　諸侯同非　會宗廟　與。非邦也　唯赤則 <sup>十二</sup>

12. *Once more, Hsî inquired,* "And was it not a state which Ch'ih proposed for himself?" *The Master again replied,* "*Yes;* who but princes have to do with ancestral temples, and with audiences but the sovereign? If Ch'ih were to be a small *assistant* in these *services,* who could be a great one?"

They were all thinking of great things, yet not greater than they were able for. Tsze-lû's fault was his levity. That was his offense against *propriety.*"

## BOOK XII.　YEN YÜAN

克己復　仁、一日　復禮爲　曰、克己　問仁。　顏淵　十二　顏淵第

CHAPTER I. 1. Yen Yüan asked about perfect virtue. The Master said, "To subdue one's self and return to propriety, is perfect virtue. If a man can for one day subdue himself and return to propriety, all under

HEADING OF THIS BOOK.—顏淵第 十二, "The twelfth Book, beginning with 'Yen Yüan.'" It contains 24 chapters, conveying lessons on perfect virtue, government, and other questions of morality and policy, addressed in conversation by Confucius chiefly to his disciples. The different answers, given about the same subject to different questioners, show well how the sage suited his instructions to the characters and capacities of the parties with whom he had to do.

1. HOW TO ATTAIN TO PERFECT VIRTUE:—A CONVERSATION WITH YEN YÜAN. 1. In Ho Yen, 克己 is explained by 約身, "to restrain the body." Chû Hsî defines 克 by 勝, "to overcome," and 己 by 身之私

勿聽、非禮勿言、
非禮勿視、非禮
請問其目子曰、
人乎哉顏淵曰、
爲仁由己、而由
禮、天下歸仁焉、

heaven will ascribe perfect virtue to him. Is the practice of perfect virtue from a man himself, or is it from others?"

2  Yen Yüan said, "I beg to ask the steps of that process." The Master replied, "Look not at what is contrary to propriety; listen not to what is contrary to propriety; speak not what is contrary to propriety;

欲, "the selfish desires of the body." In the 合 講, it is said—己 非 卽 是 私,但 私 卽 附 身 而 奪, 故 謂 私 爲 己, "己 here is not exactly selfishness, but selfishness is what abides by being attached to the body, and hence it is said that selfishness is 己." And again, 克 己 非 克 去 其 己, 乃 克 去 己 中 之 私 欲 也, "克 己 is not subduing and putting away the *self*, but subduing and putting away the selfish desires *in the self*." This "selfishness in the self" is of a threefold character: first, 氣 稟, said by Morrison to be "a person's natural constitution and disposition of mind": it is, I think, very much the ψυχικὸς ἄνθρωπος or "animal man", second, 耳, 目, 口, 鼻 之 欲, "the desires of the ears, the eyes, the mouth, the nose;" i. e., the dominating influences of the senses; and third, 爾 我, "Thou and I," i. e., the lust of superiority. More concisely, the 己 is said, in the 翼 註, to

be the 人 心 as opposed to the 道 心, "the mind of man" in opposition to "the mind of reason";—see the Shû-ching, II, ii, 15. This refractory "mind of man," it is said, 與 生 俱 生, "is innate," or, perhaps, "connate." In all these statements there is an acknowledgment of the fact—the morally abnormal condition of human nature—which underlies the Christian doctrine of original sin. With reference to the above threefold classification of selfish desires, the second paragraph shows that it was the second order of them—the influence of the senses—which Confucius specially intended 復 禮,—see note on 禮, VIII, ii. It is not here *ceremonies*. Chû Hsî defines it—天 理 之 節 文, "the specific divisions and graces of heavenly principle or reason." This is continually being departed from, on the impulse of selfishness, but there is an ideal of it as *proper to*

非禮勿動。顏淵曰、

回雖不敏、請事斯

語矣。

仲弓問仁子曰、

出門如見大賓、使

民如承大祭、己所

不欲、勿施於人、在

邦無怨、在家無怨。

make no movement which is contrary to propriety."
Yen Yüan *then* said, "Though I am deficient in
intelligence and vigor, I will make it my business to
practice this lesson."

CHAPTER II. Chung-kung asked about perfect
virtue. The Master said, *"It is,* when you go abroad,
*to behave to every one* as if you were receiving a great
guest; to employ the people as if you were assisting
at a great sacrifice; not to do to others as you would
not wish done to yourself; to have no murmuring
against you in the country, and none in the family."

man, which is to be sought—"returned to"—by overcoming that.
歸 is explained by Chû Hsî by 與,
"to allow." The gloss of the 備旨
is—稱其仁, "will praise his perfect
virtue." Perhaps 天下 is only=our
"everybody," or "anybody." Some
editors take *kwei* in the sense of "to
return,"—"the empire will return to
perfect virtue;"—supposing the ex-
emplifier to be a prince. In the next
sentence, which is designed to teach
that every man may attain to this
virtue for himself, 而 is equivalent to
our "or," and implies a strong denial
of what is asked. 2. 其 refers to 克
己復禮. 目=條件, "a list of particulars." 事 is used as an active
verb;—"I beg to make my business
these words."

2. WHEREIN PERFECT VIRTUE IS
REALIZED:—A CONVERSATION WITH
CHUNG-KUNG. Chung-kung, see VI,
i. From this chapter it appears that
reverence (敬) and reciprocity (恕),
on the largest scale, constitute perfect virtue. 使民,—"ordering the
people," is apt to be done with
haughtiness. This part of the answer
may be compared with the apostle's
precept—"Honor all men," only the
"all men" is much more comprehen-
sive there. 己所云云,—compare
V, xi. 在邦, 在家,="abroad, "at
home." Pào Hsien, in Ho Yen,

乎。

之難、言之得無訒

之仁矣乎子曰爲

曰、其言也訒斯謂

曰、仁者其言也訒。

司馬牛問仁。子

請事斯語矣。

仲弓曰、雍雖不敏、

Chung-kung said, "Though I am deficient in intelligence and vigor, I will make it my business to practice this lesson."

CHAPTER III. 1. Sze-mâ Niû asked about perfect virtue.

2. The Master said, "The man of perfect virtue is cautious and slow in his speech."

3. "Cautious and slow in his speech!" said Niû;—"is this what is meant by perfect virtue?" The Master said, "When a man feels the difficulty of doing, can he be other than cautious and slow in speaking?"

however, takes the former as denoting "the prince of a state," and the latter, "the chief of a great officer's establishment." This is like the interpretation of 歸 in the last chapter —The answer, the same as that of Hûi in the last chapter, seems to betray the hand of the compiler.

3. CAUTION IN SPEAKING A CHARACTERISTIC OF PERFECT VIRTUE:—A CONVERSATION WITH TSZE-NIÛ. 1. Tsze-niû was the designation of Sze-mâ Kǎng. *alias* Lî Kǎng (犂 耕), whose tablet is now the 7th east in the outer ranges of the disciples.

He belonged to Sung, and was a brother of Hwan T'ûi, VII, xxii. Their ordinary surname was Hsiang (向), but that of Hwan could also be used by them, as they were descended from the duke so called. The office of "master of the horse" (司 馬) had long been in the family, and that title appears here as if it were Niû's surname. 2. 訒=言 難 出, "the words coming forth with difficulty." 3. 爲 之, 言 之,—comp. on 之 in the note on VII, x, *et al.*—"Doing being difficult, can speaking be without difficulty of utterance?"

子夏曰、商聞之矣。

皆有兄弟、我獨亡。

司馬牛憂曰、人

憂何懼。

曰內省不疚、夫何

謂之君子矣乎子

懼。曰、不憂不懼斯

子曰、君子不憂不

司馬牛問君子。

CHAPTER IV. 1. Sze-mâ Niû asked about the superior man. The Master said, "The superior man has neither anxiety nor fear."

2. "Being without anxiety or fear!" said Niû;— "does this constitute what we call the superior man?"

3. The Master said, "When internal examination discovers nothing wrong, what is there to be anxious about, what is there to fear?"

CHAPTER V. 1. Sze-mâ Niû, full of anxiety, said, "*Other* men all have their brothers, I only have not."

2. Tsze-hsiâ said to him, "There is the following saying which I have heard—

4. HOW THE CHÜN-TSZE HAS NEITHER ANXIETY NOR FEAR, AND CONSCIOUS RECTITUDE FREES FROM THESE. 1. 憂 is our "anxiety," trouble about coming troubles; 懼 is "fear," when the troubles have arrived. 2. 疚 is "a chronic illness"; here it is understood with reference to the mind, *that* displaying no symptom of disease.

5. CONSOLATION OFFERED BY TSZE-HSIÂ TO TSZE-NIÛ, ANXIOUS

ABOUT THE WAYS OF HIS BROTHER. 1. Tsze-niû's anxiety was occasioned by the conduct of his eldest brother Hwan T·ûi, who, he knew, was contemplating rebellion, which would probably lead to his death. 兄弟, "elder brothers" and "younger brothers," but Tsze-niû was himself the youngest of his family. The phrase simply="brothers." "All have their brothers,"—i. e., all can rest quietly without anxiety in their

死生有命、富貴
在天君子敬而
無失、與人恭而
有禮四海之內、
皆兄弟也君子
何患乎無兄弟
也。
子張問明子
曰、浸潤之譖膚

3. "'Death and life have their determined appointment; riches and honors depend upon Heaven.'

4. "Let the superior man never fail reverentially to order his own conduct, and let him be respectful to others and observant of propriety:—then all within the four seas will be his brothers. What has the superior man to do with being distressed because he has no brothers?"

CHAPTER VI. Tsze-chang asked what constituted intelligence. The Master said, "He with whom neither slander that gradually soaks *into the mind*, nor

relation. 2. It is naturally supposed that the author of the observation was Confucius. Tsze-hsiâ, see I, vii. 4. The 翼 註 says that the expression, "all within the four seas are brothers," 不 是 通 天 譜, "does not mean that all under heaven have the same genealogical register." Chû Hsî's interpretation is that, when a man so acts, other men will love and respect him as a brother. This, no doubt, is the extent of the saying. I have found no satisfactory gloss on the phrase—"the four seas." It is found in the Shû-ching, the Shih-ching, and the Lî Chî. In the 爾 雅, a sort of lexicon, very ancient, which was once reckoned among the Ching, it is explained as a territorial designation, the name of the dwelling place of all the barbarous tribes. But the great Yü is represented as

having made the four seas as four ditches, to which he drained the waters inundating "the Middle Kingdom." Plainly, the ancient conception was of their own country as the great habitable tract, north, south, east, and west of which were four seas or oceans, between whose shores and their own borders the intervening space was not very great, and occupied by wild hordes of inferior races. See the 四 書 釋 地 續, II, xxiv.—Commentators consider this attempt at consolation altogether wide of the mark.

6. WHAT CONSTITUTES INTELLIGENCE:—ADDRESSED TO TSZE-CHANG. Tsze-chang (II, xvii), it is said, was always seeking to be wise about things lofty and distant, and therefore Confucius brings him back to things near at hand, which it was

受之愬、不行焉、可謂

明也已矣、浸潤之譖、

膚受之愬、不行焉、可

謂遠也已矣。

子貢問政子曰足

食足兵民信之矣。

貢曰必不得已而去、

於斯三者何先曰、去

statements that startle like a wound in the flesh, are successful, may be called intelligent indeed. Yea, he with whom neither soaking slander, nor startling statements, are successful, may be called farseeing."

CHAPTER VII. 1. Tsze-kung asked about government. The Master said, *"The requisites of government are* that there be sufficiency of food, sufficiency of military equipment, and the confidence of the people in their ruler."

2. Tsze-kung said, "If it cannot be helped, and one of these must be dispensed with, which of the three should be foregone first?" "The military equipment," said the Master.

---

more necessary for him to attend to. 浸潤之譖, " soaking, moistening, slander," which unperceived sinks into the mind. 膚受之愬 (=and interchanged with 訴), "statements of wrongs which startle like a wound in the flesh," to which in the surprise credence is given. He with whom these things 不行,—are "no go," is intelligent,— yea, farseeing. 遠=明 之至. So Chû Hsî. The old interpreters differ in their view of 膚受之愬. The 註疏 says—"The skin receives dust which gradually accumulates." This makes the phrase synonymous with the former.

7. REQUISITES IN GOVERNMENT: —A CONVERSATION WITH TSZE-KUNG. 1. 兵 primarily means "weapons." "A soldier," the bearer of such weapons, is a secondary meaning. There were no standing armies in Confucius's time. The term is to be taken here, as="military equipment," "preparation for war." 信之,—之 refers to 其上, "their ruler."

質而已矣、何以文
棘子成曰、君子
立。
皆有死、民無信不
何先曰、去食、自古
已而去、於斯二者
兵子貢曰、必不得

3.　Tsze-kung *again* asked, "If it cannot be helped, and one of the remaining two must be dispensed with, which of them should be foregone?" The Master answered, "Part with the food. From of old, death has been the lot of all men; but if the people have no. faith *in their rulers*, there is no standing *for the state*."

CHAPTER VIII. 1. Chî Tsze-ch'âng said, "In a superior man it is only the substantial qualities which are wanted;—why should we seek for ornamental accomplishments?"

3. The difficulty here is with the concluding clause—無 信 不 立. Transferring the meaning of 信 from paragraph 1, we naturally render as in the translation, and 不 立＝國 不 立, "the state will not stand." This is the view, moreover, of the old interpreters. Chû Hsî and his followers, however, seek to make much more of 信. On the 1st paragraph he comments,—"The granaries being full, and the military preparation complete, then let the influence of instruction proceed. So shall the people have faith in their ruler, and will not leave him or rebel." On the 3rd paragraph he says,—"If the people be without food, they must die, but death is the inevitable lot of men. If they are without 信, though they live, they have not wherewith to establish themselves. It is better for them in such case to die. Therefore it is better for the ruler to die, not losing faith to his people, so that the people will prefer death rather than lose faith to him."

8.　SUBSTANTIAL QUALITIES AND ACCOMPLISHMENTS IN THE CHÜN-TSZE. 1. Tsze-ch'ăng was an officer of the state of Wei, and, distressed by the pursuit in the times of what was merely external, made this not sufficiently well-considered remark, to which Tsze-kung replied, in, according to Chû Hsî, an equally one-sided

爲。子貢曰、惜乎夫
子之說、君子也、駟
不及舌文猶質也、
質猶文也、虎豹之
鞟、猶犬羊之鞟。
哀公問於有若
曰、年饑用不足、如
之何。有若對曰、盍

2. Tsze-kung said, "Alas! Your words, sir, show you to be a superior man, but four horses cannot overtake the tongue.

3. "Ornament is as substance; substance is as ornament. The hide of a tiger or a leopard stripped of its hair, is like the hide of a dog or a goat stripped of its hair."

CHAPTER IX. 1. The duke Âi inquired of Yû Zo, saying, "The year is one of scarcity, and *the returns for* expenditure are not sufficient;—what is to be done?"

2. Yû Zo replied to him, "Why not *simply* tithe the people?"

manner. 1. 何 以 文 爲 is thus expanded in the 註 疏,—何 用 文 章 乃 爲 君 子, "why use accomplishments in order to make a *Chün-tsze?*" 2. We may interpret this paragraph, as in the translation, putting a comma after 說. So, Chû Hsî. But the old interpreters seem to have read right on, without any comma, to 也, in which case the paragraph would be —"Alas! sir, for the way in which you speak of the superior man!" And this is the most natural construction. 3. The modern commentators seem hypercritical in condemning Tsze-kung's language here. He shows the desirableness of the ornamental accomplishments, but does not necessarily put them on the same level with the substantial qualities.

9. LIGHT TAXATION THE BEST WAY TO SECURE THE GOVERNMENT FROM EMBARRASSMENT FOR WANT OF FUNDS. 1. Duke Âi, II, xx. Yû Zo, I, ii. 2. By the statutes of the Châu dynasty, the ground was divided into allotments cultivated in common by the families located upon them, and the produce was divided equally, nine tenths being given to the farmers and one tenth being reserved as a contribution to the state. This was called the law of 徹, which term = 通, "pervading," "general," with reference, apparently, to the system of

信、從義崇德也。

辨惑子曰主中

子張問崇德、

與足。

百姓不足、君孰

足、君孰與不足、

徹也。對曰、百姓

不足、如之何其

徹乎。曰二、吾猶

3. "With two tenths," said the duke, "I find them not enough;—how could I do with that system of one tenth?"

4. Yû Zo answered, "If the people have plenty, their prince will not be left to want alone. If the people are in want, their prince cannot enjoy plenty alone."

CHAPTER X. 1. Tsze-chang having asked how virtue was to be exalted, and delusions to be discovered, the Master said, "Hold faithfulness and sincerity as first principles, and be moving continually to what is right,—this is the way to exalt one's virtue.

common labor. 3. A former duke of Lû, Hsüan (609–591 B. C.), had imposed an additional tax of another teuth from each family's portion. 4. The meaning of this paragraph is given in the translation. Literally rendered, it is,—"The people having plenty, the prince—with whom not plenty? The people not having plenty with whom can the prince have plenty?" Yû Zo wished to impress on the duke that a sympathy and common condition should unite him and his people. If he lightened his taxation to the regular tithe,

then they would cultivate their allotments with so much vigor that his receipts would be abundant. They would be able, moreover, to help their kind ruler in any emergency.

10. HOW TO EXALT VIRTUE AND DISCOVER DELUSIONS. 1. Tsze-chang, see chap. vi. The Master says nothing about the 辨, "discriminating," or "discovering," of delusions, but gives an instance of a twofold delusion. Life and death, it is said, are independent of our wishes. To desire for a man either the one or the other, therefore, is one delusion.

孔子對曰、君君、臣臣、父

臺齊景公問政於孔子。

以異。

是惑也。誠不以富、亦祇

死、既欲其生、又欲其死、

愛之欲其生、惡之欲其

2.  "You love a man and wish him to live; you hate him and wish him to die. Having wished him to live, you also wish him to die. This is a case of delusion.

3.  "'It may not be on account of her being rich, yet you come to make a difference.'"

CHAPTER XI. 1. The duke Ching, of Ch'î, asked Confucius about government.

2.  Confucius replied, *"There is government,* when the prince is prince, and the minister is minister; when the father is father, and the son is son.'"

And on the change of our feelings to change our wishes in reference to the same person, is another. 之＝此人.—But in this Confucius hardly appears to be the sage. 3. See the Shih-ching, II, iv, Ode iv, 3. I have translated according to the meaning in the Shih-ching. The quotation may be twisted into some sort of accordance with the preceding paragraph, as a case of delusion, but the commentator Ch'ăng (程) is probably correct in supposing that it should be transferred to XVI, xii. Then 祇 should be in the text, not 祇.

11.  GOOD GOVERNMENT OBTAINS ONLY WHEN ALL THE RELATIVE DUTIES ARE MAINTAINED. 1. Confucius went to Ch'î in his 36th year, 517 B. C., and finding the reigning duke—styled *ching* after his death—.overshadowed by his ministers, and thinking of setting aside his eldest son from the succession, he shaped his answer to the question about

父、子子公曰、善哉、信
如君不君、臣不臣、父
不父子不子、雖有粟、
吾得而食諸。
▣子曰片言可以折
獄者、其由也與子路
無宿諾。
▣子曰聽訟吾猶人
也、必也使無訟乎。

3. "Good!" said the duke; "if, indeed, the prince
be not prince, the minister not minister, the father
not father, and the son not son, although I have my
revenue, can I enjoy it?"

CHAPTER XII. 1. The Master said, "Ah! it is Yû,
who could with half a word settle litigations!"

2. Tsze-lû never slept over a promise.

CHAPTER XIII. The Master said, "In hearing
litigations, I am like any other body. What is necessary, *however*, is to cause *the people* to have no
litigations."

government accordingly. 3. "Although I have the grain," i. e., my
revenue, the tithe of the produce of
the country. 吾得而食諸 (食諸,
compare 行諸, XI, xxi), "shall I be
able to eat it?"—intimating the
danger the state was exposed to
from insubordinate officers.

12. WITH WHAT EASE TSZE-LÛ
COULD SETTLE LITIGATIONS. 1. We
translate here—"could," and not—
"can," because Confucius is simply
praising the disciple's character.
Tsze-lû, see II, xvii. 片言=半言,
"half a word." 2. This paragraph
is from the compilers, stating a fact
about Tsze-lû, to illustrate what the
Master said of him. 宿 is explained
by Chû Hsî by 留 "to leave," "to let

remain." Its primary meaning is—
"to pass a night." We have in
English, as given in the translation,
a corresponding idiom.—In Ho Yen,
片言 is taken as=偏言, "one-sided
words," meaning that Tsze-lû could
judge rightly on hearing half a case.
宿 again is explained by 豫, "beforehand."—"Tsze-lû made no promises
beforehand."

13. TO PREVENT BETTER THAN
TO DETERMINE LITIGATIONS. See the
大學傳, IV. 訟, as opposed to 獄
(preceding chapter), is used of civil
causes (爭財曰訟), and the other
of criminal (爭罪曰獄). Little
stress is to be laid on the "I"; much
on 使, as = "to influence to."

帥以正、孰敢不正。

孔子對曰、政者正也、子

曰季康子問政於孔子。

不成人之惡、小人反是。

曰子曰君子成人之美、

以禮亦可以弗畔矣夫。

曰子曰博學於文、約之

無倦、行之以忠。

曰子張問政。子曰、居之

CHAPTER XIV.　Tsze-chang asked about government. The Master said, *"The art of governing* is to keep *its affairs* before the mind without weariness, and to practice them with undeviating consistency."

CHAPTER XV.　The Master said, "By extensively studying all learning, and keeping himself under the restraint of the rules of propriety, *one* may thus likewise not err from what is right."

CHAPTER XVI.　The Master said, "The superior man *seeks to* perfect the admirable qualities of men, and does not *seek to* perfect their bad qualities. The mean man does the opposite of this."

CHAPTER XVII.　Chî K'ang asked Confucius about government. Confucius replied, "To govern means to rectify. If you lead on *the people* with correctness, who will dare not to be correct?"

14.　THE ART OF GOVERNING.　居, as opposed to 行, must be used as an active verb, and is explained by Chû Hsî as in the translation. 之 refers to that aspect of government about which Tsze-chang was inquiring. 無倦=始 終 如 一, "first and last the same;" 以 忠=表 裏 如 一, "externally and internally the same."

15.　HARDLY DIFFERENT FROM VI, XXV.

16.　OPPOSITE INFLUENCE UPON OTHERS OF THE SUPERIOR MAN AND THE MEAN MAN.

17.　GOVERNMENT MORAL IN ITS END AND EFFICIENT BY EXAMPLE.

上之風必偃。
德風小人之德草草
善、而民善矣、君子之
子爲政焉用殺子欲
有道、何如孔子對曰、
子曰、如殺無道以就
【畫】季康子問政於孔
之不欲、雖賞之不竊。
孔子孔子對曰苟子
【畫】季康子患盜、問於

CHAPTER XVIII. Chî K‘ang, distressed about the number of thieves *in the state*, inquired of Confucius *how to do away with them*. Confucius said, "If you, sir, were not covetous, although you should reward them to do it, they would not steal."

CHAPTER XIX. Chî K‘ang asked Confucius about government, saying, "What do you say to killing the unprincipled for the good of the principled?" Confucius replied, "Sir, in carrying on your government, why should you use killing at all? Let your *evinced* desires be for what is good, and the people will be good. The relation between superiors and inferiors is like that between the wind and the grass. The grass must bend, when the wind blows across it."

18. THE PEOPLE ARE MADE THIEVES BY THE EXAMPLE OF THEIR RULERS. This is a good instance of Confucius's boldness in reproving men in power. Chî K‘ang II, xx, had made himself head of the Chî family, and entered into all its usurpations, by taking off the infant nephew, who should have been its rightful chief. 不 欲＝不 貪, "djd not covet," i. e., a position and influence to which you have no right. 苟 子 之 不 欲＝"given the fact of your not being ambitious." 賞 之＝賞民.

19. KILLING NOT TO BE TALKED OF BY RULERS; THE EFFECT OF THEIR EXAMPLE. In 就 有 道, 就 is an active verb,＝成, or 成就, "to complete," "to perfect." 德 is used in a vague sense, not positive virtue, but＝"nature," "character." Some for 上 would read 尙＝加, "to add upon," but 上 itself must here have substantially that meaning. 草 上 之 風＝草, 加 之 以 風, "the grass, having the wind upon it."

虑以下人在邦必達、

而好義察言而觀色、

達也夫達也者、質直

必聞子曰是聞也、非

對曰、在邦必聞、在家

哉、爾所謂達者。子張

可謂之達矣子曰、何

子張問士何如、斯

CHAPTER XX. 1. Tsze-chang asked, "What must the officer be, who may be said to be distinguished?"

2. The Master said, "What is it you call being distinguished?"

3. Tsze-chang replied, "It is to be heard of through the state, to be heard of throughout his clan."

4. The Master said, "That is notoriety, not distinction.

5. "Now the man of distinction is solid and straightforward, and loves righteousness. He examines people's words, and looks at their countenances. He is anxious to humble himself to others. Such a man will be distinguished in the country; he will be distinguished in his clan.

20. THE MAN OF TRUE DISTINCTION AND THE MAN OF NOTORIETY. 1. The ideas of "a scholar" and an "officer" blend together in China. 達＝通 達, "to reach all round";—being influential, and that influence being acknowledged. 3. If 士 be "an officer," then 在 邦 assumes him to be the minister of a prince of a state, and 在 家, that he is only the minister of a great officer, who is the head of a clan. If, however, 士 be understood of "a scholar," 邦 will＝州 里, "the country," "people generally," and 家 will＝族 黨, "the circle of relatives and neighbors." 5. 下 人,—下 is the verb. The dictionary explains it by "to descend. From being on high to become low." But it is here rather more

得、非崇德與、攻其惡、無
惑。子曰、善哉問先事後
下、曰、敢問崇德修慝、辨
樊遲從遊於舞雩之
在邦必聞在家必聞。
取仁而行違居之不疑、
在家必達夫聞也者、色

6. "As to the man of notoriety, he assumes the appearance of virtue, but his actions are opposed to it, and he rests in this character without any doubts *about himself*. Such a man will be heard of in the country; he will be heard of in the clan."

CHAPTER XXI. 1. Fan Ch'ih rambling with the Master under *the trees* about the rain altars, said, "I venture to ask how to exalt virtue, to correct cherished evil, and to discover delusions."

2. The Master said, "Truly a good question!

3. "If doing what is to be done be made the first business, and success a secondary consideration:—is not this the way to exalt virtue? To assail one's own

still,="to come down below *other men*." 6. The condemnation here might be more fully and clearly expressed.

21. HOW TO EXALT VIRTUE, COR-RECT VICE, AND DISCOVER DELUSIONS. Compare chap. x. Here, as there, under the last point of the inquiry, Confucius simply indicates a case of

delusion, and perhaps that is the best way to teach how to discover delusions generally. 1. Fan Ch'ih, see II, v. 舞 雩, see XI, xxv, 7; followed here by 之 下, there must be reference to the trees growing about the altars. 慝 formed from "heart" and "to conceal,"=secret vice. 3. 先 事 後 得,—compare with

使枉者直。樊遲退見子

達子曰舉直錯諸枉能

問知。子曰知人樊遲未

樊遲問仁子曰、愛人。

親、非惑與。

朝之忿忘其身以及其

攻人之惡、非修慝與、一

wickedness and not assail that of others;—is not this the way to correct cherished evil? For a morning's anger to disregard one's own life, and involve that of his parents;—is not this a case of delusion?"

CHAPTER XXII. 1. Fan Ch'ih asked about benevolence. The Master said, "It is to love *all* men." He asked about knowledge. The Master said, "It is to know *all* men."

2. Fan Ch'ih did not immediately understand *these answers*.

3. The Master said, "Employ the upright and put aside all the crooked; in this way the crooked can be made to be upright."

4. Fan Ch'ih retired, and, seeing Tsze-hsiâ, he said

先難後獲, in VI, xx, which also is the report of a conversation with Fan Ch'ih. 其 惡,—其＝己, "himself," "his own." "A morning's anger" must be a small thing, but the consequences of giving way to it are very terrible. The case is one of great delusion.

22. ABOUT BENEVOLENCE AND WISDOM;—HOW KNOWLEDGE SUBSERVES BENEVOLENCE. Fan Ch'ih might well deem the Master's replies enigmatical, and, with the help of Tsze-hsiâ's explanations, the student still finds it difficult to understand the chapter. 1. 仁 here, be'ng opposed to, or distinct from, 知, is to be taken as meaning "benevolence," and not as "perfect virtue." 2. 未, "not yet," i. e., not immediately. 3. Compare II, xix. 4. 鄉, 4th tone, in the dictionary defined by 昔,

仁者遠矣。

有天下、選於衆擧伊尹、不

衆、擧皋陶、不仁者遠矣、湯

富哉、言乎舜有天下、選於

使枉者直、何謂也。子夏曰、

問知子曰、擧直錯諸枉能

夏曰、鄉也、吾見於夫子而

to him, "A little while ago, I had an interview with our Master, and asked him about knowledge. He said, 'Employ the upright, and put aside all the crooked;—in this way, the crooked will be made to be upright.' What did he mean?"

5. Tsze-hsiâ said, "Truly rich is his saying!

6. "Shun, being in possession of the kingdom, selected from among all the people, and employed Kâo-yâo, on which all who were devoid of virtue disappeared. T'ang, being in possession of the kingdom, selected from among all the people, and employed Î Yin, and all who were devoid of virtue disappeared."

"formerly." 6. See the names here in the Shû-ching, Parts II, III, and IV. Shun and T'ang showed their wisdom—their knowledge of men— in the selection of the ministers who were named. That was their employment of the upright, and therefore all devoid of virtue disappeared. That was their making the crooked upright;—and so their love reached to all.

輔友、以 曰、🀆自 則 之、而 曰、問 🀆
仁。以 文 君 曾 辱 止、不 善 忠 友。子
友 會 子 子 焉。毋 可 道 告、子 貢

CHAPTER XXIII.　Tsze-kung asked about friendship.　The Master said, "Faithfully admonish *your friend,* and skillfully lead him on.　If you find him impracticable, stop.　Do not disgrace yourself."

CHAPTER XXIV.　The philosopher Tsăng said, "The superior man on grounds of culture meets with his friends, and by their friendship helps his virtue."

23. PRUDENCE IN FRIENDSHIP. 告, read *kû*, as in III, xvii, implying some degree of deference. 道＝導, as in II, iii, 1.

24. THE FRIENDSHIP OF THE CHŪN-TSZE. 以 文, "by means of letters," i. e., common literary studies and pursuits.

## BOOK XIII.　TSZE-LÛ

之、 曰、 政。 路 🀆　 第 子
勞 先 子 問 子＝ 三 十 路

CHAPTER I.　1. Tsze-lû asked government.　The Master said, "Go before the people *with your example,* and be laborious in their affairs."

HEADING OF THIS BOOK.—子 路 第 十 三, "Tsze-lû, No. 13." Here, as in the last Book, we have a number of subjects touched upon, all bearing more or less directly on the government of the state, and the cultivation of the person.　The Book extends to thirty chapters.

·1. THE SECRET OF SUCCESS IN GOVERNING IS THE UNWEARIED EXAMPLE OF THE RULERS:—A LESSON TO TSZE-LÛ.　1. To what understood antecedents do the 之 refer? For the first, we may suppose 民；—先 之 ＝率 民, or 道 民, "precede the people," "lead the people," that is, do so by the example of your personal conduct.　But we cannot in the second clause bring 之 (＝民) in the same way under the regimen of 勞. 勞 之＝爲 他 勤 勞, "to be laborious for them;" that is, to set

知、人其舍諸。 爾所知、爾所不 才而舉之。曰、舉 賢才。曰、焉知賢 有司、赦小過、舉 宰問政子曰先 圖仲弓爲季氏 之請益曰、無倦。

2. He requested further instruction, and was answered, "Be not weary (in these things)."

CHAPTER II. 1. Chung-kung, being chief minister to the head of the Chî family, asked about government. The Master said, "Employ first the services of your various officers, pardon small faults, and raise to office men of virtue and talents."

2. *Chung-kung* said, "How shall I know the men of virtue and talent, so that I may raise them to office?" He was answered, "Raise to office those whom you know. As to those whom you do not know, will others neglect them?"

them the example of diligence in agriculture, etc. It is better, however, according to the idiom I have several times pointed out, to take 之 as giving a sort of neuter and general force to the preceding words, so that the expressions are="ex. ample and laboriousness."—K'ung An-kwo understands the meaning differently:—"set the people an example, and then you may make them labor." But this is not so good. 2. 無 in the old copies is 毋. The meaning comes to be the same.

2. THE DUTIES CHIEFLY TO BE ATTENDED TO BY A HEAD MINISTER: —A LESSON TO ZAN YUNG. 1. 先有 司—compare VIII, iv, 3. The 有司

are the various smaller officers. A head minister should assign them their duties, and not be interfering in them himself. His business is to examine into the manner in which they discharge them. And in doing so, he should overlook small faults. 2. 人其舍諸,—compare 山川其舍 諸, in VI, iv, though the force of 舍 here is not so great as in that chapter. Confucius's meaning is that Chung-kung need not trouble himself about *all* men of worth. Let him advance those he knew. There was no fear that the others would be neglected. Compare what is said on "knowing men," in XII, xxii.

所不知、蓋闕　也、君子於其　子曰、野哉、由　迁也、奚其正。　有是哉、子之　名乎子路曰、　政子將奚先。　君待子而爲　子路曰、衞

CHAPTER III. 1. Tsze-lû said, "The ruler of Wei has been waiting for you, in order with you to administer the government. What will you consider the first thing to be done?"

2. The Master replied, "What is necessary is to rectify names."

3. "So, indeed!" said Tsze-lû. "You are wide of the mark! Why must there be such rectification?"

4. The Master said, "How uncultivated you are, Yû! A superior man, in regard to what he does not know, shows a cautious reserve.

3. THE SUPREME IMPORTANCE OF NAMES BEING CORRECT. 1. This conversation is assigned by Chû Hsî to the 11th year of the duke Âi of Lû, when Confucius was 69, and he returned from his wanderings to his native state. Tsze-lû had then been some time in the service of the duke Ch'û of Wei, who, it would appear, had been wishing to get the services of the sage himself, and the disciple did not think that his Master would refuse to accept office, as he had not objected to *his* doing so. 2. 名 must have here a special reference, which Tsze-lû did not apprehend. Nor did the old interpreters, for Mâ Yung explains the 正 名 by 正 百 事 之 名, "to rectify the names of all things." On this view, the reply would indeed be "wide of the mark." The answer is substantially the same as the reply to Duke Ching of Ch'î about government in XII, xi, that it obtains when the prince is prince, the father father, etc.; that is, when each man in his relations is what the *name* of his relation would require. Now, the duke Ch'î held the rule of Wei against his father; see III, xiv. Confucius, from the necessity of the case and peculiarity of the circumstances, allowed his disciples, notwithstanding that, to take office in Wei; but at the time of this conversation, Ch'û had been duke for nine years, and ought to have been so established that he could have taken the course of a filial son without subjecting the state to any risks. On this account, Confucius said he would begin with rectifying the name of the duke, that is, with requiring him to resign the dukedom to his father, and be what his name of *son* required him to be. See the 翼 註. *in loc.* This view enables us to understand better the climax that follows, though its successive steps are still not without difficulty. 正 名

如也。名不正、則言不
順、言不順、則事不成。
事不成、則禮樂不興、
禮樂不興、則刑罰不
中、刑罰不中、則民無
所措手足。故君子、名
之必可言也、言之必
可行也、君子於其言、
無所苟而已矣。

5. "If names be not correct, language is not in accordance with the truth of things. If language be not in accordance with the truth of things, affairs cannot be carried on to success.

6. "When affairs cannot be carried on to success, proprieties and music will not flourish. When proprieties and music do not flourish, punishments will not be properly awarded. When punishments are not properly awarded, the people do not know how to move hand or foot.

7. "Therefore a superior man considers it necessary that the names he uses may be spoken *appropriately,* and also that what he speaks may be carried out *appropriately.* What the superior man requires is just that in his words there may be nothing incorrect."

---

平,—平 may be taken as an exclamation, or as="is it not?" 4. 奚如.—奚 is used in the same sense as in II, xviii. The *kai* is the introductory hypothetical particle. The phrase="is putting-aside-like," i. e., the superior man reserves and re- volves what he is in doubt about, and does not rashly speak. 6. "Proprieties" here are not ceremonial rules, but="*order,*" what such rules are designed to display and secure. So, "music" is equivalent to "harmony." 中, 4th tone, is the verb.

樊遲請學稼子曰、

吾不如老農請學爲

圃。曰、吾不如老圃。樊

遲出子曰、小人哉、樊

須也。上好禮則民莫

敢不敬、上好義則民

莫敢不服、上好信、則

民莫敢不用情、夫如

是、則四方之民、襁負

其子而至矣、焉用稼。

CHAPTER IV. 1. Fan Ch'ih requested to be taught husbandry. The Master said, "I am not so good for that as an old husbandman." He requested *also* to be taught gardening, and was answered, "I am not so good for that as an old gardener."

2. Fan Ch'ih having gone out, the Master said, "A small man, indeed, is Fan Hsü!

3. "If a superior love propriety, the people will not dare not to be reverent. If he love righteousness, the people will not dare not to submit *to his example*. If he love good faith, the people will not dare not to be sincere. Now, when these things obtain, the people from all quarters will come to him, bearing their children on their backs;—what need has he of a knowledge of husbandry?"

4. A RULER HAS NOT TO OCCUPY HIMSELF WITH WHAT IS PROPERLY THE BUSINESS OF THE PEOPLE. It is to be supposed that Fan Ch'ih was at this time in office somewhere, and thinking of the Master, as the villager and high officer did, IX, ii and vi, that his knowledge embraced almost every subject, he imagined that he might get lessons from him on the two subjects he specified, which he might use for the benefit of the people. 1. 稼 is properly the "seed-sowing," and 圃, "a kitchen-garden," but they are used generally, as in the translation. 3. 情, "the feelings," "desires," but sometimes, as here, in the sense of "sincerity." 襁, often joined with *páo* (made of the classifier 衣 and 保), is a cloth with strings by which a child is strapped upon the back of its mother or nurse.—This paragraph shows what people in office should learn. Confucius intended that it should be repeated to Fan Ch'ih.

兄弟也。

子曰魯衞之政、

雖令不從。

令而行其身不正、

子曰其身正不

雖多亦奚以爲。

於四方不能專對、

授之以政不達使

子曰、誦詩三百、

CHAPTER V. The Master said, "Though a man may be able to recite the three hundred odes, yet if, when intrusted with a governmental charge, he knows not how to act, or if, when sent to any quarter on a mission, he cannot give his replies unassisted, notwithstanding the extent *of his learning*, of what practical use is it?"

CHAPTER VI. The Master said, "When a prince's personal conduct is correct, his government is effective without the issuing of orders. If his personal conduct is not correct, he may issue orders, but they will not be followed."

CHAPTER VII. The Master said, "The governments of Lû and Wei are brothers."

5. LITERARY ACQUIREMENTS USE-LESS WITHOUT PRACTICAL ABILITY. 詩 三 百, —see II, 11. 誦, "to croon over," as Chinese students do; here, = "to have learned." 專 = 獨, "alone," i. e., unassisted by the individuals of his suite. 多, "many," refers to the 300 odes. 亦, "also," here and in other places, = our "yet," "after all." 奚 以 爲, —以, it is said, = 用, "use," and 爲 is a mere expletive,—是 語 助 詞. See in Wang Yan-chih's Treatise on the Particles under the heading 爲 語 助 也; chap. ii.

6' HIS PERSONAL CONDUCT ALL IN ALL TO A RULER. A translator finds it impossible here to attain to the terse conciseness of his original.

7. THE SIMILAR CONDITION OF THE STATES OF LÛ AND WEI. Compare VI, xxii. Lû's state had been directed by the influence of Châu-kung, and Wei was the fief of his brother Fung (封), commonly known as K'ang-shû (康 叔). They had, similarly, maintained an equal and brotherly course in their progress, or, as it was in Confucius's time, in their degeneracy. That portion of the present Honan, which runs up and lies between Shansi and Peichili, was the bulk of Wei.

子謂衞公子

荆善居室、始有、

曰、苟合矣、少有、

曰、苟完矣、富有、

曰、苟美矣。

子適衞、冉有

僕、子曰庶矣哉。

冉有曰既庶矣、

又何加焉、曰、富

CHAPTER VIII. The Master said of Ching, a scion of the ducal family of Wei, that he knew the economy of a family well. When he began to have means, he said, "Ha! here is a collection!" When they were a little increased, he said, "Ha! this is complete!" When he had become rich, he said, "Ha! this is admirable!"

CHAPTER IX. 1. When the Master went to Wei, Zan Yû acted as driver of his carriage.

2. The Master observed, "How numerous are the people!"

3. Yû said, "Since they are thus numerous, what more shall be done for them?" "Enrich them," was the reply.

8. THE CONTENTMENT OF THE OFFICER CHING, AND HIS INDIFFERENCE ON GETTING RICH. Chĭng was a great officer of Wei, a scion of its ducal house. 善居室 is a difficult expression. Literally it is— "dwelt well in his house." 室 implies that he was a married man, the head of a family. The 合 講 says the phrase is equivalent to 處家, "managed his family." Chû Hsî explains 苟 by 聊且粗署之意,—"it is significant of indifference and carelessness." Our word "ha!" express-

ing surprise and satisfaction corresponds to it pretty nearly. We are not to understand that Ching really made these utterances, but Confucius thus vividly represents how he felt. Compare Burns's line, "Contented wi' little, and cantie wi' mair."

9. A PEOPLE NUMEROUS, WELL-OFF, AND EDUCATED, IS THE GREAT ACHIEVEMENT OF GOVERNMENT. 1. 僕, "a servant," but here with the meaning in the translation. That, indeed, is the second meaning of the character given in the dictionary.

矣、誠哉是言也。

年、亦可以勝殘去殺

子曰善人為邦百

有成。

碁月、而已可也三年

子曰、苟有用我者、

焉。曰、教之。

之。曰、旣富矣、又何加

4.　"And when they have been enriched, what more shall be done?"　The Master said, "Teach them."

CHAPTER X.　The Master said, "If there were (any of the princes) who would employ me, in the course of twelve months, I should have done something considerable.　In three years, *the government* would be perfected."

CHAPTER XI.　The Master said, "'If good men were to govern a country *in succession* for a hundred years, they would be able to transform the violently bad, and dispense with capital punishments.'　True indeed is this saying!"

10.　CONFUCIUS'S ESTIMATE OF WHAT HE COULD DO, IF EMPLOYED TO ADMINISTER THE GOVERNMENT OF A STATE.　朞 is to be distinguished from 期, and ="a revolution of the year."　There is a comma at 月, and 而 已 可 are read together. 而 已 does not signify, as it often does, "and nothing more," but ="and have," 已 being 已 經, a sign of the perfect tense.—"Given twelve months, and there would be a pass-able result.　In three years there would be a completion."

11.　WHAT A HUNDRED YEARS OF GOOD GOVERNMENT COULD EFFECT. Confucius quotes here a saying of his time, and approves of it.　勝, 1st tone, "to be equal to."　勝 殘, "would be equal to the violent," that is, to transform them.　去 殺, "to do away with killing," that is, with capital punishments, unnecessary with a transformed people.

子曰、如有王者、
必世而後仁。
子曰、苟正其身
矣、於從政乎何有、
不能正其身、如正
人何。
冉子退朝、子曰、
何晏也。對曰、有
政。

CHAPTER XII. The Master said, "If a truly royal ruler were to arise, it would *still* require a generation, and then virtue would prevail."

CHAPTER XIII. The Master said, "If a minister make his own conduct correct, what difficulty will he have in assisting in government? If he cannot rectify himself, what has he to do with rectifying others?"

CHAPTER XIV. The disciple Zan returning from the court, the Master said to him, "How are you so late?" He replied, "We had government business."

12. IN WHAT TIME A ROYAL RULER COULD TRANSFORM THE KINGDOM. 王者, "one who was a king." The character 王 is formed by three straight lines representing the three powers of Heaven, Earth, and Man, and a perpendicular line, going through and uniting them, and thus conveys the highest idea of power and influence. See the dictionary, *sub voc.*, character 王. Here it means the highest wisdom and virtue in the highest place. 世, "a generation," or thirty years. See note on II, xxiii, 1. The old interpreters take 仁 as＝仁 政, "virtuous government."— To save Confucius from the charge of vanity in what he says, in chap. x, that he could accomplish in three years, it is said, that the perfection which he predicates there would only be the foundation for the virtue here realized.

13. THAT HE BE PERSONALLY CORRECT ESSENTIAL TO AN OFFICER OF GOVERNMENT. Compare chap. vi. That the subject is here an officer of government, and not the ruler, appears from the phrase 從 政; see note on VI, vi. With reference to the other phraseology of the chapter, the 備旨 says that 從 政 embraces 正 君, "the rectification of the prince," and 正 民, "the rectification of the people."

14. AN IRONICAL ADMONITION TO ZAN YÛ ON THE USURPING TENDENCIES OF THE CHÎ FAMILY. The point of the chapter turns on the opposition of the phrases 有 政 and 其 事

子曰其事也、如
有政雖不吾以、
吾其與聞之。
𥊑定公問一言
而可以與邦、有
諸孔子對曰言
不可以若是其
幾也人之言曰、
爲君難爲臣不

The Master said, "It must have been *family* affairs.
If there had been government business, though I am
not *now* in office, I should have been consulted about
it."

CHAPTER XV. 1. The duke Ting asked whether
there was a single sentence which could make a country
prosperous. Confucius replied, "Such an effect cannot be expected from one sentence.

2. "There is a saying, however, which people
have—'To be a prince is difficult; to be a minister is
not easy.'

也;—at the court of the Chî family,
that is, they had really been discussing matters of government, affecting the state, and proper only for
the prince's court. Confucius affects
not to believe it, and says that at
the chief's court they could only
have been discussing the affairs of
his house. 不 吾 以,—an inversion,
and 以 = 用, "although I am *now* not
employed." 與, in 4th tone.—"I
should have been present and heard
it." Superannuated officers might
go to court on occasions of emergency, and might also be consulted
on such, though the general rule was
to allow them to retire at 70. See
the Lî Chî, I, i, Pt. i, 28. The 其
after 吾 makes a double subject, and
=an emphatic I; a style more com-

mon in the Shû than in these Analects.
15. HOW THE PROSPERITY AND
RUIN OF A COUNTRY MAY DEPEND ON
THE RULER'S VIEW OF HIS POSITION,
HIS FEELING ITS DIFFICULTY, OR
ONLY CHERISHING A HEADSTRONG
WILL. 1. I should suppose that 一 言
可 以 與 邦 and the corresponding
sentence below were common sayings, about which the duke asks, in a
way to intimate his disbelief of
them,—有 諸· 幾 is not here in the
sense of "a spring," or "*primum
mobile*," but = 期, in the sense of "to
expect," "to be expected from." 一
言 = 一 句, as in II, ii. 2. It is only
the first part of the saying on which
Confucius dwells. That is called 主,
the principal sentence; the other is

幾乎一言而喪邦乎。

善乎。如不善、而莫之違也、不

也如其善、而莫之違也、不亦

樂乎爲君、唯其言而莫予違

若是其幾也、人之言曰予無

邦有諸孔子對曰言不可以

一言而興邦乎。曰、一言而喪

易。如知爲君之難也、不幾乎

3. "If a *ruler* knows this,—the difficulty of being a prince,—may there not be expected from this one sentence the prosperity of his country?"

4. *The duke then* said, "Is there a single sentence which can ruin a country?" Confucius replied, "Such an effect as that cannot be expected from one sentence. There is, *however*, the saying which people have—'I have no pleasure in being a prince, but only in that no one can offer any opposition to what I say!'

5. "If a *ruler's* words be good, is it not also good that no one oppose them? But if they are not good, and no one opposes them, may there not be expected from this one sentence the ruin of his country?"

only 帶 說, "an accessory." 3. Some put a comma at the first 乎, but it is better to take that 乎 as a preposition:—"May it not be expected that *from* this one word, etc.?" Similarly, par. 4, 乎 is a preposition＝our *in.* 其言,—言 is here used specially of the orders, rules, etc., which a ruler may issue.

黨有直躬者其父攘

一
葉公語孔子曰吾

小利則大事不成。

小利、欲速則不達、見

政子曰無欲速無見

一
子夏爲莒父宰、問

者說遠者來。

一
葉公問政子曰、近
二

CHAPTER XVI. 1. The duke of Sheh asked about government.

2. The Master said, *"Good government obtains when those who are near are made happy, and those who are far off are attracted."*

CHAPTER XVII. Tsze-hsiâ, being governor of Chü-fû, asked about government. The Master said, "Do not be desirous to have things done quickly; do not look at small advantages. Desire to have things done quickly prevents their being done thoroughly. Looking at small advantages prevents great affairs from being accomplished."

CHAPTER XVIII. 1. The duke of Sheh informed Confucius, saying, "Among us here are those who may be styled upright in their conduct. If their father

16. GOOD GOVERNMENT SEEN FROM ITS EFFECTS. 1. 葉 read *shêh;* see VII, xviii. 2. Confucius is supposed to have in view the oppressive and aggressive government of Ch'û, to which Shih belonged.

17. HASTE AND SMALL ADVANTAGES NOT TO BE DESIRED IN GOVERNING. Chù-fû (fû, 3rd tone) was a

small city in 'the western border of Lù. 無=毋, the prohibitive particle.

18. NATURAL DUTY AND UPRIGHTNESS IN COLLISION. 1. 吾黨, "our village," "our neighborhood," but 黨 must be taken vaguely, as in the translation; compare V, xxi. We cannot say whether the duke is referring to one or more actual cases,

可棄也。
人忠雖之夷狄、不
居處恭執事敬與
樊遲問仁子曰、
矣。
爲父隱直在其中
於是、父爲子隱、
曰、吾黨之直者異
羊、而子證之孔子

have stolen a sheep, they will bear witness to the fact."

2. Confucius said, "Among us, in our part of the country, those who are upright are different from this. The father conceals the misconduct of the son, and the son conceals the misconduct of the father. Unrightness is to be found in this."

CHAPTER XIX. Fan Ch'ih asked about perfect virtue. The Master said, "It is, in retirement, to be sedately grave; in the management of business, to be reverently attentive; in intercourse with others, to be strictly sincere. Though a man go among rude, uncultivated tribes, these *qualities* may not be neglected."

or giving his opinion of what his people would do. Confucius's reply would incline us to the latter view. In the 集 證, accounts are quoted of such cases, but they are probably founded on this chapter. 攘 is "to steal on occasion," i. e., on some temptation, as when another person's animal comes into my grounds, and I appropriate it. 證 seems to convey here the idea of accusation, as well as of witnessing. 2. 直在其中,—compare II, xviii, 2. The expression does not absolutely affirm that this is upright, but that in this there is a better principle than in the other

conduct.—Anybody but a Chinese will say that both the duke's view of the subject and the sage's were incomplete.

19. CHARACTERISTICS OF PERFECT VIRTUE. This is the third time that Fan Ch'ih is represented as questioning the Master about 仁, and it is supposed by some to have been the first in order. 居 處 (in 3rd tone), in opposition to 執 事="dwelling alone," "in retirement." The rude tribes here are the Î and the Ti. The Î we met with in IX, xiii. Here it is associated with Ti, the name of tribes on the north.

子貢問曰、何如
斯可謂之士矣。子
曰、行己有恥、使於
四方、不辱君命可
謂士矣。曰、敢問其
次。曰、宗族稱孝焉、
鄉黨稱弟焉曰、敢
問其次曰、言必信、

CHAPTER XX. 1. Tsze-kung asked, saying, "What qualities must a man possess to entitle him to be called an officer?" The Master said, "He who in his conduct of himself maintains a sense of shame, and when sent to any quarter will not disgrace his prince's commission, deserves to be called an officer."

2. *Tsze-kung* pursued, "I venture to ask who may be placed in the next lower rank?" and he was told, "He whom the circle of his relatives pronounce to be filial, whom his fellow villagers and neighbors pronounce to be fraternal."

3. *Again the disciple* asked, "I venture to ask about the class still next in order." *The Master* said, "They are determined to be sincere in what they say,

20. DIFFERENT CLASSES OF MEN WHO IN THEIR SEVERAL DEGREES MAY BE STYLED OFFICERS, AND THE INFERIORITY OF THE MASS OF THE OFFICERS OF CONFUCIUS'S TIME. 1. 士,—compare on XII, xx. Here it denotes—not the scholar, but the officer. 有 恥, "has shame," i. e., will avoid all bad conduct which would subject him to reproach. 2. 宗 族 is "a designation for all who form one body having the same ancestor." They are also called 九 族, "nine branches of kindred," being all of the same surname from the great-great-grandfather to the great-great-grandson. 弟＝悌, meaning "submissive," giving due honor to all older than himself. 3. 硜, "the sound of stones." 硜 硜 然, "stone-like." The dictionary, with reference

行必果、硜硜然小人哉、抑
亦可以爲次矣。曰、今之從四節
政者何如子曰、噫斗筲之
人、何足算也。
子曰不得中行而與之、
必也狂狷乎、狂者進取、狷
者有所不爲也。

and to carry out what they do. They are obstinate
little men. Yet perhaps they may make the next
class."

4. *Tsze-kung finally* inquired, "Of what sort are
those of the present day, who engage in government?"
The Master said, "Pooh! they are so many pecks and
hampers, not worth being taken into account."

CHAPTER XXI. The Master said, "Since I cannot
get men pursuing the due medium, to whom I might
communicate *my instructions,* I must find the ardent
and the cautiously-decided. The ardent will advance
and lay hold *of truth;* the cautiously-decided will keep
themselves from what is wrong."

to this passage, explains it—小 人
貌, "the appearance of a small man."
4. 斗 筲 之 人, i. e., mere utensils.
Compare on II, xii. Dr. Williams
translates the expression fairly well
by "peck-measure men."
21. CONFUCIUS OBLIGED TO CON-
TENT HIMSELF WITH THE ARDENT
AND CAUTIOUS AS DISCIPLES. Compare V, xxi, and Mencius VII,
ii, 37. 與 之 is explained as in the
translation—以 道 傳 之. The 註
疏, however, gives simply—與 之 同
處, "dwell together with them." 必
也, 狂 狷 乎,—comp. VIII, xvi, 2.
狷 is explained in the dictionary
by 褊 急, "contracted and urgent."
Opposed to 狂, it would seem to
denote caution, but yet not a
caution which may not be combined
with decision. 有 所 不 爲, "have
what they will not do."

子曰、南人有言曰、

人而無恆、不可以作

巫醫善夫不恆其德、

或承之羞子曰不占

而已矣。

子曰君子和而不

同、小人同而不和。

CHAPTER XXII. 1. The Master said, "The people of the south have a saying—'A man without constancy cannot be either a wizard or a doctor.' Good!

2. "Inconstant in his virtue, he will be visited with disgrace."

3. The Master said, "This arises simply from not attending to the prognostication."

CHAPTER XXIII. The Master said, "The superior man is affable, but not adulatory; the mean man is adulatory, but not affable."

22. THE IMPORTANCE OF FIXITY AND CONSTANCY OF MIND. 1. I translate 巫 by "wizard," for want of a better term. In the Châu Lî, Bk. XXVI, the *wû* appear sustaining a sort of official status, regularly called in . to bring down spiritual beings, obtain showers, etc. They are distinguished as men and women, though 巫 is often feminine, "a witch," as opposed to 覡, "a wizard." Confucius's use of the saying, according to Chû Hsî, is this—"Since such small people must have constancy, how much more ought others to have it!" The ranking of the doctors and wizards together sufficiently shows what was the position of the healing art in those days.—

Chang K'ang-ch'ăng interprets this paragraph quite inadmissibly:— "Wizards and doctors cannot manage people who have no constancy." 2. This is a quotation from the Yî-ching, diagram 恆; hexagram XXXII, line 3. 3. This is inexplicable to Chû Hsî. Some bring out from it the meaning in the translation.— Chăng K'ang-ch'ăng says: "By the Yî we prognosticate good and evil, but in it there is no prognostication of people without constancy."

23. THE DIFFERENT MANNERS OF THE SUPERIOR AND THE MEAN MAN. Compare II, xiv, but here the parties are contrasted in their more private intercourse with others. 同, "agreeing with," = flattering.

難說也說之不以道、

子曰君子易事而

善者惡之。

人之善者好之其不

子曰未可也不如鄉

也鄉人皆惡之何如。

好之何如子曰未可

子貢問曰鄉人皆

CHAPTER XXIV. Tsze-kung asked, saying, "What do you say of a man who is loved by all the people of his neighborhood?" The Master replied, "We may not for that accord our approval of him." "And what do you say of him who is hated by all the people of his neighborhood?" The Master said, "We may not for that conclude that he is bad. It is better than either of these cases that the good in the neighborhood love him, and the bad hate him."

CHAPTER XXV. The Master said, "The superior man is easy to serve and difficult to please. If you try to please him in any way which is not accordant

24. How, to judge of a man from the likings and dislikings of others, we must know the characters of those others. 未可,—literally, "not yet may." The general meaning of a Chinese sentence is often plain, and yet we are puzzled to supply exactly the subjects, auxiliaries, etc., which other languages require. In rendering the phrase, I have followed many of the paraphrasts, who complete it thus: 未可信其爲賢也 and 未可信其爲惡也. In the 註疏, however, the second occurrence of it is expanded in the same way as the first. Compare Luke's Gospel, 6 : 21, 26.

25. Difference between the superior and the mean man in their relation to those employed by them. 易事而難說 (＝悅),—

子曰剛、毅、木、訥、近仁。
子曰君子泰而不驕、小人驕而不泰。
其使人也求備焉。
說之雖不以道說也、及
之。小人難事而易說也、
不說也、及其使人也、器

with right, he will not be pleased. But in his employment of men, he uses them according to their capacity.
The mean man is difficult to serve, and easy to please.
If you try to please him, though it be in a way which
is not accordant with right, he may be pleased. But
in his employment of men, he wishes them to be
equal to everything.

CHAPTER XXVI. The Master said, "The superior
man has a dignified ease without pride. The mean
man has pride without a dignified ease."

CHAPTER XXVII. The Master said, "The firm, the
enduring, the simple, and the modest are near to
virtue.'"

as in the translation, or we may
render, "is easily served, but is
pleased with difficulty." 器之,—see
II, xii, 器 being here a verb. 求 備
is the opposite of 器 之, and＝以 全
材 責 備 一 人 身 上, "he requires
all capabilities from a single
man."

26. THE DIFFERENT AIR AND
BEARING OF THE SUPERIOR AND THE
MEAN MAN.

27. NATURAL QUALITIES WHICH
ARE FAVORABLE TO VIRTUE. 木,
"wood," here an adjective, but not
our "wooden." It＝質樸, "simple,"
"plain." 訥, see IV, xxiv. The
gloss on it here is—遲 鈍, "slow and
blunt." "Modest" seems to be the
idea.

棄之。　子曰以不教民戰是謂　可以卽戎矣。　子曰善人教民七年、亦　切偲偲、兄弟怡怡。　怡如也、可謂士矣、朋友切　之士矣。子曰切切偲偲、怡　子路問曰、何如斯可謂

CHAPTER XXVIII. Tsze-lû asked, saying, "What qualities must a man possess to entitle him to be called a scholar?" The Master said, "He must be thus,—earnest, urgent, and bland:—among his friends, earnest and urgent; among his brethren, bland."

CHAPTER XXIX. The Master said, "Let a good man teach the people seven years, and they may then likewise be employed in war."

CHAPTER XXX. The Master said, "To lead an uninstructed people to war, is to throw them away."

28. QUALITIES THAT MARK THE SCHOLAR IN SOCIAL INTERCOURSE. This is the same question as in chap. xx, 1, but 士 is here "the scholar," the gentleman of education, without reference to his being in office or not.

29. HOW THE GOVERNMENT OF A GOOD RULER WILL PREPARE THE PEOPLE FOR WAR. 善人, "a good man,"—spoken with reference to him as a ruler. The teaching is not to be understood of military training, but of the duties of life and citizenship; a people so taught are morally fitted to fight for their government. What military training may be included in the teaching, would merely be the hunting and drilling in the people's repose from the toils of agriculture. 戎, "weapons of war." 可以卽戎,—"they may go to their weapons."

30. THAT PEOPLE MUST BE TAUGHT, TO PREPARE THEM FOR WAR. Compare the last chapter. The language is very strong, and 教 being understood as in the last chapter, shows how Confucius valued education for all classes.

## BOOK XIV.　HSIEN WĂN

可　欲　豐　道　道　子　豐　　　憲
以　不　克　穀　穀　曰　憲　十　問
爲　行　伐　恥　邦　邦　問　四　第
仁　焉、怨、也。無　有　恥。

CHAPTER I.　Hsien asked what was shameful.　The Master said, "When good government prevails in a state, *to be thinking only of* salary; and, when bad government prevails, *to be thinking, in the same way, only of* salary;—this is shameful."

CHAPTER II.　1. "When the love of superiority, boasting, resentments, and covetousness are repressed, this may be deemed perfect virtue."

HEADING OF THIS BOOK.—憲問第十四, "Hsien asked, No. 14." The glossarist Hsing Ping (邢 昺) says, "In this Book we have the characters of the *Three Kings*, and *Two Chiefs*, the courses proper for princes and great officers, the practice of virtue, the knowledge of what is shameful, personal cultivation, and the tranquilizing of the people;—all subjects of great importance in government. They are therefore collected together, and arranged after the last Book, which commences with an inquiry about government." Some writers are of opinion that the whole Book with its 47 chapters was compiled by Hsien or Yüan Sze, who appears in the first chapter. That only the name of the inquirer is given and not his surname, is said to be our proof of this.

1. IT IS SHAMEFUL IN AN OFFICER TO BE CARING ONLY ABOUT HIS EMOLUMENT. Hsien is the Yüan Sze of VI, iii, and if we suppose Confucius's answer designed to have a practical application to himself, it is not easily reconcilable with what appears of his character in that other place. 穀 here = 祿, "emolument," but its meaning must be pregnant and intensive, as in the translation. If we do not take it so, the sentiment is contradictory to VIII, xiii. 3. K'ung Ân-kwo, however, takes the following view of the reply: "When a country is well-governed, emolument is right; when a country is ill-governed, to take office and emolument is shameful." I prefer the construction of Chû Hsî, which appears in the translation.

2. THE PRAISE OF PERFECT VIRTUE IS NOT TO BE ALLOWED FOR THE REPRESSION ON BAD FEELINGS. In Ho Yen, this chapter is joined to the preceding, and Chû Hsî also takes

孫。

危行、邦無道、危行言

子曰、邦有道危言

足以爲士矣。

子曰、士而懷居、不

仁則吾不知也。

矣。子曰、可以爲難矣、

2. The Master said, "This may be regarded as the achievement of what is difficult. But I do not know that it is to be deemed perfect virtue."

CHAPTER III. The Master said, "The scholar who cherishes the love of comfort is not fit to be deemed a scholar."

CHAPTER IV. The Master said, "When good government prevails in a state, language may be lofty and bold, and actions the same. When bad government prevails, the actions may be lofty and bold, but the language may be with some reserve."

the first paragraph to be a question of Yuǎn Hsien. 1. 克, "overcoming," i. e., here="the love of superiority." 伐, as in V, xxv, 3. 不行, "do not go," i. e., are not allowed to have their way,=are repressed. 2. 難, "difficult,"—the doing what is difficult. 仁 is quoad 仁;—"as to its being perfect virtue, that I do not know."

3. A SCHOLAR MUST BE AIMING AT WHAT IS HIGHER THAN COMFORT OR PLEASURE. Compare IV, xi. The 懷

居 here is akin to the 懷 土 there. Compare also IV, ix.

4. WHAT ONE DOES MUST ALWAYS BE RIGHT; WHAT ONE FEELS NEED NOT ALWAYS BE SPOKEN:—A LESSON OF PRUDENCE. 孫, for 遜, as in VII, xxxv. 危, "terror from being in a high position;" then "danger," "dangerous." It is used here in a good sense, meaning "lofty, and what may seem to be, or really be, dangerous," under a bad government, where good principles do not prevail.

不得其死然禹稷躬
曰羿善射奡盪舟俱
南宮适問於孔子
必有仁。
仁者必有勇、勇者不
言、有言者不必有德、
子曰、有德者必有

CHAPTER V. The Master said, "The virtuous will be sure to speak *correctly*, but those whose speech is good may not always be virtuous. Men of principle are sure to be bold, but those who are bold may not always be men of principle."

CHAPTER VI. Nan-kung Kwo, submitting an inquiry to Confucius, said, "I was skillful at archery, and Âo could move a boat along upon the land, but neither of them died a natural death. Yü and Chî personally

5. WE MAY PREDICATE THE EXTERNAL FROM THE INTERNAL, BUT NOT VICE VERSA. The 有言 must be understood of virtuous speaking and "virtuously," or "correctly," be supplied to bring out the sense. A translator is puzzled to render 仁者 differently from 有德者. I have said "men of principle," the opposition being between moral and animal courage; yet the men of principle may not be without the other, in order to their doing just ce to themselves.

6. EMINENT PROWESS CONDUCTING TO RUIN; EMINENT VIRTUE LEADING TO DIGNITY. THE MODESTY OF CONFUCIUS. Nan-kung Kwo is said by

Chû Hsî to have been the same as Nan Yung in V, 1. But this is doubtful. See on Nan Yung there. Kwo, it is said, insinuated in his remark an inquiry whether Confucius was not like Yu or Chî, and the great men of the time so many Î and Âo; and the sage was modestly silent upon the subject. Î and Âo carry us back to the 22nd century before Christ. The first belonged to a family of princelets, famous, from the time of the emperor 嚳 (2432 B. C.), for their archery, and dethroned the emperor Hâu-hsiang (后 相), 2145 B. C. Î was afterwards slain by his minister, Han Cho (寒 浞), who then married his wife, and one

乎。

勞乎、忠焉、能勿誨

■子曰、愛之能勿

小人而仁者也。

仁者有矣夫未有

■子曰、君子而不

德哉若人。

曰、君子哉若人尙

不答。南宮适出子

稼、而有天下夫子

wrought at the toils of husbandry, and they became possessors of the kingdom." The Master made no reply; but when Nan-kung Kwo went out, he said, "A superior man indeed is this! An esteemer of virtue indeed is this!"

CHAPTER VII. The Master said, "Superior men, and yet not *always* virtuous, there have been, alas! But there never has been a mean man, and, *at the same time*, virtuous."

CHAPTER VIII. The Master said, "Can there be love which does not lead to strictness with its object? Can there be loyalty which does not lead to the instruction of its object?"

of their sons (澆, *Chiâo*) was the individual here named Âo, who was subsequently destroyed by the emperor Shâo-k'ang, the posthumous son of Hâu-hsiang. Chî was the son of the emperor 嚳, of whose birth many prodigies are narrated, and appears in the Shû-ching as Hâu-chî, the minister of agriculture to Yâo and Shun, by name 棄. The Châu family traced their descent lineally from him, so that though the throne only came to his descendants more than a thousand years after his time, Nan-kung Kwo speaks as if he had got it himself, as Yü did. 君子 哉 若 人,—compare V, ii. The

name Âo in the text should be 奡.

7. THE HIGHEST VIRTUE NOT EASILY ATTAINED TO, AND INCOMPATIBLE WITH MEANNESS. Compare IV, iv. We must supply the "always," to bring out the meaning.

8. A LESSON FOR PARENTS AND MINISTERS, THAT THEY MUST BE STRICT AND DECIDED. *Lâo*, being parallel with *hûi*, is to be construed as a verb, and conveys the meaning in the translation different from the meaning of the term in XIII, i. K'ung An-kwo takes it in the sense of "to soothe," "comfort," in the 3rd tone, but that does not suit the parallelism.

也。問子西曰、彼哉彼哉。

䚛或問子產子曰惠人

色之。

羽修飾之東里子產潤

之世叔討論之行人子

子曰、爲命裨諶草創

CHAPTER IX. The Master said, "In preparing the governmental notifications, P'î Shăn first made the rough draft; Shî-shû examined and discussed its contents; Tsze-yü, the manager of foreign intercourse, then polished the style; and, finally, Tsze-ch'ân of Tung-lî gave it the proper elegance and finish."

CHAPTER X. 1. Some one asked about Tsze-ch'ân. The Master said, "He was a kind man."

2. He asked about Tsze-hsî. The Master said, "That man! That man!"

9. THE EXCELLENCE OF THE OFFICIAL NOTIFICATIONS OF CHĂNG, OWING TO THE ABILITY OF FOUR OF ITS OFFICERS. The state of Chăng, small and surrounded by powerful neighbors, was yet fortunate in having able ministers, through whose mode of conducting its government it enjoyed considerable prosperity. 命, with reference to this passage, is explained in the dictionary by 政令 盟會之辭, "the language of government orders, covenants, and conferences"; see the Châu Lî, XXV, par. 11. Tsze-ch'ân (see V, xv) was the chief minister of the state; and in preparing such documents first used the services of P'î Shăn, who was noted for his wise planning of matters. Shî-shû shows the relation of the officer indicated to the ruling family. His name was Yû-chî (游吉). The province of the 行人 was "to superintend the ceremonies of communication with other states"; see the Châu Lî, Bk. XXXVIII.

10. THE JUDGMENT OF CONFUCIUS CONCERNING TSZE-CH'ÂN, TSZE-HSÎ, AND KWAN CHUNG. 1. See V, xv. 2. Tsze-hsî was the chief minister of Ch'û. He had refused to accept the nomination to the sovereignty of the

以爲滕薛大夫。

趙魏老則優不可

臺子曰、孟公綽爲

難、富而無驕、易。

臺子曰、貧而無怨、

疏食沒齒無怨言。

伯氏駢邑三百飯

問管仲曰人也、奪

3. He asked about Kwan Chung. "For him," said the Master, "the city of Pien, with three hundred families, was taken from the chief of the Po family, who did not utter a murmuring word, though, to the end of his life, he had only coarse rice to eat."

CHAPTER XI. The Master said, "To be poor without murmuring is difficult. To be rich without being proud is easy."

CHAPTER XII. The Master said, "Măng Kung-ch'o is more than fit to be chief officer in the families of Châo and Wei, but he is not fit to be great officer to either of *the states* Tăng or Hsieh."

state in preference to the rightful heir, but did not oppose the usurping tendencies of the rulers of Ch'û. He had, moreover, opposed the wish of king Châo (of Ch'û) to employ the sage. 3. Kwan Chung,—see III, xxii. To reward his merits, the duke Hwan conferred on him the domain of the officer mentioned in the text, who had been guilty of some offense. His submitting as he did to his changed fortunes was the best tribute to Kwan's excellence.

11. IT IS HARDER TO BEAR POVERTY ARIGHT THAN TO CARRY RICHES. This sentiment may be controverted. Compare I, xv.

12. THE CAPACITY OF MĂNG KUNG-CH'O. Kung-ch'o was the head of the Măng, or Chung-sun family,

and, according to the "Historical Records," was regarded by Confucius more than any other great man of the times in Lû. His estimate of him, however, as appears here, was not very high. In the sage's time, the government of the state of Tsin (晉) was in the hands of the three families, Châo, Weî, and Han (韓), which afterwards divided the whole state among themselves; but meanwhile they were not states, and Kung-ch'o, as their *lâo*, or chief officer, could have managed their affairs. T'ăng and Hsieh were small states, whose great officers would have to look after their relations with greater states, to which function Kung-ch'o's abilities were not equal.

命、久要不忘平生
見利思義、見危授
之成人者何必然、
以爲成人矣。曰今
文之以禮樂亦可
子之勇冉求之藝、
公綽之不欲、卞莊
曰、若臧武仲之知、
子路問成人。

CHAPTER XIII. 1. Tsze-lû asked what constituted
a COMPLETE man. The Master said, "Suppose a man
with the knowledge of Tsang Wû-chung, the freedom
from covetousness of Kung-ch'o, the bravery of
Chwang of Pien, and the varied talents of Zăn Ch'iû;
add to these the accomplishments of the rules of
propriety and music;—such a one might be reckoned
a COMPLETE man."

2. *He then* added, "But what is the necessity for a
complete man of the present day to have all these
things? The man, who in the view of gain, thinks of
righteousness; who in the view of danger is prepared
to give up his life; and who does not forget an old

13. OF THE COMPLETE MAN:—A
CONVERSATION WITH TSZE-LÛ. 1.
Tsang Wû-chung had been an officer
of Lû in the reign anterior to that
in which Confucius was born. So
great was his reputation for wisdom
that the people gave him the title of
a 聖人, or "sage." Wû was his
honorary epithet, and 仲 denotes his
family place, among his brothers.
Chwang, it is said by Chû Hsî, after
Châu (周), one of the oldest commentators, whose surname only has
come down to us, was 卞邑大夫,
"great officer of the city of Pien."

According to the "Great Collection
of Surnames," a secondary branch
of a family of the state of Ts'âo
(曹) having settled in Lû, and being
gifted with Pien, its members took
their surname thence. For the history of Chwang and of Wû-chung,
see the 集證, *in loc.* 亦可云云,—
亦 implies that there was a higher
style of man still, to whom the
epithet *complete* would be more fully
applicable. 2. The 曰 is to be understood of Confucius, though some
suppose that Tsze-lû is the speaker.
要, 1st tone,=約,. "an agreement."

曰、其然豈其然乎。

然後取、人不厭其取。

然後笑、人不厭其笑義

然後言、人不厭其言樂

曰以告者過也夫子時

不笑不取乎。公明賈對

明賈曰、信乎、夫子不言、

鼂子問公叔文子於公

之言、亦可以爲成人矣。

agreement however far back it extends:—such a man
may be reckoned a COMPLETE man."

CHAPTER XIV. 1. The Master asked Kung-ming
Chiâ about Kung-shû Wăn, saying, "Is it true that
your master speaks not, laughs not, and takes not?"

2. Kung-ming Chiâ replied, "This has arisen from
the reporters going beyond *the truth.*—My master
speaks when it is the time to speak, and so men do
not get tired of his speaking. He laughs when there
is occasion to be joyful, and so men do not get tired
of his laughing. He takes when it is consistent with
righteousness to do so, and so men do not get tired of
his taking." The Master said, "So! But is it so with
him?"

"a covenant;"—"a long agreement,
he does not forget the words of his
whole life." The meaning is what
appears in the translation.

14. THE CHARACTER OF KUNG-
SHÛ WĂN, WHO WAS SAID NEITHER
TO SPEAK, NOR LAUGH, NOR TAKE.
1. Wăn was the honorary epithet of
the individual in question, by name
Chih (枝), or, as some say, Fa (發),
an officer of the state of Wei. He
was descended from the duke 獻, and

was himself the founder of the
Kung-shû family, being so designated, I suppose, because of his
relation to the reigning duke. Of
Kung-ming Chiâ nothing seems to be
known; he would seem from this
chapter to have been a disciple of
Kung-shû Wăn. 2. 其 然,—with
reference to Chiâ's account of Kung-
shû Wăn. 豈 其 然 乎 intimates
Confucius's opinion that Chiâ was
himself going beyond the truth.

而不謟。

而不正齊桓公正

臺子曰晉文公謟

也。

曰不要君吾不信

防求爲後於魯雖

臺子曰、臧武仲、以

CHAPTER XV. The Master said, "Tsang Wû-chung, keeping possession of Fang, asked of *the duke of* Lû to appoint a successor to him *in his family.* Although it may be said that he was not using force with his sovereign, I believe he was."

CHAPTER XVI. The Master said, "The duke Wăn of Tsin was crafty and not upright. The duke Hwan of Ch'î was upright and not crafty."

15. CONDEMNATION OF TSANG WÛ-CHUNG FOR FORCING A FAVOR FROM HIS PRINCE. Wû-chung (see chap. xiii) was obliged to fly from Lû, by the animosity of the Măng family, and took refuge in Chû (邾). As the head of the Tsang family, it devolved on him to offer the sacrifices in the ancestral temple, and he wished one of his half brothers to be made the head of the family, in his room, that those might not be neglected. To strengthen the application for this, which he contrived to get made, be returned himself to the city of Fang, which belonged to his family, and thence sent a message to the court, which was tantamount to a threat, that if the application were not granted, he would hold possession of the place. This was what Confucius condemned,—the 以 执 in a matter

which should have been left to the duke's grace. See all the circumstances in the 左 傳, 襄 公 二 十 三 年. 要, in 1st tone, as in chap. xiii, but with a different meaning, = 勒, "to force to do."

16. THE DIFFERENT CHARACTERS OF THE DUKES WĂN OF TSIN AND HWAN OF CH'Î. Hwan and Wăn were the two first of the five leaders of the princes of the empire, who play an important part in Chinese history, during the period of the Châu dynasty known as the Ch'un Ch'iû (春 秋). Hwan ruled in Ch'î, 681–643 B. C., and Wăn in Tsin, 636–628 B. C. Of Duke Hwan, see the next chapter. The attributes mentioned by Confucius are not to be taken absolutely, but as respectively predominating in the two chiefs.

子路曰、桓公殺公
子糾、召忽死之、管仲
不死、曰、未仁乎。子曰、
桓公九合諸侯、不以
兵車、管仲之力也、如
其仁、如其仁。

CHAPTER XVII.　1. Tsze-lû said, "The duke Hwan caused his brother Chiû to be killed, when Shâo Hû died *with his master*, but Kwan Chung did not die. May not I say that he was wanting in virtue?"

2.　The Master said, "The duke Hwan assembled all the princes together, and that not with weapons of war and chariots:—it was all through the influence of Kwan Chung.　Whose beneficence was like his? Whose beneficence was like his?"

17. THE MERIT OF KWAN CHUNG: —A CONVERSATION WITH TSZE-LÛ. 1. 公子糾, "the duke's son Ch'iû," but, to avoid the awkwardness of that rendering, I say—"his brother." Hwan (the honorary epithet; his name was 小白) and Ch'iû had both been refugees in different states, the latter having been carried into Lû, away from the troubles and dangers of Ch'î, by the ministers, Kwan Chung and Shâo Hû. On the death of the prince of Ch'î, Hwan anticipated Ch'iû, got to Ch'î, and took possession of the state. Soon after, he required the duke of Lû to put his brother to death, and to deliver up the two ministers, when Shâo (召 here=邵) Hû chose to dash his brains out, and die with his master, while Kwan Chung returned gladly to Ch'î, took service with Hwan, became his prime minister, and made him supreme arbiter among the various chiefs of the empire. Such conduct was condemned by Tsze-lû. 死之 is a peculiar expression=爲子糾而死. z. Confucius defends Kwan Chung, on the ground of the services which he rendered, using 仁 in a different acceptation from that intended by the disciple. 九, 1st tone, explained in the dictionary by 聚, synonymous with 合, though the 註 疏 makes out more than nine assemblages of princes under the presidency of Duke Hwan. 如其仁=誰如其仁者, as in the translation.

髮左衽矣。豈若匹　賜、微管仲、吾其被　下、民到于今受其　公、霸諸侯、一匡天　之。子曰、管仲相桓　子糾不能死、又相　仁者與、桓公殺公　子貢曰、管仲非

CHAPTER XVIII. 1. Tsze-kung said, "Kwan Chung, I apprehend, was wanting in virtue. When the duke Hwan caused his brother Chiû to be killed, Kwan Chung was not able to die with him. Moreover, he became prime minister to Hwan."

2. The Master said, "Kwan Chung acted as prime minister to the duke Hwan, made him leader of all the princes, and united and rectified the whole kingdom. Down to the present day, the people enjoy the gifts which he conferred. But for Kwan Chung, we should now be wearing our hair unbound, and the lappets of our coats buttoning on the left side.

3. "Will you require from him the small fidelity of

18. THE MERIT OF KWAN CHUNG: —A CONVERSATION WITH TSZE-KUNG. 1. Tsze-lû's doubts about Kwan Chung arose from his not dying with the prince Chiû; Tsze-kung's turned principally on his subsequently becoming premier to Hwan. 2. 匡=正, "to rectify," "reduce to order." — blends with 匡 its own verbal force, ="to unite." 微=無, "not," "if not." 被 (the 4th tone) 髮,—see the Lî Chî, III, iii, 14, where this is mentioned as a characteristic of the eastern barbarians. 左 衽,—see the Shû-ching, V, xxiv, 13. A note in the 集 證 says, that anciently the right was the position of honor, and the right hand, moreover, is the more convenient for use, but the practice of the barbarians was contrary to that of China in both points. The sentiment of Confucius is, that but for Kwan Chung, his countrymen would have sunk to the state of the rude tribes about them. 3. 匹 夫, 匹 婦,—see IX, xxv. 諒=小 信, "small fidelity," by which is intended the faithfulness of a married couple of

夫匹婦之爲諒
也、自經於溝瀆、
而莫之知也。

臺公叔文子之
臣、大夫僎與文
子同升諸公子。二㉑
聞之曰、可以爲
文矣。

common men and common women, who would commit
suicide in a stream or ditch, no one knowing anything
about them?"

CHAPTER XIX. 1. The great officer, Hsien, who
had been *family* minister to Kung-shû Wân, ascended
to the prince's *court* in company with Wăn.

2. The Master, having heard of it, said, "He
deserved to be considered WĂN (the accomplished)."

the common people, where the husband takes no concubine in addition
to his wife. The argument is this:—
"Do you think Kwan Chung should
have considered himself bound to
Chiû, as a common man considers
himself bound to his wife? And
would you have had him commit
suicide, as common people will do on
any slight occasion?" Commentators
say that there is underlying the
vindication this fact:—that Kwan
Chung and Shâo Hû's adherence to
Chiû was wrong in the first place,
Chiû being the younger brother.
Chung's conduct, therefore, was not
to be judged as if Chiû had been the
senior. There is nothing of this,
however, in Confucius's words. He
vindicates Chung simply on the
ground of his subsequent services, and
his reference to "the small fidelity"
of husband and wife among the
common people is very unhappy. 自

經 (3rd tone), "to strangle one's
self," but in connection with 溝 瀆,
the phrase must be understood
generally = "to commit suicide."

19. _THE MERIT OF KUNG-SHÛ
WĂN IN RECOMMENDING TO HIGH
OFFICE, WHILE IN AN INFERIOR POSI-
TION, A MAN OF WORTH. 1. Kung-
shû Wân,—see chap. xiv. This
paragraph is to be understood as
intimating that Kung-shû, seeing the
worth and capacity of his minister,
had recommended him to his
sovereign, and afterwards was not
ashamed to appear in the same
rank with him at court. 公,=our
"duke's," i. e., the duke's court. 2.
The meaning of the chapter turns on
the signification of the title Wăn. For
the conferring of this on Kung-shû,
see the Lî Chî, II, Sect. ii, Pt. ii, 13.
The name Hsien generally appears in
the form 僎.

之也難。

靈子曰其言之不怍、則爲

夫如是、奚其喪。

鮀治宗廟、王孫賈治軍旅、

孔子曰仲叔圉治賓客祝

康子曰夫如是、奚而不喪。

靈子言衞靈公之無道也、

CHAPTER XX. 1. The Master was speaking about the unprincipled course of the duke Ling of Wei, when Ch'î K'ang said, "Since he is of such a character, how is it he does not lose his state?"

2. Confucius said, "The Chung-shû Yü has the superintendence of his guests and of strangers; the litanist, T'o, has the management of his ancestral temple; and Wang-sun Chiâ has the direction of the army and forces:—with such officers as these, how should he lose his state?"

CHAPTER XXI. The Master said, "He who speaks without modesty will find it difficult to make his words good."

20. THE IMPORTANCE OF GOOD AND ABLE MINISTERS:—SEEN IN THE STATE OF WEI. 1. *Ling* was the honorary epithet of Yüan (元), duke of Wei, 533–492 B. C. He was the husband of Nan-tsze, VI, xxvi. See 莊子, Bk. XXV, 9. The Chung-shû

Yü is the K'ung Wăn of V, xiv. 仲叔 express his family position, according to the degrees of kindred. "The litanist, T'o,"—see VI, xiv. Wang-sun Chiâ,—see III, xiii.

21. EXTRAVAGANT SPEECH HARD TO BE MADE GOOD. Compare IV, xxii.

陳成子弒簡

公孔子沐浴而

朝、告於哀公曰、

陳恆弒其君、請

討之公曰、告夫

三子孔子曰以

吾從大夫之後、

不敢不告也、君

曰、告夫三子者。

CHAPTER XXII. 1. Chăn Ch'ăng murdered the duke Chien *of* Ch'î.

2. Confucius bathed, went to court, and informed the duke Ăi, saying, "Chăn Hăng has slain his sovereign. I beg that you will undertake to punish him."

3. The duke said, "Inform the chiefs of the three families of it."

4. Confucius *retired, and* said, "Following in the rear of the great officers, I did not dare not to represent such a matter, and my prince says, "Inform the chiefs of the three families of it."

22. How CONFUCIUS WISHED TO AVENGE THE MURDER OF THE DUKE OF CH'Î:—HIS RIGHTEOUS AND PUBLIC SPIRIT. 1. *Chien*,—"not indolent in a single virtue," and "tranquil, not speaking unadvisedly," are the meanings attached to 簡, as an honorary epithet, while 成 (the honorary epithet of Chăn Hăng indicates, "tranquilizer of the people, and establisher of government." The murder of the duke Chien by his minister, Chăn Hăng (恆), took place 481 B. C., barely two years before Confucius's death. 2. 沐浴 implies all the fasting and all the solemn preparation, as for a sacrifice or other great occasion. Properly, 沐 is to wash the hair with the water in which rice has been washed, and 浴 is to wash the body with hot water. 請討之,—according to the account of this matter in the 左傳, Confucius meant that the duke Ăi should himself, with the forces of Lû, undertake the punishment of the criminal. Some modern commentators cry out against this. The sage's advice, they say, would have been that the duke should report the thing to the king, and with his authority associate other princes with himself to do justice on the offender. 3. 告夫三子,—this is the use of 夫 in XI, xxiv, *et al.* 4. This is taken as the remark of Confucius, or his colloquy with himself, when he had gone out from the duke. 以吾從大夫之後,—see XI, vii. The 者 leaves the sentence

之三子告、不可、孔子曰、以

吾從大夫之後、不敢不告

也。

子路問事君子曰、勿欺

也、而犯之。

子曰君子上達、小人下

達。

5. He went to the chiefs, and informed them, but they would not act. Confucius *then* said, "Following in the rear of the great officers, I did not dare not to represent such a matter."

CHAPTER XXIII. Tsze-lû asked how a ruler should be served. The Master said, "Do not impose on him, and, moreover, withstand him to his face."

CHAPTER XXIV. The Master said, "The progress of the superior man is upwards; the progress of the mean man is downwards."

incomplete;—"my prince says, 'Inform the three chiefs of it;'—this circumstance." The paraphrasts complete the sentence by 何 耶,—"How is it that the prince, etc.?" 5. 之 三 子,—之 is the verb—"to go to." 孔 子 曰, 云 云,—this was spoken to the chiefs to reprove them for their disregard of a crime, which concerned every public man, or perhaps it is merely the reflection of the sage's own mind.

23. HOW THE MINISTER OF A PRINCE MUST BE SINCERE AND BOLDLY UPRIGHT. 犯 之 is well expressed by the phrase in the translation. Many passages in the Lî Chî show that to 犯 was required by the duty of a minister, but not allowed to a son with his father.

24. THE DIFFERENT PROGRESSIVE TENDENCIES OF THE SUPERIOR MAN AND THE MEAN MAN. Ho Yen takes 達 in the sense of 曉, "to understand." The modern view seems better.

蘧子曰、古之學者爲己、今之學

者爲人。

蘧伯玉使人於孔子孔子與

之坐而問焉曰、夫子何爲對曰、

夫子欲寡其過而未能也使者

出、子曰、使乎、使乎。

CHAPTER XXV. The Master said, "In ancient times, men learned with a view to their own improvement. Nowadays, men learn with a view to the approbation of others."

CHAPTER XXVI. 1. Chü Po-yü sent a messenger *with friendly inquiries* to Confucius.

2. Confucius sat with him, and questioned him. "What," said he, "is your master engaged in?" The messenger replied, "My master is anxious to make his faults few, but he has not yet succeeded." He then went out, and the Master said, "A messenger indeed! A messenger indeed!"

25. THE DIFFERENT MOTIVES OF LEARNERS IN OLD TIMES, AND IN THE TIMES of CONFUCIUS. 爲己, 爲人 "for themselves, for *other* men." The meaning is as in the translation.

26. AN ADMIRABLE MESSENGER. 1. Po-yü was the designation of Chü Yuan (瑗), an officer of the state of Wei, and a disciple of the sage. His place is now 1st east in the outer court of the temples. Confucius had lodged with him when in Wei, and it was after his return to Lû that Po-yü sent to inquire for him.

子貢曰、夫子自道也。

知者不惑勇者不懼。

我無能焉仁者不憂、

子曰君子道者三、

而過其行。

子曰君子恥其言

出其位。

曾子曰、君子思不

謀其政。

子曰、不在其位、不

CHAPTER XXVII. The Master said, "He who is not in any particular office has nothing to do with plans for the administration of its duties."

CHAPTER XXVIII. The philosopher Tsăng said, "The superior man, in his thoughts, does not go out of his place."

CHAPTER XXIX. The Master said, "The superior man is modest in his speech, but exceeds in his actions."

CHAPTER XXX. 1. The Master said, "The way of the superior man is threefold, but I am not equal to it. Virtuous, he is free from anxieties; wise, he is free from perplexities; bold, he is free from fear.

2. Tsze-kung said, "Master, that is what you yourself say."

27. A repetition of VIII, xiv.

28. THE THOUGHTS OF A SUPERIOR MAN IN HARMONY WITH HIS POSITION. Tsăng here quotes from the 象, or Illustrations, of the 52nd diagram of the Yi-ching, but he leaves out one character,—以 before 思, and thereby alters the meaning somewhat. What is said in the Yî, is—"The superior man is thoughtful, and so does not go out of his place."—The chapter, it is said, is inserted here, from its analogy with the preceding.

29. THE SUPERIOR MAN MORE IN DEEDS THAN IN WORDS. 恥其言,—literally, "is ashamed of his words." Compare chaps. xxi and IV, xxii.

30. CONFUCIUS'S HUMBLE ESTIMATE OF HIMSELF, WHICH TSZE-KUNG DENIES. 1. We have the greatest part of this paragraph in IX, xxviii, but the translation must be somewhat different, as 仁者, 知者, 勇者 are here in apposition with 君子. 君子道者=君子所以爲道者, "what the superior man takes to be his path." 2. 道=言, "to say."

先覺者、是賢乎。
不億不信、抑亦
罍子曰、不逆詐、
不能也。
之不已知、患其
罍子曰、不患人
夫我則不暇。
曰、賜也賢乎哉、
罍子貢方人、子

CHAPTER XXXI. Tsze-kung was *in the habit of* comparing men together. The Master said, "Tsze must have reached a high pitch of excellence! Now, I have not leisure *for this*."

CHAPTER XXXII. The Master said, "I will not be concerned at men's not knowing me; I will be concerned at my own want of ability."

CHAPTER XXXIII. The Master said, "He who does not anticipate attempts to deceive him, nor think beforehand of his not being believed, and yet apprehends these things readily (*when they occur*);—is he not a man of superior worth?"

31. ONE'S WORK IS WITH ONE'S SELF:—AGAINST MAKING COMPARISONS. 賢 乎 哉 = "Ha! is he not superior?" The remark is ironical.

32. CONCERN SHOULD BE ABOUT OUR PERSONAL ATTAINMENT, AND NOT ABOUT THE ESTIMATION OF OTHERS. See I, xvi, *et al.* A critical canon is laid down here by Chû Hsî:—"All passages, the same in meaning and in words, are to be understood as having been spoken only once, and their recurrence in the work of the compilers. Where the meaning in the same and the language a little different, they are to be taken as having been repeated by Confucius himself with the variations." According to this rule the sentiment in this chapter was repeated by the Master in four different utterances.

33. QUICK DISCRIMINATION WITHOUT SUSPICIOUSNESS IS HIGHLY MERITORIOUS. 逆, "to be disobedient," "to rebel"; also, "to meet," and here "to anticipate," i. e., in judgment. 抑 亦, see XIII, xix, but the meaning is there "perhaps," while here the 抑 is adversative, and = "but." 先 覺 者 is used in opposition to 後 覺 者, and = "a quick apprehender, one who understands things before others." So, Chû Hsî. K'ung Ân-kwo, however, takes 抑 as conjunctive, and 先 覺 in apposition with the two preceding characteristics, and interprets the conclusion—"Is such a man of superior worth?" On Chû Hsî's view, the 乎 is exclamatory.

微生畝謂孔子

曰、丘何爲是栖栖

者與、無乃爲佞乎。

孔子曰、非敢爲佞

也、疾固也。

子曰、驥不稱其

力、稱其德也。

或曰、以德報怨、

CHAPTER XXXIV. 1. Wei-shăng Mâu said to Confucius, "Ch'iû, how is it that you keep roosting about? Is it not that you are an insinuating talker?"

2. Confucius said, "I do not dare to play the part of such a talker, but I hate obstinacy."

CHAPTER XXXV. The Master said, "A horse is called a ch'î, not because of its strength, but because of its *other* good qualities."

CHAPTER XXXVI. 1. Some one said, "What do you say concerning the principle that injury should be recompensed with kindness?"

34. CONFUCIUS NOT SELF-WILLED, AND YET NO GLIB-TONGUED TALKER: —DEFENSE OF HIMSELF FROM THE CHARGE OF AN AGED REPROVER. 1. From Wei-shang's addressing Confucius by his name, it is presumed that he was an old man. Such a liberty in a young man would have been impudence. It is presumed also that he was one of those men who kept themselves retired from the world in disgust. 栖, "to perch or roost," as a bird, used contemptuously with reference to Confucius going about among the princes and wishing to be called to office. 2. 固 =執 一 不 通, "holding one idea without intelligence."

35. VIRTUE AND NOT STRENGTH, THE FIT SUBJECT OF PRAISE. 驥 was the name of a famous horse of antiquity who could run 1000 *lî* in one day. See the dictionary *in voc.* It is here used generally for "a good horse."

36. GOOD IS NOT TO BE RETURNED FOR EVIL; EVIL TO BE MET SIMPLY WITH JUSTICE. 1. 德=恩 惠, "kindness." 怨, "resentment," "hatred," here put for what awakens resentment, "wrong," "injury." The phrase 以 德 報 怨 is found in the 道 德 經 of Lâo-tsze, II, chap. lxiii, but it is possible that Confucius's questioner simply consulted him about it as a saying which he had himself heard and was inclined to approve. 2. 以 直, "with straightness," i. e., with justice.—How far the ethics of Confucius fall below our Christian

何如。子曰、何以報

德以直報怨、以德

報德。

子曰、莫我知也

夫子貢曰、何爲其

莫知子也子曰、不

怨天、不尤人、下學

2. The Master said, "With what then will you recompense kindness?"

3. "Recompense injury with justice, ·and recompense kindness with kindness."

CHAPTER XXXVII. 1. The Master said, "Alas! there is no one that knows me."

2. Tsze-kung said, "What do you mean by thus saying—that no one knows you?" The Master replied, "I do not murmur against Heaven. I do not grumble against men. My studies lie low, and my

standard is evident from this chapter, and even below Lâo-tsze. The same expressions are attributed to Confucius in the Li Chî, XXIX, xii, and it is there added 子曰、以德報怨、則寬身之仁 (＝人), which is explained,—"He who returns good for evil is a man who is careful of his person," i. e., will try to avert danger from himself by such a course. The author of the 翼註 says that the injuries intended by the questioner were only trivial matters, which perhaps might be dealt with in the way he mentioned, but great offenses, as those against a sovereign or a father, may not be dealt with by such an inversion of the principles of justice. The Master himself, however, does not fence his deliverance in any way.

37. CONFUCIUS, LAMENTING THAT MEN DID NOT KNOW HIM, RESTS IN THE THOUGHT THAT HEAVEN KNEW HIM. 1. 莫我知,—the inversion for 莫知我, "does not know me." He referred, commentators say, to the way in which he pursued his course, simply 爲己, out of his own conviction of duty, and for his own improvement, without regard to success, or the opinions of others. 2. 何爲其莫知子也, "what is that which you say—no man knows you?" 下學、上達,—"beneath I learn, above I penetrate";—the meaning appears to be that he contented himself with the study of men and things, common matters as more ambitious spirits would deem them, but from those he rose to understand the high principles involved in them,

乎。　而上達、知我者其天

翳公伯寮愬子路於

季孫子服景伯以告、

曰夫子固有惑志於

公伯寮吾力猶能肆

諸市朝子曰道之將

行也與、命也道之將

penetration rises high.　But there is Heaven;—that knows me!"

CHAPTER XXXVIII. 1. The Kung-po Liâo, having slandered Tsze-lû to Chî-sun, Tsze-fû Ching-po informed Confucius of it, saying, "Our master is certainly being led astray by the Kung-po Liâo, but I have still power enough left to cut *Liâo* off, and expose his corpse in the market and in the court."

2. The Master said, "If *my* principles are to advance, it is so ordered.　If they are to fall to the

---

—"the appointments of Heaven (天命)";—according to one commentator. 知我者, 其天乎,—"He who knows me, is not that Heaven?" The 曰 講 paraphrases this, as if it were a soliloquy,—上天, 於冥冥之中, 能知我耳.

38. How CONFUCIUS RESTED, AS TO THE PROGRESS OF HIS DOCTRINES, ON THE ORDERING OF HEAVEN:— ON OCCASION OF TSZE-LÛ'S BEING SLANDERED. 1. Liâo, called Kungpo (literally, duke's uncle), probably from an affinity with the ducal house, is said by some to have been a disciple of the sage, but that is not

likely, as we find him here slandering Tsze-lû, that he might not be able, in his official connection with the Chî family, to carry the Master's lessons into practice. 景 was the hon. epithet of Tsze-fû Ching, a great officer of Lû. 夫子 refers to Chîsun. 有惑志:—"is having his will deceived." Exposing the bodies (陳尸) of criminals, after their execution, was called 肆. The bodies of "great officers" were so exposed in the court, and those of meaner criminals in the market place. 市朝 came to be employed together, though the exposure could take place

廢也與、命也、公伯寮其

如命何。

子曰、賢者辟世其次

辟地其次辟色其次辟

言。

子曰、作者七人矣。

ground, it is so ordered.　What can the Kung-po Liâo do where such ordering is concerned?"

CHAPTER XXXIX.　1.　The Master said, "*Some* men of worth retire from the world.

2.　"Some retire from *particular* states.

3.　"Some retire because of *disrespectful* looks.

4.　"Some retire because of *contradictory* language."

CHAPTER XL.　The Master said, "Those who have done this are seven men."

only in one place, just as we have seen 兄弟 used generally for "brother."　2. 與 makes the preceding clause conditional, = "if." 命=天命, "Heaven's ordering."

39.　DIFFERENT CAUSES WHY MEN OF WORTH WITHDRAW FROM PUBLIC LIFE, AND DIFFERENT EXTENTS TO WHICH THEY SO WITHDRAW THEMSELVES.　1. 辟 *pi*, 4th tone, = 避. 2. 其次,—"the next class," but commentators say that the meaning is no more than "some," and that the terms do not indicate any comparison of the parties on the ground of their worthiness. 地, "the earth," here = territories or states.　3. The

"looks," and "language" in par. 4, are to be understood of the princes whom the worthies wished to serve —Confucius himself could never bear to withdraw from the world.

40.　THE NUMBER OF MEN OF WORTH WHO HAD WITHDRAWN FROM PUBLIC LIFE IN CONFUCIUS'S TIME. This chapter is understood in connection with the preceding;—as appears in the translation.　Chû, however, explains 作 by 起, "have arisen."　Others explain it by 爲, "have done this."　They also give the names of the seven men, which Chû calls 鑿, "chiseling."

子路宿於石門、晨門

曰、奚自子路曰、自孔氏。

曰是知其不可而爲之

者與。

子擊磬於衞、有荷蕢、

而過孔氏之門者、曰、有

心哉擊磬乎既、而曰、鄙

CHAPTER XLI. Tsze-lû happening to pass the night in Shih-măn, the gatekeeper said to him, "Whom do you come from?" Tsze-lû said, "From Mr. K'ung." "It is he,—is it not?"—said the other, "who knows the impracticable nature of the times and yet will be doing in them."

CHAPTER XLII. 1. The Master was playing, *one day*, on a musical stone in Wei, when a man, carrying a straw basket passed the door of the house where Confucius was, and said, "His heart is full who *so* beats the musical stone."

2. A little while after, he added, "How contemptible is the one-ideaed obstinacy *those sounds display!*

41. CONDEMNATION OF CON-FUCIUS'S COURSE IN SEEKING TO BE EMPLOYED, BY ONE WHO HAD WITH-DRAWN FROM PUBLIC LIFE. The site of Shih-măn is referred to the district of Ch'ang-ch'ing, department of Chi-nan, in Shantung. 晨 門, "morning gate,"—a designation of the keeper, as having to open the gate in the morning,—perhaps one of the seven worthies of the preceding chapter We might translate 石 門 by "Stony gate." It seems to have been one of the passes between Ch'i and Lû. 孔

氏, "*the* K'ung," or Mr. K'ung. Observe the force of the final 與.

42. THE JUDGMENT OF A RETIRED WORTHY ON CONFUCIUS'S COURSE, AND REMARK OF CONFUCIUS THERE-ON. 1. The *ch'ing* was one of the eight musical instruments of the Chinese; see Medhurst's dictionary, *in loc.* 過, 1st tone, "to go by." Meaning "to go beyond," "to ex-ceed," it is in the 4th tone. 有 心 哉 擊 磬 乎 is to be read as one sentence, and understood as if there were a 之 after the 哉. 2. 硜 硜 乎,—see

高宗、古之人皆然、

何謂也子曰、何必〔二節〕

宗諒陰、三年不言、

子張曰、書云、高〔一節〕

果哉、末之難矣。

則厲、淺則揭子曰、〔三節〕

也、斯已而已矣、深

哉、硜硜乎、莫己知

When one is taken no notice of, he has simply at once to give over *his wish for public employment.* "Deep water must be crossed with the clothes on; shallow water may be crossed with the clothes held up."

3. The Master said, "How determined is he in his purpose! *But* this is not difficult!"

CHAPTER XLIII. 1. Tsze-chang said, "What is meant when the Shû says that Kâo-tsung, while observing the usual imperial mourning, was for three years without speaking?"

2. The Master said, "Why must Kâo-tsung *be referred to as an example of this?* The ancients all did

XIII, xx, 3. The 備旨 interprets this clause also, as if a 之 were after the 哉, and 硜 硜 had reference to the sounds of the *ch'ing.* 深 則 云 云,—see the Shih, I, iii, 9, stanza 1. The quotation was intended to illustrate that we must act according to circumstances. 3. 末＝無. 之 seems to be a mere expletive. The case is one where the meaning is plain while the characters can hardly be construed satisfactorily. I have not found this example of 之 in Wang Yin-chih.

43. HOW GOVERNMENT WAS CAR- RIED ON DURING THE THREE YEARS OF SILENT MOURNING BY THE SOVER- EIGN. 1. 書 云,—see the Shû, IV,

viii, Sect. I, 1, but the passage there is not exactly as in the text. It is there said that Kâo-tsung, after the three years' mourning, still did not speak. 高 宗 was the honorary title of the king Wû-ting (武 丁, 1324– 1264 B. C.). 諒 (*Shû,* 亮) 陰 (read *an*), according to the dictionary, means "the shed where the mourner lived the three years." Chû Hsî does not know the meaning of the terms.—Tsze-chang was perplexed to know how government could be carried on during so long a period of silence. 2. 古 之 人,—the 人 em- braces the sovereigns, and subor- dinate princes who had their own petty courts. 總 己,—in the 備旨

君薨、百官總己、以聽於

冢宰三年。

䷖子曰、上好禮、則民易

使也。

䷖子路問君子子曰、脩

己以敬曰、如斯而已乎。

曰、脩己以安人、曰、如斯

so. When the sovereign died, the officers all attended to their several duties, taking instructions from the prime minister for three years."

CHAPTER XLIV. The Master said, "When rulers love *to observe* the rules of propriety, the people respond readily to the calls on them for service."

CHAPTER XLV. Tsze-lû asked what constituted the superior man. The Master said, "The cultivation of himself in reverential carefulness." "And is this all?" said *Tsze-lû*. "He cultivates himself so as to give rest to others," was the reply. "And is this all?"

it is said,—摠, 揔 也, 不敢放縱意 也, "揔 is to manage. The meaning is, that they did not dare to allow themselves any license." The expression is not an easy one. I have followed the paraphrasts.

44. HOW A LOVE OF THE RULES OF PROPRIETY IN RULERS FACILITATES GOVERNMENT.

45. REVERENT SELF-CULTIVATION THE DISTINGUISHING CHARACTERISTIC OF THE CHÜN-TSZE. 以 敬, it is said, are not to be taken as the *wherewith* of the *Chün-tsze* in cultivating himself, but as the chief thing which he keeps before him in the process. I translate 以, therefore, by *in*, but in

the other sentences, it indicates the realizations, or consequences, of the 修 己. 百 姓,—"the hundred sur-names," as a designation for the mass of the people, occurs as early as in the *Yâo-tien* (堯 典). It is＝百 家 姓, "the surnames of the hundred families," into which number the families of the people were perhaps divided at a very early time. The surnames of the Chinese now amount to several hundreds. The small work 百 家 姓 帖, made in the Sung dynasty, contains nearly 450. The number of them given in an appen-dix to Williams's Syllabic Diction-ary, as compiled by the Rev. Dr.

而已乎。曰、脩已
以安百姓、脩已
以安百姓、堯舜
其猶病諸。

■原壤夷俟子
曰、幼而不孫弟、
長而無述焉、老
而不死、是爲賊。

*again* asked *Tsze-lû*. *The Master* said, "He cultivates himself so as to give rest to all the people. He cultivates himself so as to give rest to all the people:—even Yâo and Shun were still solicitous about this."

CHAPTER XLVI. Yüan Zang was squatting on his heels, and so waited *the approach of* the Master, who said to him, "In youth not humble as befits a junior; in manhood, doing nothing worthy of being handed down; and living on to old age:—this is to be a pest."

Blodget, is 1863. In the 集 證, *in loc.*, we find a ridiculous reason given for the surnames being a hundred, to the effect that the ancient sages gave a surname for each of the five notes of the scale in music, and of the five great relations of life and of the four seas; consequently 5 × 5 × 4 = 100. It is to be observed that in the Shû we find "a hundred surnames," interchanged with 萬 姓, "ten thousand surnames," and it would seem needless, therefore, to seek to attach a definite explanation to the number. 堯舜其猶病諸,— see VI, xxviii.

46. CONFUCIUS'S CONDUCT TO AN UNMANNERLY OLD MAN OF HIS ACQUAINTANCE. Yuan Zang was an old acquaintance of Confucius, but had adopted the principles of Lâo-tsze, and gave himself extraordinary license in his behavior.—See an instance in the Lî Chî, II, Sect. II, iii, 24, and the note there. 夷俟,— the dictionary explains the two words together by 展 足 箕 坐, but that is the meaning of 夷 alone, and 俟=待, "to wait for." So, the commentators, old and new. The use of 夷 in this sense is thus explained:— "The 鴟 鳥 is fond of squatting, and is therefore called the squatting *ch'ih* (蹲 鴟), but it is called by some the *ch'ih i* (鴟 夷), and hence 夷 is used for 蹲, *to squat*!" See the 集 證, *in loc.* 孫 for 遜, and 弟 for 悌. 賊,— in the sense of 賊 害,=our "pest," rather than "thief." The address of Confucius might be translated in the 2nd person, but it is perhaps better to keep to the 3rd, leaving the

也。　也　也　與　於　曰　曰　將　闕
　　　欲　非　先　位　吾　益　命　黨
　　　速　求　生　也　見　者　或　童
　　　成　益　並　見　其　與　問　子
　　　者　者　行　其　居　子　之

With this he hit him on the shank with his staff.

CHAPTER XLVII. 1. A youth of the village of Ch'üeh was employed *by Confucius* to carry the messages between him and his visitors. Some one asked about him, saying, "I suppose he has made great progress."

2. The Master said, "I observe that he is fond of occupying the seat *of a full-grown man;* I observe that he walks shoulder to shoulder with his elders. He is not one who is seeking to make progress *in learning.* He wishes quickly to become a man."

application to be understood. From several references to Yuan Zang in the Li Chi, it appears he was a very old acquaintance of Confucius, and mentally somewhat weak. Confucius felt kindly to him, but was sometimes provoked by him to very candid expressions of his judgment about him,—as here.

47. CONFUCIUS'S EMPLOYMENT OF A FORWARD YOUTH. 1. 闕 黨,—there is a tradition that Confucius lived and taught in 闕 里, but it is much disputed. 將命謂傳賓主之書, "將 命 means to convey the messages between visitors and the

host." 益 者 與,—the inquirer supposed that Confucius's employment of the lad was to distinguish him for the progress which he had made. 2. According to the rules of ceremony, a youth must sit in the corner, the body of the room being reserved for full-grown men;—see the Lî Chî, II, Sect. I, i, 18. In walking with an elder, a youth was required to keep a little behind him;—see the Lî Chî, I, Sect. I, ii, chap. 4, 7. Confucius's employment of the lad, therefore, was to teach him the courtesies required by his years.

## BOOK XV. WEI LING KUNG

衛靈公第十五

衛靈公問陳於孔
子孔子對曰、俎豆之
事、則嘗聞之矣、軍旅
之事、未之學也明日
遂行。在陳絶糧、從者
病、莫能與子路愠見

CHAPTER I. 1. The duke Ling of Wei asked Confucius about tactics. Confucius replied, "I have heard
all about sacrificial vessels, but I have not learned
military matters." On this, he took his departure
the next day.

2. When he was in Chăn, their provisions were
exhausted, and his followers became so ill that they
were unable to rise.

3. Tsze-lû, with evident dissatisfaction, said, "Has

HEADING OF THIS BOOK.—衛靈公
第十五, "The duke Ling of Wei,
No. 15." The contents of the Book,
contained in forty chapters, are as
miscellaneous as those of the former.
Rather they are more so, some chapters bearing on the public administration of government, several being
occupied with the superior man, and
others containing lessons of practical
wisdom. "All the subjects," says
Hsing Ping, "illustrate the feeling of
the sense of shame and consequent
pursuit of the correct course, and
therefore the Book immediately
follows the preceding one."

1. CONFUCIUS REFUSES TO TALK
ON MILITARY AFFAIRS. IN THE MIDST

OF DISTRESS, HE SHOWS THE DIS-
CIPLES HOW THE SUPERIOR MAN IS
ABOVE DISTRESS. 1. 陳, read chăn,
in 4th tone, ' the arrangement of the
ranks of an army," here=tactics
generally. 俎豆之事,—comp. 籩
豆之事, VIII, iv, 3. The 俎 was a
dish, 18 inches long and 8 inches
broad, on a stand 8½ inches high,
upon which the flesh of victims was
laid, but the meaning is sacrificial
vessels generally,=the business of
ceremonies. It is said of Confucius,
in the "Historical Records," that
when a boy, he was fond of playing
at 俎 and 豆. He wished, by his
reply and departure, to teach the
duke that the rules of propriety, and

予一以貫之。
然、非與曰、非也、
識之者與。對曰、
以予爲多學而
子曰、賜也、女
矣。
窮、小人窮斯濫
乎。子曰君子固
曰、君子亦有窮

the superior man likewise to endure *in this way?*"
The Master said, "The superior man may indeed have
to endure want, but the mean man, when he is in
want, gives way to unbridled license."

CHAPTER II. 1. The Master said, "Ts'ze, you
think, I suppose, that I am one who learns many
things and keeps them in memory?"

2. Tsze-kung replied, "Yes,—but perhaps it is
not so?"

3. "No," was the answer; "I seek a unity all-
pervading."

not war, were essential to the government of a state. 2. From Wei, Confucius proceeded to Chăn, and there met with the distress here mentioned. It is probably the same which is referred to in XI, ii, 1, though there is some chronological difficulty about the subject. (See the note by Chû Hsî in his preface to the Analects.) 3. 固="yes, indeed," with reference to Tsze-lû's question. Some take it in its sense of "firm."—"The superior man firmly endures want."—Duke Ling,—see XIV, xx, also in Chwang-tsze, x, v, 9, *et al.*

2. HOW CONFUCIUS AIMED AT THE KNOWLEDGE OF AN ALL-PERVADING UNITY. This chapter is to be compared with IV, xv; only, says Chû Hsî, "that is spoken with reference to practice, and this with reference to knowledge." But the design of Confucius was probably the same in them both; and I understand the first paragraph here as meaning—"Ts'ze, do you think that I am aiming, by the exercise of memory, to acquire a varied and extensive knowledge?" Then the 3rd paragraph is equivalent to:—"I am not doing this. My aim is to know myself,—the mind which embraces all knowledge, and regulates all practice." This is the view of the chapter given in the 日 講:—此 一 章 書 言 學 貴 乎 知 要, "This chapter teaches that what is valuable in learning is the knowledge of that which is important."

行不篤敬雖州里行

之邦行矣言不忠信

忠信行篤敬雖蠻貊

子張問行子曰言

其舜也與夫何爲哉

恭己正南面而已矣。

子曰、無爲而治者、

矣。

子曰、由知德者鮮

CHAPTER III. The Master said, "Yû, those who know virtue are few."

CHAPTER IV. The Master said, "May not Shun be instanced as having governed efficiently without exertion? What did he do? He did nothing but gravely and reverently occupy his royal seat."

CHAPTER V. 1. Tsze-chang asked how a man should conduct himself, *so as to be everywhere appreciated.*

2. The Master said, "Let his words be sincere and truthful, and his actions honorable and careful;—such conduct may be practiced among the rude tribes of the South or the North. If his words be not sincere and truthful, and his actions not honorable and careful, will he, with such conduct, be appreciated, even in his neighborhood?

ℭ FEW REALLY KNOW VIRTUE. This is understood as spoken with reference to the dissatisfaction manifested by Tsze-lû in chapte *i.* If he had possessed a right knowledge of virtue, he would not have been so affected by distress.

4. HOW SHUN WAS ABLE TO GOVERN WITHOUT PERSONAL EFFORT. 恭 己, "made himself reverent." 正 南 面, "correctly adjusted his southwards face;" see VI, i. Shun succeeding Yâo, there were many ministers of great virtue and ability to occupy all the offices of the government. All that Shun did was by his grave and sage example. This is the lesson,—the influence of a ruler's personal character.

5. CONDUCT THAT WILL BE APPRECIATED IN ALL PARTS OF THE WORLD. 1. We must supply a good deal to bring out the meaning here. Chû Hsî compares the question with that other of Tsze-chang about the scholar who may be called 達; see XII, xx. 2. 貊 may be regarded as another name for the 北 狄, the rude

矢。君子哉遽伯玉、邦

有道如矢、邦無道如

子曰、直哉史魚、邦

張書諸紳。

於衡也、夫然後行子

前也、在輿、則見其倚

乎哉。立則見其參於

3. "When he is standing, let him see those two things, as it were, fronting him. When he is in a carriage, let him see them attached to the yoke. Then may he subsequently carry them into practice."

4. Tsze-chang wrote these counsels on the end of his sash.

CHAPTER VI. 1. The Master said, "Truly straight-forward was the historiographer Yü. When good government prevailed in his state, he was like an arrow. When bad government prevailed, he was like an arrow.

2. "A superior man indeed is Chü Po-yü! When

tribes on the North (III, v). 2500 families made up a 州, and 25 made up a 里, but the meaning of the phrase is that given in the transla-tion. 3. 其, "them," i. e., such words and actions.—Let him see them 參於前, "before him, with himself making a trio." 輿 is prop-erly "the bottom of a carriage," planks laid over wheels, a simple "hackery," but here it="a car-riage." 4. 紳 denotes the ends of the sash that hang down.

5. THE ADMIRABLE CHARACTERS OF TSZE-YÜ AND CHÜ PO-YÜ. 1. 子魚 was the designation of 魚子, the

historiographer of Wei, generally styled Shih Ch'iù. On his deathbed, he left a message for his prince, and gave orders that his body should be laid out in a place and manner likely to attract his attention when he paid the visit of condolence. It was so, and the message then delivered had the desired effect. Perhaps it was on hearing this that Confucius made this remark. 如矢, "as an arrow," i. e., straight and decided. 2. Chü Po-yü,—see XIV, xxvi. 可=能. 卷 而懷之,—之 is to be understood as referring to "his principles," or per-haps the clause="he could roll

以成仁。

求生以害仁有殺身

子曰志士仁人無

者不失人亦不失言。

言而與之言失言知

與之言失人不可與

子曰可與言而不

可卷而懷之。

有道、則仕邦無道、則

good government prevails in his state, he is to be found in office. When bad government prevails, he can roll his principles up, and keep them in his breast."

CHAPTER VII. The Master said, "When a man may be spoken with, not to speak to him is to err in reference to the man. When a man may not be spoken with, to speak to him is to err in reference to our words. The wise err neither in regard to their man nor to their words."

CHAPTER VIII. The Master said, "The determined scholar and the man of virtue will not seek to live at the expense of injuring their virtue. They will even sacrifice their lives to preserve their virtue complete."

himself up and keep himself to himself," i. e., he kept aloof from office.—Commentators say that Tsze-yü's uniform straightforwardness was not equal to Po-yü's rightly adapting himself to circumstances.—Chwang-tsze continually mentions Tsăng Shăn and Shih Yu together.

7. THERE ARE MEN WITH WHOM TO SPEAK, AND MEN WITH WHOM TO KEEP SILENCE. THE WISE KNOW THEM. 失言 may be translated, literally and properly,—"to lose our words," but in English we do not speak of "losing men."

8. HIGH NATURES VALUE VIRTUE MORE THAN LIFE. The two different classes here are much the same as in IV, ii. The first word of the second sentence may be naturally translated —"They will kill themselves." No doubt suicide is included in the expression (see K'ung Ăn-kwo's explanation, given by Ho Yen), and Confucius here justifies that act, as in certain cases expressive of high virtue.

之冕樂則韶舞。

乘殷之輅服周

子曰行夏之時。

顏淵問爲邦。

其士之仁者。

大夫之賢者、友

居是邦也、事其

事、必先利其器、

子曰工欲善其

子貢問爲仁。

CHAPTER IX. Tsze-kung asked about the practice of virtue. The Master said, "The mechanic, who wishes to do his work well, must first sharpen his tools. When you are living in any state, take service with the most worthy among its great officers, and make friends of the most virtuous among its scholars."

CHAPTER X. 1. Yen Yüan asked how the government of a country should be administered.

2. The Master said, "Follow the seasons of Hsiâ.

3. "Ride in the state carriage of Yin.

4. "Wear the ceremonial cap of Chân.

5. "Let the music be the Shâo with its panto-mimes.

9. How INTERCOURSE WITH THE GOOD AIDS THE PRACTICE OF VIRTUE. Compare "Iron sharpeneth iron; so a man sharpeneth the countenance of his friend."

10. CERTAIN RULES, EXEMPLIFIED IN THE ANCIENT DYNASTIES, TO BE FOLLOWED IN GOVERNING:— A REPLY TO YEN YÜAN. 1. The disciple modestly put his question with reference to the government of a state (邦), but the Master answers it according to the disciple's ability, as if it had been about the ruling of the kingdom (治 天 下). 2 The three great ancient dynasties began the year at different times. According to an ancient tradition, "Heaven was opened at the time 子; Earth appeared at the time 丑; and Man was born at the time 寅." 子 commences in our December, at the winter solstice; 丑 a month later; and 寅 a month after 丑. The Châu dynasty began its year with 子; the Shang with 丑; and the Hsiâ with 寅. As human life thus began, so the year, in reference to human labors, naturally proceeds from the spring, and Confucius approved the rule of the Hsiâ dynasty. His decision has been the law of all dynasties since the Ch'in. See the "Discours Preliminaire, Chap. I," in Gaubil's Shû-ching. 3. The state carriage of the Yin dynasty was plain and substantial, which Confucius preferred to the more ornamented one of Châu.

放鄭聲、遠佞人、鄭聲淫、佞

人殆。

子曰、人無遠慮、必有近

憂。

子曰、已矣乎、吾未見好

德如好色者也。

子曰、臧文仲、其竊位者

6. "Banish the songs of Chăng, and keep far from specious talkers. The songs of Chăng are licentious; specious talkers are dangerous."

CHAPTER XI. The Master said, "If a man take no thought about what is distant, he will find sorrow near at hand."

CHAPTER XII. The Master said, "It is all over! I have not seen one who loves virtue as he loves beauty."

CHAPTER XIII. The Master said, "Was not Tsang Wăn like one who had stolen his situation? He knew

4. Yet he does not object to the more elegant cap of that dynasty, "the cap," says Chŭ Hsî, "being a small thing, and placed over all the body." 5. The *shăo* was the music of *Shun*; see III, xxv. 舞,—the "dancers," or "pantomimes," who kept time to the music. See the Shû-ching, II, ii, 21. 6. 鄭聲, "the sounds of Chăng," meaning both the songs of Chăng and the music to which they were sung. Those songs form the 7th book of the 1st division of the Shih-ching, and are here characterized justly.

11. THE NECESSITY OF FORE-THOUGHT AND PRECAUTION.

12. THE RARITY OF A TRUE LOVE OF VIRTUE. 已矣乎,—see V, xxvi; the rest is a repetition of IX, xvii, said to have been spoken by Confucius when he was in Wei and saw the duke riding out openly in the same carriage with Nan-tsze.

13. AGAINST JEALOUSY OF OTHERS' TALENTS:—THE CASE OF TSANG WĂN, AND HÛI OF LIU-HSIÂ. Tsang Wăn-chung,—see V, xvii. 竊位 is explained—"as if he had got it by theft, and secretly held possession of

與、知柳下惠之賢、而不

與立也。

子曰、躬自厚而薄責

於人、則遠怨矣。

子曰不曰如之何、如

之何者、吾末如之何也

已矣。

子曰、群居終日、言不

the virtue and the talents of Hûi of Liû-hsiâ, and yet did not *procure that he should* stand with him *in court*."

CHAPTER XIV. The Master said, "He who requires much from himself and little from others, will keep himself from *being the object of* resentment."

CHAPTER XV. The Master said, "When a man is not *in the habit of* saying—'What shall I think of this? What shall I think of this?' I can indeed do nothing with him!"

CHAPTER XVI. The Master said, "When a number of people are together, for a whole day, without their conversation turning on righteousness, and when they

it." Tsang Wăn would not recommend Hûi because he was an abler and better man than himself. Hûi is a famous name in China. He was an officer of Lû, so styled after death, whose name was 展獲, and designation 禽. He derived his revenue from a town called Liû-hsiâ, or from a *liû* or willow tree, overhanging his house, which made him be called Liû-hsiâ Hûi—"Hûi that lived under the willow tree. See Mencius, II, Pt. i, chap. 9.

14. THE WAY TO WARD OFF RESENTMENTS. 責, it is said, is here "to require from," and not "to reprove."

15. NOTHING CAN BE MADE OF PEOPLE WHO TAKE THINGS EASILY, NOT GIVING THEMSELVES THE TROUBLE TO THINK. Compare VII, viii.

16. AGAINST FRIVOLOUS TALKERS AND SUPERFICIAL SPECULATORS. Chû explains 難 矣 哉 by "they have no ground from which to become virtuous, and they will meet with calamity" Ho Yen gives Chăng's explanation, "they will never complete anything." Our nearly literal translation appears to convey the

及義好行小慧難矣

哉。

子曰、君子義以爲

質、禮以行之、孫以出

之、信以成之君子哉。

子曰、君子病無能

are fond of carrying out *the suggestions of* a small shrewdness;—theirs is indeed a hard case."

CHAPTER XVII. The Master said, "The superior man *in everything* considers righteousness to be essential. He performs it according to the rules of propriety. He brings it forth in humility. He completes it with sincerity. This is indeed a superior man."

CHAPTER XVIII. The Master said, "The superior man is distressed by his want of ability. He is not distressed by men's not knowing him."

CHAPTER XIX. The Master said, "The superior

meaning. "A hard case," i. e., they will make nothing out, and nothing can be made of them.

17. THE CONDUCT OF THE SUPERIOR MAN IS RIGHTEOUS, COURTEOUS, HUMBLE, AND SINCERE. 質 is explained by Chû Hsî by "the substance and stem"; and in the "Complete Digest" by "foundation." The antecedent to all the 之 is 義, or rather the thing, whatever it be, **done righteously**.

18. OUR OWN INCOMPETENCY, AND NOT OUR REPUTATION, THE PROPER BUSINESS OF CONCERN TO US. See XIV, xxxii, *et al.*

19. THE SUPERIOR MAN WISHES TO BE HAD IN REMEMBRANCE. Not, say the commentators, that the superior man cares about fame, but fame is the invariable concomitant of merit. He cannot have been the superior man, if he be not remembered. 沒世,—see 大學傳, II. In

焉、不病人之不已知也。

子曰、君子疾沒世、而名
不稱焉。

子曰、君子求諸己、小人
求諸人。

子曰、君子矜而不爭、群
而不黨。

子曰君子不以言舉人、
不以人廢言。

man dislikes the thought of his name not being mentioned after his death."

CHAPTER XX. The Master said, "What the superior man seeks, is in himself. What the mean man seeks, is in others."

CHAPTER XXI. The Master said, "The superior man is dignified, but does not wrangle. He is sociable, but not a partisan."

CHAPTER XXII. The Master said, "The superior man does not promote a man *simply* on account of his words, nor does he put aside *good* words because of the man."

the 備 旨, 日 講, and many other paraphrases, 沒 世 is taken as＝終身; "all his life." Still, I let the translation suggested by the use of the phrase in the "Great Learning" keep its place.

20. HIS OWN APPROBATION IS THE SUPERIOR MAN'S RULE. THE APPROBATION OF OTHERS IS THE MEAN MAN'S. Compare XIV, xxv.

21. THE SUPERIOR MAN IS DIGNIFIED AND AFFABLE, WITHOUT THE FAULTS TO WHICH THOSE QUALITIES OFTEN LEAD. Compare II, xiv, and VII, xxx, 2. 矜 is here＝莊 以 持 已, "grave in self-maintenance."

22. THE SUPERIOR MAN IS DISCRIMINATING IN HIS EMPLOYMENT OF MEN AND JUDGING OF STATEMENTS.

之所以直道而行也。

有所試矣斯民也、三代

毀、誰譽、如有所譽者其

子曰、吾之於人也誰

施於人。

曰、其恕乎、己所不欲、勿

可以終身行之者乎子

子貢問曰、有一言、而

CHAPTER XXIII. Tsze-kung asked, saying, "Is there one word which may serve as a rule of practice for all one's life?" The Master said, "Is not RECIPROCITY such a word? What you do not want done to yourself, do not do to others."

CHAPTER XXIV. 1. The Master said, "In my dealings with men, whose evil do I blame, whose goodness do I praise, beyond what is proper? If I do sometimes exceed in praise, there must be ground for it in my examination *of the individual.*

2. "This people supplied the ground why the three dynasties pursued the path of straightforwardness."

23. THE GREAT PRINCIPLE OF RECIPROCITY IS THE RULE OF LIFE. Compare V, xi. It is singular that Tsze-kung professes there to act on the principle here recommended to him. *Altruism* may be substituted for *reciprocity.*

24. CONFUCIUS SHOWED HIS RESPECT FOR MEN BY STRICT TRUTH-FULNESS IN AWARDING PRAISE OR CENSURE. 1. I have not marked "beyond what is proper" with italics, because there is really that force in the verbs—毀 and 譽. "Ground for it in my examination of the individual;"—i. e., from my examination of him I believe he will yet verify my words. 2. 斯民也, resumes the 人 of the 1st paragraph, which the 也 indicates. 所以 is to be taken as="the reason why," and 行 as a neuter verb of general application. 三代, "the three dynasties," with special reference to their great founders, and the principles which they inaugurated.—The truth-approving nature of the people was a rule even to those sages. It was the same to Confucius.

子曰、吾猶及史

之闕文也、有馬者、

借人乘之今亡已

夫。

子曰、巧言亂德、

小不忍則亂大謀。

子曰衆惡之必

察焉、衆好之必察

焉。

CHAPTER XXV. The Master said, "Even in my *early* days, a historiographer would leave a blank in his text, and he who had a horse would lend him to another to ride. Now, alas! there are no such things."

CHAPTER XXVI. The Master said, "Specious words confound virtue. Want of forbearance in small matters confounds great plans."

CHAPTER XXVII. The Master said, "When the multitude hate a man, it is necessary to examine into the case. When the multitude like a man, it is necessary to examine into the case."

25. INSTANCES OF THE DEGENERACY OF CONFUCIUS'S TIMES. Most paraphrasts supply a 見 after 及;—"even in my time I have seen." The appointment of the historiographer is referred to Hwang-tî, or "The Yellow Sovereign," the inventor of the cycle. The statutes of Châu mention no fewer than five classes of such officers. They were attached also to the feudal courts, and what Confucius says is that, in his early days, a historiographer, on any point about which he was not sure, would leave a blank; so careful were they to record only truth. 吾猶及 extends on to 有馬 云云. This second sentence is explained in Ho Yen:—"If any one had a horse which he could not tame, he would lend it to another to ride and exercise it!"—The commentator Hû (胡氏) says well, that the meaning of the chapter must be left in uncertainty (the second part of it especially).

26. THE DANGER OF SPECIOUS WORDS, AND OF IMPATIENCE. 小不忍 is not "a little impatience," but impatience in little things; "the hastiness," it is said, "of women and small people."

27. IN JUDGING OF A MAN, WE MUST NOT BE GUIDED BY HIS BEING GENERALLY LIKED OR DISLIKED. Compare XIII, xxiv.

也。 無益不如學 夜不寝以思、終 終日不食、終 𦕈子曰吾嘗 矣。 不改是謂過 𦕈子曰過而 人。 弘道非道弘 𦕈子曰人能

CHAPTER XXVIII. The Master said, "A man can enlarge the principles *which he follows;* those principles do not enlarge the man."

CHAPTER XXIX. The Master said, "To have faults and not to reform them,—this, indeed, should be pronounced having faults."

CHAPTER XXX. The Master said, "I have been the whole day without eating, and the whole night without sleeping:—occupied with thinking. It was of no use. The better plan is to learn."

28. PRINCIPLES OF DUTY AN INSTRUMENT IN THE HAND OF MAN. This sentence is quite mystical in its sententiousness. The 翼 註 says: "道 here is the path of duty, which all men, in their various relations, have to pursue, and man has the three virtues of knowledge. benevolence, and fortitude, wherewith to pursue that path, and so he enlarges it. That virtue remote, occupying an empty place, cannot enlarge man, needs not to be said." That writer's account of 道 here is probably correct, and "duty unapprehended," "in an empty place," can have no effect on any man; but this is a mere truism. Duty apprehended is constantly enlarging, elevating, and energizing multitudes, who had previously been uncognizant of it. The first clause of the chapter may be granted, but the second is not in accordance with truth. Generally, however, man may be considered as the measure of the truth in morals and metaphysics which he holds; but after all, systems of men are for the most part beneath the highest capacities of the model men, the *Chun-tsze.*

29. THE CULPABILITY OF NOT REFORMING KNOWN FAULTS. Compare I, viii. Chû Hsî's commentary appears to make the meaning somewhat different. He says: "If one having faults can change them, he comes back to the condition of having no faults. But if he do not change them, then they go on to their completion, and will never come to be changed."

30. THE FRUITLESSNESS OF THINKING, WITHOUT READING. Compare II, xv, where the dependence of acquisition and reflection on each other is set forth.—Many commentators say that Confucius merely transfers the things which he here mentions to himself for the sake of others, not that it ever was really thus with himself.

必失之知及之仁
不能守之雖得之、
豐子曰知及之仁
不憂貧。
其中矣君子憂道、
其中矣學也祿在
不謀食耕也餒在
豐子曰君子謀道

CHAPTER XXXI. The Master said, "The object of the superior man is truth. Food is not his object. There is plowing;—even in that there is *sometimes* want. So with learning;—emolument may be found in it. The superior man is anxious lest he should not get truth; he is not anxious lest poverty should come upon him."

CHAPTER XXXII. 1. The Master said, "When a man's knowledge is sufficient to attain, and his virtue is not sufficient to enable him to hold, whatever he may have gained, he will lose again.

2. "When his knowledge is sufficient to attain, and

31. THE SUPERIOR MAN SHOULD NOT BE MERCENARY BUT HAVE TRUTH FOR HIS OBJECT. Here again we translate 道 by "truth," as the best term that offers. 餒, "hunger,"= want. "Want may be in the midst of plowing,"—i. e., husbandry is the way to plenty, and yet a famine or scarcity sometimes occurs. The application of this to the case of learning, however, is not apt Is the emolument that sometimes comes with learning a calamity like famine? The contrast of the two cases is not well maintained.

32. HOW KNOWLEDGE WITHOUT VIRTUE IS NOT LASTING, AND TO KNOWLEDGE AND VIRTUE A RULER SHOULD ADD DIGNITY AND THE RULES OF PROPRIETY. 1. Here the various *chih* and the two first in the other paragraphs have *le*, or principle, for their reference. In Ho Yen, however, Pâo Hsien says: "A man may have knowledge equal to the management of his office (治其官), but if he have not virtue which can hold it fast, though he get it, he will lose it." 2. In 涖之, and 動之 below, 之指民言, "the 之 have 民

也。　不可大受、而可小知　知、而可大受也、小人　蠶子曰、君子不可小　之不以禮、未善也。　能守之、莊以涖之、動　則民不敬。知及之、仁　能守之、不莊以涖之、

he has virtue enough to hold fast, if he cannot govern with dignity, the people will not respect him.

3. "When his knowledge is sufficient to attain, and he has virtue enough to hold fast; when he governs also with dignity, yet if he try to move the people contrary to the rules of propriety:—full excellence is not reached."

CHAPTER XXXIII. The Master said, "The superior man cannot be known in little matters; but he may be intrusted with great concerns. The small men may not be intrusted with great concerns, but he may be known in little matters."

or people, for their reference." 3. The phrase—"to move the people" is analogous to several others, such as 鼓 之, 舞 之, 與 之, "to drum the people," "to dance them," "to rouse them."

33. How to know the superior man and the mean man; and their capacities. Chû Hsî says—知, 我 知 之, "the knowing here is our knowing the individuals." The "little matters" are ingenious but trifling arts and accomplishments, in which a really great man may sometimes be deficient, while a small man will be familiar with them. The "knowing" is not that the parties are chun-tsze and hsiáo-zăn, but what attainments they have, and for what they are fit. The difficulty, on this view, is with the conclusion—而 可 小 知.—Ho Yen says: "The way of the chün-tsze is profound and far-reaching. He will not let his knowledge be small, and he may be trusted with what is great. The way of the hsiáo-zăn is shallow and near. He will let his knowledge be small, and he may not be trusted with what is great."

諒。　　師。　　仁而死者也。　　蹈而死者矣、未見蹈　　甚於水火、水火吾見　　子曰民之於仁也、

子曰君子貞、而不　　子曰當仁、不讓於　　子曰

CHAPTER XXXIV. The Master said, "Virtue is more to man than either water or fire. I have seen men die from treading on water and fire, but I have never seen a man die from treading the course of virtue."

CHAPTER XXXV. The Master said, "Let every man consider virtue as what devolves on himself. He may not yield the performance of it *even* to his teacher."

CHAPTER XXXVI. The Master said, "The superior man is correctly firm, and not firm merely."

34. VIRTUE MORE TO MAN THAN WATER OR FIRE; AND NEVER HURTFUL TO HIM. 民 is here＝人, "man," as in VI, xx. 民 之 於 仁 也—"the people's relation to, or dependence on, virtue." The case is easily conceivable of men's suffering death on account of their virtue. There have been martyrs for their loyalty and other virtues, as well as for their religious faith. Chû Hsî provides for this difference in his remarks: "The want of fire and water is hurtful only to man's body, but to be without virtue is to lose one's mind (the higher nature), and so it is more to him than water or fire." See on IV, viii.

35. VIRTUE PERSONAL AND OBLIGATORY ON EVERY MAN. The old interpreters take 當 in the sense of "ought." Chû Hsî certainly improves on them by taking it in the sense of 擔 當, as in the translation. A student at first takes 當 to be in the 2nd person, but the 不 following recalls him to the 3rd.

36. THE SUPERIOR MAN'S FIRMNESS IS BASED ON RIGHT. 貞 is used here in the sense which it has throughout the Yî-ching. Both it and 諒 imply firmness, but 貞 supposes a moral and intelligent basis which may be absent from 諒; see XIV, xviii, 3.

子曰、辭達而已矣。

謀。

子曰、道不同、不相爲

子曰、有敎、無類。

後其食。

子曰、事君敬其事、而

CHAPTER XXXVII. The Master said, "A minister, in serving his prince, reverently discharges his duties, and makes his emolument a secondary consideration."

CHAPTER XXXVIII. The Master said, "In teaching there should be no distinction of classes."

CHAPTER XXXIX. The Master said, "Those whose courses are different cannot lay plans for one another."

CHAPTER XL. The Master said, "In language it is simply required that it convey the meaning."

37. THE FAITHFUL MINISTER. The 其 refers not to 君, but to the individual who 事君. We have to supply the subject—"a minister." 後, as in VI, xx.

38. THE COMPREHENSIVENESS OF TEACHING. Chû Hsî says on this: "The nature of all men is good, but we find among them the different classes of good and bad. This is the effect of physical constitution and of practice. The superior man, in consequence, employs his teaching, and all may be brought back to the state of good, and there is no necessity (the language is 不當復論其類之

惡) of speaking any more of the badness of some. This is extravagant. Teaching is not so omnipotent.—The old interpretation is simply that in teaching there should be no distinction of classes.

39. AGREEMENT IN PRINCIPLE NECESSARY TO CONCORD IN PLANS. 爲 is the 4th tone, but I do not see that there would be any great difference in the meaning, if it were read in its usual 2nd tone.

40. PERSPICUITY THE CHIEF VIRTUE OF LANGUAGE. 辭 may be used both of speech and of style.

師冕見及階子曰

階也及席子曰席也。

皆坐子告之曰某在

斯某在斯師冕出子

張問曰與師言之道

與子曰然固相師之

道也。

CHAPTER XLI. 1. The music master, Mien, having called upon him, when they came to the steps, the Master said, "Here are the steps." When they came to the mat *for the guest* to sit upon, he said, "Here is the mat." When all were seated, the Master informed him, saying, "So and so is here; so and so is here."

2. The music master, Mien, having gone out, Tsze-chang asked, saying, "Is it the rule to tell those things to the music master?"

3. The Master said, "Yes. This is certainly the rule for those who lead the blind."

41. CONSIDERATION OF CONFUCIUS FOR THE BLIND. 1. 師,—i. q. 太師, III, xxiii. Anciently, the blind were employed in the offices of music, partly because their sense of hearing was more than ordinarily acute, and partly that they might be made of some use in the world; see the 集證, *in loc.* 見,—4th tone. Mien had come to Confucius's house, under the care of a guide, but the sage met him, and undertook the care of him himself. 2. 之 is governed by 言, and refers to the words of Confucius to Mien in the preceding paragraph.

## BOOK XVI. KE SHE

事於顓臾。　季氏將有　於孔子曰、　有季路見　伐顓臾。　季氏將　十六　季氏第

CHAPTER I. 1. The head of the Chî family was going to attack Chwan-yü.

2. Zan Yû and Chî-lû had an interview with Confucius, and said, *"Our chief*, Chî, is going to commence operations against Chwan-yü."

HEADING OF THIS BOOK.—季 氏 第 十 六, "The chief of the Chî, No. 16." Throughout this Book, Confucius is spoken of as 孔 子, "The philosopher K'ung," and never by the designation 子, or "The Master." Then, the style of several of the chapters (iv—xi) is not like the utterances of Confucius to which we have been accustomed. From these circumstances, one commentator, Hung Kwo (洪适),supposed that it belonged to the Ch'î (齊) *recensus* of these Analects; the other Books belonging to the Lû (魯) *recensus*. This supposition, however, is not otherwise supported.

1. CONFUCIUS EXPOSES THE PRESUMPTUOUS AND IMPOLITIC CONDUCT OF THE CHIEF OF THE CHÎ FAMILY IN PROPOSING TO ATTACK A MINOR STATE, AND REBUKES ZAN YÛ AND TSZE-LÛ FOR ABETTING THE DESIGN. 1. 季 氏 and 季 孫 below,— see III, i. Chwan-yü was a small territory in Lû, whose ruler was of the 子, or 4th order of nobility. It was one of the states called 附 庸, or "attached," whose chiefs could not appear in the presence of the sovereign, excepting in the train of the prince within whose jurisdiction they were embraced. Their existence was not from a practice like the subinfeudation, which belonged to the feudal system of Europe. They held of the lord paramount or king, but with the restriction which has been mentioned, and with a certain subservience also to their immediate superior. Its particular position is fixed by its proximity to Pî and to the Măng hill. 伐 is not merely "to attack," but "to attack and punish," an exercise of judicial authority, which could emanate only from the sovereign. The term is used here, to show the nefarious and presumptuous character of the contemplated operations. 2. There is some difficulty here, as, according to the "Historical Records," the two disciples were not in the service of the Chî family at the same time. We may suppose, however, that Tsze-lû, returning with the sage from Wei on the invitation of duke Âi, took service a second time, and for a short period, with the Chî family, of which the chief was then Chî K'ang. This brings the time of the transaction to 483, or 482 B. C. 將 有 事,—literally, "is

孔子曰、求無乃

爾是過與夫顓

臾、昔者、先王以

爲東蒙主、且在

邦域之中矣、是

社稷之臣也、何

以伐爲冉有曰、

夫子欲之吾二

臣者、皆不欲也。

3. Confucius said, "Ch'iû, is it not you who are in fault here?

4. "Now, in regard to Chwan-yü, long ago, a former king appointed its ruler to preside over *the sacrifices to the eastern Măng*; moreover, it is in the midst of the territory of our state; and its ruler is a minister in direct connection with the sovereign:—What has *your chief* to do with attacking it?"

5. Zan Yû said, "Our master wishes the thing; neither of us two ministers wishes it."

going to have an affair." 3. Confucius addresses himself only to Ch'iû, as he had been a considerable time, and very active, in the Chî service. 4. It was the prerogative of the princes to sacrifice to the hills and rivers within their jurisdictions; —here was the chief of Chwan-yü, royally appointed (the "former king" is probably 成, the second sovereign of the Chàu dynasty) to be the lord of the Măng mountain, that is, to preside over the sacrifices offered to it. This raised him high above any mere ministers or officers of Lû. The mountain Măng is in the present district of Pî, in the department of I-châu. It was called eastern, to distinguish it from another of the same name in Shensi, which was the western Măng. 且在邦域之中,—this is mentioned to show that Chwan-yü was so situated as to give Lû no occasion for apprehension. 社稷之臣, "a minister of the altars to the spirits of the land and grain." To those spirits only, the prince had the prerogative of sacrificing. The chief of Chwan-yü having this, how dared an officer of Lû to think of attacking him? The 臣 is used of his relation to the king Chû Hsî makes the phrase=公家之臣, "a minister of the ducal house," saying that the three families had usurped all the dominions proper of Lû, leaving only the chiefs of the attached states to appear in the ducal court. I prefer the former interpretation. 何以伐爲 must be understood with reference to the Chî. See Wang Yin Chih on Wei as a 語助, where he quotes this text (2nd chapter of his treatise on the Particles). 5. 夫子,

費今不取後世必爲
今夫顓臾固而近於
是誰之過與。冉有曰、
於柙龜玉毀於櫝中、
且爾言過矣虎兕出
扶、則將焉用彼相矣。
止、危而不持顚而不
曰、陳力就列不能者
孔子曰、求、周任有言

6. Confucius said, "Ch'iû, there are the words of Châu Zăn,—'When he can put forth his ability, he takes his place in the ranks *of office;* when he finds himself unable to do so, he retires from it. How can he be used as a guide to a blind man, who does not support him when tottering, nor raise him up when fallen?'

7. "And further, you speak wrongly. When a tiger or rhinoceros escapes from his cage; when a tortoise or piece of jade is injured in its repository:— whose is the fault?"

8. Zăn Yû said, "But at present, Chwan-yü is strong and near to Pî; if *our chief* do not now take it, it will hereafter be a sorrow to his descendants."

our 'master,' i. e , the chief of the Chî family. 6. Châu Zăn is by Chû Hsî simply cal'ed—"a good historiographer of ancient time." Some trace him back to tl e Shang dynasty, and others only to the early times of the Châu. There are other weighty utterances of his in vogue, besides that in the text. 7. Chû Hsî explains 兕 by 野牛, "a wild bull."

The dictionary says it is like an ox, and goes on to describe it as "one-horned " The 本草 獸部, says that 兕 and 犀 are different terms for the same animal, i. e., the rhinoceros. I cannot think that 龜 here is the living tortoise. That would not be kept in a 櫝, or "coffer," like a gem. Perhaps the character is, by mistake,

子孫憂孔子曰、求君子疾

夫舍曰欲之、而必爲之辭。

丘也、聞有國有家者、不患

寡、而患不均、不患貧而患

不安蓋均無貧、和無寡、安

9. Confucius said. "Ch'iû, the superior man hates that declining to say—'I want such and such a thing,' and framing explanations *for the conduct*.

10. "I have heard that rulers of states and chiefs of families are not troubled lest their people should be few, but are troubled lest they should not keep their several places; that they are not troubled with fears of poverty, but are troubled with fears of a want of contented repose *among the people in their several places*. For when the people keep their several places, there will be no poverty; when harmony prevails, there will be no scarcity of people; and when there is such a *contented* repose, there will be no rebellious upsettings.

for 圭. 9. The regimen of 疾 extends down to the end of the paragraph. 夫,—as in XI, xxiv. 爲之辭 is the same idiom as 爲之宰, V, vii. 10. Confucius uses the term 患 here with reference to the 憂 in par. 8. 均, "equality." 謂各得其分 means—

"every one getting his own proper name and place." From this point, Confucius speaks of the general disorganization of Lû under the management of the three families and especially of the Chî. By 邊人

而謀動干戈於邦內、吾恐
邦分崩離析、國不能守也。
子、遠人不服、而不能來也、
則安之今由與求也、相夫
則修文德以來之、既來之、
無傾。夫如是故遠人不服、

11. "So it is.—Therefore, if remoter people are not submissive, all the influences of civil culture and virtue are to be cultivated to attract them to be so; and when they have been so attracted, they must be made contented and tranquil.

12. "Now, here are you, Yû and Ch'iû, assisting your chief.   Remoter people are not submissive, and, *with your help*, he cannot attract them to him.   In his own territory there are divisions and downfalls, leavings and separations, and, *with your help*, he cannot preserve it.

13. "And yet he is planning these hostile movements within the state.—I am afraid that the sorrow

we can hardly understand the people of Chwan-yu.  11. 來 is to be understood with a special force, "to make to come," "to attract."  12. 不能 來, 不能守 are to be understood of the head of the Chî family, as controlling the government of Lû, and *as being assisted by the two disciples*, so that the reproof falls heavily on them.  13. 在蕭牆之內, Chû Hsî simply says 蕭牆, 屏 也, "*hsiâo-ch'iang* means a screen."  In the dictionary, after Ho Yen, *hsiâo* in this passage＝肅, "reverent,"

矣、自大夫出、五世希
侯出蓋十世希不失
征伐、自諸侯出、自諸
出、天下無道、則禮樂
則禮樂征伐、自天子
<ruby>孔<rt>二</rt></ruby>子曰、天下有道、
而在蕭牆之內也。
季孫之憂不在顓臾、

of the Chî-sun *family* will not be on account of Chwan-
yü, but will be found within the screen of their own
court."

CHAPTER II. 1. Confucius said, "When good
government prevails in the empire, ceremonies, music,
and punitive military expeditions proceed from the
son of Heaven. When bad government prevails in
the empire, ceremonies, music, and punitive military
expeditions proceed from the princes. When these
things proceed from the princes, as a rule, the cases
will be few in which they do not lose their power in
ten generations. When they proceed from the great
officers *of the princes, as a rule*, the cases will be few in
which they do not lose their power in five generations.

and 牆 alone means "screen," and
the phrase is thus explained;—
"Officers, on reaching the screen,
which they had only to pass to find
themselves in the presence of their
ruler, were supposed to become more
'reverential;" and hence, the expression in the text="among his own
immediate officers."

2. THE SUPREME AUTHORITY
OUGHT EVER TO MAINTAIN ITS POWER.
THE VIOLATION OF THIS RULE ALWAYS
LEADS TO RUIN, WHICH IS SPEEDIER
AS THE RANK OF THE VIOLATOR IS
LOWER. In these utterances, Con-
fucius had reference to the dis-
organized state of the kingdom,
when "the son of Heaven" was fast

去公室、五世矣、　孔子曰、祿之　人不議。　天下有道、則庶　則政不在大夫。　失矣。天下有道、　國命、三世希不　不失矣、陪臣執

When the subsidiary ministers *of the great officers* hold in their grasp the orders of the state, *as a rule*, the cases will be few in which they do not lose their power in three generations.

2. "When right principles prevail in the kingdom, government will not be in the hands of the great officers.

3. "When right principles prevail in the kingdom, there will be no discussions among the common people."

CHAPTER III. Confucius said, "The revenue *of the state* has left the ducal house now for five generations.

becoming an empty name, the princes of states were in bondage to their great officers, and those again at the mercy of their family ministers. 1. 有道, 無道,—compare XIV, i. 征伐 are to be taken together, as in the translation. We read of four 征, i. e., expeditions,— east, west, north, and south; and of nine 伐, i. e., nine grounds on which the sovereign might order such expeditions. On the royal prerogatives, see the 中庸, XXVIII. 蓋 is here＝大約, "generally speaking," "as a rule." 陪臣＝家臣, "family ministers" 國命 are the same as the previous 禮, 樂, 征, 伐, but having

been usurped by the princes, and now again snatched from them by their officers, they can no longer be spoken of as royal affairs, but only as 國之事, "state matters" 3. 議 ＝私議, "private discussions;" i. e., about the state of public affairs.

3. ILLUSTRATION OF THE PRINCIPLES OF THE LAST CHAPTER. In the year 609 B. C., at the death of Duke Wăn, his rightful heir was killed, and the son of a concubine raised to the ruler's place. He is in the annals as Duke Hsüan (宣), and after him came Ch'ăng, Hsiang, Ch'âo, and Ting, in whose time this must have been spoken. These

政逮於大夫、四世矣、故夫三桓之子孫微矣。

孔子曰、益者三友、損者三友、友直、友諒、友多聞益矣、友便辟、友善柔、友便佞、損矣。

The government has been in the hands of the great officers for four generations. On this account, the descendants of the three Hwan are much reduced."

CHAPTER IV. Confucius said, "There are three friendships which are advantageous, and three which are injurious. Friendship with the upright; friendship with the sincere; and friendship with the man of much observation:—these are advantageous. Friendship with the man of specious airs; friendship with the insinuatingly soft; and friendship with the glib-tongued:—these are injurious."

dukes were but shadows, pensionaries of their great officers, so that it might be said the revenue had gone from them. Observe that here and in the preceding chapter 世 is used for "a reign." "The three Hwan" are the three families, as being all descended from Duke Hwan; see on II, v.—Chû Hsî appears to have fallen into a mistake in enumerating the four heads of the Chî family who had administered the government of Lû as Wû, Tâo, P'ing, and Hwan, as Tâo (悼) died before his father, and would not be said, therefore, to have the government in his hands. The right enumeration is Wǎn (文), Wǔ (武), P'ing (平), and Hwan (桓). See the 拓餘說, III, xxvi.

4. THREE FRIENDSHIPS ADVANTAGEOUS, AND THREE INJURIOUS. In the 備旨 it is said—三友下各友字俱作交字看,是我去友人, "after 三友, the character 友 is always verbal and＝交, 'to have intercourse with.'" It is as well to translate the term by "friendship" throughout. 諒 is "sincere," without the subtractions required in XIV, xviii, 3, XV, xxxvi. 便, here＝習熟, "practiced" 善柔＝善柔之工, "善 is skilfulness in being bland."

子有三愆言未及

孔子曰、侍於君

樂損矣。

驕樂樂佚遊樂宴

樂多賢友益矣、樂

禮樂樂道人之善、

樂、損者三樂、樂節

孔子曰、益者三

CHAPTER V. Confucius said, "There are three things men find enjoyment in which are advantageous, and three things they find enjoyment in which are injurious. To find enjoyment in the discriminating study of ceremonies and music; to find enjoyment in speaking of the goodness of others; to find enjoyment in having many worthy friends:—these are advantageous. To find enjoyment in extravagant pleasures; to find enjoyment in idleness and sauntering; to find enjoyment in the pleasures of feasting:—these are injurious."

CHAPTER VI. Confucius said, "There are three errors to which they who stand in the presence of a man of virtue and station are liable. They may speak

5. THREE SOURCES OF ENJOYMENT ADVANTAGEOUS, AND THREE INJURIOUS. Here we have 樂 with three pronunciations and in three different meanings. The leading word is read *âo*, 4th tone, "to have enjoyment in," as in VI, xxi. In 禮 樂, it is *yo*, "music." The two others are 樂, *lo* or *lê*, "joy," "to delight in." 節 禮 樂, 一節=節 之, i. e., it is a verb, "to discriminate"; "to mark the divisions of " The idea is that ceremonies and music containing in them the principles of propriety and harmony, the study of them could not but be beneficial to the student himself, as having to exemplify both of those things. 驕, primarily, "a tall horse," often used for "proud"; here = vain and extravagant self-indulgence. 宴, "feasting," including, says a gloss, "eating, drinking, music, women, etc."

6. THREE ERRORS IN REGARD TO SPEECH TO BE AVOIDED IN THE PRESENCE OF THE GREAT. 君 子, according to Chû Hsî, denotes here "a man both of rank and virtue." "Without

血氣既衰戒之在得。

剛、戒之在鬬及其老也、

在色及其壯也、血氣方

少之時、血氣未定、戒之

孔子曰君子有三戒、

色而言謂之瞽。

而不言謂之隱未見顏

之而言謂之躁、言及之

when it does not come to them to speak;—this is
called rashness. They may not speak when it comes
to them to speak;—this is called concealment. They
may speak without looking at the countenance *of their
superior;*—this is called blindness."

CHAPTER VII. Confucius said, "There are three
things which the superior man guards against. In
youth, when the physical powers are not yet settled,
he guards against lust. When he is strong and the
physical powers are full of vigor, he guards against
quarrelsomeness. When he is old, and the animal
powers are decayed, he guards against covetousness."

looking at the countenance,"—i. e.,
to see whether he is paying attention
or not.—The general principle is that
there is a time to speak. Let that
be observed, and these three errors
will be avoided.

7. THE VICES WHICH YOUTH, MAN-
HOOD, AND AGE RESPECTIVELY HAVE
TO GUARD AGAINST. 血氣, "blood
and breath." In the 中庸, XXI, 凡
有 血 氣 者="all human beings."
Here the phrase is equivalent to
"the physical powers." On 未定,
"not yet settled," the gloss in the
備旨 is—方動之時, "the time
when they are moving most." As to

what causal relation Confucius may
have supposed to exist between the
state of the physical powers, and the
several vices indicated, that is not
developed. Hsing Ping explains the
first caution thus: "Youth embraces all the period below 29. Then
the physical powers are still weak
and the sinews and bones have not
reached their vigor, and indulgence
in lust will injure the body." By
the superior man's guarding against
these three things, I suppose it is
meant that he teaches that they are
to be guarded against

之者次也困而學
之者上也學而知
者孔子曰生而知
人之言。
畏也狎大人侮聖
人不知天命而不
人畏聖人之言小
三畏畏天命畏大
者孔子曰君子有

CHAPTER VIII. 1. Confucius said, "There are three things of which the superior man stands in awe. He stands in awe of the ordinances of Heaven. He stands in awe of great men. He stands in awe of the words of sages.

2. "The mean man does not know the ordinances of Heaven, and *consequently* does not stand in awe of them. He is disrespectful to great men. He makes sport of the words of sages."

CHAPTER IX. Confucius said, "Those who are born with the possession of knowledge are the highest class of men. Those who learn, and so, *readily*, get possession of knowledge, are the next. Those who are dull and

8. CONTRAST OF THE SUPERIOR AND THE MEAN MAN IN REGARD TO THE THREE THINGS OF WHICH THE FORMER STANDS IN AWE. 天命, according to Chû Hsî, means the moral nature of man, conferred by Heaven. High above the nature of other creatures, it lays him under great responsibility to cherish and cultivate himself. The old interpreters take the phrase to indicate Heaven's moral administration by rewards and punishments. The "great men" are men high in position and great in wisdom and virtue, the royal instructors, who have been raised up by Heaven for the training and ruling of mankind. So, the commentators; but the 狎 suggests at once a more general and a lower view of the phrase.

9. FOUR CLASSES OF MEN IN RELATION TO KNOWLEDGE. On the 1st clause, see on VII, xix, where Confucius disclaims for himself being ranked in the first of the classes here mentioned. The modern commentators say that men are differenced

義。　恣思難見得思　事思敬疑思問、　貌思恭言思忠、　聽思聰色思溫、　有九思視思明、　孔子曰君子　下矣。　而不學民斯爲　之又其次也、困

stupid, and yet compass the learning, are another class next to these. As to those who are dull and stupid and yet do not learn;—they are the lowest of the people."

CHAPTER X. Confucius said, "The superior man has nine things which are subjects with him of thoughtful consideration. In regard to the use of his eyes, he is anxious to see clearly. In regard to the use of his ears, he is anxious to hear distinctly. In regard to his countenance, he is anxious that it should be benign. In regard to his demeanor, he is anxious that it should be respectful. In regard to his speech, he is anxious that it should be sincere. In regard to his doing of business, he is anxious that it should be reverently careful. In regard to what he doubts about, he is anxious to question others. When he is angry, he thinks of the difficulties (*his anger may involve him in*). When he sees gain to be got, he thinks of righteousness."

here by the difference of their 氣 質 or 氣 禀, on which see Morrison's Dictionary, part II, vol. i, character 質. 困, in the dictionary, and by commentators, old and new, is explained by 不 通, "not thoroughly understanding." It is not to be joined with 學, as if the meaning were—"they learn with painful effort," although such effort will be required in the case of the 困.

10. NINE SUBJECTS OF THOUGHT TO THE SUPERIOR MAN:—VARIOUS INSTANCES OF THE WAY IN WHICH HE REGULATES HIMSELF. The conciseness of the text contrasts here with the verbosity of the translation, and yet the many words of the latter seem necessary.

死之日民無德而稱　齊景公有馬千駟、　語矣、未見其人也。　義以達其道吾聞其　矣。隱居以求其志行　見其人矣、吾聞其語　及、見不善如探湯、吾　孔子曰、見善如不

CHAPTER XI. 1. Confucius said, "Contemplating good, *and pursuing it*, as if they could not reach it; contemplating evil, *and shrinking from it*, as they would from thrusting the hand into boiling water:— I have seen such men, as I have heard such words.

2. "Living in retirement to study their aims, and practicing righteousness to carry out their principles:—I have heard these words, but I have not seen such men."

CHAPTER XII. 1. The duke Ching of Ch'î had a thousand teams, each of four horses, but on the day of his death, the people did not praise him for a single

11. THE CONTEMPORARIES OF CON-FUCIUS COULD ESCHEW EVIL, AND FOLLOW AFTER GOOD, BUT NO ONE OF THE HIGHEST CAPACITY HAD APPEARED AMONG THEM. 1. The two first clauses here and in the next paragraph also, are quotations of old sayings, current in Confucius's time. "Such men" were several of the sage's own disciples. 2. 求其志, "seeking for their aims;" i. e., meditating on them, studying them, fixing them, to be prepared to carry them out, as in the next clause. Such men among the ancients were the great ministers Î Yin and T'âi-kung. Such might the disciple Yen Hûi have been, but an early death snatched him away before he could have an opportunity of showing what was in him.

12. WEALTH WITHOUT VIRTUE AND VIRTUE WITHOUT WEALTH;—THEIR DIFFERENT APPRECIATIONS. This chapter is plainly a fragment. As it stands, it would appear to come from the compilers and not from Confucius. Then the 2nd paragraph implies a reference to something which has been lost. Under XII, x,

詩、無以言鯉退而學詩。

學詩乎。對曰未也。不學

嘗獨立鯉趨而過庭、曰、

亦有異聞乎對曰、未也、

圖陳亢問於伯魚曰子

斯之謂與。

之下、民到于今稱之其

爲、伯夷叔齊、餓于首陽

virtue. Po-î and Shû-ch'î died of hunger at the foot of the Shâu-yang mountain, and the people, down to the present time, praise them.

2. "Is not that saying illustrated by this?"

CHAPTER XIII. 1. Ch'ǎn K'ang asked Po-yü, saying, "Have you heard any lessons *from your father* different *from what we have all* heard?"

2. Po-yü replied, "No. He was standing alone once, when I passed below the hall with hasty steps, and said to me, 'Have you learned the Odes?' On my replying 'Not yet,' *he added*, 'If you do not learn the Odes, you will not be fit to converse with.' I retired and studied the Odes.

I have referred to the proposal to transfer to this place the last paragraph of that chapter which might be explained, so as to harmonize with the sentiment of this.—The duke Ching of Ch'î,—see XII, xi. Po-î and Shû-ch'î,—see VI, xxii. The mountain Shâu-yang is to be found probably in the department of 蒲州 in Shansi.

13. CONFUCIUS'S INSTRUCTION OF HIS SON NOT DIFFERENT FROM HIS INSTRUCTION OF THE DISCIPLES GENERALLY. 1. Ch'ǎn K'ang is the Tsze-ch'in of I, x. When Confucius's eldest son was born, the duke of Lû

子也。　聞禮又聞君子之遠其　而喜曰問一得三聞詩、　學禮聞斯二者陳亢退　不學禮無以立鯉退而　庭曰、學禮乎對曰、未也。　他日又獨立、鯉趨而過

3. "Another day, he was in the same way standing alone, when I passed by below the hall with hasty steps, and said to me, 'Have you learned the rules of Propriety?' On my replying 'Not yet,' *he added,* 'If you do not learn the rules of Propriety, your character cannot be established.' I then retired, and learned the rules of Propriety.

4. "I have heard only these two things from him."

5. Ch'ǎn K'ang retired, and, quite delighted, said, "I asked one thing, and I have got three things. I have heard about the Odes. I have heard about the rules of Propriety. I have also heard that the superior man maintains a distant reserve towards his son."

sent the philosopher a present of a carp, on which account he named the child 鯉 (the carp), and afterwards gave him the designation of 伯魚. 子亦有異聞乎, "Have you *also* (i. e., as being his son) heard different instructions?" 2. On 詩 here, and 禮 next paragraph, see on VII, xvii.

Before 不 學, here and below, we must supply a 曰. 3. 立.—see VIII, viii. 4. The force of the 者 is to make the whole = "what I have heard from him are only these two remarks." 5. Confucius is, no doubt, intended by 君 子, but it is best to translate it generally.

邦君之妻、君稱之曰

夫人、夫人自稱曰小童、

邦人稱之曰君夫人、稱

諸異邦、曰寡小君、異邦

人稱之、亦曰君夫人。

CHAPTER XIV. The wife of the prince of a state is called by him FÛ ZĂN. She calls herself HSIÂO T'UNG. The people of the state call her CHÜN FÛ ZĂN, and, to the people of other states, they call her K'WA HSIÂO CHÜN. The people of other states also call her CHÜN FÛ ZĂN.

14. APPELLATIONS FOR THE WIFE OF A RULER. This chapter may have been spoken by Confucius to rectify some disorder of the times, but there is no intimation to that effect. The different appellations may be thus explained:—妻 is 與 已 齊 者, "she who is her husband's equal.' The 夫 in 夫 人 is taken as＝扶, "to support," "to help," so that designation is equivalent to "helpmeet." 童 means either "a youth," or "a girl." The wife modestly calls herself 小 童, "the little girl." The old interpreters take—most naturally— 君 夫 人 as＝君 之 夫 人, "our prince's helpmeet," but the modern commentators take 君 adjectively, as＝主, with reference to the office of the wife to "preside over the internal economy of the palace." On this view 君 夫 人 is "the domestic helpmeet." The ambassador of a prince spoke of him by the style of 寡 君, "our prince of small virtue." After that example of modesty, his wife was styled to the people of other states, "our small prince of small virtue." The people of other states had no reason to imitate her subjects in that, and so they styled her—"your prince's helpmeet," or "the domestic helpmeet"

## BOOK XVII.　YANG HO

之。　也、　子　孔　見　𤣥　　　陽
遇　而　時　子　孔　陽　十　貨
諸　往　其　豚、　子、　貨　七　第
塗。　拜　亡　孔　不　欲　　　　
　　　　　　見、　孔　　　　
　　　　　　歸　　　　　

CHAPTER I.　1. Yang Ho wished to see Confucius, but Confucius would not go to see him. *On this,* he sent a present of a pig to Confucius, who, having chosen a time when Ho was not at home, went to pay his respects *for the gift.* He met him, *however,* on the way.

HEADING OF THIS BOOK.—陽 貨 第 十 七, "Yang Ho, No. 17."—As the last Book commenced with the presumption of the head of the Chî family, who kept his prince in subjection, this begins with an account of an officer, who did for the head of the Chî what he did for the duke of Lû. For this reason—some similarity in the subject matter of the first chapters—this Book, it is said, is placed after the former. It contains 26 chapters.

1. CONFUCIUS'S POLITE BUT DIGNIFIED TREATMENT OF A POWERFUL, BUT USURPING AND UNWORTHY, OFFICER. 1. Yang Ho, known also as Yang Hû (虎), was nominally the principal minister of the Chî family, but its chief was entirely in his hands, and he was scheming to arrogate the whole authority of the state of Lû to himself. He first appears in the Chronicles of Lû, acting against the exiled duke Châo; in 505 B. C., we find him keeping his own chief, Chî Hwan, a prisoner, and, in 501, he is driven out, on the failure of his projects, a fugitive into Ch'î. At the time when the incidents in this chapter occurred, Yang Ho was anxious to get, or appear to get, the support of a man of Confucius's reputation, and finding that the sage would not call on him, he adopted the expedient of sending him a pig, at a time when Confucius was not at home, the rules of ceremony requiring that when a great officer sent a present to a scholar, and the latter was not in his house on its arrival, he had to go to the officer's house to acknowledge it. See the Lî Chî, XI, Sect. iii, 20. 歸 is in the sense of 饋, "to present food," properly "before a superior."

論 語

曰、諾、吾將仕矣。

不可。日月逝矣、歲不我與。孔子

好從事、而亟失時、可謂知乎。曰、

寶、而迷其邦、可謂仁乎。曰、不可。

謂孔子曰、來、予與爾言、曰、懷其

2. *Ho* said to Confucius, "Come, let me speak with
you." He then asked, "Can he be called benevolent
who keeps his jewel in his bosom, and leaves his
country to confusion?" *Confucius* replied, "No."
"Can he be called wise, who is anxious to be engaged
in public employment, and yet is constantly losing the
opportunity of being so?" *Confucius again* said,
"No." "The days and months are passing away; the
years do not wait for us." Confucius said, "Right; I
will go into office."

Confucius, however, was not to be
entrapped. He also *timed* (時, as a
verb) Hû's being away from home
(亡), and went to call on him. 2. 迷
其 邦, "deludes, confuses, his country," but the meaning is only negative,="leaves his country to confusion" 亟, read *k'i*, in 4th tone,
"frequently." 日 月—我 與—all this
is to be taken as the remark of Yang
Ho, and a 曰 supplied before 日. 我
與; 與, in the dictionary, and by the
old interpreters, is here explained, as
in the translation, by 待, "to wait
for."

子曰、性相

近也、習相遠

也。

子曰、唯上

知與下愚不

移。

子之武城、

聞絃歌之聲。

CHAPTER II. The Master said, "By nature, men are nearly alike; by practice, they get to be wide apart."

CHAPTER III. The Master said, "There are only the wise of the highest class, and the stupid of the lowest class, who cannot be changed."

CHAPTER IV. 1. The Master, having come to Wû-ch'ǎng, heard *there* the sound of stringed instruments and singing.

2. THE DIFFERENCES IN THE CHARACTERS OF MEN ARE CHIEFLY OWING TO HABIT. 性, it is contended, is here not the moral constitution of man, absolutely considered, but his complex, actual nature, with its elements of the material, the animal, and the intellectual, by association with which, the perfectly good moral nature is continually being led astray. The moral nature is the same in all, and though the material organism and disposition do differ in different individuals, they are, at first, more nearly alike than they subsequently become. In the 註 疏 we read: "The nature is the constitution received by man at birth, and is *then* still. While it has not been acted on by external things, men are all like one another; they are 近. After it has been acted on by external things, then practice forms, as it were, a second nature. He who practices what is good, becomes the superior man; and he who practices what is not good, becomes the mean man:—men become 相 遠."—No doubt, it is true that many—perhaps most—of the differences among men are owing to habit. This chapter is incorporated with the San Tsze Ching at its commencement.

3. ONLY TWO CLASSES WHOM PRACTICE CANNOT CHANGE. This is a sequel to the last chapter with which it is incorporated in Ho Yen's edition. The case of the 下 愚 would seem to be inconsistent with the doctrine of the perfect goodness of the moral nature of all men. Modern commentators, to get over the difficulty, say that they are the 自 暴 者 and 自 棄 者 of Mencius, IV, Pt. I, x.

4. HOWEVER SMALL THE SPHERE OF GOVERNMENT, THE HIGHEST INFLUENCES OF PROPRIETIES AND MUSIC SHOULD BE EMPLOYED. 1. Wû-ch'ang was in the district of Pî. Tsze-yǔ appears as the commandant of it, in

子、假之言是也前言戲
之耳。
公山弗擾以費畔、召、

子學道則愛人小人學
道則易使也。子曰二三

焉用牛刀子游對曰、昔
者偃也、聞諸夫子曰、君

夫子莞爾而笑曰、割雞

2. Well pleased and smiling, he said, "Why use an ox knife to kill a fowl?"

3. Tsze-yû replied, "Formerly, Master, I heard you say,—'When the man of high station is well instructed, he loves men; when the man of low station is well instructed, he is easily ruled.'"

4. The Master said, "My disciples, Yen's words are right. What I said was only in sport."

CHAPTER V. 1. Kung-shan Fû-zâo, when he was holding Pî, and in an attitude of rebellion, invited the

VI, xii. 弦, "the silken string of a musical instrument," used here for stringed instruments generally. In the 偏旨 we read, "The town was named Wû (武), from its position, precipitous and favorable to military operations, but Tsze-yû had been able, by his course, to transform the people, and make them change their mail and helmets for stringed instruments and singing. This was what made the Master glad." 2. 莞 (read hwan, 3rd tone) 爾, "smilingly." "An ox knife," a large instrument, and not necessary for the death of a fowl. Confucius intends by it the high principles of government employed by Tsze-yû. 3. 君子 and 小人 are here indicative of rank, and not of character. 易使, "are easily employed," i. e., 安分從上, "they rest in their lot, and obey their superiors." 4. 二三子, as in VII, xxiii, et al. Observe the force of the final 耳, = "only."

5. THE LENGTHS TO WHICH CONFUCIUS WAS INCLINED TO GO, TO GET HIS PRINCIPLES CARRIED INTO PRACTICE. Kung-shan Fû-zâo, called also Kung-shan Fû-niû (狃), by designation 子洩, was a confederate of Yang Ho (ch. 1), and according to K'ung

子欲往子路不說、曰、
末之也已、何必公山
氏之之也。子曰夫召
我者、而豈徒哉、如有
用我者、吾其爲東周
乎。
子張問仁於孔子、
孔子曰能行五者於
天下爲仁矣。請問之、

Master to visit him, who was rather inclined to go.

2. Tsze-lû was displeased, and said, "Indeed, you cannot go! Why must you think of going to see Kung-shan?"

3. The Master said, "Can it be without some reason that he has invited ME? If any one employ me, may I not make an eastern Châu?"

CHAPTER VI. Tsze-chang asked Confucius about perfect virtue. Confucius said, "To be able to practice five things everywhere under heaven constitutes perfect virtue." He begged to ask what they

Ân-kwo, and the 日 講, it was after the imprisonment by them, in common, of Chî Hwan, that Fû-zâo sént this invitation to Confucius. Others make the invitation subsequent to Ho's discomfiture and flight to Ch'î. See the 歷 代 統 紀 表, 501 B. c. We must conclude, with Tszo-lû, that Confucius ought not to have thought of accepting the invitation of such a man. 2. The first and last 之 are the verb. 末＝無. 末 之 也 已 ＝"There is no going there. Indeed, there is not." 何 必 公 山 氏 之 之 也, "why must there be going to (之 here＝to) that (such is the force of

氏) Kung-shan?" 3. 夫 召 我 者,—者 is to be taken here as referring expressly to Fû-zâo, while its reference below is more general. The 我 in 用 我, and 吾, are emphatic. The original seat of the Châu dynasty lay west from Lû, and the revival of the principles and government of Wăn and Wû in Lû, or even in Pî, which was but a part of it, might make an eastern Châu, so that Confucius would perform the part of King Wăn.—After all, the sage did not go to Pî.

6. FIVE THINGS THE PRACTICE OF WHICH CONSTITUTES PERFECT VIRTUE.

不善者、君子不入也、

夫子曰親於其身爲

路曰昔者由也聞諸

佛肸召子欲往子

則足以使人。

人任焉、敏則有功、惠、

不侮、寬則得衆信則

曰、恭寬信敏惠恭則

were, and was told, "Gravity, generosity *of soul*, sincerity, earnestness, and kindness. If you are grave, you will not be treated with disrespect. If you are generous, you will win all. If you are sincere, people will repose trust in you. If you are earnest, you will accomplish much. If you are kind, this will enable you to employ the services of others."

CHAPTER VII. 1. Pî Hsî inviting him to visit him, the Master was inclined to go.

2. Tsze-lû said, "Master, formerly I have heard you say, 'When a man in his own person is guilty of doing evil, a superior man will not associate with

於 天 下, "in under heaven" is simply = "anywhere." 信 則 人 任, 一任, in 4th tone, is explained by Chû Hsî by 倚 仗, "to rely upon," a meaning of the term not found in the dictionary. See XX, i, 9.

7. CONFUCIUS, INCLINED TO RE-SPOND TO THE ADVANCES OF AN UN-WORTHY MAN, PROTESTS AGAINST HIS CONDUCT BEING JUDGED BY ORDI-NARY RULES. Compare chap. v; but the invitation of Pî Hsî was subse-quent to that of Kung-shan Fû-zâo, and after Confucius had given up

office in Lû. 1. 佛 (read Pî) Hsî was commandant of Chung-mâu, for *the* chief of the Châo family, in the state of Tsin. 2. 親 於 其 身 爲 不 善 者,—"he who himself, in his own person, does what is not good." 不 入,—according to K'ung An-kwo, = 不 入 其 國, "does not enter his state"; according to Chû Hsî, it = 不 入 其 黨, "does not enter his party." There were two places of the name of Chung-mâu, one belonging to the state of Chăng, and the other to the state of Tsin (晉), which is that

佛肸以中牟畔、子
之往也、如之何。子
曰、然有是言也、不
曰堅乎、磨而不磷、
不曰白乎、涅而不
緇。吾豈匏瓜也哉、
焉能繫而不食。
子曰、由也、女聞
六言六蔽矣乎。對
曰、未也。居、吾語女。

him.' Pî Hsî is in rebellion, holding possession of Chung-mâu; if you go to him, what shall be said?"

3. The Master said, "Yes, I did use these words. But is it not said, that, if a thing be really hard, it may be ground without being made thin? Is it not said, that, if a thing be really white, it may be steeped in a dark fluid without being made black?

4. "Am I a bitter gourd! How can I be hung up out of the way of being eaten?"

CHAPTER VIII. 1. The Master said, "Yû, have you heard the six words to which are attached six beclouding?" Yû replied, "I have not."

2. "Sit down, and I will tell them to you.

intended here, and is referred to the present district of 湯 陰, department of 彰 德, in Honan province. 3. 不 曰 is to be taken interrogatively, as in the translation, Ping's paraphrase is—人豈不曰, "do not men say?" 堅乎云云,—"Is a thing hard, then," etc. Nieh is explained—"black earth in water, which may be used to dye a black color." The application of these strange proverbial sayings is to Confucius himself, as, from his superiority, incapable of being affected by evil communications. 4. This paragraph is variously explained. By some, 匏 瓜 is taken as the name of a star; so that the meaning is—"Am I, like such

and such a star, to be hung up, etc.?" But we need not depart from the proper meaning of the characters. Chû Hsî, with Ho Yen, takes 不 食 actively:—"A gourd can be hung up, because it does not need to eat. But I must go about, north, south, east, and west, to get food." This seems to me very unnatural. The expression is taken passively, as in the translation, in the 日 講, and other works.

8. KNOWLEDGE, ACQUIRED BY LEARNING, IS NECESSARY TO THE COMPLETION OF VIRTUE, BY PRESERVING THE MIND FROM BEING BECLOUDED. 1. 六言是六字, "The six 言 are six characters"; see the

好<sub>三而</sub>仁不好學、其
蔽也愚好智不
好學、其蔽也蕩、
好信不好學、其
蔽也賊好直不
好學、其蔽也絞、
好勇不好學、其
蔽也亂好剛不
好學其蔽也狂。

3. "There is the love of being benevolent without the love of learning;—the beclouding here leads to a foolish simplicity. There is the love of knowing without the love of learning;—the beclouding here leads to dissipation of mind. There is the love of being sincere without the love of learning;—the beclouding here leads to an injurious disregard of consequences. There is the love of straightforwardness without the love of learning;—the beclouding here leads to rudeness. There is the love of boldness without the love of learning;—the beclouding here leads to insubordination. There is the love of firmness without the love of learning;—the beclouding here leads to extravagant conduct."

備旨. They are, therefore, the benevolence, knowledge, sincerity, straightforwardness, boldness, and firmness, mentioned below, all virtues, but yet each, when pursued without discrimination, tending to becloud the mind. 蔽＝遮掩, "to cover and screen"; the primary meaning of it is said to be 小草, "small plants." 2. 居＝"sit down." Tsze-lú had risen, according to the rules of propriety, to give his answer; see the Lî Chî, I, Sect. I, iii, 4, 21; and Confucius tells him to resume his seat. 3. I give here the paraphrase of the 日講 on the first virtue and its beclouding, which may illustrate the manner in which the whole paragraph is developed:—"In all matters, there is a perfectly right and unchangeable principle, which men ought carefully to study, till they have thoroughly examined and apprehended it. Then their actions will be without error, and their virtue may be perfected. For instance, loving is what rules in benevolence. It is certainly a beautiful virtue, but if you only set yourself to love men, and do not care to study to understand the principle of benevolence, then your mind will be beclouded by that loving, and you will be following a man into a well to save him, so that both he and you will perish. Will not this be foolish simplicity?"

獸草木之名。

之事君多識於鳥

以怨邇之事父遠

可以觀可以群可

學夫詩詩可以興。

子曰、小子、何莫

CHAPTER IX. 1. The Master said, "My children, why do you not study the Book of Poetry?

2. "*The Odes* serve to stimulate the mind.

3. "They may be used for purposes of self-contemplation.

4. "They teach the art of sociability.

5. "They show how to regulate feelings of resentment.

6. "From them you learn the more immediate duty of serving one's father, and the remoter one of serving one's prince.

7. "From them we become largely acquainted with the names of birds, beasts, and plants."

9. BENEFITS DERIVED FROM STUDYING THE BOOK OF POETRY. 1. 小子;—see V, xxi; VIII, iii. I translate 詩 here by the "Book of Poetry," because the lesson is supposed to have been given with reference to the compilation of the Odes. The 夫 is *that*, as in XI, ix, 1, *et al.* 2. The descriptions in them of good and evil may have this effect. 3. Their awarding of praise and blame may show a man his own character. 4. Their exhibitions of gravity in the midst of pleasure may have this effect. 羣, as in XV, xxi. 5. Their blending of pity and earnest desire with reproofs may teach how to regulate our resentments. 7. 草 木, "grasses and trees,"=plants generally.

鐘鼓云乎哉。

帛云乎哉樂云樂云、

子曰禮云禮云、玉

正牆面而立也與。

不爲周南召南、其猶

周南召南矣乎、人而

子謂伯魚曰、女爲

CHAPTER X. The Master said to Po-yü, "Do you give yourself to the Châu-nan and the Shâo-nan. The man who has not studied the Châu-nan and the Shâo-nan is like one who stands with his face right against a wall. Is he not so?"

CHAPTER XI. The Master said, "'It is according to the rules of propriety,' they say.—'It is according to the rules of propriety,' they say. Are gems and silk all that is meant by propriety? 'It is music,' they say.—'It is music,' they say. Are bells and drums all that is meant by music?"

10. THE IMPORTANCE OF STUDY-ING THE CHÂU-NAN AND SHÂO-NAN. Châu-nan and Shâo-nan are the titles of the first two books in the Songs of the States, or first part of the Shih-ching. For the meaning of the titles, see the Shih-ching, I, i, and I, ii. They are supposed to inculcate important lessons about personal virtue and family government. Chû Hsî explains 爲 by 學, "to learn," "to study." It denotes the entire mastery of the studies. 女 (for 汝) 爲 云 云 is imperative, the 乎 at the end not being interrogative. 正面牆而立 is for 正面對牆而立. In such a situation, one cannot advance a step, nor see anything. I have added—"Is he not so?" to bring out the force of the 與.—This chapter in the old editions is incorporated with the preceding one.

11. IT IS NOT THE EXTERNAL APPURTENANCES WHICH CONSTITUTE PROPRIETY, NOR THE SOUND OF INSTRUMENTS WHICH CONSTITUTES MUSIC. 禮云 = 所稱爲禮者, "as to what they say is propriety." The words approach the quotation of a common saying. So 樂云. Having thus given the common views of propriety and music, he refutes them in the questions that follow, 樂 and 禮 being present to the mind as the expressions of respect and harmony.

子曰、色厲而內荏、

譬諸小人其猶穿窬

之盜也與。

子曰、鄉原德之賊

也。

子曰、道聽而塗說、

德之棄也。

CHAPTER XII. The Master said, "He who puts on an appearance of stern firmness, while inwardly he is weak, is like one of the small, mean people;—yea, is he not like the thief who breaks through, or climbs over, a wall?"

CHAPTER XIII. The Master said, "Your good, careful people of the villages are the thieves of virtue."

CHAPTER XIV. The Master said, "To tell, as we go along, what we have heard on the way, is to cast away our virtue."

12. THE MEANNESS OF PRESUMPTION AND PUSILLANIMITY CONJOINED. 色 is here not the countenance merely, but the whole outward appearance. 小人 is explained by 細民, and the latter clause shows emphatically to whom, among the low, mean people, the individual spoken of is like—a thief, namely, who is in constant fear of being detected.

13. CONTENTMENT WITH VULGAR WAYS AND VIEWS INJURIOUS TO VIRTUE. See the sentiment of this chapter explained and expanded by Mencius, VII, Pt. II, xxxvii, 7, 8. 原, 4th tone, the same as 愿 See the dictionary, character 愿. 賊, as in XIV, xlvi, though it may be translated here, as generally, by the term "thief."

14. SWIFTNESS TO SPEAK INCOMPATIBLE WITH THE CULTIVATION OF VIRTUE. It is to be understood that what has been heard contains some good lesson. At once to be talking of it without revolving it, and striving to practice it, shows an indifference to our own improvement. 道 is "the way" or "road." 塗 is the same "way," a little farther on.—The glossarist on Ho Yen's work explains 德之棄 as meaning— "is what the virtuous do not do." But this is evidently incorrect.

狂也肆、今之狂
是之亡也。古之
有三疾、今也或
■子曰古者民
無所不至矣。
失之苟患失之、
得之既得之、患
其未得之也、患
與事君也與哉。
■子曰鄙夫、可

CHAPTER XV. 1. The Master said, "There are those mean creatures! How impossible it is along with them to serve one's prince!

2. "While they have not got their aims, their anxiety is how to get them. When they have got them, their anxiety is lest they should lose them.

3. "When they are anxious lest such things should be lost, there is nothing to which they will not proceed.'"

CHAPTER XVI. 1. The Master said, "Anciently, men had three failings, which now perhaps are not to be found.

2. "The high-mindedness of antiquity showed itself in a disregard of small things; the high-mindedness of the present day shows itself in wild license.

15. THE CASE OF MERCENARY OFFICERS, AND HOW IT IS IMPOSSIBLE TO SERVE ONE'S PRINCE ALONG WITH THEM. 1. 與字作共字看, "與=共," i. e., "together with." 與哉是深憾其不可與意, "與哉=a deep-felt lamentation on the unfitness of such persons to be associated with." So, the 備旨. But as the remaining paragraphs are all occupied with describing the mercenaries, we must understand Confucius's object as being to condemn the employment of such creatures, rather than to set forth the impossibility of serving with them. 2. The 之 here, and in par. 3, are all to be understood of place and emolument.

16. THE DEFECTS OF FORMER TIMES BECOME VICES IN THE TIME OF CONFUCIUS. 1. 疾, "bodily sickness," here used metaphorically for "errors," "vices." 或是之亡 (wú),—"perhaps there is the absence of them." The next paragraph shows that worse things had taken their

覆邦家者。
雅樂也惡利口之
朱也、惡鄭聲之亂
子曰、惡紫之奪
鮮矣仁。
子曰、巧言令色、
也詐而已矣。
之愚也直今之愚
今之矜也忿戾、古
也蕩、古之矜也廉、

The stern dignity of antiquity showed itself in grave reserve; the stern dignity of the present day shows itself in quarrelsome perverseness. The stupidity of antiquity showed itself in straightforwardness; the stupidity of the present day shows itself in sheer deceit."

CHAPTER XVII. The Master said, "Fine words and an insinuating appearance are seldom associated with virtue."

CHAPTER XVIII. The Master said, "I hate the manner in which purple takes away *the luster of* vermilion. I hate the way in which the songs of Chăng confound the music of the Yâ. I hate those who with their sharp mouths overthrow kingdoms and families "

place. 2. That 肆 is only "a disregard of smaller matters," or conventionalisms, appears from its opposition to 蕩, which has a more intense signification than in chap. viii. 矜, as in XV, xxi, also with an intenser meaning. 廉, "an angular corner," which cannot be impinged against without causing pain. It is used for "purity," "modesty," but the meaning here appears to be that given in the translation.

17. A repetition of I, iii.

18. CONFUCIUS'S INDIGNATION AT THE WAY IN WHICH THE WRONG OVERCAME THE RIGHT. 紫之奪朱, —see X, vi, 2. 朱 is here as "a correct" color, though it is not among the five such colors mentioned in the note there. 紫 I have here translated—"purple." "Black and carnation mixed," it is said, "give 紫." "The songs or sounds of Chăng,"—see XV, x. "The *yâ*,"—see on IX, xiv. 國 家 is a common designation for "a state," the 國, or kingdom of the prince, embracing the 家, "families or clans," of his great officers. For 國 we here have 邦.

子曰予欲無言。

子貢曰子如不言、

則小子何述焉。子

曰天何言哉、四時

行焉、百物生焉、天

何言哉。

孺悲欲見孔子、

孔子辭以疾、將命

CHAPTER XIX. 1. The Master said, "I would prefer not speaking."

2. Tsze-kung said, "If you, Master, do not speak, what shall we, your disciples, have to record?"

3. The Master said, "Does Heaven speak? The four seasons pursue their courses, and all things are *continually* being produced, *but* does Heaven say anything?"

CHAPTER XX. Zû Pei wished to see Confucius, but Confucius declined, on the ground of being sick, to see him. When the bearer of this message went out

19. THE ACTIONS OF CONFUCIUS WERE LESSONS AND LAWS, AND NOT HIS WORDS MERELY. Such is the scope of this chapter, according to Chû Hsî and his school. The older commentators say that it is a caution to men to pay attention to their conduct rather than to their words. This interpretation is far-fetched, but, on the other hand, it is not easy to defend Confucius from the charge of presumption in comparing himself to Heaven. 3. 天何言哉, "Does Heaven speak,"—better than "what does Heaven say?"

20. HOW CONFUCIUS COULD BE "NOT AT HOME," AND YET GIVE

INTIMATION TO THE VISITOR OF HIS PRESENCE. Of Zû Pei little is known. He was a small officer of Lû, and had at one time been in attendance on Confucius to receive his instructions. There must have been some reason—some fault in him—why Confucius would not see him on the occasion in the text; and that he might understand that it was on that account, and not because he was really sick, that he declined his visit, the sage acted as we are told;—see the Li Chî, XVIII, Sect. II, i, 22. It is said that his fault was in trying to see the Master without using the services of an

穀既升鑽燧改火、

必崩舊穀既沒新

壞三年不爲樂樂

三年不爲禮禮必

喪期已久矣君子

宰我問三年之

使之聞之。

者出戶、取瑟而歌、

at the door, (the Master) took his lute and sang to it, in order that Pei might hear him.

CHAPTER XXI. 1. Tsâi Wo asked about the three years' mourning *for parents, saying* that one year was long enough.

2. "If the superior man," said he, "abstains for three years from the observances of propriety, those observances will be quite lost. If for three years he abstains from music, music will be ruined.

3. *"Within a year* the old grain is exhausted, and the new grain has sprung up, and, in procuring fire by friction, we go through all the changes of wood for that purpose. After a complete year, the mourning may stop."

internuncius (將 命 者);—see XIV, xlvii. I translate the last 之 by *him,* but it refers generally to the preceding sentence, and might be left untranslated.

21. THE PERIOD OF THREE YEARS' MOURNING FOR PARENTS; IT MAY NOT ON ANY ACCOUNT BE SHORTENED; THE REASON OF IT. 1. We must understand a 日, either before 三, or, as I prefer, before 期, which is read *chî,* in 1st tone, the same as 朞, XIII, x. On the three years' mourning, see the 35th Book of the Lî Chî. Nominally extending to three years, that period comprehended properly but 25 months, and at most 27 months. 2. 此 以 人 事 言 之,— Tsze-wo finds here a reason for his view in the necessity of "human affairs." 3. 此 以 天 時 言 之,—he finds here a reason for his view in "the seasons of heaven." 燧 means either "a piece of metal,"—a speculum, with which to take fire from the sun, or "a piece of wood," with which to get fire by friction or "boring" (鑽). It has here the latter meaning. Certain woods were assigned to the several seasons to be employed for this purpose, the elm and willow, for instance, to spring,

也子生三年、然後免於父

之宰我出子曰予之不仁

安、故不爲也今女安、則爲

旨不甘聞樂不樂居處不

則爲之夫君子之居喪、食

夫錦、於女安乎。曰、安女安、

期可已矣子曰、食夫稻、衣

4. The Master said, "If you were, *after a year*, to eat good rice, and wear embroidered clothes, would you feel at ease?" "I should," replied Wo.

5. The Master said, "If you can feel at ease, do it. But a superior man, during the whole period of mourning, does not enjoy pleasant food which he may eat, nor derive pleasure from music which he may hear. He also does not feel at ease, if he is comfortably lodged. Therefore he does not do *what you propose*. But now you feel at ease and may do it."

6. Tsâi Wo then went out, and the Master said, "This shows Yü's want of virtue. It is not till a child is three years old that it is allowed to leave the

the date and almond trees to summer, etc. 鑽燧改火＝鑽燧以取火, 又改乎四時之木, "In boring with the 燧 to get fire, we have changed from wood to wood through the trees appropriate to the four seasons." 4. Coarse food and coarse clothing were appropriate, though in varying degree, to all the period of mourning. Tsze-wo is strangely insensible to the home-put argument of the Master. 稻 is to be understood here as 穀之美者, "the most excellent grain." The 夫 are demonstrative. 6. 予之不仁也 responds to all that has gone before,

爲之猶賢乎已。

心難矣哉不有博弈者乎、

豆子曰飽食終日、無所用

愛於其父母乎。

之通喪也予也、有三年之

母之懷、夫三年之喪、天下

arms of its parents. And the three years' mourning is universally observed throughout the empire. Did Yü enjoy the three years' love of his parents?"

CHAPTER XXII. The Master said, "Hard is it to deal with him, who will stuff himself with food the whole day, without applying his mind to anything *good!* Are there not gamesters and chess players? To be one of these would still be better than doing nothing at all."

and forms a sort of *apodosis.* Confucius added, it is said, the remarks in this paragraph that they might be reported to Tsai Wo (called also Tsze-wo), lest he should "feel at ease" to go and do as he said he could. Still the reason which the Master finds for the statute-period of mourning for parents must be pronounced puerile.

22. THE HOPELESS CASE OF GLUT-TONY AND IDLENESS. 難 矣 哉,—XV, xvi. 博 and 弈 are two things. To the former I am unable to give a name; but see some account of it quoted in the 集 證, *in loc.* 弈 is "to play at chess," of which there are two kinds,—the 圍 棋, played with 361-pieces, and referred to the ancient Yâo as its inventor, and the 象 棋, or ivory chess, played with 32 pieces, and having a great analogy to our European game. Its invention · is attributed to the emperor Wû, of the later Châu dynasty, in our 6th century. It was probably borrowed from India. 爲 之,—之 refers to 博 弈. 賢 for 勝, as in XI, xv, 1.

下流而訕上者、惡勇而無禮

曰、有惡惡稱人之惡者、惡居

醫子貢曰、君子亦有惡乎子

為盜。

無義為亂、小人有勇而無義、

君子義以為上、君子有勇而

醫子路曰、君子尚勇乎子曰、

CHAPTER XXIII. Tsze-lû said, "Does the superior
man esteem valor?" The Master said, "The superior
man holds righteousness to be of highest importance.
A man in a superior situation, having valor without
righteousness, will be guilty of insubordination; one
of the lower people, having valor without righteousness, will commit robbery."

CHAPTER XXIV. 1. Tsze-kung said, "Has the
superior man his hatreds also?" The Master said,
"He has his hatreds. He hates those who proclaim
the evil of others. He hates the man who, being in a
low station, slanders his superiors. He hates those
who have valor *merely*, and are unobservant of

23. VALOR TO BE VALUED ONLY
IN SUBORDINATION TO RIGHTEOUS-
NESS; ITS CONSEQUENCES APART FROM
THAT. The first two 君子 are to be
understood of the man superior in
virtue. The third brings in the idea
of rank, with 小人 as its correlate.

24. CHARACTERS DISLIKED BY CON-
FUCIUS AND TSZE-KUNG. 1. Tsze-
kung is understood to have intended
Confucius himself by "the superior
man." 流 is here in the sense of
"class." 下流—下位之人, "men
of low station." In 君子亦有惡乎

怨。

之則不孫、遠之則

小人爲難養也、近

子曰、唯女子與

許以爲直者。

不孫以爲勇者、惡

惡徼以爲知者、惡

曰、賜也、亦有惡乎。

者、惡果敢而窒者。

propriety. He hates those who are forward and determined, and, *at the same time*, of contracted understanding."

2. *The Master then* inquired, "Ts'ze, have you also your hatreds?" *Tsze-kung replied*, "I hate those who pry out matters, and ascribe the knowledge to their wisdom. I hate those who are *only* not modest, and think that they are valorous. I hate those who make known secrets, and think that they are straightforward."

CHAPTER XXV. The Master said, "Of all people, girls and servants are the most difficult to behave to. If you are familiar with them, they lose their humility. If you maintain a reserve towards them, they are discontented."

the force of 亦 is to oppose 惡 to 愛, "hatreds," to "loves." 2. Hsing P'ing takes 子 貢 as the nominative to 曰,—"he went on to say, *I, Ts'ze, also*," etc. The modern commentators, however, more correctly, understand 子, "the Master," as nominative to 曰, and supply another 曰 before 惡 徼.

25. THE DIFFICULTY HOW TO

TREAT CONCUBINES AND SERVANTS. 女 子 does not mean *women* generally, but girls, i. e., concubines. 小 人, in the same way, is here boys, i. e., servants. 養, "to nourish," "to keep,"=to behave to. The force of 唯, "only," is as indicated in the translation.—We hardly expect such an utterance, though correct in itself, from Confucius.

子曰、年四十而見惡焉、其終也已。

**CHAPTER XXVI.** The Master said, "When a man at forty is the object of dislike, he will always continue what he is."

26. THE DIFFICULTY OF IMPROVEMENT IN ADVANCED YEARS. According to Chinese views, at forty a man is at his best in every way. After 惡 we must understand 于 君 子,—"the object of dislike to the superior man." 其 終＝其 終 于 此, "he will end in this."—Youth is doubtless the season for improvement, but the sentiment of the chapter is too broadly stated.

## BOOK XVIII. WEI TSZE

微子第十八 微子 去之、箕子為之、奴比干、諫而死。

**CHAPTER I.** 1. The viscount of Wei withdrew *from the court.* The viscount of Chî became a slave *to Châu.* Pî-kan remonstrated with him and died.

HEADING OF THIS BOOK.—微 子 第 十 八. "The viscount of Wei, No. 18." This Book, consisting of only eleven chapters, treats of various individuals famous in Chinese history, as eminent for the way in which they discharged their duties, to their sovereign, or for their retirement from public service. It commemorates also some of the worthies of Confucius's days, who lived in retirement rather than be in office in so degenerate times. The object of the whole is to illustrate and vindicate the course of Confucius himself.

1. THE VISCOUNTS OF WEI AND CHÎ, AND PÎ-KAN:—THREE WORTHIES OF THE YIN DYNASTY. 1. Wei-tsze and Chî-tsze are continually repeated by Chinese, as if they were proper names. But Wei and Chî were the names of two small states, presided over by chiefs of the Tsze, or fourth degree of nobility, called *viscounts,* for want of a more exact term. They both appear to have been within the limits of the present Shansi, Wei being referred to the district of 潞 城, department 潞 安, and Chî' to 榆 社, department 遼 州. The chief of Wei was an elder brother by a concubine of the tyrant Châu, the last sovereign of the Yin dynasty, 1154-1122 B. C. The chief of Chî,

孔子曰、殷有三仁
焉。

二仁

柳下惠爲士師、

三黜、人曰、子未可

以去乎曰、直道而

事人、焉往而不三

黜、枉道而事人、何

必去父母之邦。

2. Confucius said, "The Yin dynasty possessed *these* three men of virtue."

CHAPTER II. Hûi of Liû-hsiâ, being chief criminal judge, was thrice dismissed from his office. Some one said to him, "Is it not yet time for you, sir, to leave this?" He replied, "Serving men in an upright way, where shall I go to, and not experience such a thrice-repeated dismissal? If I choose to serve men in a crooked way, what necessity is there for me to leave the country of my parents?"

and Pî-kan, were both uncles of the tyrant. The first, seeing that remonstrances availed nothing, withdrew from court, wishing to preserve the sacrifices of their family amid the ruin which he saw was impending. The second was thrown into prison, and, to escape death, feigned madness. He was used by Châu as a buffoon. Pî-kan, persisting in his remonstrances, was put barbarously to death, the tyrant having his heart torn out, that he might see, he said, a sage's heart. The 之 in 去 之 is explained by 其 位, "his place." Its reference may also be to 紂, the tyrant himself. On 爲 之 奴, compare 爲 之 宰, V, vii, 3, *et al.*

2. How HÛI OF LIÛ-HSIÂ, THOUGH OFTEN DISMISSED FROM OFFICE, STILL CLEAVED TO HIS COUNTRY. Liû-hsiâ Hûi,—see XV, xiii. The office of the 士 師 is described in the Châu-lî, XXXIV, iii. He was under the 司 寇, or minister of crime, but with many subordinate magistrates under him. 三, 4th tone, as in V, xix; XI, v. We may translate 黜, "was dismissed from office," or "retired from office." 人 =或 人—Some remarks akin to that in the text are ascribed to Hûi's wife. It is observed by the commentator Hû (胡) that there ought to be another paragraph, giving Confucius's judgment upon Hûi's conduct, but it has been lost.

季桓子受之三

齊人歸女樂。

孔子行。

老矣、不能用也。

之閒待之曰、吾

吾不能、以季孟

子、曰、若季氏、則

齊景公待孔

CHAPTER III. The duke Ching of Ch'î, *with reference to the manner in which* he should treat Confucius, said, "I cannot treat him as I would the chief of the Chî family. I will treat him in a manner between that accorded to the chief of the Chî, and that given to the chief of the Măng family." He *also* said, "I am old; I cannot use *his doctrines.*" Confucius took his departure.

CHAPTER IV. The people of Ch'î sent *to Lû* a present of female musicians, which Chî Hwan received,

3. HOW CONFUCIUS LEFT CH'Î, WHEN THE DUKE COULD NOT APPRECIATE AND EMPLOY HIM. It was in the year 517 B. C. that Confucius went to Ch'î. The remarks about how he should be treated, etc., are to be understood as having taken place in consultation between the duke and his ministers, and being afterwards reported to the sage. The Măng family (see II, v) was in the time of Confucius much weaker than the Chî. The chief of it was only the 下 鄉, lowest noble of Lû, while the Chî was the highest. Yet for the duke of Ch'î to treat Confucius better than the duke of Lû treated the chief of the Măng family, was not dishonoring the sage. We must suppose that Confucius left Ch'î because of the duke's concluding remarks.

4. HOW CONFUCIUS GAVE UP OFFICIAL SERVICE IN Lû. In the ninth year of the duke Ting, Confucius reached the highest point of his official service. He was minister of crime, and also, according to the general opinion, acting premier. He effected in a few months a wonderful renovation of the state, and the neighboring countries began to fear that under his administration, Lû would overtop and subdue them all. To prevent this, the duke of Ch'î sent a present to Lû of fine horses and of 80 highly accomplished beauties. The duke of Lû was induced to receive these by the advice of the head of the Chî family, Chî Sze (斯), or Chî Hwan. The sage was forgotten; government was neglected. Confucius, indignant and sorrowful, withdrew from office, and for a time,

而辟之不得與之言。 孔子下、欲與之言趨 而、今之從政者殆而。 來者猶可追已而已 德之衰往者不可諫、 孔子、曰鳳兮鳳兮、何 楚狂接輿歌而過 日不朝、孔子行。

and for three days no court was held.　Confucius took his departure.

CHAPTER V.　1. The madman of Ch'û, Chieh-yü, passed by Confucius, singing and saying, "O FĂNG! O FĂNG! How is your virtue degenerated! As to the past, reproof is useless; but the future may still be provided against. Give up *your vain pursuit.* Give up *your vain pursuit.* Peril-awaits those who now engage in affairs of government."

2.　Confucius alighted and wished to converse with him, but Chieh-yü hastened away, so that he could not talk with him.

from the country too. 歸 as in XVII, i, 1. 齊 人, "the people of Ch'î,' is to be understood of the duke and his ministers.

5. CONFUCIUS AND THE MADMAN OF CH'Û, WHO BLAMES HIS NOT RE-TIRING FROM THE WORLD. 1. Chieh-yü was the designation of one Lû T'ung (陸 通), a native of Ch'û, who feigned himself mad, to escape being importuned to engage in public service. There are several notices of him in the 集 證, *in loc.* It must have been about the year 489 B. C.

that the incident in the text occurred. By the *făng,* which we commonly translate by *phœnix,* his satirizer or adviser intended Confucius; see IX, viii. The three 而 in the song are simply expletives, pauses for the voice to help out the rhythm. 追, "to overtake," generally with reference to the past, but here it has reference to the future. In the dictionary, with reference to this passage, it is explained by 及, "to come up to," and 救, "to save,"= to provide against.

長沮桀溺耦而耕孔子

過之、使子路問津焉長沮

曰夫執輿者為誰子路曰、

為孔丘。曰、是魯孔丘與。曰、

是也。曰、是知津矣。問於桀

溺桀溺曰、子為誰。曰、為仲

由。曰、是魯孔丘之徒與。對

CHAPTER VI. 1. Ch'ang-tsü and Chieh-nî were at work in the field together, when Confucius passed by them, and sent Tsze-lû to inquire for the ford.

2. Ch'ang-tsü said, "Who is he that holds the reins in the carriage there?" Tsze-lû told him, "It is K'ung Ch'iû." "Is it not K'ung Ch'iû of Lû?" asked he. "Yes," was the reply, to which the other rejoined, "He knows the ford."

3. *Tsze-lû then* inquired of Chieh-nî, who said to him, "Who are you, sir?" He answered, "I am Chung Yû." "Are you not the disciple of K'ung Ch'iû of Lû?" asked the other. "I am," replied he,

6. CONFUCIUS AND THE TWO RE-CLUSES, CH'ANG-TSÜ AND CHIEH-NÎ; WHY HE WOULD NOT WITHDRAW FROM THE WORLD. 1. The surnames and names of these worthies are not known. It is supposed that they belonged to Ch'û, like the hero of the last chapter, and that the interview with them occurred about the same time. The designations in the text are descriptive of their character, and = "the long Rester (沮 者 止 而 不 出)" and "the firm Recluse (溺 者 沉 而 不 返)." What kind of field labor is here denoted by 耕 cannot be determined. 2. 執 輿 者, "he who holds the carriage," = 執 轡 在 車 者, as in the translation. It is supposed that it was the remarkable appearance of Confucius which elicited the inquiry. In 是 知 津, 是 = "*he*"; i. e., he, going about everywhere and seeking to be employed, ought to know the ford. 3. 滔 滔 者 天 下,—the speaker here probably pointed to the surging waters before

群、吾非斯人之徒與而

憮然曰鳥獸不可與同

不輟子路行以告夫子

若從辟世之士哉耰而

與其從辟人之士也豈

是也、而誰以易之且而

曰、然曰、滔滔者天下皆

and then Chieh-nî said to him, "Disorder, like a swell-ing flood, spreads over the whole empire, and who is he that will change its state *for you?* Than follow one who merely withdraws from this one and that one, had you not better follow those who have with-drawn from the world altogether?" *With this* he fell to covering up the seed, *and proceeded with his work,* without stopping.

4. Tsze-lû went and reported their remarks, when the Master observed with a sigh, "It is impossible to associate with birds and beasts, as if they were the same with us. If I associate not with these people,—

them, for the ford to cross which the travelers were asking. Trans-lating literally, we should say— "swelling and surging, such is all the empire." 且 而,—而＝汝, "you." 辟 人, 辟 世,—comp. XIV, xxxix. 耰, "an implement for drawing the soil over the seed." It may have been a hoe, or a rake. 4. 徒 is here—類, "class." 吾 非 斯 人 之

徒 與 而 誰 與,＝"If I am not to associate with the class of these men, i. e., with mankind, with whom am I to associate? I cannot associate with birds and beasts." 丘 不 與 易,—不 與, it is said, 作 無 用, —"there would be no use." Liter-ally, "I should not have for whom to change *the state of the empire.*"— The use of 夫子 in this paragraph is

誰與、天下有道丘

不與易也。

子路從而後、遇

丈人以杖荷蓧。

路問曰子見夫子

乎丈人曰四體不

勤、五穀不分孰爲

夫子植其杖而芸。

with mankind,—with whom shall I associate? If right principles prevailed through the empire, there would be no use for me to change its state."

CHAPTER VII. 1. Tsze-lû, following the Master, happened to fall behind, when he met an old man, carrying across his shoulder on a staff a basket for weeds. Tsze-lû said to him, "Have you seen my master, sir?" The old man replied, "Your four limbs are unaccustomed to toil; you cannot distinguish the five kinds of grain:—who is your master?" With this, he planted his staff in the ground, and proceeded to weed.

remarkable. It must mean "his Master" and not "the Master." The compiler of this chapter can hardly have been a disciple of the sage.

7. TSZE-LU'S RENCONTER WITH AN OLD MAN, A RECLUSE: HIS VINDICATION OF HIS MASTER'S COURSE. This incident in this chapter was probably nearly contemporaneous with those which occupy the two previous ones. Some say that the old man belonged to Sheh, which was a part of Ch'û. 1. 後, as in XI, xxii,—顔淵後. 丈人 is used for "an old man" as early as in the Yî-ching, hexagram 師; perhaps by taking 丈 as＝杖, "a

staff," the phrase comes to have that signification. 蓧 is simply called by Chû Hsî—竹器, "a bamboo basket." The 說文 defines it as in the translation,—芸田器. 四體, "the four bodies," i. e., the arms and legs, the four limbs of the body, "The five grains" are 稻, 黍, 稷, 麥, and 菽, "rice, millet, panicled millet, wheat, and pulse." But they are sometimes otherwise enumerated. We have also "the six kinds," "the eight kinds," "the nine kinds," and perhaps other classifications. 2. Tsze-lû, standing with his arms across his breast, indicated his respect, and won upon

之義、如之何其廢之、欲潔
長幼之節不可廢也、君臣
則行矣子路曰不仕無義、
隱者也、使子路反見之、至、
焉。明日子路行以告子曰、
鷄、爲黍而食之、見其二子
子路拱而立止子路宿、殺

2. Tsze-lû joined his hands across his breast, and stood *before him*.

3. The old man kept Tsze-lû to pass the night in his house, killed a fowl, prepared millet, and feasted him. He also introduced to him his two sons.

4. Next day, Tsze-lû went on his way, and reported *his adventure*. The Master said, "He is a recluse," and sent Tsze-lû back to see him again, but when he got to the place, the old man was gone.

5. Tsze-lû then said *to the family*, "Not to take office is not righteous. If the relations between old and young may not be neglected, how is it that he sets aside the duties that should be observed between sovereign and minister? Wishing to maintain his

the old man. 3. 食 (*tsze*), the 4th tone, "entertained," "feasted." The dictionary defines it with this meaning, 以 食 與 人, "to give food to people." 5. Tszo-lû is to be understood as here speaking the sentiments of the Master, and vindicating his course. 長 幼 之 節 refers to the manner in which the old man had introduced his sons to him the evening before, and to all the orderly intercourse between old and young,

不辱其身、伯夷叔齊

少連子曰不降其志、

仲夷逸朱張柳下惠、

逸民、伯夷、叔齊、虞

之不行、已知之矣。

之仕也、行其義也、道

其身、而亂大倫、君子

personal purity, he allows that great relation to come
to confusion.  A superior man takes office, and performs the righteous duties belonging to it.  As to the
failure of right principles to make progress, he is
aware of that."

CHAPTER VIII.  1.  The men who have retired to
privacy from the world have been Po-î, Shû-ch'î, Yü-
chung, Î-yî, Chû-chang, Hûi of Liû-hsiâ, and Shâo-
lien.

2.  The Master said, "Refusing to surrender their
wills, or to submit to any taint in their persons;—
such, I think, were Po-î and Shû-ch'î.

which he had probably seen in the
family.  何 其 廢 之,—其 refers to
the old man, but there is an indefi-
niteness about the Chinese construction, which does not make it so
personal as our "he"  So Confucius
is intended by 君 子, though that
phrase may be taken in its general
acceptation.  "He is aware of that;"
--but will not therefore shrink from
his righteous service.

8.  CONFUCIUS'S JUDGMENT OF
FORMER WORTHIES WHO HAD KEPT
FROM THE WORLD.  HIS OWN GUID-
ING PRINCIPLE.  1. 逸 民,—"retired

people."  民 is used here just as we
sometimes use *people*, without reference to the rank of the individuals
spoken of.  The 備 旨 quotes, upon
the phrase, from the 說 統 to the
following effect:—"逸 here is not
the 逸 of seclusion, but is characteristic of men of large souls, who
cannot be measured by ordinary
rules.  They may display their character by retiring from the world.
They may display it also in the
manner of their discharge of office."
The phrase is guarded in this way, I
suppose, because of its application

放言身中清廢

虞仲夷逸隱居

其斯而已矣。謂〔四章〕

言中倫行中慮、

連降志辱身矣、

與謂柳下惠少〔三章〕

3. "Ît may be said of Hûi of Liû-hsiâ, and of Shâo-lien, that they surrendered their wills, and submitted to taint in their persons, but their words corresponded with reason, and their actions were such as men are anxious to see. This is all that is to be remarked in them.

4. "It may be said of Yü-chung and Î-yî, that, while they hid themselves in their seclusion, they gave a license to their words; but in their persons, they succeeded in preserving their púrity, and, in their retirement, they acted according to the exigency of the times.

to Hûi of Liû-hsiâ, who did not obstinately withdraw from the world. Po-î and Shú-ch'î,—see V, xxii. Yu-chung should probably be Wû (吳)-chung. He was the brother of T'âi-po, called Chung-yung (仲雍), and is mentioned in the note on VIII, i. He retired with T'âi-po among the barbarous tribes, then occupying the country of Wû, and succeeded to the chieftaincy of them on his brother's death. "Î-yî and Chû-chang," says Chû Hsî, "are not found in the *ching* and *chwan* (經傳)." See, however, the 集證, *in loc.* From a passage in the Lî Chî, XVIII, ii, 14, it appears that Shâolien belonged to one of the barbarous tribes on the east but was well acquainted with, and observant of, the rules of Propriety, particularly those relating to mourning. 3. The 謂 at the beginning of this paragraph and the next are very perplexing. As there is neither 謂 nor 曰 at the beginning of par. 5, the 子曰 of par. 2 must evidently be carried on to the end of the chapter. Commentators do not seem to have felt the difficulty, and understand 謂 to be in the 3rd person.—"He, i. e., the Master, said," etc. I have made the best of it I could. 倫=義理之次第, "the order and series of righteousness and principles." 慮=人心

秦鼓方叔、入　蔡。四飯缺適　楚。三飯繚適　齊亞飯干適　大師摯適　不可。　於是、無可無　中權。我則異

5. "I am different from all these. I have no course for which I am predetermined, and no course against which I am predetermined."

CHAPTER IX. 1. The grand music master, Chih, went to Ch'î.

2. Kan, *the master of the band at* the second meal, went to Ch'û. Liâo, *the band master at* the third meal, went to Ts'âi. Chüěh, *the band master at* the fourth meal, went to Ch'in.

3. Fang-shû, the drum master, withdrew to *the north of* the river.

之思慮, "the thoughts and solicitudes of men's hearts." 4. "Living in retirement, they gave a license to their words,"—this is intended to show that in this respect they were inferior to Hûi and Shâo-lien, who 言中倫. 權,—see note on IX, xxix. 5. Confucius's openness to act according to circumstances is to be understood as being always in subordination to right and propriety.

9. THE DISPERSION OF THE MUSICIANS OF Lû. The dispersion here narrated is supposed to have taken place in the time of Duke Âi. When once Confucius had rectified the music of Lû (IX, xiv), the musicians would no longer be assisting in the prostitution of their art; and so, as the disorganization and decay proceeded, the chief among them withdrew to other states, or from society altogether. 1. 大＝太, as opposed to 少, par. 5, "grand," and "assistant." "The music master, Chih," — see VIII, xv. 2. The princes of China, it would appear, had music at their meals, and a separate band performed at each meal, or, possibly, the band might be the same, but under the superintendence of a separate officer at each meal. The king had four meals a day, and the princes of states only three, but it was the prerogative of the duke of Lû to use the ceremonies of the royal court. Nothing is said here of the band master at the first meal, perhaps because he did not leave Lû, or nothing may have been known of him. 3. "The river" is, of course, "the Yellow River." According to the 四書釋地, article LVII, the expressions 入於河, 入於漢 are to be taken as meaning simply,—"lived on the banks of the Ho, the Han."

人。故棄也無求備於一
　　故舊無大故、則不
　　使大臣怨乎不以、
　　君子不施其親、不
　〔五節〕周公謂魯公曰、
　入於海。
　漢少師陽、擊磬襄、
　〔四節〕於河播鼗武、入於

4. Wû, the master of the hand drum, withdrew to the Han.

5. Yang, the assistant music master, and Hsiang, master of the musical stone, withdrew to *an island in the sea.*

CHAPTER X. The duke of Châu addressed *his son,* the duke of Lû, saying, "The virtuous prince does not neglect his relations. He does not cause the great ministers to repine at his not employing them. Without some great cause, he does not dismiss from their offices the members of old families. He does not seek in one man talents for every employment."

The interpretation in the translation is after Chû Hsî, who follows the glossarist Hsing Ping. The ancient sovereigns had their capitals mostly north and east of "the river," hence, the country north of it was called 河內, and to the south of it was called 河外. I do not see, however, the applicability of this to the Han, which is a tributary of the Yang-tze, flowing through Hupeh. 5. It was from Hsiang that Confucius learned to play on the 琴.

10. INSTRUCTIONS OF CHÂU-KUNG TO HIS SON ABOUT GOVERNMENT; A GENEROUS CONSIDERATION OF OTHERS TO BE CHERISHED. 周公,—see VII, v. The facts of the case seem to be that the duke of Châu was himself appointed to the principality of Lû, but being detained at court by his duties to the young king 成; he sent his son 伯禽, here called "the duke of Lû," to that state as his representative. 君子 contains here the ideas both of rank and virtue. 施 is read in the 3rd tone, with the same meaning as 弛. Chû Hsî, indeed, seems to think that 弛 should be in the text, but we have 施 in Ho Yen, who gives K'ung Ân-kwo's interpretation:—施易也, 不以他人之親易己之親, "施 is *to change.* He does not substitute the relatives of other men in the room of his own relatives." 以,—here＝用, "to use," "to employ." 求備,—see XIII, xxv.

隨、叔　忽、仲　達、八　畕
季　夏、叔　突、伯　士、周
騧。季　夜、仲　适、伯　有

**CHAPTER XI.** To Châu belonged the eight officers, Po-tâ, Po-kwô, Chung-tû, Chung-hwû, Shû-yâ, Shû-hsiâ, Chî-sui, and Chî-kwa.

11. THE FRUITFULNESS OF THE EARLY TIME OF THE CHÂU DYNASTY IN ABLE OFFICERS. The eight individuals mentioned here are said to have been brothers, four pairs of twins by the same mother. This is intimated in their names, the two first being 伯, or *primi*, the next pair 仲, or *secundi*, the third 叔, or *tertii*, and the last two 季. One mother, bearing twins four times in succession, and all proving distinguished men, showed the vigor of the early days of the dynasty in all that was good.—It is disputed to what reign these brothers belonged, nor is their surname ascertained. 達, 适, 突, 云云 seem to be honorary designations.

## BOOK XIX. TSZE-CHANG

命、危　士、張　畕　九　第　子
見　致　見　曰、子　　十　張

**CHAPTER I.** Tsze-chang said, "The scholar, *trained for public duty*, seeing threatening danger, is prepared to sacrifice his life. When the opportunity of gain is

HEADING OF THIS BOOK.—子 張 第 十 九, "Tsze-chang, No. 19." Confucius does not appear personally in this Book at all. Chû Hsî says: "This Book records the words of the disciples, Tsze-hsiâ being the most frequent speaker, and Tsze-kung next to him. For in the Confucian school, after Yen Yuan there was no one of such discriminating understanding as Tsze-kung, and after Tsäng Shän no one of such firm sincerity as Tsze-hsiâ." The disciples deliver their sentiments very much after the manner of their master, and yet we can discern a falling off from him.

1. TSZE-CHANG'S OPINION OF THE CHIEF ATTRIBUTES OF THE TRUE SCHOLAR. 士.—see note on XII, xx, 1. Tsze-chang there asks Confucius about the scholar-officer. 見 危,—the danger is to be understood as threatening his country. Hsing Ping,

交
於
子
張
。
子
張
曰
、

子
夏
之
門
人
問

爲
有
、
焉
能
爲
亡
。

弘
信
道
不
篤
、
焉
能

子
張
曰
、
執
德
不

思
哀
、
其
可
已
矣
。

得
思
義
祭
思
敬
、
喪

presented to him, he thinks of righteousness. In
sacrificing, his thoughts are reverential. In mourning,
his thoughts are about the grief *which he should feel.*
Such a man commands our approbation indeed."

CHAPTER II. Tsze-chang said, "When a man holds
fast virtue, but without seeking to enlarge it, and
believes right principles, but without firm sincerity,
what account can be made of his existence or non-
existence?"

CHAPTER III. The disciples of Tsze-hsiâ asked
Tsze-chang about the principles that should charac-
terize mutual intercourse. Tsze-chàng asked, "What

indeed, confines the danger to the person of the sovereign, for whom the officer will gladly sacrifice his life. 致命 is the same as 致其身 in I, vii. 已 is not to be explained by 止, as in 而已. The combination 已矣 has occurred before, and＝也已 in I, xiv. It greatly intensifies the preceding 可.

2. TSZE-CHANG ON NARROW-MIND-EDNESS AND A HESITATING FAITH. Hsing Ping interprets this chapter in the following way:—"If a man grasp hold of his virtue, and is not widened and enlarged by it, although he may believe good principles, he cannot be sincere and generous." But it is better to take the clauses as coördinate, and not dependent on each other. With 執德不弘 we may compare XV, xxviii, which suggests the taking 弘 actively. The two last clauses are perplexing. Chû Hsî, after Ân-kwo apparently, makes them equivalent to—"is of no considera-tion in the world" (猶言不足輕重).

3. THE DIFFÉRENT OPINIONS OF TSZE-HSIÂ AND TSZE-CHANG ON THE PRINCIPLES WHICH SHOULD REGULATE OUR INTERCOURSE WITH OTHERS. On the disciples of Tsze-hsiâ, see the 集

其拒人也。

賢與、人將拒我、如之何

於人何所不容、我之不

而矜不能、我之大賢與、

君子尊賢而容衆嘉善

之。子張曰異乎吾所聞、

可者與之其不可者拒

子夏云何。對曰子夏曰、

does Tsze-hsiâ say on the subject?" They replied, "Tsze-hsiâ says: 'Associate with those who can *advantage you.* Put away from you those who cannot do so.'" Tsze-chang observed, "This is different from what I have learned. The superior man honors the talented and virtuous, and bears with all. He praises the good, and pities the incompetent. Am I possessed of great talents and virtue?—who is there among men whom I will not bear with? Am I devoid of talents and virtue?—men will put me away from them. What have we to do with the putting away of others?"

證, *in loc.* It is strange to me that they should begin their answer to Tsze-chang with the designation 子夏, instead of saying 夫 子, "our Master." 矜,—see V, xvi. In 可 者 不 可 者, the 可 is taken differently by the old interpreters and the new. Hsing Ping expounds: "If the man be worthy, fit for you to have intercourse with, then have it; but if he be not worthy," etc. On the other hand, we find:—"If the man will advantage you, he is a fit person (是 可 者); then maintain intercourse with him," etc. This seems to be merely carrying out Confucius's rule, I, viii, 3. Chû Hsî, however, approves of Tsze-chang's censure of it, while he thinks also that Tsze-chang's own view is defective.—Pâo Hsien says, "Our intercourse with friends should be according to Tsze-hsiâ's rule; general intercourse according to Tsze-chang's."

已
矣。

無忘其所能、可謂好學也

子夏曰曰知其所亡、月

子不爲也。

觀者焉、致遠恐泥、是以君

子夏曰、雖小道、必有可

CHAPTER IV. Tsze-hsiâ said, "Even in inferior studies and employments there is something worth being looked at; but if it be attempted to carry them out to what is remote, there is a danger of their proving inapplicable. Therefore, the superior man does not practice them."

CHAPTER V. Tsze-hsiâ said, "He, who from day to day recognizes what he has not yet, and from month to month does not forget what he has attained to, may be said indeed to love to learn."

4. TSZE-HSIÂ'S OPINION OF THE INAPPLICABILITY OF SMALL PURSUITS TO GREAT OBJECTS. Gardening, husbandry, divining, and the healing art are all mentioned by Chû Hsî as instances of the 小道, "small ways," here intended, having their own truth in them, but not available for higher purposes, or what is beyond themselves. 致 is imperative and emphatic, =推極, "push them to an extreme." What is intended by 遠 is the far-reaching object of the Chün-tsze, "to cultivate himself and regulate others." 泥, in the 4th tone, explained in the dictionary by 滯, "water impeded."—Ho Yen makes the 小道 to be 異端, "strange principles."

5. THE INDICATIONS OF A REAL LOVE OF LEARNING:—BY TSZE-HSIÂ.

子夏曰、博學而篤
志切問而近思、仁在
其中矣。

子夏曰、百工居肆、
以成其事、君子學以
致其道。

子夏曰、小人之過
也、必文。

CHAPTER VI. Tsze-hsiâ said, "There are learning extensively, and having a firm and sincere aim; inquiring with earnestness, and reflecting with self-application:—virtue is in such a course."

CHAPTER VII. Tsze-hsiâ said, "Mechanics have their shops tò dwell in, in order to accomplish their works. The superior man learns, in order to reach to the utmost of his principles."

CHAPTER VIII. Tsze-hsiâ said, "The mean man is sure to gloss his faults."

6. HOW LEARNING SHOULD BE PURSUED TO LEAD TO VIRTUE:—BY TSZE-HSIÂ. K'ung Ân-kwo explains 志 as if it were 識, "to remember." On 切問而近思, the 備旨 says— 所問，皆切已之事，所思，皆身心 之要, "what are inquired about are things essential to one's self; what are thought about are the important personal duties." Probably it is so; but all this cannot be put in a translation. On 近思, compare VI, xxviii. 3. 仁在其中,—compare VII, xv; XIII, xviii.

7. LEARNING IS THE STUDENT'S WORKSHOP:— BY TSZE-HSIÂ. 肆 is here "a place for the display and sale of goods." A certain quarter was assigned anciently in Chinese towns and cities for mechanics, and all of one art were required to have their shops together. This is still very much the case. A son must follow his father's profession, and, seeing nothing but the exercise of that around him, it was supposed that he would not be led to think of anything else, and become very proficient in it.

8. GLOSSING HIS FAULTS THE PROOF OF THE MEAN MAN:—BY TSZE-HSIÂ. Literally, "The faults of the mean man, must gloss," i. e., he is sure to gloss. Wǎn, in this sense, a verb, in the 4th tone.

已也。

信而後諫、未信、則以爲謗

其民、未信、則以爲厲己也、

子夏曰、君子信而後勞

也属。

之儼然、卽之也溫聽其言

子夏曰君子有三變望

CHAPTER IX. Tsze-hsiâ said, "The superior man undergoes three changes. Looked at from a distance, he appears stern; when approached, he is mild; when he is heard to speak, his language is firm and decided."

CHAPTER X. Tsze-hsiâ said, "The superior man, having obtained their confidence, may then impose labors on his people. If he have not gained their confidence, they will think that he is oppressing them. Having obtained the confidence *of his prince*, one·may then remonstrate with him. If he have not gained his confidence, *the prince* will think that he is vilifying him."

9. CHANGING APPEARANCES OF THE SUPERIOR MAN TO OTHERS:—BY TSZE-HSIÂ. Tsze-hsiâ probably intended Confucius by the *Chun-tsze*, but there is a general applicability in his language and sentiments. 望 之, 卽 之,—literally, "look towards him," "approach him."—The description is about equivalent to our "*fortiter in re, suaviter in modo.*"

10. THE IMPORTANCE OF ENJOYING CONFIDENCE TO THE RIGHT SERVING OF SUPERIORS AND ORDERING OF INFERIORS:—BY TSZE-HSIÂ. Chû Hsî gives to 信 here the double meaning of "being sincere," and "being believed in." The last is the proper force of the term, but it requires the possession of the former quality.

噫、言游過矣、君子之道、

無、如之何子夏閧之曰、

則可矣抑末也本之則

小子、當洒掃應對、進退、

子游曰子夏之門人

小德出入可也。

子夏曰、大德不踰閑、

CHAPTER XI. Tsze-hsiâ said, "When a person does not transgress the boundary line in the great virtues, he may pass and repass it in the small virtues."

CHAPTER XII. 1. Tsze-yû said, "The disciples and followers of Tsze-hsiâ, in sprinkling and sweeping the ground, in answering and replying, in advancing and receding, are sufficiently accomplished. But these are only the branches *of learning,* and they are left ignorant of what is essential.—How can they be acknowledged as sufficiently taught?"

2. Tsze-hsiâ heard of the remark and said, "Alas! Yen Yû is wrong. According to the way of the

11. THE GREAT VIRTUES DEMAND THE CHIEF ATTENTION, AND THE SMALL ONES MAY BE SOMEWHAT VIOLATED:—BY TSZE-HSIÂ. The sentiment here is very questionable. A different turn, however, is given to the chapter in the older interpreters. Hsing Ping, expanding K'ung Ân-kwo, says: "Men of great virtue never go beyond the boundary line; it is enough for those who are virtuous in a less degree to keep near to it, going beyond and coming back." We adopt the more natural interpretation of Chû Hsî. 閑, "a piece of wood, in a doorway, obstructing ingress and egress"; then, "an inclosure" generally, "a railing," whatever limits and confines.

12. TSZE-HSIÂ'S DEFENSE OF HIS OWN GRADUATED METHOD OF TEACHING:—AGAINST TSZE-YÛ. 1. 小子 is to be taken in apposition with 門人, being merely, as we have found it previously, an affectionate method of speaking of the disciples. The sprinkling, etc., are the things which boys were supposed anciently to be

而　而　臺　惟　始　焉　矣　草　後　孰
優　優　子　聖　有　可　君　木　倦　先
則　則　夏　人　卒　誣　子　區　焉　傳
仕　學　曰　乎　者　也　之　以　譬　焉
。　學　仕　。　其　有　道　別　諸　孰

superior man *in teaching*, what departments are there
which he considers of prime importance, and delivers?
what are there which he considers of secondary importance, and allows himself to be idle about? *But
as in the case of plants, which are assorted according
to their classes, *so he deals with his disciples.* How
can the way of a superior man be such as to make
fools of *any of* them? Is it not the sage alone, who
can unite in one the beginning and the consummation
*of learning?*"

CHAPTER XIII. Tsze-hsiâ said, "The officer, *having
discharged all his duties*, should devote his leisure to
learning. The student, having completed his learning,
should apply himself to be an officer."

taught, the rudiments of learning, from which they advanced to all that is inculcated in the 大 學. But as Tsze-hsiâ's pupils were not boys, but men, we should understand, I suppose, these specifications as but a contemptuous reference to his in-structions, as embracing merely what was external. 洒, read *shâi* and *shâ*, 1st tone, "to sprinkle the ground before sweeping." 應, in the 4th tone, "to answer a call." 對, "to answer a question." 抑="but," as in VII, xxxii. 本 之 is expanded by the paraphrasts—若 木 之 所 在, "as to that in which the root (or, what is essential) is." This is, no doubt, the meaning, but the phrase itself is abrupt and enigmatical. 如 之 何=

如 之 何 其 可 誣, in opposition to the 則 可 矣 above. 2. The general scope of Tsze-hsiâ's reply is suf-ficiently plain, but the old inter-preters and new differ in explaining the several sentences. After dwelling long on it, I have agreed generally with the new school, and followed Chû Hsî in the translation. 區 is explained in the dictionary by 類, "classes."

13. THE OFFICER AND THE STU-DENT SHOULD ATTEND EACH TO HIS PROPER WORK IN THE FIRST IN-STANCE:—BY TSZE-HSIÂ. 優=有 餘 力, in I, vi.—The saying needs to be much supplemented in translating, in order to bring out its meaning.

止。

子游曰、喪致乎哀而

子游曰、吾友張也、爲

難能也、然而未仁。

曾子曰、堂堂乎張也、

難與並爲仁矣。

曾子曰、吾聞諸夫子、

人未有自致者也、必也

CHAPTER XIV. Tsze-yû said, "Mourning, having been carried to the utmost degree of grief, should stop with that."

CHAPTER XV. Tsze-yû said, "My friend Chang can do things which are hard to be done, but yet he is not perfectly virtuous."

CHAPTER XVI. The philosopher Tsǎng said, "How imposing is the manner of Chang! It is difficult along with him to practice virtue."

CHAPTER XVII. The philosopher Tsǎng said, "I heard this from our Master:—'Men may not have

14. THE TRAPPINGS OF MOURNING MAY BE DISPENSED WITH:—BY TSZE-yû. The sentiment here is perhaps the same as that of Confucius in III, iv, but the sage guards and explains his utterance.—K'ung Ân-kwo, following an expression in the 孝 經, makes the meaning to be that the mourner may not endanger his health or life by excessive grief and abstinence.

15. TSZE-YÛ'S OPINION OF TSZE-CHANG, AS MINDING HIGH THINGS TOO MUCH.

16. THE PHILOSOPHER TSǍNG'S OPINION OF TSZE-CHANG, AS TOO HIGH-PITCHED FOR FRIENDSHIP. 堂 堂 is explained in the dictionary by 盛 也, 正 也, "exuberant," "correct." It is to be understood of Chang's manner and appearance, keeping himself aloof from other men in his high-pitched course.

17. HOW GRIEF FOR THE LOSS OF PARENTS BRINGS OUT THE REAL NATURE OF MAN:—BY TSǍNG SHǍN. 自 is said to indicate the ideas both of 自 己, "one's self," and 自 然,

親喪乎。

⟨圖⟩曾子曰、吾聞諸夫
子、孟莊子之孝也、其
他可能也其不改父
之臣、與父之政、是難
能也。

⟨圖⟩孟氏使陽膚爲士

shown what is in them to the full extent, and yet they will be found to do so, on occasion of mourning for their parents.'"

CHAPTER XVIII. The philosopher Tsăng said, "I have heard this from our Master:—'The filial piety of Măng Chwang, in other matters, was what other men are competent to, but, as seen in his not changing the ministers of his father, nor his father's mode of government, it is difficult to be attained to.'"

CHAPTER XIX. The chief of the Măng family having appointed Yang Fû to be chief criminal judge, the

"naturally." 自 致, "to put forth one's self to the utmost," as we should say—"to come out fully," i. e., in one's proper nature and character. On the construction of 必 也, 親 喪 乎, compare XII, xiii. 吾聞諸夫子—諸 seems to=之, it, so that 諸 and 夫 子 are like two objectives, both governed by 聞.

18. THE FILIAL PIETY OF MĂNG CHWANG:—BY TSANG SHĂN. Chwang was the honorary epithet of Sù (逸), the head of the Măng family, not long anterior to Confucius. His father, according to Chû Hsî, had

been a man of great merit, nor was he inferior to him, but his virtue especially appeared in what the text mentions.—Ho Yen gives the comment of Mâ Yung, that though there were bad men among his father's ministers, and defects in his government, yet Chwang made no change in the one or the other, during the three years of mourning, and that it was this which constituted his excellence.

19. HOW A CRIMINAL JUDGE SHOULD CHERISH COMPASSION IN HIS ADMINISTRATION OF JUSTICE:—BY

歸 惡 如 子 其 失 師
焉。 居 是 貢 情、 其 、問
 下 之 曰、 則 道、 於
 流、 甚 紂 哀 民 曾
 天 也、 之 矜 散 子。
 下 是 不 而 久 曾
 之 以 善、 勿 矣、 子
 惡 君 不 喜。 如 曰、
 皆 子  得 上

latter consulted the philosopher Tsăng. Tsăng said, "The rulers have failed in their duties, and the people consequently have been disorganized, for a long time. When you have found out the truth *of any accusation*, be grieved for and pity them, and do not feel joy *at your own ability.*"

CHAPTER XX. Tsze-kung said, "Châu's wickedness was not so great *as that name implies*. Therefore, the superior man hates to dwell in a low-lying situation, where all the evil of the world will flow in upon him."

TSĂNG SHĂN. Seven disciples o. Tsăng Shăn are more particularly mentioned, one of them being this Yang Fù. 散 is to be understood of the moral state of the people, and not, physically, of their being scattered from their dwellings. 情 has occurred before in the sense of—"the truth," which it has here.

20. THE DANGER OF A BAD NAME: —BY TSZE-KUNG. 如是之甚, "so very bad as this";—the *this* (是) is understood by Hsing Ping as referring to the epithet—紂, which cannot be called honorary in this instance. According to the rules for such terms, it means—殘忍損義, "cruel and unmerciful, injurious to righteousness." If the 是 does not in this way refer to the name, the remark would seem to have occurred in a conversation about the wickedness of Châu. 下流 is a low-lying situation, to which the streams flow and waters drain, representing here a bad reputation, which gets the credit of every vice.

賢者識其大者、不賢者

武之道、未墜於地、在人、

曰、仲尼焉學子貢曰、文

二十二 衞公孫朝問於子貢

皆見之更也、人皆仰之。

如日月之食焉、過也、人

二十一 子貢曰、君子之過也、

CHAPTER XXI. Tsze-kung said, "The faults of the superior man are like the eclipses of the sun and moon. He has his faults, and all men see them; he changes again, and all men look up to him."

CHAPTER XXII. 1. Kung-sun Ch'âo of Wei asked Tsze-kung, saying, "From whom did Chung-nî get his learning?"

2. Tsze-kung replied, "The doctrines of Wăn and Wû have not yet fallen to the ground. They are to be found among men. Men of talents and virtue remember the greater principles of them, and others,

21. THE SUPERIOR MAN DOES NOT CONCEAL HIS ERRORS, NOR PERSIST IN THEM:—BY TSZE-KUNG. Such is the lesson of this chapter, as expanded in the 日 講. The sun and the moon being here spoken of together, the 食 must be confined to "eclipses," but the term is also applied to the ordinary waning of the moon.

22. CONFUCIUS'S SOURCES OF KNOWLEDGE WERE THE RECOLLECTIONS AND TRADITIONS OF THE PRIN-CIPLES OF WĂN AND WÛ:—BY TSZE-KUNG. 1. Of the questioner here we have no other memorial. His surname indicates that he was a descendant of some of the dukes of Wei. Observe how he calls Confucius by his designation of 仲 尼 or "Nî secundus." (There was an elder brother, a concubine's son, who was called 伯 尼.) 仲 尼 焉 學, "How did Chung-nî learn?" but the "how" = "from whom?" The expression,

識其小者、莫不有
文武之道焉、夫子
焉不學、而亦何常
師之有。

叔孫武叔語大

夫於朝曰子貢賢
於仲尼。子服景伯
以告子貢子貢曰、
譬之宮牆賜之牆
也、及肩、窺見室家

not possessing such talents and virtue, remember the
smaller. *Thus,* all possess the doctrines of Wăn and
Wû. Where could our Master go that he should not
have an opportunity of learning them? And yet what
necessity was there for his having a regular master?"

CHAPTER XXIII. 1. Shû-sun Wû-shû observed to
the great officers in the court, saying, "Tsze-kung is
superior to Chung-nî."

2. Tsze-fû Ching-po reported the observation to
Tsze-kung, who said, "Let me use the comparison of
a house and its *encompassing* wall. My wall *only*
reaches to the shoulders. One may peep over it, and
see whatever is valuable in the apartments.

however, in par. 2,—夫子焉不
學. expounded as in the translation, might suggest, from "what
quarter?" rather than "from what
person?" as the proper rendering.
The last clause is taken by modern
commentators, as asserting Confucius's connate knowledge, but Ân.
kwo finds in it only a repetition of
the statement that the sage found
teachers everywhere.

23. TSZE-KUNG REPUDIATES BEING
THOUGHT SUPERIOR TO CONFUCIUS,

AND, BY THE COMPARISON OF A HOUSE
AND WALL, SHOWS HOW ORDINARY
PEOPLE COULD NOT UNDERSTAND THE
MASTER. 1. 武 was the honorary
epithet of Châu Ch'âu (州仇), one of
the chiefs of the Shû-sun family.
From a mention of him in the 家語,
顏回 篇, we may conclude that he
was given to envy and detraction.
賢,—used here as in XI, xv, 1. 2.
Tsze-fû Ching-po,—see XIV, xxxviii.
譬之宮牆,—宮 is to be taken
generally for a house or building,

人之賢者、丘陵也、猶可踰也、
無以爲也、仲尼不可毁也、他
叔孫武叔毁仲尼子貢曰、
之云不亦宜乎、
之富得其門者或寡矣、夫子
門而入、不見宗廟之美、百官
之好夫子之牆、數仞、不得其

3. "The wall of my Master is several fathoms high. If one do not find the door and enter by it, he cannot see the ancestral temple with its beauties, nor all the officers in their rich array.

4. "But I may assume that they are few who find the door. Was not the observation of the chief only what might have been expected?"

CHAPTER XXIV. Shû-sun Wû-shû having spoken revilingly of Chung-nî, Tsze-kung said, "It is of no use doing so. Chung-nî cannot be reviled. The talents and virtue of other men are hillocks and mounds, which may be stepped over. Chung-nî is

and not in its now common accepta-tion of "a palace." It is a poor house, as representing the disciple, and a ducal mansion as representing his master. Many commentators make the wall to be the sole object in the comparison, and 宮牆＝宮之牆. It is better, with the 合講, to take both the house and the wall as members of the comparison, and 宮牆＝宮與牆. The wall is not a part of the house, but one inclosing it.

3.—仞 means 7 cubits. I have trans-lated it—"fathoms." 4. The 夫子 here refers to Wû-shû.

24. CONFUCIUS IS LIKE THE SUN OR MOON, HIGH ABOVE THE REACH OF DEPRECIATION:—BY TSZE-KUNG. 無以爲 is explained by Chû Hsî (and the gloss of Hsing Ping is the same) as＝無用爲此, "it is of no use to do this." 他人之賢者,—他人 is to be understood, according to the 備旨, as embracing all other sages. 自

也夫子之不可及也、　爲不知言不可不愼　一言以爲知、一言以　於子乎子貢曰、君子　子爲恭也、仲尼豈賢　〇陳子禽謂子貢曰、　其不知量也。　何傷於日月乎、多見　踰焉、人雖欲自絕、其　仲尼、日月也、無得而

the sun or moon, which it is not possible to step over. Although a man may wish to cut himself off *from the sage*, what harm can he do to the sun or moon? He only shows that he does not know his own capacity."

CHAPTER XXV. 1. Ch'ǎn Tsze-ch'in, addressing Tsze-kung, said, "You are too modest. How can Chung-nî be said to be superior to you?"

2. Tsze-kung said to him, "For one word a man is *often* deemed to be wise, and for one word he is *often* deemed to be foolish. We ought to be careful indeed in what we say.

3. "Our Master cannot be attained to, just in the same way as the heavens cannot be gone up to by the steps of a stair.

絕,—I have supplied *"from the sage,"* after most modern paraphrasts. Hsing Ping, however, supplies *"from the sun and moon."* The meaning comes to the same. Chû Hsî says that 多 here is the same with 祇, "only"; and Hsing Ping takes it as = 適, "just." This meaning of the character is not given in the dictionary, but it is necessary here;—see supplement to Hsing Ping's 疏, *in loc.*

25. CONFUCIUS CAN NO MORE BE EQUALED THAN THE HEAVENS CAN BE CLIMBED:—BY TSZE-KUNG. We find it difficult to conceive of the sage's disciples speaking to one another, as Tsze-ch'in does here to Tsze-kung, and Hsing Ping says that this was not the disciple Tsze-ch'in, but another man of the same surname and designation. But this is inadmissible, especially as we find the same parties, in I, x, talking about the character of their Master. 1. 子爲恭, "you are doing the modest." 2. 君子 has here its lightest meaning. The 備旨 makes it =

也。如之何其可及也榮其死也哀動之斯和其生斯行綏之斯來立之斯立道之得邦家者所謂而升也夫子之猶天之不可階

4. "Were our Master in the position of the ruler of a state or the chief of a family, we should find verified the description *which has been given of a sage's rule:* — he would plant the people, and forthwith they would be established; he would lead them on, and forthwith they would follow him; he would make them happy, and forthwith *multitudes* would resort to *his dominions;* he would stimulate them, and forthwith they would be harmonious. While he lived, he would be glorious. When he died, he would be bitterly lamented. How is it possible for him to be attained to?"

學者, "a student," but "a man," as in the translation, is quite as much as it denotes. Compare its use in I, viii, *et al.* 4. 夫子之得邦家者 must be understood hypothetically, because he never was in the position here assigned to him. 斯,—as in X, x, 1. 道 is for 導, as in I, v. 來,— as in XVI, i, II. 動之,—as in XV, xxxii, 3. 之, *them,* "the people" being always understood.

## BOOK XX.  YÂO YÜEH

終舜亦以命禹。　海困窮、天祿永　躬、允執其中、四　天之曆數在爾　堯曰、咨、爾舜、　堯曰第二十

CHAPTER I.  I. Yâo said, "Oh! you, Shun, the Heaven-determined order of succession now rests in your person.  Sincerely hold fast the due Mean.  If there shall be distress and want within the four seas, the Heavenly revenue will come to a perpetual end."

2. Shun also used the same language in giving charge to Yü.

HEADING OF THIS BOOK.— 堯曰第 二十, Yâo said, No. 20.  Hsing Ping says: "This Book records the words of the two sovereigns, the three kings, and of Confucius, throwing light on the excellence of the ordinances of Heaven, and the transforming power of government.  Its doctrines are all those of sages, worthy of being transmitted to posterity.  On this account, it brings up the rear of all the other Books, without any particular relation to the one immediately preceding."

1. PRINCIPLES AND WAYS OF YÂO, SHUN, YÜ, T'ANG, AND WÛ.  The first five paragraphs here are mostly compiled from different parts of the Shû-ching.  But there are many variations of language.  The compiler may have thought it sufficient, if he gave the substance of the original in his quotations, without seeking to observe a verbal accuracy, or, possibly, the Shû-ching, as it was

in his days, may have contained the passages as he gives them, and the variations be owing to the burning of most of the classical books by the founder of the Ch'in dynasty, and their recovery and restoration in a mutilated state. 1. We do not find this address of Yâo to Shun in the Shû-ching, Pt. I, but the different sentences may be gathered from Pt. II, ii, 14, 15, where we have the charge of Shun to Yü.  Yâo's reign commenced 2357 B. C., and after reigning 73 years, he resigned the administration to Shun.  He died 2257 B. C., and, two years after, Shun occupied the throne, in obedience to the will of the people.  天 之 曆 數, literally, "the represented and calculated numbers of heaven," i. e., the divisions of the year, its terms, months, and days, all described in a calendar, as they succeed one another with determined regularity.  Here, ancient and modern

曰、予小子履、敢

用玄牡、敢昭告

于皇皇后帝有

罪不敢赦帝臣

不蔽、簡在帝心、

朕躬有罪、無以

萬方、萬方有罪、

3. *T'ang* said, "I, the child Lî, presume to use a dark-colored victim, and presume to announce to Thee, O most great and sovereign God, that the sinner I dare not pardon, and thy ministers, O God, I do not keep in obscurity. The examination of them is by thy mind, O God. If, in my person, I commit offenses, they are not to be attributed to you, *the people of* the myriad regions. If you in the myriad regions commit offenses, these offenses must rest on my person."

interpreters agree in giving to the expression the meaning which appears in the translation. I may observe here, that Chû Hsî differs often from the old interpreters in explaining these passages of the Shû-ching, but I have followed him, leaving the correctness or incorrectness of his views to be considered in the annotations on the Shû-ching. 3. Before 曰 here we must understand 湯, the designation of the founder of the Shang dynasty. The sentences here may in substance be collected from the Shû-ching, Pt. IV, iii, 4, 8. Down to 簡在帝心 is a prayer addressed to God by T'ang, on his undertaking the overthrow of the Hsiâ dynasty, which he rehearses to his nobles and people, after the completion of his work. T'ang's name was 履. We do not find in the Shû-ching the remarkable designation of God—皇皇后帝. For the grounds on which I translate 帝 by *God*, see my work on "The Notions of the Chinese Concerning God and Spirits." 后, now generally used for "empress," was anciently used for "sovereign," and applied to the kings. Here it is an adjective, or in apposition with 帝. The sinner is Chieh (桀), the tyrant, and last sovereign of the Hsiâ dynasty. "The ministers of God" are the able and virtuous men, whom T'ang had called, or would call, to office. By 簡在帝心, T'ang indicates that, in his punishing or rewarding, he only wanted to act in harmony with the mind of God. 無以萬方＝萬方小民何預焉, as in the translation. In the dictionary, it is said that 以 and 與 are interchanged. This is a case

之民歸心焉。所重民食、

國繼絕世、舉逸民、天下

官、四方之政行焉興滅

人謹權量審法度、修廢

仁人、百姓有過、在予一

人是富雖有周親不如

罪在朕躬周有大賚善

4.　Châu conferred great gifts, and the good were enriched.

5.　"Although he has his near relatives, they are not equal to *my* virtuous men.　The people are throwing blame upon me, the One man."

6.　He carefully attended to the weights and measures, examined the body of the laws, restored the discarded officers, and the good government of the kingdom took its course.

7.　He revived states that had been extinguished, restored families whose line of succession had been broken, and called to office those who had retired into obscurity, so that throughout the kingdom the hearts of the people turned towards him.

8.　What he attached chief importance to were the food of the people, the duties of mourning, and sacrifices.

in point.　4. In the Shû-ching, Pt. V, ιιi, 9, we find King Wû saying 大 賚 於 四 海 而 萬 姓 悅 服. "I distributed great rewards through the kingdom, and all the people were pleased and submitted."　5. See the Shû-ching, Pt. V, i, sect. II, 6, 7.

The subject in 雖 有 周 親 is 受 or 紂, tyrant of the Yin dynasty.　周, ―in the sense of 至.　過 is used in the sense of 咎, "to blame."　The people found fault with him, because he did not come to save them from their sufferings by destroying their

政矣子張曰何謂

屏四惡斯可以從

政矣子曰尊五美、

曰、何如斯可以從

子張問於孔子、

功、公則說。

則民任焉、敏則有

喪、祭寬、則得眾信、

9. By his generosity, he won all. By his sincerity, he made the people repose trust in him. By his earnest activity, his achievements were great. By his justice, all were delighted.

CHAPTER II. 1. Tsze-chang asked Confucius, saying, "In what way should *a person in authority* act in order that he may conduct government properly?" The Master replied, "Let him honor the five excellent, and banish away the four bad, things;—then may he conduct government properly." Tsze-chang said, "What are meant by the five excellent things?" The

oppressor. The remaining paragraphs are descriptive of the policy of King Wû, but cannot, excepting the 8th one, be traced in the present Shû-ching. 任, paragraph 9, is in the 4th tone. See XVII, vi, which chapter, generally, resembles this paragraph.

2. HOW GOVERNMENT MAY BE CONDUCTED WITH EFFICIENCY, BY HONORING FIVE EXCELLENT THINGS, AND PUTTING AWAY FOUR BAD THINGS:—A CONVERSATION WITH TSZE-CHANG. It is understood that this chapter, and the next, give the ideas of Confucius on government, as a sequel to those of the ancient sages

and emperors, whose principles are set forth in the preceding chapter, to show how Confucius was their proper successor. 1. On 從 政, see VI, vi, but the gloss of the 備 旨 says—從 政只泛說行政, 不作爲大夫, "從 政 here denotes generally the practice of government. It is not to be taken as indicating a minister." We may, however, retain the proper meaning of the phrase, Confucius describing principles to be observed by all in authority, and which will find in the highest their noblest embodiment. The 日 講 favors this view. See its paraphrase *in loc.* I

五美子曰君子惠而不

費、勞而不怨、欲而不貪、

泰而不驕、威而不猛。二節

張曰何謂惠而不費子

曰、因民之所利而利之、

斯不亦惠而不費乎、擇

可勞而勞之又誰怨欲

仁而得仁又焉貪君子

Master said, "When the person in authority is beneficent without great expenditure; when he lays tasks *on
the people* without their repining; when he *pursues
what he* desires without being covetous; when he
maintains a dignified ease without being proud; when
he is majestic without being fierce."

2.  Tsze-chang said, "What is meant by being
beneficent without great expenditure?" The Master
replied, "When *the person in authority* makes more
beneficial to the people the things from which they
naturally derive benefit;—is not this being beneficent
without *great* expenditure? When he chooses the
labors which are proper, and makes them labor on
them, who will repine? When his desires are set on
benevolent *government*, and he secures it, who will
accuse him of covetousness? Whether he has to do

have therefore translated 君子 by—
"a person in authority." 勞而不怨、
—see IV, xviii, though the application of the terms there is different.
泰而不驕,—see XIII, xxvi. 威而
不猛,—see VII, xxxvii. 2. 因民云
云 is instanced by the promotion of

agriculture. 擇可勞云云 is in-
stanced by the employment of the
people in advantageous public works.
欲仁云云 is explained:—"Desire
for what is not proper is covetousness, but if, while the wish to have
the kingdom overshadowed by his

殺、謂之虐、不戒視成、謂

何謂四惡子曰、不教而

亦威而不猛乎子張曰、

儼然人望而畏之、斯不

子正其衣冠尊其瞻視、

斯不亦泰而不驕乎、君

無衆寡、無小大、無敢慢、

with many people or few, or with things great or small, he does not dare to indicate any disrespect;—is not this to maintain a dignified ease without any pride?  He adjusts his clothes and cap, and throws a dignity into his looks, so that, thus dignified, he is looked at with awe;—is not this to be majestic without being fierce?"

3.  Tsze-chang then asked, "What are meant by the four bad things?"  The Master said, "To put the people to death without having instructed them;—this is called cruelty.  To require from them, *suddenly*, the full tale of work, without having given them warning;—this is called oppression.  To issue orders

benevolence has not reached to universal advantaging, his desire does not cease, then, with a heart impatient of people's evils, he administers a government impatient of those evils.  What he desires is benevolence; and what he gets is the same;—how can he be regarded as covetous?"  3. 視 is explained here by 責, "to require from."  We may get that meaning out of the character, which="to examine," "to look for."  A good deal has to be supplied, here and in the sentences below, to bring out the meaning as in the

知人也。

以立也。不知言、無以

為君子也。不知禮、無以

子曰不知命、無以

之咎謂之有司。

賊、猶之與人也、出納

之暴、慢令致期、謂之

as if without urgency, *at first*, and, when the time comes, *to insist on them with severity;*—this is called injury. And, generally, in the giving *pay or rewards* to men, to do it in a stingy way;—this is called acting the part of a mere official."

CHAPTER III. 1. The Master said, "Without recognizing the ordinances *of Heaven*, it is impossible to be a superior man.

2. "Without an acquaintance with the rules of Propriety, it is impossible for the character to be established.

3. "Without knowing *the force of* words, it is impossible to know men."

translation. 猶之 is explained by 均之, and seems to me to be nearly = our "on the whole." 出 納,—"giving out," i. e., *from this*, and "presenting," i. e., *to that*. The whole is understood to refer to rewarding men for their services, and doing it in an unwilling and stingy manner.

3. THE ORDINANCES OF HEAVEN, THE RULES OF PROPRIETY, AND THE FORCE OF WORDS, ALL NECESSARY TO BE KNOWN. 1. 知 here is not only "knowing," but "believing and resting in." 命 is the will of Heaven regarding right and wrong, of which man has the standard in his own moral nature. If this be not recognized, a man is the slave of passion, or the sport of feeling. 2. Compare VIII, viii, 2. 3. 知 here supposes much thought and examination of principles. Words are the voice of the heart. To know a man, we must attend well to what and how he thinks.

# THE GREAT LEARNING

大學

可　也、　德　初　遺　孔　曰、　子　　　
見　於　之　學　書、　氏　大　程　　　
古　今　門　入　而　之　學、　子　　　

*My master, the philosopher Ch'ǎng, says: "The Great Learning is a Book transmitted by the Confucian School, and forms the gate by which first learners enter into virtue. That we can now perceive the order in which the*

TITLE OF THE WORK.—大學, "The Great Learning." I have pointed out, in the prolegomena, the great differences which are found among Chinese commentators on this Work, on almost every point connected with the criticism and interpretation of it. We encounter them here on the very threshold. The name itself is simply the adoption of the two commencing characters of the treatise, according to the custom noticed at the beginning of the Analects; but in explaining those two characters, the old and new schools differ widely. Anciently, 大 was read as 太, and the oldest commentator whose notes on the work are preserved, Chǎng K'ang-ch'ǎng, in the last half of the 2nd century, said that the Book was called 大學, 以其記博學, 可以爲 政, "because it recorded that extensive learning, which was available for the administration of government." This view is approved by K'ung Ying-tâ (孔穎達), whose expansion of K'ang-ch'ǎng's notes, written in the first half of the 7th century, still remains. He says—大 學, 至道矣, "大學 means the highest principles." Chû Hsî's definition, on the contrary, is—大學者大人 之學也, "大學 means the Learning of Adults." One of the paraphrasts who follow him says—大是大人, 與 小子對, "大 means adults, in op-

position to children " The grounds of Chû Hsî's interpretation are to be found in his very elegant preface to the Book, where he tries to make it out, that we have here the subjects taught in the advanced schools of antiquity. I have contented myself with the title—"The Great Learning," which is a literal translation of the characters, whether read as 太 學 or 大學.

THE INTRODUCTORY NOTE.—I have thought it well to translate this, and all the other notes and supplements appended by Chû Hsî to the original text, because they appear in nearly all the editions of the work, which fall into the hands of students, and his view of the classics is what must be regarded as the orthodox one. The translation, which is here given, is also, for the most part, according to his views, though my own differing opinion will be found freely expressed in the notes. Another version, following the order of the text, before it was transposed by him and his masters, the Ch'ǎng, and without reference to his interpretations, will be found in the translation of the Lî Chî.—子程子, —see note to the Analects, I, i, 1. The Ch'ǎng here is the second of the two brothers, to whom reference is made in the prolegomena. 孔氏, "Confucius,"=the K'ung, as 季氏 is

德、在親民、在止於
大學之道、在明明
差矣。
爲、則庶乎其不
者必由是而學
而論孟次之、學
獨賴此篇之存、
人爲學次第者、

*ancients pursued their learning is solely owing to the preservation of this work, the Analects and Mencius coming after it. Learners must commence their course with this, and then it may be hoped they will be kept from error."*

## THE TEXT OF CONFUCIUS

1. What the Great Learning teaches, is—to illustrate illustrious virtue; to renovate the people; and to rest in the highest excellence.

found continually in the Analects for *the* Chî, i. ə., the chief of the Chî family. For how can we say that "The Great Learning" is a work left by Confucius? Even Chû Hsî ascribes only a small portion of it to the Master, and makes the rest to be the production of the disciple Tsăng, and before his time, the whole work was attributed generally to the sage's grandson. I must take 孔 氏 as＝孔 門, the Confucian school.

THE TEXT OF CONFUCIUS. Such Chû Hsî, as will be seen from his concluding note, determines this chapter to be, and it has been divided into two sections (段), the first containing three paragraphs, occupied with the *heads* (綱 領) of the Great Learning, and the second containing four paragraphs, occupied with the *particulars* (條 目) of those.

*Par. 1. The heads of the Great Learning.* 大 學 之 道,—"the way of the Great Learning," 道 being＝修 爲 之 方 法, "the methods of cultivating and practicing it,"—the Great Learning, that is. 在, "is in." The first 明 is used as a verb; the second as an adjective, qualifying 德. The illustrious virtue is the virtuous nature which man derives from Heaven. This is perverted as man grows up, through defects of the physical constitution, through inward lusts, and through outward seductions; and the great business of life should be, to bring the nature back to its original purity.—"To renovate the people,"—this object of the Great Learning is made out, by changing the character 親 of the old text into 新. The Ch'ăng first proposed the alteration, and Chû

至善。知止、
而后有定、
定、而后能
靜、靜而后
能安、安而
后能慮、慮、
而后能得。

2. The point where to rest being known, the object of pursuit is then determined; and, that being determined, a calm unperturbedness may be attained to. To that calmness there will succeed a tranquil repose. In that repose there may be careful deliberation, and that deliberation will be followed by the attainment *of the desired end.*

Hsî approved of it. When a man has entirely illustrated his own illustrious nature, he has to proceed to bring about the same result in every other man, till "under heaven" there be not an individual, who is not in the same condition as himself.— "The highest excellence" is understood of the two previous matters. It is not a third and different object of pursuit, but indicates a perseverance in the two others, till they are perfectly accomplished.—According to these explanations, the objects contemplated in the Great Learning are not three, but two. Suppose them realized, and we should have the whole world of mankind perfectly good, every individual what he ought to be!

Against the above interpretation, we have to consider the older and simpler. 德 is there not the *nature*, but simply virtue, or virtuous conduct, and the first object in the Great Learning is the making of one's self more and more illustrious in virtue, or the practice of benevolence, reverence, filial piety, kindness, and sincerity. See the 故本大學註辨, *in loc.*—There is nothing, of course, of the *renovating of the people*, in this interpretation. The second object of the Great Learning is 親民＝親愛於民, "to love the people."—The third object is said by Ying-tâ to be "in resting in conduct which is perfectly good (在止處於至善之行)," and here also, there would seem to be only two objects, for what essential distinction can we make between the first and third? There will be occasion below to refer to the reasons for changing 親 into 新, and their unsatisfactoriness. "To love the people" is, doubtless, the second thing taught by the Great Learning.—Having the heads of the Great Learning now before us, according to both interpretations of it, we feel that the student of it should be a sovereign, and not an ordinary man.

*Par. 2. The mental process by which the point of rest may be attained.* I confess that I do not well understand this paragraph, in the relation of its parts in itself, nor in relation to the rest of the chapter. Chû Hsî says: "止 is the ground where we ought to rest";—namely, the highest excellence mentioned above. But if this be known in the outset, where is the necessity for the 慮, or "careful deliberation," which issues in its attainment? The para-

物有本末、<sup>三節</sup>
事有終始、
知所先後、
則近道矣。
古之欲明<sup>四節</sup>
明德於天
下者、先治
其國、欲治
其國者、先

3. Things have their root and their branches. Affairs have their end and their beginning. To know what is first and what is last will lead near to what is taught *in the Great Learning.*

4. The ancients who wished to illustrate illustrious virtue throughout the kingdom, first ordered well their own states. Wishing to order well their states, they

phrasts make 知 止 to embrace even all that is understood by 格 物 致 知 below —Ying-tâ is perhaps rather more intelligible. He says: "When it is known that the rest is to be in the perfectly good, then the mind has fixedness. So it is free from concupiscence, and can be still, not engaging in disturbing pursuits. That stillness leads to a repose and harmony of the feelings. That state of the feelings fits for careful thought about affairs (能 思 慮 於 事), and thence it results that what is right in affairs is attained." Perhaps, the paragraph just intimates that the objects of the Great Learning being so great, a calm, serious thoughtfulness is required in proceeding to seek their attainment.

*Par. 3. The order of things and methods in the two preceding paragraphs.* So, according to Chû Hsî, does this paragraph wind up the two preceding. "The illustration of virtue," he says, "is the *root,* and the renovation of the people is the *completion* (literally, *the branches*).

Knowing where to rest is the *beginning,* and being able to attain is the end. The root and the beginning are *what is first.* The completion and end are *what is last.*"—The adherents of the old commentators say, on the contrary, that this paragraph is introductory to the succeeding ones. They contend that the illustration of virtue and renovation of the people are *doings* (事), and not *things* (物). According to them, the *things* are the person, heart, thoughts, etc., mentioned below, which are "the root," and the family, kingdom, and empire, which are "the branches." The *affairs* or *doings* are the various processes put forth on those things.—This, it seems to me, is the correct interpretation.

*Par. 4. The different steps by which the illustration of illustrious virtue throughout the kingdom may be brought about.* 明 明 德 於 天 下 is understood by the school of Chû Hsî as embracing the two first objects of the Great Learning, the illustration,

者、
先
正
其

欲
脩
其
身

先
脩
其
身、

齊
其
家
者、

齊
其
家、
欲

first regulated their families.　Wishing to regulate their families, they first cultivated their persons. Wishing to cultivate their persons, they first rectified

namely, of virtue, and the renovation of the people. We are not aided in determining the meaning by the synthetic arrangement of the different steps in the next paragraph, for the result arrived at there is simply—天 下 平, "the whole kingdom was made tranquil."—Ying-tâ's comment is—章 明 己 之 明 德 使 徧 於 天 下, "to display illustriously their own illustrious virtue (or virtues), making them reach through the whole kingdom." But the influence must be very much transformative. Of the several steps described, tne central one is 脩 身, "the cultivation of the person," which, indeed, is called 本, "the root," in par. 6. This requires "the heart to be correct," and that again "that the thoughts be sincere." Chû Hsî defines 心 as 身 之 所 主, "what the body has for its lord," and 意 as 心 之 所 發, "what the 心 sends forth." Ying-tâ says: 總 包 萬 慮 謂 之 心, "that which comprehends and embraces all considerings is called the 心"; 爲 情 所 意 念 謂 之 意, "the thoughts under emotion are what is called 意." 心 is then the metaphysical part of our nature, all

that we comprehend under the terms of mind or soul, heart, and spirit. This is conceived of as quiescent, and when its activity is aroused, then we have thoughts and purposes relative to what affects it. The "being sincere" is explained by 實, "real." The sincerity of the thoughts is to be obtained by 致 知, which means, according to Chû Hsî, carrying our knowledge to its utmost extent, with the desire that there may be nothing which it shall not embrace." This knowledge, finally, is realized 在 格 物. The same authority takes 物, "things," as embracing, 事, "affairs," as well. 格 sometimes = 至, "to come or extend to," and assuming that the "coming to" here is by study, he makes it = 窮 究 "to examine exhaustively," so that "格 物 means exhausting by examination the principles of things and affairs, with the desire that their uttermost point may be reached."— We feel that this explanation cannot be correct, or that, if it be correct, the teaching of the Chinese sage is far beyond and above the condition and capacity of men. How can we suppose that, in order to secure

心、
欲正其

心者、
先誠

其意、
欲誠

其意者、先

致其知、致

知、
在格
物。

their hearts. Wishing to rectify their hearts, they first sought to be sincere in their thoughts. Wishing to be sincere in their thoughts, they first extended to the utmost their knowledge. Such extension of knowledge lay in the investigation of things.

sincerity of thought and our self-cultivation. there is necessarily the study of all the phenomena of physics and metaphysics, and of the events of history? Moreover, Chû Hsi's view of the two last clauses is a consequence of the alterations which he adopts in the order of the text. As that exists in the Lî Chî, the 7th paragraph of this chapter is followed by 此為知本, 此為知之至也, which he has transferred and made the 5th chapter of annotations. Ying-tâ's comment on it is: "*The root* means *the person*. The person (i. e., personal character) being regarded as the root, if one can know his own person, this is the knowledge of the root; yea, this is the very extremity of knowledge." If we apply this conclusion to the clauses under notice, it is said that wishing to make our thoughts sincere we must first carry to the utmost our self-knowledge, and this extension of self-knowledge 在格物. Now, the change of the style indicates that the relation of 致知 and 格物 is different from that of the parts in the other clauses. "It is not said that to get the one thing we must first do the other. Rather it seems to me that the 格物 is a consequence of 致知, that in it is seen the other. Now, 式, "a rule or pattern," and 正 "to correct," are accepted meanings of 格, and 物 being taken generally and loosely as =*things*, 在格物 will tell us that, when his self-knowledge is complete, a man is a law to himself, measuring, and measuring correctly, all. things with which he has to do, not led astray or beclouded by them. This is the interpretation strongly insisted on by 羅仲藩, the author of the 古本大學註辨. It is the only view into any sympathy with which I can bring my mind. In harmony with it, I would print 致知在格物 as a paragraph by itself, between the. analytic and synthetic processes described in paragraphs 4, 5. Still there are difficulties connected with it, and I leave the vexed questions, regretting my own inability to clear them up.

於庶人、壹是皆以脩．

天下平。<sub>六節</sub>自天子以至

而后國治國治而后

身脩、而后家齊家齊、

心正、心正而后身脩、

而后意誠意誠、而后

物格而后知至、知至、<sub>五節</sub>

5. Things being investigated, knowledge became complete. Their knowledge being complete, their thoughts were sincere. Their thoughts being sincere, their hearts were then rectified. Their hearts being rectified, their persons were cultivated. Their persons being cultivated, their families were regulated. Their families being regulated, their states were rightly governed. Their states being rightly governed, the whole kingdom was made tranquil and happy.

6. From the Son of Heaven down to the mass of the people, all must consider the cultivation of the person the root of *everything besides*.

*Par. 5. The synthesis of the preceding processes.* Observe the 致 of the preceding paragraph is changed into 至, and how 治 (the second, or lower first tone) now becomes 治, the 4th tone. 治 is explained by 政 理, "the work of ruling," and 治 by 理 效, "the result." 后 is used for 後, as in par. 2.

*Par. 6. The cultivation of the person is the prime, radical thing required from all.* I have said above that the Great Learning is adapted only to a sovereign, but it is intimated here that *the people* also may take part in it in their degree. 天子, "Son of Heaven," a designation of the sovereign 以 其 命 于 天, "because he is ordained by Heaven." 壹 是 = 一 切, "all." Chăng K'ang-ch'ăng, however, says: 壹 是, 專 行 是 也, "壹 是 means that they uniformly do this."

身爲本。

其七本亂、
曰

而末治

者否矣。

其所厚

者薄而

其所薄

者厚、未

之有也。

7. It cannot be, when the root is neglected, that what should spring from it will be well ordered. It never has been the case that what was of great importance has been slightly cared for, and, at the same time, that what was of slight importance has been greatly cared for.

*Par. 7. Reiteration of the importance of attending to the root.* Chû Hsî makes the *root* here to be the person, but according to the preceding paragraph, it is "the cultivation of the person" which is intended. By the 末 or "branches" is intended the proper ordering of the family, the state, the kingdom. "The family," however, must be understood in a wide sense, as meaning not a household, but a *clan*, embracing all of the same surname. 厚薄, "thick" and "thin,"—used here metaphorically. 所厚, according to Chû Hsî, means "the family," and 所薄, "the state and the kingdom," but that I cannot understand. 所厚 is the same as the *root*. Mencius has a saying which may illustrate the second part of the paragraph.—於所厚者薄, 無所不薄, "He who is careless in what is important will be careless in everything."

右經一

章、蓋孔

子之言、

而曾子

述之、其

傳十章、

則曾子

之意、而

門人記

之也、舊

*The preceding chapter of classical text is in the words of Confucius, handed down by the philosopher Tsǎng. The ten chapters of explanation which follow contain the views of Tsǎng, and were recorded by his disciples. In*

CONCLUDING NOTE. It has been shown in the prolegomena that there is no ground for the distinction made here between so much *ching* attributed to Confucius, and so much 傳, or commentary, ascribed to his disciple Tsǎng. The invention of paper is ascribed to Ts'âi Lun (蔡倫), an officer of the Han dynasty, in the time of the emperor Hwo (和), A. D. 89–105. Before that time, and long after also, slips of wood and of bamboo (簡) were used to write and engrave upon. We can easily conceive how a collection of them might get disarranged, but whether those containing the Great Learning did so is a question vehemently disputed. 右經一章, "the chapter of classic on the right"; 如左, "on the left";

本頗有錯
簡、今因程
子所定、而
更考經文、
別爲序次
如左。
釁康誥曰、克 一節
明德。大甲曰、二節
顧諟天之明

*the old copies of the work, there appeared considerable confusion in these, from the disarrangement of the tablets. But now, availing myself of the decisions of the philosopher Ch'ăng, and having examined anew the classical text, I have arranged it in order, as follows:*

## COMMENTARY OF THE PHILOSOPHER TSĂNG

CHAPTER I. 1. In the Announcement to K'ang, it is said, "He was able to make his virtue illustrious."

2. In the Tâi Chiâ, it is said, "He contemplated and studied the illustrious decrees of Heaven."

—these are expressions = our "preceding," and "as follows," indicating the Chinese method of writing and printing from the right side of a manuscript or book on to the left.

COMMENTARY OF THE PHILOSOPHER TSĂNG

1. THE ILLUSTRATION OF ILLUSTRIOUS VIRTUE. The student will do well to refer here to the text of "The Great Learning," as it appears in the Lî Chî. He will then see how a considerable portion of it has been broken up, and transposed to form this and the five succeeding chapters. It was, no doubt, the occurrence of 明, in the four paragraphs here, and of the phrase 明 德, which determined Chû Hsî to form them into one chapter, and refer them to the first head in the classical text. The old commentators connect them

with the great business of making the thoughts sincere. 1. See the Shû-ching, V, ix, 3. The words are part of the address of King Wû to his brother Făng (封), called also K'ang-shû (康 叔; 康, the honorary epitheton appointing him to the marquisate of 衛. The subject of 克 is King Wăn, to whose example K'ang-shû is referred.—We cannot determine, from this paragraph, between the old interpretation of 德, as = "virtues," and the new which understands by it,—"the heart or nature, all-virtuous." 2. See the Shû-ching, IV, v, Sect. I, 2. Chû Hsî takes 諟 as = 此, "this," or 審, "to judge," "to examine." The old interpreters explain it by 正, "to correct." The sentence is part of the address of the premier, Î Yin, to T'âi-chiâ, the second emperor of the Shang dynasty, 1753–1719 B. C. The subject of 顧 is T'âi-chiâ's

新康誥曰、作新民。

日新、日日新、又日

〔盤〕湯之盤銘曰、茍

明明德。

右傳之首章、釋

德皆自明也、

命帝典曰、克明峻

3. In the Canon of the emperor (Yâo), it is said, "He was able to make illustrious his lofty virtue."

4. These *passages* all *show how those sovereigns* made themselves illustrious.

*The above first chapter of commentary explains the illustration of illustrious virtue.*

CHAPTER II. 1. On the bathing tub of T'ang, the following words were engraved: "If you can one day renovate yourself, do so from day to day. Yea, let there be daily renovation."

2. In the Announcement to K'ang, it is said, "To stir up the new people."

father, the great T'ang. Chû Hsî understands by 明命, the Heaven-given, illustrious nature of man. The other school take the phrase more generally, the 顯道, "displayed ways" of Heaven. 3. See the Shû-ching, I, i, 2. It is of the emperor Yâo that this is said. 4. The 皆 must be referred to the three quotations.

2. THE RENOVATION OF THE PEOPLE. Here the character 新, "new," "to renovate," occurs five times, and it was to find something corresponding to it at the commencement of the work, which made the Ch'ang change the 親 of 親民 into 新. But the 新 here have nothing to do with the renovation of the people. This is self-evident in the 1st and 3rd paragraphs. The description of the chapter, as above, is a misnomer. 1. This fact about T'ang's bathing tub had come down by tradition. At least, we do not now find the mention of it anywhere but here. It was customary among the ancients, as it is in China at the present day, to engrave, all about them, on the articles of their furniture, such moral aphorisms and lessons. 2. See the *K'ang Kâo*, par. 7, where K'ang-shû is exhorted to assist the king "to settle the decree of Heaven, and 作新民," which may mean to make the bad people of Yin into good

千里、惟民所

詩云邦畿

章、釋新民。

右傳之二

所不用其極。

是故君子無

邦、其命維新。

詩曰、周雖舊

3. In the Book of Poetry, it is said, "Although Châu was an ancient state, the ordinance which lighted on it was new."

4. Therefore, the superior man in everything uses his utmost endeavors.

*The above second chapter of commentary explains the renovating of the people.*

CHAPTER III. I. In the Book of Poetry, it is said, "The royal domain of a thousand li is where the people rest."

people, or to stir up the new people, i. e., *new*, as recently subjected to Châu. 3. See the Shih-ching, III, i, Ode I, st. 1. The subject of the ode is the praise of King Wăn, whose virtue led to the possession of the kingdom by his house, more than a thousand years after its first rise. 4. 君子 is here the man of rank and office probably, as well as the man of virtue; but I do not, for my own part, see the particular relation of this to the preceding paragraphs, nor the work which it does in relation to the whole chapter.

3. ON RESTING IN THE HIGHEST EXCELLENCE. The frequent occurrence of 止 in these paragraphs, and of 至 善, in par. 4, led Chû Hsî to combine them in one chapter, and connect them with the last clause in the opening paragraph of the work. 1. See the Shih-ching, IV, iii, Ode III, st. 4. The ode celebrates the rise and establishment of the Shang or Yin dynasty. 畿 is the 1,000 *li* around the capital, and constituting the royal demesne. The quotation shows, according to Chû Hsî, that 物 各 有 所 當 止 之 處, "everything has the place where it ought to rest." But that surely is a very sweeping conclusion from the words. 2. See the Shih-ching, II, viii, Ode VI, st. 2, where we have the complaint of a downtrodden man, contrasting his position with that of a bird. For 綿 here, we have 綿 in the Shih-ching. 綿 蠻 are intended to express the sound of the bird's singing or chattering. "The yellow bird" is known by a variety of names. A common one is 倉 庚, or, properly, 鶬 鶊 (*ts'ang kăng*). It is a species of oriole. The 子 曰 are worthy of observation. If the first chapter of the classical text, as Chû Hsî calls it, really contains the words of Confucius, we might have expected it to be headed by these characters. 於

孝、爲人父、止於慈、與國人交、

爲人臣、止於敬、爲人子、止於

於緝熙敬止、爲人君、止於仁、

而不如鳥乎詩云、穆穆文王、

子曰、於止、知其所止、可以人

止詩云、緡蠻黃鳥、止于丘隅。

2.　In the Book of Poetry, it is said, "The twitter-
ing yellow bird rests on a corner of the mound." The
Master said, "When it rests, it knows where to rest.
Is it possible that a man should not be equal to this
bird?"

3.　In the Book of Poetry, it is said, "Profound
was King Wăn. With how bright and unceasing a
feeling of reverence did he regard his resting places!"
As a sovereign, he rested in benevolence. As a minister, he rested in reverence. As a son, he rested in
filial piety. As a father, he rested in kindness. In
communication with his subjects, he rested in good
faith.

---

止, literally, "in resting." 3. See
the Shih-ching, III, i, Ode I, st. 4.
All the stress is here laid upon the
final 止, which does not appear to
have any force at all in the original,
Chû Hsî himself saying there that it
is 語詞, "a mere supplemental particle." In 於緝, 於 is read wû, and

恂慄也、赫兮喧兮者、威
者、自脩也瑟兮僩兮者、
磋者道學也、如琢如磨
子、終不可諠兮。如切如
僩兮赫兮喧兮有斐君
切如磋如琢如磨瑟兮
菉竹猗猗、有斐君子、如
止於信詩云、瞻彼淇澳、

4. In the Book of Poetry, it is said, "Look at that winding course of the Ch'î, with the green bamboos so luxuriant! Here is our elegant and accomplished prince! As we cut and then file; as we chisel and then grind: *so has he cultivated himself*. How grave is he and dignified! How majestic and distinguished! Our elegant and accomplished prince never can be forgotten." *That expression*—"As we cut and then file," indicates the work of learning. "As we chisel and then grind," indicates that of self-culture. "How grave is he and dignified!" indicates the feeling of cautious reverence. "How commanding and distinguished!" indicates an awe-inspiring deportment.

is an interjection. 4. See the Shih-ching, I, v, Ode I, st. 1. The ode celebrates the virtue of the duke *Wu* (武) of Wei (衛), in his laborious endeavors to cultivate his person. There are some verbal differences between the ode in the Shih-ching, and as here quoted; namely, 奧 for

澳; 綠 for 菉; 匪 for 斐. 猗, here, *poetic*, read *o*. 道 is used as = 言, "says," or "means." It is to be understood before 自修, 恂慄, and 威儀.—The transposition of this paragraph by Chû Hsî to this place does seem unhappy. It ought evi-dently to come in connection with

儀也、有斐君子、終不可

諠兮者、道盛德至善、民

之不能忘也。詩云、於戲、

前王不忘、君子賢其賢、

而親其親、小人樂其樂、

而利其利、此以沒世不

忘也。

右傳之三章、釋止於

至善。

"Our elegant and accomplished prince never can be forgotten," indicates how, when virtue is complete and excellence extreme, the people cannot forget them.

5. In the Book of Poetry, it is said, "Ah! the former kings are not forgotten." *Future* princes deem worthy what they deemed worthy, and love what they loved. The common people delight in what delighted them, and are benefited by their beneficial arrangements. It is on this account that the former kings, after they have quit the world, are not forgotten.

*The above third chapter of commentary explains resting in the highest excellence.*

the work of 脩身. 5. See the Shih-ching, IV, i, Sect. I, Ode IV, st. 3. The former kings are Wăn and Wŭ, the founders of the Châu dynasty. 於戲 are an interjection, read *wû hû*. In the Shih-ching we have 於乎. 烏呼 are found with the same meaning. I translate 其賢, 其親, by "what they deemed worthy," "what they loved." When we try to determine *what* that what was, we are perplexed by the varying views of the old and new schools. 沒世,—see Analects' XV, xix.—According to Ȳing-tâ, "this paragraph illustrates the business of having the thoughts sincere." According to Chù Hsî, it tells that how the former kings renovated the people was by their resting in perfect excellence, so as to be able, through out the kingdom and to future ages, to effect that there should not be a single thing but got its proper place.

子曰、聽訟吾猶人也、必也、使

無訟乎。無情者不得盡其辭、大

畏民志、此謂知本。

右傳之四章、釋本末。

CHAPTER IV. The Master said, "In hearing litigations, I am like any other body. What is necessary to cause the people to have no litigations?" *So*, those who are devoid of principle find it impossible to carry out their speeches, and a great awe would be struck into men's minds;—this is called knowing the root.

*The above fourth chapter of commentary explains the root and the issue.*

4. EXPLANATION OF THE ROOT AND THE BRANCHES. See the Analects, XII, xiii, from which we understand that the words of Confucius terminate at 訟 乎, and that what follows is from the compiler. According to the old commentators, this is the conclusion of the chapter on having the thoughts made sincere, and that 誠 其 意 is the root. But according to Chû, it is the illustration of illustrious virtue which is the root, while the renovation of the people is the *result* therefrom. Looking at the words of Confucius, we must conclude that *sincerity* was the subject in his mind.

此
謂
知
本
。
此
謂
知
之
至
也
。

右
傳
之
五
章
、
蓋
釋
格
物
致
知

之
義
、
而
今
亡
矣
、
閒
嘗
竊
取
程

子
之
意
、
以
補
之
曰
、
所
謂
致
知

在
格
物
者
、
言
欲
致
吾
之
知
、
在

即
物
而
窮
其
理
也
、
蓋
人
心
之

靈
莫
不
有
知
、
而
天
下
之
物
莫

不
有
理
、
惟
於
理
有
未
窮
、
故
其

知
有
不
盡
也
、
是
以
大
學
始
教
、

CHAPTER V.　1. This is called knowing the root.
2.　This is called the perfecting of knowledge.

*The above fifth chapter of the commentary explained the meaning of "investigat-*
*ing things and carrying knowledge to the utmost extent," but it is now lost.*
*I have ventured to take the views of the scholar Ch'ăng to supply it, as*
*follows · The meaning of the expression, "The perfecting of knowledge*
*depends on the investigation of things," is this:—If we wish to carry our*
*knowledge to the utmost, we must investigate the principles of all things we*
*come into contact with, for the intelligent mind of man is certainly formed*
*to know, and there is not a single thing in which its principles do not*
*inhere. But so long as all principles are not investigated, man's knowledge*
*is incomplete. On this account, the Learning for Adults, at the outset of*

5. ON THE INVESTIGATION OF THINGS, AND CARRYING KNOWLEDGE TO THE UTMOST EXTENT. 1. This is said by one of the Ch'ăng to be 衍文, "superfluous text." 2. Chû Hsî considers this to be the conclusion of a chapter which is now lost. But we have seen that the two sentences come in, as the work stands in the Lî Chî, at the conclusion of what is deemed the classical text. It is not necessary to add anything here to what has been said there, and in the prolegomena, on the new dispositions of the work from the time of the Sung scholars, and the manner in which Chû Hsî has supplied this supposed missing chapter.

惡惡臭、如好好色、此之謂自謙、

所謂誠其意者、毋自欺也、如

謂物格此謂知之至也。

心之全體大用、無不明矣、此

物之表裏精粗、無不到、而吾

久、而一旦豁然貫通焉、則衆

以求至乎其極、至於用力之

不因其已知之理、而益窮之、

必使學者卽凡天下之物、莫

*its lessons, instructs the learner, in regard to all things in the world, to proceed from what knowledge he has of their principles, and pursue his investigation of them, till he reaches the extreme point. After exerting himself in this way for a long time, he will suddenly find himself possessed of a wide and far-reaching penetration. Then, the qualities of all things, whether external or internal, the subtle or the coarse, will all be apprehended, and the mind, in its entire substance and its relations to things, will be perfectly intelligent. This is called the investigation of things. This is called the perfection of knowledge.*

CHAPTER VI. 1. What is meant by "making the thoughts sincere," is the allowing no self-deception, as *when* we hate a bad smell, and as *when* we love what is beautiful. This is called self-enjoyment.

6. ON HAVING THE THOUGHTS SINCERE. 1. *The sincerity of the thoughts obtains, when they move without effort to what is right and wrong, and, in order to this, a man must be* specially on his guard in his solitary moments. 自謙 is taken as if it were 自慊, =repose or enjoyment in one's self. 慊, according to Chû Hsî, is in the entering tone, but the dictionary

故君子必愼其獨也。小人

閒居爲不善、無所不至、見

君子、而后厭然揜其不善、

而著其善、人之視己、如見

其肺肝然、則何益矣、此謂

誠於中、形於外、故君子必

Therefore, the superior man must be watchful over himself when he is alone.

2. There is no evil to which the mean man, dwelling retired, will not proceed, but when he sees a superior man, he instantly tries to disguise himself, concealing his evil, and displaying what is good. The other beholds him, as if he saw his heart and reins;— of what use *is his disguise?* This is an instance of the saying—"What truly is within will be manifested without." Therefore, the superior man must be watchful over himself when he is alone.

makes it in the 2nd. 2. *An enforcement of the concluding clause in the last paragraph.* 厭, 3rd tone, the same as 掩, meaning 閉藏貌, "the appearance of concealing." 人之視己,—人 refers to the superior man mentioned above, ="the other." 己 =他, "him," and not=*himself*, which is its common signification. 肺肝,—

literally, "the lungs and liver," but with the meaning which we attach to the expression substituted for it in the translation. The Chinese make the lungs the seat of righteousness, and the liver the seat of benevolence. Compare 今予其敷心腹腎腸 in the Shû-ching, IV. vii, Sect. III, 3.

愼其獨也。曾子
曰、十目所視、十
手所指、其嚴乎。
富潤屋、德潤身、
心廣體胖、故君
子必誠其意。
右傳之六章、
釋誠意。

3. The disciple Tsăng said, "What ten eyes behold, what ten hands point to, is to be regarded with reverence!"

4. Riches adorn a house, and virtue adorns the person. The mind is expanded, and the body is at ease. Therefore, the superior man must make his thoughts sincere.

*The above sixth chapter of commentary explains making the thoughts sincere.*

3. The use of 曾子 at the beginning of this paragraph (and extending, perhaps, over to the next) should suffice to show that the whole work is not his, as assumed by Chû Hsî. "Ten" is a round number, put for *many.* The recent commentator, Lo Chung-fan, refers Tsăng's expressions to the multitude of spiritual beings, servants of Heaven or God, who dwell in the regions of the air, and are continually beholding men's conduct. But they are probably only an emphatic way of exhibiting what is said in the preceding paragraph. 4. This paragraph is commonly ascribed to Tsăng Shăn, but whether correctly so or not cannot be positively affirmed. It is of the same purport as the two preceding, showing that hypocrisy is of no use. Compare Mencius, VII, Pt. I, xxi, 4. Chăng K'ang-ch'ăng explains 胖 (read *p'ang*) by 大, "large," and Chû

Hsî by 安 舒, as in the translation. The meaning is probably the same. —It is only the first of these paragraphs from which we can in any way ascertain the views of the writer on making the thoughts sincere. The other paragraphs contain only illustration or enforcement. Now the gist of the first paragraph seems to be in 毋自欺, "allowing no self-deception." After knowledge has been carried to the utmost, this remains to be done, and it is not true that, when knowledge has been completed, the thoughts become sincere. This fact overthrows Chû Hsî's interpretation of the vexed passages in what he calls the text of Confucius. Let the student examine his note appended to this chapter, and he will see that Chû was not unconscious of this pinch of the difficulty.

見聽而不聞、食而不知

其正。二而心不在焉、視而不

其正、有所憂患、則不得

其正、有所好樂、則不得

其正、有所恐懼、則不得

者、身有所忿懥、則不得

一而所謂脩身、在正其心

CHAPTER VII. 1. What is meant by, "The cultivation of the person depends on rectifying the mind," *may be thus illustrated:*—If a man be under the influence of passion, he will be incorrect in his conduct. He will be the same, if he is under the influence of terror, or under the influence of fond regard, or under that of sorrow and distress.

2. When the mind is not present, we look and do not see; we hear and do not understand; we eat and do not know the taste of what we eat.

7. ON PERSONAL CULTIVATION AS DEPENDENT ON THE RECTIFICATION OF THE MIND. 1. Here Chû Hsî, following his master Ch'ăng, would again alter the text, and change the second 身 into 心. But this is unnecessary. The 身 in 脩身 is not the mere material body, but the person, the individual man, in contact with things, and intercourse with society, and the 2nd paragraph shows that the evil conduct in the first is a consequence of the mind not being under control. In 忿懥,

恐懼, 好樂 (*as*), 憂患, the 2nd term rises on the signification of the first, and intensifies it. Thus, 忿 is called "a burst of anger," and 懥, "persistence in anger," etc., etc.—I have said above that 身 here is not the material body. Lo Chung-fan, however, says that it is:—身謂肉身, "身 is the body of flesh." See his reasonings, *in loc.*, but they do not work conviction in the reader. 2. 心不在焉,—this seems to be a case in point, to prove that we cannot tie 心 in this Work to any very

其味此謂脩身在正其
心。

右傳之七章、釋正心

脩身。

所謂齊其家、在脩其
身者人之其所親愛而
辟焉、之其所賤惡而辟
焉、之其所畏敬、而辟焉、

3. This is what is meant by saying that the cultivation of the person depends on the rectifying of the
mind.

*The above seventh chapter of commentary explains rectifying the mind and cultivating the person*

CHAPTER VIII. 1. What is meant by "The regulation of one's family depends on the cultivation of his
person," is this:—Men are partial where they feel
affection and love; partial where they despise and
dislike; partial where they stand in awe and reverence;

definite application. Lo Chung-fan
insists that it is "the God-given
*moral* nature," but 心 不 在 焉 is
evidently="when the thoughts are
otherwise engaged."

8. THE NECESSITY OF CULTIVAT-
ING THE PERSON, IN ORDER TO THE
REGULATION OF THE FAMILY. The
lesson here is evidently that men
are continually falling into error, in
consequence of the partiality of their
feelings and affections. How this
error affects their personal cultivation, and interferes with the regulating of their families, is not specially

indicated. 1. The old interpreters
seem to go far astray in their interpretation. They take 之 in 之 其 所
親 愛, and the other clauses, as = 適,
"to go to," and 辟 as synonymous
with 譬, "to compare." Ying-tâ
thus expands K'ang-ch'ǎng on 人 之
其 所 親 愛 而 辟 焉:—"Suppose I
go to that man. When I see that he
is virtuous, I feel affection for, and
love him. I ought then to turn
round and compare him with myself.
Since he is virtuous and I love him,
then, if I cultivate myself and be
virtuous, I shall so be able in like

齊家。

右傳之八章、釋脩身

脩、不可以齊其家。

知其苗之碩。此謂身不

曰人莫知其子之惡莫

者、天下鮮矣。故諺有之

而知其惡、惡而知其美

其所敖惰、而辟焉、故好

之其所哀矜、而辟焉、之

partial where they feel sorrow and compassion; partial where they are arrogant and rude. Thus it is that there are few men in the world who love and at the same time know the bad qualities of *the object of their love*, or who hate and yet know the excellences of *the object of their hatred*.

2. Hence it is said, in the common adage, "A man does not know the wickedness of his son; he does not know the richness of his growing corn."

3. This is what is meant by saying that if the person be not cultivated, a man cannot regulate his family.

*The above eighth chapter of commentary explains cultivating the person and regulating the family.*

manner to make all men feel affection for, and love me." In a similar way the other clauses are dealt with. Chŭ Hsî takes 之 as = 於, "in regard to," and 辟 (read p'i) as = 偏, "partial," "one-sided." Even his opponent, Lo Chung-fan, interprets here in the same way. But 之 is evidently the common sign of possession, the clause that follows it being construed as the regent after 人之. 敖 = 傲, "proud," "uncivil." 2. 碩,—"great," "tall"; 苗之碩,—"the tallness (richness, abundance) of his growing crop." Farmers were noted, it would appear, in China, so long ago, for grumbling about their crops.

事長也、慈者、所以使眾

所以事君也、弟者、所以

出家、而成教於國孝者、

教人者、無之故君子不

家者、其家不可教而能

醫所謂治國、必先齊其

CHAPTER IX.  1. What is meant by "In order rightly to govern the state, it is necessary first to regulate the family," is this:—It is not possible for one to teach others, while he cannot teach his own family.  Therefore, the ruler, without going beyond his family, completes the lessons for the state.  There is filial piety:—therewith the sovereign should be served.  There is fraternal submission:—therewith elders and superiors should be served.  There is kindness:—therewith the multitude should be treated.

9.  ON REGULATING THE FAMILY AS THE MEANS TO THE WELL-ORDERING OF THE STATE.  1. *There is here implied the necessity of self-cultivation to the rule both of the family and of the state, and that being supposed to exist,—which is the force of the* 故,—*it is shown how the virtues that secure regulation of the family have their corresponding virtues in the wider* sphere of the state.  君子 has here both the moral and the political meaning; it is 治國之君子, "the superior man with whom is the government of the state."  It being once suggested to Chû Hsî that 不可教 should be 不能教, he replied— 彼之不可教, 即我之不能教, "The *impossibility* of another's being taught is just my *inability* to teach."

此謂一言僨事、一人定

戾、一國作亂、其機如此、

家讓、一國興讓、一人貪

也一家仁、一國興仁、一

未有學養子、而后嫁者

誠求之雖不中不遠矣、

也康誥曰、如保赤子心

2. In the Announcement to K'ang, it is said, "*Act
as if you were watching over an infant.*" If (*a mother*)
is really anxious about it, though she may not hit
*exactly the wants of her infant,* she will not be far from
doing so. There never has been *a girl* who learned to
bring up a child, that she might afterwards marry.

3. From the loving *example* of one family a whole
state becomes loving, and from its courtesies the
whole state become courteous, while, from the ambition and perverseness of the One man, the whole state
may be led to rebellious disorder;—such is the nature
of the influence. This verifies the saying, "Affairs may
be ruined by a single sentence; a kingdom may be
settled by its One man."

2. See the Shû-ching, V, x, 7. Both
in the Shû and here, some verb, like
*act*, must be supplied. This paragraph seems designed to show that
*the ruler must be carried on to his
object by an inward, unconstrained
feeling, like that of the mother for her
infant.* Lo Chung-fan insists on
this as harmonizing with 親民, "to
love the people," as the second
object proposed in the Great Learning. 3. *How certainly and rapidly
the influence of the family extends to
the state.* 一家 is the one family of
the ruler, and 一人 is the ruler. 一
人,="I, the One man," is a way in
which the sovereign speaks of himself; see Analects, XX, i, 5. 一言=
一句, as in Analects, II, ii. 一言僨
事, 一人定國,—compare Analects,

所藏乎身不恕、而能喻
人、無諸己而后非諸人、
君子有諸己而后求諸
其所好、而民不從、是故
暴、而民從之其所令反
民從之桀紂帥天下以
國堯舜帥天下以仁、而

4. Yâo and Shun led on the kingdom with benevolence, and the people followed them. Chieh and Châu led on the kingdom with violence, and the people followed them. The orders which these issued were contrary to the practices which they loved, and so the people did not follow them. On this account, the ruler must himself be possessed of the *good* qualities, and then he may require them in the people. He must not have *the bad qualities* in himself, and then he may require that they shall not be in the people. Never has there been a man, who, not having reference to his own character and wishes in dealing with others, was able effectually to instruct them.

XIII, xv. 仁 and 讓 have reference to the 孝, 弟 (＝悌), 慈, in par. 1. 4. *An illustration of the last part of the last paragraph.* But from the examples cited, the sphere of influence is extended from the state to the kingdom, and the family, moreover, does not intervene between the kingdom and the ruler. In 其所令, 其 must be understood as referring to the tyrants Chieh and Châu. Their orders were good, but unavailing, in consequence of their own contrary example 諸＝於. 所藏乎身, "what is kept in one's own person," i. e., his character and mind. 恕,—see Analects, V, xi; XV, xxiii. Ying-tâ seems to take 不恕 as simply＝

以教國人。詩云、其儀

弟宜兄宜弟。而后可

教國人。詩云、宜兄宜

宜其家人、而后可以

之子于歸宜其家、

桃之夭夭、其葉蓁蓁、

治國、在齊其家。詩云、

諸人者、未之有也。故

5. Thus we see how the government of the state depends on the regulation of the family.

6. In the Book of Poetry, it is said, "That peach tree, so delicate and elegant! How luxuriant is its foliage! This girl is going to her husband's house. She will rightly order her household." Let the household be rightly ordered, and then the people of the state may be taught.

7. In the Book of Poetry, it is said, "They can discharge their duties to their elder brothers. They can discharge their duties to their younger brothers." Let the ruler discharge his duties to his elder and younger brothers, and then he may teach the people of the state.

8. In the Book of Poetry, it is said, "In his deportment there is nothing wrong; he rectifies all the

"good." 6. See the Shih-ching, I, i, Ode VI, st. 3. The ode celebrates the wife of King Wăn, and the happy influence of their family government. 之 子＝是 子. Observe 子 is feminine, as in Analects, V, i. 歸, "going home," a term for marriage, used by women. 7. See the Shih, II, ii, Ode VI, st. 3. The ode was sung at entertainments. when the king feasted the princes. It celebrates their

釁所謂平天下、

釋齊家治國、

右傳之九章、

在齊其家。

之也。此謂治國

足法、而后民法

其為父子兄弟

不忒、正是四國、

people of the state." *Yes;* when the ruler, as a father, a son, and a brother, is a model, then the people imitate him.

9. This is what is meant by saying, "The government of his kingdom depends on his regulation of the family."

*The above ninth chapter of commentary explains regulating the family and governing the kingdom.*

CHAPTER X. 1. What is meant by "The making

virtues. 8. See the Shih, I, xiv, Ode III, st. 3. It celebrates, according to Chû Hsî, the praises of some *chun-tsze,* or ruler. 四國.—not "four states," but the four quarters of the state, the whole of it.

10. ON THE WELL-ORDERING OF THE STATE, AND MAKING THE WHOLE KINGDOM PEACEFUL AND HAPPY. The key to this chapter is in the phrase 絜矩之道, the principle of reciprocity, the doing to others as we would that they should do to us, though here, as elsewhere, it is put forth negatively. It is implied in the expression of the last chapter,— 所藏乎身不恕, but it is here discussed at length, and shown in its highest application. The following analysis of the chapter is translated freely from the 四書輯要: "This chapter explains the well-ordering of the state, and the tranquilization of the kingdom. The greatest stress is

to be laid on the phrase—*the measuring square.* That, and the expression in the general commentary —*loving and hating what the people love and hate, and not thinking only of the profit,* exhaust the teaching of the chapter. It is divided into five parts. The *first,* embracing the first two paragraphs, teaches that the way to make the kingdom tranquil and happy is in the principle of the measuring square. The *second* part embraces three paragraphs, and teaches that the application of the measuring square is seen in loving and hating, in common with the people. The consequences of *losing* and *gaining* are mentioned for the first time in the 5th paragraph, to wind up the chapter so far, showing that the decree of Heaven goes or remains, according as the people's hearts are lost or gained. The *third* part embraces eight paragraphs, and

倍、　恤　而　與　上　在
是　孤、　民　孝、　老　治
以　而　與　上　老、　其
君　民　弟、　長、　而　國
子、　不　上　長、　民　者、

the whole kingdom peaceful and happy depends on the
government of his state," is this:—When the sovereign
behaves to his aged, as the aged should be behaved
to, the people become filial; when the sovereign
behaves to his elders, as the elders should be behaved
to, the people learn brotherly submission; when the
sovereign treats compassionately the young and helpless, the people do the same.　Thus the ruler has a

teaches that the most important
result of loving and hating in common with the people is seen in
making the *root* the primary subject,
and the *branch* only secondary.
Here, in par. 11, mention is again
made of *gaining* and *losing*, illustrating the meaning of the quotation in
it, and showing that to the collection
or dissipation of the people the
decree of Heaven is attached.　The
*fourth* part consists of five paragraphs,
and exhibits the extreme results of
loving and hating, as shared with
the people, or on one's own private
feeling, and it has special reference
to the sovereign's employment of
ministers because there is nothing
in the principle more important than
that.　The 19th paragraph speaks of
*gaining* and *losing*, for the third time,
showing that from the 4th paragraph
downwards, in reference both to the
hearts of the people and the decree
of Heaven, the application or non-
application of the principle of the
*measuring square* depends on the

mind of the sovereign.　The *fifth*
part embraces the other paragraphs.
Because the root of the evil of a
sovereign's not applying that principle lies in his not knowing how
wealth is produced, and employing
mean men for that object, the distinction between righteousness and
profit is here much insisted on, the
former bringing with it all advantages, and the latter leading to all
evil consequences.　Thus the sovereign is admonished, and it is seen
how to be careful of his virtue is
the root of the principle of the
*measuring square*, and his loving and
hating, in common sympathy with
the people, is its reality."
1.　There is here no progress of
thought, but a repetition of what
has been insisted on in the two last
chapters.　In 老老, 長長, the first
characters are verbs, with the meaning which it requires so many words
to bring out in the translation.　弟 =
悌. 孤,—properly, "fatherless"; here
="the young and helpless."　倍,

有絜矩之道也所惡於

上、毋以使下、所惡於下、

毋以事上、所惡於前、毋

以先後、所惡於後、毋以

從前、所惡於右、毋以交

於左、所惡於左、毋以交

於右、此之謂絜矩之道。

principle with which, as with a measuring square, he may regulate his conduct.

2. What a man dislikes in his superiors, let him not display in the treatment of his inferiors; what he dislikes in inferiors, let him not display in the service of his superiors; what he hates in those who are before him, let him not therewith precede those who are behind him; what he hates in those who are behind him, let him not therewith follow those who are before him; what he hates to receive on the right, let him not bestow on the left; what he hates to receive on the left, let him not bestow on the right:—this is what is called "The principle with which, as with a measuring square, to regulate one's conduct."

read as, and＝背, "to rebel," "to act contrary to." 君子, here and throughout the chapter, has reference to office, and specially to the royal or highest. 絜矩之道,—絜 is a verb, read *hsieh*, according to Chû Hsî, 度, "to measure"; 矩,—the mechanical instrument, "the carpenter's square." It having been seen that the ruler's example is so influential, it follows that the minds of all men are the same in sympathy and tendency. He has then only to take his own mind, and measure therewith the minds of others. If he act accordingly, the grand result—the kingdom tranquil and happy—will ensue. 2. *A lengthened description of the principle of reciprocity.* 先,—4th tone,

詩云、樂只君子、民之父母、

民之所好好之、民之所惡

惡之此之謂民之父母。四節詩

云、節彼南山、維石巖巖、赫

赫師尹、民具爾瞻、有國者、

不可以不愼、辟則爲天下

3. In the Book of Poetry, it is said, "How much to be rejoiced in are these princes, the parents of the people!" When *a prince* loves what the people love, and hates what the people hate, then is he what is called the parent of the people.

4. In the Book of Poetry, it is said, "Lofty is that southern hill, with its rugged masses of rocks! Greatly distinguished are you, O *grand*-teacher Yin, the people all look up to you." Rulers of states may not neglect to be careful. If they deviate *to a mean selfishness*, they will be a disgrace in the kingdom.

"to precede." 3. See the Shih-ching, II, ii, Ode V, st. 3. The ode is one that was sung at festivals, and celebrates the virtues of the princes present. Chû Hsî makes 只 (read *chih*, 3rd tone) an expletive. Chăng's gloss, in 毛詩註疏, takes it as=是, and the whole is—"I gladden these princes, the parents of the people." 4. See the Shih-ching, II, iv, Ode VII, st. 1. The ode complains of the king Yû (幽), for his employing unworthy ministers. 節, read *ts'ieh*, meaning "rugged and lofty-looking." 具=俱, "all." 辟, read *p'i*, as in chap. viii. 僇 is explained in the dictionary by 辱, "disgrace." Chû Hsî seems to take it as=戮, "to kill," as did the old commentators. They say: "He will be put to death by the people, as were the

傲矣。詩云、殷之未

喪師、克配上帝、儀

監于殷、峻命不易、

道得衆、則得國、失

衆、則失國。是故君

子、先愼乎德有德、

此有人、有人、此有

土、有土、此有財、有

5. In the Book of Poetry, it is said, "Before the sovereigns of the Yin *dynasty* had lost the *hearts of the* people, they could appear before God. Take warning from *the house of* Yin. The great decree is not easily *preserved*." This shows that, by gaining the people, the kingdom is gained, and, by losing the people, the kingdom is lost.

6. On this account, the ruler will first take pains about *his own* virtue. Possessing virtue will give him the people. Possessing the people will give him the territory. Possessing the territory will give him its wealth. Possessing the wealth, he will have resources for expenditure.

tyrants Chieh and Châu." 5. See the Shih, III, i, st. 6, where we have 宜 for 儀, and 駿 for 峻. The ode is supposed to be addressed to King Ch'ăng (成), to stimulate him to imitate the virtues of his grandfather Wăn. 殷,="the sovereigns of the Yin dynasty." The capital of the Shang dynasty was changed to Yin by P'an-kăng, about 1400 B. C., after which the dynasty was so denominated. 配上帝, according to Chû Hsî, means "they were the sover-

eigns of the realm, and corresponded to (fronted) God." K'ang-ch'ăng says: "Before they lost their people, from their virtue, they were also able to appear before Heaven; that is, Heaven accepted their sacrifices." Lo Chung-fan makes it:—"They harmonized with God; that is, in loving the people." K'ang-ch'ăng's interpretation is, I apprehend, the correct one. 6. 愼乎德,—德 here, according to Chû·Hsî, is the "illustrious virtue" at the beginning of the

悖而入貨悖而出入者、

是故言悖而出者、亦<sup>十節</sup>

則民散財散則民聚。

爭民施奪是故財聚、<sup>九節</sup>

財者、末也。外本內末、<sup>八節</sup>

財、此有用德者、本也、<sup>七節</sup>

7. Virtue is the root; wealth is the result.

8. If he make the root his secondary object, and the result his primary, he will *only* wrangle with his people, and teach them rapine.

9. Hence, the accumulation of wealth is the way to scatter the people; and the letting it be scattered among them is the way to collect the people.

10. And hence, the ruler's words going forth contrary to right, will come back to him in the same way, and wealth, gotten by improper ways, will take its departure by the same.

book. His opponents say that it is the exhibition of virtue; that is, of filial piety, brotherly submission, etc. This is more in harmony with the first paragraph of the chapter. 8. 外 and 內 are used as verbs, = 輕 重, "to consider slight," "to consider important." 爭 民, — "will wrangle the (i. e., with the) people." The ruler will be trying to take, and the people will be trying to hold. 施 奪, —"he will give"—(i. e., lead the people to, = teach them)—"rapine." The two phrases = he will be against the people, and will set them against himself, and against one another. Ying-tâ explains them—"people wrangling for gain will give reins to their rapacious disposition." 9. 財 散, "wealth being scattered,"—that is, diffused, and allowed to be so by the ruler, among the people. The collecting and scattering of the people are to be understood with reference to their feelings towards their ruler. 10. The "words" are to be understood of governmental orders and enactments. 悖, read

無以爲寶、仁親
寶舅犯曰亡人、°十三節
爲寶惟善以爲
書曰、楚國、無以
善則失之矣楚°十二節
道善則得之不
曰、惟命不于常、
亦悖而出康誥。°十一節

11. In the Announcement to K'ang, it is said, "The decree indeed may not always rest on *us;*" that is, goodness obtains the decree, and the want of goodness loses it.

12. In the Book of Ch'û, it is said, "The kingdom of Ch'û does not consider that to be valuable. It values, *instead*, its good men."

13. *Duke Wăn's* uncle, Fan, said, "Our fugitive does not account that to be precious. What he considers precious is the affection due to his parent."

*pei,*=逆, "to act contrary to," "to rebel," that which is outraged being 理, "what is right," or, in the first place, 民 心, "the people's hearts," and, in the second place, 君 心, "the ruler's heart." Our proverb— "goods ill-gotten go ill-spent"— might be translated by 貨 悖 而 入 者, 亦 悖 而 出, but those words have a different meaning in the text. 11. See the *K'ang Kâo*, par. 23. The only difficulty is with 于. K'ang-ch'ăng and Ying-tâ do not take it as an expletive, but say it=於, "in," or "on"; —"The appointment of Heaven may not constantly rest on one family." Treating 于 in this way, the supplement in the Shû should be "us." 12. The Book of Ch'û is found in the 國 語, "Narratives of the States," a collection purporting to be of the Châu dynasty, and, in relation to the other states, what Confucius's "Spring and Autumn" is to Lû. The exact words of the text do not occur, but they could easily be constructed from the narrative. An officer of Ch'û being sent on an embassy to Tsin, the minister who received him asked about a famous girdle of Ch'û, called 白 珩, how much it was worth. The officer replied that his country did not look on such things as its treasures, but on its able and virtuous ministers. 13. 舅 犯, "Uncle Fan"; that is, uncle to Wăn, subsequently marquis, commonly described as duke, of Tsin. Wăn is the 亡 人, or, "fugitive." In the early part of his life, he was a fugitive, and suffered many vicissitudes of fortune.

以爲寶秦誓曰若有一个臣、
斷斷兮、無他技其心休休焉、
其如有容焉人之有技若己
有之人之彥聖其心好之不
啻若自其口出實能容之以
能保我子孫黎民尙亦有利
哉。人之有技媢疾以惡之人

14. In the Declaration *of the duke of* Ch'in, it is said, "Let me have but one minister, plain and sincere, not *pretending to* other abilities, but with a simple, upright, mind; and possessed of generosity, *regarding* the talents of others as if he himself possessed them, and, where he finds accomplished and perspicacious men, loving them in his heart more than his mouth expresses, and really showing himself able to bear them *and employ them:*—such a minister will be able to preserve my sons and grandsons and black-haired people, and benefits likewise to the kingdom may well be looked for from him. But if *it be his character,* when he finds men of ability, to be jealous and hate

Once, the duke of Ch'in (秦) having offered to help him, when he was in mourning for his father who had expelled him, to recover Tsin, his uncle Fan gave the reply in the text. The *that* in the translation refers to 得 國, "getting the kingdom." 14.

"The declaration *of the duke of* Ch'in" is the last book in the Shû-ching. It was made by one of the dukes of Ch'in to his officers, after he had sustained a great disaster, in consequence of neglecting the advice

之彥聖、而違之俾不

通實不能容以不能

保我子孫黎民、亦曰

殆哉。〇十五節 唯仁人放流之、

迸諸四夷、不與同中

國、此謂唯仁人爲能

愛人、能惡人。〇十六節 見賢、而

them; and, when he finds accomplished and perspicacious men, to oppose them and not allow their advancement, showing himself really not able to bear them:—such a minister will not be able to protect my sons and grandsons and black-haired people; and may he not also be pronounced dangerous *to the state?*"

15.　It is only the truly virtuous man who can send away such a man and banish him, driving him out among the barbarous tribes around, determined not to dwell along with him in the Middle Kingdom. This is in accordance with the saying, "It is only the truly virtuous man who can love or who can hate others."

16.　To see men of worth and not be able to raise

of his most faithful minister. Between the text here, and that which we find in the Shû, there are some differences, but they are unimportant. 15. 仁人 is here, according to Chû Hsî and his followers, the prince who applies the principle of reciprocity, expounded in the second paragraph. Lo Chung-fan contends that it is 親民者, "the lover of the people." The paragraph is closely connected with the preceding. In 放流之, 之 refers to the bad minister, there described. The 四夷, "four I"; see the Lî Chî, III, iii, 14. 不與同中國＝不與之同處中國, "will not dwell together with him in the Middle Kingdom." China is evidently so denominated, from its being thought to be surrounded by barbarous tribes. 惟仁人能云云, —see Analects, IV, iii. 16. I have

子、有大道必忠信以

菑必逮夫身是故君
〇十八節

所好、是謂拂人之性、

好人之所惡惡人之
十七節

退、退、而不能遠過也。

命也見不善、而不能

不能舉舉、而不能先、

them to office; to raise them to office; but not to do so quickly:—this is disrespectful. To see bad men and not be able to remove them; to remove them, but not to do so to a distance:—this is weakness.

17. To love those whom men hate, and to hate those whom men love;—this is to outrage the natural feeling of men. Calamities cannot fail to come down on him who does so.

18. Thus *we see that* the sovereign has a great course *to pursue*. He must show entire self-devotion

translated 命 as if it were 慢, which K'ang-ch'ăng thinks should be in the text. Ch'ăng Î (頤) would substitute 怠, "idle," instead of 慢, and Chû Hsî does not know which suggestion to prefer. Lo Chung-fan stoutly contends for retaining 命, and interprets it as="fate," but he is obliged to supply a good deal himself, to make any sense of the passage. See his argument, *in loc.* The paraphrasts all explain 先 by 早, "early." 遠, 3rd tone, but with a hiphil force. 退 is referred to 放 流 in the last paragraph, and 遠 to 不 與 同 中 國. 17. This is spoken of the ruler not

having respect to the common feelings of the people in his employment of ministers, and the consequences thereof to himself. 夫, 1st tone, is used as in Analects, XI, ix, 4, or = the preposition 乎. *This paragraph speaks generally of the primal cause of gaining and losing, and shows how the principle of the measuring square must have its root in the ruler's mind.* So, in the 日 講. The great course is explained by Chû as—"the art of occupying the throne, and therein cultivating himself and governing others." Ying-tâ says it is—"the course by which he practices filial

財。〇廿一節 財發身不仁者以身發 舒、則財恆足矣。〇二十節 仁者以 者寡爲之者疾用之者 有大道、生之者眾食之 得之驕泰以失之。〇十九節 生財
未有上好仁、而下不

and sincerity to attain it, and by pride and extravagance he will fail of it.

19. There is a great course *also* for the production
of wealth. Let the producers be many and the
consumers few. Let there be activity in the production, and economy in the expenditure. Then the
wealth will always be sufficient.

20. The virtuous *ruler*, by means of his wealth,
makes himself more distinguished. The vicious ruler
accumulates wealth, at the expense of his life.

21. Never has there been a case of the sovereign

piety, fraternal duty, benevolence,
and righteousness." 驕 and 泰 are
here qualities of the same nature.
They are not contrasted as in the Analects, XIII, xxvi. 19. This is understood by K'ang-ch'ăng as requiring
the promotion of agriculture, and
that is included, but does not exhaust the meaning. The consumers
are the salaried officers of the government. The sentiment of the whole
is good;—where there *is* cheerful in-
dustry in the people, and an economical administration of the government, the finances will be flourishing.
20. The sentiment here is substantially the same as in paragraphs 7, 8.
The old interpretation is different:—
"The virtuous man uses *his* wealth
so as to make his person distinguished. He who is not virtuous, toils
with his body to increase his wealth."
21. This shows how the people
respond to the influence of the ruler,
and that benevolence, even to the
scattering of his wealth on the part

聚斂之臣、與其有聚斂之

不畜牛羊、百乘之家不畜

乘、不察於雞豚、伐冰之家、

其財者也。孟獻子曰、畜馬 二十二節

不終者也、未有府庫財、非

好義者也、未有好義其事

loving benevolence, and the people not loving righteousness. Never has there been a case where the
people have loved righteousness, and the affairs of the
sovereign have not been carried to completion. And
never has there been a case where the wealth in such
a state, collected in the treasuries and arsenals, did
not continue in the sovereign's possession.

22. The officer Măng Hsien said, "He who keeps
horses and a carriage does not look after fowls and
pigs. The family which keeps its stores of ice does
not rear cattle or sheep. *So*, the house which possesses a hundred chariots should not keep a minister to look out for imposts that he may lay them
on the people. Than to have such a minister, it were

of the latter, is the way to permanent
prosperity and wealth. 22. Hsien
was the honorary epithet of Chung-
sun Mieh (蔑), a worthy minister of
Lû under the two dukes, who ruled
before the birth of Confucius. His
sayings, quoted here, were preserved
by tradition, or recorded in some
Work which is now lost. 畜 (read
ch'ŭ) 乘 馬,—on a scholar's being

臣、寧有盜臣、此謂國不以

利爲利、以義爲利也〇廿三節長國

家、而務財用者必自小人

矣、彼爲善之、小人之使爲

國家、菑害竝至、雖有善者、

亦無如之何矣、此謂國不

以利爲利、以義爲利也。

better for that house to have one who should rob it *of its revenues*." This is in accordance whith the saying:—"In a state, *pecuniary* gain is not to be considered to be prosperity, but its prosperity *will* be found in righteousness."

23. When he who presides over a state or a family makes his revenues his chief business, he must be under the influence of some small, mean man. He may consider this man to be good; but when such a person is employed in the administration of a state or family, calamities *from Heaven*, and injuries *from men*, will befall it together, and, though a good man may take his place, he will not be able to remedy the evil. This illustrates *again* the saying, "In a state, gain is not to be considered prosperity, but its prosperity will be found in righteousness."

first called to office, he was gifted by his prince with a carriage and four horses. He was then supposed to withdraw from petty ways of getting wealth. The 殯, or high officers of a state, kept ice for use in their funeral rites and sacrifices. 伐 冰,— with reference to the *cutting* the ice to store it; see the Shih, I, xv, Ode I, 8. 聚 斂 之 臣,—see Analects, XI, xvi. 23. 彼爲善之,—善 is used as a verb,=以 爲 善, "considers to be good." 不 以 利 爲 利, 以 義 爲 利, —see Mencius, 1, Pt. I, i, *et passim*.

右傳之十章、釋治國平
天下。凡傳十章、前四章、
統論綱領指趣、後六章、
細論條目工夫其第五
章、乃明善之要、第六章、
乃誠身之本、在初學、尤
爲當務之急讀者不可
以其近而忽之也。

The above tenth chapter of commentary explains the government of the state,
and the making the kingdom peaceful and happy.

There are thus, in all, ten chapters of commentary, `the first four of which
discuss, in a general manner, the scope of the principal topic of the Work;
while the other six go particularly into an exhibition of the work required in
its subordinate branches. The fifth chapter contains the important subject
of comprehending true excellence, and the sixth, what is the foundation of
the attainment of true sincerity. Those two chapters demand the especial
attention of the learner. Let not the reader despise them because of their
simplicity.

# THE DOCTRINE OF THE MEAN

中庸

子程子曰、不偏

之謂中、不易之

謂庸、中者、天下

之正道、庸者、天

下之定理、此篇

*My master, the philosopher Ch'ăng, says—"Being without inclination to either side is called CHUNG; admitting of no change is called YUNG. By CHUNG is denoted the correct course to be pursued by all under heaven; by YUNG is denoted the fixed principle regulating all under heaven. This work contains*

THE TITLE OF THE WORK.—中庸, "The Doctrine of the Mean." I have not attempted to translate the Chinese character 庸, as to the exact force of which there is considerable difference of opinion, both among native commentators, and among previous translators. Chǎng K'ang-ch'ǎng said ~名曰中庸者、以其記中和之為用也, "The Work is named 中庸, because it records the practice of the non-deviating mind and of harmony." He takes 庸 in the sense of 用, "to use," "to employ," which is the first given to it in the dictionary, and is found in the Shû-ching, I, i, par. 9. As to the meaning of 中 and 和, see chap. i, par. 4. This appears to have been the accepted meaning of 庸 in this combination, till Ch'ăng Î introduced that of 不 易, "unchanging," as in the introductory note, which, however, the dictionary does not acknowledge. Chû Hsî himself says—中者不偏不倚, 無過不及之名, 庸, 平常也, "*Chung* is the name for what is without inclination or deflection, which neither exceeds nor comes short. *Yung* means ordinary, constant. The dictionary gives another meaning of *Yung*, with special reference to the point before us. It is said—又 和 也, "It also means harmony;" and then reference is made to K'ang-ch'ǎng's words given above, the compilers not having observed that he immediately subjoins—庸, 用 也, showing that he takes *Yung* in the sense of "to

其味無窮、皆實學也、善

六合、卷之則退藏於密、

復合爲一理、放之則彌

言一理、中散爲萬事、末

於書以授孟子、其書始

恐其久而差也、故筆之

乃孔門傳授心法子思

*the law of the mind, which was handed down from one to another, in the*
*Confucian school, till Tsze-sze, fearing lest in the course of time errors*
*should arise about it, committed it to writing, and delivered it to Mencius.*
*The Book first speaks of one principle; it next spreads this out, and*
*embraces all things; finally, it returns and gathers them all up under the one*
*principle.  Unroll it, and it fills the universe; roll it up, and it retires and*
*lies hid in mysteriousness.  The relish of it is inexhaustible.  The whole of*
*it is solid learning.  When the skillful reader has explored it with delight*

employ," and not of "harmony."
Many, however, adopt this meaning
of the term in chap. ii, and my own
opinion is decidedly in favor of it,
here in the title.  The work then
treats of the human mind:—in its
state of *chung*, absolutely correct, as
it is in itself; and in its state of *hwo*,
or harmony, acting *ad extra*, accord-·
ing to its correct nature.—In the
version of the work, given in the
collection of "*Memoires concernant l'
histoire, les sciences, etc., des Chinois*,"
vol. i, it is styled—"*Juste Milieu*."
Rémusat calls it "*L'invariable
Milieu*," after Ch'ăng Ï.  Intorcetta
and his coadjutors call it—"*Medium
constans vel sempiternum*."  The Book
treats, they say, "*De MEDIO SEMPI-
TERNO, sive de durea mediocritate illa,
quæ est, ut ait Cicero, inter nimium et*

*parum, constanter et omnibus in rebus
tenenda*."  Morrison, character 庸,
says, "*Chung Yung*, the constant
(golden) Medium."  Collie calls it—
"*The golden Medium*."  The objection which I have to all these names
is, that from them it would appear
as if 中 were a noun, and 庸 a qualifying adjective, whereas they are
coordinate terms.  My own version
of the title in the translation published in "The Sacred Books of the
East" is "*The State of Equilibrium
and Harmony*."

INTRODUCTORY NOTE.  子程子,—
see on introductory note to the 大
學.  On Tsze-sze, and his authorship
of this work, see the prolegomena.
六合 is a phrase denoting—"the
zenith and nadir, and the four cardinal points,"=the universe. 善讀

性之謂道、修道之

天命之謂性、率

矣。

之、有不能盡者

得焉、則終身用

讀者、玩索而有

*till he has apprehended it, he may carry it into practice all his life, and will find that it cannot be exhausted."*

CHAPTER I. 1. What Heaven has conferred is called THE NATURE; an accordance with this nature is called THE PATH *of duty;* the regulation of this path is called INSTRUCTION.

者,—not our "good reader," but as in the translation.—I will not here anticipate the judgment of the reader on the eulogy of the enthusiastic Ch'ăng.

1. It has been stated, in the prolegomena, that the current division of the Chung Yung into chapters was made by Chû Hsî, as well as their subdivision into paragraphs. The thirty-three chapters which embrace the work are again arranged by him in five divisions, as will be seen from his supplementary notes. The first and last chapters are complete in themselves, as in the introduction and conclusion of the treatise. The second part contains ten chapters; the third, nine; and the fourth, twelve.

*Par. 1. The principles of duty have their root in the evidenced will of Heaven, and their full exhibition in the teaching of sages.* By 性, or "nature," is to be understood the nature of man, though Chû Hsî generalizes it so as to embrace that of brutes also; but only *man* can be cognizant of the *tâo* and *chiâo*. 命 he defines by 令, "to command," "to order." But we must take it as in a gloss on a passage from the Yî-ching, quoted in the dictionary.— 命 者 人 所 稟 受, "*Ming* is what men are endowed with." Chû also says that 性 is just 理, the "principle," characteristic of any particular nature. But this only involves the subject in mystery. His explanation of 道 by 路, "a path," seems to be correct, though some modern writers object to it.—What is taught seems to be this:—To man belongs a moral nature, conferred on him by Heaven or God, by which he is constituted a law to himself. But as he is prone to deviate from the path in which, according to his nature, he should go, wise and good men—sages—have appeared, to explain and regulate this, helping all by their instructions to walk in it.

故君子愼其燭也。

見乎隱莫顯乎微、

懼乎其所不聞莫○三郎

愼乎其所不睹恐

道也、是故君子戒

須臾離也、可離、非

謂教道也者、不可 ○二

2. The path may not be left for an instant. If it could be left, it would not be the path. On this account, the superior man does not wait till he sees things, to be cautious, nor till he hears things, to be apprehensive.

3. There is nothing more visible than what is secret, and nothing more manifest than what is minute. Therefore the superior man is watchful over himself, when he is alone.

*Par. 2. The path indicated by the nature may never be left, and the superior man*—體道之人, *he who would embody all principles of right and duty—exercises a most sedulous care that he may attain thereto.* 須臾 is a name for a short period of time, of which there are thirty in the twenty-four hours; but the phrase is commonly read for "a moment," "an instant." K'ung-Ying-tâ explains 可離非道,—"what may be left is a wrong way," which is not admissible. 離, 4th tone,=去, "to be, or go, away from." If we translate the two last clauses literally, it "is cautious and careful in regard to what he does not see; is fearful and apprehensive in regard to what he does not hear,"—they will not be intelligible to an English reader. A question arises, moreover, whether 其所不睹. 其所不聞, ought not to be understood passively,="where he is not seen," "where he is not heard." They are so understood by Ying-tâ, and the 大學傳. chap vi, is much in favor, by its analogy, of such an interpretation.

*Par. 3.* Chû Hsî says that 隱 is "a dark place"; that 細 means "small matters"; and that 獨 is "the place which other men do not know, and is known only to one's self." There would thus hardly be here any advance from the last paragraph. It seems to me that the secrecy must be in the recesses of one's own heart, and the minute things, the springs of thought and stirrings of purpose there. The full development of what is intended here is probably to be found in all the subsequent passages about 誠, or "sincerity." See 四河合集, 中庸說, *in loc.*

喜、怒哀樂之未

發、謂之中發而

皆中節謂之和、

中也者、天下之

大本也、和也者、

天下之達道也。

致中和、天地位

4. While there are no stirrings of pleasure, anger, sorrow, or joy, the mind may be said to be in the state of EQUILIBRIUM. When those feelings have been stirred, and they act in their due degree, there ensues what may be called the state of HARMONY. This EQUILIBRIUM is the great root *from which grow all the human actings* in the world, and this HARMONY is the universal path *which they all should pursue.*

5. Let the states of equilibrium and harmony exist in perfection, and a happy order will prevail

*Par. 4.* "This," says Chû Hsî, "speaks of the virtue of the nature and passions, to illustrate the meaning of the statement that the path may not be left." It is difficult to translate the paragraph because it is difficult to understand it. 謂 之 is different from 之 謂 in par. 1. That *defines;* this *describes.* What is described in the first clause, seems to be 性, "the nature," capable of all feelings, but unacted on, and in equilibrium.

*Par. 5.* On this Intorcetta and his colleagues observe:—*Quis non videt eo dumtaxat collimasse philosophum, ut hominis naturam, quam ab origine sua rectam, sed deinde lapsam et depravatam passim Sinenses docent, ad primœvum innocentiœ statum reduceret? Atque ita reliquas 'res creatas, homini jam rebelles, et in ejusdem ruinam armatas, ad pristinum obsequium veluti revocaret. Hoc caput primum libri Ta Heŏ, hoc item hic et alibi non semel indicat. Etsi autem nesciret philosophus nos a prima felicitate propter peccatum primi parentis excidisse, tamen et tot rerum quæ adversantur et infestæ sunt homini, et ipsius naturæ humanæ ad deteriora tam pronæ, longo usu et contemplatione didicisse videtur, non posse hoc universum, quod homo vitiatus quodam modo vitiarat, connaturali suæ integritati et ordini restitui, nisi prius ipse homo per victoriam sui ipsius, cam, quam amiserat, integritatem et ordinem recuperaret."* I fancied something of the same kind, before reading their note. According to Chû Hsî, the

焉、萬物育焉。

右第一章、子思述所傳之
意以立言首明道之本原
出於天、而不可易其實體
備於己、而不可離次言存
養省察之要、終言聖神功
化之極、蓋欲學者於此、反

throughout heaven and earth, and all things will be nourished and flourish.

*In the first chapter, which is given above, Tsze-sze states the views which had been handed down to him, as the basis of his discourse. First, it shows clearly how the path of duty is to be traced to its origin in Heaven, and is unchangeable, while the substance of it is provided in ourselves, and may not be departed from. Next, it speaks of the importance of preserving and nourishing this, and of exercising a watchful self-scrutiny with reference to it. Finally, it speaks of the meritorious achievements and transforming influence of sage and spiritual men in their highest extent. The wish of Tsze-sze was that hereby the learner should direct his thoughts*

paragraph describes the work and influence of sage and spiritual men in their highest issues. The subject is developed in the 4th part of the work, in very extravagant and mystical language. The study of it will modify very much our assent to the views in the above passage. There is in this whole chapter a mixture of sense and mysticism,—of what may be grasped, and what tantalizes and eludes the mind. 位, according to Chû Hsî, = 安其位, "will rest in their positions." K'ang-ch'äng explained it by 正,—"will be rectified." "Heaven and Earth" are here the parent powers of the universe. Thus Ying-tâ expounds: "Heaven and Earth will get their correct place, and the processes of production and completion will go on according to their principles, so that all things will be nourished and fostered."

CONCLUDING NOTE. The writer Yang, A. D. 1053–1135, quoted here, was a distinguished scholar and

仲尼曰、君子中庸、小人反

夫子之言、以終此章之義。

是也、其下十章蓋子思引

善、楊氏所謂一篇之體要

外誘之私、而充其本然之

求諸身、而自得之以去夫

*inwards, and by searching in himself, there find these truths, so that he might put aside all outward temptations appealing to his selfishness, and fill up the measure of the goodness which is natural to him. This chapter is what the writer Yang called it,—"The sum of the whole work." In the ten chapters which follow, Tsze-sze quotes the words of the Master to complete the meaniny of this.*

CHAPTER II. 1. Chung-nî said, "The superior man *embodies* the course of the Mean; the mean man acts contrary to the course of the Mean.

author in the Sung dynasty. He was a disciple of Ch'ăng Hâo, and a friend both of him and his brother Î. 體 要, "the substance and the abstract," = the sum.

2. ONLY THE SUPERIOR MAN CAN FOLLOW THE MEAN; THE MEAN MAN IS ALWAYS VIOLATING IT. 1. Why Confucius should here be quoted by his designation, or marriage name, is a moot-point. It is said by some that disciples might in this way refer to their teacher, and a grandson to his grandfather, but such a rule is constituted probable on the strength of this instance, and that in chap.

xxx. Others say that it is the honorary designation of the sage, and = the 尼 父, which Duke Âi used in reference to Confucius, in eulogizing him after his death. See the Lî Chî, II, Sect. I, iii, 44. Some verb must be understood between 君 子 and 中 庸, and I have supposed it to be 體, with most of the paraphrasts. Nearly all seem to be agreed that 中 庸 here is the same as 中 和 in the last chapter. On the change of terms, Chû Hsî quotes from the scholar Yû (遊), to the effect that 中 和 is said with the nature and feelings in view, and 中 庸, with reference to virtue

乎、民鮮能久矣。 子曰中庸其至矣 憚也。 中庸也、小人而無忌 君子而時中小人之 中庸。君子之中庸也、

2. "The superior man's embodying the course of the Mean is because he is a superior man, and so always maintains the Mean. The mean man's acting contrary to the course of the Mean is because he is a mean man, and has no caution."

CHAPTER III. The Master said, "Perfect is the virtue which is according to the Mean! Rare have they long been among the people, who could practice it!"

and conduct. 2. 君子而時中 is explained by Chû:—"Because he has the virtue of a superior man, and moreover is able always to manage the *chung*." But I rather think that the *chun-tsze* here is specially to be referred to the same as described in I, ii, and 中＝正 中. Wang Sû, the famous scholar of the Wei (魏) dynasty, in the first part of the third century, quotes 小 人 之 中庸, with 反 before 中, of which Chû Hsî approves. If 反 be not introduced into the text, it must certainly be understood. 忌 憚 is the opposite of 戒 慎, 恐 懼, in 1, ii.—This, and the

ten chapters which follow, all quote the words of Confucius with reference to the 中 庸, to explain the meaning of the first chapter; and "though there is no connection of composition between them," says Chû Hsî, "they are all related by their meaning."

3. THE RARITY, LONG EXISTING IN CONFUCIUS'S TIME, OF THE PRACTICE OF THE MEAN. See the Analects, VI, xxvii. K'ang-ch'ăng and Ying-tâ take the last clause as="few can practice it long." But the view in the translation is better. The change from 仲 尼 曰 to 子 曰 is observable.

也。

人莫不飲食也、鮮能知　味

賢者過之、不肖者不及也、

也、道之不明也、我知之矣、

之矣、知者過之、愚者不及

子曰、道之不行也、我知

CHAPTER IV. 1. The Master said, "I know how it is that the path *of the Mean* is not walked in:—The knowing go beyond it, and the stupid do not come up to it. I know how it is that the path of the Mean is not understood:—The men of talents and virtue go beyond it, and the worthless do not come up to it.

2. "There is no body but eats and drinks. But they are few who can distinguish flavors."

4. HOW IT WAS THAT FEW WERE ABLE TO PRACTICE THE MEAN. 1. 道 may be referred to the 道 in the first chapter; immediately following 中庸 in the last, I translate it here—"the path of the Mean." 知者 and 賢者 are not to be understood as meaning the truly wise and the truly worthy, but only those who in the degenerate times of Confucius deemed themselves to be such. The former thought the course of the Mean not worth their study, and the latter thought it not sufficiently exalted for their practice. 肖,—"as," "like."

不肖 following 賢, indicates individuals of a different character, not equal to them. 2. We have here not a comparison, but an illustration, which may help to an understanding of the former paragraph, though it does not seem very apt. People do not know the true flavor of what they eat and drink, but they need not go beyond that to learn it. So the Mean belongs to all the actions of ordinary life, and might be discerned and practiced in them, without looking for it in extraordinary things.

子曰、道其不行

矣夫。

子曰、舜其大知

也與、舜好問而好

察邇言隱惡而揚

善、執其兩端、用其

中於民、其斯以為

舜乎。

CHAPTER V. The Master said, "Alas! How is the path of the Mean untrodden!"

CHAPTER VI. The Master said, "There was Shun:— He indeed was greatly wise! Shun loved to question *others*, and to study their words, though they might be shallow. He concealed what was bad *in them,* and displayed what was good. He took hold of their two extremes, *determined* the Mean, and employed it in *his government of* the people. It was by this that he was Shun!"

5. Chû Hsî says: "From not being understood, therefore it is not practiced." According to K'ang-ch'ăng, the remark is a lament that there was no intelligent sovereign to teach the path. But the two views are reconcilable.

6. How SHUN PURSUED THE COURSE OF THE MEAN. This example of Shun, it seems to me, is adduced in opposition to the knowing of chap. iv. Shun, though a sage, invited the opinions of all men, and found truth of the highest value in their simplest sayings, and was able to determine from them the course of the Mean. 執其兩端,— "the two extremes," are understood by K'ang-ch'ăng of the two errors of exceeding and coming short of the Mean. Chû Hsî makes them—"the widest differences in the opinions which he received." I conceive the meaning to be that he examined the answers which he got, in their entirety, from beginning to end. Compare 扣其兩端, Analects, IX, vii. His concealing what was bad, and displaying what was good, was alike to encourage people to speak freely to him. K'ang-ch'ăng makes the last sentence to turn on the meaning of 舜, when applied as an honorary epithet of the dead,= "Full, all-accomplished"; but Shun was so named when he was alive.

子曰、人皆曰予知、驅

而納諸罟擭陷阱之中、

而莫之知辟也人皆曰

予知、擇乎中庸、而不能

期月守也。

子曰、回之爲人也、擇

乎中庸、得一善、則拳拳

服膺、而弗失之矣。

CHAPTER VII. The Master said, "Men all say, 'We are wise'; but being driven forward and taken in a net, a trap, or a pitfall, they know not how to escape. Men all say, 'We are wise'; but happening to choose the course of the Mean, they are not able to keep it for a round month."

CHAPTER VIII. The Master said, "This was the manner of Hûi:—he made choice of the Mean, and whenever he got hold of what was good, he clasped it firmly, as if wearing it on his breast, and did not lose it."

7. THEIR CONTRARY CONDUCT SHOWS MEN'S IGNORANCE OF THE COURSE AND NATURE OF THE MEAN. The first 予 知 is to be understood with a general reference,—"We are wise," i. e., we can very well take care of ourselves. Yet the presumption of such a profession is seen in men's not being able to take care of themselves. The application of this illustration is then made to the subject in hand, the second 予 知 requiring to be specially understood with reference to the subject of the Mean. The conclusion in both parts is left to be drawn by the reader for himself. 擭, read hwâ, 4th tone, "a trap for catching animals." 期, read ch'î, like 朞, in Analects, XIII, x, though it is here applied to a month, and not, as there, to a year.

8. HOW HÛI HELD FAST THE COURSE OF THE MEAN. Here the example of Hûi is likewise adduced, in opposition to those mentioned in chap. iv. All the rest is exegetical of the first clause—回 之 爲 人 也, "Hûi's playing the man." 一 善 is not "one good point," so much as any one. 拳 is "the closed fist"; 拳 拳,—"the appearance of holding firm."

子曰、天下國
家、可均也、爵祿、
可辭也、白刃、可
蹈也、中庸、不可
能也。

子路問強。

曰、南方之強與、

北方之強與抑

CHAPTER IX. The Master said, "The kingdom, its states, and its families, may be perfectly ruled; dignities and emoluments may be declined; naked weapons may be trampled under the feet;—but the course of the Mean cannot be attained to."

CHAPTER X. 1. Tsze-lû asked about energy.

2. The Master said, "Do you mean the energy of the South, the energy of the North, or the energy which you should cultivate yourself?

9. THE DIFFICULTY OF ATTAINING TO THE COURSE OF THE MEAN. 天下,—"the kingdom"; we should say —"kingdoms," but the Chinese know only of *one* kingdom, and hence this name for it—"all under the sky," embracing by right, if not in fact, all kingdoms. The kingdom was made up of states, and each state of families. See the Analects, V, vii; XII, xx. 均, "level"; here a verb= 平治, "to bring to perfect order." 刃,—"a sharp, strong weapon," used of swords, spears, javelins, etc. 不可能,—literally. "cannot be *canned.*"

10. ON ENERGY IN ITS RELATION TO THE MEAN. In the Analects we find Tsze-lû, on various occasions, putting forward the subject of his valor (勇), and claiming, on the ground of it, such praise as the Master awarded to Hûi. We may suppose, with the old interpreters, that hearing Hûi commended, as in chap. viii, he wanted to know whether Confucius would not allow that he also could, with his forceful character, seize and hold fast the Mean. 1. For 強 I have been disposed to coin the term "forcefulness." Chû defines it correctly—力足以勝人之名, "the name of strength sufficient to overcome others." 2. 而 (=汝) 強 must be— "the energy which you should cultivate," not "which you have." If the latter be the meaning, no further notice of it is taken in Confucius's reply, while he would seem, in the three following paragraphs, to describe the three kinds of energy which he specifies. K'ang-ch'ǎng and Ying-tâ say that 而 強 means the energy of the Middle Kingdom, the North being "the sandy desert," and the South, "the country south of the Yangtze." But this is not

不流、強哉矯中立

居之故君子、和而

方之強也、而強者

金革、死而不厭、北

強也、君子居之衽

不報無道、南方之

而強與寬柔以教、

3. "To show forbearance and gentleness in teaching others; and not to revenge unreasonable conduct:—this is the energy of southern regions, and the good man makes it his study.

4. "To lie under arms; and meet death without regret:—this is the energy of northern regions, and the forceful make it their study.

5. "Therefore, the superior man cultivates *a friendly* harmony, without being weak.—How firm is he in his energy! He stands erect in the middle,

allowable. 3. That climate and situation have an influence on character is not to be denied, and the Chinese notions on the subject may be seen in the amplification of the 9th of the K'ang-hsî celebrated Precepts (聖諭廣訓). But to speak of their effects as Confucius here does is extravagant. The barbarism of the South, according to the interpretation mentioned above, could not have been described by him in these terms. The energy of mildness and forbearance, thus described, is held to come short of the Mean; and therefore 君子 is taken with a low and light meaning, far short of what it has in par. 5. This practice of determining the force of phrases from the context makes the reading of the Chinese classics perplexing to a student. 居之,—see the Analects, XII, xiv. 4. 衽, "the lapel in front of a coat"; also "a mat." 衽金革, "to make a mat of the leather dress (革) and weapons (金)." This energy of the North, it is said, is in excess of the Mean, and the 故, at the beginning of par. 5, "therefore," = "those two kinds of energy being thus respectively in defect and excess." 矯 is 強貌, "the appearance of being energetic." This illustrates the energy which is in exact accord

爲之矣。君子遵道　後世有述焉、吾弗　子曰、素隱行怪、　不變、強哉矯。　哉矯、國無道至死　有道不變塞焉、強　而不倚、強哉矯、國

without inclining to either side.—How firm is he in his energy! When good principles prevail in the government of his country, he does not change from what he was in retirement.—How firm is he in his energy! When bad principles prevail in the country, he maintains his course to death without changing.—How firm is he in his energy!"

CHAPTER XI. 1. The Master said, "To live in obscurity, and yet practice wonders, in order to be mentioned with honor in future ages:—this is what I do not do.

2. "The good man tries to proceed according to

with the Mean, in the individual's treatment of others, in his regulation of himself, and in relation to public affairs. 有道, 無道;—often in the Analects. I have followed Chû Hsî in translating 塞. Ying-tâ paraphrases: 守直不懇德行充實, "He holds to what is upright, and does not change, his virtuous conduct being all-complete." A modern writer makes the meaning: "He does not change through being puffed up by the fullness of office." Both of these views go on the interpretation of 塞 as＝實.

11. ONLY THE SAGE CAN COME UP TO THE REQUIREMENTS OF THE MEAN.

1. 素 is found written 索, "to examine," "to study," in a work of the Han dynasty, and Chû adopts that character as the true reading, and explains accordingly:—"To study what is obscure and wrong (隱僻)." K'ang-ch'äng took it as＝傃, "towards," or, "being inclined to," and both he and Ying-tâ explain as in the translation. It is an objection to Chû's view, that, in the next chapter, 隱 is given as ·one of the characteristics of the Mean. The 遯世 云 云, in par. 3, moreover, agree well with the older view. 2. 君子 is here the same as in the last chapter, par. 3. A distinction is made between

道費而隱。　量君子之　能之。　悔唯聖者　見知、而不　庸遯世不　子依乎中　能已矣。君　而廢吾弗　而行、半塗

the right path, but when he has gone halfway, he abandons it:—I am not able *so* to stop.

3. "The superior man accords with the course of the Mean. Though he may be all unknown, unregarded by the world, he feels no regret.—It is only the sage who is able for this."

CHAPTER XII. 1. The way which the superior man pursues, reaches wide and far, and yet is secret.

遵 道 here and 依 道 below. The former, it is said, implies endeavor, while the latter is natural and unconstrained accordance. 3. 君 子 here has its very highest signification, and = 聖 者 in the last clause. 遯 世 is said to be different from 避 世, the latter being applicable to the recluse who withdraws from the world, while the former may describe one who is in the world, but does not act with a reference to its opinion of him. It will be observed how Confucius declines saying that he had himself attained to this highest style—"With this chapter," says Chû Hsî, "the quotations by Tsze-sze of the Master's words, to explain the meaning of the first chapter, stop. The great object of the work is to set forth wisdom, benevolent virtue, and valor, as the three grand virtues whereby entrance is effected into the path of the Mean, and therefore, at its commencement, they are illustrated by reference to Shun, Yen Yuan, and Tsze-lû; Shun possessing the wisdom, Yen Yüan the benevolence, and Tsze-lû the valor. If one of these virtues be absent, there is no way of advancing to the path, and perfecting the virtue. This will be found fully treated of in the 20th chapter." So, Chû Hsî. The student forming a judgment for himself, however, will not see very distinctly any reference to these cardinal virtues. The utterances of the sage illustrate the phrase 中 庸, showing that the course of the Mean had fallen out of observance, some overshooting it, and others coming short of it. When we want some precise directions how to attain to it, we come finally to the conclusion that only the sage is capable of doing so. We greatly want teaching, more practical and precise.

12. THE COURSE OF THE MEAN REACHES FAR AND WIDE, BUT YET IS SECRET. With this chapter, the third part of the work commences, and the first sentence,—君 子 之 道，費 而 隱，may be regarded as its text. If we could determine satisfactorily the signification of those two terms, we

君子語大天下莫
也人猶有所憾故
不能焉、天地之大
也、雖聖人亦有所
以能行焉、及其至
焉、夫婦之不肖、可
聖人亦有所不知
知焉、及其至也、雖
夫婦之愚、可以與

2. Common men and women, however ignorant, may intermeddle with the knowledge of it; yet in its utmost reaches, there is that which even the sage does not know. Common men and women, however much below the ordinary standard of character, can carry it into practice; yet in its utmost reaches, there is that which even the sage is not able to carry into practice. Great as heaven and earth are, men still find some things in them with which to be dissatisfied. Thus it is that, were the superior man to speak of his way in all its greatness, nothing in the world would be

should have a good clue to the meaning of the whole, but it is not easy to do so. The old view is inadmissible. K'ang-ch'ăng takes 費 as＝佹, "doubly involved," "perverted," and both he and Ying-tâ explain:—"When right principles are opposed and disallowed, the superior man retires into obscurity, and does not hold office." On this view of it, the sentence has nothing to do with the succeeding chapters. The two meanings of 費 in the dictionary are —"the free expenditure of money," and "dissipation," or "waste." According to Chû, in this passage, 費 即 用 之 廣 也, "費 indicates the wide range of the tâo in practice."

Something like this must be its meaning:—the course of the Mean, requiring everywhere to be exhibited. Chû then defines 隱 as 體 之 微, "the minuteness of the tâo in its nature or essence." The former answers to the *what* of the tâo, and the latter to the *why*. But it rather seems to me that the 隱 here is the same with the 隱 and 微, i, 4, and that the author simply intended to say that the way of the superior man reaching everywhere,—embracing all duties,—yet had its secret spring and seat in the Heaven-gifted nature, the individual consciousness of duty in every man    2. 夫 婦＝匹 夫, 匹 婦, Analects, XIV, xviii, 3. But

察乎天地。

道、造端乎夫婦、及其至也、

淵、言其上下察也君子之

焉。詩云、鳶飛戻天、魚躍于

能哉焉、語小、天下莫能破

found able to embrace it, and were he to speak of it in its minuteness, nothing in the world would be found able to split it.

3.　It is said in the Book of Poetry, "The hawk flies up to heaven; the fishes leap in the deep." This expresses how this *way* is seen above and below.

4.　The way of the superior man may be found, in its simple elements, in the intercourse of common men and women; but in its utmost reaches, it shines brightly through heaven and earth.

I confess to be all at sea in the study of this paragraph Chû quotes from the scholar Hâu (侯 氏), that what the superior man fails to know was exemplified in Confucius's having to ask about ceremonies and offices, and what he fails to practice was exemplified in Confucius not being on the throne, and in Yâo and Shun's being dissatisfied that they could not make every individual enjoy the benefits of their rule. He adds his own opinion, that what men complained of in Heaven and Earth, was the partiality of their operations in overshadowing and supporting, producing and completing, the heat of summer, the cold of winter, etc. If such things were intended by the writer, we can only regret the vagueness of his language, and the want of coherence in his argument. In translating 君子語大云云, I have followed Mâo Hsî-ho.　3. See the Shih, III, i, Ode V, st. 3.　The ode is in praise of the virtue of King Wăn. 察 is in the sense of 昭 著, "brightly displayed." The application of the words of the ode does appear strange.

柯、睨而視之猶以爲遠、故君
柯伐柯、其則不遠、執柯以伐
而遠人、不可以爲道。詩云、伐
子曰、道不遠人、人之爲道
之言以明之。
意也、其下八章、雜引孔子
以申明首章道不可離之
右第十二章子思之言、蓋

*The twelfth chapter above contains tne words of Tsze-sze, and is designed to illustra'e what is said in the first chapter, that "The path may not be left." In the eight chapters which follow, he quotes, in a miscellaneous way, the words of Confucius to illustrate it.*

CHAPTER XIII. 1. The Master said, "The path is not far from man. When men try to pursue a course, which is far from the common indications of consciousness, this course cannot be considered THE PATH.

2. "In the Book of Poetry, it is said, 'In hewing an ax handle, in hewing an ax handle, the pattern is not far off.' We grasp one ax handle to hew the other; and yet, if we look askance from the one to the other, we may consider them as apart. Therefore,

13. THE PATH OF THE MEAN IS NOT FAR TO SEEK. EACH MAN HAS THE LAW OF IT IN HIMSELF, AND IT IS TO BE PURSUED WITH EARNEST SINCERITY. 1. 人之爲道而遠人, "When men practice a course, and *wish to be* far from men." The meaning is as in the translation. 2. See the Shih-ching, I, xv, Ode V, st. 2. The object of the paragraph seems to be to show that the rule for dealing with men, according to the principles of the Mean, is nearer to us than the one ax is to the other. The branch

子以人治人、改而止忠。

恕違道不遠、施諸己而

不願、亦勿施於人君子

之道四、丘未能一焉、所

求乎子、以事父、未能也、

所求乎臣、以事君、未能

the superior man governs men, according to their nature, with what is proper to them, and as soon as they change *what is wrong,* he stops.

3. "When one cultivates to the utmost the principles of his nature, and exercises them on the principle of reciprocity, he is not far from the path. What you do not like when done to yourself, do not do to others.

4. "In the way of the superior man there are four things, to not one of which have I as yet attained.— To serve my father, as I would require my son to serve me: to this I have not attained; to serve my prince, as I would require my minister to serve me: to

is hewn, and its form altered from its natural one. Not so with man. The change in him only brings him to his proper state. 3. Compare Analects, IV, xv. 違 is here a neuter verb="to be distant from." 4. The admissions made by Confucius here are remarkable, and we do not think the less of him because of them. Those who find it necessary to insist, with the Chinese, on his having been, like other men, compassed with infirmity, dwell often on them: but it must be allowed that the cases, as put by him, are in a measure hypothetical, his father having died when

慥
爾。

行、行顧言君子胡不慥

不勉有餘不敢盡言顧

言之謹、有所不足不敢

之未能也庸德之行、庸

能也、所求乎朋友、先施

也、所求乎弟以事兄、未

this I have not attained; to serve my elder brother, as
I would require my younger brother to serve me: to
this I have not attained; to set the example in
behaving to a friend, as I would require him to behave
to me: to this I have not attained. Earnest in
practicing the ordinary virtues, and careful in speaking
about them, if, in his practice, he has anything
defective, the superior man dares not but exert himself;
and if, in his words, he has any excess, he dares not
allow himself such license. Thus his words have
respect to his actions, and his actions have respect to
his words; is it not just an entire sincerity which
marks the superior man?"

he was a child. He passes from
speaking of himself by his name (丘),
to speak of the *chün-tsze*, and the
change is most naturally made after
the last 能也. 庸德之行, 庸言之
謹,—"in the practice of ordinary
virtues," i. e., the duties of a son,
minister, etc., mentioned above, and
"in the carefulness of ordinary
speech," i. e., speaking about those
virtues. To the practice belong the
clauses 有所不足, 不敢不免, and
to the speaking, the two next clauses.
爾,—as a final particle, =耳, "simply," "just."

子無入而不自得

患難行乎患難、君

夷狄行乎夷狄、素

貧賤行乎貧賤、素

富貴行乎富貴、素

行、不願乎其外。二前 素

㊀ 君子素其位而 一前

CHAPTER XIV.　1. The superior man does what is proper to the station in which he is; he does not desire to go beyond this.

2.　In a position of wealth and honor, he does what is proper to a position of wealth and honor.　In a poor and low position, he does what is proper to a poor and low position.　Situated among barbarous tribes, he does what is proper to a situation among barbarous tribes.　In a position of sorrow and difficulty, he does what is proper to a position of sorrow and difficulty. The superior man can find himself in no situation in which he is not himself.

14. How the superior man, in every varying situation, pursues the Mean, doing what is right, and finding his rule in himself. 1. Chû Hsî takes 素 as = 見 在, "at present," "now"; but that meaning was made to meet the exigency of the present passage. K'ang-ch'ǎng takes it, as in chap. xi, as = 傃, "being inclined to." Mâo endeavors to establish this view:— 素位者, 卽本來故有之位, "素 位 is the proper station in which he has been." The meaning comes to much the same in all these interpretations. 不 願 乎 其 外,—compare Analects, XIV, xxviii. 2. 行 乎 富 貴 = 行 乎 富 貴 所 當 行 之 道, "He pursues the path, which ought to be pursued amid riches and honors." So, in the other clauses. 自 得,—literally = "self-possessing." The paraphrasts make it—"happy in conforming himself to his position." I consider it equivalent to what is said in chap. ii,—君 子 之 中 庸 也, 君 子 而 時 中

失諸正鵠、反求諸其身。

幸子曰、射有似乎君子、

以俟命、小人行險以徼

下不尤人、故君子居易

於人、則無怨、上不怨天、

位、不援上、正己而不求

焉。在上位、不陵下、在下

3.　In a high situation, he does not treat with contempt his inferiors.　In a low situation, he does not court the favor of his superiors.　He rectifies himself, and seeks for nothing from others, so that he has no dissatisfactions.　He does not murmur against Heaven, nor grumble against men.

4.　Thus it is that the superior man is quiet and calm, waiting for the appointments *of Heaven*, while the mean man walks in dangerous paths, looking for lucky occurrences.

5.　The Master said, "In archery we have something like the way of the superior man.　When the archer misses the center of the target, he turns round and seeks for the cause of his failure in himself."

3. 援 is explained in the dictionary, after K'ang-ch'ǎng, by 牽持, "to drag and cling to." The opposition of the two clauses makes the meaning plain. 4. 易, according to K'ang-ch'ǎng, 猶平安, "is equivalent to peaceful and tranquil." Chû Hsî says,—易, 平地也, "易 means level ground." This is most correct, but we cannot so well express it in the translation. 5. 正, the 1st tone, and 鵠 are both names of birds, small and alert, and difficult to be hit. On this account, a picture of the former was painted on the middle of the target, and a figure of the latter was attached to it in leather. It is not meant, however, by this, that they were both used in the same target, at the same time. For another illustration of the way of the superior man from the customs of archery, see Analects, III, vii.

母其順矣乎。

耽宜爾室家樂

爾妻帑子曰父

弟既翕和樂且

合如鼓瑟琴、

卑詩曰妻子好

辟如登高必自

如行遠必自邇、

君子之道、辟

CHAPTER XV. 1. The way of the superior man may be compared to what takes place in traveling, when to go to a distance we must first traverse the space that is near, and in ascending a height, when we must begin from the lower ground.

2. It is said in the Book of Poetry, "Happy union with wife and children is like the music of lutes and harps. When there is concord among brethren, the harmony is delightful and enduring. *Thus* may you regulate your family, and enjoy the pleasure of your wife and children."

3. The Master said, "In such a state of things, parents have entire complacence!"

15. IN THE PRACTICE OF THE MEAN THERE IS AN ORDERLY ADVANCE FROM STEP TO STEP. 1. 辟 is read as, and = 譬. 2. See the Shih, II, i, Ode IV, st. 7, 8. The ode celebrates, in a regretful tone, the dependence of brethren on one another, and the beauty of brotherly harmony. Mâo says: "Although there may be the happy union of wife and children, like the music of lutes and harps, yet there must also be the harmonious concord of brethren, with its exceeding delight, and then may wife and children be regulated and enjoyed. Brothers are near to us, while wife and children are more remote. Thus it is that from what is near we proceed to what is remote." He adds that anciently the relationship of husband and wife was not among the five relationships of society, because the union of brothers is from Heaven, and that of husband and wife is from man! 3. This is understood to be a remark of Confucius on the ode. From wife, and children, and brothers, parents at last are reached, illustrating how from what is low we ascend to what is high.—But all this is far-fetched and obscure.

而不可　聞、體物　之而弗　弗見、聽　視之而　盛矣乎。　為德、其　鬼神之　子曰、

CHAPTER XVI. 1. The Master said, "How abundantly do spiritual beings display the powers that belong to them!

2. "We look for them, but do not see them; we listen to, but do not hear them; yet they enter into all things, and there is nothing without them.

16. AN ILLUSTRATION, FROM THE OPERATION AND INFLUENCE OF SPIRITUAL BEINGS, OF THE WAY OF THE MEAN. What is said of the *kwei-shăn* in this chapter is only by way of illustration. There is no design, on the part of the sage, to develop his views on those beings or agencies. The key of it is to be found in the last paragraph, where the 夫微之顯 evidently refers to 莫顯乎微 in chap. i. This paragraph, therefore, should be separated from the others, and not interpreted specially of the *kwei-shăn*. I think that Dr. Medhurst, in rendering it ("Theology of the Chinese," p. 22)—"How great then is the manifestation of *their* abstruseness! Whilst displaying their sincerity, they are not to be concealed," was wrong, notwithstanding that he may be defended by the example of many Chinese commentators. The second clause of par. 5,—誠之不可揜如此, appears altogether synonymous with the 誠於中必形於外, in the 大學 何, chap. vi, 2, to which chapter we have seen that the whole of chap. i, pars. 2, 5, has a remarkable similarity. However we may be driven to find a recondite, mystical, meaning for 誠, in the 4th part of this work, there is no necessity to do so here. With regard to what is said of the *kwei-shăn*, it is only the first two paragraphs which occasion difficulty. In the 3rd par., the sage speaks of the spiritual beings that are sacrificed to. 齊,—read *chái*; see Analects, VII, xii. The same is the subject of the 4th par.; or rather, spiritual beings generally, whether sacrificed to or not, invisible themselves and yet able to behold our conduct See the Shih-ching, III, iii, Ode II, st. 7, which is said to have been composed by one of the dukes of Wei, and was repeated daily in his hearing for his admonition. In the context of the quotation, he is warned to be careful of his conduct, when alone as when in company. For in truth we are never alone. "Millions of spiritual beings walk the earth," and can take note of us. The 思 is a final particle here, without meaning. It is often used so in the Shih-ching. 度, read *to*, 4th tone, "to conjecture," "to surmise." 射, read *yî*, 4th tone, "to dislike." What now are the *kwei-shăn* in the first two paragraphs. Are we to understand by them something different from what they are in the third par., to which they run on from the first as the nominative or subject of 使? I think not. The precise meaning of what is said of them in 體物而不可遺 cannot be

矧　不　神　左　上　乎　祭　之　遺
可　可　之　右　如　如　祀　人　使
射　度　格　。四　在　在　洋　齊　天
思　思　思　詩　其　其　洋　明　下
。　。　、　曰　　　　　　　。三
　　　　　、　　　盛　　　注
　　　　　　　　　服　　　明
　　　　　　　　　以　　　
　　　　　　　　　承　　　

3. "They cause all the people in the kingdom to fast and purify themselves, and array themselves in their richest dresses, in order to attend at their sacrifices. Then, like overflowing water, they seem to be over the heads, and on the right and left *of their worshipers*.

4. "It is said in the Book of Poetry, 'The approaches of the spirits, you cannot surmise;—and can you treat them with indifference?'

determined. The old interpreters say that 體=生, "to give birth to"; that 可=所, "that which"; that 不可遺=不有所遺, "there is nothing which they neglect"; and that the meaning of the whole is—"that of all things there is not a single thing which is not produced by the breath (or energy; 氣) of the *kwei-shăn*." This is all that we learn from them. The Sung school explain the terms with reference to their physical theory of the universe, derived, as they think, from the Yi-ching. Chŭ's master, Ch'ăng, explains:—"The *kwei-shăn* are the energetic operations of Heaven and Earth, and the traces of production and transformation." The scholar Chăng (張 氏) says: "The *kwei-shăn* are the easily acting powers of the two breaths of nature (二 氣)." Chŭ Hsî's own account is:—"If we speak of two breaths, then by *kwei* is denoted the efficaciousness of the secondary or inferior one, and by *shăn*, that of the superior one. If we speak of one breath, then by *shăn* is denoted its advancing and developing, and by *kwei*, its returning and reverting. They are really only one thing." It is difficult—not to say impossible—to conceive to one's self exactly what is meant by such descriptions. And nowhere else in the Four Books is there an approach to this meaning of the phrase. Mâo Hsî-ho is more comprehensible: though, after all, it may be doubted whether what he says is more than a play upon words. His explanation is:—"But is truth, the *kwei-shăn* are 道. In the Yi-ching the 陰 and 陽 are considered to be the *kwei-shăn;* and it is said—"*one* 陰 and *one* 陽 *are called* 道." Thus the *kwei-shăn* are the 道, embodied in Heaven (體 天) for the nourishment of things. But in the text we have the term 德 instead of 道, because the latter is the name of the absolute as embodied in Heaven, and the former denotes the same not

海之內、宗廟

天子、富有四

爲聖人尊爲

大孝也與、德

子曰、舜其

此夫。

之不可揜、如

夫微之顯、誠

5. "Such is the manifestness of what is minute! Such is the impossibility of repressing the outgoings of sincerity!"

CHAPTER XVII. 1. The Master said, "How greatly filial was Shun! His virtue was that of a sage; his dignity was the throne; his riches were all within the four seas. He offered his sacrifices in his ancestral

only embodied, but operating to the nourishing of things, for Heaven considers the production of things to be 德." See the 中庸說, *in loc.*
Rémusat translates the first paragraph:—"*Que les vertus des esprits sont sublimes!*" His Latin version is:—"*Spirituum geniorumque est virtus: ea capax!*" Intorcetta renders:—"*Spiritibus inest operativa virtus et efficacitas, et hæc o quam præstans est! quam multiplex! quam sublimis!*" In a note, he and his friends say that the dignitary of the kingdom who assisted them, rejecting other interpretations, understood by *kwei-shăn* here—"those spirits for the veneration of whom and imploring their help, sacrifices were instituted." 神 signifies "spirits," "a spirit," "spirit"; and 鬼, "a ghost," or "demon." The former is used for the *animus*, or intelligent soul separated from the body, and the latter for the *anima*, or animal, grosser, soul, so separated. In the text, however, they blend together, and are not to be separately translated. They are together equivalent to 神 in par. 4, "spirits," or "spiritual beings."

17. THE VIRTUE OF FILIAL PIETY, EXEMPLIFIED IN SHUN AS CARRIED TO THE HIGHEST POINT, AND REWARDED BY HEAVEN. 1. One does not readily see the connection between Shun's great filial piety, and all the other predicates of him that follow. The paraphrasts, however, try to trace it in this way:—"A son without virtue is insufficient to distinguish his parents. But Shun was born with all knowledge and acted without any effort;—in virtue, a sage. How great was the distinction which he thus conferred on his parents!" And so with regard to the other predicate. See the 日講. 四海之內;—on this expression it is said in the encyclopædia called 博物志:—"The four cardinal points of heaven and earth are connected together by the waters of seas, the earth being a small space in the midst of them. Hence, he who rules over the kingdom (天下) is said to govern all within the four seas." See also note on Analects, XII, v, 4. The characters 宗廟 are thus explained:—"*Tsung* means honorable. *Miâo* means figure. The two together mean the place where the figures of one's ancestors

饗之子孫保之。

故大德、必得其

位、必得其祿、必

得其名、必得其

壽故天之生物、

必因其材而篤

焉、故栽者培之、

temple, and his descendants preserved the sacrifices to himself.

2. "Therefore having such great virtue, it could not but be that he should obtain the throne, that he should obtain those riches, that he should obtain his fame, that he should attain to his long life.

3. "Thus it is that Heaven, in the production of things, is sure to be bountiful to them, according to their qualities. Hence the tree that is flourishing, it

are." Chû Hsi says nothing on 宗廟饗之, because he had given in to the views of some who thought that Shun sacrificed merely in the ancestral temple of Yâo. But it is capable of proof that he erected one of his own, and ascended to Hwang-tî, as his great progenitor. See Mâo Hsî-ho's 中庸說, *in loc.* 饗,—"to entertain a guest"; and sometimes for 享, "to enjoy." So we must take it here,—"enjoyed him"; that is, his sacrifices. As Shun resigned the throne to Yü, and it did not run in the line of his family, we must take 保之 as in the translation. In the time of the Châu dynasty, there were descendants of Shun, possessed of the state of Ch'ăn (陳), and of course

sacrificing to him. 2. The 其 must refer in every case to 大德,—"its place, its emolument," etc.; that is, what is appropriate to such great virtue. The whole is to be understood with reference to Shun. He died at the age of one hundred years. The word "virtue" takes here the place of "filial piety," in the last paragraph, according to Mâo, because that is the root, the first and chief, of all virtues. 3. 材 and 篤 (according to Chú=厚, "thick," "liberal") are explained by most commentators as equally capable of a good and bad application. This may be said of 材, but not of 篤, and the 生 in 天之生物 would seem to determine the meaning of both to be only good.

受命。申之。故大德者、必天、保佑命之自天宜民宜人、受祿于樂君子、憲憲令德、傾者覆之。詩曰嘉

nourishes, while that which is ready to fall, it over-throws.

4. "In the Book of Poetry, it is said, 'The admirable, amiable prince displayed conspicuously his excelling virtue, adjusting his people, and adjusting his officers. *Therefore*, he received from Heaven the emoluments of dignity. It protected him, assisted him, decreed him the throne; sending from Heaven these favors, *as it were* repeatedly.'

5. "*We may say* therefore that he who is greatly virtuous will be sure to receive the appointment of Heaven."

If this be so, then the last clause 傾者覆 之 is only an after-thought of the writer, and, indeed, the sentiment of it is out of place in the chapter. 栽 is best taken, with K'ang-ch'ăng, as = 哉, and not, with Chû Hsî, as merely = 植. 4. See the Shih-ching, III, ii, Ode V, st. 1, where we have two slight variations of 假 for 嘉 and 顯 for 憲. The prince spoken of is King Wăn, who is thus brought forward to confirm the lesson taken from Shun. That lesson, however, is stated much too broadly in the last paragraph. It is well to say that only virtue is a solid title to eminence, but to hold forth the certain attainment of wealth and position as an inducement to virtue is not favorable to morality. The case of Confucius himself, who attained neither to power nor to long life, may be adduced as inconsistent with these teachings.

之顯名、尊爲天子、富有四

衣而有天下、身不失天下・

大王王季文王之緒壹戎

子、父作之、子述之。武王纘

乎、以王季爲父以武王爲

子曰、無憂者、其惟文王

CHAPTER XVIII. 1. The Master said, "It is only King Wăn of whom it can be said that he had no cause for grief! His father was King Chî, and his son was King Wû. His father laid the foundations of his dignity, and his son transmitted it.

2. "King Wû continued the enterprise of King T'âi, King Chî, and King Wăn. He once buckled on his armor, and got possession of the kingdom. He did not lose the distinguished personal reputation which he had throughout the kingdom. His dignity was the royal throne. His riches were the possession of all

18. ON KING WĂN, KING WÛ, AND THE DUKE OF CHÂU. 1. Shun's father was bad, and the fathers of Yâo and Yü were undistinguished. Yâo and Shun's sons were both bad, and Yü's not remarkable. But to Wăn neither father nor son gave occasion but for satisfaction and happiness. King Chî was the duke Chî-lî (季歷), the most distinguished by his virtues, and prowess, of all the princes of his time. He prepared the way for the elevation of his family. In 父作之, 子述之, the 之 is made to refer to 基業, "the foundation of the kingdom," but it may as well be referred to Wăn himself. 2. 大王.— this was the duke T'an-fû (亶父), the father of Chî-lî, a prince of great eminence, and who, in the decline of the Yin dynasty, drew to his family the thoughts of the people. 緒,— "the end of a cocoon." It is used here for the beginnings of supreme sway, traceable to the various progenitors of King Wû. 壹戎衣 is interpreted by K'ang-ch'ăng:—"He destroyed the great Yin"; and recent commentators defend his view. It is not worth while setting forth what

海之內、宗廟饗之、子
孫保之武王末受命、
周公成文武之德、追
王大王王季、上祀先
公以天子之禮、斯禮
也、達乎諸侯大夫、及
士庶人父爲大夫子
爲士、葬以大夫、祭以

within the four seas. He offered his sacrifices in his ancestral temple, and his descendants maintained the sacrifices to himself.

3. "It was in his old age that King Wû received the appointment *to the throne*, and the duke of Châu completed the virtuous course of Wăn and Wû. He carried up the title of king to T'âi and Chî, and sacrificed to all the former dukes above them with the royal ceremonies. And this rule he extended to the princes of the kingdom, the great officers, the scholars, and the common people. If the father were a great officer and the son a scholar, then the burial was that due to a great officer, and the sacrifice that due to

may be said for and against it. "He did not lose his distinguished reputation;" that is, though he proceeded against his rightful sovereign, - the people did not change their opinion of his virtue. 3. 末＝老, "when old." Wû was eighty-seven when he became emperor, and he only reigned seven years. His brother Tan (旦), the duke of Châu (see Analects, VI, xxii; VII, v) acted as his chief minister. In 追王. 王 is in the 4th tone, in which the character means—"to exercise the sovereign power." 上祀先公云云,—the house of Châu traced their lineage up to the Tî K'û (帝嚳), 2432 B.C. But in various passages of the Shû, King T'âi and King Chî are spoken of, as if the conference of those titles had been by King Wû. On this there are very long discussions. See the 中庸說, *in loc*. The truth seems to be, that Châu-kung, carrying out his brother's wishes by laws of state, confirmed the titles, and made the general rule about burials and sacrifices which is described. From 斯禮也 to the end, we are at first inclined to translate in the present tense, but the past with

之志、善述人之事者也。

孝矣乎夫孝者善繼人

〔二〕子曰武王周公其達

賤、一也。

乎天子、父母之喪、無貴

達乎大夫、三年之喪、達

以士、祭以大夫、期之喪、

士、父爲士、子爲大夫、葬

a scholar. If the father were a scholar and the son a great officer, then the burial was that due to a scholar, and the sacrifice that due to a great officer. The one year's mourning was made to extend *only* to the great officers, but the three years' mourning extended to the Son of Heaven. In the mourning for a father or mother, he allowed no difference between the noble and the mean."

CHAPTER XIX. 1. The Master said, "How far-extending was the filial piety of King Wû and the duke of Châu!

2. "Now filial piety is seen in the skillful carrying out of the wishes of our forefathers, and the skillful carrying forward of their undertakings.

a reference to Châu-kung is more correct. The "year's mourning" is that principally for uncles, and it did not extend beyond the great officers, because their uncles were the subjects of the princes and the sovereign, and feelings of kindred must not be allowed to come into collision with the relation of governor and governed. On the "three years' mourning," see Analects, XVII, xxi.

19. THE FAR-REACHING FILIAL PIETY OF KING WÛ, AND OF THE DUKE OF CHÂU. 1. 達 is taken by Chû as meaning — "universally acknowledged"; "far-extending" is better, and accords with the meaning of the term in other parts of the Work. 2. This definition of 孝, or "filial piety," is worthy of notice. Its operation ceases not with the lives of parents and parents' parents. 人 = 前 人, "antecedent men"; but English idiom seems to require the

昭穆也、序爵、　之禮、所以序　其時食。<sub></sub>宗廟　設其裳衣、薦　廟、陳其宗器、　春秋、脩其祖

3. "In spring and autumn, they repaired and beautified the temple halls of their fathers, set forth their ancestral vessels, displayed their various robes, and presented the offerings of the several seasons.

4. "By means of the ceremonies of the ancestral temple, they distinguished the royal kindred according to their order of descent. By ordering the parties

addition of *our*. 3. 春秋,—the sovereigns of China sacrificed, as they still do, to their ancestors every season Reckoning from the spring, the names of the sacrifices appear to have been—祠, 禴 or 礿, 嘗, and 烝. Others, however, give the names as 礿, 禘, 嘗, 烝, while some affirm that the spring sacrifice was 禘. Though spring and autumn only are mentioned in the text, we are to understand that what is said of the sacrifices in those seasons applies to all the others. 祖廟,—"halls or temples of ancestors," of which the sovereign had seven (see the next paragraph), all included in the name of 宗廟. 宗器, "ancestral," or "venerable, vessels." Chû Hsî understands by them relics, something like our regalia. Chăng K'ang-ch'ăng makes them, and apparently with more correctness, simply "the sacrificial vessels." 裳衣,—"lower and upper garments," with the latter of which the parties personating the deceased were invested. 4. It was an old interpretation that the sacrificed and accompanying services,

spoken of here, were not the seasonal services of every year, which are the subject of the preceding paragraph, but the great 禘 and 祫 sacrifices; and to that view I would give in my adhesion. The sovereign, as mentioned above, had seven 廟. One belonged to the remote ancestor to whom the dynasty traced its origin. At the great sacrifices, his spirit tablet was placed fronting the east, and on each side were ranged, three in a row, the tablets belonging to the six others, those of them which fronted the south being, in the genealogical line, the fathers of those who fronted the north As fronting the south, the region of *brilliancy*, the former were called 昭; the latter, from the north, the *somber* region, were called 穆. As the dynasty was prolonged, and successive sovereigns died, the older tablets were removed, and transferred to what was called the 祧廟, yet so that one in the 昭 line displaced the topmost 昭, and so with the 穆. At the sacrifices, the royal kindred arranged themselves as they were descended from

禮、奏其樂、敬

踐其位、行其

所以序齒也。

逮賤也、燕毛、

下爲上、所以

辨賢也、旅酬、

也、序事、所以

所以辨貴賤

present according to their rank, they distinguished the more noble and the less.　By the arrangement of the services, they made a distinction of talents and worth. In the ceremony of general pledging, the inferiors presented the cup to their superiors, and thus something was given the lowest to do.　At the *concluding* feast, places were given according to the hair, and thus was made the distinction of years.

5.　"They occupied the places of their forefathers, practiced their ceremonies, and performed their music.

a 昭 on the left, and from a 穆 on the right, and thus a genealogical correctness of place was maintained among them.　The ceremony of "general (族=衆) pledging" occurred towards the end of the sacrifice. Chû Hsî takes 爲 in the 3d tone, saying that to have anything to do at those services was accounted honorable, and after the sovereign had commenced the ceremony by taking "a cup of blessing," all the juniors presented a similar cup to the seniors, and thus were called into employment.　Ying-tâ takes 爲 in its ordinary tone, 下 爲 上, "the inferiors were the superiors," i. e., the

juniors did present a cup to their elders, but had the honor of drinking first themselves.　The 燕 was a concluding feast confined to the royal kindred.　5. 踐 其 位, according to K'ang-ch'ǎng, is—"ascended their thrones"; according to Chû, it is "trod on—i. e., occupied—their places in the ancestral temple."　On either view, the statement must be taken with allowance.　The ancestors of King Wû had not been kings, and their places in the temples had only been those of princes.　The same may be said of the four particulars which follow.　By "those whom they"—i. e., their progenitors—

上帝也宗廟之禮、

郊社之禮所以事

如事存、孝之至也。

事死如事生、事亡

其所尊、愛其所親、

They reverenced those whom they honored, and loved those whom they regarded with affection. Thus they served the dead as they would have served them alive; they served the departed as they would have served them had they been continued among them.

6. "By the ceremonies of the sacrifices to Heaven and Earth they served God, and by the ceremonies of

"honored" are intended their ancestors, and by "those whom they loved," their descendants, and indeed all the people of their government. The two concluding sentences are important, as the Jesuits mainly based on them the defense of their practice in permitting their converts to continue the sacrifices to their ancestors. We read in "*Confucius Sinarum philosophus,*"—the work of Intorcetta and others, to which I have made frequent reference:— "*Ex plurimis et clarissimis textibus Sinicis probari potest, legitimum prædicti axiomatis sensum esse, quod eadem intentione et formali motivo Sinenses naturalem pietatem et politicum obsequium erga defunctos exerceant, sicuti erga eosdem adhuc superstites exercebant, ex quibus et ex infra dicendis prudens lector facile deducet, hos ritus circa defunctos fuisse mere civiles, institutos dumtaxat in honorem et obsequium parentum, etiam post mortem non intermittendum; nam si quid illic divinum agnovissent, cur diceret Confucius — Priscos servire solitos defunctis, uti iisdem serviebant viventibus.*" This is ingenious reasoning, but does it meet the fact that sacrifice is an entirely new element introduced into the service of the dead? 6. What is said about the sacrifices to God, however, is important, in reference to the views which we should form about the ancient religion of China. K'ang-ch'ang took 郊 to be the sacrifice to Heaven, offered, at the winter solstice, in the southern suburb (郊) of the imperial city; and 社 to be that offered to the Earth, at the summer solstice, in the northern. Chû agrees with him. Both of them, however, add that after 上帝 we are to understand 后 土, "Sovereign Earth" (不言后土者省文). This view of 社 here is vehemently controverted by Mâo and many others.

所以祀乎其

先也、明乎郊

社之禮、禘嘗

之義、治國其

如示諸掌乎。

魯哀公問政。

the ancestral temple they sacrificed to their ancestors. He who understands the ceremonies of the sacrifices to Heaven and Earth, and the meaning of the several sacrifices to ancestors, would find the government of a kingdom as easy as to look into his palm!''

CHAPTER XX. 1. The duke Âi asked about government.

But neither the opinion of the two great commentators that 后 土 is suppressed for the sake of brevity, nor the opinion of others that by 社 we are to understand the tutelary deities of the soil, affects the judgment of the Sage himself, that the service of one being—even of God —was designed by all those ceremonies. See my "Notions of the Chinese Concerning God and Spirits," pp. 50–52. The ceremonies of the ancestral temple embrace the great and less frequent services of the 禘 and 祫 (see the Analects, III, x, 11) and the seasonal sacrifices, of which only the autumnal one (嘗) is specified here. The old commentators take 示 as＝寘, with the meaning of 置, "to place," and interpret—"the government of the kingdom would be as easy as to place anything in the palm." This view is defended in the 中 庸 說. It has the advantage of accounting better for the 諸. We are to understand "the meaning of the sacrifices to ancestors," as including all the uses mentioned in par. 4. It is not easy to understand the connection between the first part of this paragraph and the general object of the chapter. Taking the paragraph by itself, it teaches that a proper knowledge and practice of the duties of religion and filial piety would amply equip a ruler for all the duties of his government.

20. ON GOVERNMENT: SHOWING PRINCIPALLY HOW IT DEPENDS ON THE CHARACTER OF THE OFFICERS ADMINISTERING IT, AND HOW THAT DEPENDS ON THE CHARACTER OF THE SOVEREIGN HIMSELF. We have here one of the fullest expositions of Confucius's views on this subject, though he unfolds them only as a description of the government of the kings Wăn and Wŭ. In the chapter there is the remarkable intermingling, which we have seen in "The Great Learning," of what is peculiar to a ruler, and what is of universal application. From the concluding paragraphs, the transition is easy to the next and most difficult part of the Work. This chapter is found also in the 家 語, but with considerable additions. 1. 哀 公,—see Analects,

為政在人、取
者蒲盧也。故
敏樹夫政也、
道敏政、地道
則其政息。人
政舉、其人亡、
其人存、則其
政布在方策、
子曰、文武之

2. The Master said, "The government of Wăn and Wû is displayed in *the records*,—the tablets of wood and bamboo. Let there be the men and the government will flourish; but without the men, their government decays and ceases.

3. "With the *right* men the growth of government is rapid, just as vegetation is rapid in the earth; and, moreover, *their* government *might be called* an easily-growing rush.

4. "Therefore the administration of government lies in *getting proper* men. Such men are to be got by

II, xix, *et al.* 2. The 方 were tablets of wood, one of which might contain up to 100 characters. The 策 were 簡, or slips of bamboo tied together. In 其人, 其＝*such*, i. e., rulers like Wăn and Wû, and ministers such as they had. 3. K'ang-ch'ăng and Ying-tă take 敏 as＝勉, "to exert one's self," and interpret:—"A ruler ought to exert himself in the practice of government, as the earth exerts itself to produce and to nurture" (樹＝殖) Chù Hsî takes 敏 as＝速, "hasty," "to make haste." 人道敏政,—"man's way hastens government"; but the 人 must be taken with special reference to the preceding paragraph, as in the translation. The old commentators took 蒲

盧 as the name of an insect (so it is defined in the 爾雅), a kind of bee, said to take the young of the mulberry caterpillar, and keep them in its hole, where they are transformed into bees. So, they said, does government transform the people. This is in accordance with the paragraph, as we find it in the 家語,—天道敏生, 人道敏政,地道敏樹,夫政者猶蒲盧也,待化以成. This view is maintained also in the 中庸說 But we cannot hesitate in preferring Chù H i's, as in the translation. The other is too absurd. He takes 盧, as if it were 盧＝蘆, which, as well as 蒲, is the name of various rushes or sedges. 4. In the 家語, for 在人, we have 在於得人, which is, no

上、民不可得
下位不獲乎
禮所生也。在
殺尊賢之等、
爲大、親親之
者、宜也、尊賢
親親爲大義
仁。仁者、人也、
以道脩道以
人以身脩身

means of *the ruler's own* character. That character is to be cultivated by his treading in the ways *of duty*. And the treading those ways of duty is to be cultivated by the cherishing of benevolence.

5. "Benevolence is *the characteristic element of* humanity, and the great exercise of it is in loving relatives. Righteousness is *the accordance of actions with what is* right, and the great exercise of it is in honoring the worthy. The decreasing measures of the love due to relatives, and the steps in the honor due to the worthy, are produced by *the principle of* propriety.

6. "When those in inferior situations do not possess the confidence of their superiors, they cannot retain the government of the people.

doubt, the meaning. By 道 here, says Chû Hsî, are intended "tne duties of universal obligation," in par 8, "which," adds Mâo, "are the ways of the Mean, in accordance with the nature." 5. 仁者人也. "Benevolence is man." We find the same language in Mencius, VII, Pt, ii, 16. This virtue is called MAN, "because loving, feeling, and the forbearing nature, belong to man, as he is born. They are that whereby man is man." See the 中庸說,

*in loc.* 殺,—in the 3rd tone, read *shâi.* It is opposed to 隆, and means "decreasing," "growing less." For 禮所生 we have, in the 家語, 禮所以生, which would seem to mean— "are that whereby ceremonies are produced." But there follow the words—禮者政之本也. The "produced" in the translation can only = "distinguished" Ying-tâ explains 生 by 辨明. 6. This has crept into the text here by mistake. It belongs to par. 17, below. We do not find

也父子也、夫婦也、昆弟

所以行之者三曰君臣

不知天天下之達道五、

不知人思知人不可以

不事親思事親不可以

不脩身思脩身不可以

而治矣故君子、不可以

7. "Hence the sovereign may not neglect the cultivation of his own character.. Wishing to cultivate his character, he may not neglect to serve his parents. In order to serve his parents, he may not neglect to acquire a knowledge of men. In order to know men, he may not dispense with a knowledge of Heaven.

8. "The duties of universal obligation are five, and the virtues wherewith they are practiced are three. The duties are those between sovereign and minister, between father and son, between husband and wife,

it here in the 家語. 7. 君子 is here the *ruler* or *sovereign*. I fail in trying to trace the connection between the different parts of this paragraph. "He may not be without knowing men."—Why? "Because," we are told, "it is by honoring, and being courteous to the worthy, and securing them as friends, that a man perfects his virtue, and is able to serve his relatives." "He may not be without knowing Heaven."—Why? "Because," it is said, "the gradations in the love of relatives and the honoring the worthy are all heavenly arrangements and a heavenly order,—natural, necessary, principles." But in this explanation, 知人 has a very different meaning from what it has in the previous clause. 親, too, is here *parents*, its meaning being more restricted than in par. 5. 8. From this down to par. 11, there is brought before us the character of the "*men*," mentioned in par. 2, on whom depends the flourishing of "*government*," which government is exhibited in paragraphs 12–15. 天下之達道,—"the paths proper to be trodden by all

也、朋友之交也、五
者、天下之達道也、
知仁勇三者、天下
之達德也、所以行
之者一也。或生而
知之、或學而知之、
或困而知之、及其

between elder brother and younger, and those belonging to the intercourse of friends. Those five are the duties of universal obligation. Knowledge, magnanimity, and energy, these three, are the virtues universally binding. And the means by which they carry *the duties* into practice is singleness.

9. "Some are born with the knowledge *of those duties;* some know them by study; and some acquire the knowledge after a painful feeling of their ignorance. But the knowledge being possessed, it comes to the

under heaven,"=the path of the Mean. 知=智, is the *knowledge* necessary to choose the detailed course of duty. 仁(=心之公, "the unselfishness of the heart") is the *magnanimity* (so I style it for want of a better term) to pursue it. 勇 is the *valiant energy*, which maintains the permanence of the choice and the practice. 所以行之者一也,—this, according to Ying-tâ, means—"From the various kings (百王) downwards, in the practicing of these five duties and three virtues there has been but one method. There has been no change in modern times and an-

cient." This, however, is not satisfactory. We want a substantive meaning for 一. This Chû Hsî gives us. He says: 一 則 誠 而 已, "一 is simply sincerity;" the sincerity, that is, on which the rest of the work dwells with such strange predication. I translate, therefore, 一 here by *singleness.* There seems a reference in the term to 獨, chap. i, p. 3. The singleness is that of the soul in the apprehension and practice of the duties of the Mean, which is attained to by watchfulness over one's self, when *alone.* 行之 I understand as in the second clause

知之一也、或安
而行之、或利而
行之、或勉強而
行之及其成功、
一也。子曰、好學
近乎知、力行近
乎仁、知恥近乎
勇。知斯三者、則
知所以脩身、知

same thing.　Some practice them with a natural ease; some from a desire for their advantages; and some by strenuous effort.　But the achievement being made, it comes to the same thing."

10.　The Master said, "To be fond of learning is to be near to knowledge.　To practice with vigor is to be near to magnanimity.　To possess the feeling of shame is to be near to energy.

11.　"He who knows these three things knows how to cultivate his own character.　Knowing how to

of the paragraph. 9. Compare Analects, XVI, ix. 利,—compare Analects, XX, ii. 強, 2nd tone, "to force," "to employ violent efforts." Chû Hsî says: "The 之 in 知 之, and 行 之, refers to the duties of universal obligation." But is there the threefold difference in the *knowledge* of those duties? And who are they who can practice them with entire ease? 10. Chû Hsî observes that 子曰 is here superfluous. In the 家 語, however, we find the last paragraph followed by—"The duke said, Your words are beautiful and perfect, but I am stupid, and unable to accomplish this." Then comes

this paragraph, "Confucius said," etc. The 子 曰, therefore, prove that Tsze-sze took this chapter from some existing document, that which we have in the 家 語, or some other. Confucius's words were intended to encourage and stimulate the duke, telling him that the three grand virtues might be nearly, if not absolutely, attained to 知 恥,—"knowing to be ashamed," i. e., being ashamed at being below others, leading to the determination not to be so. 11. "These three things", are the three things in the last paragraph, which makes an approximation at least, to the three virtues

羣臣也、子庶民也、　親也、敬大臣也、體　脩身也、尊賢也、親　下國家有九經、曰、　下國家矣。凡爲天　人、則知所以治天　以治人、知所以治　所以脩身、則知所

十二節

cultivate his own character, he knows how to govern other men. Knowing how to govern other men, he knows how to govern the kingdom with all its states and families.

12. "All who have the government of the kingdom with its states and families have nine standard rules to follow;—viz., the cultivation of their own characters; the honoring of men of virtue and talents; affection towards their relatives; respect towards the great ministers; kind and considerate treatment of the whole body of officers; dealing with the mass of the people

which connect with the discharge of duty attainable by every one. What connects the various steps of the climax is the unlimited confidence in the power of the example of the ruler, which we have had occasion to point out so frequently in "The Great Learning." 12. These nine standard rules, it is to be borne in mind, constitute the government of Wăn and Wŭ, referred to in par. 2. Commentators arrange the 4th and 5th rules under the second; and the 6th, 7th, 8th, and 9th under the third, so that after "the cultivation of the person," we have here an expansion of 親 親 and 尊 賢, in par. 5. 凡爲,—爲=治, "to govern." The student will do well to understand a 者 after 家. 尊賢,—by the 賢 here are understood specially the

officers called 師, 傅, and 保, the 三 公 and the 三 孤, who, as teachers and guardians, were not styled 臣, "ministers," or "servants." See the Shŭ-ching, V, xxi, 5, 6. 敬大臣,—by the 大 臣 are understood the six 卿,—the minister of Instruction, the minister of Religion, etc. See the Shŭ, V, xxi, 7–13. 體羣臣,—the 羣 臣 are the host of subordinate officers after the two preceding classes. K'ang-ch'ǎng says,—體 猶 接 納, "體 =to receive," to which Ying-tâ adds 一 與 之 同 體, "being of the same body with them." Chû Hsî brings out the force of the term in this way:—體 謂 設 以 身 處 其 地, 而 察 其 心 也, "體 means that he places himself in their place, and so examines their feelings." 子庶民,— 子 is a verb, "to make children of,"

不惑、親親、　立尊賢、則　脩身、則道　懷諸侯也。　柔遠人也、　來百工也、

as children; encouraging the resort of all classes of artisans; indulgent treatment of men from a distance; and the kindly cherishing of the princes of the states.

13. "By the ruler's cultivation of his own character, the duties *of universal obligation* are set forth. By honoring men of virtue and talents, he is preserved from errors of judgment. By showing affection to his

"to treat kindly as children." 來百 工,—來=招 來, "to call to come," ="to encourage." The 百 工, or "various artisans," were, by the statutes of Châu, under the superintendence of a special officer, and it was his business to draw them out and forth from among the people. See the Châu-lì, XXXIX. 1-5. 柔 遠 人,—Chû Hsî by 遠 人 understands 賓 旅, "guests or envoys, and travelers, or traveling merchants"; K'ang-ch'ǎng understands by them 蕃 國 之 諸 侯, "the princes of surrounding kingdoms," i. e., of the tribes that lay beyond the six *fû* (服), or feudal tenures of the Châu rule. But these would hardly be spoken of before the 諸 侯. And among *them*, in the 9th rule, would be included the 賓, or guests, the princes themselves at the royal court, or their envoys. I doubt whether any others beside the 旅, or traveling merchants, are intended by the 遠 人. If we may adopt,

however, K'ang-ch'ǎng's view, this is the rule for the treatment of foreigners by the government of China. 13. This paragraph describes the happy effects of observing the above nine rules. 道 立,—by 道 are understood the five duties of universal obligation. We read in the 日 講:—"About these nine rules, the only trouble is that sovereigns are not able to practice them strenuously. Let the ruler be really able to cultivate his person, then will the universal duties and universal virtues be all-complete, so that he shall be an example to the whole kingdom, with its states and families. Those duties will be set up (道 立), and men will know what to imitate." 不 惑 means, according to Chû Hsî, 不 疑 於 理, "he will have no doubts as to principle." K'ang-ch'ǎng explains it by 謀 者 良, "his counsels will be good." This latter is the meaning, the worthies being those specified in the note on the preceding

則諸父昆弟不怨、

敬大臣則不眩、體

羣臣則士之報禮

重、子庶民則百姓

勸、來百工、則財用

足、柔遠人、則四方

歸之懷諸侯、則天

relatives, there is no grumbling nor resentment among his uncles and brethren.　By respecting the great ministers, he is kept from errors in the practice of government.　By kind and considerate treatment of the whole body of officers, they are led to make the most grateful return for his. courtesies.　By dealing with the mass of the people as his children, they are led to exhort one another to what is good.　By encouraging the resort of all classes of artisans, his resources for expenditure are rendered ample.　By indulgent treatment of men from a distance, they are brought to resort to him from all quarters.　And by kindly cherishing the princes of the states, the whole kingdom is brought to revere him.

paragraph, their sovereign's counselors and guides. The addition of 諸 determines the 父 to be uncles. See the 爾雅, I, iv. 昆弟 are all the younger branches of the ruler's kindred. 不眩＝不惑; but the deception and mistake will be in the affairs in charge of those great ministers. 羣臣 and 士 are the same parties. 勸,—as in Analects, II, xx.　Ying-tâ explains it here—"They will exhort and stimulate one another to serve their ruler."　On 財用足, Chû Hsî says: "The resort of all classes of artisans being encouraged, there is an intercommunication of the pro-

ductions of labor, and an interchange of men's services, and the husbandman and the trafficker" (it is this class which is designed by 末), "are aiding to one another.　Hence the resources for expenditure are sufficient."　I suppose that Chû felt a want of some mention of agriculture in connection with these rules, and thought to find a place for it here.　Mâo would make 財＝材, and 用＝器物.　See the 中庸說, in loc. Compare also 大學傳, x 19. K'ang-ch'ăng understands 四方 as meaning 蕃國, "frontier kingdoms," but the usage of the phrase is against such

使、所以勸大臣也、

勸親親也官盛任

祿、同其好惡所以

賢也尊其位重其

貨而貴德所以勸

身也去讒遠色、賤

非禮不動、所以脩

下畏之齊明盛服、
十四　章

14. "Self-adjustment and purification, with careful regulation of his dress, and the not making a movement contrary to the rules of propriety:—this is the way for a ruler to cultivate his person. Discarding slanderers, and keeping himself from *the seductions of* beauty; making light of riches, and giving honor to virtue:—this is the way for him to encourage men of worth and talents. Giving them places *of honor* and large emolument, and sharing with them in their likes and dislikes:—this is the way for him to encourage his relatives to love him. Giving them numerous officers to discharge their orders and commissions:— this is the way for him to encourage the great

an interpretation. 14. After 天下畏 之, we have in the 家語,—公曰, 爲 之 奈 何, "The duke said, *How are these rules to be practiced?*" and then follows this paragraph, preceded by 孔子曰, "Confucius said." 齊明盛 服,—as in chap. xvi, 3. The blending together, as equally important, attention to inward purity and to dress, seems strange enough to a Western reader. 勸, throughout,= "to stimulate in a friendly way." I

have translated 親 親 after the 合 講, which says 勸 親 親 謂 親 之 親 我, the upper 親 being the noun, and the second the verb. The use of 忠 in reference to the prince's treatment of the officers is strange, but the translation gives what appears to be the meaning K'ang-ch'ang explained:—"Making large the emolument of the loyal and sincere;" but, according to the analogy of all the other clauses, 忠 and 信 must be

忠信重祿、所以勸

士也、時使薄斂、所

以勸百姓也、日省

月試、既稟稱事、所

以勸百工也、送往

迎來嘉善而矜不

能、所以柔遠人也、

ministers. According to them a generous confidence, and making their emoluments large:—this is the way to encourage the body of officers. Employing them only at the proper times, and making the imposts light:—this is the way to encourage the people. By daily examinations and monthly trials, and by making their rations in accordance with their labors:—this is the way to encourage the classes of artisans. To escort them on their departure and meet them on their coming; to commend the good among them, and show compassion to the incompetent:—this is the way to treat indulgently men from a distance. To restore

descriptive of the ruler. 時使,—compare Analects, I, v. For 既稟 we have in the 家語, 餼廩, which K'ang-ch'äng explains by 稍食, "rations allowed by government;"—see Morrison, character 稍. Chû follows K'ang-ch'äng, but I agree with Mâo, that 稟 and not 餼 is to be substituted here for 既. 稱, 4th tone, "to weigh," "to be according to." The trials and examinations, with these rations, show that the artisans are not to be understood as dispersed among the people. Ambassadors from foreign countries have been received up to the present century, according to the rules here prescribed, and the two last regulations are quite in harmony with the superiority that China claims over the countries which they may represent. But in the case of travelers, and traveling ·merchants, passing from one state to another, there were anciently regulations, which may be

事、豫則立不豫則

以行之者一也。〇十六節凡

下國家有九經、所

懷諸侯也凡爲天 〇十五節

厚往而薄來、所以

亂持危、朝聘以時、

繼絕世、舉廢國治

families whose line of succession has been broken, and to revive states that have been extinguished; to reduce to order states that are in confusion, and support those which are in peril; to have fixed times for their own reception at court, and the reception of their envoys; to send them away after liberal treatment, and welcome their coming with small contributions:—this is the way to cherish the princes of the states.

15. "All who have the government of the kingdom with its states and families have the above nine standard rules. And the means by which they are carried into practice is singleness.

16. "In all things success depends on previous preparation, and without such previous preparation there is sure to be failure. If what is to be spoken be previously determined, there will be no stumbling. If

adduced to illustrate all the expressions here:—see the 中庸說, and the 日講, *in loc.* 繼絕世,舉廢國, as in Analects, XX, , 7. 15. We naturally understand the last clause as meaning—"the means·by which they are carried into practice is one and the same." Then this means

will be the 豫, or "previous preparation" of the next paragraph. This is the interpretation of K'ang-ch'ăng and Ying-tâ, who take the two paragraphs together. But according to Chû, "the one thing" is *sincerity*, as in par. 8  16. The "all things" has

順乎親有道、反諸身不誠、
不順乎親、不信乎朋友矣、
獲乎上矣信乎朋友有道、
乎上有道、不信乎朋友、不
乎上、民不可得而治矣、獲
前定、則不窮在下位、不獲
則不困、行前定則不疚、道
廢、言前定、則不跲、事前定、

十七

affairs be previously determined, there will be no
difficulty with them. If one's actions have been
previously determined, there will be no sorrow in
connection with them. If principles of conduct have
been previously determined, the practice of them will
be inexhaustible.

17. "When those in inferior situations do not
obtain the confidence of the sovereign, they cannot
succeed in governing the people. There is a way to
obtain the confidence of the sovereign;—if one is not
trusted by his friends, he will not get the confidence
of his sovereign. There is a way to being trusted by
one's friends;—if one is not obedient to his parents,
he will not be true to friends. There is a way to
being obedient to one's parents;—if one, on turning
his thoughts in upon himself, finds a want of sincerity,

reference to the above duties, virtues, and standard rules. 17. The
object here seems to be to show that
the singleness, or sincerity, lies at
the basis of that previous preparation, which is essential to success
in any and every thing. The steps
of the climax conduct us to it, and
this sincerity is again made dependent on the understanding of what is
good, upon which point see the next
chapter. 不獲乎上,=according to

誠之者、擇善而固執

得、從容中道聖人也、

者、不勉而中、不思而

誠之者、人之道也、誠

身矣。誠者、天之道也、

道、不明乎善、不誠乎

不順乎親矣誠身有

he will not be obedient to his parents. There is a way to the attainment of sincerity in one's self;—if a man do not understand what is good, he will not attain sincerity in himself.

18. "Sincerity is the way of Heaven. The attainment of sincerity is the way of men. He who possesses sincerity is he who, without an effort, hits what is right, and apprehends, without the exercise of thought;—he is the sage who naturally and easily embodies the *right* way. He who attains to sincerity is he who chooses what is good, and firmly holds it fast.

Ying-tâ, "do not get the mind—pleased feeling—of the sovereign." We use "to gain," and "to win," sometimes, in a similar way. 18. Prémare (p. 156) says: "誠 者 *est in abstracto, et* 誠 之 者 *est in concreto.*" 誠 者 is in the concrete, as much as the other, and is said, below, to be characteristic of the sage. 誠 者 is the quality possessed absolutely. 誠 之 者 is the same acquired. "The way of Heaven,"—this, according to Ying-tâ, = "the way which Heaven pursues." Chû Hsî explains it, "the fundamental, natural course of heavenly principle." Mâo says: "This is like the accordance of nature in the Mean, considered to be THE PATH, having its root in Heaven." We might acquiesce in this, but for the opposition of 人 之 道, on which Mâo says: 此 猶 中 庸 之 修 道 以 爲 道 者 也, 成 乎 人 也:—"This is like the cultivation of the path in the Doctrine of the Mean, considered to be THE PATH, having its completion from man." But this takes the second and third utterances in the Work as independent sentiments, which they are not. I do not see my way to rest in any but the old interpretation, extravagant as it is. —At this point, the chapter in the 家 語 ceases to be the same with that

有弗辨辨之弗明、弗

思、思之弗得弗措也

之弗知弗措也、有弗

能、弗措也、有弗問、問

行之有弗學、學之弗

之愼思之明辨之篤

之者也。博學之審問

19. "To this attainment there are requisite the extensive study of what is good, accurate inquiry about it, careful reflection on it, the clear discrimina-tion of it, and the earnest practice of it.

20. "The superior man, while there is anything he has not studied, or while in what he has studied there is anything he cannot understand, will not intermit his labor. While there is anything he has not inquired about, or anything in what he has inquired about which he does not know, he will not intermit his labor. While there is anything which he has not reflected on, or anything in what he has reflected on which he does not apprehend, he will not intermit his labor. While there is anything which he has not discriminated, or his discrimination is not clear, he will not intermit his

before us, and diverges to another subject. 19. The different processes which lead to the attainment of sincerity. The gloss in the 備 旨 says that "the five 之 all refer to the *what is good* in the last chapter, the five universal duties and the nine standard rules being included there-in." Rather it seems to me, that the 之, according to the idiom pointed out several times in the Analects, simply intensifies the meaning of the different verbs, whose regimen it is. 20. Here we

自明誠、謂之教、誠

龜自誠明、謂之性、

雖柔必強。

此道矣、雖愚必明、

能之己千之果能
廿一郡

能之己百之人十

弗篤、弗措也人一

措也、有弗行、行之

labor.  If there be anything which he has not practiced,
or his practice fails in earnestness, he will not intermit
his labor.  If another man succeed by one effort, he
will use a hundred efforts.  If another man succeed
by ten efforts, he will use a thousand.

21.  "Let a man proceed in this way, and, though
dull, he will surely become intelligent; though weak,
he will surely become strong."

CHAPTER XXI.  When we have intelligence resulting from sincerity, this condition is to be ascribed to
nature; when we have sincerity resulting from intelligence, this condition is to be ascribed to instruction.

have the determination which is
necessary in the prosecution of the
above processes, and par. 21 states
the result of it.  Chû Hsî makes a
pause at the end of the first clause
in each part of the paragraph, and
interprets thus:—"If he do not
study, well.  But if he do, he will
not give over till he understands
what he studies," and so on.  But
it seems more natural to carry the
supposition in 有 over the whole of
every part, as in the translation,
which, moreover, substantially agrees
with Ying-tâ's interpretation.—Here
terminates the third part of the
Work.  It was to illustrate, as Chû
Hsî told us, how "the path of the
Mean cannot be left."  The author

seems to have kept this point before
him in chapters xiii–xvi, but the
next three are devoted to the one
subject of filial piety, and the 20th,
to the general subject of government.  Some things are said worthy
of being remembered, and others
which require a careful sifting; but,
on the whole, we do not find ourselves advanced in an understanding
of the argument of the Work.

21.  THE RECIPROCAL CONNECTION
OF SINCERITY AND INTELLIGENCE.
With this chapter commences the
fourth part of the Work, which, as
Chû observes in his concluding note,
is an expansion of the 18th paragraph of the preceding chapter.  It
is, in a great measure, a glorification

則
明矣、
明則
誠矣。

右第二十
一章、子思
承上章、夫
子天道人
道之意、而
立言也、自
此以下十
二章、皆子
思之言、以
反覆推明
此章之意。

But given the sincerity, and there shall be the intelligence; given the intelligence, and there shall be the sincerity.

*The above is the twenty-first chapter. Tsze-sze takes up in it, and discourses the subjects of "the way of Heaven" and "the way of men," mentioned in the preceding chapter. The twelve chapters that follow are all from Tsze-sze, repeating and illustrating the meaning of this one.*

of the sage, finally resting in the person of Confucius; but the high character of the sage, it is maintained, is not unattainable by others. He realizes the ideal of humanity, but by his example and lessons, the same ideal is brought within the reach of many, perhaps of all. The ideal of humanity,—the perfect character belonging to the sage, which ranks him on a level with Heaven,—is indicated by 誠, and we have no single term in English, which can be considered as the complete equivalent of that character. The Chinese themselves had great difficulty in arriving at that definition of it which is now generally acquiesced in. In the 四書通 (quoted in the 匯參, 中庸, xvi, 5), we are told that "the Han scholars were all ignorant of its meaning. Under the Sung dynasty, first came 李邦直, who defined it by 不欺, *freedom from all deception.* After him, 徐仲車 said that it meant 不息, *ceaselessness.* Then, one of the Chăng called it 無妄, *freedom from all moral error;* and finally, Chû Hsî added to this the positive element of 眞實, *truth and reality,* on which the definition of 誠 was complete." Rémusat calls it—*la perfection,* and

*la perfection morale.* Intorcetta and his friends call it—*vera solidaque perfectio.* Simplicity or singleness of soul seems to be what is chiefly intended by the term;—the disposition to, and capacity of, what is good, without any deteriorating element, with no defect of intelligence, or intromission of selfish thoughts. This belongs to Heaven, to Heaven and Earth, and to the Sage. Men, not naturally sages, may, by cultivating the intelligence of what is good, raise themselves to this elevation. 性 and 教 carry us back to the first chapter, but the terms have a different force, and the longer I dwell upon it, the more am I satisfied with Chû Hsî's pronouncement in his 語類, that 性 is here 性之, "possessing from nature," and 教＝學之, "learning it," and therefore I have translated 謂 之 by—"is to be ascribed to." When, however, he makes a difference in the connection between the parts of the two clauses —誠則明矣, 明則誠矣, and explains—誠則無不明, 明則可以至誠, "sincerity is invariably intelligent, and intelligence may arrive at sincerity," this is not dealing fairly with his text.

性、　能　　盡　　盡　　至　　　臺
能　　盡　　其　　其　　誠、　　唯
盡　　人　　性、　性、　爲　　天
人　　之　　則　　能　　能　　下

CHAPTER XXII.    It is only he who is possessed of
the most complete sincerity that can exist under
heaven, who can give its full development to his
nature.    Able to give its full development to his own
nature, he can do the same to the nature of other
men.    Able to give its full development to the nature

Here, at the outset, I may observe that, in this portion of the Work, there are specially the three following dogmas, which are more than questionable:— 1st, That there are some men — sages — naturally in a state of moral perfection; and, 2nd, That the same moral perfection is attainable by others, in whom its development is impeded by their material organization, and the influence of external things; and 3rd, That the understanding of what is good will certainly lead to such moral perfection.

22. THE RESULTS OF SINCERITY; AND HOW THE POSSESSOR OF IT FORMS A TERNION WITH HEAVEN AND EARTH. On 天下至誠, Chû Hsî says that it denotes "the reality of the virtue of the Sage, to which there is nothing in the world that can be added." This is correct, and if we were to render—"It is only the most sincere man under heaven," the translation would be wrong. 盡 means simply "to exhaust," but, by what processes and in what way, the character tells us nothing about. The "giving full development to his nature," however, may be understood, with Mâo, as = "pursuing THE PATH in accordance with his nature, so that what Heaven has conferred on him is displayed without shortcoming or let." The "giving its development to the nature of other men" indicates the Sage's helping them, by his example and lessons, to perfect themselves. "His exhausting the nature of things," i. e., of all other beings, animate and inanimate, is, according to Chû, "knowing them completely, and dealing with them correctly," "so," add the paraphrasts, "that he secures their prosperous increase and development according to their nature." Here, however, a Buddhist idea appears in Chû's commentary. He says: "The nature of other men and things ( =animals) is the same with my nature," which, it is observed in Mâo's Work, is the same with the Buddhist sentiment, that "a dog has the nature of Buddha," and with that of the philosopher Kâo, that "a dog's nature is the same as a man's."    Mâo himself

參矣。

則可以與天地

贊天地之化育、

地之化育可以

性、則可以贊天

之性、能盡物之

之性、則能盡物

of other men, he can give their full development to
the natures of animals and things. Able to give their
full development to the natures of creatures and
things, he can assist the transforming and nourishing
powers of Heaven and Earth. Able to assist the
transforming and nourishing powers of Heaven and
Earth, he may with Heaven and Earth form a ternion.

illustrates the "exhausting the nature of things," by reference to the
Shû-ching, IV, iii, 2, where we are
told that under the first sovereigns
of the Hsiâ dynasty, "the mountains and rivers all enjoyed tranquillity, and the birds and beasts,
the fishes and tortoises, all realized
the happiness of their nature." It
is thus that the sage "assists Heaven
and Earth." K'ang-ch'ǎng, indeed,
explains this by saying:—"The sage,
receiving Heaven's appointment to
the throne, extends everywhere a
happy tranquillity." Evidently there
is a reference in the language to the
mystical paragraph in the 1st chapter—致中和,天地位焉,萬物育
焉. "Heaven and Earth" take the
place here of the single term—
"Heaven," in chap. xx, par. 18. On
this Ying-tâ observes: "It is said
above, *sincerity is the way of Heaven,*
and here mention is made also of
*Earth.* The reason is, that the reference above was to the principle of
sincerity in its spiritual and mysterious origin, and thence the expression
simple,—*The way of Heaven;* but
here we have the transformation and
nourishing seen in the production of
things, and hence *Earth* is associated
with *Heaven.*" This is not very
intelligible, but it is to bring out
the idea of a *ternion,* that the great,
supreme, ruling Power is thus dual-
ized. 參 is "a file of three," and
I employ "ternion" to express the
idea, just as we use "quaternion"
for a file of four. What is it but
extravagance thus to file man with
the supreme Power?

至誠爲能化。

變、則化、唯天下

明、則動、動、則變、

形、則著、著、則明、

能有誠誠、則形、

🖲其次致曲、曲

CHAPTER XXIII. Next to the above is he who cultivates to the utmost the shoots *of goodness* in him. From those he can attain to the possession of sincerity. This sincerity becomes apparent. From being apparent, it becomes manifest. From being manifest, it becomes brilliant. Brilliant, it affects others. Affecting others, they are changed by it. Changed by it, they are transformed. It is only he who is possessed of the most complete sincerity that can exist under heaven, who can transform.

23. THE WAY OF MAN;—THE DEVELOPMENT OF PERFECT SINCERITY IN THOSE NOT NATURALLY POSSESSED OF IT. 其次, "the next," or "his next," referring to the 自誠明者, of chap. xxi. 曲 is defined by Chû Hsî as 一偏, "one half," "a part." K'ang-ch'ăng explains it by 小小之事, "very small matters." Mâo defines it by 隅, "a corner," and refers to Analects, VII, viii, 舉一隅不以三隅反, as a sentiment analogous to the one in 致曲. There is difficulty about the term. It properly means "crooked," and with a bad application, like 偏, often signifies "deflec-

tion from what is straight and right." Yet it cannot have a bad meaning here, for if it have, the phrase, 致曲, will be, in the connection, unintelligible. One writer uses this comparison: "Put a stone ·on a bamboo shoot, or where the shoot would show itself, and it will travel round the stone, and come out *crookedly* at its side." So it is with the good nature, whose free development is repressed.˙ It shows itself in shoots, but if they be cultivated and improved, a moral condition and influence may be attained, equal to that of the Sage.

前知、國家將興、必
有禎祥、國家將亡、
必有妖孽、見乎蓍
龜、動乎四體、禍福
將至、善、必先知之、

至誠之道、可以

CHAPTER XXIV. It is characteristic of the most entire sincerity to be able to foreknow. When a nation or family is about to flourish, there are sure to be happy omens; and when it is about to perish, there are sure to be unlucky omens. *Such events are seen in the milfoil and tortoise, and affect the movements of the four limbs.* When calamity or happiness is about to come, the good shall certainly be foreknown

24. THAT ENTIRE SINCERITY CAN FOREKNOW. 至誠之道 is the quality in the abstract, while 至 誠 at the end is the entirely sincere individual,—the Sage, by nature, or by attainment. 禎祥, "lucky omens." In the dictionary 祥 is used to define 禎. 祥 may be used also of inauspicious omens, but here it cannot embrace such. Distinguishing between the two terms, Ying-tâ says that unusual appearances of things existing in a country are 祥, and appearances of things new are 禎. 妖 孽 are "unlucky omens," the former being spoken of "prodigies of plants, and of strangely dressed boys singing ballads," and the latter of "prodigious animals." The subject of the verbs 見 and 動 is the events, not the omens. For the milfoil and tortoise, see the Yî-ching, App. III, ii, 73. They are there called 神 物, "spiritual things." Divination by the milfoil was called 筮; that by the tortoise was called 卜. They were used from the highest antiquity. See the Shû-ching, II, ii, 18; V, iv, 20–30. 四 體, "four limbs," are by K'ang-ch'ǎng interpreted of the feet of the tortoise, each foot being peculiarly appropriate to divination in a particular season. Chû Hsî interprets them of

是故君子誠之爲

之終始、不誠無物、

道、自道也。誠者、物

誠者、自成也、而

至誠如神。

不善、必先知之、故

by him, and the evil also. Therefore the individual possessed of the most complete sincerity is like a spirit.

CHAPTER XXV. 1. Sincerity is that whereby self-completion is effected, and *its* way is that by which man must direct himself.

2. Sincerity is the end and beginning of things; without sincerity there would be nothing. On this account, the superior man regards the attainment of sincerity as the most excellent thing.

the four limbs of the human body. 如 神 must be left as indefinite in the translation as it is in the text.— The whole chapter is eminently absurd, and gives a character of ridiculousness to all the magniloquent teaching about "entire sincerity." The foreknowledge attributed to the Sage,—the mate of Heaven, —is only a guessing by means of augury, sorcery, and other follies.

25. HOW FROM SINCERITY COMES SELF-COMPLETION, AND THE COMPLETION OF OTHERS AND OF THINGS. I have had difficulty in translating this chapter, because it is difficult to understand it. We wish that we had the writer before us to question him; but, if we had, it is not likely that he would be able to afford us much satisfaction. Persuaded that what he denominates *sincerity* is a figment, we may not wonder at the extravagance of its predicates. 1. All the commentators of the Sung school say that 誠 is here 天命之性, "the Heaven-conferred nature," and that 道 is 率性之道, "the path which is in accordance with the nature." They are probably correct, but the difficulty comes when we go on with this view of 誠 to the next paragraph. 2. I translate the expansion of this in the 日 講:—"All that fill up the space between heaven and earth are things (物). They end and they begin again; they begin and proceed to an end; every change being accomplished by sincerity, and every phenomenon having sincerity unceasingly in it. So far as the mind of man (人之心) is concerned, if there be not sincerity, then every movement of it is vain and false.

之宜也。

之道也、故時措

之德也、合外內

也、成物、知也、性

成物也、成己、仁

己而已也、所以

貴誠者、非自成

3. The possessor of sincerity does not merely
accomplish the self-completion of himself. With this
quality he completes *other men and* things *also.* The
completing himself *shows his* perfect virtue. The
completing *other men and* things *shows his* knowledge.
*Both these are* virtues belonging to the nature, and *this
is* the way by which a union is effected of the external
and internal. Therefore, whenever he—*the entirely
sincere man*—employs them,—*that is, these virtues,*—
*their action will be* right.

How can an unreal mind accomplish real things? Although it may do something, that is simply equivalent to nothing. Therefore the superior man searches out the source of sincerity, and examines the evil of insincerity, chooses what is good, and firmly holds it fast, so seeking to arrive at the place of truth and reality." Mâo's explanation is:—"Now, since the reason why the sincerity of spiritual beings is so incapable of being repressed, and why they foreknow, is because they enter into things, and there is nothing without them:—shall there be anything which is without the entirely sincere man, who is as a spirit?" I have given these specimens of commentary, that the reader may, if he can, by means of them, gather some apprehensible meaning from the text. 3. I have translated 成物 by—"complete *other men and* things *also,*" with a reference to the account of the achievements of sincerity, in chap. xxii. On 性之德也, 合外內之道也, the 日講 paraphrases:—"Now both this perfect virtue and knowledge are virtues certainly and originally belonging to our nature, to be referred for their bestowment to Heaven;—what distinction is there in them of external and internal?"—All this, so far as I can see, is but veiling ignorance by words without knowledge.

故至誠無息不息

則久、久則徵徵則悠

遠、悠遠則博厚、博厚、

則高明博厚、所以載

物也、高明、所以覆物

也、悠久、所以成物也。

CHAPTER XXVI. 1. Hence to entire sincerity there belongs ceaselessness.

2. Not ceasing, it continues long. Continuing long, it evidences itself.

3. Evidencing itself, it reaches far. Reaching far, it becomes large and substantial. Large and substantial, it becomes high and brilliant.

4. Large and substantial;—this is how it contains *all* things. High and brilliant;—this is how it overspreads *all* things. Reaching far and continuing long;—this is how it perfects *all* things.

26. A PARALLEL BETWEEN THE SAGE POSSESSED OF ENTIRE SINCERITY, AND HEAVEN AND EARTH, SHOWING THAT THE SAME QUALITIES BELONG TO THEM. The first six paragraphs show the way of the Sage; the next three show the way of Heaven and Earth; and the last brings the two ways together, in their essential nature, in a passage from the Shih-ching. The doctrine of the chapter is liable to the criticisms which have been made on the 22nd chapter. And, moreover, there is in it a sad confusion of the visible heavens and earth with the immaterial power and reason which govern them; in a word, with God. 1. Because of the 故, "hence," or "therefore," Chû Hsî is condemned by recent writers for making a new chapter to commence here. Yet the matter is sufficiently distinct from that of the preceding one. Where the 故 takes hold of the text above, however, it is not easy to discover. The gloss in the 備旨 says that it indicates a conclusion from all the preceding predicates about sincerity. 至誠 is to be understood, now in the

博厚配地、高明配天、悠
久無疆。如此者、不見而
章、不動而變、無爲而成。
天地之道、可一言而盡
也、其爲物不貳、則其生
物不測。天地之道、博也、
厚也、高也、明也、悠也、久

5. So large and substantial, *the individual possessing it* is the co-equal of Earth. So high and brilliant, it makes him the co-equal of Heaven. So far-reaching and long-continuing, it makes him infinite.

6. Such being its nature, without any display, it becomes manifested; without any movement, it produces changes; and without any effort, it accomplishes its ends.

7. The way of Heaven and Earth may be completely declared in one sentence.—They are without any doubleness, and so they produce things in a manner that is unfathomable.

8. The way of Heaven and Earth is large and substantial, high and brilliant, far-reaching and long-enduring.

abstract, and now in the concrete. But the 5th paragraph seems to be the place to bring out the personal idea, as I have done. 無疆, "without bounds,"=our *infinite*. Surely it is strange to apply that term in the description of any created being. 7. What I said was the prime idea in 誠, viz., "simplicity," "singleness of soul," is very conspicuous here. 其爲物不貳,一爲 is the substantive verb. It surprises us, however, to find Heaven and Earth called "*things*," at the same time that they are represented as by their entire sincerity producing all things. 9.

振河海而不洩、
載華嶽而不重、
之多、及其廣厚、
今夫地、一撮土
繫焉、萬物覆焉、
窮也、日月星辰
昭之多、及其無
也。今夫天、斯昭

9. The heaven now before us is only this bright shining spot; but when viewed in its inexhaustible extent, the sun, moon, stars, and constellations of the zodiac, are suspended in it, and all things are overspread by it. The earth before us is but a handful of soil; but when regarded in its breadth and thickness, it sustains mountains like the Hwâ and the Yo, without feeling their weight, and contains the rivers and seas, without their leaking away. The mountain

This paragraph is said to illustrate the unfathomableness of Heaven and Earth in producing things, showing how it springs from their sincerity, or freedom from doubleness. I have already observed how it is only the material heavens and earth which are presented to us. And not only so;—we have mountains, seas, and rivers, set forth as acting with the same unfathomableness as those entire bodies and powers. The 備旨 says on this:—"The hills and waters are what Heaven and Earth produce, and that they should yet be able themselves to produce *other* things, shows still more how Heaven and Earth, in the producing of things, are unfathomable." The use of 多 in the several clauses here perplexes the student. On 斯昭昭之多, Chû Hsî says—此 指 其 一 處 而 言 之, "This is speaking of it",—heaven— "as it appears in one point." In the 中庸說, *in loc.*, there is an attempt to make this out by a definition of 多:—多 餘 也, 言 少 許 耳, "多 is overplus, meaning a small overplus." 日 月 星 辰,—compare the Shú-ching, 1, 3. In that passage, as well as here, many take 星 as meaning the planets, but we need not depart from the meaning of "stars" generally. 辰 is applied variously, but used along with the other terms, it denotes the conjunctions of the sun and moon, which divide the circumference of the heavens into twelve parts. 華 嶽,—there are five peaks, or 嶽, celebrated in China, the western one of which is called 華 (lower 3rd tone) 嶽. Here, however, we are to understand by each term a particular mountain. See the 集證 and 中庸 說, *in loc.* In the 集證, the Yellow River, and that only, is understood by 河, but both it and 海 must be

已、蓋曰天之所以爲天也、

焉、詩云、維天之命、於穆不

黿、蛟、龍、魚、鼈生焉、貨財殖

水、一勺之多、及其不測、黿、

禽獸居之寶藏興焉、今夫

之多、及其廣大、草木生之、

萬物載焉、今夫山、一卷石

now before us appears only a stone; but when contemplated in all the vastness of its size, we see how the grass and trees are produced on it, and birds and beasts dwell on it, and precious things which men treasure up are found on it. The water now before us appears but a ladleful; yet extending our view to its unfathomable depths, the largest tortoises, iguanas, iguanodons, dragons, fishes, and turtles, are produced in them, articles of value and sources of wealth abound in them.

10. It is said in the Book of Poetry, "The ordinances of Heaven, how profound are they and unceasing!" The meaning is, that it is thus that Heaven is

taken generally. 卷 read *ch'üan*, the 2nd tone, is in the dictionary, with reference to this passage, defined by 區, "a place," "a small plot." In the 中庸說, 黿 is defined as 介蟲之元, "the first-produced of the Chelonia"; 龍 as 鱗蟲之長, "the chief of scaly animals"; 鼈 as being "a kind of 黿"; 蛟 as being "a kind of 龍," while the 鼉 "has scales like a fish, feet like a dragon, and is related to the 黿." By 貨 are intended pearls and valuable shells; by 財, fish, salt, etc. 10. See the Shih-ching, IV, i, Bk. I, Ode II, st. 1. The attributes of the ordinances of Heaven, and the virtue

三百、威儀三<br>千。

優優大哉、禮儀

萬物、峻極于天。

道。洋洋乎、發育

大哉聖人之

文也、純亦不已、

文王之所以爲

之德之純、蓋曰、

於乎不顯文王

Heaven. *And again,* "How illustrious was it, the singleness of the virtue of King Wăn!" indicating that it was thus that King Wăn was what he was. Singleness likewise is unceasing.

CHAPTER XXVII. 1. How great is the path proper to the Sage!

2. Like overflowing water, it sends forth and nourishes all things. and rises up to the height of heaven.

3. All-complete is its greatness! It embraces the three hundred rules of ceremony, and the three thousand rules of demeanor.

of King Wăn, are here set forth, as substantially the same. 純 = "fine and pure," "unmixed." The dictionary gives it the distinct meaning of "ceaselessness," quoting the last clause here,—純 亦 不 已, as if it were definition, and not description.

27. THE GLORIOUS PATH OF THE SAGE; AND HOW THE SUPERIOR MAN ENDEAVORS TO ATTAIN TO IT. The chapter thus divides itself into two parts, one containing five paragraphs, descriptive of the SAGE, and the other two descriptive of the *superior man,* which two appellations are to be here distinguished. 1. "This paragraph," says Chù Hsî, "embraces the two that follow." They are, indeed, to be taken as exegetical of it. 道, it is said, is here, as everywhere else in the Work (see the 翼 注, *in loc.*),

"*the path which is in accordance with the nature.*" The student tries to believe so, and goes on to par. 2, when the predicate about *the nourishing of all things* puzzles and confounds him. 2. 極 is not here the adverb, but = 至, "reaching to." 3. By 禮儀 we are to understand the greater and more general principles of propriety, "such," says the 備旨, "as capping, marriage, mourning, and sacrifice"; and by 威 儀 are intended all the minuter observances of those. The former are also 經禮, 禮經, and 正 經; the latter, 曲 禮 and 動 禮. See the 集 證, *in loc.* 300 and 3,000 are round numbers. Reference is made to these rules and their minutiæ, to show how, in every one of them, as proceeding from the Sage, there is a principle, to be referred to

庸、溫故而知新、敦厚

精微、極高明而道中

道問學、致廣大而盡

焉。故君子尊德性而

苟不至德、至道不凝

待其人而後行故曰、

4. It waits for the proper man, and then it is trodden.

5. Hence it is said, "Only by perfect virtue can the perfect path, in all its courses, be made a fact."

6. Therefore, the superior man honors his virtuous nature, and maintains constant inquiry and study, seeking to carry it out to its breadth and greatness, so as to omit none of the more exquisite and minute points which it embraces, and to raise it to its greatest height and brilliancy, so as to pursue the course of the Mean. He cherishes his old knowledge, and is continually acquiring new. He exerts an honest, generous earnestness, in the esteem and practice of all propriety.

the Heaven-given nature. 4. Compare chap. xx, 2. In "*Confucius Sinarum Philosophus*," it is suggested that there may be here a prophecy of the Savior, and that the writer may have been "under the influence of that spirit, by whose moving the Sibyls formerly prophesied of Christ." There is nothing in the text to justify such a thought.

5. 凝, "to congeal"; then = 成, "to complete," and 定, "to fix." The whole paragraph is merely a repetition of the preceding one, in other words. 6. 道 in both cases here = 由, "to proceed from," or "by." It is said correctly, that 首句是一節頭腦, "the first sentence,—尊德性而道問學, is the brains of the whole paragraph." 溫故而知新,—see

乎今之世反古之
用、賤而好自專生
鼇子曰愚而好自
謂與。
以保其身其此之
容詩曰既明且哲、
國無道其默足以
有道其言足以興、國
不驕爲下不倍、
以崇禮是故居上

7. Thus, when occupying a high situation he is not proud, and in a low situation he is not insubordinate. When the kingdom is well governed, he is sure by his words to rise; and when it is ill governed, he is sure by his silence to command forbearance to himself. Is not this what we find in the Book of Poetry,—"Intelligent is he and prudent, and so preserves his person?"

CHAPTER XXVIII. 1. The Master said, "Let a man who is ignorant be fond of using his own judgment; let a man without rank be fond of assuming a directing power to himself; let a man who is living in the present age go back to the ways of antiquity;—

Analects, II, xi. 7. This describes the superior man, largely successful in pursuing the course indicated in the preceding paragraphs. 倍＝背.. 詩曰,—see the Shih, III, iii, Ode VI, st. 4.

28. AN ILLUSTRATION OF THE SENTIMENT IN THE LAST CHAPTER—"IN A LOW SITUATION HE IS NOT INSUBORDINATE." There does seem to be a connection of the kind thus indicated between this chapter and the last, but the principal object of what is said here is to prepare the way for the eulogium of Confucius below,—the eulogium of him, a Sage without the throne. 1. The different clauses here may be understood generally, but they have a special reference to the general scope of the chapter. Three things are required to give law to the kingdom: virtue (including intelligence), rank, and the right time. 愚 is he who wants the virtue, 賤 is he who wants the rank, and the last clause describes the absence of the right time.— In this last clause, there would seem to

書同文、行
下、車同軌、
考文。今天<sup>三師</sup>
不制度、不
子、不議禮、
者也。非天<sup>三師</sup>
道、如此者、

on the persons of all who act thus calamities will be sure to come.

2. To no one but the Son of Heaven does it belong to order ceremonies, to fix the measures, and to determine the written characters.

3. Now, over the kingdom, carriages have all wheels of the same size; all writing is with the same characters; and all conduct there are the same rules.

be a sentiment, which should have given course in China to the doctrine of Progress. 2. This and the two next paragraphs are understood to be the words of Tsze-sze, illustrating the preceding declarations of Confucius. We have here the royal prerogatives, which might not be usurped. "Ceremonies" are the rules regulating religion and society; "the measures" are the prescribed forms and dimensions of buildings, carriages, clothes, etc.; 文 is said by Chû Hsî, after K'ang-ch'ăng, to be 書名, "the names of the characters." But 文 is properly the form of the character, representing, in the original characters of the language, the 形, or figure of the object denoted. The character and name together are styled 字; and 書 is the name appropriate to many characters, written or printed. 文, in the text, must denote both the form and sound of the character. 議, "to discuss," and 考, "to examine," but implying, in each case, the consequent ordering and settling. There is a long and eulogistic note here, in "Confucius Sinarum Philosophus," on the admirable uniformity secured by these prerogatives throughout the Chinese Empire. It was natural for Roman Catholic writers to regard Chinese uniformity with sympathy. But the value, or, rather, small value, of such a system in its formative influence on the characters and institutions of men may be judged, both in the empire of China, and in the Church of Rome. 3. 今, "now." is said with reference to the time of Tsze-sze. The paragraph is intended to account for Confucius's not giving law to the kingdom. It was not the time. 軌,

同倫。雖有其位苟無其德、

不敢作禮樂焉、雖有其德、

苟無其位、亦不敢作禮樂

焉○五而子曰吾說夏禮杞不足

徵也、吾學殷禮有宋存焉、

吾學周禮、今用之、吾從周。

4. One may occupy the throne, but if he have not the proper virtue, he may not dare to make ceremonies or music. One may have the virtue, but if he do not occupy the throne, he may not presume to make ceremonies or music.

5. The Master said, "I may describe the ceremonies of the Hsiâ dynasty, but Chî cannot sufficiently attest my words. I have learned the ceremonies of the Yin dynasty, and in Sung they still continue. I have learned the ceremonies of Châu, which are now used, and I follow Châu."

"the rut of a wheel." 4. 禮樂;— but we must understand also "the measures" and "characters" in par. 2. This paragraph would seem to reduce most sovereigns to the condition of *rois faineants*. 5. See the Analects, III, ix, xiv, which chapters are quoted here; but in regard to what is said of Sung, with an important variation. The paragraph illustrates how Confucius himself 下爲 不倍, "occupied a low station, without being insubordinate."

焉者雖善不尊、

不信民弗從、

無徵無徵不信、

乎上焉者雖善

重焉、其寡過矣

王天下有三

CHAPTER XXIX. 1. He who attains to the sovereignty of the kingdom, having *those* three important things, shall be able to effect that there shall be few errors *under his government*.

2. However excellent may have been the regulations of those of former times, they cannot be attested. Not being attested, they cannot command credence, and not being credited, the people would not follow them. However excellent might be the regulations made by one in an inferior situation, he is not in a

29. AN ILLUSTRATION OF THE SENTENCE IN THE TWENTY-SEVENTH CHAPTER—"WHEN HE OCCUPIES A HIGH SITUATION HE IS NOT PROUD"; OR RATHER, THE SAGE AND HIS INSTITUTIONS SEEN IN THEIR EFFECT AND ISSUE. 1. Different opinions have obtained as to what is intended by the 三重, "three important *things.*" K'ang-ch'ăng says they are 三王之禮, "the ceremonies of the three kings," i. e.; the founders of the three dynasties, Hsiâ, Yin, and Châu. This view we may safely reject. Chû Hsî makes them to be the royal prerogatives, mentioned in the last chapter, par. 2. This view may, possibly, be correct. But I incline to the view of the commentator Lû (陸 氏), of the T'ang dynasty, that they refer to the virtue, station, and time, which we have seen, in the notes on the last chapter, to be necessary to one who would give law to the kingdom. Mâo mentions this view, indicating his own approval of it. 寡 is used as a verb, "to make few."—"He shall be able to effect that there shall be few errors," i. e., few errors among his officers and people. 2. By 上焉者 and 下焉者, K'ang-ch'ăng understands "sovereign and minister," in which, again, we must pronounce him wrong. The translation follows the interpretation of Chû Hsî, it being understood that the subject of the paragraph is the regulations to be followed by the people. 上焉者 having a reference both to *time* and to *rank*, 下焉者 must have the same. Thus there is in it an allusion to Confucius, and the way is still further prepared for

質諸鬼神而無疑、

建諸天地而不悖、

考諸三王而不繆、

本諸身、徵諸庶民、

弗從故君子之道、

不尊不信、不信民

position to be honored.　Unhonored, he cannot command credence, and not being credited, the people would not follow his rules.

3.　Therefore the institutions of the Ruler are rooted in his own character and conduct, and sufficient attestation of them is given by the masses of the people.　He examines them *by comparison* with those of the three kings, and finds them without mistake. He sets them up before heaven and earth, and finds nothing in them contrary to their mode of operation. He presents himself with them before spiritual beings, and no doubts about them arise.　He is prepared to

his eulogium. 3. By 君子 is intended the 王天下者 in par. 1,—the ruling-sage. By 道 must be intended all his institutions and regulations. "Attestation of them is given by the masses of the people;" i. e., the people believe in such a ruler, and follow his regulations, thus attesting their adaptation to the general requirements of humanity. "The three kings" must be taken here as the founders of the three dynasties, viz., the great Yû, T'ang, the Completer, and Wăn and Wŭ, who are so often joined together, and spoken of as one. 繆＝謬, and should be read in the 4th tone. I hardly know what to make of 建諸天地. Chû, in his 語類, says: 此天地只是道耳, 謂吾建於此, 而與道不相悖也, "Heaven and Earth here simply mean right reason. The meaning is—I set up *my institutions* here, and there is nothing in them contradictory to right reason." This, of course, is explaining the text away. But who can do anything better with it? I interpret 質諸鬼神 (the 諸 is unfortunately

則、遠之則有望、近之則

天下法言而世爲天下

世爲天下道行而世爲

知人也。是故君子、動而

百世以俟聖人而不惑、

質鬼神而無疑、知天也、

百世以俟聖人而不惑。

wait for the rise of a sage a hundred ages after, and has no misgivings.

4. His presenting himself *with his institutions* before spiritual beings, without any doubts arising about them, shows that he knows Heaven. His being prepared, without any misgivings, to wait for the rise of a sage a hundred ages after, shows that he knows men.

5. Such being the case, the movements of such a ruler, *illustrating his institutions,* constitute an example to the world for ages. His acts are for ages a law to the kingdom. His words are for ages a lesson to the kingdom. Those who are far from him look longingly for him; and those who are near him are never wearied with him.

left out in the text) as the general trial of a ruler's institutions by the efficacy of his sacrifices, in being responded to by the various spirits whom he worships. This is the view of a Ho Hi-chan (何屺瞻), and is preferable to any other I have met with. 百世以俟聖人而不惑,—compare Mencius, II, Pt. I, ii, 17.

舜、憲章文武、上
▩仲尼、祖述堯
譽於天下者也。
不如此、而蚤有
終譽君子未有
庶幾夙夜、以永
無惡、在此無射、
不厭。詩曰、在彼

6. It is said in the Book of Poetry,—"Not disliked there, not tired of here, from day to day and night to night, will they perpetuate their praise." Never has there been a ruler, who did not realize this description, that obtained an early renown throughout the kingdom.

CHAPTER XXX. 1. Chung-nî handed down the doctrines of Yâo and Shun, as if they had been his ancestors, and elegantly displayed the regulations of Wăn and Wû, taking them as his model. Above, he

6. See the Shih-ching, IV, i, Bk. II, Ode III, st. 2. It is a great descent to quote that ode here, however, for it is only praising the feudal princes of Châu. 在彼, "there," means their own states; and 在此, "here," is the royal court of Châu. For 射, the Shih-ching has 斁.

30. THE EULOGIUM OF CONFUCIUS, AS THE BEAU IDEAL OF THE PERFECT- LY SINCERE MAN, THE SAGE, MAKING A TERNION WITH HEAVEN AND EARTH. 1. 仲尼,—see chap. ii. The various predicates here are explained by K'ang-ch'ăng and Ying-tâ, with ref- erence to the "Spring and Autumn," making them descriptive of it, but such a view will not stand examina- tion. In translating the two first clauses, I have followed the editor of the 參匯, who says: 祖述者、以 爲祖而樷述之、憲章者、奉爲憲 而表章之. In the 紹聞編, it is observed that in what he handed down, Confucius began with Yâo and Shun, because the times of Fû- hsî and Shăn-năng were very remote. Was not the true reason this, that he knew of nothing in China more remote than Yâo and Shun? By "the times of heaven" are denoted the ceaseless regular movement, which appears to belong to the heavens; and by the "water and the land," we are to understand the earth, in contradistinction from heaven, supposed to be fixed and unmovable. Liŭ, "a statute," "a

大也。

敦化、此天地之所以爲

不相悖、小德川流、大德

育、而不相害、道並行而

如日月之代明。萬物並

覆幬、辟如四時之錯行、

天地之無不持載無不

律天時、下襲水土辟如

harmonized with the times of heaven, and below, he
was conformed to the water and land.

2. He may be compared to heaven and earth in
their supporting and containing, their overshadowing
and curtaining, all things. He may be compared to
the four seasons in their alternating progress, and to
the sun and moon in their successive shining.

3. All things are nourished together without their
injuring one another. The courses *of the seasons, and
of the sun and moon,* are pursued without any collision
among them. The smaller energies are like river
currents; the greater energies are seen in mighty
transformations. It is this which makes heaven and
earth so great

law"; here used as a verb, "to take
as a law." 襲＝因, "to follow," "to
accord with." The scope of the
paragraph is that the qualities of
former Sages, of Heaven, and of
Earth, were all concentrated in
Confucius. 2. 辟 read as, and＝譬.
錯, read *ts'oh,＝tieh,* "successively,"
"alternatingly." "This describes"
says Chû Hsî, "the virtue of the
Sage." 3. The wonderful and mysterious course of nature, or—as the
Chinese express it—of the operations
of Heaven and Earth, are described
to illustrate the previous comparison
of Confucius.

容　柔　也　足　聰　至　鼉唯一
也　足　寬　以　明　聖　天<br>
發　以　裕　有　睿　爲　下<br>
強　有　溫　臨　知　能

CHAPTER XXXI. 1. It is only he, possessed of all sagely qualities that can exist under heaven, who shows himself quick in apprehension, clear in discernment, of far-reaching intelligence, and all-embracing knowledge, fitted to exercise rule; magnanimous, generous, benign, and mild, fitted to exercise forbearance; impulsive, energetic, firm, and enduring, fitted to maintain a firm hold; self-adjusted, grave, never

31. THE EULOGIUM ON CONFUCIUS CONTINUED. Chû Hsî says that this chapter is an expansion of the clause in the last paragraph of the preceding.—"The smaller energies are like river currents." Even if it be so, it will still have reference to Confucius, the subject of the preceding chapter. K'ang-ch'ăng's account of the first paragraph is:—音 德 不 如 此, 不 可 以 君 天 下 也, 蓋 傷 孔 子 有 其 德 而 無 其 命. "It describes how no one, who has not virtue such as this, can rule the kingdom, being a lamentation over the fact that while Confucius had the virtue, he did not have the appointment;" that is, of Heaven, to occupy the throne. Mâo's account of the whole chapter is:—"Had it been that Chung-nî possessed the throne, then Chung-nî was a perfect Sage. Being a perfect Sage, he would certainly have been able to put forth the greater energies, and the smaller energies, of his virtue,

so as to rule the world, and show himself the co-equal of Heaven and Earth, in the manner here described." Considering the whole chapter to be thus descriptive of Confucius, I was inclined to translate in the past tense,—"It *was* only he, who could," etc. Still the author has expressed himself so indefinitely, that I have preferred translating the whole, that it may read as the description of the ideal man, who found, or might have found, his realization in Confucius. 1. 唯 天 下 至 聖,—see chap. xxi. 聖 here takes the place of 誠. Collie translates:—"It is only the most HOLY man " Rémusat:—"*Il n'y a dans l'univers qu'un* SAINT, *qui . . .*" So the Jesuits:—"*Hic commemorat et commendat summe* SANCTI *virtutes.*" But *holiness* and *sanctity* are terms which indicate the humble and pious conformity of human character and life to the mind and will of God. The Chinese idea of the 聖 人 is far

民莫不說。是以聲名洋溢乎

莫不敬、言而民莫不信、行而

溥博如天、淵泉如淵、見而民

有別也。溥博淵泉、而時出之、

足以有敬也、文理密察、足以

剛、毅足以有執也、齊、莊、中、正、

swerving from the Mean, and correct, fitted to command reverence; accomplished, distinctive, concentrative, and searching, fitted to exercise discrimination.

2. All-embracing is he and vast, deep and active as a fountain, sending forth in their due season his virtues.

3. All-embracing and vast, he is like heaven. Deep and active as a fountain, he is like the abyss. He is seen, and the people all reverence him; he speaks, and the people all believe him; he acts, and the people all are pleased with him.

4. Therefore his fame overspreads the Middle

enough from this. 臨,—以尊適卑 曰 臨, "the approach of the honorable to the mean is called *lin*." It denotes the high drawing near to the low, to influence and rule. 2. "An abyss, a spring," equal, according to Chû Hsî, to—靜 深 而 有 本, "still and deep, and having a source." 時 出 之, "always,"—or, in season—"puts them forth," the

之, "them," having reference to the qualities described in par. 1. 3. "He is seen;"—with reference, says the 備 旨, to "the robes and cap," the visibilities of the ruler. "He speaks;" —with reference to his "instructions, declarations, orders." "He acts;"— with reference to his "ceremonies, music, punishments, and acts of government." 4. This paragraph is

天下之大經、立天下之大

𧰼唯天下至誠、爲能經綸

曰配天。

凡有血氣者、莫不尊親、故

所載日月所照、霜露所隊、

人力所通天之所覆、地之

中國施及蠻貊、舟車所至、

Kingdom, and extends to all barbarous tribes. Wherever ships and carriages reach; wherever the strength of man penetrates; wherever the heavens overshadow and the earth sustains; wherever the sun and moon shine; wherever frosts and dews fall:—all who have blood and breath unfeignedly honor and love him. Hence it is said,—"He is the equal of Heaven."

CHAPTER XXXII. 1. It is only the individual possessed of the most entire sincerity that can exist under heaven, who can adjust the great invariable relations of mankind, establish the great fundamental

the glowing expression of grand conceptions. 蠻, the general name for the rude tribes south of the Middle Kingdom. 貊 is another name for the 狄, or rude tribes on the north. The two stand here, like 夷 狄, Analects, III, v, and like 四 夷, in the *Great Learning*, x, 15, as representatives of all barbarous tribes. 隊, read *chûi*, 4th tone, = 墜, "to fall."

32. THE EULOGIUM OF CONFUCIUS CONCLUDED. "The chapter," says Chû Hsî, "expands the clause in the last paragraph of chap. xxix, that the greater energies are seen in mighty transformations." 1. 經 and 綸 are processes in the manipulation of silk, denoting the first separating of the threads, and the subsequent bringing of them together, according to their kinds. 天下之大經,—"the great invariabilities of the world"; explained of the 達道 and 九經, in chap. xx, 8, 12. 天下之大本,—"the great root of the world"; evidently with reference to the same

本、知天地
之化育、夫
焉有所倚。
肫肫其仁、
淵淵其淵、
浩浩其天。
苟不固聰

virtues of humanity, and know the transforming and nurturing operations of Heaven and Earth;—shall this individual have any being or anything beyond himself on which he depends?

2.　Call him man in his ideal, how earnest is he! Call him an abyss, how deep is he!　Call him Heaven, how vast is he!

3.　Who can know him, but he who is indeed quick

expression in chap. i, 4. 知 is taken as emphatic;—有默契焉, 非但聞見之知而已, "he has an intuitive apprehension of, and agreement with, them.　It is not that he knows them merely by hearing and seeing." 夫焉有所倚. This is joined by K'ang-ch'äng with the next paragraph, and he interprets it of the Master's virtue, universally affecting all men, and not partially deflected, reaching only to those near him or to few.　Chû Hsî more correctly, as it seems to me, takes it as = 倚靠, "to depend on."　I translate the expansion of the clause which is given in *"Confucius Sinarum Philosophus:"*—"The perfectly holy man of this kind therefore, since he is such and so great, how can it in any way be, that there is anything in the whole universe, on which he leans, or in which he inheres, or on which he behooves to depend, or to be assisted by it in the first place, that he may afterwards operate?"　2. The three clauses refer severally to the three in the preceding paragraph.　仁 is virtuous humanity in all its dimensions and capacities, existing perfectly in the Sage.　Of 淵 I do not know what to say.　The old commentators interpret the second and third clauses, as if there were a 如 before 淵 and 天, against which Chû Hsî reclaims, and justly.　In the 紹聞編 we read:—天人本無二, 人只有此形體, 與天便隔, 視聽思慮, 動作, 皆曰由我, 各我其我, 可知其小也, 除却形體, 便渾是天. 形體如何除得, 只克去有我之私, 便是除也, 天這般廣大, 吾心亦這般廣大, 而造化無間於我, 故曰浩浩其天. "Heaven and man are not properly two, and man is separate from Heaven only by his having this body.　Of their seeing and hearing, their thinking and revolving, their moving and acting, men all say—*It is from* ME.　Every one thus brings out his SELF, and his smallness becomes known.　But let the body be taken away, and all would be Heaven.　How can the body be taken away?　Simply by

明聖知達天

德者、其孰能

知之。

一
豐詩曰、衣錦

尚絅、惡其文

之著也、故君

子之道、闇然

而日章、小人

in apprehension, clear in discernment, of far-reaching intelligence, and all-embracing knowledge, possessing all heavenly virtue?

CHAPTER XXXIII. 1. It is said in the Book of Poetry, "Over her embroidered robe she puts a plain, single garment;" intimating a dislike to the display of the elegance of the former. Just so, it is the way of the superior man to prefer the concealment *of his virtue*, while it daily becomes more illustrious, and it

subduing and removing that self-having of the *ego*. This is the taking it away. That being done, so wide and great as Heaven is, my mind is also so wide and great, and production and transformation cannot be separated from me. Hence it is said—*How vast is his Heaven.*" Into such wandering mazes of mysterious speculation are Chinese thinkers conducted by the text:—only to be lost in them. As it is said, in par. 3, that only the sage can know the sage, we may be glad to leave him.

33. THE COMMENCEMENT AND THE COMPLETION OF A VIRTUOUS COURSE. The chapter is understood to contain a summary of the whole Work, and to have a special relation to the first chapter. There, a commencement is made with Heaven, as the origin of our nature, in which are grounded the laws of virtuous conduct. This ends with Heaven, and exhibits the progress of virtue, advancing step by step in man, till it

is equal to that of High Heaven. There are eight citations from the Book of Poetry, but to make the passages suit his purpose, the author allegorizes them, or alters their meaning, at his pleasure. Origen took no more license with the Scriptures of the Old and New Testaments than Tsze-sze and even Confucius himself do with the Book of Poetry. 1. *The first requisite in the pursuit of virtue is, that the learner think of his own improvement, and do not act from a regard to others.* 詩曰, —see the Shih-ching, I, v, Ode III, st. 1, where we read, however, 衣錦 褧衣. 褧 and 絅 are synonyms 惡 (the 4th tone) 其云云 is a gloss by Tsze-sze giving the spirit of the passage. The ode is understood to express the condolence of the people with the wife of the duke of Wei, worthy of, but denied, the affection of her husband. 君子之道, 小人 之道,—道 seems here to correspond exactly to our English *way*, as in the

故君子內省不
伏矣亦孔之昭、
德矣。詩云、潛雖
微之顯可與入
近知風之自知
溫而理知遠之
而不厭簡而文、
亡、君子之道淡
之道、的然而日

is the way of the mean man to seek notoriety, while he daily goes more and more to ruin. It is characteristic of the superior man, appearing insipid, yet never to produce satiety; while showing a simple negligence, yet to have his accomplishments recognized; while seemingly plain, yet to be discriminating. He knows how what is distant lies in what is near. He knows where the wind proceeds from. He knows how what is minute becomes manifested. Such a one, we may be sure, will enter into virtue.

2. It is said in the Book of Poetry, "Although *the fish* sink and lie at the bottom, it is still quite clearly seen." Therefore the superior man examines his heart,

translation. 的 然,—the primary meaning of 的 is 明, "bright," "displayed." 的 然, "displayed-like," in opposition to 闇然, "concealed-like." 知遠之近,—what is *distant*, is the nation to be governed, or the family to be regulated; what is *near*, is the person to be cultivated. 知風之自, —the *wind* is the influence exerted upon others, the *source* of which is one's own virtue. 知微之顯,— compare chap. i, 3. 可與＝"it may be granted to such an one," 與 being in the sense of 許. 2. *The superior man going on to virtue, is watchful over himself when he is alone.* 詩云, —see the Shih-ching, II, iv, Ode VIII, st. 11. The ode appears to have been written by some officer who was bewailing the disorder and misgovernment of his day. This is one of the comparisons which he uses;—the people are like fish in a shallow pond, unable to save themselves by diving to the bottom. The application of this to the superior man, dealing with himself, in the bottom of his soul, so to speak, and thereby realizing what is good and right, is very far-fetched. 志, "the will," is here＝心, "the whole mind," the self. 3. We have here substantially the same subject as in the last paragraph. The ode is the same which is quoted in chap. xvi, 4, and the citation is from the same stanza

時靡有爭、是故君子不賞

不言而信詩曰、奏假無言、

於屋漏、故君子不動而敬、

乎詩云、相在爾室尙不愧

可及者、其唯人之所不見

疚、無惡於志君子之所不

that there may be nothing wrong there, and that he may have no cause for dissatisfaction with himself. That wherein the superior man cannot be equaled is simply this,—his *work* which other men cannot see.

3. It is said in the Book of Poetry, "Looked at in your apartment, be there free from shame as being exposed to the light of heaven." Therefore, the superior man, even when he is not moving, has *a feeling of* reverence, and while he speaks not, he has *the feeling of* truthfulness.

4. It is said in the Book of Poetry, "In silence is the offering presented, and *the spirit* approached to; there is not the slightest contention." Therefore the superior man does not use rewards, and the people are

of it. 屋漏, according to Chû Hsî, was the northwest corner of ancient apartments, the spot most secret and retired. The single panes, in the roofs of Chinese houses, go now by the name, the light of heaven leaking in (漏) through them. Looking at the whole stanza of the ode, we must conclude that there is reference to the light of heaven, and the inspection of spiritual beings, as specially connected with the spot intended. 4. *The result of the processes described in the two preceding paragraphs.* 詩曰,—see the Shih-ching, IV, iii, Ode II, st. 2, where for 奏 we have 鬷. 假 read as, and =格. The ode describes the royal worship of T'ang, the founder of the Shang dynasty. The first clause

聲以色子曰、聲色之

詩云予懷明德不大

君子、篤恭而天下平。

德、百辟其刑之、是故

於鈇鉞。詩曰不顯惟

而民勸、不怒而民威

stimulated *to virtue*. He does not show anger, and the people are awed more than by hatchets and battle-axes.

5. It is said in the Book of Poetry, "What needs no display is virtue. All the princes imitate it." Therefore, the superior man being sincere and reverential, the whole world is conducted to a state of happy tranquillity.

6. It is said in the Book of Poetry, "I regard with pleasure your brilliant virtue, making no great display of itself in sounds and appearances." The Master said, "Among the appliances to transform the people,

belongs to the sovereign's act and demeanor: the second to the effect of these on his assistants in the service. They were awed to reverence, and had no striving among themselves. The 鈇鉞 were anciently given by the sovereign to a prince, as symbolic of his investiture with a plenipotent authority to punish the rebellious and refractory. The 鉞 is described as a large-handled ax, eight catties in weight. I call it a battle-ax, because it was with one that King Wû dispatched the tyrant Châu. 5. *The same subject continued.* 詩 曰,—see the Shih-

ching, IV, i, Bk. I, Ode IV, st. 3. But in the Shih-ching we must translate,—"There is nothing more illustrious than the virtue *of the sovereign*, all the princes will follow it." Tsze-sze puts another meaning on the words, and makes them introductory to the next paragraph. 君子 must here be the 王天下者 of chap. xxix. Thus it is that a constant shuffle of terms seems to be going on, and the subject before us is all at once raised to a higher, and inaccessible platform. 6. *Virtue in its highest degree and influence.* 詩 云,—see the Shih-ching, III, i,

於以化民、末也、詩曰、德輶
如毛、毛猶有倫、上天之載、
無聲無臭、至矣。
右第三十三章、子思因
前章極致之言反求其
本復自下學爲己謹獨
之事推而言之、以馴致
乎篤恭而天下平之盛、
又贊其妙、至於無聲無

sounds and appearances are but trivial influences. It is said in another ode, 'His virtue is light as a hair.' Still, a hair will admit of comparison *as to its size*. 'The doings of the supreme Heaven have neither sound nor smell.'—That is perfect virtue."

*The above is the thirty-third chapter. Tsze-sze having carried his descriptions to the extremest point in the preceding chapters, turns back in this, and examines the source of his subject; and then again from the work of the learner, free from all selfishness, and watchful over himself when he is alone, he carries out his description, till by easy steps he brings it to the consummation of the whole kingdom tranquilized by simple and sincere reverentialness. He further eulogizes its mysteriousness, till he speaks of it at last as*

Ode VII, st. 7. The "*I*" is God, who announces to King Wăn the reasons why he had called him to execute his judgments. Wăn's virtue, not sounded nor emblazoned, might come near to the 不顯 of last paragraph, but Confucius fixes on the 大 to show its shortcoming. It had *some*, though not *large*, exhibition. He therefore quotes again from III, iii, Ode VI, st. 6, though away from the original intention of the words. But it does not satisfy him that virtue should be likened even to a *hair*. He therefore finally quotes III, i, Ode I, st. 7, where the imperceptible working of Heaven (載＝事), in producing the overthrow of the Yin dynasty, is set forth as without sound or smell. That is his highest conception of the nature and power of virtue.

其可不盡心乎。

至深切矣學者

丁寧示人之意、

約言之其反復

舉一篇之要、而

臭、而後已焉蓋

without sound or smell.  He here takes up the sum'of his whole Work, and speaks of it in a compendious manner.  Most deep and earnest was he in thus going again over his ground, admonishing and instructing men:—shall the learner not do his utmost in the study of the Work?

# THE WORKS OF MENCIUS

## BOOK I

### KING HWUY OF LEANG.　PART I

曰、叟、不遠　　梁惠王。王　　孟子見　　章句上　　梁惠王　　孟子

**CHAPTER I.　1.** Mencius *went to* see King Hwuy of Leang.

2.　The king said, "Venerable sir, since you have

TITLE OF THE WORK. 孟子,— "The philosopher Măng." The Work thus simply bears the name, or surname rather, of him whose conversations and opinions it relates, and is said to have been compiled in its present form by the author himself. On the use of 子, after the surname, see on Ana., I, i. The surname and this 子 were combined by the Romish missionaries, and Latinized into Mencius, which it is well to adopt throughout the translation, and thereby avoid the constant repetition of the word "philosopher," Măng not being distinguished, like K'ung (Confucius), by the crowning epithet of "The Master."

TITLE OF THIS BOOK. 梁惠王章句上,—"King Hwuy of Leang, in chapters and sentences. Part I." Like the books of the Confucian Analects, those of this Work are headed by two or three characters at or near their commencement. Each Book is divided into two parts, called 上 下, "Upper and Lower." This arrangement was made by Chaou K'e (趙歧), a scholar of the Eastern Han dynasty (died A.D. 202), by whom the chapters and sentences were also divided, and the 章句上, 章句下, remain to the present day, a memorial of his work.

CH. I. BENEVOLENCE AND RIGHTEOUSNESS MENCIUS' ONLY TOPICS WITH THE PRINCES OF HIS TIME; AND THE ONLY PRINCIPLES WHICH CAN MAKE A COUNTRY PROSPEROUS. 1. "King Hwuy of Leang."—In the time of Confucius, Tsin (晉) was one of the great States of the empire, but the power of it was usurped by six great families. By 452 B.C., three of those were absorbed by the other three, viz., Wei, Chaou, and Han (魏, 趙, and 韓), which continued to encroach on the small remaining power of their prince, until at last they extinguished the royal house, and divided the whole territory among themselves. The emperor Wei Lëě (威烈), in his 23rd year, 402 B.C., conferred on the chief of each family the title of prince (侯). Wei, called likewise, from the name of its capital,

義而已矣。 利、亦有仁 王何必曰 孟子對曰、 利吾國乎。 亦將有以 千里而來、

not counted it far to come here, a distance of a thousand li, may I presume that you are likewise provided
with counsels to profit my kingdom?"

3. Mencius replied, "Why must Your Majesty·use
that word 'profit'? What I am 'likewise' provided
with, are *counsels* to benevolence and righteousness,
and these are my only topics.

Leang, occupied the southeastern part of Tsin, Han and Chaou lying to the west and northwest of it. The Leang, where Mencius visited King Hwuy, is said to have been in the present department of Kaifeng. Hwuy—"The Kindly"—is the post-humous epithet of the king, whose name was Yung (罃). The title of *king* had been usurped by Ying, at some time before Mencius first visited him, which, it is said, he did in the 35th year of his government, 335 B.C. Mencius visited him on invitation, it must be supposed, and the simple 見 ＝被招往見.

2. Mencius was a native of Tsow (鄒), in Loo, the name of which is still retained in the Tsow district of the department of Yenchow (兗州), in Shantung. The king, in compli-mentary style, calls the distance from Tsow to Leang a thousand li. It is difficult to say what was the exact length of the ancient li. At present, it is a little more than one third of an English mile. The 亦, "also," occasions some difficulty.— With reference to what is it spoken?

Some compare the 亦乎 with 不亦乎, Analects, I, i. But the cases are not parallel. Others say that the king refers to the many scholars who at the time made it their business to wander from country to country, as advisers to the princes —"You *also*, like other scholars," etc. Then, when Mencius, in par. 3, replies—亦有仁義, they say that he refers to Yaou, Shun, etc., as his models.—"I, like them," etc. But this is too far-fetched. The king's 亦, I suppose, follows the clause—"You have come a thousand li," and means:—"That is one favor, but you probably have others to confer also. Then Mencius' 亦 refers to the king's, and ＝"You say I likewise have counsels to profit you. What I likewise have, is benevolence," etc.· Observe the force of 將, delicately and sugges-tively putting the question. 3. 對, —marking the answer of an inferior, used from respect to the king. 曰 is "to say," followed directly by the words spoken. It is not "to speak of." 而已矣 mark very decidedly Men-cius' purpose to converse only of 仁

取千焉、千取百焉、不爲不

弒其君者、必百乘之家、萬

者、必千乘之家千乘之國、

國危矣、萬乘之國弒其君

以利吾身、上下交征利、而

何以利吾家士庶人曰、何

王曰、何以利吾國、大夫曰、 <sup>四莭</sup>

4. "If Your Majesty say, 'What is to be done to profit my kingdom?' the great officers will say, 'What is to be done to profit our families?' and the inferior officers and the common people will say, 'What is to be done to profit our persons?' Superiors and inferiors will try to snatch this profit the one from the other, and the kingdom will be endangered. In the kingdom of ten thousand chariots, the murderer of his sovereign shall be *the chief of* a family of a thousand chariots. In a kingdom of a thousand chariots, the murderer of his prince shall be *the chief of* a family of a hundred chariots. To have a thousand in ten thousand, and a hundred in a thousand, cannot

and 義. 4. 征,—here＝取, "to take." 交 征, "mutually to take"; *i.e.*, superiors from inferiors, and inferiors from superiors. 乘, low. 3rd tone, "a carriage or chariot." The emperor's domain,＝1,000 li square, produced 10 000 war chariots. A kingdom producing 1,000 chariots was that of a how, or prince. He is here called 百乘之家, instead of 百乘之君, because the emperor has just been denominated by that term.

立　　孟　必　亦　義　而　利　多
於　　子　曰　曰　而　遺　不　矣
沼　　見　利　仁　後　其　奪　苟
上　　梁　。　義　其　親　不　爲
顧　　惠　　而　君　者　饜　後
鴻　　王　　已　者　也　未　義
鴈　　王　　矣　也　未　有　而
麋　　　　　何　王　有　仁　先

be said not to be a large allotment, but if righteousness be put last, and profit be put first, they will not
be satisfied without snatching *all*.

5. "There never has been a man trained to benevolence who neglected his parents. There never has
been a man trained to righteousness who made his
sovereign an after consideration.

6. "Let Your Majesty also say, 'Benevolence and
righteousness, and these shall be the only themes.'
Why must you use that word—'profit'?"

CHAPTER II. I. Mencius, *another day*, saw King
Hwuy of Leang. The king *went and* stood *with him*
by a pond, and, looking round at the large geese and

後 and 先 are verbs. See Ana., VI,
xx. 5. The 仁 and 義 here are supposed to result from the sovereign's
example.
CH. 2. RULERS MUST SHARE THEIR
PLEASURE WITH THE PEOPLE. THEY
CAN ONLY BE HAPPY WHEN THEY
RULE OVER HAPPY SUBJECTS. 1. 王
立,—"The king stood"; and the
meaning is not that Mencius found

him by the pond. The king seems
to have received him graciously, and
to have led him into the park. 於
沼 上,—comp. Ana., VI, vii, but for
which passage I should translate
here—";over a pond," i. e., in some
building over the water, such as is
still very common in China. 鴻
means "large geese," and 麋 is the
name for a large kind of deer, but

庶民子來、王在靈

日成之經始勿亟、

營之庶民攻之不

云、經始靈臺經之

雖有此不樂也。詩

而後樂此不賢者、

乎孟子對曰賢者

鹿、曰賢者亦樂此

deer, said, "Do wise and good *princes* also find pleasure in these things?"

2. Mencius replied, "Being wise and good, they have pleasure in these things. If they are not wise and good, though they have these things, they do not find pleasure.

3. "It is said in the 'Book of Poetry,'

'He measured out and commenced his spirit-tower;
He measured it out and planned it.
The people addressed themselves to it,
And in less than a day completed it.
When he measured and began it, *he said to them* — Be not so earnest:
But the multitudes came as if they had been his children.
The king was in his spirit-park;

they are joined here, as adjectives, to 鷹 and 鹿. 賢者＝賢者之君, "worthy princes." It does not refer to Mencius, as some make it out. The reply makes this plain. The king's inquiry is prompted by a sudden dissatisfaction with himself, for being occupied so much with such material gratifications, and = "Amid all their cares of govt. do these pleasures find a place with good princes?" 3. See the She-king, III, i, Ode VIII, stt. 1, 2. The ode tells how his people delighted in King

囿、麀鹿攸伏、麀鹿濯濯、

白鳥鶴鶴、王在靈沼、於

牣魚躍文王以民力爲

臺爲沼、而民歡樂之謂

其臺曰靈臺謂其沼曰

靈沼樂其有麋鹿魚鼈、

古之人與民偕樂故能

樂也湯誓曰時日害喪、

> The does reposed about,
> The does so sleek and fat;
> And the white birds shone glistening.
> The king was by his spirit-pond;
> How full was it of fishes leaping about!'

"King Wăn used the strength of the people to make his tower and his pond, and yet the people rejoiced to do the work, calling the tower 'the spirit-tower,' calling the pond 'the spirit-pond,' and rejoicing that he had his large deer, his fishes, and turtles. The ancients caused the people to have pleasure as well as themselves, and therefore they could enjoy it.

4. "In the Declaration of T'ang it is said, 'O sun,

Wăn. For 鶴 the She-king reads 翯. 於 is read *woo*, an interjection. 古之人 referring to King Wăn, but put generally. 4. See the Shoo-king, III, i, 3;—"T'ang's announcement of his reasons for proceeding against the tyrant, Keĕ. The words quoted are those of the people. Keĕ had pointed to the sun, saying that, as surely as the sun was in heaven, so firm was he on his throne. The people took up his words, and pointing to th sun, thus expressed their hatred of the tyrant, preferring death with him to life under him. 時=是. 害 read *hĕă*. 喪, up. 3rd tone. Chaou

其民於河東、移其
耳矣、河內凶、則移
之於國也、盡心焉
梁惠王曰、寡人
哉。
池鳥獸豈能獨樂
與之偕亡、雖有臺
予及女偕亡、民欲

when wilt thou expire? We will die together with thee.' The people wished *for Kĕĕ's death,* though they should die with him. Although he had towers, ponds, birds, and animals, how could he have pleasure alone?"

CHAPTER III. 1. King Hwuy of Leang said, "Small as my virtue is, in the government of my kingdom, I do indeed exert my mind to the utmost. If the year be bad on the inside of the river, I remove *as many of the people as I can* to the East of the river, and convey

K'e gives quite another turn to the quotation, making the words _an address of the people to T'ang:—"This day he [Kĕĕ] must die. We will go with you to kill him." Choo He's view is to be preferred. I don't think that the last two clauses are to be understood generally:—"When the people wish to die with a prince," etc. They must specially refer to Kĕĕ.

CH. 3. HALF MEASURES ARE OF LITTLE USE. THE GREAT PRINCIPLES OF ROYAL GOVERNMENT MUST BE FAITHFULLY AND IN THEIR SPIRIT CARRIED OUT. 1. The combination of particles—焉 耳 矣 gives great emphasis to the king's profession of his own devotedness to his kingdom. 寡 人 was the designation of themselves used by the princes in speaking to their people, = 寡 德 之 人, "I, the man of small virtue." I shall hereafter simply render it by "I." Leang was on the south of the river, i. e., the *Ho,* or Yellow River, but portions of the Wei territory lay on the other side, or north of the river. This was called the Inside of the river, because the ancient imperial capitals had mostly been there, in the province of K'e (冀 州), comprehending the present Shanse; and the country north of the Ho, looked at from them, was of course "within," or on this side of it. 粟,—now used

既接、棄甲曳兵而走、或百步

戰、請以戰喻、填然鼓之、兵刃

不加多、何也○孟子對曰、王好

鄰國之民不加少、寡人之民

國之政、無如寡人之用心者、

粟於河內、河東凶亦然、察鄰

grain to the country in the Inside. When the year is bad on the East of the river, I act on the same plan. On examining the government of the neighboring kingdoms, I do not find that there is any prince who employs his mind as I do. And yet the people of the neighboring kingdoms do not decrease, nor do my people increase. How is this?"

. 2. Mencius replied, "Your Majesty is fond of war; —let me take an illustration from war.—*The soldiers move forward to* the sound of the drums; and after their weapons have been crossed, *on one side* they throw away their coats of mail, trail their arms behind them, and run. Some run a hundred paces and stop;

commonly for millet and maize, but here for grain generally. 加少,加多; lit., "add few, add many." To explain the 加, it is said the expressions＝分外少,分外多, "not fewer, nor larger, than they should for such states be." 2. 填然 is said to express the sound of the drum. In 鼓之, 鼓 is used as a verb, and 之 refers to 戰士, or soldiers. It was the rule

入洿池、魚鼈不可勝食也、

時穀不可勝食也、數罟不

民之多於鄰國也不違農

走也。曰、王如知此、則無望

曰、不可、直不百步耳、是亦

以五十步笑百步、則何如。

而後止、或五十步而後止、

some run fifty paces and stop. What would you think if those who run fifty paces were to laugh at those who run a hundred paces?" The king said, "They may not do so. They only did not run a hundred paces; but they also ran away." "Since Your Majesty knows this," replied Mencius, "you need not hope that your people will become more numerous than those of the neighboring kingdoms.

3. "If the seasons of husbandry be not interfered with, the grain will be more than can be eaten. If close nets are not allowed to enter the pools and ponds, the fishes and turtles will be more than can be

of war to advance at the sound of the drum, and retreat at the sound of the gong. 是亦走也,—lit., "this also," i. e., the fifty paces, "was running away." 3. Here we have an outline of the first principles of royal government, in contrast with the measures on which the king plumes himself in the 1st par. The 不 is not imperative = "do not." The first clauses of the various sentences are conditional. In spring there was the sowing; in summer, the weeding; and in autumn, the harvesting:— those were the seasons and works of husbandry, from which the people might not be called off. 勝, up. 1st tone. The dict. explains it by "to bear," "to be adequate to." 穀不可勝食 = "there is no eating power adequate to eat the grain." 數, here read ts'uh, "close-meshed." The

斧斤以時入山
林、材木不可勝
用也、穀與魚鼈
不可勝食材木
不可勝用是使
民養生喪死無
憾也、養生喪死
無憾、王道之始
也。五畞之宅、樹
之以桑、五十者、

consumed. If the axes and bills enter the hills and forests *only* at the proper time, the wood will be more than can be used. When the grain and fish and turtles are more than can be eaten, and there is more wood than can be used, this enables the people to nourish their living and bury their dead, without any feeling against any. This condition, in which the people nourish their living and bury their dead without any feeling against any, is the first step of Royal Government.

4. "Let mulberry trees be planted about the homesteads with their five *mow*, and persons of fifty years

meshes of a net were anciently required to be large, of the size of 4 inches. People might only eat fish a foot long. 山 = wooded hills. 林 = forests in the plains. The time to work in the forests was, according to Choo He, in the autumn, when the growth of the trees for the year was stopped. But in the Chow-le, we find various rules about cutting down trees,—those on the south of the hill for instance, in midwinter, those on the north, in summer, etc., which may be alluded to. 無憾 I have translated, "without any feeling against any," the ruler being specially intended. 4. The higher principles which complete royal government. We can hardly translate 畞 by "an acre," it consisting, at present at least, only of 240 square paces, or 1200 square cubits, and anciently it was much smaller, 100 square paces, of 6 cubits each, making a *mow*. The ancient theory for allotting the land was to mark it off in squares of 900 mow, the middle square being called the 公田, or "government fields." The other eight were assigned to eight husbandmen and their families, who cultivated the public field in common. But from this 20 *mow* were cut off, and, in portions of 2½ *mow*, assigned to the farmers to build on, who had also the same amount of ground in their towns or villages, making 5 mow in all for their houses. And to have the ground all for growing grain, they were required

不負戴於道路矣、七十者衣

教、申之以孝悌之義頒白者、

之家、可以無飢矣謹庠序之

矣、百畝之田、勿奪其時數口

無失其時、七十者可以食肉

可以衣帛矣、雞豚狗彘之畜、

may be clothed with silk. In keeping fowls, pigs, dogs, and swine, let not their times of *breeding* be neglected, and persons of seventy years may eat flesh. Let there not be taken away the time that is proper for the cultivation of the farm with its hundred *mow*, and the family of several mouths that is supported by it shall not suffer from hunger. Let careful attention be paid to education in schools, inculcating in it especially the filial and fraternal duties, and gray-haired men will not be seen upon the roads, carrying burdens on their backs or on their heads. It never has been that the ruler of a state, where such results were seen, — persons of seventy wearing silk and

to plant mulberry trees about their houses, for the nourishment of silk-worms. 雞 豚 (a young pig) 狗 (the grain-fed, or edible dog) 彘 (the sow) 之 畜, —lit., "as to the nourishing of the fowl," etc. 數 口 之 家—the ground was distinguished into three kinds; — best, medium, and inferior, feeding a varying number of mouths. To this the expression alludes. 庠 序, See on Book III, Pt. I, iii, 10. 王 "low. 3rd tone, to come to reign,"

帛食肉、黎民不飢不寒、然

而不王者、未之有也。狗彘<sub>五而</sub>

食人食而不知檢、塗有餓

莩、而不知發人死、則曰、非

我也、歲也、是何異於刺人

而殺之曰、非我也兵也、王

無罪歲、斯天下之民至焉。

eating flesh, and the black-haired people suffering neither from hunger nor cold,—did not attain to the imperial dignity.

5. "Your dogs and swine eat the food of men, and you do not know to make any restrictive arrangements. There are people dying from famine on the roads, and you do not know to issue the stores *of your granaries* for them. When people die, you say, 'It is not owing to me; it is owing to the year.' In what does this differ from stabbing a man and killing him, and then saying—'It was not I; it was the weapon'? Let Your Majesty cease to lay the blame on the year, and instantly from all the empire the people will come to you."

"to become regnant emperor." 5. Mencius now boldly applies the subject, and presses home his faults upon the king. 食人食,—the second 食 is read *tsze*, low, 3rd tone. 檢=制

"to regulate." The phrase 不知檢 is not easy. The translation given accords with the views of most of the commentators.

梁惠王曰寡人願安承教。

孟子對曰殺人以梃與刃、有

以異乎。曰、無以異也。以刃與

政、有以異乎、曰、無以異也。曰、

庖有肥肉、廄有肥馬、民有飢

色、野有餓莩、此率獸而食人

CHAPTER IV. 1. King Hwuy of Leang said, "I wish quietly to receive your instructions."

2. Mencius replied, "Is there any difference between killing a man with a stick and with a sword?" *The king* said, "There is no difference."

3. "Is there any difference between doing it with a sword and with *the style of* government?" "There is no difference," was the reply.

4. *Mencius then* said, "In your kitchen there is fat meat; in your stables there are fat horses. *But* your people have the look of hunger, and on the wilds there are those who have died of famine. This is leading on beasts to devour men.

CH. 4. A CONTINUATION OF THE FORMER CHAPTER, CARRYING ON THE APPEAL, IN THE LAST PARAGRAPH, ON THE CHARACTER OF KING HWUY'S OWN GOVERNMENT. 1. 安, "quietly," i. e , sincerely and without constraint. It is said 安對勉強, 看見其出于誠意. 2, 3. 有以異 乎,=有所以異乎, lit., "Is there whereby they are different?" 4. 野, —outside a town were the 郊 (*keaou*), *suburbs*, but without buildings; outside the *keaou* were the 牧 (*muh*), *pasture-grounds;* and outside the *muh* were the 野 (*yay*), *wilds.* 5.

斯民飢而死也。
而用之也、如之何其使
者、其無後乎、爲其象人
父母也。仲尼曰始作俑
獸而食人惡在其爲民
民父母行政不免於率
也。獸相食且人惡之爲

5. "Beasts devour one another; and men hate them *for doing so.* When *a prince,* being the parent of his people, administers his government so as to be chargeable with leading on beasts to devour men, where is that parental relation to the people?"

6. Chung-ne said, "Was he not without posterity who first made wooden images *to bury with the dead? So he said,* because that man made the semblances of men, and used them *for that purpose:*—what shall be thought of him who causes his people to die of hunger?"

且 has the force of "and yet," i. e., though they are beasts. So that a "how much more" is carried on, in effect, to the rest of the par. 人惡之,—惡, up. 3rd tone, the verb. 惡在,—惡, up. 1st tone, = 何. "Being the parent of the people,"—i. e., this is his designation, and what he ought to be. 6. 俑,—in ancient times, bundles of straw were made, to represent men imperfectly, called 芻靈, and carried to the grave, and buried with the dead, as attendants upon them. In middle antiquity, i. e., after the rise of the Chow dynasty, for those bundles of straw, wooden figures of men were used, having springs in them, by which they could move. Hence they were called 俑, as if 俑 = 踊. By and by, came the practice of burying living persons with the dead, which Confucius thought was an effect of this invention, and therefore he branded the inventor as in the text. 其無後乎,—the 乎 is partly interrogative, and partly an exclamation = *nonne.* 爲,—low. 3rd tone, = *because* 如之何 is by some taken as = "what would he (viz., Confucius) have thought," etc.? I prefer taking it as in the translation. The designation of Confucius by *Chung-ne* is to be observed. See Doctrine of the Mean, ii, I.

者一洒之如之何
寡人恥之願比死
七百里南辱於楚、
死焉、西喪地於秦
身東敗於齊長子
所知也及寡人之
天下莫強焉叟之
梁惠王曰晉國

CHAPTER V. 1. King Hwuy of Leang said, "There was not in the empire a stronger state than Tsin, as you, venerable sir, know. But since it descended to me, on the east we have been defeated by Ts'e, and then my eldest son perished; on the west we have lost seven hundred le of territory to Ts'in; and on the south we have sustained disgrace at the hands of Ts'oo. I have brought shame on my departed predecessors, and wish on their account to wipe it away, once for all. What course is to be pursued to accomplish this?"

CH. 5. HOW A RULER MAY BEST TAKE SATISFACTION FOR LOSSES WHICH HE HAS SUSTAINED. THAT BENEVOLENT GOVERNMENT WILL RAISE HIM HIGH ABOVE HIS ENEMIES. 1. After the partition of the state of Tsin by the three families of Wei, Chaou, and Han (note, ch. I), they were known as the three Tsin, but King Hwuy would here seem to appropriate to his own principality the name of the whole State. He does not, however, refer to the strength of Tsin before its partition, but under his two predecessors in the state of Wei. It was in the 30th year of his reign, and 340 B.C., that the defeat was received from Ts'e, when his oldest son was taken captive, and afterwards died. That from Ts'in was in the year 361 B.C., when the old capital of the state was taken, and afterwards peace had to be secured by various surrenders of territory. The disgrace from Ts'oo was also attended with the loss of territory;—some say 7, some say 8, towns or districts. The nominative to the verbs 敗, 喪, and 辱, does not appear to be 寡人 so much as 晉. 寡人恥之 may be translated—"I am ashamed of these things," but most comm. make 之 refer to 先人, Hwuy's predecessors when Tsin was strong; as in the translation. The same reference they also give to 死者, as not said generally of "the dead,"—those who had died in the various wars. This view is on the whole preferable to the other, and it gives a better antecedent for the 之 in 洒之. 一 =by one blow, one great movement. 洒=洗. 比 low. 3rd tone,

則可。孟子對
曰、地方百里、
而可以王王
如施仁政於
民、省刑罰、薄
稅斂深耕易
耨、壯者以暇
曰、脩其孝弟

2. Mencius replied, "With a territory which is only a hundred li square, it is possible to attain the imperial dignity.

3. "If Your Majesty will *indeed* dispense a benevolent government to the people, being sparing in the use of punishments and fines, and making the taxes and levies light, so causing that the fields shall be plowed deep, and the weeding of them be carefully attended to, and that the strong-bodied, during their days of leisure, shall cultivate their filial piety, fraternal respectfulness, sincerity, and truthfulness, serving thereby, at home, their fathers and elder brothers,

=爲, "for." 2. See Pt. II; ii, 1; but it seems necessary to take the 方 in this and similar cases as in the transl. There is a pause at 地:—"with territory, which is," etc. This is the reply to the king's wish for counsel to wipe away his disgraces. He may not only avenge himself on Ts'e, Ts'in, and Ts'oo, but he may make himself chief of the whole empire. How, is shown in the next par. 3. 省刑罰, 薄稅斂, are the two great elements of benevolent govt., out of which grow the other things specified. 刑罰 can hardly be separated. The dictionary says that 刑 is the general name of 罰. If we make a distinction, it must be as in the translation; 罰 is the redemption fine for certain crimes. So 稅 斂 together represent all taxes. Great differences of opinion obtain as to the significance of the individual terms. Some make 稅 to be the proportion of the land produce paid to the govt., and 斂 all other contributions. By some this explanation is just reversed. A third party makes 稅 to be the tax of produce, and 斂 the graduated *collection* thereof. This last view suits the connection here. 易, read *e*, low, 3rd tone,＝治. 壯者,—at 30, a man is said to be 壯. Translators have rendered it here by "the young,"

溺其民、王往而征之夫誰與

母凍餓、兄弟妻子離散彼陷

使不得耕耨以養其父母、父

之堅甲利兵矣、彼奪其民時、

其長上、可使制梃以達秦楚

忠信、入以事其父兄、出以事

and, abroad their elders and superiors;—you will then have a people who can be employed, with sticks which they have prepared, to oppose the strong mail and sharp weapons of the troops of Ts'in and Ts'oo.

4. "The *rulers of those states* rob their people of their time, so that they cannot plow and weed their fields, in order to support their parents. Their parents suffer from cold and hunger. Brothers, wives, and children are separated and scattered abroad.

5. "Those *rulers, as it were*, drive their people into pitfalls, or drown them. Your Majesty will go to punish them. In such a case, who will oppose Your Majesty?

but the meaning is the strong-bodied,—those who could be employed to take the field against the enemy. 可使 does not appear to be—"you can make or employ," but to be passive with special reference to the 壯者 above. 耆, read *sang*. 撻,—"to strike," "to smite," here="to oppose." 4. 彼,—"they" or "those," i. e., the rulers of Ts'in and Ts'oo. 養, low. 3rd tone. It is so toned in the case of children supporting their parents, and inferiors their superior. See in Ana. II, vii. 5. 夫, low. 1st

王敵故曰仁者無敵。

王請勿疑。

孟子見梁襄王出

語人曰望之不似人

君就之而不見所畏

焉卒然問曰天下惡

乎定吾對曰定于一。

6. "In accordance with this is the saying,—'The benevolent has no enemy.' I beg Your Majesty not to doubt *what I say*."

CHAPTER VI. 1. Mencius went to see the King Seang of Leang.

2. On coming out *from the interview*, he said to some persons, "When I looked at him from a distance, he did not appear like a sovereign; when I drew near to him, I saw nothing venerable about him. Abruptly he asked me, 'How can the empire be settled?' I replied, 'It will be settled by being united under one *sway*.'

tone, here = 則. 6. 故,—not "therefore"; it may indicate a *deduction* from what precedes, or be simply an illustration of it. 勿 疑, "Do not doubt." It is strange that Julien, in his generally accurate version, should translate this by "*ne cuncteris*." Hesitancy would, indeed, be an effect of doubting Mencius' words, not the proverb just quoted, but specially the affirmation in par. 2. But the words may not be so rendered.

CH. 6. DISAPPOINTMENT OF MEN-CIUS WITH KING SEANG. BY WHOM THE TORN EMPIRE MAY BE UNIT-ED UNDER ONE SWAY. 1. On the death of King Hwuy, he was succeeded by his son *Hih* (赫), called here by his honorary epithet, Seang, = "The land enlarger, and virtuous." The interview here recorded seems to have taken place immediately after Hih's accession, and Mencius, it is said, was so disappointed by it that he soon left the country. 2. 語,—low. 3rd tone. The 人 probably refers to

孰能禦之今夫天下之人牧未

下雨則苗浡然與之矣其如是、

旱、則苗槁矣天油然作雲沛然

與也、王知夫苗乎、七八月之閒、

一之孰能與之對曰天下莫不

孰能一之對曰、不嗜殺人者能

3.　"'Who can so unite it?'

4.　"I replied, 'He who has no pleasure in killing men can so unite it.'

5.　"'Who can give it to him?'

6.　"I replied, 'All the people of the empire will unanimously give it to him. Does Your Majesty understand the way of the growing grain? During the seventh and eighth months, when drought prevails, the plants become dry. Then the clouds collect densely in the heavens, they send down torrents of rain, and the grain erects itself, as if by a shoot. When it does so, who can keep it back? Now among the shepherds of men throughout the empire, there is not one

some friends of the philosopher, and is not to be taken generally. 卒, read *ts'uh*. 卒然,—comp. 率 爾, Analects, XI, xxiv, 4. On 望 之, 就 之, comp. Ana. XIX, 14. Chaou K'e makes

定 于 一 to = "It will be settled by him who makes benevolent government his one object." But this is surely going beyond the text. 5. The 與 is here explained, by Choo

有不嗜殺人者<br>
也、如有不嗜殺<br>
人者、則天下之<br>
民、皆引領而望<br>
之矣、誠如是也、<br>
民歸之、由水之<br>
就下、沛然誰能<br>
禦之。<br>
齊宣王問曰、

who does not find pleasure in killing men.  If there were one who did not find pleasure in killing men, all the people in the empire would look towards him with outstretched necks.  Such being indeed the case, the people would flock to him, as water flows downwards with a rush, which no one can repress.'"

CHAPTER VII.  1.  King Seuen of Ts'e asked,

He and others, as equivalent to 歸, founding, no doubt, on the 民歸之 in the end.  But in Book V, Pt. I, v, we have a plain instance of 與, used in connection with the bestowment of the empire, as in the translation which I have ventured to give, which seems to me, moreover, to accord equally well, if not better, with the rest of the chapter.  6. The 7th and 8th months of Chow were the 5th and 6th of the Hea dynasty, with which the months of the present dynasty agree.  今 夫,—夫, in lower 1st tone, is used as in the Ana. XI, ix, 3.  The 之 at the end is to be referred to 水, the whole, from 由 (＝猶), being an illustration of the people's turning with resistless energy to a benevolent ruler.

CH. 7.  LOVING AND PROTECTING THE PEOPLE IS THE CHARACTERISTIC OF IMPERIAL GOVERNMENT, AND THE SURE PATH TO THE IMPERIAL DIGNITY.  This long and interesting chapter has been arranged in five parts.  In the first part, pars. 1–5, Mencius unfolds the principle of imp. govt., and tells the king of Ts'e that he possesses it.  In the second part, pars. 6–8, he leads the king on to understand his own mind, and apprehend how he might exercise an imp. govt.  In the third, pars. 9–12, he unfolds how the king may and ought to carry out the kindly heart which he possessed.  In the fourth part, pars. 13–17, he shows the absurdity of the king's expecting to gain his end by the course he was pursuing, and how rapid would be the response to an opposite one.  In the last part, he shows the government that loves and protects the people in full development, and crowned with Imperial sway.  1. King Seuen ("The distinguished," 聖善周聞曰 宣), the second of his family, who governed in Ts'e, by surname T'ëen (田), and named P'eih-keang (辟彊), began his reign, 332 B. C.  By some the date of this event is placed 9 years earlier.  The time of Mencius' visit to him is also matter of dispute. See "Life of Mencius," in the *proleg.*

齊桓晉文之事、

可得聞乎孟子

對曰仲尼之徒、

無道桓文之事

者、是以後世無

傳焉臣未之聞

也、無以、則王乎。

曰、德何如、則可

以王矣、曰保民

而王莫之能禦

saying, "May I be informed by you of the transactions of Hwan of Ts'e, and Wǎn of Tsin?"

2. Mencius replied, "There were none of the disciples of Chung-ne who spoke about the affairs of Hwan and Wǎn, and therefore they have not been transmitted to these after ages;—your servant has not heard them. If you will have me speak, let it be about imperial government."

3. The king said, "What virtue must there be in order to the attainment of imperial sway?" Mencius answered, "The love and protection of the people; with this there is no power which can prevent a ruler from attaining it."

The ruler of Ts'e was properly only a duke (公), or a prince (侯); the title of *king* was a usurpation. Hwan and Wǎn,—see Ana., XIV, xvi. They were the greatest of the five leaders of the princes, who had played so conspicuous a part in the earlier time of the Chow dynasty, but to whom Confucius and Mencius so positively refused their approval. 2. 道 is a verb,="to speak of," in which sense it had formerly a tone different from its usage as a noun. 無 以, 則 王 乎,—以 is taken by Choo He as=巳, which it is as well to acquiesce in. See Chaou K'e's comm. for the all but impossibility of making any sense of the passage in any other way. 王,—low. 3rd tone, and

so generally throughout the chap. As an imperial title, it is low. 2nd tone, the simple name of dignity; as implying the attainment or exercise of that dignity, it is the 3rd tone. By translating it by "imperial government," "imperial sway," we come nearer to giving Mencius's meaning than if we were to use the term "royal." 3. Here the nominatives of "king" and "Mencius" are dropped before 曰, as frequently afterwards. The 曰 just serves the purpose of our points of quotation. 保,—"to preserve," "to protect." I translate it, according to Choo He's account, as= 愛 護. A pause is to be made at 民, and 而 王 joined to the remainder of

曰、舍之吾不忍其觳觫、若無

曰牛何之。對曰、將以釁鐘。

有牽牛而過堂下者、王見之、

臣聞之胡齕曰、王坐於堂上

哉。曰可曰、何由知吾可也曰、

也。曰、若寡人者、可以保民乎

4. *The king* asked again, "Is such a one as I competent to love and protect the people?" *Mencius* said, "Yes." "From what do you know that I am competent to that?" "I heard the following incident from Hoo Heih:—'The king,' said he, 'was sitting aloft in the hall, when a man appeared, leading an ox past the lower part of it. The king saw him, and asked, "Where is the ox going?" The man replied, "We are going to consecrate a bell with its blood." The king said, "Let it go. I cannot bear its frightened appearance, as if it were an innocent person going to

the sentence. 4. The hall, or *t'ang*, here mentioned, was probably that where the king was giving audience, and attending to the affairs of govt. 牛何之,—the 之 is the verb,=往。舍,—also a verb, up. 2nd tone. 諸=之, and at the same time with an indirect interrogative force. Choo He explains 釁鐘 from the meaning of 釁 as "a crack," "a crevice," saying·

"After the casting of a bell, they killed an animal, took its blood, and smeared over the crevices." But the first meaning of 釁 is—"a sacrifice by blood," and anciently "almost all things," connected with their religious worship, were among the Chinese purified with blood;—their temples, and the vessels in them. See the Le-ke, XXI, ii, Pt. II, 32.

誠有百姓者、齊國雖褊小、吾

臣固知王之不忍也王曰、然、

以王矣、百姓皆以王爲愛也、

不識有諸曰、有之曰、是心足

鐘與。曰、何可廢也、以羊易之。

罪而就死地、對曰、然則廢釁

the place of death." The man answered, "Shall we then omit the consecration of the bell?" *The king* said, "How can that be omitted? Change it for a sheep."' I do not know whether this incident really occurred."

5. *The king* replied, "It did," and *then Mencius* said, "The heart seen in this is sufficient to carry you to the imperial sway. The people all supposed that Your Majesty grudged *the animal,* but your servant knows surely, that it was Your Majesty's not being able to bear *the sight, which made you do as you did.*"

6. *The king* said, "You are right. And yet there really was an appearance of what the people condemned. But though Ts'e be a small and narrow state,

The reference here is to the religious rite. The only thing is that, in using an ox to consecrate his bell, the prince of Ts'e was usurping an imperial privilege. 5. 愛 may be taken as the finite verb—"you loved, i. e., grudged the animal," or as = "to be niggardly,"—"you were parsimonious." 6. It is better to make a pause after 然, and give the meaning as in the translation. Chaou K'e runs it on to the next clause. 誠有百姓者 is elliptical, and the particle

羊也宜乎百姓之謂我愛也。

心哉我非愛其財而易之以

牛羊何擇焉。王笑曰是誠何

王若隱其無罪而就死地、則

爲愛也以小易大彼惡知之、

也曰王無異於百姓之以王

無罪而就死地、故以羊易之

何愛一牛、卽不忍其觳觫、若

how should I grudge one ox. Indeed it was because I
could not bear its frightened appearance, as if it were
an innocent person going to the place of death, that
therefore I changed it for a sheep."

7. *Mencius* pursued, "Let not Your Majesty deem
it strange that the people should think you were grudg-
ing *the animal*. When you changed a large one for a
small, how should they know *the true reason?* If · you
felt pained by its being led without guilt to the place
of death, what was there to choose between an ox and
a sheep?" The king laughed and said, "What really
was my mind in the matter? I did not grudge the
expense of it, and changed it for a sheep!—There was
reason in the people's saying that I grudged it."

者 denotes this, requiring the supplement which I have given. 卽 ac-
knowledges the truth of Mencius's
explanation. 7. 隱＝痛. 是誠何心
哉 expresses the king's quandary.
He is now quite perplexed by the

曰、無傷也是乃仁術也、見

牛、未見羊也、君子之於禽

獸也、見其生不忍見其死、

聞其聲不忍食其肉、是以

君子遠庖廚也。王說曰、詩

云、他人有心予忖度之、夫

子之謂也、夫我乃行之、反

8. "There is no harm *in their saying so*," said *Mencius*. "Your conduct was an artifice of benevolence. You saw the ox, and had not seen the sheep. So is the superior man affected towards animals, that, having seen them alive, he cannot bear to see them die; having heard their dying cries, he cannot bear to eat their flesh. Therefore he keeps away from his cookroom."

9. The king was pleased, and said, "It is said in the Book of Poetry, 'The minds of others, I am able by reflection to measure';—this is verified, my Master, in your discovery of my motive. I indeed did the thing, but when I turned my thoughts inward,

way in which Mencius has put the case. 8. 仁術,—comp. Ana., VI, xxviii, 2,—仁之方. 庖 ind. the killing place of the animals more especially, but we must take the two words 庖 廚 together. 9. 說=悅. For the ode, see the Book of Poetry, II, iv, Ode IV, st. 4, where the 他人 has a special reference. 夫子之謂也,—lit., "This was a speaking about

而功不至於百姓者、獨何與、

之乎曰否。今恩足以及禽獸、

毫之末、而不見輿薪、則王許

不足以舉一羽、明足以察秋

王者曰吾力足以舉百鈞、而

以合於王者何也。曰有復於

於我心有戚戚焉、此心之所

而求之、不得吾心、夫子言之、

and examined into it, I could not discover my own mind. When you, Master, spoke those words, the movements of compassion began to work in my mind. How is it that this heart has in it what is equal to the imperial sway?"

10. *Mencius* replied, "Suppose a man were to make this statement to Your Majesty: 'My strength is sufficient to lift three thousand catties, but it is not sufficient to lift one feather;—my eyesight is sharp enough to examine the point of an autumn hair, but I do not see a wagonload of fagots;'—would Your Majesty allow what he said?" "No," *was the answer, on which Mencius proceeded*, "Now here is kindness sufficient to reach to animals, and no benefits are extended from it to the people.—How is this? Is an

you, my master." 10. 復, read *fuh*, up. 4th tone, often meaning to report the execution of a mission, as in the phrase—復命. Here it is="to inform." 獨何與,—in order to bring out the force of the 獨, "only," it is

何以異曰、挾太山以超北海、

也曰不爲者與不能者之形、

故王之不王不爲也非不能

百姓之不見保爲不用恩焉、

焉、與薪之不見爲不用明焉、

然則一羽之不舉爲不用力

exception to be made here? The truth is, the feather's not being lifted, is because the strength is not used; the wagonload of firewood's not being seen, is because the vision is not used; and the people's not being loved and protected, is because the kindness is not employed. Therefore Your Majesty's not exercising the Imperial sway, is because you do not do it, not because you are not able to do it."

11. *The king* asked, "How may the difference between the not doing a thing, and the not being able to do it, be represented?" *Mencius* replied, "In such a thing as taking the T'ae Mountain under your arm, and leaping over the north sea with it, if you say to

necessary to make two sentences of this in English. 不爲也, it is said, ＝不肯爲, "not wi''ng to do it," but it is better to add nothing to the simple text. We have here, indeed, the famous distinction of "moral" and "physical" ability. 11. 形,— "the form," "or figure";—lit., "How

語人曰、我不能是誠不

能也、爲長者折枝語人

曰、我不能、是不爲也、非

不能也、故王之不王、非

挾太山以超北海之類

也、王之不王、是折枝之

類也。十一老吾老、以及人之

老、幼吾幼、以及人之幼、

people — 'I am not able to do it,' that is a real case of
not being able. In such a matter as breaking off a
branch from a tree at the order of a superior, if you
say to people — 'I am not able to do it,' that is a case
of not doing it, it is not a case of not being able to do
it. Therefore Your Majesty's not exercising the imperial sway, is not such a case as that of taking the
T'ae Mountain under your arm, and leaping over the
north sea with it. Your Majesty's not exercising
the imperial sway is a case like that of breaking off a
branch from a tree.

12. "Treat with the reverence due to age the elders
in your own family, so that the elders in the families
of others shall be similarly treated; treat with the
kindness due to youth the young in your own family,

may the figure . . . be differenced?"
語人.—語, low. 3rd tone,＝告.　12.
Chacu K'e makes the opening here＝

"Treat as their age requires your
own old (Eng. idiom seems to require
the 2nd person), and treat the old of

者無他焉善推其所爲

子古之人所以大過人

四海不推恩無以保妻

彼而已故推恩足以保

于家邦言舉斯心加諸

于寡妻至于兄弟以御

天下可運於掌詩云刑

so that the young in the families of others shall be similarly treated:—do this, and the empire may be made to go round in your palm.　It is said in 'The Book of Poetry,' 'His example affected his wife. It reached to his brothers, and his family of the state was governed by it.'—The language shows how *King Wăn* simply took this *kindly* heart, and exercised it towards those parties.　Therefore the carrying out his kindly heart *by a prince* will suffice for the love and protection of all within the four seas, and if he do not carry it out, he will not be able to protect his wife and children.　The way in which the ancients came greatly to surpass other men, was no other than this:—simply that they knew well how to carry out, so as to affect

others in the same way," but there seems to be a kind of *constructio pregnans*, conveying all that appears in the translation.　天下可運於掌 is made by most comm. to mean— "you may pervade the empire with your kindness so easily."　But I must believe that it is the *effect*, and not the *means*, which is thus represented. For the ode, see the She-king, III, i, Ode VI, st. 2.　The original celebrates the virtue of King Wăn, and we must translate in the third person, and not in the first."　御＝迓, but the meaning is disputed.　Here Choo He explains it by 治.　The philosopher now introduces a new element into his discourse.　It is no longer the 不忍之心, "the heart that cannot bear," i. e., the humane heart, which is necessary to raise to the imperial sway, but it is 推此心, "the *carrying out* of this heart."　All may have the heart, but all may not be gifted,

而已矣、今恩足以及禽獸、

而功不至於百姓者獨何

與。十三節權然後知輕重度然後

知長短、物皆然心爲甚、王

請度之抑王興甲兵、危士十四節

臣、構怨於諸侯、然後快於

others, what they themselves did. Now your kindness is sufficient to reach to animals, and no benefits are extended from it to reach the people. — How is this? Is an exception to be made here?

13. "By weighing, we know what things are light, and what heavy. By measuring, we know what things are long, and what short. The relations of all things may be thus determined, and it is of the greatest importance to estimate *the motions of* the mind. I beg Your Majesty to measure it.

14. "You collect your equipments of war, endanger your soldiers and officers, and excite the resentment of the other princes; — do these things cause you pleasure in your mind?"

so to carry it out that it shall affect all others. We cannot wonder that the princes whom Mencius lectured should have thought his talk 迂闊, *transcendental*. 13. The 1st 度 is low. 3rd tone, *too*, "a measure," the instrument for measuring. But both it and 權 are equivalent to active verbs. 心爲甚 means that the mind, as affected from without, and going forth to affect, may be light or heavy, long or short, i. e., may be right or wrong, and that in different degrees;—and that it is more important to estimate the character of its action, than to weigh or measure other things. 14. Here Mencius helps the king to measure his mind. 抑,—about the same as our "come,

心與王曰、否、吾何快於是、將

以求吾所大欲也。曰王之所

大欲可得聞與。王笑而不言。

曰、爲肥甘不足於口與、輕煖

不足於體與、抑爲采色不足

視於目與聲音不足聽於耳

與、便嬖不足使令於前與、王

15. The king replied: "No. How should I derive pleasure from these things? My object in them is to seek for what I greatly desire."

16. *Mencius* said, "May I hear from you what it is that you greatly desire?" The king laughed and did not speak. *Mencius* resumed, "*Are you led to desire it,* because you have not enough of rich and sweet food for your mouth? Or because you have not enough of light and warm *clothing* for your body? Or because you have not enow of beautifully colored objects to delight your eyes? Or because you have not voices and tones enow to please your ears? Or because you have not enow of attendants and favorites to stand before you and receive your orders? Your Majesty's

now," or "well then." 16. The 與 are all interrog., low. 1st tone, and │ the 爲 are all low. 3rd tone. 便, read *p'een*, low. 1st tone, joined with the

甚焉、緣木求魚雖不得魚、無後

魚也王曰、若是其甚與曰殆有 〇十七節

若所爲、求若所欲猶緣木而求

朝秦楚莅中國而撫四夷也、以

王之所大欲可知已、欲辟土地、

是哉。曰否、吾不爲是也。曰然則

之諸臣、皆足以供之、而王豈爲

various officers are sufficient to supply you with those
things. How can Your Majesty be led to entertain
such a desire on account of them?" "No," said *the
king;* "my desire is not on account of them?" *Mencius*
added, "Then, what Your Majesty greatly desires may
be known. You wish to enlarge your territories, to
have Ts'in and Ts'oo wait at your court, to rule the
Middle Kingdom, and to attract to you the barbarous
tribes that surround it. But to do what you do to
seek for what you desire, is like climbing a tree to seek
for fish."

17. *The king* said, "Is it so bad as that?" "It is
even worse," was the reply. "If you climb a tree to
seek for fish, although you do not get the fish, you will

next char. 可 知 已,—已 gives a
positiveness to the assertion. 辟,
read as, and＝闢. 緣 木, from the
use of the phrase here, has come to

be used for "to climb a tree," but it
simply is—"from a tree." 17. The
殆, an introduct. part., ＝ "yes, and."

災、以若所爲、求若所欲、盡心力

而爲之、後必有災。曰、可得聞與、

曰、鄒人與楚人戰、則王以爲孰

勝。曰、楚人勝曰、然則小固不可

以敵大寡固不可以敵衆弱固

不可以敵彊、海內之地方千里

者九、齊集有其一、以一服八、何

not suffer any subsequent calamity. But if you do what you do to seek for what you desire, doing it moreover with all your heart, you will assuredly afterwards meet with calamities." *The king* asked, "May I hear *from you the proof of* that?" *Mencius* said, "If the people of Tsow should fight with the people of Ts'oo, which of them does Your Majesty think would conquer?" "The people of Ts'oo would conquer." "Yes;—and so it is certain that a small country cannot contend with a great, that few cannot contend with many, that the weak cannot contend with the strong. The territory within the *four* seas embraces nine divisions, each of a thousand li square. All Ts'e together is but one of them. If with one part you try to subdue the other eight,

以異於鄒敵楚哉、蓋亦反其
本矣〇十八章今王發政施仁使天下
仕者皆欲立於王之朝耕者、
皆欲耕於王之野商賈皆欲
藏於王之市行旅皆欲出於
王之塗天下之欲疾其君者、
皆欲赴愬於王其若是孰能

what is the difference between that and Tsow's contending with Ts'oo? For, *with the desire which you
have,* you must likewise turn back to the radical course
*for its attainment.*

18. "Now, if Your Majesty will institute a government whose action shall all be benevolent, this will
cause all the officers in the empire to wish to stand in
Your Majesty's court, and the farmers all to wish to
plow in Your Majesty's fields, and the merchants,
both traveling and stationary, all to wish to store their
goods in Your Majesty's market places, and traveling
strangers all to wish to make their tours on Your
Majesty's roads, and all throughout the empire who
feel aggrieved by their rulers to wish to come and
complain to Your Majesty. And when they are so
bent, who will be able to keep them back?"

蓋亦反其本, is spoken with reference to the king's object of ambition:
—"By the course you are pursuing
you cannot succeed, for, if you wish
to do so, you must also turn back
to the root of success." 18. 野一
"fields," here; not "wilds." 出於一
"to come forth in," i. e., to pass from

及陷於罪、然後從而刑之是罔民

心、苟無恆心放辟邪侈無不爲已、

惟士爲能若民則無恆產因無恆

請嘗試之曰無恆產、而有恆心者、 二十節

夫子輔吾志明以教我我雖不敏、

禦之王曰、吾惛、不能進於是矣、願 ○十九節

19. The king said, "I am stupid, and not able to advance to this. I wish you, my Master, to assist my intentions. Teach me clearly; although I am deficient in intelligence and vigor, I will essay and try to carry your instructions into effect."

20. *Mencius* replied, "They are only men of education, who, without a certain-livelihood, are able to maintain a fixed heart. As to the people, if they have not a certain livelihood, it follows that they will not have a fixed heart. And if they have not a fixed heart, there is nothing which they will not do, in the way of self-abandonment, of moral deflection, of depravity, and of wild license. When they thus have been involved in crime, to follow them up and punish them;—this is to entrap the people. How can such

their own states into yours. 欲疾,— " wishing to be aggrieved, but must | restrain their feelings." 20. 辟, read as, and＝僻. 罔,—"en-net," i. e., to

之從之也輕今也、制民
亡、然後驅而之善、故民
歲終身飽凶年免於死
父母、俯足以畜妻子樂
民之產、必使仰足以事
而可爲也。是故明君制
也、焉有仁人在位罔民

a thing as entrapping the people be done under the
rule of a benevolent man?''

21. "Therefore an intelligent ruler will regulate the
livelihood of the people, so as to make sure that,
above, they shall have sufficient wherewith to serve
their parents, and, below, sufficient wherewith to
support their wives and children; that in good years
they shall always be abundantly satisfied, and that in
bad years they shall escape the danger of perishing.
After this he may urge them, and they will proceed to
what is good, for in this case the people will follow
after that with ease.

22. "Now, the livelihood of the people is so

entrap. 無所不爲已─已, see on
par. 17. 21. 終身, gen. means "the
whole life." Perhaps we should
translate, "If some years be good,
they will all their lives have plenty";
i. e., they will in those years lay by a
sufficient provision for bad years.
This supposes that the people have
felt the power of the instruction and
moral training that is a part of royal
govt., which, however, is set forth as
consequent on the regulation of the
livelihood. Similarly, below. 之
善,─之 is the verb,＝從, 民之從之
也輕,─Julien censures Noel here for
rendering 從之 by *ipsi* (*principi*)

五十者、可以衣帛矣、雞豚

本矣。〔廿四節〕五畝之宅、樹之以桑、

義哉。〔廿三節〕王欲行之、則盍反其

救死、而恐不贍奚暇治禮

苦、凶年不免於死亡、此惟

不足以畜妻子、樂歲終身

之產、仰不足以事父母、俯

regulated, that, above, they have not sufficient wherewith to serve their parents, and, below, they have not
sufficient wherewith to support their wives and
children. *Notwithstanding* good years, their lives are
continually embittered, and, in bad years, they do not
escape perishing. In such circumstances they only try
to save themselves from death, and are afraid they will
not succeed. What leisure have they to cultivate
propriety and righteousness?

23. "If Your Majesty wishes to effect this *regulation
of the livelihood of the people*, why not turn to that
which is the essential step to it?

24. "Let mulberry trees be planted about the
homesteads with their five *mow*, and persons of fifty
years may be clothed with silk. In keeping fowls,

*obsequentur,*" and rightly. But I am
not sure that the error is not rather
in the rendering of 從 than in that
of 之. The prince is supposed to exemplify, as well as to urge to, the
good course, and the well-off people
have no difficulty in following him.
23. 反其本, as in par. 17, but with
reference to the immediate subject.
24. See ch. iii, the only difference

狗彘之畜無失其時、七十者、
可以食肉矣、百畝之田勿奪
其時、八口之家、可以無飢矣、
謹庠序之教、申之以孝悌之
義、頒白者不負戴於道路矣、
老者衣帛食肉、黎民不飢不
寒、然而不王者、未之有也。

pigs, and swine, let not their times of breeding be
neglected, and persons of seventy years may eat flesh.
Let there not be taken away the time that is proper
for the cultivation of the farm with its hundred *mow*,
and the family of eight mouths that is supported by it
shall not suffer from hunger.　Let careful attention be
paid to education in schools, — the inculcation in it
especially of the filial and fraternal duties, and gray-
haired men will not be seen upon the roads, carrying
burdens on their backs or on their heads.　It never
has been that the ruler of a state where such results
were seen, — the old wearing silk and eating flesh, and
the black-haired people suffering neither from hunger
nor cold, — did not attain to the imperial dignity."

being that, for 數口之家 there, we have 八口之家, eight mouths being the number which 100 *mow* of medium land were computed to feed.

## BOOK I

### KING HWUY OF LEANG.　PART II

之好樂甚、則齊國其

好樂何如。孟子曰、王

樂、暴未有以對也。曰、

見於王、王語暴以好

莊暴見孟子曰、暴

梁惠王章句下

CHAPTER I.　1.　Chwang Paou, seeing Mencius, said to him, "I had an audience of the king.　His Majesty told me that he loved music, and I was not prepared with anything to reply to him.　What do you pronounce about that love of music?"　Mencius replied, "If the king's love of music were very great, the kingdom of Ts'e would be near to *a state of good government*."

CH. 1.　HOW THE LOVE OF MUSIC MAY BE MADE SUBSERVIENT TO GOOD GOVERNMENT, AND TO A PRINCE'S OWN ADVANCEMENT.　The chapter is a good specimen of Mencius's manner,—how he slips from the point in hand to introduce his own notions, and would win princes over to benevolent government by their very vices.　He was no stern moralist, and the Chinese have done well in refusing to rank him with Confucius. 1.　hwang Paou appears to have been a minister at the court of Ts'e.

The 曰 preceding 好 樂 如 何 is unnecessary.　If we translate it, we must render—"He then said."　But the paraphrasts all neglect it.　庶 幾 (up. 1st tone) is a phrase, signifying "near to"; sometimes we find 庶 alone, as in Ana. XI, xviii, i.　The subject, nearness to which is indicated, is often left to be gathered from the context, as here.　The 王 之 好 樂 甚 is a platitude.　It should be the text of the chap., but Mencius proceeds to substitute 樂 *loh* for 樂

曰、獨樂樂、與人樂樂、孰樂。曰、

樂、由古之樂也。曰、可得聞與。

好樂甚、則齊其庶幾乎、今之

也、直好世俗之樂耳。曰、王之

色曰、寡人非能好先王之樂

語莊子以好樂、有諸。王變乎

庶幾乎他日見於王曰、王嘗

2. Another day, *Mencius*, having an audience of the king, said, "Your Majesty, *I have heard*, told the officer Chwang that you love music;—was it so?" The king changed color, and said, "I am unable to love the music of the ancient sovereigns; I only love the music that suits the manners of the *present* age."

3. *Mencius* said, "If Your Majesty's love of music were very great, Ts'e would be near to *a state of good government!* The music of the present day is just like the music of antiquity, *in regard to effecting that.*"

4. *The king* said, "May I hear from you the proof of that?" *Mencius* asked, "Which is the more pleasant,—to enjoy music by yourself alone, or to enjoy it along with others?" "To enjoy it along with

*ngŏh*, in his own manner. 2. 直, as in last Pt., ch. iii, 3; observe how the final 耳 adds to the force of "only." "Ancient sovereigns," i. e., Yaou, | Shun, Yu, T'ang, Wän, and Woo, is a better translation of 先王 than "former kings." 3. 由=猶. 4. 司 得聞與, as in prec. ch. 獨樂樂,一

何使我至於此極也父子

相告曰吾王之好鼓樂、夫

管籥之音舉疾首蹙頞而

於此、百姓聞王鐘鼓之聲、

臣請爲王言樂今王鼓樂

衆樂樂孰樂。樂曰不若與衆。

不若與人曰、與少樂樂與

others," was the reply. "And which is the more pleasant,— to enjoy music along with a few, or to enjoy it along with many?" "To enjoy it along with many."

5. *Mencius proceeded*, "Your servant begs to explain *what I have said about* music to Your Majesty.

6. "Now, Your Majesty is having music here.—The people hear the noise of your bells and drums, and the notes of your fifes and pipes, and they all, with aching heads, knit their brows, and say to one another, 'That's how our king likes his music! But why does he reduce us to this extremity *of distress?*—Fathers

the second 樂 is *loh*, "joy," "pleasure." So, in the next clause, and after 孰. 5. 爲 (low. 3rd tone) 王, "for the sake of Your Majesty." 6. 鼓 樂.—鼓 is a verb,=作. The ancient dict., the 說 文, makes a difference between this, and the same word for "drum," saying this is formed from 攴, named *p‘ŭh*, while the other is formed from 支. The difference of form is now not regarded. 於 此, "here," used as we use *here* in English, putting a case with little local reference. 舉=俱 or 皆, "all." 蹙 頞 expresses anguish, not anger. 夫 is here the introd. particle, and is better rendered by *but* than *now*. It will be seen that the preced. 吾 王 之 好 鼓 樂 is incomplete. The paraphrasts add, to

子離散、此無他、不與民同
極也、父子不相見、兄弟妻
好田獵、夫何使我至於此
首蹙頞而相告曰吾王之
馬之音、見羽旄之美、舉疾
王田獵於此、百姓聞王車
不相見、兄弟妻子離散、今

and sons cannot see one another. Elder brothers and younger brothers, wives and children, are separated and scattered abroad. Now, Your Majesty is hunting here.—The people hear the noise of your carriages and horses, and see the beauty of your plumes and streamers, and they all, with aching heads, knit their brows, and say to one another, 'That's how our king likes his hunting! But why does he reduce us to this extremity *of distress?*—Fathers and sons cannot see one another. Elder brothers and younger brothers, wives and children, are separated and scattered abroad. Their feeling thus is from no other reason but that you do not give the people to have pleasure as well as yourself.

complete it, 固然已. 田 is used synonymously with 畋, "to hunt." 聲 and 音 are to each other much as our sound or noise and tone or note. 音 is applied appropriately to the

fifes and pipes, and also to the carriages and horses, having reference to the music of the *bells* with which these were adorned. Of 羽旄 Choo He simply says that they were 旌屬,

樂也。今王鼓樂於此、百姓聞王

鐘鼓之聲管籥之音舉欣欣然

有喜色而相告曰吾王庶幾無

疾病與、何以能鼓樂也、今王田

獵於此、百姓聞王車馬之音、見

羽旄之美舉欣欣然有喜色而

相告曰吾王庶幾無疾病與、何

以能田獵也、此無他、與民同樂

7. "Now, Your Majesty is having music here. The people hear the noise of your bells and drums, and the notes of your fifes and pipes, and they all, delighted, and with joyful looks, say to one another, 'That sounds as if our king were free from all sickness! If he were not, how could he enjoy this music?' Now, Your Majesty is hunting here. The people hear the noise of your carriages and horses, and see the beauty of your plumes and streamers, and they all, delighted, and with joyful looks, say to one another, 'That looks as if our king were free from all sickness! If he were not, how could he enjoy this hunting?' Their feeling thus is from no other reason but that you cause them to have their pleasure as you have yours.

"belonging to the banners." The 羽 were feathers adorning the top of the flagstaff; the 旄, a number of cows'-tails suspended from the top. 與民同樂, see Pt. I, ch. ii.

大何也曰文王之囿方七

之囿方四十里民猶以爲

曰民猶以爲小也曰寡人

於傳有之曰若是其大乎

方七十里有諸孟子對曰

齊宣王問曰文王之囿

矣。

也今王與百姓同樂則王

8. "If Your Majesty now will make pleasure a thing common to the people and yourself, the imperial sway awaits you."

CHAPTER II. I. The king, Seuen, of Ts'e asked, "Was it so, that the park of King Wăn contained seventy square li?" Mencius replied, "It is so in the records."

2. "Was it so large as that?" exclaimed *the king*. "The people," said *Mencius*, "still looked on it as small." *The king* added, "My park contains *only* forty square li, and the people still look on it as large. How is this?" "The park of King Wăn," was the

CH. 2. HOW A RULER MUST NOT INDULGE HIS LOVE FOR PARKS AND HUNTING TO THE DISCOMFORT OF THE PEOPLE. 1. 傳, low. 3rd tone, "a record," an historical narration handing down events to futurity (傳於後人). 方七十里, must be understood—"containing seventy square li," not "seventy li square." · In the

日講, the meaning of 方 here (not similarly, however, in Pt. I, v, 2; vii, 17) is given by 囘圍, "in circumference." The glossarist on Chaou K'e explains it by 方闊, which, I think, confirms the meaning I have given. The book or books giving account of this park of King Wăn

中民以爲大不亦宜乎。

則是方四十里爲阱於國

殺其麋鹿者如殺人之罪、

郊關之內有囿方四十里、

國之大禁然後敢入臣聞

不亦宜乎臣始至於境問

往焉與民同之民以爲小、

十里芻蕘者往焉雉兔者

reply, "contained seventy square li, but the grass-cutters and fuel gatherers had the privilege of entrance into it; so also had the catchers of pheasants and hares. He shared it with the people, and was it not with reason that they looked on it as small?

3. "When I first arrived at the borders *of your state*, I inquired about the great prohibitory regulations, before I would venture to enter it; and I heard, that inside the border gates there was a park of forty square li, and that he who killed a deer in it, was held guilty of the same crime as if he had killed a man. — Thus those forty square li are a pitfall in the middle of the kingdom. Is it not with reason that the people look upon them as large?"

are now lost. 2. 芻者蕘者 are distinguished thus:—"gatherers of grass to feed animals, and gatherers of grass for fuel." Observe how those nouns, and 雉 and 兔 that follow are made verbs by the 者;—the fodderers, the pheasanters, etc. 3. 郊 is used here in the sense simply of "borders," and on the borders of the various states there were "passes" or "gates," for the taxa-tion of merchandise, the examination of strangers, etc. 麋鹿, see Pt. I, ii. These forest laws of Ts'e were hardly worse than those enacted by the first Norman sovereigns of England, when whoever killed a deer, a boar, or even a hare, was punished with the loss of his eyes, and with death if the statutes were repeatedly violated.

故太王事獯鬻、句踐事

惟智者爲能以小事大、

故湯事葛、文王事昆夷、

仁者爲能以大事小、是

有道乎。孟子對曰、有惟

齊宣王問曰、交鄰國

CHAPTER III. 1. The King Seuen of Ts'e asked, saying, "Is there any way *to regulate one's maintenance of* intercourse with neighboring kingdoms?" Mencius replied, "There is. But it requires a perfectly virtuous *prince* to be able, with a great *country*, to serve a small one,—as, for instance, T'ang served Kŏ, and King Wăn served the Kwăn barbarians. And it requires a wise *prince* to be able, with a small *country*, to serve a large one,—as the King T'ae served the Heun-yuh, and Kow-tseen served Woo.

CH. 3. How FRIENDLY INTERCOURSE WITH NEIGHBORING KINGDOMS MAY BE MAINTAINED, AND THE LOVE OF VALOR MADE SUBSERVIENT TO THE GOOD OF THE PEOPLE, AND THE GLORY OF THE PRINCE. 1. The two first 事 differ in meaning considerably from the two last, and they are explained by 撫字周恤 and 聽從服役, i. e., "cherishing," and "obeying," respectively, but the translation need not be varied. For the affairs of T'ang with Kŏ, see III, Pt. II, v. Of those of King Wăn with the Kwăn tribes we have nowhere an account, which satisfies Mencius's reference to them. Both Chaou K'e and Choo He make refer. to the She-king, III, i, Ode III, st. 8; but what is there said would seem to be of things antecedent to King Wăn. Of King T'ae and the Heun-yuh, see below, ch. xv. A very readable, though romanced account of Kow-Tseen's service of Woo is in the Lĕé Kwŏ Che (列國志), Bk. lxxx. 是故 and 故, "therefore," introducing illustrations of what has been said,

言矣、寡人有疾、寡人好

威于時保之。王曰、大哉

者、保其國詩云、畏天之

也、樂天者保天下、畏天

也、以小事大者畏天者

吳以大事小者樂天者

2. "He who with a great *state* serves a small one, delights in Heaven. He who with a small *state* serves a large one, stands in awe of Heaven. He who delights in Heaven, will affect with his love and protection the whole empire. He who stands in awe of Heaven, will affect with his love and protection his own kingdom.

3. "It is said in the 'Book of Poetry,' 'I fear the majesty of Heaven, and will thus preserve its favoring decree.'"

4. The king said, "A great saying! But I have an infirmity;— I love valor."

are=our "as." 2. 天, says Choo He, 理 而 已 矣, "Heaven is just principle, and nothing more." It is a good instance of the way in which he and others often try to expunge the idea of a governing Power and a personal God from their classics. Heaven is here evidently the superintending, loving Power of the universe Chaou K'e says on the whole paragraph: "The sage delights to pursue the way of Heaven, just as Heaven overspreads every thing;— as was evidenced in T'ang and Wăn's protecting the whole empire. The wise measure the time and revere Heaven, and so preserve their states; — as was evidenced in King T'ae and Kow-tseen." This view gives to 天 a positive, substantial meaning, though the personality of the Power is not sufficiently prominent. The commentator 王 觀 濤 says: "The Heaven here is indeed the Supreme Heaven, but after all it is equivalent to principle and nothing more!" 保, as in Pt. I, vii. 3. See the She-king, IV, i, Bk. I, Ode VII, st. 3. 保, "to preserve," "to keep." 時 is here taken=是; not so in the ode. The final 之 refers to the decree or favor

也文王一怒而安天下
對于天下此文王之勇
以遏徂莒以篤周祜以
云王赫斯怒爰整其旅
一人者也王請大之詩
當我哉此匹夫之勇敵
夫撫劍疾視曰彼惡敢
勇對曰王請無好小勇

5. "I beg Your Majesty," was the reply, "not to love small valor. If a man brandishes his sword, looks fiercely, and says, 'How dare he withstand me?'—this is the valor of a common man, who can be the opponent only of a single individual. I beg Your Majesty to greaten it.

6. "It is said in the 'Book of Poetry,'

> 'The king blazed with anger,
> And he marshaled his hosts,
> To stop the march to Keu,
> To consolidate the prosperity of Chow,
> To meet the expectations of the empire.'

This was the valor of King Wăn. King Wăn, in one burst of his anger, gave repose to all the people of the empire.

of Heaven. 5. Observe the verbal meaning of 大. 6. See the She-king, III, i, Ode VII, st. 5, where we have 按 for 遏, and 旅 for 莒. 莒 is the name of a state or place, the same probably that in the ode is called 共. 以遏徂莒, "to stop the march to Keu," unless we take, with some, 徂 also to be the name of a place.

也而武王亦一怒而安天下

天下武王恥之此武王之勇

曷敢有越厥志一人衡行於

四方有罪無罪惟我在天下

作之師惟曰其助上帝寵之

之民書曰天降下民作之君、七節

7. "In the 'Book of History' it is said, 'Heaven, having produced the inferior people, appointed for them rulers and teachers, with the purpose that they should be assisting to God, and therefore distinguished them throughout the four quarters of the empire. Whoever are offenders, and whoever are innocent, here am I *to deal with them.* How dare any under heaven give indulgence to their refractory wills?' There was one man pursuing a violent and disorderly course in the empire, and King Woo was ashamed of it. This was the valor of King Woo. He also, by one display of his anger, gave repose to all the people of the empire.

7. See the Shoo-king, V, i, Sect. I, 7, but the passage as quoted by Mencius is very different from the original text. 惟 曰 其 助 上 帝,—lit., "just saying, They shall be aiding to God." The sentiment is that of Paul, in Rom. 13 : 1-4. "The powers ordained of God are the ministers of God." In 天 下 曷 敢 有 越 厥 志, there is an allusion to the

人不得、則非其上矣。

此樂乎。孟子對曰、

雪宮、王曰賢者亦有

齊宣王見孟子於

王之不好勇也。

安天下之民、民惟恐

之民。今王亦一怒、而

8. "Let now Your Majesty also, in one burst of anger, give repose to all the people of the empire. The people are only afraid that Your Majesty does not love valor."

CHAPTER IV. 1. The King Seuen of Ts'e had an interview with Mencius in the Snow palace, and said to him, "Do men of talents and worth likewise find pleasure in these things?" Mencius replied, "They do, and if people *generally* are not able *to enjoy themselves*, they condemn their superiors.

tyrant Këĕ, who is the 一人 in Mencius's subjoined explanation. 8. 惟恐 is, by some, taken—"The people would only be afraid," the prec. clause being="If Your Majesty," etc. I think the present tense is preferable.

CH. 4. A RULER'S PROSPERITY DEPENDS ON HIS EXERCISING A RESTRAINT UPON HIMSELF, AND SYMPATHIZING WITH THE PROPER IN THEIR JOYS AND SORROWS. 1. "The Snow palace" was a pleasure palace of the princes of Ts'e, and is said to have been in the present district of Lintszo, in the department of Tsingchow. Most comm. say that King Seuen had lodged Mencius there, and went to see him, but it may not have been so. Perhaps they only had their interview there. 賢者亦有此樂乎, is different from the question in nearly the same words, in Pt. I, ii, 賢者 being there "worthy princes," and here "scholars," men of worth generally, with a reference to Mencius himself. 人不得,一人 is to be taken as=民,

天下、然而不王者、未
其憂樂以天下、憂以
憂民之憂者民亦憂
之樂者、民亦樂其樂、
同樂者、亦非也。樂民
也、爲民上、而不與民
不得而非其上者非

2. "For them, when they cannot enjoy themselves, to condemn their superiors is wrong, but when the superiors of the people do not make enjoyment a thing common to the people and themselves, they also do wrong.

3. "When a ruler rejoices in the joy of his people, they also rejoice in his joy; when he grieves at the sorrow of his people, they also grieve at his sorrow. A sympathy of joy will pervade the empire; a sympathy of sorrow will do the same:—in such a state of things, it cannot be but that the ruler attain to the imperial dignity.

"the people," men generally, and 不得, it is said, 是不得安居之樂, 非指雪宮, "is=do not get the pleasure of quiet living and enjoyment, not referring to the Snow palace." 非其上,—非 is used as a verb,="to blame," "to condemn." So in the next par. 3. I have given the meaning of the phrases 樂以天下, 憂以天下, which sum up the preceding part of the par., and are not to be understood as spoken of the ruler only. The 合講 says:— "These two sentences are to be explained from the four prec. sentences. The phrase 天下 is only a forcible way of saying what is said by 民. The 以 is to be explained as if we read—不以一身, 乃以天下耳, the joy and sorrow is not with (i. e., from) one individual, but from the whole empire." 王, low. 3rd tone.

朝于天子曰述職、述職者、述

巡狩、巡狩者巡所守也、諸侯

曰、善哉問也、天子適諸侯曰

可以比於先王觀也。晏子對

海而南放于琅邪、吾何脩、而

子曰、吾欲觀於轉附朝儛、遵

之有也。昔者、齊景公問於晏

4. "Formerly, the duke, King, of Ts'e, asked the minister Ngan, saying, 'I wish to pay a visit of inspection to Chuen-foo, and Chaou-woo, and then to bend my course southward along the shore, till I come to Lang-yay. What shall I do that my tour may be fit to be compared with the visits of inspection made by the ancient emperors?'

5. "The minister Ngan replied, 'An excellent inquiry! When the emperor visited the princes, it was called a tour of inspection, that is, he surveyed the *states* under their care. When the princes attended at the court of the emperor, it was called a report of office,

4. 晏子, see Conf. Ana., V, xvi. The duke King occupied the throne for 58 years, from 546–488 B. C. Chuen-foo and Chaou-woo were two hills, which must have been on the north of Ts'e, and looking on the waters now called the Gulf of Pe-chili. Langyay was the name

both of a mountain and an adjacent city, referred to the present department of Chooshing, in Ts'ingchow. 脩＝作 爲, "to do." 5. 狩巡,—see the Shoo-king, II, i, 8, 9. 狩 is used as＝守. It does not seem necessary to repeat the 巡狩 and 述職 in the translation. This tour of

諸侯度今也不然師行

吾何以助一遊一豫爲

遊吾何以休吾王不豫

助不給夏諺曰吾王不

耕而補不足秋省斂而

所職也無非事者春省

that is, they reported their administration of their
offices.  Thus, neither of the proceedings was without
a purpose.  *And moreover,* in the spring they examined
the plowing, and supplied any deficiency *of seed;* in
the autumn they examined the reaping, and supplied
any deficiency of yield.  There is the saying of the
Hea dynasty,—"If our king do not take his ramble,
what will become of our happiness?  If our king do
not make his excursion, what will become of our
help?"  That ramble and that excursion were a
pattern to the princes.

6.　"'Now, the state of things is different.—A host

inspection appears to have been
made, under the Chow dynasty,
once in 12 years, while the princes
had to present themselves at court,
(朝, read *ch'aou*) once in 6 years.
From 春, "in the spring," the practices appropriate to the various
princes, as well as the emperor, are
described, though, as appears from
the last clause, with special reference
to the latter. 豫 or 預＝遊. By 一遊

一預 the spring and autumn visita-
tions are intended, each called 一.
6. 師, properly a body of 2,500 men,
but here generally＝a host, a multitude. 睊睊胥讒, 民乃作慝, are
referred to the people, and the next
two clauses to the princes.  Yet the
乃 after 民, would rather indicate a
different subject for the clause before. 諸侯憂,—諸侯, by Choo He
and others, is explained as in the

忘反謂之連從獸無　反謂之流從流上而　諸侯憂從流下而忘　食若流流連荒亡爲　乃作慝方命虐民飲　者弗息眈眈胥讒民　而糧食飢者弗食勞

marches *in attendance on the ruler,* and stores of provisions are consumed. The hungry are deprived of their food, and there is no rest for those who are called to toil. Maledictions are uttered by one to another with eyes askance, and the people proceed to the commission of wickedness. Thus the *imperial* ordinances are violated, and the people are oppressed, and *the supplies of* food and drink flow away like water. *The rulers* yield themselves to the current, or they urge their way against it; they are wild; they are utterly lost:—these things proceed to the grief of their subordinate governors.

7. "'Descending along with the current, and forgetting to return, is what I call yielding to it. Pressing up against it, and forgetting to return, is what I call urging their way against it. Pursuing the chase

translation. This view certainly puts force on the characters, yet we seem driven to it. Chaou K'e makes them refer to the princes proper, who also are with him the subject in the clause 眈眈, but how can it be said that these things in which they delighted were a "grief" to them?

相說之樂蓋徵招角招是也、

不足、召太師曰爲我作君臣

國出舍於郊於是始與發補

惟君所行也景公說大戒於

先王無流連之樂荒亡之行。

厭謂之荒、樂酒無厭、謂之亡。

without satiety is what I call being wild.   Delighting
in wine without satiety is what I call being lost.

8.　"'The ancient emperors had no pleasures to
which they gave themselves as on the flowing stream;
no doings which might be so characterized as wild
and lost.

9.　"'It is for you, my prince, to pursue your
course.' "

10.　"The duke King was pleased.   He issued a
proclamation throughout his state, and went out and
occupied a shed in the borders.   From that time he
began to open his granaries to supply the wants of the
people, and calling the grand music master, he said
to him—'Make for me music to suit a prince and his
minister pleased with each other.'   And it was then
that the Che-shaou and Kĕŏ-shaou were made, in the

10. 太 師.—see Ana., VIII, xv. 徵 | the name of two of the 5 notes in the
(read che, up. 2nd tone) and 角 are | Chinese scale, the 4th and the 3rd. 招

子對曰夫明堂

堂、毀諸已乎孟二

人皆謂我毀明

齊宣王問曰、

也。

尤、畜君者、好君

其詩曰畜君何

poetry to which it was said, 'What fault is it to restrain one's prince?' He who restrains his prince loves his prince."

CHAPTER V. 1. The king Seuen of T'se said, "People all tell me to pull down and remove the Brilliant palace. Shall I pull it down, or stop *the movement for that object?*"

2. Mencius replied, "The Brilliant palace is a palace

is used for 韶, the name given to the music of Shun. This was said to be preserved in Ts'e, and the same name was given to all Ts'e music. The Che-shaou and Kĕŏ-shaou were, I suppose, two tunes or pieces of music, starting with the notes 徵 and 角, respectively.

CH. 5. TRUE ROYAL GOVERNMENT WILL ASSUREDLY RAISE TO THE IMPERIAL DIGNITY, AND NEITHER GREED OF WEALTH, NOR LOVE OF WOMAN, NEED INTERFERE WITH ITS EXERCISE. However his admirers may try to defend him, here, and in other chapters, Mencius,. if he does not counsel to, yet suggests, rebellion. In his days, the Chow dynasty was nearly a century distant from its extinction. And then his accepting the princes, with all their confirmed habits of vice and luxury, and telling them those need. not interfere with the benevolence of their government,

shows very little knowledge of man, or of men's affairs. 1. 明 堂,—not "the *Ming* or Brilliant *Hall*." It was the name given to the palaces occupied in different parts of the country by the emperors in their tours of inspection mentioned in the last chapter. See the Book of Rites, Bk. XIV. The name *Ming* was given to them, because royal government, etc., were "displayed" by means of them. The one in the text was at the foot of the T'ae Mountain in Ts'e, and as the emperor no longer made use of it, the suggestion on which he consulted Mencius, was made to King Seuen. In 毀 諸 已 乎, we have two questions,—"Shall I destroy it (諸, the interrog. of hesitancy, so common in Mencius), or, Shall I stop?" 2. the 1st and 2nd 王 here have the low. 1st tone; they quite differ from the 2nd, which is merely the style of King Seuen. I

梁無禁罪人不孥、
關市譏而不征澤
者九一、仕者世祿、
文王之治岐也、耕
得聞與對曰昔者
之矣○王曰、王政可
欲行王政、則勿毀
者、王者之堂也、王

appropriate to the emperors. If Your Majesty wishes to practice the true royal government, then do not pull it down.''

3. The king said, ''May I hear from you what the true royal government is?'' ''Formerly,'' was, the reply, ''King Wăn's government of K'e was as follows: — The husbandmen *cultivated for the government* one ninth of the land; the descendants of officers were salaried; at the passes and in the markets, *strangers* were inspected, but *goods* were not taxed: there were no prohibitions respecting the ponds and weirs; the wives and children of criminals were not involved in

may give here a note from the 集 證 (Pt. I, i, 1) on the force of the terms 君 and 王.—''He who is followed by the people till they form *a flock* (羣) is a *keun*. He to whom they turn and go (往 之) is a *wang*. Thus the title *wang* expresses the idea of the people's turning and resorting to him who holds it, but the possessor of a state can barely be called a *keun*. It is only the possessor of the empire, who can be styled *wang*.'' 3. K'e was a double peaked hill, giving its name to the adjoining country, the old state of Chow. Its

name is still retained in the district of K'eshan, in Fungtseang, the most western department of Shense, bordering on Kansu. 耕 者 九 一，—A square li was divided into 9 parts, each containing 100 *mow*: eight farming families were located upon them, one part being reserved for govt., which was cultivated by the joint labors of the husbandmen. See III, Pt. I, iii, 仕 者 世 祿.— ''officers, hereditary emolument''; that is, descendants of meritorious officers, if men of ability, received office, and, even if they were not,

行。王曰、寡人有疾、寡人好貨。對、

哉言乎。曰王如善之、則何爲不

云、哿矣富人、哀此煢獨王曰、善

文王發政施仁、必先斯四者、詩

此四者、天下之窮民、而無告者、

老而無子曰獨、幼而無父曰孤、

老而無妻曰鰥、老而無夫曰寡、

their guilt. There were the old and wifeless, or widowers; the old and husbandless, or widows; the old and childless, or solitaries; the young and fatherless, or orphans:—these four classes are the most destitute of the people, and have none to whom they can tell their wants, and King Wăn, in the institution of his government with its benevolent action, made them the first objects of his regard, as it is said in the 'Book of Poetry,'

> 'The rich may get through.
> But alas! for the miserable and solitary!'"

4. The king said, "O excellent words!" *Mencius* said, "Since Your Majesty deems them excellent, why do you not practice them?" "I have an infirmity," said the king; "I am fond of wealth." The reply was,

they had pensions, in reward of the merit of their fathers. "Ponds and weirs,"—it is not to be understood that the *ponds* were artificial. 先斯

四.—先 is the verb. For the ode, see the She-king, II, iv, Ode VIII, st. 13, where for 辇 we find 惸.

日、昔者公劉好貨、詩

云、乃積乃倉乃裹餱

糧、于橐于囊思戢用

光弓矢斯張干戈戚

揚爰方啟行故居者

有積倉行者有裹糧

也、然後可以爰方啟

"Formerly, Kung-lew was fond of wealth.　It is said in the 'Book of Poetry':

> 'He reared his ricks, and filled his granaries,
> He tied up dried provisions and grain,
> In bottomless bags, and sacks,
> That he might gather his people together, and glorify
> *his state.*
> With bows and arrows all-displayed,
> With shields, and spears, and battle-axes, large and
> small, '
> He commenced his march.'

In this way those who remained in their old seat had their ricks and granaries, and those who marched had their bags of provisions.　It was not till after this that he thought he could commence his march.　If

4. 公劉, "The duke Lew," was the great-grandson of How-tseih, the high ancestor of the Chow family. By him the waning fortunes of his house were revived, and he founded a settlement in 豳 (*Pin*), the present Pinchow (邠 州), in Shense. The account of his doing so is found in the ode quoted, She-king, III, ii, Ode IV, st. 1. For 乃 we have in the She-king, 廼 and for 戢, 輯 積, read *ts'ze*, up. 3rd tone, "to store up," "stores." Choo He explains: "stores in the open air." The King

行、王如好貨與百姓同之、

於王何有王曰寡人有疾、

寡人好色對曰昔者大王

好色愛厥妃詩云古公亶

父、來朝走馬率西水滸至

于岐下、爰及姜女聿來胥

Your Majesty loves wealth, let the people be able to gratify the same feeling, and what difficulty will there be in your attaining the imperial sway?"

5. The king said, "I have an infirmity; I am fond of beauty." The reply was, "Formerly, King T'ae was fond of beauty, and loved his wife. It is said in the 'Book of Poetry':

'Koo-kung T'an-foo
Came in the morning, galloping his horse,
By the banks of the western waters,
As far as the foot of K'e hill,
Along with the lady of Keang;
They came and together chose the site of settlement.'

T'ae (see the Doctrine of the Mean, ch. xviii) was the 9th in descent from Kung Lew, by name T'an-foo (up. 2nd tone). He removed from Pin to K'e, as is celebrated in the ode, She-king, III, i, Ode III, st. 2. 古公 = 先公, "the ancient duke." T'an-foo's title, before it was changed into 大王, "the king, or emperor, T'ae."

餒其妻子、則如之何。王曰、
之楚遊者比其反也、則凍
臣、有託其妻子於其友、而
🔳孟子謂齊宣王曰、王之
同之於王何有。
無曠夫、王如好色、與百姓
宇、當是時也、內無怨女、外

At that time, in the seclusion of the house, there were
no dissatisfied women, and abroad, there were no un-
married men. If Your Majesty loves beauty, let the
people be able to gratify the same feeling, and what
difficulty will there be in your attaining the imperial
sway?''

CHAPTER VI. 1. Mencius said to the King Seuen
of Ts'e, "Suppose that one of Your Majesty's ministers
were to intrust his wife and children to the care of his
friend, while he himself went into Ts'oo to travel, and
that, on his return, *he should find that* the friend had
caused his wife and children to suffer from cold and
hunger;—how ought he to deal with him?" The
king said, "He should cast him off."

CH. 6 BRINGING HOME HIS BAD
GOVERNMENT TO THE KING OF TS'E. 1.
之楚,一之 is the verb=往. 比, low;
3rd tone,=及, as in Ana., XI, xxv,
4, 5. 凍 and 餒 are active, *hiphil*
verbs. It is better to prefix "suppose that," or "if," to the whole
sentence, in the translation, as the
cases in the remaining par. cannot
well be put directly, as this might
be. The replies suggest the render-
ings of 如之何, which I have given.

棄之曰士師不能治士、

則如之何王曰已之曰、

四境之內不治則如之

何。王顧左右而言他。

孟子見齊宣王曰所

謂故國者非謂有喬木

之謂也有世臣之謂也、

2. *Mencius* proceeded, "Suppose that the chief criminal judge could not regulate the officers *under him*, how would you deal with him?" The king said, "Dismiss him."

3. *Mencius again* said, "If within the four borders *of your kingdom* there is not good government, what is to be done?" The king looked to the right and left, and spoke of other matters.

CHAPTER VII.   1. Mencius, having an interview with the King Seuen of Ts'e, said to him: "When men speak of 'an ancient kingdom,' it is not meant thereby that it has lofty trees in it, but that it has ministers *sprung from families which have been noted in it* for

2. 士師, see on Ana. XVIII, ii. 治 is low. 1st tone. In the next par. it is low. 3rd. The two instances well illustrate the difference of signification, which the tone makes.

CH. 7.  THE CARE TO BE EMPLOYED BY A PRINCE IN THE EMPLOYMENT OF MINISTERS; AND THEIR RELATION TO HIMSELF, AND THE STABILITY OF HIS KINGDOM. 1. On the idiom 之 謂,

see Premare, on char. 之; but the examples which he adduces are not quite similar to those in this passage. Lit., the opening sentence would be:— "That which is said—an ancient kingdom, is not the saying (之 謂) of saying it has lofty trees; it is the saying of—it has hereditary ministers." The 謂 in 非 謂 might be omitted, and yet it adds something

右皆曰賢未可也、諸大夫
踰尊、疏踰戚、可不愼與、左
君進賢、如不得已、將使卑
以識其不才而舍之曰國
日不知其亡也。王曰吾何
王無親臣矣、昔者所進、今

generations. Your Majesty has no intimate ministers *even*. Those whom you advanced yesterday are gone to-day, and you do not know it."

2. The king said, "How shall I know that they have not ability, and so avoid employing them at all?"

3. The reply was, "The ruler of a state advances to office men of talents and virtue, only as a matter of necessity. Since he will thereby cause the low to overstep the honorable, and strangers to overstep his relatives, may he do so but with caution?

4. "When all those about you say, — 'This is a man of talents and worth,' you may not for that believe it. When your great officers all say, — 'This

in the turn of the sentence. As opposed to 今 日, 昔 者＝"yesterday." Chaou K'e strangely mistakes the meaning of the last clause, which he makes to be:—"Those whom you advanced on the past day, do evil to-day, and you do not know to cut them off!" 2. 舍＝捨, up. 2nd tone, "to let go," "to dismiss." 3. 如不得已, —lit., "as a thing in which he cannot stop." Comp. the Chung Yung, xx, 13. 4. 未 可, "you may

曰可殺勿聽諸大夫皆曰可殺、

之見不可焉、然後去之左右皆

可、勿聽、國人皆曰不可、然後察

皆曰不可、勿聽諸大夫皆曰不

後察之、見賢焉、然後用之、左右

皆曰賢、未可也、國人皆曰賢、然

is a man of talents and virtue,' neither may you for
that believe it. When all the people say, — 'This is
a man of talents and virtue,' then examine into the
case, and when you find that the man is such, employ
him. When all those about you say, — 'This man
won't do,' don't listen to them. When all your great
officers say, — 'This man won't do,' don't listen to
them. When the people all say, — 'This man won't
do,' then examine into the case, and when you find
that the man won't do, send him away.

5. "When all those about you say, — 'This man
deserves death,' don't listen to them. When all your
great officers say, — 'This man deserves death,' don't

not *yet* believe that the man is so
and so." See on Ana., XIII, xxiv, 6.
Compare the Great Learning, Comm.

x, 3. We may use the second person
in translating, or more indefinitely,
the third.

傳有之。曰臣弑其君可乎。

王伐紂、有諸孟子對曰、於

齊宣王問曰湯放桀、武

後可以爲民父母。

故曰國人殺之也。如此然

察之見可殺焉、然後殺之、

勿聽、國人皆曰可殺、然後

listen to them. When the people all say, — 'This man deserves death,' then inquire into the case, and when you see that the man deserves death, put him to death. In accordance with this we have the saying, 'The people killed him.'

6. "You must act in this way in order to be the parent of the people."

CHAPTER VIII. 1. The king Seuen of Ts'e asked, saying, "Was it so, that T'ang banished Kĕĕ, and that King Woo smote Chow?" Mencius replied, "It is so in the records."

2. *The king* said, "May a minister *then* put his sovereign to death?"

CH. 8. KILLING A SOVEREIGN IS NOT NECESSARILY REBELLION NOR MURDER. 1. Of T'ang's banishment of Kĕĕ, see the Shoo-king, IV, 11, iii; and of the smiting of Chow, see the same, V. i. 2. 弑 is the word appropriated to regicide, which Mencius in his reply exchanges for 誅.

則王喜、以爲能勝其
求大木工師得大木、
爲巨室、則必使工師
孟子見齊宣王曰、
夫紂矣、未聞弑君也。
人謂之一夫、聞誅一
義者謂之殘、殘賊之
曰、賊仁者、謂之賊、賊

3. *Mencius* said, "He who outrages the benevolence *proper to his nature* is called a robber; he who outrages righteousness is called a ruffian. The robber and ruffian we call a mere fellow. I have heard of the cutting off of the fellow Chow, but I have not heard of the putting a sovereign to death, *in his case*."

Chapter IX. 1. Mencius, having an interview with the king Seuen of Ts'e, said to him: "If you are going to build a large mansion, you will surely cause the master of the workmen to look out for large trees, and when he has found such large trees, you will be glad, thinking that they will answer for the intended

臣.—"a minister," i. e., here, a subject. 3. 賊, as a verb,＝傷害, "to hurt and injure," as in the Analects, several times. "To outrage" answers well for it here. In the use of 夫, Mencius seems to refer to the expression 獨夫紂, Shoo-king, V, i, Section III, 4.

Ch. 9. The absurdity of a ruler's not acting according to the counsel of the men of talents and virtue, whom he calls to aid in his government, but requiring them to follow his ways. In one important point Mencius's illustrations fail. A prince is not supposed to understand either housebuilding or stonecutting; he must delegate those matters to the men who do. But government he ought to understand, and he may not delegate it to any scholars or officers. 1. The 工師 was a special officer having charge of all the artisans, etc. See the Le-ke, VI, 11, 29; vi, 17. 勝, upper 1st tone,—see Pt. I, iii, 3. 其任 (low. 3rd tone),—"its use," i. e., the building of the house.

鎰、必使玉人彫琢之、至於

何如。今有璞玉於此、雖萬

曰、姑舍女所學而從我、則

幼而學之、壯而欲行之、王

怒、以爲不勝其任矣、夫人

任矣、匠人斲而小之、則王

object. Should the workmen hew them so as to make them too small, then Your Majesty will be angry, thinking that they will not answer for the purpose. Now, a man spends his youth in learning *the principles of right government*, and, being grown up to vigor, he wishes to put them in practice;—if Your Majesty says to him, 'For the present put aside what you have learned, and follow me,' what shall we say?

2. "Here now you have a gem unwrought, *in the stone*. Although it may be worth 240,000 *taels*, you will surely employ a lapidary to cut and polish it. But when you come to the government of the state,

The 之 after 學 and 行 are to be understood as referring to 仁 and 義, or as in the translation. 壯 denotes the maturity of 30 years, when one was supposed to be fit for office. 2. The 鎰 was 24 Chinese ounces or *taels* (of gold). Choo He, after Chaou K'e. erroneously makes it 20 ounces. The gem in question, worth so much, would be very dear to the king, *and yet* he would certainly confide to another the polishing of it:—why would he not do so with the state?

取、或謂寡人取之以
王問曰、或謂寡人勿
齊人伐燕勝之宣
哉。
異於教玉人彫琢玉
所學而從我、則何以
治國家、則曰、姑舍女

then you say,—'For the present put aside what you have learned, and follow me." How is it that you herein act so differently from your conduct in calling in the lapidary to cut the gem!"

CHAPTER X. 1. The people of Ts'e attacked Yen, and conquered it.

2. The king Seuen asked, saying, "Some tell me not to take possession of it for myself, and some tell me to take possession of it. For a kingdom of ten

國家,—the kingdom, embracing the families and possessions of the nobles. 女=汝. 教, up. 1st tone=使 or 令, "to make," not "to teach." From 至 於, however, was explained by Chaou K'e (and many still follow him) thus:—"But in the matter of the government of your state, you say,—For the present put aside what you have learned, and follow me. In what does this differ from your teaching—i. e., wishing to teach—the lapidary to cut the gem?" This is the interpretation which Julien adopts in his translation. The other upon the whole appears to me the better. The first 則 is a difficulty in Chaou K'e's view; the second, in the other. But the final 哉 turns the balance in its

favor, and accordingly I have adopted it.

CH. 10. THE DISPOSAL OF KINGDOMS RESTS WITH THE MINDS OF THE PEOPLE. VOX POPULI, VOX DEI. We shall find this doctrine often put forth very forcibly by Mencius. Here the king of Ts'e insinuates that it was the will of Heaven that he should take Yen, and Mencius sends him to the will of the people, by which only the other could be ascertained. 1. The state of Yen (up. 1st tone) lay northwest from Ts'e, forming part of the present province of Chihli. Its prince, a poor weakling, had resigned his throne to his prime minister, and great confusion ensued, so that the people welcomed the appearance of the troops of Ts'e, and made no resistance to them. 2.

悅、則勿取、古之人有行之者、文

之者、武王是也、取之而燕民不

而燕民悅、則取之、古之人有行

天殃、取之何如孟子對曰取之

舉之、人力不至於此、不取、必有

萬乘之國、伐萬乘之國、五旬而

thousand chariots, attacking another of ten thousand chariots, to complete the conquest of it in fifty days, is an achievement beyond *mere* human strength. If I do not take possession of it, calamities from Heaven will surely come upon me. What do you say to my taking possession of it?"

3. Mencius replied, "If the people of Yen will be pleased with your taking possession of it, then do so. —Among the ancients there was *one* who acted on this principle, namely, King Woo. If the people of Yen will not be pleased with your taking possession of it, then do not do so.—Among the ancients there was *one* who acted on this principle, namely, King Wǎn.

舉之 is explained as＝勝之, "to conquer it"; but 舉 has not this signification. Lit., we might render "and *up* with it." 3. The common saying is that King Wǎn 三分天下有其二, "had possession of two of the three parts of the empire." Still he did not think that the people were prepared for the entire extinction of the Yin dynasty, and left the completion of the fortunes of his house to

侯將謀救燕宣王曰、
齊人伐燕取之諸
已矣。
深、如火益熱亦運而
哉、避水火也、如水益
漿、以迎王師豈有他
伐萬乘之國簞食壺
王是也。以萬乘之國

4. "When, with *all the strength of* your country of ten thousand chariots, you attacked another country of ten thousand chariots, and *the people brought* baskets of rice and vessels of congee, to meet Your Majesty's host, was there any other reason for this but that they hoped to escape out of fire and water? If you make the water more deep and the fire more fierce, they will just in like manner make *another* revolution."

CHAPTER XI. 1. The people of Ts'e, having smitten Yen, took possession of it, *and upon this*, the princes of the various states deliberated together, and resolved to deliver Yen *from their power*. The king

his son, King Woo. 4. 食 read *tsze*, low. 3rd tone, "rice." 漿 is properly congee, but here used generally for beverages; some say wine. 壺, "a goblet," "a jug," "a vase," a vessel for liquids generally.—The first par. is constructed according to the rules of composition employed by Confucius in his "Spring and Autumn." The 人 refuses honor to the king of. Ts'e. 伐 expresses the ill deserts of Yen. And 勝 之 intimates that the conquest was from the disinclination of Yen to fight, not from the power of Ts'e.

CH. 11. AMBITION AND AVARICE ONLY RAISE ENEMIES AND BRING DISASTERS. SAFETY AND PROSPERITY LIE IN A BENEVOLENT GOVERNMENT. 1. 將 before 謀 救 indicates the execution of the plans to be still in the future. 者 in 諸侯 . . . 者 makes the

而征、北狄怨曰奚爲後我、

之、東面而征、西夷怨南面

曰、湯一征、自葛始、天下信

未聞以千里畏人者也書二

里、爲政於天下者、湯是也、

待之。孟子對曰臣聞七十

諸侯多謀伐寡人者、何以

Seuen said *to Mencius,* "The princes have formed many plans to attack me:—how shall I prepare myself for them?" Mencius replied, "I have heard of one who with seventy li exercised all the functions of government throughout the empire. That was T'ang. I have never heard of a *prince* with a thousand li standing in fear of others.

2. "It is said in the 'Book of History,' 'As soon as T'ang began his work of executing justice, he commenced with Kŏ. The whole empire had confidence in him. When he pursued his work in the east, the rude tribes on the west murmured. So did those on the north, when he was engaged in the south. Their cry was—"Why does he make us last?" *Thus,*

clause like one in English beginning with a nominative absolute. 待之, —lit., "await them." 2. See the Shoo-king, IV, ii, 6. Mencius has introduced the clause 天下信之, and there are some other differences from the orig. text. Kŏ was a small territory, which is referred to the

中也簞食壺漿以迎王

以爲將拯己於水火之

虐其民王往而征之民

徯我后后來其蘇今燕

若時雨降民大悅書曰、

不變誅其君而弔其民、

霓也歸市者不止耕者

民望之若大旱之望雲

the locking of the people to him was like the looking
in a time of great drought to clouds and rainbows.
The frequenters of the markets stopped not. The
husbandmen made no change *in their operations*.
While he punished their rulers, he consoled the
people. *His progress* was like the falling of opportune
rain, and the people were delighted. It is said *again*
in the 'Book of History,' 'We have waited for our
prince *long;* the prince's coming will be our re-
viving!'

3. "Now *the ruler of* Yen was tyrannizing over his
people, and Your Majesty went and punished him.
The people supposed that you were going to deliver
them out of the water and the fire, and brought
baskets of rice and vessels of congee, to meet Your

present district of Ningling (寧陵)
in Kweitih (歸德), in Honan. 望雲
霓.—the modern comm. ingeniously
interpret:—"The people look for
rain in drought, and murmured at
his not coming, as they dread the
appearance of a rainbow, on which

the rain will stop." This is perhaps,
overrefining, and making too much
of the 望. Chaou K'e says: "The
rainbow appears when it rains, so
people, in time of drought, long to
see it." The second quotation is
from the same paragraph of the

師、若殺其父兄、係累其子弟、
毀其宗廟、遷其重器、如之何
其可也、天下固畏齊之彊也、
今又倍地、而不行仁政、是動
天下之兵也。○四 王速出令、反其
旄倪、止其重器、謀於燕衆、置

Majesty's host. But you have slain their fathers and elder brothers and put their sons and younger brothers in chains. You have pulled down the ancestral temple *of the state,* and are removing *to Ts'e* its precious vessels. How can such a course be deemed proper? *The rest of* the empire is indeed *jealously* afraid of the strength of Ts'e, and now, when with a doubled territory you do not put in practice a benevolent government;—it is this which sets the arms of the empire in motion.

4. "If Your Majesty will make haste to issue an ordinance, restoring *your captives,* old and young, stopping *the removal of* the precious vessels, *and saying that, after* consulting with the people of Yen,

Shoo-king, where we have 予 for 我. 3. Comp. last ch. 若, in 若殺云云, is not our "if," but rather "since." They say 是指數之詞, 不作設詞 看, "it is demonstrative, not conditional." 父 兄,—父 is not *fathers*

only, but *uncles* as well. 其 宗 廟, 其 宗 器,—其＝"its or his," i. e., the kingdom's or the prince's, not their, the people's. 4. 旄, low. 3rd tone, used for 耄, "people of 80 and 90." The clauses after the first are to be

不救如之何則可
視其長上之死而
可勝誅、不誅則疾
之死也、誅之則不
三十三人、而民莫
問曰、吾有司死者、
臺鄒與魯鬨、穆公
可及止也。
君而後去之、則猶

you will appoint them a ruler, and withdraw from the country;—in this way you may still be able to stop *the threatened attack*."

CHAPTER XII. 1. There had been a brush between Tsow and Loo, when the duke Muh asked *Mencius*, saying, "Of my officers there were killed thirty-three men, and none of the people would die in their defense. If I put them to death *for their conduct*, it is impossible to put such a multitude to death. If I do not put them to death, then there is *the crime unpunished of* their looking angrily on at the death of their officers, and not saving them. How is the exigency of the case to be met?"

understood as the substance of the order or ordinance, which Mencius advised the king to issue.

CH. 12. THE AFFECTIONS OF THE PEOPLE CAN ONLY BE SECURED THROUGH A BENEVOLENT GOVERN- MENT. AS THEY ARE DEALT WITH BY THEIR SUPERIORS, SO WILL THEY DEAL BY THEM. 1. Tsow, the native state of Mencius, was a small terri- tory, whose name is still retained, in the district of Tsow-heen, in Yen- chow, in Shantung. 鬨 is explained —"the noise of a struggle." It is a

brush, a skirmish. Tsow could not stand long against the forces of Loo. Muh,—"the dispenser of virtue, and maintainer of righteousness, out- wardly showing inward feeling,"—is the posthumous epithet of the duke. 有 司 are to be taken together,= "officers"; see Con. Analects, VIII, iv. 莫 之 死 is to be completed 莫 (or 莫肯) 爲 之 死; comp. Analects, XIV, xvii. 則 疾 視 云 云 is not to be translated,—"they will hereafter look angrily on, etc."; the reference is to the crime that had taken place.

而後得反之也、君無尤焉。

爾者、反乎爾者也、夫民今

也、曾子曰戒之戒之出乎

司莫以告、是上慢而殘下

而君之倉廩實府庫充、有

散而之四方者、幾千人矣、

之民、老弱轉乎溝壑、壯者

也。孟子對曰凶年饑歲君

2. Mencius replied, "In calamitous years and years of famine, the old and weak of your people, who have been found lying in the ditches and water channels, and the able-bodied who have been scattered about to the four quarters, have amounted to several thousands. All the while, your granaries, O prince, have been stored with grain, and your treasuries and arsenals have been full, and not one of your officers has told you *of the distress.* Thus negligent have the superiors *in your state* been, and cruel to their inferiors. The philosopher Tsăng said, 'Beware, beware. What proceeds from you will return to you again.' Now at length the people have returned their conduct to the officers. Do not you, O prince, blame them.

2. 凶 年=years of pestilence,. and other calamities. 轉 乎 溝 壑=have tossed and *turned about* in, etc. 夫, low. 1st tone, indicates the application of the saying. 今 而 後="now at last."—They had long been wishing to show their feeling, but only now had they found the opportunity. 反 之,—之 refers to the 有 司. 3. 其

君行仁政、斯民親其上、死
其長矣。

滕文公問曰、滕、小國也、
間於齊楚、事齊乎、事楚乎。

孟子對曰、是謀非吾所能
及也、無已、則有一焉、鑿斯
池也、築斯城也、與民守之、

3. "If you will put in practice a benevolent government, this people will love you and all above them, and will die for their officers."

CHAPTER XIII. 1. The duke Wăn of T'ăng asked *Mencius*, saying, "T'ăng is a small kingdom, and lies between Ts'e and Ts'oo. Shall I serve Ts'e? Or shall I serve Ts'oo?"

2. Mencius replied, "This plan *which you propose* is beyond me. If you will have me counsel you, there is one thing *I can suggest*. Dig deeper your moats; build higher your walls; guard them along with your people.

上,—embracing the prince and officers generally; 其 長 (up. 2nd tone), the officers only. 死 其 長,—to be supplemented, as in par. 1.

CH. 13. IT IS BETTER FOR A PRINCE TO DEPEND ON HIMSELF, THAN TO RELY ON, OR TRY TO PROPITIATE OTHER POWERS. 1. T'ang still gives its name to a district of Yenchow in the south of Shantung. North of it was Ts'e, and, in the time of Mencius, Ts'oo had extended its power so far north as to threaten it from the south. 間, up. 3rd tone, "to occupy a space between." 2. 無 已, 則 有 一 焉,—comp. Pt. I, vii, 2, 一 無 以, 則 王 乎. 斯 池—"these"

者、大王居邠、狄人侵

何則可孟子對曰、昔

將築薛、吾甚恐、如之

滕文公問曰、齊人

可爲也。

效死而民弗去、則是

*In case of attack*, be prepared to die *in your defense*, and have the people so that they will not leave you;— this is a proper course."

CHAPTER XIV. 1. The duke Wăn of T'ăng asked *Mencius*, saying, "The people of Ts'e are going to fortify Sëë. *The movement* occasions me great alarm. What is the proper course for me to take in the case?"

2. Mencius replied, "Formerly, when King T'ae dwelt in Pin, the barbarians of the north were *continually* making incursions upon it. He *therefore* left

= your moats. 效 死,一效=致, as that is used in Ana., I, vii, *et al.* A good deal must be supplied here in the translation, to bring out Mencius's counsel.

Ch. 14. A PRINCE, THREATENED BY HIS NEIGHBORS, WILL FIND HIS BEST DEFENSE AND CONSOLATION IN DOING WHAT IS GOOD AND RIGHT. Mencius was at his wit's end, I suppose, to give Duke Wăn an answer. It was all very well to tell him to do good, but the promise of an imperial descendant would hardly be much comfort to him. The re-

ward to be realized in this world in the person of another, and the reference to Heaven, as to a fate more than to a personal God,—are melancholy. Contrast Psalm 37 : 3.— "Trust in the Lord and do good; *so* shalt thou dwell in the land, and verily thou shalt be fed." 1. 薛 was the name of an ancient principality, adjoining T'ăng. It had long been incorporated with Ts'e, which now resumed an old design of fortifying it,—that is, I suppose, of repairing the wall of its principal town, as a basis of operations against T'ăng. 2.

則天也、君如彼何哉、彊爲善

業垂統爲可繼也、若夫成功、

世子孫必有王者矣、君子創

而取之、不得已也。苟爲善、後

之去之岐山之下居焉、非擇

而已矣。

it, went to the foot of Mount K'e, and there took up
his residence. He did not take that situation, as
having selected it. It was a matter of necessity with
him.

3. "If you do good, among your descendants, in
after generations, there shall be one who will attain to
the imperial dignity. A prince lays the foundation of
the inheritance, and hands down the beginning *which
he has made,* doing what may be continued *by his
successors.* As to the accomplishment of the great
result, that is with Heaven. What is that *T'se* to you,
O prince? Be strong to do good. That is all your
business."

See ch. iii, and also the next. 去之
岐山下,—it is best to take 之 here
as the verb,＝往. 3. 君子,—generally, "a prince." 垂統—統; "the
end of a cocoon, or clue," "a begin-

ning." 若夫, the 夫 is not a mere
expletive, but is used as in Ana., XI,
ix, 3, *et al.*: "as to this—the accom-
plishing," etc.＝彊, low. 2nd tone,
the verb.

焉、乃屬其耆老而告之曰、狄

得免焉、事之以珠玉、不得免

幣、不得免焉、事之以犬馬、不

王居邠、狄人侵之、事之以皮

之、何則可。孟子對曰、昔者太

力以事大國、則不得免焉、如

騰文公問曰、騰小國也、竭

CHAPTER XV. 1. The duke Wăn of T'ăng asked
Mencius, saying, "T'ăng is a small kingdom. Though
I do my utmost to serve those large kingdoms *on
either side of it*, we cannot escape *suffering from them*.
What course shall I take that we may do so?" Mencius replied, "Formerly, when King T'ae dwelt in Pin,
the barbarians of the north were *constantly* making
incursions upon it. He served them with skins and
silks, and still he suffered from them. He served
them with dogs and horses, and still he suffered from
them. He served them with pearls and gems, and still
he suffered from them. Seeing this, he assembled the
old men, and announced to them, saying, 'What the

CH. 15. TWO COURSES OPEN TO A
PRINCE PRESSED BY HIS ENEMIES;—
FLIGHT OR DEATH. 1. Comp. ch. iii,
屬,—read *chuh*, up. 4th tone, "to
assemble," "meet with." 耆,—"a
sexagenarian." 二三子,—see Ana.

VII, xxiii, *et al.* 何患乎無君 seems
to mean:—"If I remain here, I am
sure to die from the barbarians. I
will go and preserve your ruler for
you." So, the paraphrast in the 備
旨. The 日講, however, says:—"My

從之者如歸市。或曰、世守也、非

居焉、邠人曰、仁人也、不可失也、

之去邠踰梁山邑於岐山之下

人二三子、何患乎無君、我將去

也、君子不以其所以養人者害

人之所欲者、吾土地也吾聞之

barbarians want is my territory. I have heard this,—
that a ruler does not injure his people with that
wherewith he nourishes them. My children, why
should you be troubled about having no prince? I
will leave this.'- *Accordingly,* he left Pin, crossed the
mountain Leang, *built* a town at the foot of Mount
K'e, and dwelt there. The people of Pin said, 'He is
a benevolent man. We must not lose him.' Those
who followed him looked like crowds hastening to
market.

2. *"On the other hand,* some say, '*The kingdom* is a
thing to be kept from generation to generation. One

children, why need you be troubled
about having no prince?' When I
am gone, whoever can secure your
repose, will be your prince and chief.
I will leave this, and go elsewhere."

歸 市 is different rather from the
same phrase in ch. vii. There it
means traders, here market-goers
generally. 2. This par. is to be
understood as spoken *to* a ruler, in

今乘輿已駕矣、有司

出、則必命有司所之、

臧倉者請曰、他日君

魯平公將出、嬖人

者。

勿去君請擇於斯二

身之所能爲也、效死

individual cannot undertake to dispose of it in his own person. Let him be prepared to die for it. Let him not quit it.'

3. "I ask you, prince, to make your election between these two courses."

CHAPTER XVI. 1. The duke P'ing of Loo was about to leave *his palace*, when his favorite, one Tsang Ts'ang, made a request to him, saying, "On other days, when you have gone out, you have given instructions to the officers as to where you were going. But now, the horses have been put to the carriage,

his own person. Comp. ch. vii. 爲 =專, "to take the whole disposal of," to deal with. It is not to be referred to the 守. The paraphrasts make the whole spoken by the ruler;— thus:—"The territory of the state was handed down by my ancestors to their descendants, that they should keep it from generation to generation. It is not what I can assume in my person the disposal of. If calamities and difficulties come, my course is to fight to the death to keep it. I may not abandon it, and go elsewhere." The meaning comes to the same. But the 勿 is against this construction.

CH. 16. A MAN'S WAY IN LIFE IS ORDERED BY HEAVEN. THE INSTRUMENTALITY OF OTHER MEN IS ONLY SUBORDINATE. 1. The duke P'ing (i. e., "The Pacificator") had been informed of Mencius's worth, it appears, by Gŏ-ching, and was going out, half-ashamed at the same time to do so, to offer the due respect to him as a professor of moral and political science, by visiting him and asking his services. The author of the 四書撫餘說 approves of the

後喪踰前喪、君無見焉。公

禮義由賢者出、而孟子之

以先於匹夫者、以爲賢乎、

孟子。曰、何哉、君所爲輕身、

未知所之、敢請。公曰、將見

and the officers do not yet know where you are going. I venture to ask." The duke said, "I am going to see the scholar Măng." "How is this!" said the other. "That you demean yourself, prince, in paying the honor of the first visit to a common man, is, I apprehend, because you think that he is a man of talents and virtue. By such men the rules of ceremonial proprieties and right are observed. But on the occasion of this Măng's second mourning, his observances exceeded those of the former. Do not go to see him, my prince." The duke said, "I will not."

view that the incident in this chapter is to be referred to the 4th year of the emperor 根, 310 B. C., but the chronology of the duke P'ing is very confused. 所之,一之＝徃. 何哉 is an exclamation of surprise, extending as far as 前喪. In 以爲賢乎, the 乎 is hardly so much as an interrogation. I have given its force by —"I apprehend." 出 does not indicate the origin of rites and right, but only their exhibition. The first occasion of Mencius's mourning referred to was that, it is said, for his father. But his father died, according to the received accounts, when he was only a child of three years old. We must suppose that the favorite invented the story. I have retained the surname Măng here, as suiting the paragraph better

謂棺椁衣衾之美也。曰

鼎、而後以五鼎與。曰否、

以士、後以大夫前以三

曰、何哉君所謂踰者、前

踰前喪、是以不往見也。

告寡人曰、孟子之後喪

奚爲不見孟軻也。曰、或

曰、諾樂正子入見曰、君

. 2. The officer Gŏ-ching entered *the court*, and had an audience. He said, "Prince, why have you not gone to see Măng K'o?" *The duke* said, "One told me that on the occasion of the scholar Măng's second mourning, his observances exceeded those of the former. It is on that account that I have not gone to see him." "How is this!" answered Gŏ-ching. "By what you call 'exceeding,' you mean, I suppose, that, on the first occasion, he used the rites appropriate to a scholar, and, on the second, those appropriate to a great officer; that he first used three tripods, and afterwards five tripods."— *The duke* said, "No; I refer to the greater excellence of the coffin, the shell, the graveclothes, and the shroud." Gŏ-ching said, "That

than Mencius. 2. 樂 正 is a double surname. This individual, whose name was K'ih (克) (See par. 3), was a disciple of Mencius. The surname probably arose from one of his ancestors having been the music master of some state, and so the name of his office passing over to become the designation of his descendants. The tripods contained the offerings of meat used in sacrifice. The emperor used nine, the prince

非所謂踰也、貧富不同

也樂正子見孟子曰克

告於君君爲來見也嬖

人有臧倉者沮君君是

以不果來也曰行或使

之止或尼之行止非人

所能也吾之不遇魯侯、

cannot be called 'exceeding.' That was the difference between being poor and being rich.''

3. *After this,* Gŏ-ching saw Mencius, and said to him, "I told the prince about you, and he was consequently coming to see you, when one of his favorites, named Tsang Ts'ang, stopped him, and therefore he did not come according to his purpose." *Mencius* said, "A man's advancement is effected, it may be, by others, and the stopping him is, it may be, from the efforts of others. *But* to advance a man or to stop his advance is *really* beyond the power of other men. My not finding *in* the prince of Loo *a ruler who would confide in me, and put my counsels into practice,*

of a state seven, a great officer five, and a scholar three. To each tripod belonged its appropriate kind of flesh. 3. 君爲來，一爲, low. 3rd tone,＝"therefore," i. e., in couse- | quence of what Gŏ-ching had said, the duke was going to visit Mencius. 尼 is read low. 2nd tone, and low. 3rd tone, both with the same meaning, ＝止, "to stop." 不遇魯君 is not

哉。　予不遇　焉能使　氏之子、　天也、臧

is from Heaven.　How could that scion of the Tsang family cause me not to find *the ruler that would suit me?*"

spoken merely with reference to the duke's not coming, as he had purposed, to meet him.　The phrase 不遇 really conveys all the meaning in the translation, however periphrastic that may seem.　With this reference of Mencius to Heaven, compare the language of Confucius, Ana., VII, xxi; IX, v; XIV, xxxviii.

## BOOK II
## KUNG-SUN CH'OW. PART I

知管仲晏子而
曰子誠齊人也、
可復許乎孟子
管仲晏子之功、
夫子當路於齊、
霊公孫丑問曰、
上
公孫丑章句

CHAPTER I. 1. Kung-sun Ch'ow asked *Mencius,* saying, "Master, if you were to obtain the ordering of the government in Ts'e, could you promise yourself to accomplish anew such results as those realized by Kwan Chung and Gan?"

2. Mencius said, "You are indeed a *true* man of Ts'e. You know about Kwan Chung and Gan, and nothing more.

TITLE OF THIS BOOK. The name of Kung-sun Ch'ow, a disciple of Mencius, heading the first chapter, the book is named from him accordingly. On 章 句 上, see note on the title of the first Book.

CH. 1. WHILE MENCIUS WISHED TO SEE A TRUE IMPERIAL GOVERNMENT AND SWAY IN THE EMPIRE, AND COULD EASILY HAVE REALIZED IT, FROM THE PECULIAR CIRCUMSTANCES OF THE TIME, HE WOULD NOT, TO DO SO, HAVE HAD RECOURSE TO ANY WAYS INCONSISTENT WITH ITS IDEA.
1. Kung-sun Ch'ow, one of Mencius's disciples, belonged to Ts'e, and was probably a cadet of the ducal family.

The sons of the princes were generally 公 子; their sons again, 公 孫, "ducal grandsons," and those two characters, became the surname of *their* descendants, who mingled with the undistinguished classes of the people. 當 路, lit., "in a way." Chaou K'e says, 當 仕 路, "in an official way," and Choo He, 居 要 地, "to occupy an important position." The gloss in the 備 旨 says: "當 路 is 操 政 柄, to grasp the handle of government." The analogous phrase 一當 道 is used now to describe an officer's appointment. 管 仲,—see Con. Ana., III, xxii; XIV, x, xvii, xviii. 晏 子,—see Con. Ana., V, xvi;

如彼其卑也、爾何曾比
國政、如彼其久也、功烈
得君、如彼其專也、行乎
何曾比予於管仲、管仲
賢、曾西艴然不悅曰、爾
曰、然則吾子與管仲孰
然曰吾先子之所畏也、
子與子路孰賢、曾西蹵
已矣。或問乎曾西曰、吾

3. "Some one asked Tsăng Se, saying, 'Sir, to which do you give the superiority,—to yourself or to Tsze-loo?' Tsăng Se looked uneasy, and said, 'He was an object of veneration to my grandfather.' 'Then,' pursued the other, 'Do you give the superiority to yourself or to Kwan Chung?' Tsăng Se, flushed with anger and displeased, said, 'How dare you compare me with Kwan Chung? Considering how entirely Kawn Chung possessed *the confidence of* his prince, how long he enjoyed the direction of the government of the kingdom, and how low, *after all*, was what he accomplished,—how is it that you liken me to him?'·

Men., I, Pt. II, iv. 3. Tsăng Se was the grandson, according to Chaou K'e and Choo He, of Tsăng Sin, the famous disciple of Confucius. Others say he was Sin's son. It is a mooted point. 孰賢,—comp. Ana., XI, xv. 蹵然, acc. to Choo, is 不安貌, as in the translation. The dict. gives it, 一敬貌, "the appearance of reverence." 先子,—we see what a wide application this character 子 has. 何曾一曾 is not to be taken as if it were the sign of the present complete tense, though in the dict. this passage is quoted under that signif. of the character. It is here = 則 or 乃. For more than 40 years Kwan Chung possessed the entire confidence of

手也。曰若是、則弟子之惑滋甚、

子、猶不足爲與。曰以齊王由反

其君霸晏子以其君顯管仲晏

也、而子爲我願之乎。曰、管仲以

予於是曰、管仲、曾西之所不爲

4. "Thus," concluded Mencius, "Tsăng Se would not play Kwan Chung, and is it what you desire for me, that I should do so?"

5. *Kung-sun Ch'ow* said, "Kwan Chung raised his prince to be the leader of all the other princes, and Gan made his prince illustrious, and do you still think it would not be enough for you to do what they did?"

6. *Mencius* answered, "To raise Ts'e to the imperial dignity would be as easy as it is to turn round the hand."

7. "So!" returned the other. "The perplexity of your disciple is hereby very much increased. There

the duke Hwăn. 4. 爲我，一爲, low. 3rd tone, "on my behalf." Sun Shih (孫奭), the paraphrast of Chaou K'e, takes it as＝以 爲:—"Do you think that I desire to do-so?" This

does not appear to be K'e's own interpretation. 5. 管仲晏子猶不足爲與,—lit., "and are Kwan Chung and Gan still not sufficient to be played?" 7. 若是—"in this

之君六七作、天下歸殷久矣、

可當也、由湯至於武丁、賢聖

則文王不足法與曰文王何

之、然後大行、今言王若易然、

猶未洽於天下、武王周公繼

且以文王之德、百年而後崩、

was King Wăn, with all the virtue which belonged to him; and who did not die till he had reached a hundred years:—and still *his influence* had not penetrated throughout the empire. It required King Woo and the duke of Chow to continue his course, before that influence greatly prevailed. Now you say that the imperial dignity might be so easily obtained:—is King Wăn then not a sufficient object for imitation?"

8. Mencius said, "How can King Wăn be matched? From T'ang to Woo-ting there had appeared six or seven worthy and sage sovereigns. The empire had been attached to Yin for a long time, and this length

case"; but by using our exclamatory *So!* the spirit of the remark is brought out. 且 introduces a new subject, and a *stronger one* for the point in hand. King Wăn died at 97.—Ch'ow uses the round number, 今言王若易然。=今言王齊若是 之易然, "Now you say that Ts'e might be raised to the imperial sway thus easily." 8. From T'ang to Woo-ting (1765–1323 B. C.), there were altogether 18 emperors, exclusive of themselves, and from Woo-ting to Chow (1323–1153) seven. 朝, *ch'aou*,

久、則難變也、武丁朝諸
侯、有天下、猶運之掌也、
紂之去武丁未久也、其
故家遺俗流風善政猶
有存者、又有微子、微仲、
王子比干、箕子、膠鬲、皆
賢人也、相與輔相之、故
久而後失之也、尺地、莫

of time made a change difficult. Woo-ting had all the princes coming to his court, and possessed the empire as if it had been a thing which he moved round in his palm. *Then,* Chow was removed from Woo-ting by no great interval of time. There were still remaining some of the ancient families and of the old manners, of the influence also which had emanated *from the earlier sovereigns,,* and of their good government. Moreover, there were the viscount of Wei and his second son, their Royal Highnesses Pe-kan and the viscount of Ke, and Kaou-kih, all, men of ability and virtue, who gave their joint assistance to Chow *in his government.* In consequence of these things, it took a long time for him to lose *the empire.* There was not a foot of

low. 1st tone, used as in I, Pt. I, vi, 6, *et al.* 微子, 比干, 箕子,—see Con. Ana., XVIII, ï. The latter two are 王子, as being uncles of Chow, "imperial sons." 微仲 was the second son (some say brother) of 微

子. Kaou-kih was a distinguished man and minister of the time,— whose worth was first discovered by King Wăn, but who continued loyal to the house of Yin. 輔相,—相, up. 3rd tone. 失之,—之 refers to the

過千里者也、而齊有其地

也。夏后殷周之盛地未有

基、不如待時、今時則易然

有智慧、不如乘勢、雖有鎡

是以難也。齊人有言曰、雖

也、然而文王猶方百里起、

非其有也、一民莫非其臣

ground which he did not possess. There was not one of all the people who was not his subject. So it was on *his side*, and King Wăn made his beginning from a territory of *only* one hundred square li. On all these accounts, it was difficult for him *immediately to attain the imperial dignity*.

9. "The people of Ts'e have a saying—'A man may have wisdom and discernment, but that is not like embracing the favorable opportunity. A man may have instruments of husbandry, but that is not like waiting for the *farming* seasons.' The present time is one in which *the imperial dignity* may be easily attained.

10. "In the flourishing periods of the Hea, Yin, and Chow dynasties, *the imperial* domain did not exceed a thousand li, and Ts'e embraces so much

empire. 文王猶方云云、一猶、the opp. of former cases, takes the place of 由. 9. 鎡基、—written variously, 兹基、鎡錤、—was the name for *a hoe*. 10. 夏后、殷、周, see Con. Ana., III, xxi. 辟＝闢. The last sentence,

矣、雞鳴狗吠相聞、而達乎四
境、而齊有其民矣、地不改辟
矣、民不改聚矣、行仁政而王、
莫之能禦也。且王者之不作、
未有疏於此時者也、民之憔
悴於虐政、未有甚於此時者
也、饑者易為食、渴者易為飲。

territory. Cocks crow and dogs bark to each other, all the way to the four borders of the state:—so Ts'e possesses the people. No change is needed for the enlarging of its territory: no change is needed for the collecting of a population. If its ruler will put in practice a benevolent government, no power will be able to prevent his becoming emperor.

11. "Moreover, never was there a time further removed than the present from the appearance of a true sovereign: never was there a time when the sufferings of the people from tyrannical government were more intense than the present. The hungry are easily supplied with food, and the thirsty are easily supplied with drink.

as in I, Pt. I, vii, 3. 11. The 爲 in 易爲食, 易爲飲 is perplexing. We might put it, in the 3rd tone, and 食 and 飲 in the same. But in VII, Pt. I, xxiv, we have the expressions 飢者甘食, 渴者甘飲, where 食 and 飲 must have their ordinary tones. Stress therefore is not to be laid on the 爲. Perhaps the expressions = "easily do eating, easily do drinking."

惟此時爲然。

也、故事半古之人、功必倍之、

行仁政民之悅之、猶解倒懸

而傳命當今之時、萬乘之國、

孔子曰、德之流行、速於置郵

12. "Confucius said, 'The flowing progress of virtue is more rapid than the transmission of *imperial* orders by stages and couriers.'

13. "At the present time, in a country of ten thousand chariots, let benevolent government be put in practice, and the people will be delighted with it, as if they were relieved from hanging by the heels. With half the merit of the ancients, double their achievements is sure to be realized. It is only at this time that such could be the case."

12. The distinction between 置 and 郵 is much disputed. Some make the former a foot post, but that is unlikely. It denotes the slower conveyance of dispatches, and the other the more rapid. So much seems plain. See the 集證, *in loc.* 13. 猶解倒懸,—Choo He simply says: 倒懸喩困苦, "倒懸 expresses bitter suffering." Lit., it is—"as if they were loosed from being turned upside down and suspended."

焉、雖由此

相、得行道

加齊之卿

問曰、夫子

公孫丑

**CHAPTER II.** 1. Kung-sun Ch'ow asked *Mencius*, saying, "Master, if you were to be appointed a high noble and the prime minister of Ts'e, so as to be able to carry *your* principles into practice, though you

CH. 2. THAT MENCIUS HAD ATTAINED TO AN UNPERTURBED MIND; THAT THE MEANS BY WHICH HE HAD DONE SO WAS HIS KNOWLEDGE OF WORDS AND THE NOURISHMENT OF HIS PASSION-NATURE; AND THAT IN THIS HE WAS A FOLLOWER OF CONFUCIUS. The chapter is divided into four parts:—the 1st, pars. 1–8, showing generally that there are various ways to attain an unperturbed mind; the 2nd, pars. 9, 10, exposing the error of the way taken by the philosopher Kaou; the 3rd, pars. 11–17, unfolding Mencius's own way; and the 4th, pars. 18–28, showing that Mencius followed Confucius, and praising the sage as the first of mortals. It is chiefly owing to what Mencius says in this chapter about the nourishment of the passion nature, that a place has been accorded to him among the sages of China, or in immediate proximity to them. His views are substantially these,—Man's nature is composite. He possesses moral and intellectual powers (comprehended by Mencius under the term 心 "heart," "mind," interchanged with 志, "the will"), and active powers (summed up under the term 氣, and embracing generally the emotions, desires, appetites). The moral and intellectual powers

should be supreme and govern, but there is a close connection between them and the others which give effect to them. The active powers may not be stunted, for then the whole character will be feeble. But, on the other hand, they must not be allowed to take the lead. They must get their tone from the mind, and the way to develop them in all their completeness is to do good. Let them be vigorous, and the mind clear and pure, and we shall have the man whom nothing external to himself can perturb,—Horace's *justum et tenacem propositi virum.* In brief, if we take the *sanum corpus* of the Roman adage, as not expressing the mere physical *body*, but the emotional and physical nature, what Mencius exhibits here, may be said to be "*mens sana in corpore sano.*" The attentive reader will, I think, find the above thoughts dispersed through this chapter, and be able to separate them from the irrelevant matter (that especially relating to Confucius), with which they are put forth. 1. 加, "to add," and generally "to confer upon," is here to be taken passively,—"If on you were conferred the dignity of, etc." 相, up. 3rd tone. 卿相 are not to be

我不動心曰不動心有道

賁遠矣曰是不難告子先

動心。曰若是則夫子過孟

否乎孟子曰否我四十不

霸王不異矣如此則動心

should thereupon raise the prince to the headship of all the other princes, or *even* to the imperial dignity, it would not be to be wondered at.—In such a position would your mind be perturbed or not?" Mencius replied, "No. At forty, I attained to an unperturbed mind."

2. *Ch'ow* said, "Since it is so with you, my master, you are far beyond Măng Pun." "The *mere* attainment," said *Mencius*, "is not difficult. The scholar Kaou had attained to an unperturbed mind, at an earlier period of life than I did."

3. *Ch'ow* asked, "Is there any way to an unperturbed mind?" The answer was, "Yes."

separated by an *or*, as 霸王 must be. See on 公卿, Ana., IX, xv. Ch'ow's meaning is that, with so great an office and heavy a charge, the mind might well be perturbed:—would it be so with his master? With Mencius's reply, comp. Confucius's account of himself, Ana., II, iv, 3. 2. Măng Pun was a celebrated bravo, probably of Ts'e, who could pull the horn from an ox's head, and feared no man. Kaou is the same who gives name to the 6th Book of Mencius, which see. 是不難 is not to be understood so much with reference to the case of Măng Pun, as to the *mere* attainment of an unperturbed mind, without reference to the way of attaining to it. 3. 道 here = 方法, "way," or "method."

嚴諸侯、惡聲至、必反之。

萬乘之君、若刺褐夫、無

不受於萬乘之君、視刺

市朝、不受於褐寛博、亦

一毫挫於人、若撻之於

也、不膚撓、不目逃、思以

乎曰、有北宮黝之養勇

4. "Pih-kung Yew had this way of nourishing his valor:—He did not flinch from any strokes at his body. He did not turn his eyes aside from any thrusts at them. He considered that the slightest push from any one was the same as if he were beaten *before the crowds* in the market place, and that what he would not receive from *a common man* in his loose large garments of hair, neither should he receive from a prince of ten thousand chariots. He viewed stabbing a prince of ten thousand chariots just as stabbing a fellow dressed in cloth of hair. He feared not any of all the princes. A bad word addressed to him he always returned.

4. Pih-kung Yew was a bravo, belonging probably to Wei (衛), and connected with its ruling family. 不膚撓, (low. 1st tone), 不目逃, lit., "not skin bend, not eye avoid." The meaning is not that he had first been wounded in those parts, and still was indifferent to the pain, but that he would press forward, careless of all risks. 思 covers down to 視. 一毫挫, = "the least push," = disgrace. Chaou K'e says—"to have

a hair pulled from his body," but 挫 does not agree with this. 市朝 (ch'aou, low. 1st tone) are not to be separated, and made—"the market place or the court." The latter char. is used, because anciently the diff. parties in the markets were arranged in their respective ranks and places, as the officers in the court. But comp. Ana., XIV, xxxviii, 1. 褐寛博 = 褐寛博之夫 (or 賤). 5. There

其孰賢然而孟施舍守

子夏夫二子之勇、未知

施舍似曾子北宮黝似

勝哉、能無懼而已矣。孟

三軍者也、舍豈能爲必

後進、慮勝而後會是畏

視不勝猶勝也、量敵而

孟施舍之所養勇也、曰、

5. "Măng She-shay had this way of nourishing his valor:—He said, 'I look upon not conquering and conquering in the same way. To measure the enemy and then advance; to calculate the chances of victory and then engage:—this is to stand in awe of the opposing force. How can I make certain of conquering? I can only rise superior to all fear.'

6. "Măng She-shay resembled the philosopher Tsăng. Pih-kung Yew resembled Tsze-hea. I do not know to the valor of which of the two the superiority should be ascribed, but yet Măng She-shay attended to what was of the greater importance.

is a difficulty with the 施, in 孟施舍, as this gentleman in the end of the par. simply calls himself 舍. Hence the 施 is made like our "h'm";—Măng H'm-shay. The use of A before the name, especially in the south of China, is analogous to this. Notwithstanding the 所 in the 1st clause of this par., we need not translate diff'tly from the 1st clause of the preceding. 三軍,—see Ana., VII, x; used here simply for "the enemy." 6. 孰賢,—as in last ch. Pih-kung Yew thought of others,— of conquering; Măng Shay of himself,—of not being afraid. It is on this account that Men. gives him the preference. The basis of the ref. to the two disciples is the commouly received idea of their several characters. Tsăng Sin was reflective, and dealt with himself. Tsze-hea

施舍之守氣又不如

雖千萬人吾往矣。八而

吾不惴焉自反而縮、

反而不縮雖褐寬博、

聞大勇於夫子矣自

襄曰子好勇乎吾嘗

約也。昔者曾子謂子七而

7. "Formerly, the philosopher Tsăng said to Tsze-seang, 'Do you love valor? I heard an account of great valor from the Master. *It speaks thus:*—"If, on self-examination, I find that I am not upright, shall I not be in fear even of a poor man in his loose garments of haircloth? If, on self-examination, I find that I am upright, I will go forward against thousands and tens of thousands."'"

8. "*Yet*, what-Măng She-shay maintained, being his *merely* physical energy, was after all inferior to what

was ambitious, and would not willingly be inferior to others. 7. Tsze-seang was a disciple of Tsăng. 縮, —properly, the straight seams, from the top to the edge, with which an ancient cap was made, metaphorically used for "straight," "upright." 吾不惴焉=吾豈不惴焉, the interrogation being denoted by the tone of the voice. Still the 焉 is the final particle, and not the initial "how," with a different tone, as Julien supposes. 8. Here we first meet the character 氣, so important in this chapter. Its different meanings may be seen in the dictionaries of Morrison and Medhurst. Originally it was the same as 气, "cloudy vapor." With the addition of 米, "rice," or 火, "fire," which was an old form, it should indicate "steam of rice," or "steam" generally. The sense in which Mencius uses it is indicated in the translation and in the preliminary note. That sense springs from its being used as correlate to 心, "the mind," taken in connection with the idea of "energy" inherent in it, from its composition. Thus it signifies the lower, but active, portion of man's constitution; and in this paragraph, that lower part in its lowest sense,—animal vigor or courage. Observe the force of

曾子之守約也。

曰、敢問夫子之

不動心、與告子

之不動心、可得

聞與。告子曰、不

得於言勿求於

心、不得於心勿

求於氣不得於

心、勿求於氣可、

the philosopher Tsăng maintained, which was *indeed* of the most importance."

9. *Kung-sun Ch'ow* said, "May I venture to ask an explanation from you, Master, of how you maintain an unperturbed mind, and how the philosopher Kaou does the same?" *Mencius answered,* "Kaou says,— 'What is not attained in words is not to be sought for in the mind; what produces dissatisfaction in the mind, is not to be helped by passion effort.' *This last,*—when there is unrest in the mind, not to seek for relief from passion effort, may be conceded. But

the 又, referring to what had been conceded to Shay in par. 6. I translate as if there were a comma or pause after the two 守. 9. Kaou's principle seems to have been this,— utter indifference to everything external, and entire passivity of mind. Modern writers are fond of saying that in his words is to be found the essence of Buddhism,— that the object of his attainment was the Buddhistic *nirvana*, and perhaps this helps us to a glimpse of his meaning. Comm. take sides on 不得於言, whether the "words" are Kaou's own words, or those of others. To me it is hardly doubtful that they must be taken as the words of others. Mencius's account of

himself below, as "knowing words," seems to require this. At the same time, a reference to Kaou's arguments with Mencius in Bk. VI, where he changes the form of his assertions, without seeming to be aware of their refutation, gives some plausibility to the other view.—Chaou K'e is all at sea in his interpretation of the text here. He understands it thus: —"If men's words are bad, I will not inquire about their hearts; if their hearts are bad, I will not inquire about their words!" The 可 is not an approval of Kaou's second proposition, but a concession of it simply is not so bad as his first. Mencius goes on to show wherein he considered it as defective. From

不得於言、勿求於心不可、

夫志、氣之帥也、氣體之充

也、夫志至焉、氣次焉、故曰、

持其志、無暴其氣。既曰、志

至焉、氣次焉、又曰、持其志、

無暴其氣者、何也。曰、志壹、

not to seek in the mind for what is not attained in words cannot be conceded. The will is the leader of the passion nature. The passion nature pervades and animates the body. The will is *first and* chief, and the passion nature is subordinate to it. Therefore *I* say,—'Maintain firm the will, and do no violence to the passion nature.'"

10. *Ch'ow observed,* "Since you say—'The will is chief, and the passion nature is subordinate,' how do you also say,—'Maintain firm the will, and do no violence to the passion nature?'" *Mencius* replied, "When it is the will alone which is active, it moves

his language here, and in the next paragraph, we see that he uses 志 and 心 synonymously. 氣,體之充, —"the 氣 is the filling up of the body." 氣 might seem here to be little more than the "breath," but that meaning would come altogether short of the term throughout the chapter. 10. Ch'ow did not understand what his master had said about the relation between the mind and the passion nature, and as the latter was subordinate, would have had it disregarded altogether:—hence his question. Mencius shows that the passion-nature is really a part of our constitution, acts upon the mind, and is acted on by it, and may not be disregarded. 壹＝專 一.

則動氣、氣壹、則動志也、

今夫蹶者、趨者是氣也、

而反動其心敢問夫子

惡乎長曰、我知言、我善

養吾浩然之氣。敢問何

謂浩然之氣曰、難言也。

the passion nature. When it is the passion nature alone which is active, it moves the will. For instance now, in the case of a man falling or running;—that is from the passion nature, and yet it moves the mind."

11. "I venture to ask," *said Ch'ow again*, "wherein you, Master, surpass *Kaou*." *Mencius* told him, "I understand words. I am skillful in nourishing my vast, flowing passion nature."

12. *Ch'ow* pursued, "I venture to ask what you mean by your vast, flowing passion nature!" The reply was, "It is difficult to describe it.

The 反 meets Ch'ow's disregard of the passion nature, as not worth attending to. 11. The illustration here is not a very happy one, leading us to think of 氣 in its merely material signification, as in the last par. On 知言, see par. 17. On 浩然之氣 there is much vain babbling in the Comm., to show how the 氣 of heaven and earth is the 氣 also of man. Mencius, it seems to me, has before his mind the ideal of a perfect man, complete in all the parts of his constitution. It is this which gives its elevation to his

其爲氣也、至大至剛以直養

而無害、則塞于天地之間其

爲氣也、配義與道、無是餒也。

是集義所生者、非義襲而取

之也、行有不慊於心、則餒矣、

我故曰、告子未嘗知義以其

13. "This is the passion nature: — It is exceedingly great, and exceedingly strong. Being nourished by rectitude, and sustaining no injury, it fills up all between heaven and earth.

14. "This is the passion nature: — It is the mate and assistant of righteousness and reason. Without it, *man* is in a state of starvation.

15. "It is produced by the accumulation of righteous deeds; it is not to be obtained by incidental acts of righteousness. If the mind does not feel complacency in the conduct, *the nature* becomes starved. I therefore said, 'Kaou has never understood righteousness, because he makes it something external.'

language. 13. 以直養,—as in paragraphs 7, 15; 無害,—as in the latter part of par. 15. 塞 is here in the sense of "to fill up," not "to stop up." Still the 塞乎天地之間 is one of those *heroic* expressions, which fill the ear, but do not inform the mind. 14. A pause must be made after the 是, which refers to the 浩然之氣. 餒 refers to 體, in 體之充, in par. 9. It is better, however, in the translation, to supply "man," than "body." 15. 襲, — "to take an enemy by surprise"; and 義襲 = "incidental acts of righteousness." 餒 here refers to the passion nature itself. The analysis of conduct and feeling here is very good. Mencius's sentiment is just—'*Tis conscience makes cowards of us all.* On the

天下之不助苗長者寡

趨而往視之苗則槁矣、

病矣予助苗長矣其子

芒然歸謂其人曰今日

苗之不長、而揠之者芒

若宋人然宋人有閔其

正、心勿忘勿助長也、無

外之也必有事焉而勿

〇十六章

16. "There must be the *constant* practice *of this righteousness,* but without the object *of thereby nourishing the passion nature.* Let not the mind forget *its work,* but let there be no assisting the growth *of that nature.* Let us not be like the man of Sung. There was a man of Sung, who was grieved that his growing corn was not longer, and so he pulled it up. *Having done this,* he returned home, looking very stupid, and said to his people, 'I am tired to-day. I have been helping the corn to grow long.' His son ran to look at it, and found the corn all withered. There are few in the world *who do not deal with their passion nature,*

latter sentence, see Bk. VI, v, *et al.* 16. I have given the meaning of the text—必有事焉, 而勿正心勿忘, 勿助長 after Chaou K'e, to whom Choo He also inclines. But for their help, we should hardly know what to make of it. 正 is taken in the sense of 預期, "to do with anticipation of, or a view to, an ulterior object." This meaning of the term

is supported by an example from the 春秋傳. 病 = "tired." 17. Here, as sometimes before, we miss the preliminary 曰, noting a question by Mencius's interlocutor, and the same omission is frequent in all the rest of the chapter. I have supplied the lacunæ after Choo He, who himself follows Lin Che-k'e (林之奇), a scholar, who died A.D. 1176. Chaou

所陷邪辭知其所離遁

辭知其所蔽淫辭知其

又害之何謂知言曰詖

揠苗者也非徒無益而

不耘苗者也助之長者

矣以爲無益而舍之者

*as if* they were assisting the corn to grow long. Some
indeed consider it of no benefit to them, and let it
alone: — they do not weed their corn. They who
assist it to grow long, pull out their corn. *What they
do is* not only of no benefit *to the nature*, but it also
injures it."

17. *Kung-sun Ch'ow further asked,* "What do you
mean by saying that you understand *whatever* words
*you hear?*" *Mencius* replied, "When words are one-
sided, I know how *the mind of the speaker* is clouded
over. When words are extravagant, I know how
*the mind* is fallen and sunk. When words are all-
depraved, I know how *the mind* has departed *from*

K'e sometimes errs egregiously in
the last part, through not distinguishing the speakers. With regard
to the first ground of Mencius's
superiority over Kaou,—his "knowledge of words," as he is briefer than
on the other, so he is still less satisfactory;—to my mind, at least.
Perhaps he means to say, that,
however great the dignity to which

he might be raised, his knowledge
of words, and ability in referring
incorrect and injurious speeches to
the mental defects from which they
sprang, would keep him from being
deluded, and preserve his mind
unperturbed. One of the scholars
Ch'ing uses this illustration:—"Mencius with his knowledge of words
was like a man seated aloft on the

辭、知其所窮、生於其心、害

於其政、發於其政、害於其

事、聖人復起、必從吾言矣。

宰我子貢、善爲說辭、冉牛、

閔子、顏淵、善言德行、孔子

*principle.* When words are evasive, I know how *the mind* is at its wit's end. *These evils* growing in the mind, do injury to government, and, displayed in the government, are hurtful to the conduct of affairs. When a sage shall again arise, he will certainly follow my words.''

18. *On this Ch'ow observed,* "Tsae Go and Tszekung were skillful in speaking. Yen New, the disciple Min, and Yen Yuen, while their words were good, were distinguished for their virtuous conduct. Confucius united the qualities of the disciples in himself,

dais, who can distinguish all the movements of the people below the hall, which he could not do, if it were necessary for him to descend and mingle with the crowd." The concluding remark gives rise to the rest of the chapter, it seeming to Ch'ow that Mencius placed himself by it on the platform of sages. 18. Comp. Ana., XL, ii, 2, to the enumeration in which of the excellencies of several of Confucius's disciples there seems to be here a reference. There, however, it is said that Yen New, Min, and Yen Yuen were distinguished for 德行, and here we have the addition of 善言, which give a good deal of trouble. Some take 言 as a verb,— "were skillful to speak of virtuous conduct." So the Tartar version, according to Julien. Sun Shih makes it a noun, as I do. The references to the disciples are quite inept. The point of Ch'ow's inquiry lies in Confucius's remark, found nowhere else, and obscure enough. He thinks

夫子既聖矣、夫聖孔子不居、是

不厭、智也、教不倦仁也、仁且智、

學不厭而教不倦也子貢曰、學

聖矣乎、孔子曰聖則吾不能、我

也昔者子貢問於孔子曰夫子

則夫子既聖矣乎。曰惡、是何言
十九節

兼之曰、我於辭命、則不能也、然

*but still* he said, 'In the matter of speeches, I am not
competent.'—Then, Master, have you attained to be
a sage?''

19. *Mencius* said, "Oh! what words are these?
Formerly Tsze-kung asked Confucius, saying, 'Master,
are you a sage?' Confucius answered him, 'A sage
is what I cannot rise to. I learn without satiety,
and teach without being tired.' Tsze-kung said, 'You
learn without satiety:—that shows your wisdom.
You teach without being tired:—that shows your
benevolence. Benevolent and wise:—Master, you
ARE a sage.' Now, since Confucius would not have
himself regarded a sage, what words were those?''

Mencius is taking more to himself
than Confucius did. Chaou K'e, however, takes 我 於 辭 云 云, as a remark of Mencius, but it is quite
unnatural to do so. Observe the
force of the 既,—*you have come to be.*

19. 惡, up. 1st tone; an exclamation,
not interrogative. This convers. with
Tsze-kung is not found in the Analects. Compare Ana., VII, ii; xxxiii,
which latter chapter may possibly be
another version of what Mencius

何言也。昔者竊聞之子
夏子游子張皆有聖人
之一體、冉牛閔子顏淵、
則具體而微、敢問所安。
曰、姑舍是。曰、伯夷伊尹
何如。曰、不同道、非其君
不事、非其民不使、治則

20. *Ch'ow said,* "Formerly, I once heard this:— Tsze-hea, Tsze-yew, and Tsze-chang had each one member of the sage.　Yen New, the disciple Min, and Yen Yuen, had all the members, but in small proportions.　I venture to ask,— With which of these are you pleased to rank yourself?"

21. *Mencius* replied, "Let us drop speaking about these, if you please."

22. *Ch'ow then* asked, "What do you say of Pih-e and E-yun?"　"Their ways were different *from mine,*" said *Mencius.*　"Not to serve a prince whom he did not esteem, nor command a people whom he did not approve; in a time of good government to take office,

says here.　20. 竊, is used with other verbs to give a deferential tone to what they say.　21. Comp. Bk. I, Pt. II, ix.　Does Mencius here indicate that he thought himself superior to all the worthies referred to—even to Yen Yuen?　Hardly so much as that; but that he could not be content with them for his model.　22. Pih-e,—see Con. Ana., V, xxii.　E-yun,—see Con. Ana., XII, xxii.　非 其 君, 非 其 民,—the emphatic *his,* i. e., as paraphrased in the translation.　何 事 非 君 何 使 非 民＝得 君 則 事, 何 所 事 而 非 我 君, 得 民 則 使, 何 所 使 而 非 我 民. I have

有行焉、乃所願則學孔子也。

孔子也、皆古聖人也吾未能

止、可以久則久、可以速則速、

尹也、可以仕則仕、可以止則

何使非民、治亦進、亂亦進、伊

進、亂則退、伯夷也何事非君、

and on the occurrence of confusion to retire:—this
was *the way of* Pih-e. *To say*—'Whom may I not
serve? My serving him makes him my prince. What
people may I not command? My commanding them
makes them my people.' In a time of good government to take office, and when disorder prevailed, also
to take office:—that was *the way of* E-yun. When it
was proper to go into office, then to go into it; when
it was proper to keep retired from office, then to keep
retired from it; when it was proper to continue in it
long, then to continue in it long; when it was proper
to withdraw from it quickly, then to withdraw
quickly:—that was *the way of* Confucius. These were
all sages of antiquity, and I have not attained to do
what they did. But what I wish to do is to learn to
be like Confucius."

given the meaning, but the conciseness of the text makes it difficult to
a learner. The different ways of
Pih-e, E-yun, and Confucius are
thus expressed: "The principle of
the first was purity—以清爲其道；
that of the second was office—以任
爲其道; that of the third was what
the time required—以時爲其道。"

下、皆不爲也、是則同曰、敢問其

下、行一不義、殺一不辜、而得天

地而君之、皆能以朝諸侯、有天

曰、然則有同與曰、有得百里之

否、自有生民以來、未有孔子也。

伯夷伊尹於孔子、若是班乎。曰、

23. *Ch'ow said*, "Comparing Pih-e and E-yun with Confucius, are they to be placed in the same rank?" *Mencius* replied, "No. Since there were living men until now, there never was *another* Confucius."

24. *Ch'ow* said, "Then, did they have *any points of* agreement *with him?*" The reply was,—"Yes. If they had been sovereigns over a hundred li of territory, they would, all of them, have brought all the princes to attend in their court, and have obtained the empire. And none of them, in order to obtain the empire, would have committed one act of unrighteousness, or put to death one innocent person. In those things they agreed with him."

25. *Ch'ow* said, "I venture to ask wherein he

23. 於 is to be taken as＝與, the connective. 25. 汙,—*woo*, or *wa*, | "low-lying water," used here simply for "low," with reference to the

等百世之王莫之能違也、
樂而知其德由百世之後、
曰見其禮而知其政聞其
夫子賢於堯舜遠矣子貢 ｡廿七節
其所好宰我曰、以予觀於 ｡廿六節
智足以知聖人、汙不至阿
所以異曰、宰我子貢有若、

differed from them." *Mencius* replied, "Tsae Go, Tsze-kung, and Yew Jŏ had wisdom sufficient to know the sage. *Even had they been ranking themselves low, they would not have demeaned themselves to* flatter their favorite.

26. "*Now,* Tsae Go said, 'According to my view of our Master, he is far superior to Yaou and Shun.'

27. "Tsze-kung said, 'By viewing the ceremonial ordinances *of a prince,* we know *the character of* his government. By hearing his music, we know *the character of* his virtue. From the distance of a hundred ages after, I can arrange, according to their merits, the kings of a hundred ages; — not one of

wisdom of Tsae Go and Tsze-kung, in their own estimation. 阿 in the sense of "partial," = "to flatter." 26. With this and the two next pars., comp. the eulogium of Confucius, in tho *Chung Yung,* Ch. 30–32, and

Con. Ana., XIX, xxiii–xxv. It is in vain the Western reader tries to quicken himself to any corresponding appreciation of Confucius. We look for the being his disciples describe, as vainly as we do for the fabulous

來、未有盛於孔子也。類、拔乎其萃、自生民以之於民亦類也、出於其海之於行潦類也、聖人飛鳥泰山之於丘垤河麟之於走獸鳳凰之於也有若曰豈惟民哉、麒 ○廿八節 自生民以來、未有夫子

them can escape me. From the birth of mankind till now, there has never been *another* like our Master.'

28. "Yew Jŏ said, 'Is it only among men that it is so? There is the K'e-lin among quadrupeds; the Fêng-hwang among birds, the T'ae Mountain among mounds and ant hills, and rivers and seas among rain pools. *Though different in degree*, they are the same in kind. So the sages among mankind are also the same in kind. But they stand out from their fellows, and rise above the level, and from the birth of mankind till now, there never has been one so complete as Confucius.'"

K'e-lin and Fêng-hwang, to which they compare him. 鳳凰,—see Con. Ana., XI, viii. The *k'e* is properly the male, and the *lin*, the female of the animal referred to;—a monster, with a deer's body, an ox's tail, and a horse's feet, which appears to greet the birth of a sage, or the reign of a sage sovereign. Both in 麒麟 and 鳳凰, the names of the male and female are put together, to indicate one individual of either sex. The image in 拔乎其萃 is that of stalks of grass or grain, shooting high above the level of the waving field. 未有盛於孔子,—"there has not been one more complete than Confucius." But this would be no more than putting Confucius on a level with other sages. I have therefore translated after the example of Choo He, who says—自古聖人、固皆異於衆人、然未有如孔子之盛者也.

非心服也、力不贍也、

以百里以力服人者、

大湯以七十里文王

德行仁者王、王不待

者霸、霸必有大國、以

孟子曰、以力假人

CHAPTER III. 1. Mencius said, "He who, using force, makes a pretense to benevolence, is the leader of the princes. A leader *of the* princes requires a large kingdom. He who, using virtue, practices benevolence—is the sovereign of the empire. To become the sovereign of the empire, *a prince* need not wait for a large *kingdom.* T'ang did it with *only* seventy li, and King Wăn with only a hundred.

2. "When one by force subdues men, they do not submit to him in heart. *They submit, because* their strength is not adequate *to resist.* When one subdues

CH. 3. THE DIFFERENCE BETWEEN A CHIEFTAIN OF THE PRINCES AND A SOVEREIGN OF THE EMPIRE; AND BETWEEN SUBMISSION SECURED BY FORCE AND THAT PRODUCED BY VIRTUE. 1. 霸 and 王 are here the recognized titles and not="to acquire the chieftaincy," "to acquire the sovereignty." In the 集 註, we find much said on the meaning of the two characters. 王 is from three strokes (三), denoting heaven, earth, and man, with a fourth stroke, 一 or unity, going through them, grasping and uniting them together, thus affording the highest possible conception of power or ability. 霸 is synonymous with 伯, and of kindred meaning with the words, of nearly the same sound, 把, "to grasp with the hand," and 迫, "to urge," "to press." 2. 力不贍 is translated by Julien,—"*quia nempe vires* (*i. e., vis armorum*) *ad id obtinendum non sufficiunt.*" Possibly some Chi. comm. may have sanctioned such an interpretation, but it has nowhere come under my notice. The "seventy

則辱、今惡辱而居不仁、

孟子曰仁則榮不仁

之謂也。

自南自北、無思不服、此

孔子也詩云、自西、自東、

誠服也、如七十子之服

以德服人者、中心悦而

men by virtue, in their hearts' core they are pleased,
and sincerely submit, as was the case with the seventy
disciples in their submission to Confucius.　What is
said in the 'Book of Poetry,'

> 'From the west, from the east,
> From the south, from the north,
> There was not one who thought of refusing sub-
> mission,'

is an illustration of this."

CHAPTER IV.　1. Mencius said, "Benevolence brings
glory *to a prince*, and the opposite of it brings disgrace.　For *the princes of* the present day to hate
disgrace and yet live complacently doing what is not

disciples" is giving a round number,
the enumeration of them differing
in different works. We find them
reckoned at 73, 76, etc. See in the
prolegomena to Vol. I. For the ode
see the She-king, III, i, Ode IX, st.
6, celebrating the influence of the
kings Wăn and Woo.　The four
quarters are to be viewed from
Kaou, (鎬), King Woo's capital.　思
is not to be taken as an abstract
noun, = "thought."　鄒浩, a statesman and scholar of the 11th cent.,
says on this chapter: "He who

subdues men by force has the intention of subduing them, and they
dare not but submit.　He who subdues men by virtue, has no intention
to subdue them, and they cannot
but submit.　From antiquity downwards, there have been many disser-
tations on the leaders of the princes,
and the true sovereign, but none so
deep, incisive, and perspicuous as
this chapter."

CH. 4.　GLORY IS THE SURE RESULT
OF BENEVOLENT GOVERNMENT.　CA-
LAMITY AND HAPPINESS ARE MEN'S
OWN SEEKING.　1. 居不仁, lit., "to

之未陰雨徹彼桑土、

必畏之矣。三詩云迨天

時明其政刑雖大國、

在職國家閒暇及是

尊士賢者在位能者

如惡之莫如貴德而二

是猶惡溼而居下也。

benevolent, is like hating moisture and yet living in a low situation.

2. "If *a prince* hates disgrace, the best course for him to pursue is to esteem virtue and honor *virtuous* scholars, giving the worthiest among them places *of dignity*, and the able offices *of trust*. When throughout his kingdom there is leisure and rest *from external troubles*, taking advantage of such a season, let him clearly *digest* the principles of his government with its legal sanctions, and then even great kingdoms will be constrained to stand in awe of him.

3. "It is said in the 'Book of Poetry,'

'Before the heavens were dark with rain,
I gathered the bark from the roots of the mulberry trees,

dwell in not-benevolence," i. e., complacently to go on in the practice of what is not benevolent. 2. 莫如 covers as far as to 政刑, and 賢者 在位 and the next clause are to be taken as in apposition simply with the one preceding. See the Doctrine of the Mean, ch. xx. The 賢者在位 here corresponds to the 尊賢 there, and the 能者在職 may embrace both the 敬大臣 and the 體羣臣. 刑,—not punishments, but penal laws. 3. See the She-king, I, xv,

綢繆牖戶、今此下民、

或敢侮予、孔子曰、爲

此詩者其知道乎、能

治其國家、誰敢侮之。

今國家閒暇、及是時、

般樂怠敖、是自求禍

也。禍福無不自己求

And wove it closely to form the window and
　door *of my nest;*
Now, *I thought,* ye people below,
Perhaps ye will not dare to insult me.'

Confucius said, 'Did not he who made this ode understand the way *of governing?*' If a prince is able
rightly to govern his kingdom, who will dare to insult
him?

4. "*But* now *the princes* take advantage of the
time when throughout their kingdoms there is leisure
and rest *from external troubles,* to abandon themselves
to pleasure and indolent indifference;—they in fact
seek for calamities for themselves.

5. "Calamity and happiness in all cases are men's
own seeking.

Ode II, st. 2, where for 今 此 下 民
we have 今 女 下 民, the difference
not affecting the sense. The ode is
an appeal by some small bird to an
owl not to destroy its nest, which
bird, in Mencius's application of the
words, is made to represent a wise
prince taking all precautionary measures. 4. 般,—read *p'wan,* low. 1st
tone, nearly synonymous with the
next character,-- 樂, *loh.* 6. Fo. the

士、皆悅而願立於其
俊傑在位、則天下之
孟子曰、尊賢使能、
不可活、此之謂也、
作孽猶可違、自作孽、
自求多福、太甲曰、天
之者。詩云、永言配命、

6. "This is illustrated by what is said in the 'Book of Poetry,'—

'Be always studious to be in harmony with the ordinances *of God*,
So you will certainly get for yourself much happiness;'

and by the passage of the Ta'e Keă,—'When Heaven sends down calamities, it is still possible to escape from them; when we occasion the calamities ourselves, it is not possible any longer to live.'"

CHAPTER V. Mencius said, "If *a ruler* give honor to men of talents and virtue and employ the able, so that offices shall all be filled by individuals of distinction and mark;—then all the scholars of the empire will be pleased, and wish to stand in his court.

ode see the She-king, III, i, Ode I, st. 6. 言＝念, "to think of." For the other quotation, see the Shoo-king, IV, v, Sect. II, 3, where we have 道, "to escape," for 活, but the meaning is the same.

CH. 5. VARIOUS POINTS OF TRUE ROYAL GOVERNMENT NEGLECTED BY THE PRINCES OF MENCIUS'S TIME, ATTENTION TO WHICH WOULD SURELY CARRY ANY ONE OF THEM TO THE IMPERIAL THRONE. 1. Comp. last ch., par. 2. The wisest among 1,000 men is called 俊; the wisest among 10 is called 傑. Numbers, however, do not enter into the signification of the terms here. 天下之士云云,一

朝矣。市、廛而不征、
法而不廛、則天下
之商、皆悅而願藏
於其市矣。關、譏而
不征則天下之旅、
皆悅而願出於其

2. "If, in the market place *of his capital*, he levy a ground rent on the shops but do not tax the goods, or enforce the proper regulations without levying a ground rent;—then all the traders of the empire will be pleased, and wish to store their goods in his market place.

3. "If, at his frontier passes, there be an inspection of persons, but no taxes charged *on goods or other articles*, then all the travelers of the empire will be pleased, and wish to make their tours on his roads.

comp. I, Pt. I, vii, 18. 2. 廛, "a shop, or market place," is used here as a verb, "to levy ground rent for such a shop." Acc. to Choo He, in the 語類, we are to understand the market place here as that in the capital, which was built on the plan of the division of the land, after the figure of the character 井. The middle square behind was the 市; the center one was occupied by the palace; the front one by the ancestral and other temples, govt. treasuries, arsenals, etc.; and the three squares on each side were occupied by the people. He adds that, when traders became too many, a ground rent was levied; when they were few, it was remitted, and only a surveillance was exercised of the markets by the proper officers. That surveillance extended to the inspection of weights and measures, regulation of the price, etc. See its duties detailed in the Chow-le, XIV, vii. 3. Comp. I, Pt. II, v, 3; Pt. I, vii, 18. All comm. refer for the illustration of this rule to the account of the duties of the 司關, in the Chow-le, XV, xi. But from that it would appear that the levying no duties at the passes was only in bad years, and hence some have argued that Mencius's lesson was only for the emergency of the time. To avoid that conclusion, the author of the 四書撫餘說 contends that the Chow-le has been interpolated in the place,—rightly,

路矣。<sub>四句</sub>耕者、助而不税、
則天下之農皆悅而
願耕於其野矣。<sub>五句</sub>塵無
夫里之布、則天下之
民、皆悅而願爲之氓

4. "If he require that the husbandmen give their mutual aid *to cultivate the public field*, and exact no *other* taxes from them;—then all the husbandmen of the empire will be pleased, and wish to plow in his fields.

5. "If from the occupiers of the shops in his market place he do not exact the fine of the individual idler, or of the hamlet's quota of cloth, then all the people of the empire will be pleased, and wish to come and be his people.

as it seems to me. 4. The rule of 助而不税·is the same as that of 耕者九一, I, Pt. II, v, 3. 5. It is acknowledged by commentators that it is only a vague notion which we can obtain of the meaning of this paragraph. Is 廛 to be taken as in the translation, or verbally as in the 2nd par.? What was the 夫布? And what the 里布? It appears from the Chow-le, that there was a fine, exacted from idlers or loafers in the towns, called 夫布, and it is said that the family which did not plant mulberry trees and flax according to the rules, was condemned to pay one hamlet, or 25 families', quota of cloth. But 布 may be taken in the sense of money, simply＝錢, which is a signification attaching to it. We must leave the passage in the obscurity which has always rested on it. Mencius is evidently protesting against some injurious exactions' of the time. 氓＝民, but the addition of the character 亡 seems intended to convey the idea of the people of other states coming to put

矣。信能行此五者、則鄰國

之民、仰之若父母矣、率其

子弟、攻其父母、自生民以

來、未有能濟者也、如此則

無敵於天下、無敵於天下

者、天吏也、然而不王者、未

之有也

6. "If *a ruler* can truly practice these five things, then the people in the neighboring kingdoms will look up to him as a parent. From the first birth of mankind till now, never has any one led children to attack their parent, and succeeded in his design. Thus, such a ruler will not have an enemy in all the empire, and he who has no enemy in the empire is the minister of Heaven. Never has there been a ruler in such a case who did not attain to the imperial dignity."

themselves under a new rule. 6. 信 二實, "truly." "Observe the reciprocal influence of 其 in 率其子弟 ("sons and younger brothers" = children) and 攻其父母. 天吏,—— "The minister or officer of Heaven." On this designation the comm. 饒 雙峰 observes: "An officer is one commissioned by his sovereign; the officer of Heaven is he who is commissioned by Heaven. He who bears his sovereign's commission can punish men and put them to death. He may deal so with all criminals. He who bears the commission of Heaven can execute judgment on men, and smite them. With all who are oppressing and misgoverning their kingdoms, he can deal so."

下可運之掌上。
忍人之政、治天
忍人之心行不
人之政矣、以不
之心、斯有不忍
先王有不忍人
有不忍人之心。
孟子曰、人皆

CHAPTER VI. 1. Mencius said, "All men have a mind which cannot bear *to see the sufferings of* others.

2. "The ancient kings had this commiserating mind, and they, as a matter of course, had likewise a commiserating government. When with a commiserating mind was practiced a commiserating government, the government of the empire was *as easy a matter* as the making anything go round in the palm.

CH. 6. THAT BENEVOLENCE, RIGHT-EOUSNESS, PROPRIETY, AND KNOWL-EDGE, BELONG TO MAN AS NATURALLY AS HIS FOUR LIMBS, AND MAY AS EASILY BE EXERCISED. The assertions made in this chapter are universally true, but they are to be understood as spoken here with special reference to the oppressive ways and government of the princes of Mencius's time. 1. 不忍 alone is used in Bk. I, Pt. I, vii, 4, 5, 6. 人 is added here, because the discourse is entirely of a man's feelings, as exercised towards other men. 心,—"the mind," embracing the whole mental constitution. The 備旨, after

Chaou K'e, says that 不忍人 means —"cannot bear to injure others." But it is not only cannot bear to inflict suffering, but cannot bear to see suffering. The examples in I, Pt. II, vii, make this plain. 2. 斯, —used adverbially, as in Ana., X, x, 1. 運之,—之 must be taken generally,="a thing," or as giving a passive signification to the verb.— "The government of the empire could be made to go round," etc. Perhaps the latter construction is to be preferred. See the 四書味根錄, *in loc.* The whole is to be translated in the past sense, being descriptive of the ancient kings.

之、無惻隱之心、非人也、
惡其聲而然也。由是觀
要譽於鄉黨朋友也、非
孺子之父母也、非所以
隱之心、非所以內交於
將入於井、皆有怵惕惻
之心者、今人乍見孺子
所以謂人皆有不忍人

3. "When I say that all men have a mind which cannot bear *to see the sufferings of* others, my meaning may be illustrated thus:—even nowadays, if men suddenly see a child about to fall into a well, they will without exception experience a feeling of alarm and distress. *They will feel so,* not as a ground on which they may gain the favor of the child's parents, nor as a ground on which they may seek the praise of their neighbors and friends, nor from a dislike to the reputations of *having been unmoved by* such a thing.

4. "From this case we may perceive that the feeling of commiseration is essential to man, that the

3. 孺, "an infant at the breast," here = "a very young child." 內 read as, and = 納. 內交,—"to form a friendship with," "to get the favor of." 要,—up. 1st tone,= 求. 鄉 黨,—comp. Con. Ana., VI, iii, 4. The object of this par. is to show that the feeling of commiseration is instinctive and natural. 今 is to be joined to 人,— "men of the present time," in opp. "to the former kings." 4. The two negatives 無 — 非 in the difft. clauses make the strongest possible affirmation. Lit., "Without the feeling of commiseration there would not be *man,*" etc , or "if a person be without this, he is not a man," etc. 惻 隱, "pain and distress," but as it is

是義之惻非人無
非之端惻心之羞
之心也隱非心惡
心禮羞之人非之
智之惡心也人心
之端之仁無也、非
　也、心之是無
　辭　　　辭
　讓　　　讓
　　　　　之

feeling of shame and dislike is essential to man, that
the feeling of modesty and complaisance is essential
to man, and that the feeling of approving and disapproving is essential to man. ·

5. "The feeling of commiseration is the principle
of benevolence. The feeling of shame and dislike is
the principle of righteousness. The feeling of modesty
and complaisance is the principle of propriety. The
feeling of approving and disapproving is the principle
of knowledge.

in illustration of the 不忍之心, we
may render it by "commiseration."
"Shame and dislike,"—the *shame* is
for one's own want of goodness, and
the *dislike* is of the want of it in
other men. "Modesty and complaisance,"—*modesty* is the unloosing
and separating from one's self, and
*complaisance* is outgiving to others.
"Approving and disapproving,"—
*approving* is the knowledge of goodness, and the approbation of it
accordingly, and *disapproving* is the
knowledge of what is evil, and disapprobation of it accordingly. Such
is the account of the terms in the
text, given by Choo He and others.
The feelings described make up, he
says, the mind of man, and Mencius
"discoursing about commiseration

goes on to enumerate them all."
This seems to be the true account
of the introduction of the various
principles. They lie together, merely
in apposition. In his 或問 and 語
類, however, Choo He labors to
develop the other three from the
first.—Observe that "the feeling of
shame and dislike," etc., in the
original, is—"the mind that feels
and dislikes," etc. 5. 端 is explained
by 端緒, "the end of a clue," that
point outside, which may be laid
hold of, and will guide us to all
within. From the feelings which he
has specified, Mencius reasons to
the moral elements of our nature.
It will be seen how to 智, "knowledge," "wisdom," he gives a moral
sense. Comp. Gen. 2:17; 3:5, 6;

火之始然泉之始達、苟能充

於我者、知皆擴而充之矣、若

能者、賊其君者也。凡有四端

不能者、自賊者也、謂其君不

有四體也、有是四端而自謂

端也人之有是四端也、猶其

6. "Men have these four principles just as they have their four limbs. When men, having these four principles, yet say of themselves that they cannot *develop them*, they play the thief with themselves, and he who says of his prince that he cannot *develop them*, plays the thief with his prince.

7. "Since all men have these four principles in themselves, let them know to give them all their development and completion, and the issue will be like that of fire which has begun to burn, or that of a spring which has begun to find vent. Let them have their complete development, and they will suffice

Job. 38 : 28. 6. 賊,—comp. I, Pt. II, viii, 3, but we can retain its primitive meaning in the translation. 7. 凡有四端於我者, not "all who have," etc., but "all having," etc., 於 我,—*quasi dicat*, "in their ego-ity." 知皆,—皆 belongs to the 擴

亦然、故術不可不
人、惟恐傷人巫匠
人、惟恐不傷人函
不仁於函人哉、矢
孟子曰、矢人、豈
父母。
不充之、不足以事
之、足以保四海、苟

to love and protect all within the four seas. Let them be denied that development, and they will not suffice for a man to serve his parents with."

CHAPTER VII. 1. Mencius said, "Is the arrow maker less benevolent than the maker of armor of defense? *And yet,* the arrow maker's only fear is lest men should not be hurt, and the armor maker's only fear is lest men should be hurt. So it is with the priest and the coffin maker. *The choice of* a profession, therefore, is a thing in which great caution is required.

below, and refers to the 四端.—The 備旨 says: 知字重看, "the character 知 is to have weight attached to it." This is true, Mencius may well say—"Let men know," or "If men know." How is it that after all his analyses of our nature to prove its goodness, the application of his principles must begin with an IF?

CH. 7. AN EXHORTATION TO BENEVOLENCE FROM THE DISGRACE WHICH MUST ATTEND THE WANT OF IT, LIKE THE DISGRACE OF A MAN WHO DOES NOT KNOW HIS PROFESSION. 1.

矢人豈不仁於,—the 不 belongs not to the 豈, but to the 仁. If we might construe it with the 豈, we should have an instance parallel to 盛於 in ii, 28,—"benevolent as," the 於 being＝如. 函,—in the sense of 鎧, "all armor of defense." 巫,—see Con. Ana., XIII, xxii, where I have translated it "wizard." As opposed to 匠 (here＝"a coffin maker"), one who makes provision for the death of men, it indicates one who prays for men's life and prosperity. But Mencius pursues his illustration too far. An arrow maker need not be

由弓人而恥爲弓、矢人而恥

無義、人役也、人役而恥爲役、

仁、是不智也。不仁不智、無禮

也、人之安宅也、莫之禦而不

處仁、焉得智夫仁、天之尊爵

愼也。孔子曰、里仁爲美擇不

2. "Confucius said, 'It is virtuous manners which constitute the excellence of a neighborhood. If a man, in selecting a residence, do not fix on one where such prevail, how can he be wise?' Now, benevolence is the most honorable dignity conferred by Heaven, and the quiet home in which man should dwell. Since no one can hinder us from being so, if yet we are not benevolent;—this is being not wise.

3. "From the want of benevolence and the want of wisdom will ensue the entire absence of propriety and righteousness;—he who is in such a case must be the servant of other men. To be the servant of men and yet ashamed of such servitude is like a bow maker's being ashamed to make bows, or an arrow maker's being ashamed to make arrows.

inhumane. 2. See Con. Ana., IV, i. The comm. begin to bring in the idea of a profession at 擇 不 處 仁, but the whole quotation must be taken first in its proper sense. The 不 智 at the end refer to the same characters in the quotation. 3. 無 succeeding 不 shows that the second clause ensues from the first. 由,一

大舜有大焉善與人同、舍
有過、則喜禹聞善言則拜。
■■孟子曰、子路、人告之以
反求諸己而已矣。
發發而不中、不怨勝己者、
仁者如射射者正己而後
爲矢也。如恥之莫如爲仁。

4. "If he be ashamed of his case, his best course is to practice benevolence.

5. "The man who would be benevolent is like the archer. The archer adjusts himself and then shoots. If he misses, he does not murmur against those who surpass himself. He simply turns round and seeks *the cause of his failure* in himself."

CHAPTER VIII. 1. Mencius said, "When any one told Tsze-loo that he had a fault, he rejoiced.

2. "When Yu heard good words, he bowed *to the speaker.*

3. "The great Shun had a still greater *delight in what was good. He regarded* virtue as the common property of himself and others, giving up his own

used for 猶. 5. 仁者＝欲爲仁之人. Comp. Ana., III, vii; III, xvi.
CH. 8. HOW SAGES AND WORTHIES DELIGHTED IN WHAT IS GOOD. 1. Tsze-loo's ardor in pursuing his self-improvement appears in the Ana. V. xiii; XI, xx. But the par-

ticular point mentioned in the text is nowhere else related of him. 2. In the Shoo-king, II, iii, I, we have an example of this in Yu. It is said,—禹拜昌言, "Yu bowed at these excellent words." 3. 善與人同, is explained by Choo He 公天下之善

孟子

己從人、樂取於人以爲

善自耕稼陶漁以至爲

帝、無非取於人者取諸

人以爲善、是與人爲善

者也、故君子莫大乎與

人爲善。

way to follow that of others, and delighting to learn from others to practice what was good.

4. "From the time when he plowed and sowed, exercised the potter's art, and was a fisherman, to the time when he became emperor, he was continually learning from others.

5. "To take example from others to practice virtue is to help them in the same practice. Therefore, there is no attribute of the superior man greater than his helping men to practice virtue."

而不爲私也, "He considered as public—common—the good of the whole world, and did not think it private to any." Shun's distinction was that he did not think of himself, as Tsze-loo did, nor of others, as Yu did, but only of what was good, and unconsciously was carried to it, wherever he saw it. 4. Of Shun in his early days it is related in the "Historical Records," that "he plowed at the Leih (歷) mountain, did potter's work on the banks of the Yellow River, fished in the Luy lake (雷澤), and made various implements on the Show hill (壽丘), and often resided at Foô-hea (負夏)." There will be occasion to consider where these places were, in connection with some of Mencius's future references to Shun. Dr. Medhurst supposes them to have been in Shanse. See his Translation of the Shoo-king, p. 332. 5. 與 is here in the sense of 助, "to help." The meaning is that others, seeing their virtue so imitated, would be stimulated to greater diligence in the doing of it.

不正望望然去之若將浼焉、是

推惡惡之心思與鄉人立其冠

人言、如以朝衣朝冠坐於塗炭、

與惡人言、立於惡人之朝、與惡

其友不友不立於惡人之朝、不

■章孟子曰、伯夷非其君不事、非

CHAPTER IX. 1. Mencius said, "Pih-e would not serve a prince whom he did not approve, nor associate with a friend whom he did not esteem. He would not stand in a bad prince's court, nor speak with a bad man. To stand in a bad prince's court, or to speak with a bad man, would have been to him the same as to sit with his court robes and court cap amid mire and ashes. Pursuing the examination of his dislike to what was evil, *we find* that he *thought it necessary*, if he happened to be standing with a villager whose cap was not rightly adjusted, to leave him with a high air, as if he were going to be defiled. Therefore,

CH. 9. PICTURES OF PIH-E AND HWUY OF LEW-HEA, AND MENCIUS'S JUDGMENT CONCERNING THEM. 1. Comp. ch. ii, 22. In 惡人之朝, 人 refers to the prec. 君, and may be translated *prince*, but in 與惡人 立, 人 refers to the prec. 友, and must be translated *man*. 塗炭, "mire and charcoal." 推惡惡之 心,—推 is Mencius's speaking in his own person. 思 is the "thought" of Pih-e. 望望然, acc. to Choo He,

故諸侯雖有善其辭命而至

者、不受也、不受也者、是亦不

屑就已柳下惠、不羞汙君、不

卑小官、進不隱賢、必以其道、

遺佚而不怨阨窮而不憫、故

曰、爾爲爾、我爲我、雖袒裼裸

裎於我側、爾焉能浼我哉、故

although some of the princes made application to him
with very proper messages, he would not receive their
gifts.—He would not receive their gifts, counting it
inconsistent with his purity to go to them.

2. "Hwuy of Lew-hea was not ashamed to *serve*
an impure prince, nor did he think it low to be an
inferior officer. When advanced to employment, he
did not conceal his virtue, but made it a point to
carry out his principles. When neglected and left
without office, he did not murmur. When straitened
by poverty, he did not grieve. Accordingly, he had a
saying, 'You are you, and I am I. Although you
stand by my side with breast and arms bare, or with
your body naked, how can you defile me?' Therefore,

is "the appearance of going away
without looking round." Chaou K'e
makes it "the appearance of being
ashamed;"—not so well. The final

已 gives positiveness to the affirmation of the preceding clause. 2.
Hwuy of Lew-hea,—see Con. Ana.,

君子不由也。　柳下惠不恭隘與不恭、　屑去已○三孟子曰伯夷隘、　而止之而止者、是亦不　失焉、援而止之而止援　由由然與之偕、而不自

self-possessed, he companied with men indifferently, at the same time not losing himself. *When he wished to leave,* if pressed to remain in office, he would remain.—He would remain in office, when pressed to do so, not counting it required by his purity to go away."

3. Mencius said, "Pih-e was narrow-minded, and Hwuy of Lew-hea was wanting in self-respect. The superior man will not follow either narrow-mindedness, or the want of self-respect."

XV, xiii; XVIII, ii, viii. 與之偕, —the 之 properly refers to the party addressed,—"you are you." 3. Comp. ii, 22. 君子,—by this term we must suppose that Mencius makes a tacit reference to himself, as having proposed Confucius as his model. The comm. 韓元少 says:

"Elsewhere Mencius advises men to imitate E and Hwuy, but he is there speaking to the weak and the mean. When here he advises not to follow E and Hwuy, he is speaking for those who wish to do the right thing at the right time."

## BOOK II

### KUNG-SUN CH'OW.　PART II

環而攻之、而不 之城、七里之郭、 不如人和。三里 不如地利、地利、 鼞孟子曰、天時、 下 公孫丑章句

CHAPTER I. 1. Mencius said, "Opportunities of time *vouchsafed by* Heaven are not equal to advantages of situation *afforded by* the Earth, and advantages of situation afforded by the Earth are not equal to *the union arising from* the accord of Men.

2. *"There is a city*, with an inner wall of three li in circumference, and an outer wall of seven.—*The enemy* surround and attack it, but they are not able to take

CH. 1. No ADVANTAGES WHICH A RULER CAN OBTAIN TO EXALT HIM OVER OTHERS ARE TO BE COMPARED WITH HIS GETTING THE HEARTS OF MEN. Because of this chapter Mencius has got a place in China among the writers on the art of war, which surely he would not have wished to claim for himself, his design evidently boing to supersede the necessity of war,—the recourse to arms altogether. 1. In the 天, 地, 人, we have the doctrine of the 三 才, or "Three Powers," which is brought out so distinctly in the 4th part of the *Chung Yung*, and to show this in a translation requires it to be diffuse. As to what is said at much length in Chinese commentaries about ascertaining the "time of Heaven" by divination and astrology, it is to be set aside, as foreign to the mind of Mencius in the text, though many examples which resort to it may be adduced from the records of antiquity. 2. The city here supposed, with its double circle of fortification, is a small one, the better to illustrate the superiority of advantage of situation, just as

勝、夫環而攻之、必有得天

時者矣、然而不勝者、是天

時不如地利也。城、非不高

也、池、非不深也、兵革、非不

堅利也、米粟、非不多也、委

而去之、是地利不如人和

it. Now, to surround and attack it, there must have been vouchsafed to them by Heaven the opportunity of time, and in such case their not taking it is because opportunities of time vouchsafed by Heaven are not equal to advantages of situation afforded by the Earth.

3. "*There is a city, whose* walls are distinguished for their height, and whose moats are distinguished for their depth, where the arms *of its defendants*, offensive and defensive, are distinguished for their strength and sharpness, and the stores of rice and other grain are very large. *Yet it is obliged to* be given up and abandoned. This is because advantages of situation afforded by the Earth are not equal to the union arising from the accord of Men.

the next is a large one, to bring out the still greater superiority of the union of men. As to the evidence that a city of the specified dimensions must be the capital of a baronial state (子男之城), see the 集證, *in loc.* 3. 非不, the repeated negation, not only affirms, but with emphasis.—城非不高, "the wall is not not (but) high," i.e., is high indeed. 兵,—sharp weapons of offense. 革,—"leather," intending, principally, the buff coat, but including all other armor of defense. 米,—"rice," without the husk. 粟,—"grain," generally, in

也。故曰、域民、不以封疆

之界、固國不以山谿之

險、威天下、不以兵革之

利、得道者多助、失道者

寡助、寡助之至、親戚畔

之、多助之至、天下順之。

4. "In accordance with these principles it is said, 'A people is bounded in, not by the limits of dikes and borders; a kingdom is secured, not by the strengths of mountains and rivers; the empire is overawed, not by the sharpness *and strength* of arms.' He who finds the proper course has many to assist him. He who loses the proper course has few to assist him. When this,—the being assisted by few, —reaches its extreme point, his own relations revolt from *the prince.* When the being assisted by many reaches its highest point, the whole empire becomes obedient to *the prince.*

the husk. 4. 域, "a boundary," "a border," is used verbally. 域民,— "to bound a people," i. e., to separate them from other states. 封 is "a dike," or "mound." The common. 金仁山 says: "Anciently, in every state, they made a dike of earth to show its boundary (封 土為疆)." 谿,—"a valley with a stream in it"; here, in opposition to 山,=*rivers* or *streams.* The 道, or "proper course," intended is that style of government,—benevolence and righteousness,—which will secure the "union of men." 親戚,— relatives by blood and by affinity.

人如就見者也、

王使人來曰寡

☒孟子將朝王、

戰必勝矣。

故君子有不戰、

攻親戚之所畔、

以天下之所順、

5. "When one to whom the whole empire is prepared to be obedient, attacks those from whom their
own relations revolt, *what must be the result?* Therefore, the true ruler will prefer not to fight; but if he
do fight, he must overcome."

CHAPTER II. 1. As Mencius was about to go to
court *to see* the king, the king sent a person to him
*with this message,*—"I was wishing to come and see

5. The case put in the two first
clauses is here left by Mencius to
suggest its own result. The *keun-
tsze* is the prince intended above,
"who finds the proper course."
Choo He and others complete 有不
戰 by 則已, "If he do not fight,
well"; but the translation gives, I
think, a better meaning.

CH. 2. HOW MENCIUS CONSIDERED
THAT IT WAS SLIGHTING HIM FOR A
PRINCE TO CALL HIM BY MESSENGERS
TO GO TO SEE HIM, AND THE SHIFTS
HE WAS PUT TO TO GET THIS UNDER-
STOOD. It must be understood that,
at the time to which this chapter
refers, Mencius was merely an hon-
ored guest in Ts'e, and had no
official situation or emolument. It

was for him to pay his respects at
court, if he felt inclined to do so;
but if the king wished his counsel,
it was for him to show his sense of
his worth by going to him, and
asking him for it. 1. The 1st, 3rd,
and 4th 朝 are *ch'aou*, lower 1st
tone,="to go to, or wait upon, at
court." So in all the other paragraphs. The 2nd is *chaou*, upper 1st
tone, "the morning." The morning,
as soon as it was light, was the
regular time for the emperor and
princes, to give audience to their
nobles and officers, and proceed to
the administration of business. The
modern practice corresponds with
the ancient in this respect. 如 is
said to be here=欲, "to wish,"

有寒疾、不可以風朝、將視

朝、不識可使寡人得見乎。

對曰不幸而有疾、不能造

朝明日出弔於東郭氏、公

孫丑曰、昔者辭以病、今日

you. But I have got a cold, and may not expose myself to the wind. In the morning I will hold my court. I do not know whether you will give me the opportunity of seeing you *then*." *Mencius* replied, "Unfortunately, I am unwell, and not able to go to the court."

2. Next day, he went out to pay a visit of condolence to some one of the Tung-kwŏh family, when Kung-sun Ch'ow said to him, "Yesterday, you declined *going to the court* on the ground of being unwell, and to-day you are going to pay a visit of condolence.

which sense seems to be necessary, though we don't find it in the dict. 造, read *ts'aou*, up. 3rd tone, "to go to." The king's cold was merely a pretense. He wanted Mencius to wait on him. Mencius's cold was equally a pretense. Comp. Confucius's conduct, Ana., XVII, xx. 2. Tung-kwŏh is not exactly a surname. The individual intended was a descendant of the duke Hwan, and so surnamed Keang (姜), but that branch of Hwan's descendants to which he belonged having their possessions in the "eastern" part of the kingdom, the style of Tung-kwŏh appears to have been given to them to distinguish them from the other branches. In going to pay the visit of condolence, Mencius's idea was that the king might hear of it, and understand that he had merely feigned sickness, to show his sense of the disrespect done to him in

於路曰、請必無歸、而造

識能至否乎使數人要

病小愈趨造於朝、我不

釆薪之憂、不能造朝、今

子對曰、昔者有王命、有

王使人問疾、醫來、孟仲

疾、今日愈、如之何不弔。

弔、或者不可乎曰、昔者

May this not be regarded as improper?" "Yesterday," said *Mencius*, "I was unwell; to-day, I am
better:—why should I not pay this visit?"

3. *In the meantime*, the king sent a messenger
to inquire about his sickness, and also a physician.
Măng Chung replied to them, "Yesterday, when the
king's order came, he was feeling a little unwell, and
could not go to the court. To-day he was a little
better, and hastened to go to court. I do not know
whether he can have reached it *by this time* or not."
*Having said this*, he sent several men to look for
*Mencius* on the way, and say to him, "I beg that,
before you return home, you will go to the court."

trying to inveigle him to go to
court. 3. It is a moot point, whether
Mang Chung was Mencius's son, or
merely his nephew. The latter is
more likely. 釆薪之憂,—lit.,
"sorrow of gathering firewood," = a
little sickness. See a similar expression in the Le-ke, I, Pt. II, i, 8,—
君使士射,不能, 則辭以疾, 言曰
某有負薪之憂. On this the 正義
says:—"Carrying firewood was the
business of the children of the common people. From the lips of an
officer, such language was indicative
of humility." 要, upper 1st tone, =
求. Măng Chung, having committed
himself to a falsehood, in order to
make his words good, was anxious
that Mencius should go to court. 4.

見所以敬王也曰惡是何言

臣主敬丑見王之敬子也未

臣人之大倫也父子主恩君

焉景子曰內則父子外則君

於朝不得已而之景丑氏宿

4. *On this,* Mencius felt himself compelled to go to King Ch'ow's, and there stop the night. King said to him, "In the family, there is *the relation of* father and son; abroad, there is *the relation of* prince and minister. These are the two great relations among men. Between father and son the ruling principle is kindness. Between prince and minister the ruling principle is respect. I have seen the respect of the king to you, sir, but I have not seen in what way you show respect to him." *Mencius* replied, "Oh! what

What compelled Mencius to go to King Ch'ow's was his earnest wish that the king should know that his sickness was merely feigned, and that he had not gone to court, only because he *would not be* CALLED to do so. As Măng Chung's falsehood interfered with his first plan, he wished that his motive should get to the king through King Ch'ow who was an officer of Ts'e. After 宿 焉, Chaou K'e appends a note,—"when he told him all the previous incidents." No doubt, he did so. 至, up.

陳於王前、故齊人莫如我敬王

大乎是、我非堯舜之道不敢以

足與言仁義也云爾、則不敬莫

以仁義爲不美也、其心曰、是何

也、齊人無以仁義與王言者、豈

words are these? Among the people of Ts'e there
is no one who speaks to the king about benevolence
and righteousness. Are they thus silent because they
do not think that benevolence and righteousness are
admirable? *No, but* in their hearts they say, 'This
man is not fit to be spoken with about benevolence
and righteousness." Thus they manifest a disrespect
than which there can be none greater. I do not
dare to set forth before the king any but the ways
of Yaou and Shun. There is therefore no man of
Ts'e who respects the king so much as I do."

1st tone, "oh!" as in Pt. I, ii, 19.
齊人 ... 者, observe the force of the
者, carrying on the clause to those
following for an explanation of it,
as if there were a 所以 after 人. 云
爾,—see Con. Ana., VII, xvii. 5.

晋楚之富、不可及也、彼以

似然曰豈謂是與、曾子曰、
〔六節〕

遂不果、宜與夫禮若不相

俟駕、固將朝也、聞王命而

禮曰、父召無諾、君命召不

也景子曰、否、非此之謂也、
〔五節〕

5. King said, "Not so. That was not what I meant. In the 'Book of Rites' it is said, 'When a father calls, the answer must be without a moment's hesitation. When the prince's order calls, the carriage must not be waited for.' You were certainly going to the court, but when you heard the king's order, then you did not carry your purpose out. This does seem as if it were not in accordance with that rule of propriety."

6. Mencius answered him, "How can you give that meaning to my conduct? The philosopher Tsăng said, 'The wealth of Tsin and Ts'oo cannot be equaled. Let their rulers have their wealth:—I

Different passages are here quoted together from the "Book of Rites." 父 召 無 諾,—see Bk. I, Pt. I, iii, 14,—"A son must cry 唯 to his father, and not 諾," which latter is a lingering response. 君 命 召 不 俟 駕 is found substantially in Bk. XIII, iii, 2. 夫, low. 1st tone,=斯, as in Ana., XI, ix, 3, et al. 6. 豈 謂 是 與 (low. 1st tone),—lit., "how

齒、輔世長民莫如德、惡

朝廷莫如爵鄉黨莫如

達尊三、爵一、齒一、德一、

之、是或一道也、天下有

哉、夫豈不義而曾子言

爵、我以吾義吾何慊乎

其富、我以吾仁、彼以其

have my benevolence.　Let them have their nobility:
—I have my righteousness.　Wherein should I be
dissatisfied *as inferior to them?*'　Now shall we say
that these sentiments are not right?　Seeing that the
philosopher Tsăng spoke them, there is in them, I
apprehend, a *real* principle.—In the empire there are
three things universally acknowledged to be honorable.　Nobility is one of them; age is one of them;
virtue is one of them.　In courts, nobility holds the
first place of the three; in villages, age holds the first
place; and for helping one's generation and presiding
over the people, the other two are not equal to virtue.

means (it) this?"　慊 has two opposite meanings, either "dissatisfied,"
or "satisfied," in which latter sense,
it is also *hĕ̆.*　Choo He explains this
by making it the same as 嗛, "something held in the mouth," according
to the nature of which will be the
internal feeling.　In the text, the
idea is that of dissatisfaction.　夫豈

不義, 一義 is here 當 然 之 理,=
"what is proper and right," the
subject being the remarks of Tsăng.
而曾子言之云云 is expanded thus
in the 備 旨:—"And, Tsăng-tsze
speaking them, they contain perhaps
another principle different from the
vulgar view."　鄉黨, see Con. Ana.,

學焉而後臣之、故不勞而

與有爲也。故湯之於伊尹、

其尊德樂道、不如是、不足

召之臣、欲有謀賢、則就之、

將大有爲之君、必有所不

得有其一、以慢其二哉。故

How can the possession of *only* one of these *be presumed on* to despise one who possesses the other two?

7. "Therefore a prince who is to accomplish great deeds will certainly have ministers whom he does not call to go to him. When he wishes to consult with them, he goes to them. The prince who does not honor the virtuous, and delight in their ways of doing, to this extent, is not worth having to do with.

8. "Accordingly, there was the behavior of T'ang to E-yun:—he first learned of him, and then employed him as his minister; and so without difficulty

X, i. 齒, "teeth,"=age. 7. 不足
與有爲 is by some interpreted—
"is not fit to have to do with them,"
i. e , the virtuous, but I prefer the
meaning adopted in the translation.
8. In the "Historical Records," 殷
本記, one of the accounts of E-yun's

becoming minister to T'ang is, that
it was only after being five times
solicited by special messengers that
he went to the prince's presence.
See the 集註, on Ana., XII, xxii.
The confidence reposed by the duke
Hwan in Kwan Chung appears in Pt.

王、桓公之於管仲、學焉

而後臣之、故不勞而霸。

今天下、地醜德齊、莫能

相尚、無他、好臣其所教、

而不好臣其所受教湯

之於伊尹、桓公之於管

仲、則不敢召、管仲且猶

he became emperor. There was the behavior of the
duke Hwan to Kwan Chung:—he first learned of him,
and then employed him as his minister; and so without difficulty he became chief of all the princes.

9. "Now throughout the empire, the territories
*of the princes* are of equal extent, and in their
achievements they are on a level. Not one of them
is able to exceed the others. This is from no other
reason but that they love to make ministers of
those whom they teach, and do not love to make
ministers of those by whom they might be taught.

10. "So did T'ang behave to E-yun, and the duke
Hwan to Kwan Chung, that they would not venture
to call them to go to them. If Kwan Chung might

I, ii, 3. Kwan was brought to Ts'e
originally as a prisoner to be put to
death, but the duke, knowing his
ability and worth, had determined to
employ him, and therefore, having
first caused him to be relieved of
his fetters, and otherwise honorably
treated, he drove himself out of his
capital to meet and receive him with
all distinction, listening to a long
discourse on government. See the
集證, on Ana., III, xxii. 9. 臣,—
used as a verb. 10. Comp. Pt.
I, i.

十鎰而受、前日之不受是、

餽七十鎰而受於薛餽五

餽兼金一百而不受、於宋

陳臻問曰前日於齊王

乎。

不可召而況不爲管仲者

not be called to him by his prince, how much less may he be called, who would not play the part of Kwan Chung!"

CHAPTER III. 1. Ch'in Tsin asked *Mencius*, saying, "Formerly, when you were in Ts'e, the king sent you a present of 2,400 taels of fine silver, and you refused to accept it. When you were in Sung, 1,680 taels were sent to you, which you accepted; and when you were in Sëĕ, 1,200 taels were sent, which you *likewise* accepted. If your declining to accept the

CH. 3. BY WHAT PRINCIPLES MENCIUS WAS GUIDED IN DECLINING OR ACCEPTING THE GIFTS OF PRINCES. 1. Ch'in Tsin was one of Mencius's disciples, but this is all that is known of him. At what time of the philosopher's life this conversation occurred, we are unable to say. 餽—"to present an offering of food"; here, more generally, "to send a gift,"=送. 兼金,—"double metal" (I suppose 白金, or silver), called "double, as being worth twice as much as the ordinary." See Ana., XI, xxi. — 百, i. e., 100 *yih* (鎰), which, as in I, Pt. II, ix, 2, I estimate at 24 taels. Sung,—the present Kweitih in Honan. Sëĕ,—see Bk. I, Pt. II, x, iv.

則今日之受非也今日之受

是、則前日之不受非也、夫子

必居一於此矣。孟子曰、皆是

也當在宋也予將有遠行、行

者必以贐辭曰餽贐、予何爲

gift in the first case was right, your accepting it in the latter cases was wrong. If your accepting it in the latter cases was right, your declining to do so in the first case was wrong. You must accept, master, one of these alternatives."

2. Mencius said, "I did right in all the cases.

3. "When I was in Sung, I was about to take a long journey. Travelers must be provided with what is necessary for their expenses. The prince's message was—'A present against traveling expenses.' Why should I have declined the gift?

The reference here, however, is inconsistent with what is stated in the note there, that Sëë had long been incorporated with Ts'e. 前日, 今日, mark the relation of time between the cases simply. 今日 is not to be taken as = "to-day." 必居—於 此, lit., "must occupy (dwell in) one in these (places)." The meaning is that on either of the suppositions, he would be judged to have done *wrong*. 3. 贐 or 賮, "a gift to a traveler against the expenses of his journey." 必以贐,—it is difficult to assign its precise force to the 以. I consider the whole clause to be written as from the point of view of the prince of Sung;—in regard to travelers, he considered it was requisite to use the ceremony of 贐.

貨取乎。

之是貨之也、爲有君子、而可以

若於齊、則未有處也、無處而餽

聞戒、故爲兵餽之、予何爲不受。

不受當在薛也、予有戒心、辭曰

4. "When I was in Sëë, I was apprehensive for my safety, and taking measures for my protection. The message was, 'I have heard that you are taking measures to protect yourself, and send this to help you in procuring arms.' Why should I have declined the gift?

5. "But when I was in Ts'e, I had no occasion for money. To send a man a gift when he has no occasion for it is to bribe him. How is it possible that a superior man should be taken with a bribe?"

4. We must paraphrase 戒 心 considerably, to bring out the meaning. 爲, low. 3rd tone. 兵, "a weapon of war," or the character may be taken here for "a weapon bearer," "a soldier." 5. 未 有 處 也,—Julien says,—"*sicut nos Gallice; il n'y a pas lieu a*, but if it were so, 處 would be the noun, in the 3rd tone, whereas it is the verb in the 2nd, = "to manage," "to dispose of." 未 有 處 = 未 有 所 處.

歲子之民、老羸轉於溝

失伍也、亦多矣凶年饑

乎。曰不待三然則子之

日而三失伍、則去之否

夫曰子之持戟之士、一

孟子之平陸、謂其大

CHAPTER IV. 1. Mencius having gone to P'ing-luh, addressed the governor of it, saying, "If *one of* your spearmen should lose his place in the ranks three times in one day, would you, sir, put him to death or not?" "I would not wait for three times *to do so,*" was the reply.

2. *Mencius* said, "Well then, you, sir, have like-wise lost your place in the ranks many times. In bad calamitous years, and years of famine, the old and feeble of your people, who have been found lying in the ditches and water channels, and the able-bodied,

CH. 4. How MENCIUS BROUGHT CONVICTION OF THEIR FAULTS HOME TO THE KING AND AN OFFICER OF TS'E. 1. 之 is the verb=往. P'ing-luh was a city on the southern border of Ts'e. It is referred to the present department of Yenchow in Shantung, though some, with less reason, find it in P'ingyang in Shanse. The officer's name, as we learn from the last par., was K'ung Keu-sin. 大 夫 here=宰, "gov-ernor" or "commandant." The 戟 is variously described. Some say it had three points; others, that it had a branch or blade on one side. No doubt, its form varied. 去, up. 2nd tone, "to away with." Comm. concur in the meaning given in the trans-lation. 2. 凶 年 云 云,—comp. Bk. I, Pt. II, xii, 2. Julien finds a diffi-culty in the "several thousand," as not applicable to the population of P'ingluh. But it was Mencius's way

視其死與。曰此則距心

反諸其人乎抑亦立而

矣、求牧與芻而不得則

者、則必爲之求牧與芻

人之牛羊、而爲之牧之

之所得爲也。曰、今有受

幾千人矣曰、此非距心

壑、壯者散而之四方者、

who have been scattered about to the four quarters, have amounted to several thousands." *The* governor replied, "That is a state of things in which it does not belong to me Keu-sin to act."

3. "Here," said *Mencius*, "is a man who receives charge of the cattle and sheep of another, and undertakes to feed them for him;—of course he must search for pasture ground and grass for them. If, after searching for those, he cannot find them, will he return *his charge to* the owner? or will he stand by and see them die?" "Herein," said the officer, "I am guilty."

to talk roundly. To make 千 人 "one thousand," we must read 幾, up. 1st tone, and suppose the preposition 乎 suppressed. The meaning of the officer's reply is—that to provide for such a state of things, by opening the granaries and other measures, devolved on the supreme authority of the state, and not on him. 3. Comp. 非 身 之 所 能 爲, I, Pt. II, xv, 2. The first 牧 is the verb: the 2nd, a noun, =pasture grounds. 諸 =於. 其 人,—"the man," i.e., their owner. 抑 亦,—the force of the 亦 is—"or—here is another supposition—will he, etc.?" Mencius means that Keu-sin should not hold office in such circumstances

之罪也。他日、見於王曰、

王之爲都者、臣知五人、

焉、知其罪者、惟孔距心、

爲王誦之。王曰、此則寡

人之罪也。

孟子謂蚳鼃曰、子之

4. Another day, *Mencius* had an audience of the king, and said to him, "Of the governors of Your Majesty's cities I am acquainted with five, but the only one of them who knows his faults is K'ung Keu-sin." He then repeated the conversation to the king, who said, "In this matter, I am the guilty one."

CHAPTER V. 1. Mencius said to Ch'e Wa, "There seemed to be reason in your declining the governor-

4. 見, low. 3rd tone. 爲都者,—爲 has the sense of "to administer," "to govern"; comp. Ana., IV, xiii. 都,—properly "a capital city," but also used more generally. In the dict., we find:—(1) Where the emperor has his palace is called 都. (2) The cities conferred on the sons and younger brothers of the princes were called 都; in fact, every city with an ancestral temple containing the tablets of former rulers. (3) The

cities from which nobles and great officers derived their support were called 都. 爲王,—爲 low. 3rd tone.

CH. 5. THE FREEDOM BELONGING TO MENCIUS IN RELATION TO THE MEASURES OF THE KING OF TS'E FROM HIS PECULIAR POSITION, AS UNSALARIED. 1. Of Ch'e Wa we only know what is stated here. Lingk'ew is supposed to have been a city on the borders of Ts'e, remote from the court, Ch'e Wa having

辭靈丘、而請士師、似也、
爲其可以言也、今既數
月矣、未可以言與、蚳䵷
諫於王而不用、致爲臣
而去。齊人曰、所以爲蚳
䵷則善矣、所以自爲、則
吾不知也。公都子以告。

ship of Ling-k‘ew, and requesting to be appointed chief criminal judge, because *the latter office* would afford you the opportunity of speaking *your views*. Now several months have elapsed, and have you yet found nothing of which you might speak?"

2. *On this,* Ch‘e Wa remonstrated *on some matter* with the king, and, his counsel not being taken, resigned his office, and went away.

3. The people of Ts‘e said, "In the course which he marked out for Ch‘e Wa, he did well, but we do not know as to the course which he pursues for himself."

4. His disciple Kung-too told him *these remarks.*

declined the governorship of it, that he might be near the king. 士師,— see Bk. I, Pt. II, vi, 2. 爲其可以言,—lit., "because of the possibility to speak." As criminal judge, Ch‘e Wa would be often in communication with the king, and could remonstrate on any failures in the admin- istration of justice that came under his notice. 2. 致, "to resign," "give up," as in Con. Ana., I, vii, *et al.* 3. 所以爲 (low. 3rd tone), lit., "whereby for,"=所以爲之道, as in the trans- lation. 4. Kung-too was a disciple of Mencius. See Bk. III, Pt. II, ix,

曰、吾聞之也、有官守者、不得

其職則去、有言責者、不得其

言則去、我無官守、我無言責

也、則吾進退豈不綽綽然有

餘裕哉。

孟子爲卿於齊、出弔於滕、

5. *Mencius* said, "I have heard that he who is in charge of an office, when he is prevented from fulfilling its duties, ought to take his departure, and that he on whom is the responsibility of giving his opinion, when he finds his words unattended to, ought to do the same. But I am in charge of no office; on me devolves no duty of speaking out my opinion:—may not I therefore act freely and without any constraint, either in going forward or in retiring?"

CHAPTER VI. 1. Mencius, occupying the position of a high dignitary in Ts'e, went on a mission of condolence to T'ăng. The king *also* sent Wang

*et al.* 5. We find the phrase 綽綽 有裕, with the same meaning as the more enlarged form in the text.

CH. 6. MENCIUS'S BEHAVIOR WITH AN UNWORTHY ASSOCIATE. 1. "Oc-cupied the position of a high digni-

tary:"—so I translate here 爲 鄉. Mencius's situation appears to have been only honorary, without emolu-ment, and the king employed him on this occasion to give weight by his character to the mission. The

王使蓋大夫、王驩爲輔行、王驩朝暮見、反齊滕之路、未嘗與之言行事也。二節公孫丑曰、齊卿之位、不爲小矣、齊滕之路、不爲近矣、反之、而未嘗與言行事何也。曰、夫既或治之、予何言哉。

Hwan, the governor of Ka, as assistant commissioner. Wang Hwan, morning and evening, waited upon Mencius, who, during all the way to T'ang and back, never spoke to him about the business of their mission.

2. Kung-sun Ch'ow said to Mencius, "The position of a high dignitary of Ts'e is not a small one; the road from Ts'e to T'ang is not short. How was it that during all the way there and back, you never spoke to Hwan about the matters of your mission?" Mencius replied, "There were the proper officers who attended to them. What occasion had I to speak to him about them?"

officer of 蓋 (read *kă*) was an unworthy favorite of the king. 輔行, not "to assist him on the journey," but with reference to what was the business (所行) of it. 見,—low. 3rd tone. 反 implies the 往, or "going," as well as "returning." 2. 齊卿之位 refers to Wang Hwan, who had been temporarily raised to that dignity for the occasion. 夫 (low. 1st tone) 旣或,—"Now there were some,"—i. e., the proper officers—治之, "who attended to them." The glossarist of Chaou K'e understands this as spoken of Wang:—"He perhaps attended to them," i. e., he thought that he knew all about them, and never put any questions to me; but the view adopted is more natural, and gives more point to Mencius's explanation of his conduct.

今願竊有請也、木若以　虞敦匠事、嚴虞不敢請、　前日、不知虞之不肖、使　於齊、止於嬴、充虞請曰、　孟子自齊葬於魯、反

CHAPTER VII. 1. Mencius *went* from Ts'e to Loo to bury *his mother*. On his return to Ts'e, he stopped at Ying, where Ch'ung Yu begged to put a question to him, and said, "Formerly, in ignorance of my incompetency, you employed me to superintend the making of the coffin. As *you were then pressed by* the urgency *of the business*, I did not venture to put any question to you. Now, however, I wish to take the liberty to submit the matter. The wood *of the coffin*, it appeared to me, was too good."

CH. 7. THAT ONE OUGHT TO DO HIS UTMOST IN THE BURIAL OF HIS PARENTS;—ILLUSTRATED BY MENCIUS'S BURIAL OF HIS MOTHER. Comp. I, Pt. II, xvi. 1. The tradition is that Mencius had his mother with him in Ts'e, and that he carried her body to the family sepulcher in Loo. How long he remained in Loo is uncertain;—perhaps the whole three years proper to the mourning for a parent. Whether his stopping at Ying was for a night merely, or a longer period, is also disputed. Ch'ung Yu was one of his disciples. It has appeared strange that Yu should have cherished the matter so long, and submitted it to his master after a lapse of three years. (This is on the supposition that Mencius's return to Ts'e was after the completion of the three years' mourning.) But it is replied in the 四書釋地, that this only illustrates how fond Mencius's disciples were of applying to him for a solution of their doubts, and the instance of Ch'in Tsin, ch. iii, is another case in point of the length of time they would keep things in mind. 請,—as in I, Pt. II, xvi, I, "to beg to put a question." 敦=董治, "to attend to." 匠, as in Pt. I, vii, 1. 不肖;—see Chung Yung, ch. iv. 嚴, is explained as in the translation. But for the comm., I should render,—"In the gravity of your sorrow." 竊,—see Pt. I,

不<sub>三</sub>得不可以爲悅、無財、

觀美也、然後盡於人心。

天子達於庶人、非直爲

中古棺七寸、椁稱之、自

美然曰、古者棺椁無度、<sub>二</sub>

2. *Mencius* replied, "Anciently, there was no rule for the size of either the inner or the outer coffin. In middle antiquity, the inner coffin was made seven inches thick, and the outer one the same. This was *done by all*, from the emperor to the common people, and not simply for the beauty of the appearance, but because they thus satisfied *the natural feelings of* their hearts.

3. "If prevented *by statutory regulations from making their coffins in this way*, men cannot have the feeling of pleasure. If they have not the money

ii, 20. 2. "Middle antiquity" commences with the Chow dynasty. 稱, up. 3rd tone, "to correspond, or be equal, to." 盡 於 人 心,—於 is not what they call an "empty character," merely connecting the rhythm of the sentence. The whole = "they felt complete (that they had done their utmost) in their human hearts."

Mencius's account of the equal dimensions of the outer and inner coffin does not agree with what we find in the Le-ke, XXII, ii, 31. It must be borne in mind also, that the seven inches of the Chow dynasty were only = rather more than four inches of the present day. 3. 不 得, being opposed to 無 財, requires to be

親。 之也君子不以天下儉其 膚於人心獨無恔乎吾聞 不然且比化者無使土親 古之人皆用之吾何爲獨 不可以爲悅得之爲有財、

to make them, *in this way*, they cannot have the feeling of pleasure. When they were not prevented, and had the money, the ancients all used this style. Why should I alone not do so?

4. "And moreover, is there no satisfaction to the natural feelings of a man, in preventing the earth from getting near to the bodies of his dead?

5. "I have heard that the superior man will not for all the world be niggardly to his parents."

supplemented, so in the translation. For 爲有財, some would give 而有財. The 而 reads better, but the meaning is the same. 4. 比 (low. 3rd tone), 化者,—the same as 比死者 in I, Pt. I, v, 1. 化 is used appropriately with reference to the dissolution of the bodies of the dead. 膚, "skin"＝the bodies. 恔, low. 3rd tone, *heoou*. 獨無恔乎,—the meaning is—"shall this thing *alone* give no satisfaction to a son's feelings?" 5. 不以天下云云,—Chaou K'e interprets this:—"will not deny anything in all the world which he can command to his parents." So, substantially, the modern paraphrasts.

之祿爵、夫士也、亦無王命、

不告於王、而私與之吾子

子噲、有仕於此、而子悅之、

與人燕子之不得受燕於

伐與孟子曰可子噲不得

沈同以其私問曰、燕可

CHAPTER VIII. 1. Shin T'ung, on his own impulse, asked *Mencius*, saying, "May Yen be smitten?" Mencius replied, "It may. Tsze-k'wae had no right to give Yen to another man, and Tsze-che had no right to receive Yen from Tsze-k'wae. *Suppose* there were an officer here, with whom you, sir, were pleased, and that, without informing the king, you were privately to give to him your salary and rank; and suppose that this officer, also without the king's

CH. 8. DESERVED PUNISHMENT MAY NOT BE INFLICTED BUT BY PROPER AUTHORITY. A NATION MAY ONLY BE SMITTEN BY THE MINISTER OF HEAVEN. The incidents in the history of Yen referred to are briefly these:—Tsze-k'wae, a weak silly man, was wrought upon to resign his throne to his prime minister Tsze-che, in the expectation that Tsze-che would decline the honor, and that thus he would be praised as acting the part of the ancient Yaou while he retained his kingdom. Tsze-che, however, accepted the tender, and Tsze-k'wae was laid upon the shelf. By and by, his son endeavored to wrest back the throne, and great confusion and suffering to the people ensued. Comp. Bk. I, Pt. II, x, xi. 1. Shin (so read, as a surname) T'ung appears to have been a high minister of the state. It is difficult to find a word by which to translate 伐, which implies the idea of Yen's deserving to be punished. 吾子,—referring to Shin T'ung, but we can't translate it literally in English. 夫 士 也 夫,—

以伐之、今有殺人者、或問之
之、則將應之曰、爲天吏、則可
而伐之也、彼如曰、孰可以伐
燕可伐與、吾應之曰、可、彼然
齊伐燕有諸曰、未也、沈同問
異於是齊人伐燕或問曰、勸
而私受之於子、則可乎、何以

orders, were privately to receive them from you:—
would *such a transaction* be allowable? And where
is the difference between *the case of Yen and
this?*"

.2. The people of Ts'e smote Yen. Some one
asked Mencius, saying, "Is it really the case that
you advised Ts'e to smite Yen?" He replied, "No.
Shin T'ung asked me whether Yen might be smitten,
and I answered him, 'It may.' They accordingly
went and smote it. If he had asked me—'Who
may smite it?' I would have answered him, 'He
who is the minister of Heaven may smite it.' Suppose the case of a murderer, and that one asks me—

low. 1st tone,＝斯; 士 is the same
person as 仕 above, "a scholar seeking official employment." 2. 應, up-
3rd tone. 彼然,—彼 refers to the
king and people of Ts'e. 彼如曰,—
彼 refers only to Shin T'ung. 天吏,
see Pt. I, v, 6. The one Yen is of
course Ts'e, as oppressive as Yen
itself.

曰、人可殺與、則將應之曰、可、

彼如曰、孰可以殺之、則將應

之曰、爲士師、則可以殺之今

以燕伐燕、何爲勸之哉。

燕人畔、王曰、吾甚慙於孟

子陳賈曰王無患焉王自以

爲與周公孰仁且智王曰、惡、

'May this man be put to death?' I will answer
him—'He may,' If he ask me—'Who may put
him to death?'. I will answer him,—'The chief
criminal judge may put him to death.' But now
with *one* Yen to smite *another* Yen:—how should I
have advised this?''

CHAPTER IX. 1. The people of Yen having rebelled,
the king *of T'se* said, "I feel very much ashamed
*when I think* of Mencius."

2. Ch'in Kea said to him, "Let not Your Majesty
be grieved. Whether does Your Majesty consider
yourself or Chow-kung the more benevolent and
wise?" The king replied, "Oh! what words are

CH. 9. HOW MENCIUS BEAT DOWN
THE ATTEMPT TO ARGUE IN EXCUSE
OF ERRORS AND MISCONDUCT. 1. The
people of Yen set up the son of
Tsze-k'wae as king, and rebelled
against the yoke which Ts'e had
attempted to impose on them.
"Ashamed when I think of Mencius,"—i. e., because of the advice
of Mencius in regard to Yen, which

he had neglected. See Bk. I, Pt. II,
x, xi. 2. Ch'in Kea was an officer
of Ts'e. Chow-kung,—see Con. Ana.,
VII, v, *et al.* The case Kea refers
to was this:—On King Woo's extinction of the Yin dynasty, sparing the
life of Chow's son, he conferred on
him the small state of Yin from
which the dynasty had taken its
name, but placed him under the

孟子問曰周公何人
也。

王乎、賈請見而解之。見三
而

周公未之盡也、而況於

而使之、是不智也、仁智、

而使之、是不仁也、不知

叔監殷、管叔以殷畔、知

是何言也。曰周公使管

those?"  "The duke of Chow," said *Kea*, "appointed
Kwan-shuh to oversee *the heir of* Yin, but Kwan-shuh
with the power of the Yin state rebelled.  If knowing
that this would happen he appointed Kwan-shuh, he
was deficient in benevolence.  If he appointed him,
not knowing that it would happen, he was deficient
in knowledge.  If the duke of Chow was not completely benevolent and wise, how much less can Your
Majesty be expected to be so!  I beg to go and see
Mencius, and relieve Your Majesty from that feeling."

3.  *Ch'in Kea* accordingly saw Mencius, and asked
him, saying, "What kind of man was the duke of

surveillance of his own two brothers,
*Seen* (鮮) and *Too* (度), one of them
older, and the other younger, than
his brother Tan (旦), who was Chow-
kung. Seen has come down to us
under the title of Kwan-shuh, Kwan
being the name of the principality
which he received for himself. After
Woo's death, and the succession of
his son, Seen and Too rebelled, when
Chow-kung took action against them,
put the former to death, and banished the other. 監 (up. 1st tone) 殷,
—the 殷 here is the son of the
name of the state. 解之,—I take
解 in the sense of "to loose," "to
free from," with reference to the
feeling of shame, not "to explain."
3. Before 然 則, there should be a

乎。且古之君子、過則改之、今之

也、管叔、兄也、周公之過、不亦宜

然則聖人且有過與。曰、周公、弟

知其將畔而使之與曰、不知也。

叔以殷畔也、有諸曰、然。曰、周公

曰、古聖人也曰、使管叔監殷、管

Chow?" "An ancient sage," was the reply. "Is it the fact that he appointed Kwan-shuh to oversee the heir of Yin, and that Kwan-shuh with the state of Yin rebelled?" "It is." "Did the duke of Chow know that he would rebel, and *purposely* appoint him to that office?" *Mencius* said, "He did not know." "Then, though a sage, he still fell into error?" "The duke of Chow," answered *Mencius*, "was the younger brother. Kwan-shuh was his elder brother. Was not the error of Chow-kung in accordance with what is right?

4. "Moreover, when the superior men of old had errors, they reformed them. The superior men of the

曰, as it is the retort of Ch'in Kea. 聖人且有過與,—且 implies a succeeding clause—"how much more may one inferior to him!"—況下于公者乎. What Mencius means in conclusion is that brother ought not to be suspicious of brother; that it is better to be deceived than to impute evil. 4. In 今之君子, the 君子 must be taken vaguely. 更.

君子、過則順之、古之

君子、其過也、如日月

之食、民皆見之、及其

更也、民皆仰之、今之

君子、豈徒順之、又從

爲之辭。

釐孟子致爲臣而歸。

present time, when they have errors, persist in them. The errors of the superior men of old were like eclipses of the sun and moon. All the people witnessed them, and when they had reformed them, all the people looked up to them *with their former admiration.* *But* do the superior men of the present day only persist in their errors? They go on to raise apologizing discussions about them likewise."

CHAPTER X. 1. Mencius gave up his office, and *made arrangements for* returning *to his native state.*

up. 1st tone,=改. Shall we refer it to the sun and moon, or to the ancient worthies? Primarily, its application is to the heavenly bodies. 爲之辭, the double object after 爲. The remark was a severe thrust at Ch'in K'ea's own conduct.

CH. 10. MENCIUS IN LEAVING A COUNTRY OR REMAINING IN IT WAS NOT INFLUENCED BY PECUNIARY CONSIDERATIONS, BUT BY THE OPPORTUNITY DENIED OR ACCORDED TO HIM

OF CARRYING HIS PRINCIPLES INTO PRACTICE. 1. 致爲臣.—致 as in ch. v, 2, only it is here simply "resignation," with little of the idea of sacrifice. 而歸, "and returned."— Chaou K'e says "to his house," and in accordance with this, he interprets 不敢請耳 below, "I do not venture to ask you to come in person to see me," which is surely absurd enough. The meaning must be what

我欲中國而受孟子室、

願也他日王謂時子曰、

乎。對曰、不敢請耳、固所

不識可以繼此而得見

甚喜、今又棄寡人而歸、

見而不可得、得侍、同朝

王就見孟子曰、前日願

2.  The king came to visit him, and said, "Formerly, I wished to see you, but in vain.  Then, I got the opportunity of being by your side, and all my court joyed exceedingly along with me.  Now again you abandon me, and are returning home.  I do not know if hereafter I may expect to have another opportunity of seeing you."  Mencius replied, "I dare not request permission to visit you *at any particular time*, but, indeed, it is what I desire."

3.  Another day, the king said to the officer She, "I wish to give Mencius a house, somewhere in the middle of the kingdom, and to support his disciples

I have given.  2. 前日,—referring to the time before Mencius first came to Ts'e.  同朝 (*ch'aou*, low. 1st tone)＝同朝之臣, "all the officers of the court with himself."  繼此＝繼此見, "in continuation of this seeing."  Mencius sees that the king with his complimentary expressions is really bidding him adieu, and answers, accordingly, in as complimentary a way, intimating his purpose to be gone.  3. The king after all does not like the idea of Mencius's going, and thinks of this plan to retain him, which was in reality

養弟子以萬鍾、使諸大
夫國人皆有所矜式子
盡爲我言之。時子因陳
子而以告孟子、陳子以
時子之言告孟子孟子
曰、然、夫時子惡知其不
可也、如使予欲富辭十

with *an allowance of* 10,000 *chung,* that all the officers and the people may have *such an example* to reverence and imitate. Had you not better tell him this for me?"

4. She took advantage to convey this message by means of the disciple Ch'in, who reported his words to Mencius.

5. Mencius said, "Yes; but how should the officer She know that the thing may not be? Suppose that I wanted to be rich, having formerly declined 100,000

what Mencius, in ch. iii, calls "bribing" him. 爲, low. 3rd tone. 3. Ch'in here is the Ch'in Tsin of ch. iii. 因 is explained by 依託, "intrusted to." But it is more, and = "to take advantage of," with reference to Ch'in's being a disciple of Mencius. 4. Mencius does not find it convenient to state plainly his real reason for going,—that he was not permitted to see his principles carried into practice, and therefore repels simply the idea of his being accessible to pecuniary considerations. 100,000 *chung* was the fixed allowance of a 卿, which Mencius had declined to receive. 5. Of Ke-sun and Tsze-shuh E we know only what is mentioned here. Chaou K'e says that they were disciples of Mencius, and that Ke-sun made his remark with a view to induce Mencius to push forward his disciples into the employment which he could

萬而受萬是爲欲富乎季

孫曰異哉子叔疑使已爲

政、不用、則亦已矣、又使其

子弟爲卿、人亦孰不欲富

貴、而獨於富貴之中、有私

龍斷焉。古之爲市者、以其

*chung,* would my now accepting 10,000 be the conduct of one desiring riches?

6. "Ke-sun said, 'A strange man was Tsze-shuh E. He pushed himself into the service of government. *His prince* declining to employ him, he had to retire indeed, but he again schemed that his son or younger brother should be made a high officer. Who, indeed, is there of men but wishes for riches and honor? But he only, among the seekers of these, tried to monopolize the conspicuous mound.

7. "Of old time, the market dealers exchanged the

not get for himself. But such a view is inadmissible. 使已, 使其子弟,—the 1st 使, it is said, merely refers to the prince's employment of him, and the 2nd to his contriving and bringing about the employment of his son or younger brother, but why should we not give the character the same force in both cases? 龍, low. 2nd tone, read as and =壟, "a mound." 斷, up. 2nd tone, "cut," "abrupt," "well defined." 6. 治, low. 1st tone. Observe the force of 耳, "only," which also belongs to it

所有、易其所無者、有

司者治之耳、有賤丈

夫焉、必求龍斷而登

之、以左右望而罔市

利、人皆以爲賤、故從

而征之、征商自此賤

丈夫始矣。

🔳孟子去齊、宿於畫。

articles which they had for others which they had not, and simply had certain officers to keep order among them. It happened that there was a mean fellow, who made it a point to look out for a conspicuous mound, and get up upon it. Thence he looked right and left, to catch in his net the whole gain of the market. The people all thought his conduct mean, and therefore they proceeded to lay a tax upon his wares. The taxing of traders took its rise from this mean fellow."

CHAPTER XI. 1. Mencius, having taken his leave of Ts'e, was passing the night in Chow.

in par. 2, weakening the 不敢請. 征 之, the 之 should be referred to the mean individual spoken of.

CH. 11. HOW MENCIUS REPELLED A MAN, WHO, OFFICIOUSLY AND ON HIS OWN IMPULSE, TRIED TO DETAIN HIM IN TS'E. 1. 畫 was a city on the southern border of Ts'e. Some think it should be written 畫, and refer it to a place in the pres. distr.

of 臨淄, but this would place it north from Loo, whither Mencius was retiring. Mencius withdrew leisurely, hoping that the king would recall him and pledge himself to follow his counsels. 爲 (low. 3rd tone), 王,—"for the king," i. e., knowing it would please the king. 應,—upper 3rd tone. 隱,—upper 3rd tone, "to lean upon." The 几 was

有欲爲王留行者坐而

言不應隱几而臥。客不

悅曰弟子齊宿而後敢

言夫子臥而不聽請勿

復敢見矣。曰坐我明語

子昔者魯繆公無人乎

2. A person who wished to detain him on behalf of the king, *came and* sat down, and began to speak to him. *Mencius* gave him no answer, but leaned upon his stool and slept.

3. ‚ The stranger was displeased, and said, "I passed the night in careful vigil, before I would venture to speak to you, and you, master, sleep and do not listen to me. Allow me to request that I may not again presume to see you." *Mencius* replied, "Sit down, and I will explain the case clearly to you. Formerly, if the duke Muh had not kept a person by the side of

a stool or bench, on which individuals might lean forward, or otherwise, as they sat upon their mats. It could be carried in the hand. See the Le-ke, I, Pt. I, i, 1,—謀於長者，必操几杖以從之. 3. 齊, *chae*, upper 1st tone＝齋 "to keep a vigil," "to fast." 齊宿,—"fasted and passed the night." 請勿復 (low. 3rd tone) 敢見 is merely the complimentary way of complaining of what the guest considered the rudeness of his reception. 語, low. 3rd tone＝告. 繆, here read *Muh*, was the honorary

者乎、長者絕子乎。

而不及子思子絕長

安其身子爲長者慮、

乎繆公之側、則不能

子思泄柳申詳、無人

子思之側、則不能安

Tsze-sze, he could not have induced Tsze-sze to remain with him. If Sëë Lew and Shin Ts'eang had not had a *remembrancer* by the side of the duke Muh, he would not have been able to make them feel at home and remain with him.

4. "You anxiously form plans with reference to me, but you do not treat me as Tsze-sze was treated. Is it you, sir, who cut me? Or is it I, who cut you?"

epithet of the duke Heen (顯), 408–375 B. C. Tsze-sze,—the grandson of Confucius. Shin Ts'eang,—the son of Tsze-chang (子張), one of Confucius's disciples. Sëë Lew was a native of Loo, a disciple of the Confucian school. See the Le-ke, II, Pt. I, ii, 34; Pt. II, iii, 26. 平=在 or 在乎. 安 is said to=留, simply "to detain," but its force is more than that, and = "to make contented, and so induce to remain." Great respect, it seems, was shown to Tsze-sze, and he had an attendant from the duke to assure him continually of the respect with which he was cherished. Sëë Lew and Shin Ts'eang had not such attendants, but they knew that there were one or more officers by the duke's side, to admonish him not to forget them and other worthies. The stranger calls himself 弟子, "your disciple." 4. 爲, low. 3rd tone. Mencius calls himself 長 (up. 2nd tone) 者, "the elder." 子爲長者云云,—the stranger was anxious for (慮) Mencius to remain in Ts'e, but the thing was entirely from himself, not from the king; and his thinking that he could detain him by such a visit showed the little store he set by him;—was, in fact, a *cutting* him.

出晝是何濡滯也、士、則茲
見王、不遇故去、三宿而後
且至、則是干澤也、千里而
則是不明也、識其不可、然
不識王之不可以爲湯武、
孟子去齊。尹士語人曰、

CHAPTER XII. 1. When Mencius had left Ts'e, Yin Sze spoke about him to others, saying, "If he did not know that the king could not be made a T'ang or a Woo, that showed his want of intelligence. If he knew that he could not be made such, and came notwithstanding, that shows he was seeking his own benefit. He came a thousand li to wait on the king; because he did not find in him a ruler to suit him, he took his leave, but how dilatory and lingering was his departure, stopping three nights before he quit Chow! I am dissatisfied on account of this."

CH. 12. HOW MENCIUS EXPLAINED HIS SEEMING TO LINGER IN TS'E, AFTER HE HAD RESIGNED HIS OFFICE, AND LEFT THE COURT. '1· All that we know of Yin Sze is that he was a man of Ts'e. Julien properly blames Noel for translating 尹士 by "literatus cognomine Yin," as if 士 were here the noun—"a scholar."

But when he adds that it is here to be pronounced che, to mark that it is a name, this is what neither the dictionary nor any commentary mentions. 語,—low. 3rd tone,=告. 干澤, "to seek for favors," i. e., his own benefit. See Ana., II, xviii. 不遇, see Bk. I, Pt. II, xvi, 3. 茲=此, "this." What Sze chiefly means to

反予。五章<br>
予夫<br>
出畫而王不予<br>

幾改之、王如改諸、則必<br>

於予心猶以爲速、王庶<br>

已也予三宿而後出畫、<br>

去豈予所欲哉予不得<br>

王、是予所欲也、不遇故<br>

士惡知予哉、千里而見<br>

不悅高子以告曰夫尹<br>

2. The disciple Kaou informed Mencius *of these remarks.*

3. *Mencius* said, "How should Yin Sze know me! When I came a thousand li to wait on the king, it was what I desired to do. When I went away because I did not find in him a ruler to suit me, was that what I desired to do? I felt myself constrained to do it.

4. "When I stopped three nights before I quit Chow, in my own mind I still considered my departure speedy. I was hoping that the king might change. If the king had changed, he would certainly have recalled me.

5. "When I quit Chow, and the king had not sent after me, then, and only till then, was my mind

charge against Mencius is the lingering character of his departure. 3. Mencius was constrained to leave by the conviction forced on him that he could not in Ts'e carry his principles into practice. 王 庶 幾 (up. 1st tone) 改 之, lit., "The king fortunately near to change it." This was

the thought at the time in Mencius's mind, and 庶 幾 = "I hoped," "I was looking for." 諸 = 之. 4. = 然 後 "then, and not till then." 5. 浩 然, —see Part 1, ii, 11. 舍 = 捨, up. 2nd tone. 由 = 猶. 用 is by many taken as simply = 以 ;—"the king is after all competent to do good," but 用

然哉諫於其君而不受則怒

予日望之予豈若是小丈夫

天下之民舉安王庶幾改之、

善、王如用予、則豈徒齊民安、

雖然、豈舍王哉、王由足用爲

追也予然後浩然有歸志、予

resolutely bent on returning *to Tsow*. But, notwithstanding that, how can *it be said that* I give up the
king? The king, after all, is one who may be made
to do what is good. If he were to use me, would it
be for the happiness of the people of Ts'e only? It
would be for the happiness of the people of the whole
empire. I am hoping that the king will change.
I am daily hoping for this.

6. "Am I like one of your little-minded people?
They will remonstrate with their prince, and on *their*
remonstrance *not* being accepted, they get angry, and,
with their passion displayed in their countenance,

expresses more than that. 予 日 望
之, conveys in itself no more than
the translation, but the king's change
of course involved Mencius's recall to
Ts'e. I am inclined to think that
the verbs in this par. should be
translated in the past tense, and
that we have in it merely an amplification of Mencius's thoughts before
he quit Chow. 5. Compare with
this par. Confucius's defense of Kwan
Chung, Ana., XIV, 18.

悴悴然見於其面去則窮

日之力而後宿哉尹士聞

之曰士誠小人也。

蠆孟子去齊充虞路問曰、

夫子若有不豫色然前日

虞聞諸夫子曰君子不怨

天不尤人曰彼一時此一

they take their leave, and travel with all their strength for a whole day, before they will stop for the night."

7. When Yin Sze heard this explanation, he said, "I am indeed a small man."

CHAPTER XIII. 1. When Mencius left Ts'e, Ch'ung Yu questioned him upon the way, saying, "Master, you look like one who carries an air of dissatisfaction in his countenance. But formerly I heard you say— 'The superior man does not murmur against Heaven, nor grudge against men.'"

2. *Mencius* said, "That was one time, and this is another.

CH. 13. MENCIUS'S GRIEF AT NOT FINDING AN OPPORTUNITY TO DO THE GOOD WHICH HE COULD. 1. Ch'ung | Yu,—the same mentioned in ch. vii. Though Ch'ung Yu attributes the maxim 不怨天不尤人 to his

平治天下也、如欲平治
考之則可矣夫天未欲
以其數則過矣以其時
周而來、七百有餘歲矣、
與、其間必有名世者由
時也。五百年、必有王者

3. "It is a rule that a true imperial sovereign should arise in the course of five hundred years, and that during that time there should be men illustrious in their generation."

4. "From the commencement of the Chow dynasty till now, more than 700 years have elapsed. Judging numerically, the date is past. Examining the *character of the present* time, we might *expect the rise of such individuals in it.*"

5. "But Heaven does not yet wish that the empire should enjoy tranquillity and good order. If it wished

master, we find it in Confucius: see Ana., XIV, xxxvi. 3. "500 years," —this is speaking in very round and loose numbers, even if we judge from the history of China prior to Mencius. 其間, "during them," but the meaning is—at the same time with the sovereign shall arise men able to assist him. 名世＝有 or 著 名于世. 4. The Chow dynasty lasted altogether 867 years, and Mencius died, according to some accounts, at the age of 102, in the 2nd year of the last century, little more than 50 years removed from the extinction of the dynasty. 以其時考之則可矣, *lit.*, "By the time examining it, then may," i.e., such

退而有去志不欲變、故不

乎曰非也、於崇、吾得見王、

問曰、仕而不受祿古之道

䆟孟子去齊居休公孫丑

也、吾何爲不豫哉。

天下、當今之世、舍我其誰

this, who is there besides me to bring it about? How should I be otherwise than dissatisfied?"

CHAPTER XIV. 1. When Mencius left Ts'e, he dwelt in Hew. *There* Kung-sun Ch'ow asked him, saying, "Was it the way of the ancient to hold office without receiving salary?"

2. *Mencius replied*, "No; when I first saw the king in Ts'ung, it was my intention, on retiring from the interview, to go away. Because I did not wish to change this intention, I declined to receive any salary.

things may be. 5. 舍我其誰, *lit*, "Letting me go, then who?" Comp. last chap., p. 4, and many other places, where Mencius speaks of what he could accomplish. On the reference to the will of Heaven, comp. Ana., VIII, v, 3.

CH. 14. THE REASON OF MENCIUS'S HOLDING AN HONORARY OFFICE IN TS'E WITHOUT SALARY, THAT HE WISHED TO BE FREE IN HIS MOVE-MENTS. 1. Hew was in the present district of T'ang (藤) in the department of Yenchow. Kung-sun Ch'ow's inquiry was simply for information. This appears from the 非 with which it is answered. 2. Ts'ung must be the name of a place in Ts'e, which cannot be more exactly determined. It is not to be confounded with the ancient principality or barony of the same name. 得見 is

我　　　於　　　以　　　命、　　而　　　受
志　　　齊、　　請、　　不　　　有　　　也、
也。　　非　　　久　　　可　　　師　　　繼三
　　　　　　　　　　　　　　　　　　　　　　三四

3. "Immediately after, came orders for the collection of troops, when it would have been improper for me to beg permission to leave. But to remain *so* long in Ts'e was not my purpose."

evidently＝始 見. 3. 師 命 may be as in the translation, or—"the appointment to the position of a tutor," i. e., honorary adviser to the king. This is the interpretation of the glossarist of Chaou K'e, and is perhaps preferable to the former.

## BOOK III

### T'ĂNG WĂN KUNG.　PART I

滕文公章
句上
滕文公為
世子、將之楚、
過宋、而見孟
子孟子道性
善言必稱堯

CHAPTER I.　1. When the duke Wăn of T'ăng was crown prince, having to go to Ts'oo, he went by way of Sung, and visited Mencius.

2.　Mencius discoursed to him how the nature *of man* is good, and, when speaking, always made laudatory reference to Yaou and Shun.

TITLE OF THIS BOOK.—滕文公, "The Duke Wăn of T'ăng." The Book is so named from the duke Wăn, who is prominent in the first three chapters. Chaou K'e compares this with the title of the 15th Book of the Analects.

CH. 1. HOW ALL MEN BY DEVELOPING THEIR NATURAL GOODNESS MAY BECOME EQUAL TO THE ANCIENT SAGES. 1. The duke Wăn of T'ăng,—see I, Pt. II, xiii. Wăn is the posthumous title. The crown prince's name appears to have been Hwang (宏). Previous to the Han dynasty, the heirs apparent of the emperors and the princes of states were called indifferently 世子 and 太子. Since then, 太子 has been confined to the imperial heir. The title of 世子 was given, it is said, 欲其世世不絕, "to indicate the wish that the succession should be unbroken *from genera-* tion to generation." Ts'oo and T'ăng bordering on each other, the prince must have gone out of his way to visit Mencius. In the "Topography of the Four Books, Cont.," it is said: "Since T'ăng and Ts'oo ádjoined, so that one had only to lift his feet to pass into Ts'oo, why must the crown prince go round about, a distance of more than 350 li, to pass by the capital of Sung? The reason was that Mencius was there, and the prince's putting himself to so much trouble, in going and returning, shows his worthiness." 2. 道=言, a verb, "to speak or discourse about." 必, not "necessarily," but "he made it a point." 稱 is taken by Choo He and others in the sense of "to appeal to." This is supported by par. 3, but the word itself has only the meaning in the translation, with which, moreover, Chaou K'e agrees.

文王、我師也、周公豈欺我哉。

也、有爲者亦若是。公明儀曰、

哉。顏淵曰、舜何人也、予何人

丈夫也、我丈夫也、吾何畏彼

而已矣。成覸謂齊景公曰、彼

子曰、世子疑吾言乎、夫道、一

舜世子自楚反復見孟子。孟

3. When the crown prince was returning from Ts'oo, he again visited Mencius. Mencius said to him, "Prince, do you doubt my words? The path is one, and only one.

4. "Shing Kan said to the duke of Ts'e, 'They were men. I am a man. Why should I stand in awe of them?' Yen Yuen said, 'What kind of man was Shun? What kind of man am I? He who exerts himself will also become such as he was.' Kung-ming E said, 'King Wăn is my teacher. How should the duke of Chow deceive me *by those words?*'

3. 道一而已,—道 seems here to be used as in the Chung Yung, i, 1,— "an accordance with this nature is called the Path," but viewed here more in the consummation of high sageship and distinction to which it leads, which may be reached by treading it, and which can be reached in no other way. We have here for the first time the statement of Mencius's doctrine, which he subsequently dwells so much on, that "the nature of man is good." 4. Of Shing Kan we only know what is here said. 彼 丈 夫,—彼 referring to the sages. 丈 夫,—used for "man" or "men," with the idea of vigor and capability. Kung-ming E was a disciple first of Tsze-chang, and then of Tsăng Sin. 文王我師 would appear to have been a remark originally of Chow-kung, which E appropriates

故、吾欲使子問於孟子、然後

心終不忘今也不幸、至於大

昔者孟子嘗與我言於宋、於

滕定公薨、世子謂然友曰、

瞑眩、厥疾不瘳。

猶可以爲善國書 曰若藥不

今滕絕長補短、將五十里也、

5. "Now, T'ăng, taking its length with its breadth, will amount, I suppose, to fifty li. *It is small, but* still sufficient to make a good kingdom. It is said in the 'Book of History,' 'If medicine do not raise a commotion in the patient, his disease will not be cured by it.'"

CHAPTER II. 1. When the duke Ting of T'ăng died, the crown prince said to Yen Yew, "Formerly, Mencius spoke with me in Sung, and in my mind I have never forgotten *his words*. Now, alas! this great duty to my father devolves upon me; I wish to send you to ask the advice of Mencius, and then to proceed to its *various* services."

and vindicates on that high authority. 5. 絕長補短,—"cutting the long to supplement the short." Observe the force of 將, as in the translation. 猶—implying—"It is small, but still." 善國, comp. ch. iii—"a good kingdom" is such an one as is there described. 若藥云云,—see the Shoo-king, IV, viii, Sect. I, 8. 瞑, read *mĕen*, low. 3rd tone.

CH. 2. HOW MENCIUS ADVISED THE DUKE OF T'ANG TO CONDUCT THE MOURNING FOR HIS FATHER. 1. 薨 is the proper term to express the death of any of the princes of the empire. Yen Yew had been the prince's grand tutor (太 傅); I suppose that 然 is the surname. 大故 is a phrase applied to the funeral of, and mourning for, parents;—"the great cause,

矣三年之喪齊疏之服飦

未之學也雖然吾嘗聞之

禮可謂孝矣諸侯之禮吾

所自盡也曾子曰生事之

以禮死葬之以禮祭之以

孟子曰不亦善乎親喪固

行事然友之鄒問於孟子。二節

2. Yen Yew *accordingly* proceeded to Tsow, and
consulted Mencius. Mencius said, "Is this not good?
In discharging the funeral duties to parents, men
indeed feel constrained to do their utmost. The philosopher Tsăng said, 'When parents are alive, they
should be served according to propriety; when they
are dead, they should be buried according to propriety; and they should be sacrificed to according to
propriety:—this may be called filial piety.' The
ceremonies to be observed by the princes I have not
learned, but I have heard *these points:*—that the
three years' mourning, the garment of coarse cloth

or matter." 2. 之 鄒,—之 is the
verb, ＝往. 不 亦 善 乎,—spoken
with reference to the prince's sending
to consult him on such a subject.
親 喪 固 所 自 盡,—comp. Ana., XIX,
xvii. The words attributed to Tsăng
Sin were originally spoken by Confucius; see Ana., II, v. Tsăng may
have appropriated them, and spoken
them, so as to make them be
regarded as his own, or, what is
more likely, Mencius here makes a
slip of memory. 齊, up. 1st tone,
read *tsze*. See Con. Ana., IX, ix. 飦,

粥之食、自天子達於

庶人、三代共之然友

反命定爲三年之喪、

父兄百官皆不欲曰、

吾宗國魯先君莫之

行、吾先君亦莫之行

也、至於子之身而反

with its lower edge even, and the eating of congee, were equally prescribed by three dynasties, and binding on all, from the emperor to the mass of the people."

3. Yen Yew reported the execution of his commission, and *the prince* determined that the three years' mourning should be observed. His aged relatives, and the body of the officers, did not wish that it should be so, and said, "The former princes of Loo, that kingdom which we honor, have, none of them, observed this practice, neither have any of our own former princes observed it. For you to act contrary

as used in the text, read like and = 饘, denotes congee, like 粥, but made thicker. 3. 反命, "returned the commission," i. e., reported his execution of it and the reply. 世子 must be understood as the subject of 定. 父兄, "his fathers and brethren," i. e., his uncles and elderly ministers of the ducal family. The phrase is commonly applied by Chinese to the elders of their own surname, whatever be the degrees of their relationship. 吾宗國,—the ducal house of T'ang was descended from one of the sons of King Wăn (Shuh-sew, 叔繡), but by an inferior wife, while Chow-kung, the ancestor of Loo, was in the true imperial line, the author of all the civil institutions of the dynasty, and hence all the other states ruled by descendants of King Wăn were supposed to look up to Loo. That Chow-kung and the first rulers of T'ang had not observed

大事、子爲我問孟子。然友

不我足也、恐其不能盡於

馳馬試劍、今也父兄百官、

友曰、吾他日未嘗學問、好

祖、曰、吾有所受之也。謂然

之、不可、且志曰、喪祭從先

to their example is not proper. Moreover, the History says,—'In the observances of mourning and sacrifice, ancestors are to be followed,' meaning that they received those things from a *proper* source *to hand them down*."

4. *The prince said again* to Yen Yew; "Hitherto, I have not given myself to the pursuit of learning, but have found my pleasure in horsemanship and sword exercise and now I don't come up to the wishes of my aged relatives and the officers. I am afraid I may not be able to discharge my duty in the great business *that I have entered on;* do you *again* consult Mencius for me." *On this,* Yen Yew went

the three years' mourning is not to be supposed. The crown prince's remonstrants are wrong in attributing to them the neglect of later dukes. 志,—what particular "history" they refer to is not known. 吾有所受之,—吾 is to be understood as spoken in the person of the ancestors, and I have therefore rendered it by "they." Chaou K'e, however, says that some made this a reply of the prince:—"The prince said, *I have one (i. e., Mencius) from whom I received it.*" 4. 不我足=不以我足滿其意, as in the translation. 恐其不能,—"I am afraid of the not being able, etc." It is the sentiment of the prince himself, and 恐 must be translated in the first person, and not in the third, as

德風也、小人之德草也、草

下必有甚焉者矣、君子之

敢不哀先之也、上有好者、

墨、即位而哭、百官有司莫

君薨、聽於冢宰、歠粥、面深

不可以他求者也、孔子曰、

復之鄒、問孟子。孟子曰、然、

again to Tsow, and consulted Mencius. Mencius said,
"It is so, but he may not seek *a remedy* in others *but
only in himself.* Confucius said, 'When a prince dies,
his successor intrusts the administration to the prime
minister. He sips the congee. His face is of a deep
black. He approaches the place *of mourning*, and
weeps. Of all the officers and inferior ministers there
is not one who will presume not to join in the lamentation, he setting them this example. What the superior
loves, his inferiors will be found to love exceedingly.
The relation between superiors and inferiors is like
that between the wind and grass. The grass must

Julien does. In the 其 there is a
reference to his antecedents, as
occasioning the present difficulty.
不 可 以 他 求 is taken by Chaou
K'e, "You may not seek (to overcome their opposition) by any other
way, (but carrying out what you
have begun)." Choo He's view, as
in the translation, is better. In the
quotations from Confucius, Mencius

has blended different places of the
Analects together, and enlarged them
to suit his own purpose, or, it may
be, the text of the Ana. was different
in his time. See Con. Ana., XIV,
xviii, XII, xiv. 即 位 而 哭,—the
位 is the place where the coffin lay,
during the five months that elapsed
between the death and interment,

知、官族誠命在尚
及人在世世之
至可未我子子風
葬謂有五曰、曰、必
四曰命月然然偃、
方戒、居是友是
　　　百　　反

bend, when the wind blows upon it.' The business
depends on the prince."

5. Yen Yew returned with this answer to his commission, and the prince said, "It is so. The matter
does indeed depend on me." So for five months he
dwelt in the shed, without issuing an order or a
caution. All the officers and his relatives said, "He
may be said to understand *the ceremonies*." When
the time of interment arrived, from all quarters of the

5. The 盧 was a shed, built of
boards and straw, outside the center
door of the palace, against the surrounding wall, which the mourning
prince tenanted till the interment:
see the Le-ke, XXII, ii, 16. 可謂曰
知, is supposed by Choo He, with
reason, to be corrupted or defective.
I have translated as if it were 曰可
謂 知.—Choo He introduces here,
the following remarks from the commentator Lin (林):—"In the time of
Mencius, although the rites to the
dead had fallen into neglect, yet
the three years' mourning, with the
sorrowing heart and afflictive grief,
being the expression of what really
belongs to man's mind, had not
quite perished. Only, sunk in the

slough of manners becoming more
and more corrupt, men were losing
all their moral nature without being
conscious of it. When Duke Wăn
saw Mencius, and heard him speak
of the goodness of man's nature, and
of Yaou and Shun, that was the
occasion of moving and bringing
forth his better heart, and on this
occasion,—of the death of his father,
—he felt sincerely all the stirrings of
sorrow and grief. Then, moreover,
when his older relatives and his
officers wished not to act as he
desired, he turned inwards to reprove himself, and lamented his
former conduct which made him not
be believed in his present course,
not presuming to blame his officers

乘屋其始播百穀。
茅宵爾索綯亟其
緩也詩云畫爾于
孟子曰、民事不可
膝文公問爲國。
悅。
哭泣之哀弔者大
來觀之顏色之戚、

state, they came to witness it.　Those who had come *from other states* to condole with him, were greatly pleased with the deep dejection of his countenance and the mournfulness of his wailing and weeping.

CHAPTER III.　1.　The duke Wăn of T'ăng asked *Mencius* about *the proper way of* governing a kingdom.

2.　Mencius said, "The business of the people may not be remissly attended to.　It is said in the 'Book of Poetry,'

> 'In the daylight go and gather the grass,
> And at night twist your ropes;
> Then get up quickly on the roofs;—
> *Soon* must we begin sowing *again* the grain.'

and relatives:—although we must concede an extraordinary natural excellence and ability to him, yet his energy in learning may not be impeached.　Finally, when we consider how with what decision he finally acted, and how all, near and far, who saw and heard him, were delighted to acknowledge and admire his conduct, we have an instance of how, when that which belongs to all men's minds is in the first place exhibited by one, others are brought, without any previous purpose, to the pleased acknowledgment and approval of it:—is not this a proof that, it is indeed true that *the nature of man is good?*"

CH. 3.　MENCIUS'S COUNSELS TO THE DUKE OF T'ANG FOR THE GOVERNMENT OF HIS KINGDOM.　AGRICULTURE AND EDUCATION ARE THE CHIEF THINGS TO BE ATTENDED TO, AND THE FIRST AS AN ESSENTIAL PREPARATION FOR THE SECOND.　1.　爲, in the sense of 治, "to govern."　2.　By 民事, "the business of the people," is intended husbandry.　For the ode, see the She-king, I, xv, Ode 1, st. 7, written, it is said, by Chow-kung, to impress the emperor Ching with a sense of the importance and toils of

民之爲道也、有恆產者有恆心、

無恆產者、無恆心、苟無恆心、放

辟邪侈、無不爲已、及陷乎罪、然

後從而刑之、是罔民也、焉有仁

人在位、罔民而可爲也、是故賢

3. "The way of the people is this.—If they have a certain livelihood, they will have a fixed heart. If they have not a certain livelihood, they have not a fixed heart. And if they have not a fixed heart, there is nothing which they will not do in the way of self-abandonment, of moral deflection, of depravity, and of wild license. When they have thus been involved in crime, to follow them up and punish them:—this is to entrap the people. How can such a thing as entrapping the people be done under the rule of a benevolent man?

4. "Therefore, a ruler who is endowed with talents

husbandry. 3. Comp. I, Pt. I, vii, 19. In 民之爲道, the 道 is to be taken lightly, as if the expression were 民之爲民也,="As to the people's being the people," i. e., the character of the people is as follows. 4. 必,—not "must be," which would be inconsistent with the 賢,

助周人百畝而
貢殷人七十而
夏后氏五十而
矣、爲仁不富矣。
虎曰、爲富不仁
取於民有制。陽
君必恭儉禮下、

and virtue will be gravely complaisant and economical, showing a respectful politeness to his ministers,
and taking from the people only in accordance with
regulated limits.

5. "Yang Hoo said, 'He who seeks to be rich will
not be benevolent. He who wishes to be benevolent
will not be rich.'

6. "The sovereign of the Hea dynasty enacted the
fifty *mow* allotment, and the payment of a tax. The
founder of the Yin enacted the seventy *mow* allotment, and the system of mutual aid. The founder of
the Chow enacted the hundred *mow* allotment, and

but "will be," i. e., will be sure to be.
The two last clauses are exegetical
of 恭 and 儉. 下 must be understood
of 臣, "ministers," in contradistinction from the 民, "people," in the
next clause, though all are of course
"beneath" the ruler. 5. This Yang
Hoo is the Yang Ho, of the Con.
Ana., XVII, i. To accord with his
unworthy character, the observation
is taken in a bad sense, as a dis-
suasive against the practice of benevolence, while Mencius quotes it to
show the incompatibility of the two
aims. Great stress is laid on the
爲. 爲富, 爲仁,—"He who makes
riches,—benevolence,—his busi-

ness." This force of the character
would be well brought out by putting
it low. 3rd tone, but that would give
the observation a good meaning. 6.
夏后氏, 殷人, 周人,—see Con. Ana.,
III, xx. By the Hea statutes, every
husbandman,—head of a family,—
received 50 *mow*, and paid the produce of five of them to the government. This payment was the 貢.
By those of Yin, 630 *mow* were
divided into 9 equal allotments of
70 *mow* each, the central one being
reserved for the government, and 8
families on the other allotments uniting in its cultivation. By those of
Chow, to one family 100 *mow* were

爲虐、則寡取之、凶年、糞其

歲粒米狼戾、多取之、而不

者、校數歲之中以爲常、樂

莫善於助、莫不善於貢、貢

也、助者、藉也。龍子曰治地

徹其實、皆什一也、徹者、徹

the share system. In reality, *what was paid* in all these was a tithe. The share system means mutual division. The aid system means mutual dependence.

. 7. "Lung said, 'For regulating the lands, there is no better system than that of mutual aid, and none which is not better than that of taxing. By the tax system, the regular amount was fixed by taking the average of several years. In good years, when the grain lies about in abundance, much might be taken without its being oppressive, and the actual exaction would be small. But in bad years, the produce being

assigned, and ten families cultivated 1,000 acres in common, dividing the produce, and paying a tenth to government. Such is the account here given by Mencius, but it is very general, and not to be taken, especially as relates to the system of the Chow dynasty, as an accurate exposition of it. More in accordance with the accounts in the *Chow Le* is his own system recommended below to Peih Chen. 7. Of the Lung quoted here, all that Chaou K'e and Choo

He say, is that he was "an ancient worthy." 狼戾 is said to be synonymous with 狼藉, meaning "abundant." That this is the signification is plain enough, but how the characters come to indicate it is not clear. 狼 means "a wolf," and 藉 is given in connection with that character as meaning "the appearance of things scattered about in confusion." I can't find any signification of 戾, "crooked, perverse, etc.," from which, as joined to 狼,

田而不足、則必取盈焉、爲
民父母、使民盻盻然、將終
歲勤動、不得以養其父母、
又稱貸而益之、使老稚轉
乎溝壑、惡在其爲民父母
也。夫世祿滕固行之矣詩
云、雨我公田、遂及我私、惟

not sufficient to repay the manuring of the fields, this system still requires the taking of the full amount. When the parent of the people causes the people to wear looks of distress, and, after the whole year's toil, yet not to be able to nourish their parents, so that they proceed to borrowing to increase their means, till the old people and children are found lying in the ditches and water channels:—where, *in such a case,* is his parental relation to the people?'

8. "As to the system of hereditary salaries, that is already observed in T'ăng.

9. "It is said in the 'Book of Poetry,'

'May the rain come down on our public field,
And then upon our private fields!'

we can well bring out the meaning. 盻盻然 is taken by Chaou K'e as in the translation, and by Choo He, ="an angry-looking appearance," which does not suit so well. 稱=舉, "to lift up,"="to proceed to." 惡 (up. 1st tone) 在其爲民父母,—see I, Pt. I, iv, 15. 8. 夫,—low. 1st tone. 世祿,—see I, Pt. II, v, 3. 9. See the She-king, II, vi, Ode VIII, st. 3, a description of husbandry under the Chow dynasty. 雨,—the

助爲有公田、由此觀
之、雖周亦助也。設爲
庠、序、學、校、以教之庠
者、養也、校者、教也序
者、射也、夏曰校、殷曰
序、周曰庠、學則三代
共之、皆所以明人倫

It is only in the system of mutual aid that there is a public field, and from this passage we perceive that even in the Chow dynasty this system has been recognized.

10. "Establish *ts'ëang, seu, heŏ,* and *heaou,—all those educational institutions,*—for the instruction of *the people.* The name *ts'ëang* indicates nourishing *as its object; heaou* indicates teaching; and *seu* indicates archery. By the Hea dynasty, the name *heaou* was used; by the Yin, that of *seu;* and by the Chow, that of *ts'ëang.* As to the *heŏ,* they belonged to the three dynasties, *and by that name.* The object of them all

verb, up. 3rd tone. The object of the quotation is to show that the system of mutual aid obtained under the Chow as well as under the Yin dynasty, and the way is prepared for the instructions given to Peih Chen below. 10. After the due regulation of husbandry, and provision for the "certain livelihood" of the people, must come the business of education. The *heŏ* mentioned were schools of a higher order in the capital of the empire and other chief cities of the various states. The others (校, *heaou,* low. 3rd tone) were schools in the villages and smaller towns. In the Le Ke, V, v, 10, we find the *ts'ëang* mentioned in connection with the time of Shun; *seu,* in connection with the Hea dynasty; *heŏ,* in connection with the Yin; and *Keaou* (膠), in connection with the *Chow.* There is thus a want of harmony between that passage and the account in the text. Entertainments were given to the aged at different times, and in the schools, as an example to the young of the

子力行之亦以新子之國。

邦、其命維新、文王之謂也、

爲王者師也。詩云、周雖舊

下。有王者起、必來取法、是

也、人倫明於上、小民親於

is to illustrate the human relations. When those are *thus* illustrated by superiors, kindly feeling will prevail among the inferior people below.

11. "Should a real sovereign arise, he will certainly come and take an example *from you;* and thus you will be the teacher of the true sovereign.

12. "It is said in the 'Book of Poetry,'

> 'Although Chow was an old country,
> It received a new destiny.'

That is said with reference to King Wăn. Do you practice those things with vigor, and you also will by them make new your kingdom."

reverence accorded by the govt. to age. So the schools were selected for the practice of archery, as a trial of virtue and skill. 人倫明於上,—this can hardly mean, "when the human relations have been illustrated by the example of superiors," but must have reference to the inculca-tion of those relations by the institution of schools. The pith of Mencius's advice is—"Provide the means of education for all, the poor as well as the rich." 12. See the She-king, III, i, Ode I, st. 1. 其命,—"the appointment," i. e., which lighted on

均、穀祿不平、是故暴君汙

經界始、經界不正井地不

子、子必勉之夫仁政必自

之君、將行仁政選擇而使

十三節
使畢戰、問井地孟子曰子

13. *The duke afterwards* sent Peih Chen to consult *Mencius* about the nine-squares system of dividing the land. Mencius said to him, "Since your prince, wishing to put in practice a benevolent government, has made choice of you and put you into this employment, you must exert yourself to the utmost. Now, the first thing towards a benevolent government must be to lay down the boundaries. If the boundaries be not defined correctly, the division of the land into squares will not be equal, and the produce *available for* salaries will not be evenly distributed. On this account, oppressive rulers and impure ministers are

it from Heaven. 13. To understand the "nine-squares division of the land," the form of the character 井 needs only to be looked at. If we draw lines to inclose it—thus, 田一, we have a square portion of ground divided into nine equal and smaller squares. But can we suppose it possible to divide a territory in this way? The natural irregularities of the surface would be one great obstacle. And we find below the

吏、必慢其經界、經界

既正、分田制祿、可坐

而定也。夫滕壤地褊
○十四節

小、將爲君子焉、將爲

野人焉、無君子、莫治

野人、無野人、莫養君

子請野、九一而助、國
○十五節

sure to neglect this defining of the boundaries. When
the boundaries have been defined correctly, the division of the fields and the regulation of allowances may
be determined by you, sitting at your ease.

14. "Although the territory of T'ăng is narrow
and small, yet there must be in it men of a superior
grade, and there must be in it countrymen. If there
were not men of a superior grade, there would be
none to rule the countrymen. If there were not
countrymen, there would be none to support the men
of superior grade.

15. "I would ask you, in the remoter districts,
observing the nine-squares division, to reserve one
division to be cultivated on the system of mutual aid,

"holy field," and other assignments,
which must continually have been
requiring new arrangement of the
boundaries. 14. 君子,—here, generally, for officers, men not earning
their bread by the sweat of their
brow, and the toil of their hands;
see next chapter. 野人,—"countrymen," = by their toil self-support-
ing people generally. 將=殆;將爲

=殆必有. 15. Here the systems of
all the three dynasties would seem
to be employed, as the nature of the
country permitted, or made advis-
able, their application. 野 as opposed
to 國中 must be understood, as
in the translation, = "the country,"
"the remoter districts." The 九
refers to 公田 in par. 13, and the 一
to 制祿. The former would be the

中、什一使自賦。

卿以下、必有圭【十六節】

田、圭田、五十畝。

餘夫二十五畝。【十七節】

死徙、無出鄉、鄉【十八節】

田同井、出入相

友、守望相助、疾

and in the more central parts of the kingdom, to make the people pay for themselves a tenth part of their produce.

16. "From the highest officers down to the lowest, each one must have his holy field, consisting of fifty *mow*.

17. "Let the supernumerary males have their twenty-five *mow*.

18. "On occasions of death, or removal from one dwelling to another, there will be no quitting the district. In the fields of a district, those who belong. to the same nine squares render all friendly offices to one another in their going out and coming in, aid one another in keeping watch and ward, and

best way in such positions of supporting the 野人, and the latter of supporting the 君子. Similarly, the other clause. 16. 圭 is explained by Chaou K'e by 潔, and Choo He follows him, though we do not find this meaning of the term in the dictionary. The 圭田 then is "the clean field," and as its produce was intended to supply the means of sacrifice, I translate it by "the holy field." It was in addition to the hereditary salary mentioned in par.

8. 17. A family was supposed to embrace the grandfather and grandmother, the husband, wife, and children, the husband being the grandparents' eldest son. The extra fields were for other sons whom they might have, and were given to them when they were sixteen. When they married and became heads of families themselves, they received the regular allotment for a family. This is Choo He's account of this paragraph. 18. The moral benefits

與子矣。

略也、若夫潤澤之、則在君

事、所以別野人也。此其大

公田公事畢、然後敢治私

公田、八家皆私百畝、同養

里而井、井、九百畝其中爲

病相扶持、則百姓親睦方

sustain one another in sickness. Thus the people are brought to live in affection and harmony.

19. "A square li covers nine squares of land, which nine squares contain nine hundred *mow*. The central square is the public field, and eight families, each having its private hundred *mow*, cultivate in common the public field. And not till public work is finished, may they presume to attend to their private affairs. This is the way by which the countrymen are distinguished *from those of a superior grade.*

20. "Those are the great outlines of the system. Happily to modify and adapt it depends on the prince and you."

flowing from the nine-squares division of the land. "On occasions of death," i. e., in burying. 19. Under the Chow dynasty, 100 *poo* or "paces" made a *mow's* length, but the exact amount of the pace can hardly be ascertained. Many contend that the 50 *mow* of Hea, the 70 of Yin, and the 100 of Chow, were actually of the same dimensions. 養,—low. 3rd tone, so spoken always, when the subject is the support of a superior by an inferior. 20. 若夫 (low. 1st tone),＝至於. 潤澤, "the softening and moistening," i. e., the modifying and adapting.

願受一廛而　聞君行仁政、　曰、遠方之人、　門而告文公　自楚之滕、踵　之言者、許行、　有爲神農

CHAPTER IV. 1. There came from Ts‘oo to T‘áng one Heu Hing, who gave out that he acted according to the words of Shin-nung. Coming right to his gate, he addressed the duke Wăn, saying, "A man of a distant region, I have heard that you, prince, are practicing a benevolent government, and I wish to receive a site for a house, and to become one of your

CH. 4. MENCIUS'S REFUTATION OF THE DOCTRINE THAT THE RULER OUGHT TO LABOR AT HUSBANDRY WITH HIS OWN HANDS. HE VINDICATES THE PROPRIETY OF THE DIVISION OF LABOR, AND OF A LETTERED CLASS CONDUCTING GOVERNMENT. The first three paragraphs, it is said, relate how Hing, the heresiarch, and Seang, his follower, wished secretly to destroy the arrangements advised by Mencius for the division of the land. The next eight pars. expose the head error of Hing, that the ruler must labor at the toils of husbandry as well as the people. From the 12th par. to the 16th, Seang is rebuked for forsaking his master, and taking up with Hing's heresy. In the last two pars., Mencius proceeds, from the evasive replies of Seang, to give the *coup de grâce* to the new pernicious teachings. 1. 爲 is explained, by Chaou K‘e, by 治爲, and 言 as =道, so that 爲

... 言 者 = "one who cultivated the doctrines." Most others take 爲=假託, "making a false pretense of." Shin-nung, "wonderful husbandman," is the style of the 2nd of the five famous 帝, or "emperors," of Chinese history. He is also called Yen (炎) Te, "the blazing emperor." He is placed between Fuh-he, and Hwang Te, though separated from the latter by an intervention of seven reigns, extending with his own over 515 years. If any faith could be reposed in this chronology, it would place him 3272 B.C. In the appendix to the Yih-king, he is celebrated as the Father of husbandry. Other traditions make him the Father of medicine also. 之滕, —之 is the verb, =往. 踵, in the dict., after Chaou K‘e, is explained by 至, "came to." Choo He says that 踵門=足至門. 廛 and 垠, see Pt. II, v, 5, but the meaning of 廛 here is different, denoting the ground

是亦聖人也、願爲聖

曰、聞君行聖人之政、

負耒耜、而自宋之滕、

之徒陳相以其弟辛、

屨織席以爲食。陳良

徒數十人、皆衣褐、捆

爲氓。文公與之處、其

people." The duke Wăn gave him a dwelling place. His disciples, amounting to several tens, all wore clothes of haircloth, and made sandals of hemp and wove mats for a living.

2. *At the same time,* Ch'in Seang, a disciple of Ch'in Leang, and his younger brother, Sin, with their plow handles and shares on their backs, came from Sung to T'ang, saying, "We have heard that you, prince, are putting into practice the government of the *ancient* sages, *showing that* you are likewise a sage. We wish to become the subjects of a sage."

assigned for the dwelling of a husbandman. 衣 (up. 3rd tone) 褐,—it would appear from par. 4, that this "haircloth" was a very inartificial structure, not woven at least with any art. 屨,—"sandals of hemp," opposed to 扉, which were made of grass, and 履 which were made of leather. 捆 is explained by 扣椓, "to beat and hammer." 席 properly denotes single mats made of rushes (莞蒲). This manufacture of sandals and mats is supposed in the 備旨 to have been only a temporary employment of Hing's followers till lands should be assigned them. 2. Of the individuals mentioned here, we know nothing more than can be gathered from this chapter. The 耜, or share, as originally made by Shin-nung, was of wood. In Mencius's time, it had come to be made of iron; see

殫而治今也、滕有倉廩府

也、賢者、與民並耕而食饔

則誠賢君也、雖然、未聞道

孟子、道許行之言曰、滕君、

盡棄其學而學焉。陳相見

人氓。陳相見許行而大悅、

3. When Ch'in Seang saw Heu Hing, he was greatly pleased with him, and, abandoning entirely whatever he had learned, became his disciple. Having an interview with Mencius, he related to him *with approbation* the words of Heu Hing to the following effect:—"The prince of T'ang is indeed a worthy prince. He has not yet heard, however, the *real* doctrines *of antiquity*. Now, wise and able princes should cultivate the ground equally and along with their people, and eat *the fruit of their labor*. They should prepare their own meals, morning and evening, while at the same time they carry on their government. But now, *the prince of* T'ang has his granaries,

par. 4. 之滕,—之 as above. 3. 道許行之言,—道 is the verb,=稱述. 賢者,—as in I, Pt. I, ii, 1. 饔飧 denote the morning and evening meals, but must be taken here as verbs, signifying the preparation of those meals. If 倉 and 廩 are to be distinguished, the latter is a granary

庫、則是厲民而以自養也、

惡得賢孟子曰許子必種

粟而後食乎。曰、然許子必

織布而後衣乎。曰否、許子

衣褐。曰、許子冠乎。曰、冠。曰、

奚冠。曰冠素。曰自織之與。

曰否以粟易之曰許子奚

為不自織。曰害於耕。曰、許

treasuries, and arsenals, which is an oppressing of the people to nourish himself.—How can he be deemed a *real* worthy prince ? "

4. Mencius said, "I suppose that Heu Hing sows grain and eats the produce. Is it not so?" "It is so," was the answer. "I suppose *also* he weaves cloth, and wears his own manufacture. Is it not so?" "No, Heu wears clothes of haircloth." "Does he wear a cap?" "He wears a cap." "What kind of cap?" "A plain cap." "Is it woven by himself?" "No, he gets it in exchange for grain." "Why does Heu not weave it himself?" "That would injure his husbandry." "Does Heu cook his

for rice, the former for other grain. 養, low. 3rd tone. The object of Heu Hing in these remarks would be to invalidate Mencius's doctrine given in the last chap., par. 14, that the ruler must be supported by the countrymen. 4. Observe the force of 必 ... 乎, as in the translation. 粟,—"millet," but here = grain generally. 衣,—up. 3rd tone. 冠素, "his cap is plain," i. e., undyed and unadorned. The distinction given by Choo He

然、與百工交易、何許子之
其宮中而用之、何爲紛紛
子何不爲陶冶舍皆取諸
粟者豈爲厲農夫哉、且許
陶冶、陶冶亦以其械器易
之以粟易械器者、不爲厲
然。自爲之與。曰否以粟易
子以釜甑爨、以鐵耕乎曰、

food in boilers and earthenware pans, and does he plow with an iron share?" "Yes." "Does he make those articles himself?" "No, he gets them in exchange for grain."

5. *Mencius then said*, "The getting those various articles in exchange for grain, is not oppressive to the potter and the founder, and the potter and the founder in their turn, in exchanging their various articles for grain are not oppressive to the husband-man. How should such a thing be supposed? And moreover, why does not Heu act the potter and founder, supplying himself with the articles which he uses solely from his own establishment? Why does he go confusedly dealing and exchanging with the handicraftsmen? Why does he not spare himself so

between 釜 and 甑 is, that the former was used for boiling, and the latter for steaming. Their composition indicates that they were made of iron and clay, respectively. The 釜 was distinguished from other iron boilers by having no feet. 5. 以 . . . 者 = "he who gets, etc." 械,—prop. erly "stocks," but also used synony- mously with 器. I have added a sentence to bring out the force of 豈 in 豈爲厲 云云. Choo He puts a point at 冶, and taking 舍 (up. 3rd tone) in the sense of 止, "only," construes it with what follows. This is better than to join it, in the sense of house or shop, with 陶冶. Seang is here forced to make an admission,

如必自爲而後用之、

身、而百工之所爲備、

小人之事且一人之

爲與、有大人之事有

則治天下、獨可耕且

固不可耕且爲也。然 六郡

不憚煩曰、百工之事、

much trouble?"　*Ch'in Seang replied,* "The business of the handicraftsman can by no means be carried on along with the business of husbandry."

6.　*Mencius resumed,* "Then, is it the government of the empire which alone can be carried on along with the practice of husbandry? Great men have their proper business, and little men have their proper business. Moreover, in the case of any single individual, *whatever articles he can require* are ready to his hand, being produced by the various handicraftsmen:—if he must first make them for his own use,

fatal to his new master's doctrine, that every man should do every thing for himself. The only difficulty is with the 且, which here="but." The two preceding sentences are Mencius's affirmations, and he proceeds—"But Heu Hing denies this. Why then does he not himself play the potter and founder, etc.?" 6. In 一人之身, 而百工之所作備, the construction is not easy. The correct meaning seems to be that given in the translation. Some take 備 in the sense of "are all required," which would make the construction simpler:—"for a single person even, all the productions of the handicraftsmen are necessary." So, in the paraphrase of the 日講:—"Reckoning in the case of a single individual, for his clothes, his food, and his dwelling place, the productions of the various workers must all be completed in sufficiency, and then he has abundantly every thing for profitable employment, and can without anxiety support his children and parents." This gives a good enough meaning in the connection, but the signification attached to 備 is hardly otherwise authorized. 而路,—"and

是率天下而路也、故
曰、或勞心、或勞力、勞
心者治人、勞力者治
於人、治於人者食人、
治人者食於人、天下
之通義也。當堯之時、
天下猶未平、洪水橫
流、氾濫於天下、草木

this way of doing would keep the whole empire running about upon the roads.   Hence, there is the saying, 'Some labor with their minds, and some labor with their strength.   Those who labor with their minds govern others; those who labor with their strength are governed by others.   Those who are governed by others support them; those who govern others are supported by them.'   This is a principle universally recognized.

7.   "In the time of Yaou, when the world had not yet been perfectly reduced to order, the vast waters, flowing out of their channels, made a universal inundation.   Vegetation was luxuriant, and birds and

road them"＝奔走道路.　食,—low. 3rd tone, *tsze*.　7.　天下猶未平 carries us back to the time antecedent to Yaou, and 天下 is to be taken in the sense of "world," or "earth." There is the idea of a wild, confused, chaotic state, on which the successive sages had been at work, without any great amount of success.   Then in the next par. we have How-tseih doing over again the work of Shin-nung and teaching men husbandry.

We can hardly go beyond Yaou for the founding of the Chinese Empire. The various questions which would arise here, however, will be found discussed in the first part of the Shoo-king.   It is only necessary to observe in reference to the calamity here spoken of, that it is not presented as the consequence of a deluge, or sudden accumulation of water, but from the natural river channels being all broken up and

烈山澤而焚之、禽獸逃匿、

而敷治焉、舜使益掌火、益

交於中國、堯獨憂之、舉舜

禽獸偪人、獸蹄鳥跡之道、

暢茂、禽獸繁殖、五穀不登、

beasts swarmed. The various kinds of grain could not be grown. The birds and beasts pressed upon men. The paths marked by the feet of beasts and prints of birds, crossed one another throughout the Middle Kingdom. To Yaou alone this caused anxious sorrow. He raised Shun to office, and measures to regulate the disorder were set forth. Shun committed to Yih the direction of the fire to be employed, and Yih set fire to, and consumed, *the forests and vegetation on* the mountains and *in* the marshes, so that the birds and beasts fled away to hide themselves. Yu

disordered 橫,—low. 3rd tone, "disobedient," "unreasonable." 五穀, "the five kinds of grains," are 稻, 黍, 稷, 麥, and 菽, "paddy, millet, panicled millet, wheat, and pulse," but each of these terms must be taken as comprehending several varieties under it. 中國, in opposition to 天下, is the portion of country which was first settled, and regarded as a center to all surrounding territories. 堯獨憂之,—the 獨 seems to refer to Yaou's position as emperor, in which it belonged to him to feel this anxiety. For the labors of Shun, Yih, and Yu, see

乎。后稷教民稼穡、樹藝五

過其門而不入、雖欲耕得

當是時也、禹八年於外、三

江、然後中國可得而食也、

海、決汝漢、排淮泗、而注之

禹疏九河、瀹濟漯而注諸

separated the nine streams, cleared the courses of the Tse and T'ăh, and led them all to the sea. He opened a vent also for the Joo and Han, and regulated the course of the· Hwae and Sze, so that they all flowed into the Këang. When this was done, it became possible for the people of the Middle Kingdom to *cultivate the ground and* get food for themselves. During that time, Yu was eight years away from his home, and though he thrice passed the door of it, he did not enter. · Although he had wished to cultivate the ground, could he have done so?

8. "The minister of agriculture taught the people to sow and reap, cultivating the five kinds of grain.

the Shoo-king, Parts I, II, III. 濟,— up. 2nd tone. 漯,＝read T'ăh. The nine streams all belonged to the Ho, or Yellow River. By them Yu led off a portion of its vast surging waters. The Këang is the Yangtze. Choo He observes that of the rivers mentioned as being led into the Këang only the Han flows into that stream, while the Hwae receives the Joo and the Sze, and makes a direct course to the sea. He supposes an error on the part of the recorder of Mencius's words. 8. How-tseih, now received as a proper name, is properly the official title of Shun's minister of agriculture, K'e (棄). 契, (read Sëĕ) was the name of his minister of instruction. For these men and their works, see the Shoo-king, Pt. II. 藝,—used synonymously with 蓺,＝種, "to plant," or

君臣有義夫婦有別、長

徒教以人倫父子有親、

聖人有憂之使契爲司

居而無教則近於禽獸、

之有道也、飽食煖衣、逸

穀、五穀熟而民人育、人

When the five kinds of grain were brought to maturity, the people all enjoyed a comfortable subsistence. Now men possess a moral nature; but if they are well fed, warmly clad, and comfortably lodged, without being taught at the same time, they become almost like the beasts. This was a subject of anxious solicitude to the sage *Shun*, and he appointed Seĕ to be the minister of instruction, to teach the relations of humanity:—how, between father and son, there should be affection; between sovereign and minister, righteousness; between husband and wife, attention to their separate functions; between old and

"sow." 人之有道也, I have translated according to Choo He's view of the meaning, in which he is now universally followed, so far as I know. It requires the understanding, however, of 然 or 但 before the next clause, which does not appear to me to be admissible. Chaou K'e, or at least his paraphrast, understands it thus:—"Thus, men were provided with a proper course for their nourishment. They might be well fed and clothed, but with all this, if they are not taught, they

become, etc." This avoids the harshness of understanding any thing before 飽, but the interpretation, otherwise, is not natural. May we not take 人之有道也 as synonymous with the clause 民之爲道也, in ch. iii, par. 2? The translation would then be—"Now, the way of men is this:—if they are well fed, etc." 聖人 is supposed to be plural,—"the sages." This, however, cannot be, as the 使 immediately following must be understood with reference to Shun only. What has made 聖人 be taken

幼有序、朋友有信放動
曰、勞之來之匡之直之、
輔之翼之使自得之、又
從而振德之聖人之憂
民如此、而暇耕乎堯以
不得舜爲己憂、舜以不
得禹皐陶爲己憂、夫以
百畝之不易爲己憂者、

young, a proper order; and between friends, fidelity. The highly meritorious *emperor* said to him, 'Encourage them; lead them on; rectify them; straighten them; help them; give them wings:—thus causing them to become possessors of themselves. Then follow this up by stimulating them, and conferring benefits on them.' When the sages were exercising their solicitude for the people in this way, had they leisure to cultivate the ground?

9. "What Yaou felt giving him anxiety, was the not getting Shun. What Shun felt giving him anxiety was the not getting Yu and Kaou-yaou. But he whose anxiety is about his hundred *mow* not being properly cultivated, is a *mere* husbandman.

as plural, is that the instructions addressed to Seĕ are said to be from 放 (up. 2nd tone) 勳, which are two of the epithets applied to Yaou in the opening sentence of the Shoo-king, who is therefore supposed to be the speaker. Yet it was Shun who appointed Seĕ, and gave him his instructions, and may not Mencius intend *him* by "The highly meritorious"? The address itself is not found in the Shoo-king: 勞 and

來 are both low. 3rd tone. In 夫婦 有 別, 別 is the up. 4th tone,="separate functions," according to which the husband is said to preside over all that is external, and the wife over all that is internal, while to the former it belongs to lead, and to the latter to follow. 9. An illustration of the 有大人之事, 有小人之事, in par. 6. 易,—read low. 3rd tone, in the sense of 治 (low. 1st tone).

則之蕩蕩乎、民無能名焉君
哉、堯之爲君惟天爲大惟堯
易、爲天下得人難孔子曰、大
者、謂之仁、是故以天下與人
人以善、謂之忠爲天下得人
農夫也分人以財謂之惠教

10. "The imparting by a man to others of his wealth is called 'a kindness.' The teaching others what is good is called 'the exercise of fidelity.' The finding a man who shall benefit the empire is called 'benevolence.' Hence to give the empire to another man would be easy; to find a man who shall benefit the empire is difficult.

11. "Confucius said, 'Great indeed was Yaou as a sovereign. It is only heaven that is great, and only Yaou corresponded to it. How vast was his virtue! The people could find no name for it. Princely

10. 爲,—low. 3rd tone, "on behalf of,"=who shall benefit. 易,—read as above, but meaning "easy." The difficulty spoken of arises from this, that to find the man in question requires the finder to go out of himself, is beyond what is in his own power. The reader must bear in mind that 仁 is the name for the highest virtue, the combination of all possible virtues. Comp. Ana., VI, xxviii. 11. See Con. Ana., VIII, xviii and xix, which two chapters Mencius blends together with omissions and

尼之道、北學於中國、北方之

者也、陳良楚產也、悅周公仲

聞用夏變夷者、未聞變於夷

用其心哉、亦不用於耕耳吾
<br>〇十二
節

與焉、堯舜之治天下、豈無所

哉、舜也、巍巍乎、有天下而不

indeed was Shun! How majestic was he, having possession of the empire, and yet seeming as if it were
nothing to him!' In their governing the empire,
were there no subjects on which Yaou and Shun
employed their minds? There were subjects, only
they did not employ their minds on the cultivation of
the ground.

12. "I have heard of men using *the doctrines of* our
great land to change barbarians, but I have never yet
heard of any being changed by barbarians. Ch'in
Leang was a native of Ts'oo. Pleased with the
doctrines of Chow-kung and Chung-ne, he came
northwards to the Middle Kingdom and studied them.
Among the scholars of the northern regions, there was

alterations. Observe the force of 亦
in the last clause. It = "there were
subjects, on which they employed

their minds, but still, etc." 12. 夏
and 夷,—used as in Con. Ana., III,

於子貢、相嚮而哭、皆失聲、然後

三年之外、門人治任將歸入揖

年、師死而遂倍之昔者、孔子沒、

傑之士也、子之兄弟、事之數十

學者、未能或之先也、彼所謂豪

perhaps none who excelled him. He was what you call a scholar of high and distinguished qualities. You and your brother followed him some tens of years, and when your master died, you have forthwith turned away from him.

13. "Formerly, when Confucius died, after three years had elapsed, his disciples collected their baggage, and prepared to return to their several homes. But on entering to take their leave of Tsze-kung, as they looked towards one another, they wailed, till they all lost their voices. After this they returned

v. 先.—the verb; up. 3rd tone. 子之兄弟,—not "your brothers," but as in the translation; comp. par. 2. 倍＝背.—Observe how Ts'oo is here excluded from "The Middle Kingdom of Mencius's time." 13. On the death of Confucius, his disciples remained by his grave for three years, mourning for him as for a father, but without wearing the mourning dress. 治任,—both low. 1st tone, "looked after their burdens." Tsze-kung had acted

秋陽以暴之皜皜乎不可

曾子曰不可江漢以濯之、

以所事孔子事之彊曾子、

張子游、以有若似聖人、欲

三年、然後歸他日子夏、

歸、子貢反築室於場獨居

to their homes, but Tsze-kung went back, and built a
house for himself on the altar ground, where he lived
alone *other* three years, before he returned home.
On another occasion, Tsze-hea, Tsze-chang, and
Tsze-yew, thinking that Yew Jŏ resembled the sage,
wished to render to him the same observances which
they had rendered to Confucius. They tried to force
the disciple Tsǎng to join with them, but he said,
'This may not be done. What has been washed
in the waters of the Këang and Han, and bleached
in the autumn sun:—how glistening is it! Nothing
can be added to it.'

to all his codisciples as master of
the ceremonies. Hence they took a
formal leave of him. 場 is a flat
place, an area scooped out upon the
surface, and used primarily to sacrifice upon. Here it denotes such an
area formed upon the sage's grave.

On Yew Jŏ's resemblance to Confucius, see the Book of Rites, II, Pt.
I, iii, 4. 彊,—low. 2nd tone. 暴,—
low. 4th tone, *puh*. 皜,—read *haou*,
low. 2nd tone, or *kaou*, up. 2nd. 尚＝
加. Comp. 無以尚之, Ana., IV, vii, 1.

膺之子是之學、亦爲不善變

狄是膺、荆舒是懲周公方且

木而入於幽谷者魯頌曰、戎

幽谷、遷于喬木者、未聞下喬

之、亦異於曾子矣吾聞出於

先王之道子倍子之師而學

尙已今也、南蠻鴃舌之人、非

14. "Now here is this shrike-tongued barbarian of the south, whose doctrines are not those of the ancient kings. You turn away from your master and become his disciple. Your conduct is different indeed from that of the philosopher Tsăng.

15. "I have heard of *birds* leaving dark valleys to remove to lofty trees, but I have not heard of their descending from lofty trees to enter into dark valleys.

16. "In the Praise Songs of Loo it is said,

'He smote the barbarians of the west and the
    north,
He punished King and Seu.'

Thus Chow-kung would be sure to smite them, and you become their disciple again; it appears that your change is not good."

14. 鴃,—"the shrike, or butcher bird," a strong epithet of contempt or dislike, as applied to Heu Hing. 倍,—as above. 15. 下,— used as a verb, low. 3rd tone. 16. See the Book of Poetry, IV, ii, Ode IV, st. 6. The two clauses quoted refer to the achievements of the duke He. Mencius uses them as if they expressed the approbation of

物之不齊、物之情也、或相倍

若、屨大小同、則賈相若曰夫

賈相若、五穀多寡同、則賈相

賈相若、麻縷絲絮輕重同、則

市、莫之或欺、布帛長短同、則

國中無偽、雖使五尺之童適

矣從許子之道、則市賈不貳、

17. *Ch'in Seang said,* "If Heu's doctrines were followed, then there would not be two prices in the market; nor any deceit in the kingdom. If a body of five cubits were sent to the market, no one would impose on him; linen and silk of the same length would be of the same price. So it would be with *bundles of* hemp and silk, being of the same weight; with the different hanks of grain, being the same in quantity; and with shoes which were of the same size."

18. *Mencius* replied, "It is the nature of things to be of unequal quality. Some are twice, some

his ancestor Chow-kung. 17. 賈,— read *kea,* up. 3rd tone＝價. 五尺之童,—see Con. Ana., VIII, vi. 麻縷絲絮 must be joined together, I think, in pairs, in opposition to the 布帛 above, the manufactured articles. 縷 is explained, in the 說 文, by 綫, "threads," and may be used of silk or flax. 絮 is explained, also in the 說 文, by 敝 綿, "spoiled, or bad, floss." Its general application is to floss of an inferior quality. 18. 倍,—different from that in pars. 12, 15, meaning "as much again." 相＝

徙、或相什伯、或相千
萬、子比而同之、是亂
天下也、巨屨小屨同
賈、人豈爲之哉、從許
子之道、相率而爲僞
者也惡能治國家。
墨者夷之、因徐辟
而求見孟子。孟子曰、

five times, some ten times, some a hundred times,
some a thousand times, some ten thousand times as
valuable as others. If you reduce them all to the
same standard, that must throw the empire into
confusion. If large shoes and small shoes were of
the same price, who would make them? For people
to follow the doctrines of Heu, would be for them
to lead one another on to practice deceit. How can
they avail for the government of a state?"

CHAPTER V. 1. The Mihist, E Che, sought,
through Seu Peih, to see Mencius. Mencius said,

相去, "are separated from each
other," or "are to each other as."
The size of the shoes is mentioned
as a thing more palpable than their
quality, and exposing more easily
the absurdity of Heu's proposition.
　CH. 5. HOW MENCIUS CONVINCED
A MĪHIST OF HIS ERROR, THAT ALL
MEN WERE TO BE LOVED EQUALLY,
WITHOUT DIFFERENCE OF DEGREE. 1.
Mih, by name 翟 (read Teih), was a
heresiarch between the times of Con.
and Men. His distinguishing principle was that of universal and equal
love, which he contended would
remedy all the evils of society. See
next part, ch. ix, et al. (It has been
contended lately, however, by the
Rev. Joseph Edkins, that Mencius's
account of Mih's views is unfair. See
Journal of the North China Branch
of the Royal Asiatic Society, No. II.
Some of Mih's writings remain, and
I hope to be able to procure a copy,
in time to give some notice of them
in the prolegomena.) 徐辟 (read
Peih or P'eih) was a disciple of
Mencius. The philosopher, acc. to

喪也、以薄爲其道也、夷

吾聞夷子墨者墨之治

直、則道不見、我且直之、

曰、吾今則可以見矣、不

他日又求見孟子孟子

愈、我且往見夷子不來。

吾固願見今吾尚病、病

"I indeed wish to see him, but at present I am still unwell. When I am better, I will myself go and see him. E need not come here *again*."

2. Next day, *E Che* again sought to see Mencius. Mencius said, "To-day I am able to see him. But if I do not correct his errors, the *true* principles will not be fully evident. Let me first correct him. I have heard that E is a Mĭhist. Now Mih considers that in the regulation of funeral matters a spare simplicity should be the rule. E thinks with *Mih's doctrines*

the opinion of Choo He, was well enough, but feigned sickness, and told E Che that he need not come again to see him to try his sincerity. It is to be understood that Che had intimated that he was dissatisfied with his Mĭhism, and Mencius would be guided in his judgment of his really being so, by testing his desire to get an interview with him. It is difficult to express the force of the particle 且. "Myself" comes near it. 夷子不來 is Mencius's remark, and Chaou K'e is wrong, when he carries it on to the next par., and construes —"E in consequence did not then come, but another day, etc." 2. 他日, "another day," probably, "next day." The repetition of the application satisfied Mencius that Che was really anxious to be instructed. 直, Choo He says,＝盡言以相正, "to expound the truth fully to correct him." 不見,—見, low. 3rd tone. 我且直之,—且 is here＝將, "will." The 備旨 says that 對未遽見言, "it is used with reference to the not readily granting E an interview." Mencius wanted to put the applicant right, before conversing with him. We are to suppose that, after the acknowledgment in the concl.

愛無差等、施由親始。徐子

子、此言何謂也、之則以爲

儒者之道古之人若保赤

也。徐子以告夷子夷子曰、

其親厚、則是以所賤事親

是而不貴也、然而夷子葬

子思以易天下、豈以爲非

to change *the customs of* the empire;—how does he
regard them as if they were wrong, and not honor
them?　Notwithstanding his views, E buried his
parents in a sumptuous manner, and so he served
them in the way which *his doctrines* discountenance."

3.　The disciple Seu informed E of these remarks.
E said, "*Even according to* the principles of the learned,
we find that the ancients *acted towards the people*, 'as if
they were watching over an infant.'　What does this
expression mean?　To me it sounds that we are to
love *all* w'thout difference of degree; but the manifestation *of love* must begin with our parents."　Seu

par., he admitted E to his presence.
This principle about conducting
funerals, or mourning generally, in
a spare and inexpensive manner,
was a subordinate point of Mih's
teaching, and Mencius knowing that
E Che had not observed it, saw how
he could lead him on from it to see
the error of the chief principle of
the sect.　貴 and 賤 are both verbs.
3. Che attempts to show that the
classical doctrine likewise had the
principle of equal and universal love.
See the 若保赤子, quoted in the
"Great Learning," Comm. ix, 2.　之
則,—之 is the name of the speaker.
差, read *ts'ze*, "uneven."　差等,—
"uneven degrees."　E Che does not
attempt to vindicate the sumptuous
interment of his parents;—he says
施由始親, not knowing what to

以告孟子、孟子曰夫夷子、

信以爲人之親其兄之子、

爲若親其鄰之赤子乎、彼

有取爾也、赤子匍匐將入

井、非赤子之罪也、且天之

生物也使之一本、而夷子

二本、故也蓋上世嘗有不

reported this reply to Mencius, who said, "Now, does E really think that a man's affection for the child of his brother is *merely* like his affection for the infant of a neighbor? What is to be laid hold of in that *expression* is simply this:—that if an infant crawling about is about to fall into a well, it is no crime in the infant. Moreover, Heaven gives birth to creatures in such a way that they have one root, and E makes them to have two roots. This is the cause *of his error*.

4. "And, in the most ancient times, there were

say. 夫,—low. 1st tone. 彼有取爾 (＝耳) 也, with what follows, requires to be supplemented by the reader:—'The child's falling into the well being thus from no perverse intent, but the consequence of its helplessness, people will all try to save it; and the people, liable to offend in ignorance, are to be dealt with in the same way;—to be instructed and watched over. This is all that we can find in the words which he quotes.' Chaou K'e makes 彼 refer to E Che:—"he only takes a part of the meaning. He loses the scope of the whole, and clings to the word infant." This is ingenious, but does not seem sound. The "one root" is the parents (and the seed in reference to inanimate things, but the subject is all about men, and hence the 備旨 says that 物 is to be taken as＝人), to whom therefore should be given a peculiar affection. Mih saying that other men should be loved as much, and in the same way, as parents, made two roots. The 故 is quite enigmatic, but it is explained as I have done. 4. 蓋, not exactly "for," but as a more general continuative. Julien translates the first

葬其親者、其親死、則
舉而委之於壑、他日
過之狐狸食之、蠅蚋
姑嘬之其顙有泚、睨
而不視、夫泚也、非爲
人泚、中心達於面目、

some who did not inter their parents. When their
parents died, they took them up and threw them into
some water channel. Afterwards, when passing by
them, *they saw* foxes and wild cats devouring them,
and flies and gnats biting at them. The perspiration
started out upon their foreheads, and they looked
away, unable to bear the sight. It was not on account of other people that this perspiration flowed.
The emotions of their hearts affected their faces and
eyes, and instantly they went home, and came back

clause:—"*Porro in superioribus sec-
ulis nondum erant qui sepelirent suos
parentes,*" and he blames Noel for
rendering—"*quidam filii parentes
suos tumulo non mandabant.*" Mencius, he says, "is treating of all men,
and not of some only." I cannot,
however, get over the 者, which
would seem to require the rendering
given by Noel. Reference is made
indeed to the highest antiquity (上
世), when the sages had not yet
delivered their rules of ceremonies,
but from the clause 非爲人泚, we
may infer that even then all were
not equally unobservant of what
was proper. 過,—up. 1st tone. The
passing by is not to be taken as
fortuitous. Their natural solicitude
brought them to see how it was with
the bodies. The 狐 is "the fox." 狸
or 貍 is a name given to diff. animals.
We have the 貓 狸, or "wild cat";
the 風 狸, which appears to be the
"raccoon"; and others. 姑, says
Choo He, has no meaning, but is a
drawl between the words before and
after it. Some would take it for 蛄,
a kind of cricket. 非爲人泚,—
comp. 非所以要譽云云, II, Pt.
I, vi, 3. 中 心,—"their middle
heart," the very center of their

蓋歸反虆梩而

掩之、掩之誠是

也、則孝子仁人

之掩其親、亦必

有道矣。徐子以五節

告夷子夷子憮

然爲閒曰、命之

矣。

with baskets and spades and covered the bodies. If *the covering them thus* was indeed right, you may see that the filial son and virtuous man, in interring *in a handsome manner* their parents, act according to a proper rule."

5. The disciple Seu informed E of what Mencius had said. E was thoughtful for a short time, and then said, "He has instructed me."

being. 蓋 歸,—蓋="and forthwith," but what follows contains a proof of what is said before—中 心 云 云. 反 虆 梩,—"overturned baskets and shovels," i. e., of earth. 虆,—read *lo* (not *lui*, as enjoined in the tonal notes in most edd. of Mencius), low. 1st tone. The meaning of 梩 is obscure; that of a spade or shovel (wooden, of course) is given, however, to it. The conclusion of the argument is this, that what affection prompted in the first case, was prompted similarly in its more sumptuous exhibition in the progress of civilization. If any interment was right, a handsome one must be right also. 5. 憮 然, in the dict., is explained, as "the appearance of being surprised." In Ana., XVIII, vi, 4, Choo He explains the phrase by 悵 然, "vexedlike." I have there translated—"with a sigh." 命 之,—之 is again the speaker's name. 命 is in the sense of 敎, "to instruct."

## BOOK III

### T'ĂNG WĂN KUNG.　PART II

滕文公章句

下

蠢陳代曰不見

諸侯宜若小然

今一見之大則

以王小則以霸

且志曰枉尺而

直尋宜若可爲

CHAPTER I.　1. Ch'in Tae said *to Mencius*, "In not *going to* wait upon any of the princes, you seem to me to be standing on a small point. If now you were once to wait upon them, the result might be so great that you would make one of them emperor, or, if smaller, that you would make one of them chief of all the other princes. Moreover, the History says, 'By bending *only* one cubit, you make eight cubits straight.'. It appears to me like a thing which might be done."

CH. 1. HOW MENCIUS DEFENDED THE DIGNITY OF RESERVE, BY WHICH HE REGULATED HIS INTERCOURSE WITH THE PRINCES OF HIS TIME. To understand the chapter, it must be borne in mind, that there were many wandering scholars in the days of Mencius, men who went from court to court, recommending themselves to the various princes, and trying to influence the course of events by their counsels. They would stoop for place and employment. Not so with our philosopher. He required that there should be shown to him- self a portion of the respect which was due to the principles of which he was the expounder. 1. Ch'in Tae was one of Mencius's disciples. 不見 ＝不往見. 宜若小然,＝"in reason is as if it were small-like." 大 is said to be 大用, "if you were greatly employed," and 小＝小用. It is better to take these terms as in the translation. The clauses must be expanded—大則以其君王. 小則 以其君霸. 王,—low. 3rd tone. 志,—see Pt. I, ii, 3. The "thing that might be done" is Mencius's

喪其元、孔子奚

溝壑、勇士不忘

之、志士不忘在

以旌、不至、將殺

景公田、招虞人

也孟子曰、昔、齊

2. Mencius said, "Formerly, the duke King of
Ts'e, once when he was hunting, called his forester
to him by a flag. *The forester* would not come, *and
the duke* was going to kill him. *With reference to this
incident, Confucius said,* 'The determined officer never
forgets *that his end may be* in a ditch or a stream; the
brave officer never forgets that he may lose his head.'
What was it *in the forester* that Confucius thus

going to wait on the princes. 2. The
虞 人 was an officer as old as the
time of Shun, who appoints Yih (益),
Shoo-king, II, i, 22, saying that "he
could rightly superintend the birds
and beasts of the fields and trees on
his hills, and in his forests." In the
Chow Le, XVII, vi, we have an
account of the office, where it
appears, that, on occasion of a great
hunting, the forester had to clear
the paths, and set up flags for the
hunters to collect around. There
the charges are the "hills," and
"marshes," and here, acc. to Chaou
K'e and Choo He, they were the "preserves and parks." In those times,
the various officers had their several
tokens, which the prince's messenger
bore when he was sent to call any
of them. A forester's token was a
fur cap, and the one in the text
would not answer to a summons

with a flag. See the incident in the
左 傳, 昭 公, 二 十 年, where the de-
tails however, and Confucius' judgment on it, are different. It is there
said:—"The prince of Ts'e was
hunting in P'ei and summoned the
forester with *a bow*. As the forester
did not come, the prince had him
seized, when he excused himself
saying, *In the huntings of former
princes,* 大 夫 *have been summoned
with a banner;* 士, *with a bow; and
the forester with a fur cap. As I did
not see the fur cap, I did not venture
to approach.* The duke on this dismissed the man. Chung-ne said, *He
observed the law of his office, rather
than the ordinary rule of answering
the summons. Superior men will
approve of his act."* 田,—used for
畋 or 佃. The observations which
must be taken as made by Confucius
are found nowhere else. 元,—here

取爲、取非其招不
往也、如不待其招
而往、何哉。且夫枉
尺而直尋者、以利
言也、如以利、則枉
尋直尺而利、亦可
爲與。昔者趙簡子
使王良與嬖奚乘、

approved? He approved his not going *to the duke*, when summoned by the article which was not appropriate to him. If one go *to see the princes* without waiting to be invited, what can be thought of him?

3. "Moreover, *that sentence,* 'By bending *only* one cubit, you make eight cubits straight,' is spoken with reference to the gain *that may be got.* If gain be the object, then, if it can be got by bending eight cubits to make one cubit straight, may we likewise do that?

4. "Formerly, the officer Chaou Keen made Wang Leang act as charioteer for his favorite He, when, in

=首, "the head." 不忘 is a difficult phrase in the connection. I have made the best of it I could. The first 其招 is plain enough—the summons appropriate to him, i. e., to a forester. We cannot lay so much stress, however, on the 其 in the same phrase in the last sentence, the subject of the chapter being the question of Mencius's waiting on the princes without being called by them at all. 3. 且夫 (low. 1st tone) is more forcible and argumentative than 且 alone. 如以利=如以計利爲心. The question in 亦可爲與 is an appeal to Tae's own sense of what was right. Admit what he asked in par. 1, any amount of evil might be done that good might come. Was he prepared to allow that? 4. Chaou Keen (簡 was the posthumous epithet. His name was 鞅, Yang) was a noble of Tsin, in the times of Confucius, and Wang Leang was his charioteer, famous for his skill. Leang appears in the histories of the time—the 左傳, and 國語—by difft. names. He is called 郵無恤, 郵無正, 郵良, as well as 王良. See the 四書撫餘說' *in loc.* 與=爲, "for," and 乘 (low. 3rd tone), "a

良、良不可曰、吾爲之範我馳驅、

也。簡子曰、我使掌與女乘、謂王

十禽嬖奚反命曰天下之良工

曰、請復之、彊而後可、一朝而獲

天下之賤工也。或以告王良、良

終日而不獲一禽嬖奚反命曰、

the course of a whole day, they did not get a single
bird. The favorite He reported this result, saying,
'He is the poorest charioteer in the world.' Some
one told this to Wang Leang, who said, 'I beg leave
to *try* again.' By dint of pressing, this was accorded
to him, when in one morning they got ten birds. The
favorite, reporting this result, said, 'He is the best
charioteer in the world.' Keen said, 'I will make
him always drive your carriage for you.' When he
told Wang Leang so, *however,* Leang refused, saying,
'I *drove* for him, strictly observing the proper rules

carriage," is used as a verb, "to
drive a carriage." 反命,—see Pt.
I, ii, 3. It is a phrase of form. 工,
—"a mechanic," "an artist"; here=
"a charioteer." 請復 (low. 3rd tone)
之—"I beg to *again* it." 彊,—low.

2nd tone. 掌與女 (=汝) 乘,—"to
manage the chariot-driving for you."
It is not common in Chinese to
separate, as here, the verb and its
object. 良不可, "Leang might not,"
i. e., might not be induced to take

獸、雖若丘陵、弗爲也、如

羞與射者比、比而得禽

與小人乘、請辭御者、且
五節。

其馳、舍矢如破、我不貫

一朝而獲十詩云不失

終日不獲一、爲之詭遇、

for driving, and in the whole day he did not get one
*bird*. I *drove* for him so as deceitfully to intercept
*the birds*, and in one morning he got ten. It is said
in the "Book of Poetry,"

"There is no failure in the management of their horses;
The arrows are discharged surely, like the blows of an
ax."

I am not accustomed to drive for a mean man. I
beg leave to decline the office.'

5. "*Thus* this charioteer even was ashamed to
bend improperly to the will of *such an* archer.
Though, by bending to it, they would have caught
birds and animals enow to form a hill, he would not

the office. 吾 爲 (low. 3rd tone) 之
範 我 馳 驅, "I for him *law-ed* my
racing my horses and whipping
them." 詩 云,—see the She-king,
II, iii, Ode V, st. 6. Literally the
two lines are "They err not in the

galloping; they l go the arrows, as
if rending." 舍,—upper 3rd tone.
貫,—uséd for 慣. 5. 比,—low. 3rd
tone, in the sense of "to flatter."
丘 陵,—to be taken together, "a
mound," "a hill." The 彼,—"that,

枉道而從彼、何也、且子

過矣、枉己者、未有能直

人者也。

景春曰、公孫衍、張儀、

豈不誠大丈夫哉、一怒、

而諸侯懼、安居而天下

熄。孟子曰是為得為大

丈夫乎、子未學禮乎丈

do so. If I were to bend my principles and follow those *princes*, of what kind would my conduct be? And you are wrong. Never has a man who has bent himself been able to make others straight."

CHAPTER II. 1. King Ch'un said *to Mencius*, "Are not Kung-sun Yen and Chang E really great men? Let them once be angry, and all the princes are afraid. Let them live quietly, and the flames of trouble are extinguished throughout the empire."

2. Mencius said, "How can such men be great men? Have you not read the Ritual *Usages?*—'At

or those," referring to 諸侯 in par. 1. We must supply *I*, as the nominative to 枉. The concluding remark is just, but hardly consistent with the allowances for their personal misconduct which Mencius was prepared to make to the princes.

CH. 2. MENCIUS'S CONCEPTION OF THE GREAT MAN. 1. King Ch'un was a man of Mencius's days, "a practicer of the art of up-and-across" (爲縱橫之術者), i. e., one who plumed himself on his versatility. Kung-sun Yen and Chang E were also men of that age, natives of Wei (魏), and among the most celebrated of the ambitious scholars, who went from state to state, seeking employment, and embroiling the princes. See the "Historical Records," Book C, 列傳, ch. x. 丈夫,—see Pt. I, i, 4. The phrase is used, however, in the next par., for "a grown-up youth." 熄 has the opposite meanings of "feeding a fire," and "extinguishing a fire." The latter is its meaning here. 2. 是,—referring to Yen and E with what is said about them

廣居、立天下之正位、
婦之道也。居天下之
夫子、以順爲正者妾
女家必敬必戒無違
送之門、戒之曰、往之
子之嫁也、母命之往
夫之冠也、父命之女

the capping of a young man, his father admonishes him. At the marriage of a young woman, her mother admonishes her, accompanying her to the door on her leaving, and cautioning her with these words, *You are going to your home. You must be respectful; you must be careful. Do not disobey your husband.'* Thus, to look upon compliance as their correct course is the rule for women.

3. "To dwell in the wide house of the world, to stand in the correct seat of the world, and to walk in

above. 爲,—the interrogative, up. 1st tone. The "Rites" or "Book of Rites," to which Mencius here chiefly refers, is not the compilation now received among the higher classics, under the name of the Le Ke, but the Le E (禮儀). He throws various passages together, and, according to his wont, is not careful to quote correctly. In the Le E, not only does her mother admonish the bride, but her father also, and his concubines, and all to the effect that she is to be obedient, though the husband (here called 夫子) is not expressly mentioned. See the 儀禮

註疏, Bk. 11, pp. 49, 50. For the ceremonies of capping, see the same, Bk. I. In 送之門, and, more especially, in 往之女 (汝) 家 the 之 joins the verbs and nouns, as if it were= "to," or the verb,=往. 妾婦 are to be taken together,—"a concubine-woman." Mencius uses the term 妾, in his contempt for Yen and E, who, with all their bluster, only pandered to the passions of the princes. Obedience is the rule for all women, and specially so for secondary wives. 3. "The wide house of the world" is *benevolence* or *love,* the chief and home of all the virtues; "the correct

子仕乎。孟子曰、仕、傳

周霄問曰、古之君

能屈、此之謂大丈夫。

貧賤不能移、威武不

行其道、富貴不能淫、

與民由之、不得志、獨

行天下之大道、得志、

the great path of the world; when he obtains his desire *for office,* to practice his principles for the good of the people; and when that desire is disappointed, to practice them alone; to be above the power of riches and honors to make dissipated, of poverty and mean condition to make swerve from principle, and of power and force to make bend—these characteristics constitute the great man."

CHAPTER III. 1. Chow Seaou asked *Mencius,* saying, "Did superior men of old time take office?" Mencius replied, "They did. The Record says, 'If

seat" is *propriety;* and "the great path" is *righteousness.* 與 民 由 之 (the 之 refers to the virtues so metaphorically indicated),—"walks according to them, along with the people." The paraphrase in the 日 講 says: "Getting his desire, and being employed in the world, he comes forth, and carries out these principles of benevolence, propriety, and righteousness, towards the people, and pursues them along with them." 此 之 謂,—"this is what is called."

CH. 3. OFFICE IS TO BE EAGERLY DESIRED, AND YET IT MAY NOT BE SOUGHT BUT BY ITS PROPER PATH. It will be seen that the questioner of Mencius in this chapter, a man of Wei, and one of the wandering scholars of the time, wished to condemn the philosopher for the dignity of reserve which he maintained in his intercourse with the various princes. Mencius does not evade any of his questions, and very satisfactorily vindicates himself. 1. 傳, —low. 3rd tone, the "Record";

無君則弔不以急乎。

三月無君則弔三月

質、公明儀曰古之人、

皇皇如也、出疆必載

曰、孔子三月無君、則

Confucius was three months without *being employed by some* sovereign, he looked anxious and unhappy. When he passed from the boundary of a state, he was sure to carry with him his proper gift of introduction.' Kung-ming E said, 'Among the ancients, if an officer was three months unemployed by a sovereign, he was condoled with.'"

2. *Seaou said,* "Did not this condoling, on being three months unemployed by a sovereign, show a too great urgency?"

whatever it was, it is now lost. 無君,—"without a sovereign," i. e., without office. 皇皇如 is "the appearance of one who is seeking for something and can't find it." It is appropriate to a mourner in the first stages of grief after bereavement. 齊,—read *che*, up. 3rd tone, synonymous with 齎. Every person waiting on another,—a superior,—was supposed to pave his way by some introductory gift, and each official rank had its proper article to be used for that purpose by all belonging to it. See the Le-ke, I,

Pt. II, iii. 18. Confucius carried this with him, that he might not lose any opportunity of getting to be in office again. Kung-ming E, we are told by Chaou K'e, was "a worthy," but of what time and what state, we do not know. An individual of the same surname is mentioned, Ana., XIV, xiv. Julien translates 不弔 incorrectly by—"*tunc in luctu erant.*" The paraphrase of the 日講 says:—"Then people all came to condole with and to comfort them." 2. 以 is to be taken as

不　成　以　供　禮　諸　曰
備　粢　爲　粢　曰　侯　士
不　盛　衣　盛　諸　之　之
敢　不　服　夫　侯　失　失
以　潔　犧　人　耕　國　位
祭　衣　牲　蠶　助　家　也
惟　服　不　繰　以　也　猶

3. *Mencius* answered, "The loss of his place to an officer is like the loss of his kingdom to a prince. It is said in the 'Book of Rites,' 'A prince plows himself, and is assisted *by the people*, to supply the millet *for sacrifice*. His wife keeps silkworms, and unwinds their cocoons, to make the garments *for sacrifice*.' If the victims be not perfect, the millet not pure, and the dress not complete, he does not presume to sacrifice. 'And the scholar who, *out of office*, has no

synonymous with 已. 3. 國家,—the state embracing the families of the nobles. In his quotations from the Le Ke, Mencius combines and adapts to his purpose, with more, however, than his usual freedom, different passages. See Bk. XXIV, ii, pars. 5, 7, and Bk. V, iii, par. 9. Choo He, to illustrate the text, gives another summary of the passages in the Le Ke, thus:—"It is said in the Book of Rites, 'The princes had their special field of 100 *mow*, in which, wearing their crown, with its blue flaps turned up, they held the plow to commence the plowing, which was afterwards completed with the help of the common people. The produce of this field was reaped and stored in the ducal granary, to supply the vessels of millet in the ancestral temple. They also caused the family women (世 婦) of their harem to attend to the silkworms, in the silkworm house attached to the state mulberry trees, and to bring the cocoons to them. These were then presented to their wives, who received them in their sacrificial headdress and robe, soaked them, and thrice drew out a thread. They then distributed the cocoons among the ladies of the three palaces, to prepare the threads for the ornaments on the robes to be worn in sacrificing to the former kings and dukes." 盛. —low. 1st tone, "the millet placed

士無田、則亦不祭、牲殺

器皿、衣服不備、不敢以

祭、則不敢以宴亦不足

弔乎。出疆必載質、何也。

曰、士之仕也、猶農夫之

*holy* field, in the same way, does not sacrifice.' The victims for slaughter, the vessels, and the garments, not being all complete, he does not presume to sacrifice, and then neither may he dare to feel happy. Is there not here sufficient ground also for condolence?"

4. *Seaou again asked,* "What was the meaning of *Confucius's* always carrying his proper gift of introduction with him, when he passed over the boundaries *of the state where he had been?*"

5. "An officer's being in office," was the reply, "is like the plowing of a husbandman. Does a

in the sacrificial vessel. 犧 牲,—牲, the victim, whatever it might be; 犧, the victim, as pure and perfect. The officer's field is the 圭 field, Pt. I, iii, 16. 器 皿 together=vessels. Choo He says the 皿 were the covers of the 器. 以 宴,—"to feast,"=to feel happy.—The argument is that it was not the mere loss of office which was a proper subject for grief and condolence, but the consequences of it, especially in not being able to continue his proper sacrifices, as here

父母之心、人皆有之不待父母

之有室女子生、而願爲之有家、

之難仕何也曰、丈夫生、而願爲

如此其急仕如此其急也、君子

哉。曰晉國、亦仕國也、未嘗聞仕
六郡

耕也、農夫豈爲出疆、舍其耒耜

husbandman part with his plow, because he goes from one state to another?"

6. *Seaou* pursued, "The kingdom of Tsin is one, as well as others, of official employments, but I have not heard of any being thus earnest about being in office. If there should be this urgency about being in office, why does a superior man make any difficulty about the taking it?" *Mencius* answered, "When a son is born, what is desired for him is that he may have a wife; when a daughter is born, what is desired for her is that she may have a husband. This feeling of the parents is possessed by all men. If *the young people*, without waiting for the orders of their parents,

set forth. 5. 舍,—up. 2nd tone. 耒耜,—see Pt. I, iv, p. 3. 6. "The kingdom of Tsin,—see I, Pt. I, v, 1. 君子之難仕,—by the 君子 Seaou evidently intends Mencius himself, who, however, does not notice the insinuation. 丈夫 and 女子,—here simply "a son," "a daughter." 爲, low. 3rd tone. A man marrying is said 有室, "to have an apartment," and a woman marrying 有家, "to

之命、媒妁之言、鑽穴隙相

窺、踰牆相從、則父母國人

皆賤之、古之人未嘗不欲

仕也、又惡不由其道、不由

其道而往者、與鑽穴隙之

類也。

彭更問曰、後車數十乘、

從者數百人、以傳食於諸

and the arrangements of the go-betweens, shall bore holes to steal a sight of each other, or get over the wall to be with each other, then their parents and all other people will despise them. The ancients did indeed always desire to be in office, but they also hated being so by any improper way. To go *to get office* by an improper way is of a class with *young people's* boring holes."

CHAPTER IV. 1. P'ang Kăng asked *Mencius*, saying, "Is it not an extravagant procedure to go from one prince to another and live upon them, followed by several tens of carriages, and attended by several

have a family," or "home." 媒妁之言'—see the Chow Le, XIV, vii; the She-king, I, viii, Ode VI, st. 6. The law of marriage here referred to by Mencius still obtains, and seems to have been the rule of the Chinese race from time immemorial. 相從,—從＝就. 踰,—up. 3rd tone, the verb. 而往,—往＝往見諸侯.
CH. 4. THE LABORER IS WORTHY OF HIS HIRE, AND THERE IS NO LABORER SO WORTHY AS THE SCHOLAR WHO INFORMS MEN TO VIRTUE. 1. P'ang Kăng was a disciple of Mencius. His object in addressing him, as in this chapter, seems to have been to stir him up to visit the princes, and go into office. 乘,—low. 3rd tone, following 車, as a numeral or classifier. 從者,—從

食不可也曰子不通功

爲泰乎曰否士無事而

之天下不以爲泰子以

於人如其道則舜受堯

其道則一簞食不可受

侯、不以泰乎孟子曰、非

hundred men?" Mencius replied, "If there be not a proper ground *for taking it*, a single bamboo cup of rice may not be received from a man. If there be such a proper ground, then Shun's receiving the empire from Yaou is not to be considered excessive. Do you think it was excessive?"

2. *Kăng* said, "No. But for a scholar *performing* no service to receive his support notwithstanding is improper."

3. *Mencius* answered, "If you do not have an inter-communication of the productions of labor, and an

low. 3rd tone, "an attendant," "a follower," not in a moral sense. 傳, ～low. 3rd tone, explained in the diction. by 繼, "to connect," "succeed to." 以傳, "by succession."— The phrase is felt to be a difficult one. Sun Shih explains it thus:— "Mencius got his support from the princes, and his chariots and disciples got their support from Mencius. It came to this that the support of all was from the contributions of the princes, and hence it is said that by their mutual connection they all lived on the princes." 簞食—食, *tsze*, low. 3rd tone, "rice cooked." Comp Ana., VI, ix. 堯之天下, "Yaou's empire," i. e., the empire from Yaou. 舜 may be construed very well as the nominative

輪輿、而輕爲仁義者哉。
得食於子、子何尊梓匠
道以待後之學者、而不
則孝、出則弟、守先王之
食於子、於此有人焉、入
通之、則梓匠輪輿、皆得
有餘粟、女有餘布、子如
易事、以羨補不足、則農

interchange of *men's* services, so that *one 'from his* overplus may supply the deficiency *of another,* then husbandmen will have a superfluity of grain, and women will have a superfluity of cloth. If you have such an interchange, carpenters and carriage wrights may all get their food from you. ´Here now is a man, who, at home, is filial, and abroad, respectful to his elders; who watches over the principles of the ancient kings, awaiting *the rise of* future learners:— and yet you will refuse to support him. How is it that you give honor to the carpenter and carriage wright, and slight him who practices benevolence and righteousness?''

to 以爲. 3. 守先王之道以待後 之學者,—the paraphrase in the 合 講 is:—"He firmly guards the principles of benevolence and righteousness transmitted by the ancient kings, so that they do not get obscured or obstructed by perverse discourses, but hereby await future learners, and secure their having matter of instruction and models of imitation, whereby they may enter into truth and right. Thus he continues the past and opens the way for the future, and does service to the world." 以 待, then, = "for the benefit of." The 梓 and 匠 are both workers in wood, the 梓 人's work being in smaller things, such as vessels, and articles of furniture, and the 匠 人's in large, such as building houses, etc. The 輪 人 made the wheels and also the cover of a carriage; the 輿 人, the other parts.

曰、梓匠輪輿、其志將以求食

也、君子之爲道也、其志亦將

以求食與。曰、子何以其志爲

哉、其有功於子、可食而食之

矣、且子食志乎、食功乎。曰、食

志。曰、有人於此毀瓦畫墁、其

4. *P'ang Kăng* said, "The aim of the carpenter and carriage wright is *by their trades* to seek for a living. Is it also the aim of the superior man in his practice of principles thereby to seek for a living?" "What have you to do," returned *Mencius*, "with his purpose? He is of service to you. He deserves to be supported, and should be supported. And *let me ask*,—Do you remunerate a man's intention, or do you remunerate his service." *To this Kăng* replied, "I remunerate his intention."

5. *Mencius* said, "There is a man here, who breaks your tiles, and draws *unsightly* figures on your walls;

4. Observe how appropriately 將, expressive of futurity or object, follows 志. 可食而食之,—here 食 and the three that follow, are read as in—簞食, but with a different meaning, being = "to feed" (active or passive), "to give rice to." 5. 畫 (low. 3rd tone) 墁.—墁 means "ornaments on walls." He must therefore take 畫 in a bad sense, to correspond to the 毀. A man wishes to mend the roof, but he only breaks it; to

則如之何。孟子曰、湯居亳、

將行王政、齊楚惡而伐之、

萬章問曰、宋小國也、今

也、食功也。

乎。曰、否。曰、然則子非食志

志將以求食也、則子食之

—his purpose may be thereby to seek for his living, but will you indeed remunerate him?" "No," said Kăng; *and Mencius then* concluded, "That being the case, it is not the purpose which you remunerate, but the work done."

CHAPTER V. 1. Wan Chang asked *Mencius*, saying, "Sung is a small state. *Its ruler* is now setting about to practice the *true* royal government, and Ts'e and Ts'oo hate and attack him. What in this case is to be done?"

2. *Mencius* replied, "When T'ang dwelt in Pŏ, he

ornament the wall, but he only disfigures it.

CH. 5. THE PRINCE WHO WILL SET HIMSELF TO PRACTICE A BENEVOLENT GOVERNMENT ON THE PRINCIPLES OF THE ANCIENT KINGS HAS NONE TO FEAR. 1. Wan Chang was a disciple of Mencius, the fifth book of whose Works is named from him. What he says here may surprise us, because we know that the duke of Sung (its capital was in the pres. district of Shanghew [商 邱], in the Kweitih department of Honan), or king, as he styled himself, was entirely worthless and oppressive. See the "Historical Records," Book XXXVIII, 宋 微 子 世 家, towards the end. 2. Comp. I, Pt. II, iii, 1, and xi, 2. Pŏ, the capital of T'ang (though there

使亳眾往爲之耕、老弱饋
不祀。曰、無以供粢盛也、湯
祀湯又使人問之曰、何爲
之牛羊葛伯食之又不以
曰、無以供犧牲也、湯使遺
湯使人問之曰、何爲不祀。
與葛爲隣、葛伯放而不祀、

adjoined to *the state of* Kŏ, the chief of which was
living in a dissolute state and neglecting *his proper*
sacrifices. T'ang sent messengers to inquire why he
did not sacrifice. He replied, 'I have no means of
supplying the *necessary* victims.' *On this,* T'ang
caused oxen and sheep to be sent to him, but he ate
them, and still continued not to sacrifice. T'ang
again sent messengers to ask him the same question
as before, when he replied, 'I have no means of
obtaining the *necessary* millet.' *On this,* T'ang sent
the mass of the people of Pŏ to go and till the ground
for him, while the old and feeble carried their food

were three places of the same name),
is referred to the same department
of Honan as the country of Kŏ, viz.,
that of Kweitih. Its site is said to
have been distant from the site of
the supposed capital of Kŏ only
about 100 li, so that T'ang might
easily render the services here mentioned to the 伯, chief or baron, of
Kŏ. 無以供,—"no means of supplying," i. e., of obtaining. 遺, low.
3rd tone.＝饋. 粢盛 (low. 1st tone),
—see last ch. 爲之,—爲, low. 3rd
tone. 饋食,—食, *tsze*, low. 3rd tone.
要, up. 1st tone. We find it defined
in the dict., by "to meet with," "to

食葛伯率其民、要其有酒
食黍稻者奪之不授者殺
之有童子以黍肉餉、殺而
奪之、書曰、葛伯仇餉、此之
謂也。爲其殺是童子而征
之、四海之內、皆曰、非富天
下也、爲匹夫匹婦復讐也。

to them.　The chief of Kŏ ied his people to intercept those who were thus charged with wine, cooked rice, millet, and paddy, and took their stores from them, while they killed those who refused to give them up.　There was a boy who had some millet and flesh for the laborers, who was thus slain and robbed. What is said in the 'Book of History,' 'The chief of Kŏ behaved as an enemy to the provision carriers,' has reference to this.

3.　"Because of his murder of this boy, T'ang proceeded to punish him.　All within the four seas said, 'It is not because he desires the riches of the empire, but to avenge a common man and woman.'

extort," which approximate to the meaning here.　酒食, 一食, as above, low. 3rd tone.　書曰,—see the Shoo-king, IV, ii, 6.—In the 四書撂餘 說, in loc., 王厚齊 is quoted, to the effect that if Mencius had not been thus particular in explaining what is alluded to in the words of the Shoo-king, the interpretations of them would have been endless.　But that in his time there were ancient books which could be appealed to.　3. 爲, —low. 3rd tone.　匹夫匹婦,—"common men and women"; see Ana., XIV, xviii, 3.　The phrases are understood here, however, with a special application to the father and mother of the murdered boy.　4.

其君弔其民如時雨降民大

也歸市者弗止芸者不變誅

我民之望之若大旱之望雨

南面而征北狄怨曰奚爲後

敵於天下東面而征西夷怨

湯始征自葛載十一征而無

4. "When T'ang began his work of executing justice, he commenced with Kǒ, and *though* he punished eleven *princes*, he had not an enemy in the empire. When he pursued his work in the east, the rude tribes in the west murmured. So did those on the north, when he was engaged in the south. Their cry was—'Why does he make us last?' *Thus,* the people's longing for him was like their longing for rain in a time of great drought. The frequenters of the markets stopped not. Those engaged in weeding *in the fields* made no change *in their operations.* While he punished their rulers, he consoled the people. *His progress* was like the falling of opportune rain, and

Compare I, Pt. II, xi, 2. There are, however, some variations in the phrases. 載=始. The quotation in the end is from a different part of the Shoo-king. See IV, v, Section II, 6. The eleven punitive expeditions of T'ang cannot all be determined. From the She-king and

迎其君子、其小人篚

君子實玄黃于匪以

惟臣附于大邑周、其

玄黃、紹我周王見休、

東征、綏厥士女、匪厥

其無罰。有攸不爲臣、

悅、書曰徯我后、后來

the people were delighted.  It is said in the 'Book of History,' 'We have waited for our prince.  When our prince comes, we may escape from the punishments *under which we suffer.*'

5.  "There being some who would not become the subjects *of Chow, King Woo* proceeded to punish them on the east.  He gave tranquillity to their people, who *welcomed him* with baskets full of their black and yellow silks, *saying*—'From henceforth we shall serve the sovereign of *our dynasty of* Chow, that we may be made happy by him.'  So they joined themselves, as subjects, to the great city of Chow.  Thus, the men of station *of Shang* took baskets full of black and yellow *silks* to meet the men of station of *Chow,* and the lower classes of the one met those of the other,

Shoo-king six only are made out, while by some their number is given as 22 and 27.  See the 集證, *in loc.* 5.  Down to 大邑周,—the substance of this par. is found in the Shoo-king.  See V, iii, 7, but this book of the Shoo-king is confessed to require much emendation in its arrangement. 士女＝男女.  匪,—used for 篚.  匪 厥玄黃,—"basketed their azure and yellow *silks.*"  It is said:—"Heaven is azure, and Earth is yellow.  King Woo was able to put away the evils of the Yin rule, and gave the people rest.  He might be compared to Heaven and Earth, overshadowing and sustaining all things in order to nourish men."  紹 (we have 昭 in the Shoo-king),—"to continue."  We must understand a "saying," and bring out the meaning of 紹 thus:— "Formerly we served Shang, and now we continue to serve, but our service is to Chow."  大邑周,—lit., "great city (or citied) Chow, is an irregular phrase.  From 其君子 to

何畏焉。

首而望之、欲以爲君、齊楚雖大、

云爾苟行王政四海之內皆舉

殺伐用張于湯有光不行王政

我武惟揚侵于之疆、則取于殘、

火之中、取其殘而已矣。太誓曰、

食壺漿、以迎其小人、救民於水

with baskets of rice and vessels of congee. *Woo* saved the people from the midst of fire and water, seizing only their oppressors, *and destroying them.*

6. "In the Great Declaration it is said, 'My power shall be put forth, and invading the territories *of Shang*, I will seize the oppressor. I will put him to death to punish him:—so shall the greatness of my work appear, more glorious than that of T'ang.'

7. "*Sung* is not, as you say, practicing *true* royal government, and so forth. If it were practicing royal government, all within the four seas would be lifting up their heads, and looking for *its prince*, wishing to have him for their sovereign. Great as Ts'e and Ts'oo are, what wculd there be to fear from them?"

the end, Mencius explains the meaning of the Shoo-king. 6. This quotation from the Shoo-king, V, i, Sect. II, 8, is to illustrate the last clause of the preceding par. 7. 云爾,—see Confucian Ana., VII, xviii. 云, however, does not here simply act as a particle closing the sentence, but also refers to the whole of Wan Chang's statement at the commencement of the conversation.

之衆楚人咻之雖日撻而求

曰使齊人傅之曰一齊人傅

則使齊人傅諸使楚人傅諸。

大夫於此欲其子之齊語也、

之王之善與、我明告子、有楚

孟子謂戴不勝曰子欲子

CHAPTER VI. 1. Mencius said to Tae Puh-shing, "I see that you are desiring your king to be virtuous, and I will plainly tell you *how he may be made so.* Suppose that there is a great officer of Ts'oo here, who wishes his son to learn the speech of Ts'e. Will he in that case employ a man of Ts'e as his tutor, or a man of Ts'oo?" "He will employ a man of Ts'e to teach him," said *Puh-shing. Mencius* went on, "If *but* one man of Ts'e be teaching him, and there be a multitude of men of Ts'oo continually shouting out about him, although *his father* beat him every day,

CH. 6. THE INFLUENCE OF EXAMPLE AND ASSOCIATION. THE IMPORTANCE OF HAVING VIRTUOUS MEN ABOUT A SOVEREIGN'S PERSON. 1. Tae Puh-shing was a minister of Sung, the descendant of one of its dukes who had received the posthumous epithet of Tae, which had been adopted as their surname by a branch of his posterity. 子欲 . . .

與,—與, low. 1st tone, the interrog., implying an affirmative reply. 欲其子之齊語, "wishes the Ts'e speech of his son," i. e., wishes his son to learn Ts'e. 諸,—interrog. as elsewhere in Mencius. 咻, read *hew*, =譁, "shouting," "clamorous." Chwang and Yŏ were two well-known quarters in the capital of Ts'e, the former being the name of a street, and the

居州也、王誰與爲不善、

王所者、長幼卑尊皆薛

也、使之居於王所、在於

得矣○子謂薛居州善士

日撻而求其楚、亦不可

置之莊嶽之間、數年、雖

其齊也、不可得矣、引而

wishing him to learn the speech of Ts'e, it will be impossible for him to do so. But in the same way, if he were to be taken and placed for several years in Chwang or Yŏh, though *his father* should beat him, wishing him to speak the language of Ts'oo, it would be impossible for him to do so.

2. "You supposed that Sëë Keu-chow was a scholar of virtue, and you have got him placed in attendance on the king. Suppose that all in attendance on the king, old and young, high and low, were Sëë Keu-chows, whom would the king have to do evil

latter the name of a neighborhood; see the 四書撫餘說 *in loc.* 2. Sëë Keu-chow was also a minister of Sung, a descendant of one of the princes of Sëë, whose family had adopted the name of their original state as their surname. In the 萬姓通譜 we read:—"Tae Puh-shing said to Sëë Keu-chow, '*It is only the virtuous scholar* (善 士) *who can set forth what is virtuous, and shut up* the way of what is corrupt. *You are a scholar of virtue; cannot you make the king virtuous?*'" But this and what follows was probably constructed from Mencius's remark, and so I prefer to take 謂 as="supposed," "believed," not "said." 長, —up. 2nd tone. 居 於 王 所,—"to dwell in the king's place," i. e., to be about him.

而辟之泄柳閉門而不
爲臣不見段干木踰垣
侯、何義孟子曰古者不
鬱公孫丑問曰、不見諸
何。
善、一薛居州、獨如宋王
非薛居州也、王誰與爲
在王所者、長幼卑尊皆

with? And suppose that all in attendance on the king, old and young, high and low, are not Sëĕ Keu-chows, whom will the king havé to do good with? What can one Sëĕ Keu-chow do alone for the king of Sung?"

CHAPTER VII. 1. Kung-sun Chow asked *Mencius*, saying, "What is the point of righteousness involved in your not going to see the princes?" *Mencius* replied, "Among the ancients, if one had not been a minister *in a state*, he did not go to see *the sovereign*.

2. "Twan Kan-muh leaped over his wall to avoid the prince. Sëĕ Lew shut his door, and would not

CH. 7. MENCIUS DEFENDS HIS NOT GOING TO SEE THE PRINCES BY THE EXAMPLE AND MAXIMS OF THE ANCIENTS. 1. 何 義 is not simply—"what is the meaning?" but "what is the rightness?" Mencius, however, does not state distinctly the principle of the thing, but appeals to prescription and precedent. 不爲臣＝未爲臣, or 未仕於其國. In the Con. Ana., XIV, xxii, we have an example of how Confucius, not then actually in office, but having been so, went to see the duke of Loo. 2. Twan Kan-muh was a scholar of Wei (魏), who refused to see the prince Wăn (文). Wăn was the posthumous title of 斯, 426–386 B. C. In the "Historical Records," it is mentioned that he received the writings of Tsze-hea, and never drove past Kan-muh's house, without bowing forward to the front bar of his carriage. 辟＝避, low. 3rd tone. 之 refers to the

內、是皆已甚迫斯可以

見矣陽貨欲見孔子而

惡無禮、大夫有賜於士、

不得受於其家、則往拜

其門、陽貨瞷孔子之亡

也、而饋孔子蒸豚、孔子

亦瞷其亡也而往拜之、

當是時、陽貨先、豈得不

admit the prince. These two, however, *carried their scrupulosity* to excess. When *a prince* is urgent, it is not improper to see him.

3. "Yang Ho wished to get Confucius to go to see him, but disliked doing so by any want of propriety. *As it is the rule, therefore, that* when a great officer sends a gift to a scholar, if the latter be not at home to receive it, he must go to the *officer's* to pay his respects, Yang Ho watched when Confucius was out, and sent him a roasted pig. Confucius, in his turn, watched when Ho was out, and went to pay his respects to him. At that time, Yang Ho had taken the initiative;—how could *Confucius* decline *going* to see him?

prince Wăn. Sëë Lew was a scholar of Loo, who refused to admit (內＝納) the duke Muh (繆); see II, Pt. II, xi, 3. The incident referred to here must have been previous to the time spoken of there. 迫斯可以見矣,—lit., "being urgent, this (or, then) may be seen. 3. 欲見.—見, it is

noted here, should be read low. 3rd tone, with a *hiphil* sense. Comp. Con. Ana., XVII, i. 惡,—the verb, up. 3rd tone. 大夫有賜云云,—see the Le-ke, XIII, iii, 20. Mencius, however, does not quote the exact words. 亡＝無, and so read. 4. 瞷

見曾子曰、脅肩諂笑、

病于夏畦。子路曰、未

同而言、觀其色赧赧

然、非由之所知也。由

是觀之、則君子之所

養可知已矣。

戴盈之曰、什一、去

關市之征、今茲未能、

4. "The philosopher Tsăng said, 'They who shrug up their shoulders, and laugh in a flattering way, toil harder than the summer *laborer in the* fields.' Tszeloo said, 'There are those who talk with people with whom they have no *great* community *of feeling*. If you look at their countenances, they are full of blushes. I do not *desire to* know such persons.' By considering these *remarks*, the *spirit* which the superior man nourishes may be known."

CHAPTER ·VIII. 1. Tae Ying-che said to *Mencius*, "I am not able at present and immediately to do with the levying of a tithe *only*, and abolishing the duties charged at the passes and in the markets. With your leave I will lighten, however, both the tax

肩, "to rib," i. e., to shrug, "the shoulders." 病, as in II, Pt. I, ii, p. 16. 夏畦＝夏月治畦之人. Choo He makes 君子 to mean "those two superior men," referring to Tsăng and Tsze-loo, but this seems to be unnecessary.

CH. 8. WHAT IS WRONG SHOULD BE PUT AN END TO AT ONCE, WITHOUT RESERVE AND WITHOUT DELAY. 1. Tae Ying-che was a great officer of Sung supposed by some to be the same with Tae Puh-shing, ch. vi. Mencius had no doubt been talking

上

盡。

如知其非義斯速已矣、何

攘一雞、以待來年、然後已。

非君子之道、曰請損之、月

其鄰之雞者、或告之曰、是

何如。孟子曰、今有人日攘

請輕之、以待來年、然後已、

and the duties, until next year, and will then make an end of them. What do you think of such a course?"

2. Mencius said, "Here is a man, who every day appropriates some of his neighbor's strayed fowls. Some one says to him, 'Such is not the way of a good man'; and he replies, 'With your leave I will diminish my appropriations, and will take only one fowl a month, until next year, when I will make an end of the practice.'

3. "If you know that the thing is unrighteous, then use all dispatch in putting an end to it:—why wait till next year?"

with him on the points indicated; see I, Pt. II, v, 3; II, Pt. I, v, 3; III, Pt. I, iii. 請, here and below, is simply the speaker's polite way of indicating his resolution. 2. 攘, —here as in Con. Ana., XIII, xviii.

君子,—here,="a good man." 損之, "diminish it," i. e., the amount of his captures. 3. 斯 is used adverbially,—"at once." 已 in all the paragraphs is the verb="have done with it," "put an end to it."

矣、一治一亂。 天下之生久 予不得已也。 予豈好辯哉、 何也。孟子曰、 子好辯、敢問 外人皆稱夫 公都子曰、

CHAPTER IX. 1. The disciple Kung-too said to *Mencius*, "Master, the people beyond *our school* all speak of you as being fond of disputing. I venture to ask whether it be so." *Mencius* replied, "Indeed, I am not fond of disputing, but I am compelled to do it.

2. "A long time has elapsed since this world *of men* received its being, and there has been *along its history* now a period of good order, and now a period of confusion.

CH. 9. MENCIUS DEFENDS HIMSELF AGAINST THE CHARGE OF BEING FOND OF DISPUTING. WHAT LED TO HIS APPEARING TO BE SO WAS THE NECESSITY OF THE TIME. Comp. II, Pt. I, ii. Mencius would appear from this chapter to have believed that the mantle of Confucius had fallen upon him, and that his position was that of a sage, on whom it devolved to live and labor for the world. 1. 外人,—"outside men," i. e., people in general, all beyond his school, as the representative of orthodoxy in the empire. 敢問何, acc. to the gloss in the 備旨,="I venture to ask why you are so fond of disputing," as if Kung-too admitted the charge of the outside people. But it is better to interpret as in the translation. The spirit of 予豈好辯哉 seems to be better given in English by dropping the interrogation. 2. Commentators are unanimous in understanding 天下之生 not of the material world, and taking 生 as＝生民. It is remarkable, then, that Mencius, in his review of the history of mankind, does not go beyond the time of Yaou (comp. Pt. I, iv.), and that at its commencement he places a period not of good order (治, low. 3rd tone),

當堯之時、水逆行、氾濫於
中國、蛇龍居之民無所定、
下者爲巢上者爲營窟、書
曰、洚水警余、洚水者、洪水
也。使禹治之、禹掘地而注
之海、驅蛇龍而放之菹、水

3. "In the time of Yaou, the waters, flowing out of their channels, inundated the Middle Kingdom. Snakes and dragons occupied it, and the people had no place where they could settle themselves. In the low grounds they made nests for themselves, and in the high grounds they made caves. It is said in the 'Book of History,' 'The waters in their wild course warned me.' Those 'waters in their wild course' were the waters of the great inundation.

4. "*Shun* employed Yu to reduce the waters to order. Yu dug open *their obstructed channels,* and conducted them to the sea. He drove away the snakes and dragons, and forced them into the grassy

but of confusion. 3. Mark the variations of phraseology here from Pt. I, iv, 7. 書曰,––see the Shoo-king, II, iii, 14, where for 警 we have 儆. The "nests" were huts on high-raised platforms. In the Le-ke, IX, i, par. 8, these are said to have been the summer habitations of the earliest men, and 營窟, the winter. 營窟＝ "artificial caves," i.e., caves hollowed out from heaps of earth raised upon the ground. 洚水 is the same as the 水逆水 above. Choo He explains it by "deep and shoreless." 4. 掘地,––"dug the earth," but with the meaning in the translation. 菹 is

息棄田以爲園囿、使民

室以爲汙池、民無所安

之道衰、暴君代作、壞宮

而居之。堯舜旣沒、聖人
　　　　　五節

人者消、然後人得平土

也、險阻旣遠、鳥獸之害

由地中行、江淮河漢、是

marshes. *On this,* the waters pursued their course
through the country, even the waters of the Keang,
the Hwae, the Ho, and the Han, and the dangers and
obstructions which they had occasioned were removed.
The birds and beasts which had injured the people
*also* disappeared, and after this men found the plains
*available for them,* and occupied them.

5. "After the death of Yaou and Shun, the principles that mark sages fell into decay. Oppressive
sovereigns arose one after another, who pulled down
houses to make ponds and lakes, so that the people
*knew* not where they could rest in quiet, and threw
fields out of cultivation to form gardens and parks, so

read by Choo He *tseu,* but wrongly.
With the meaning in the text, it is
read *keay.* 水由地中行,—"the
waters traveled in the middle or
bosom of the earth," i. e., were no
longer spread abroad over its surface.
Choo He makes 地中＝兩涯之間,

"between their banks," but that is
not so much the idea, as that the
waters pursued a course to the sea,
through the land, instead of being
spread over its surface. 5. In describing this period of confusion,
Mencius seems to ignore the sageship

五十、驅虎豹犀象而
海隅而戮之滅國者
年討其君驅飛廉於
相武王誅紂伐奄三
身、天下又大亂周公
多而禽獸至及紂之
又作園囿汙池沛澤
不得衣食、邪說暴行

that the people could not get clothes and food. *Afterwards*, corrupt speakings and oppressive deeds became more rife; gardens and parks, ponds and lakes, thickets and marshes, became more numerous, and birds and beasts swarmed. By the time of Chow, the empire was again in a state of great confusion.

6. "Chow-kung assisted King Woo, and destroyed Chow. He smote Yen, and after three years put its sovereign to death. He drove Fei-leen to a corner by the sea, and slew him. The states which he extinguished amounted to fifty. He drove far away also the tigers, leopards, rhinoceroses, and elephants;

of T'ang, and of the kings Wăn and Woo;—especially that of T'ang, 行, —low. 3rd tone. 沛, as associated with 澤, means thick marshy jungles, where beasts could find shelter. The 水 in its composition requires that we recognize the marshiness of the thickets or cover. But this account of the empire down to the rise of the Chow dynasty implies that it was thinly peopled. 6. The kingdom of

Yen is referred to a portion of the present district of K'euh-fow (曲阜) in Yenchow in Shantung. Chaou K'e connects 三年討其君 with 誅紂, but it seems to belong more naturally to 伐奄. Fei-leën was a favorite minister of Chow, who aided him in his enormities. In the "Historical Records," Book IV, 秦本記, at the beginning, he appears as 蜚廉, but without mention of his banish-

父者有之。孔子懼、作春秋、

臣弒其君者有之、子弒其

世衰道微、邪說暴行有作、

佑啟我後人、咸以正無缺。

哉文王謨、丕承哉武王烈、

遠之、天下大悅、書曰、丕顯

—and the empire was greatly delighted. It is said in the 'Book of History,' 'Great and splendid were the plans of King Wăn. Greatly were they carried out by the energy of King Woo! They are for the assistance and instruction of us who are of an after day. They are all in principle correct, and deficient in nothing.'

7. "*Again* the world fell into decay, and principles faded away. Perverse speakings and oppressive deeds waxed rife again. There were instances of ministers who murdered their sovereigns, and of sons who murdered their fathers.

8. "Confucius was afraid, and made the 'Spring

ment and death. The place called "a corner by the sea" cannot be determined. And it would be vain to try to enumerate the "fifty kingdoms," which Chow-kung extinguished. The 夷狄, in par. 11, must be supposed to have been among them. The "tigers, leopards, etc.," are the animals kept by Chow, not those infesting the country, as in the more ancient periods. 書曰,—see the Shoo-king, V, xxiv, 6. 7. 行, low. 3rd tone. 有 作,—有 read as, and = 又. 8. "Spring and Autumn," --annals of Loo for 242 years (721–479 B. C.), with Confucius's annotations, or rather all adapted by him to express a correct judgment on

春秋、天子之事
也、是故孔子曰、
知我者、其惟春
秋乎、罪我者、其
惟春秋乎。聖王
不作、諸侯放恣、
處士橫議、楊朱
墨翟之言盈天

and Autumn.' What the 'Spring and Autumn' contains are matters proper to the emperor. On this account Confucius said, 'Yes! It is the "Spring and Autumn" which will make men know me, and it is the "Spring and Autumn" which will make men condemn me.'

9. *Once more*, sage emperors cease to arise, and the princes of the states give the reins to their lusts. Unemployed scholars indulge in unreasonable discussions. The words of Yang Choo and Mih Teih fill

every event and actor. They are composed as an emperor would have composed them. As Confucius was a sage without the imperial throne, had one of the imperial sages written annals, he would have done so, as Confucius has done. Choo He quotes from the commen. Hoo (胡 安 國):— "Chung-ne made the 'Spring and Autumn,' to lodge in it the true royal laws. There are the firm exhibition of the constant duties; the proper use of ceremonial distinctions; the assertion of *Heaven's* decree of *favor* to the virtuous; and the punishment of the guilty—all these things, of which it may be said in brief that they are the business of the emperor." (Comp. on Hoo's language the Shoo-king, II, iii, 7.) It was by the study of this book, therefore, that Confucius wished himself to be known, though he knew that he exposed himself to presumption on account of the imperial point of view from which he looked at everything in it. This is the meaning of 罪 我 者 其 惟 春 秋 乎, and not—"Those who condemn me (i. e., bad ministers and prince) will do so on account of my condemnations of them in it," which is the view of Chaou K'e I have dropped the interrogations in the translation. 9. 處,—up. 2nd tone, applied to a virgin dwelling in the seclusion of her apartments, and here to a scholar without public employment. Yang Choo, called also Yang Shoo (戌) and Yang Tsze-keu (子 居), was

色、野有餓莩、此率獸而食
有肥肉、廄有肥馬、民有饑
君、是禽獸也、公明儀曰、庖
氏兼愛是無父也、無父無
墨、楊氏爲我是無君也、墨
下、天下之言不歸楊、則歸

the empire. *If you listen to* people's discourses throughout it, *you will find that* they have adopted the views either of Yang or of Mih. *Now*, Yang's principle is—'each one for himself,' which does not acknowledge *the claims of* the sovereign. Mih's principle is—'to love all equally,' which does not acknowledge *the peculiar affection due to* a father. But to acknowledge neither king nor father is to be in the state of a beast. Kung-ming E said, 'In their kitchens, there is fat meat. In their stables, there are fat horses. But their people have the look of hunger, and on the wilds there are those who have died of famine. This is leading on beasts to devour men.'

---

an heresiarch of the times of Confucius and Lao-tse, of which last he is said to have been a disciple. In the days of Mencius, his principles appear to have been very rife. We may call his school the *selfish* school of China (爲我,—爲, low. 3rd tone), as Mih's was the *transcendental*. 庖有肥肉云云,—see I, Pt. I, iv, 4.

不得作、作於其心、害於其事、

之道、距楊墨放淫辭邪說者

人將相食吾爲此懼閑先聖
○十
而

義也、仁義充塞則率獸食人、

道不著是邪說誣民充塞仁

人也、楊墨之道不息孔子之

If the principles of Yang and Mih are not stopped, and
the principles of Confucius not set forth, then those
perverse speakings will delude the people, and stop up
*the path* of ·benevolence and righteousness.　When
benevolence and righteousness are stopped up, beasts
will be led on to devour men, and men will devour one
another.

·10· "I am alarmed by ·these things, and address
myself to the defense of the·doctrines of the former
sages; and to oppose Yang and Mih.　I drive away
their licentious expressions, so that such perverse.
speakers may not be able to show themselves.　*Their
delusions* spring up in men's minds, and do injury
to their practice of affairs.　Shown in their practice

10. 爲,—low. 3rd tone. 作於其心云 | 云, see II, Pt. I, ii, 17.

膺、荆舒是懲、則莫我敢承、無

而亂臣賊子懼詩云、戎狄是

猛獸而百姓寧孔子成春秋、

水、而天下平周公兼夷狄驅

起、不易吾言矣昔者、禹抑洪

作於其事、害於其政、聖人復

of affairs, they are pernicious to their government.
When sages shall rise up again, they will not change
my words.

11. "In former times, Yu repressed the vast waters
*of the inundation,* and the empire was reduced to
order. Chow-kung's achievements extended even to
the barbarous tribes of the west and north, and he
drove away all ferocious animals, and the people
enjoyed repose. Confucius completed the 'Spring
and Autumn,' and rebellious ministers and villainous
sons were struck with terror.

12. "It is said in the 'Book of Poetry,'

    'He smote the barbarians of the west and the north;
    He punished King and Seu;
    And no one dared to resist us.'

11. 兼,—"embraced," "comprehended," i. e., among the fifty
states referred to above. 賊子,

—the parricides, mentioned in par.
7. 12. See Pt. I, iv, 13. The remark in the note there is equally

不誠廉士哉、居於陵、
匡章曰、陳仲子豈
也。
距楊墨者、聖人之徒
哉、予不得已也。能言
以承三聖者豈好辯
邪說距詖行放淫辭、
也。我亦欲正人心息
父無君、是周公所膺

These father deniers and king deniers would have been smitten by Chow-kung.

13. "I also wish to rectify men's hearts, and to put an end to those perverse doctrines, to oppose their one-sided actions and banish away their licentious expressions;—and thus to carry on the work of the three sages. Do I do so because I am fond of disputing? I am compelled to do it.

14. "Whoever is able to oppose Yang and Mih is a disciple of the sages."

CHAPTER X. 1. K'wang Chang said *to Mencius,* "Is not Ch'an Chung a man of true self-denying purity? He was living in Wooling, and for three

applicable to the quotation here. 13. 詖 行,—行, low. 3rd tone. Comp. II, Pt. I, ii, 17. 14. This concluding remark is of a piece with the hesitancy shown by Mencius in II, Pt. I, ii, to claim boldly his place in the line of sages along with Confucius.

CH. 10. THE MAN WHO WILL AVOID ALL ASSOCIATION WITH, AND OBLIGA-TION TO, THOSE OF WHOM HE DOES NOT APPROVE, MUST NEEDS GO OUT OF THE WORLD. 1. Kw'ang Chang and Ch'an Chung, called also Ch'an Tsze-chung (子 終), were both men of Ts'e, the former high in the employment and confidence of the prince, the latter, as we learn from this chapter, belonging to an old and noble family of the state. His

三日不食耳無聞目無

見也井上有李螬食實

者、過半矣匍匐往將食

之三咽、然後耳有聞目

有見。孟子曰、於齊國之

士、吾必以仲子爲巨擘

焉、雖然仲子惡能廉、充

仲子之操、則蚓而後可

days without food, till he could neither hear nor see. Over a well there grew a plum tree, the fruit of which had been more than half eaten by worms. He crawled to it, and tried to eat *some of the fruit*, when, after swallowing three mouthfuls, he recovered his sight and hearing.

2. Mencius replied, "Among the scholars of Ts'e, I must regard Chung as the thumb *among the fingers*. But still, where is the self-denying purity *he pretends to?* To carry out the principles which he holds, one must become an earthworm, for so only can it be done.

principles appear to have been those of Heu Hing (Pt. I, iv), or even more severe. We may compare him with the *recluses* of Confucius's time. Woo-ling (於 read *voo*) appears to have been a poor wild place, where Chung and his wife, like-minded with himself, lived retired. It is referred either to the district of Ch'ang-shan or that of Tsze-ch'uen in the department of Ts'enan. The 螬 is a worm proper to excrementitious matter. The term here is used, I suppose, to heighten our sense of the strait to which Chung was reduced by his self-denial. 咽, read *yen*, up. 3rd tone, ≒吞, "to swallow." 2. 充=推 而 滿 之, "to carry out fully." 3.

彼身織屨妻辟纑以易之

是未可知也曰是何傷哉、

樹與抑亦盜跖之所樹與、

築與、所食之粟、伯夷之所

之所築與抑亦盜跖之所

黃泉仲子所居之室、伯夷

者也夫蚓、上食槁壤、下飲

3. "Now, an earthworm eats the dry mold above and drinks the yellow spring below. Was the house in which Chung dwells built by a Pih-e? or was it built by a robber like Chih? Was the millet which he eats planted by a Pih-e? or was it planted by a robber like Chih? These are things which cannot be known."

4. "But," said *Chang*, "what does that matter? He himself weaves sandals of hemp, and his wife twists hempen threads, to barter them."

Pih-e,—see Con. Ana., V, xxi, *et al.* Chih was a famous robber chief of Confucius's time, a younger brother of Hwuy of Lew-hea. There was, however, it is said, in high antiquity in the times of Hwang-te, a noted robber of the same name, which was given to Hwuy's brother, because of the similarity of his course. Taou Chih (the robber Chih) has come to be like a proper name.—As Chung withdrew from human society, lest he should be defiled by it, Mencius shows that, unless he were a worm, he could not be independent of other men. Even the house he lived in, and the millet he ate, might be the result of the labor of a villain like Taou-chih, or of a worthy like Pih-e, for anything he could tell. 4. 何傷, —see I, i, Pt. I, vii, 8. 織屨,—see Pt. I, iv. 辟, read *peih*,=纑, "to twist," as threads of hemp on the knee. This meaning is not found in

他日、其母殺是鵝也、與之食之、

己頻顣曰惡用是鶃鶃者爲哉、

陵、他日歸、則有饋其兄生鵝者、

室、而不居也辟兄離母、處於於

而不食也以兄之室爲不義之

祿萬鍾以兄之祿爲不義之祿、

也曰仲子、齊之世家也兄戴、蓋

5.　Mencius rejoined, "Chung belongs to an ancient
and noble family of Ts'e. His elder brother Tae
received from Kŏ a revenue of 10,000 *chung* but he
considered his brother's emolument to be unrighteous,
and would not eat of it, and in the same way he
considered his brother's house to be unrighteous, and
would not dwell in it. Avoiding his brother and
leaving his mother, he went and dwelt in Woo-ling.
One day afterwards, he returned *to their house*, when
it happened that some one sent his brother a present
of a live goose. He, knitting his eyebrows, said,
'What are you going to use that cackling thing for?'
By and by his mother killed the goose, and gave him

the dict. 5. 蓋,—up. 4th tone, as in II, Pt. II, vi, 1. 祿萬鍾,—see II, Pt. II, x, 3. 辟,—the same as 避. 頻顣, used for 顰蹙. 鶃,—read *neih*, the sound made by a goose. 是鶃鶃者,—"this cackler."

後充其操者也。
類也乎、若仲子者蚓而
則居之、是尚爲能充其
兄之室、則弗居以於陵
則不食以妻則食之、以
之肉也、出而哇之以母
其兄自外至曰、是鶃鶃

some of it to eat. Just then his brother came into the house, and said, 'It's the flesh of that cackling thing,' upon which he went out and vomited it.

6. "Thus, what his mother gave him he would not eat, but what his wife gives him he eats. He will not dwell in his brother's house, but he dwells in Woo-ling. How can he in such circumstances complete the style of life which he professes? With such principles as Chung holds, a man must be an earth-worm, and then he can carry them out."

6. 以母則不食 is expanded by Choo He,—以母之食爲不義而不食, "he considered what his mother gave him to eat not to be righteous, and would not eat it. Similarly he brings out the force of the 以 in the other clauses. The glossarist of Chaou K'e treats it more loosely, as in the translation.

## BOOK IV

## LE LOW.    PART I

六律、不能
之聰、不以
方員、師曠
矩、不能成
巧、不以規
公輸子之
離婁之明、
孟子曰、
句上
離婁章

CHAPTER I.    1. Mencius said, "The power of vision of Le Low, and the skill of hand of Kung-shoo, without the compass and square, could not form squares and circles.    The acute ear of the music master K'wang, without the pitch tubes, could not determine correctly

With this Book commences what is commonly called the second or lower part of the works of Mencius, but that division is not recognized in the critical editions.    It is named Le Low, from its commencing with those two characters, and contains twenty-eight chapters, which are most of them shorter than those of the preceding Books.

CH. 1. THERE IS AN ART OF GOVERNMENT, AS WELL AS A WISH TO GOVERN WELL, TO BE LEARNED FROM THE EXAMPLE AND PRINCIPLES OF THE ANCIENT KINGS, AND WHICH REQUIRES TO BE STUDIED AND PRACTICED BY RULERS AND THEIR MINISTERS.    1. Le Low, called also Le Choo (朱), carries us back to the highest Chinese antiquity.    He was, it is said, of the time of Hwang-te, and so acute of vision, that, at the distance of 100 paces, he could discern the smallest hair.    The authority for this is the philosopher Chwang (莊).    Some say that Le Low was a disciple of Mencius, but this is altogether unlikely.    Kung-shoo, named Pan (written 班 and 般), was a celebrated mechanist of Loo, of the times of Confucius.    He is fabled to have made birds of bamboo, that could continue flying for three days, and horses of wood, moved by springs, which could draw carriages.    He is now the god of carpenters, and is worshiped by them.    See the Le-ke, III, Pt. II, ii, 21.    There are some, however, who make two men of the name, an earlier and a later.    K'wang, styled Tsze-yay (子野), was music master and a wise counselor of Tsin, a little prior to the time of Confucius.    See the 左傳襄公十四年.    六律, "six pitch tubes," put by *synecdoche* for 十二律, or "twelve tubes," invented, it is said, in the earliest times, to determine by their various adjusted lengths the notes of the musical scale.    Six of them go by the name of *leu* (呂), which are to be understood as comprehended

正五音堯舜之道、

不以仁政不能平

治天下今有仁心○二節

仁聞而民不被其

澤不可法於後世

者不行先王之道

the five notes. The principles of Yaou and Shun,
without a benevolent government, could not secure
the tranquil order of the empire.

2. "There are now *princes* who have benevolent
hearts and a reputation for benevolence, while yet the
people do not receive any benefits from them, nor will
they leave any example to future ages;—all because
they do not put into practice the ways of the ancient
kings.

under the phrase in the text. The
five notes are the five full notes of
the octave, neglecting the semitones.
They are called 宮, 商, 角, 徵 (*che*),
羽. See on the Shoo-king, II, i, 24.
堯 舜 之 道,—道, is to be taken
"emptily," meaning the benevolent
wish to govern well, such as animated
Yaou and Shun. 仁 政 is the same
finding its embodiment,＝the right
art of government, having the same
relation to it as the compass to
circles, etc. 2. 聞,—low. 3rd tone.
Observe the correlation of 者 and 也,
the last clause assigning the reason

of what is said in the preceding ones.
先 王 之 道,—here, and below, the
道 must be taken differently from
its applica. in the last par., and ＝
the 仁 政 of that. The commen. 范
refers to king Seuen of Ts'e (see I,
Pt. I, vii), as an instance of the
princes who have a benevolent heart,
and to the first emperor of the Leang
dynasty (A. D. 502–557), whose Buddhistic scrupulosity about taking life
made him have a benevolent reputation. Yet the heart of the one did
not advantage the state, nor the
reputation of the other the empire.

為方員平直不可勝用

焉繼之以規矩準繩以

之有也。聖人既竭目力

遵先王之法而過者、未

云、不愆不忘率由舊章、

政、徒法、不能以自行詩

也。故曰、徒善、不足以爲

3. "Hence we have the saying: 'Virtue alone is not sufficient for the exercise of government; laws alone cannot carry themselves into practice.'

4. "It is said in the 'Book of Poetry,'

'Without transgression, without forgetfulness,
Following the ancient canons.'

Never has any one fallen into error, who followed the laws of the ancient kings.

5. "When the sages had used the vigor of their eyes, they called in to their aid the compass, the square, the level, and the line, to make things square, round, level, and straight:—the use of the *instruments*

3. 徒善,—here "simply being good," i. e., virtue without laws, and 徒法 =laws without virtue; the virtue, however, being understood of the "benevolent heart." 4. See the She-king, Pt. III, ii, Ode v, st. 2. 繼之 以,—lit., "continued it with." The line must be understood of the plumb line, as well as of the marking line. 準 is rightly translated,—"the level," but I have not been able to ascertain its original form in China. In the 前漢書, 本志, Bk. I, we read: "From the adjustment of weights and things sprang the *lever* (衡). The lever revolving produced the *circle*. The circle produced the *square*. The square produced the *line*. The line produced the *level*." On the last sentence 韋昭 says: "They set up the level to look at the line, using water as the equalizer." 不可勝 (up. 1st tone) 用,—see I, Pt. I, iii, 3. The nominative to 可 is the

不因先王之道、可謂智

陵、爲下、必因川澤爲政、

下矣。故曰、爲高必因丘
六邸

不忍人之政、而仁覆天

也、既竭心思焉、繼之以

六律、正五音不可勝用

也、既竭耳力焉、繼之以

is inexhaustible. When they had used their power of hearing to the utmost, they called in the pitch tubes to their aid to determine the five notes:—the use of those *tubes* is inexhaustible. When they had exerted to the utmost the thoughts of their hearts, they called in to their aid a government that could not endure to witness the sufferings of men:—and their benevolence overspread the empire.

6. "Hence we have the saying: 'To raise a thing high, we must begin from *the top of* a mound or a hill; to dig to a *great* depth, we must commence in *the low ground of* a stream or a marsh.' Can he be pronounced wise, who, in the exercise of government, does not proceed according to the ways of the former kings?

whole of what precedes from 繼. 不 忍人, see II, Pt. II, vi, 1. 6. 因 = 依. "to conform to," i. e., here to take advantage of. The saying is

小人犯刑、國之所存者

道工不信度君子犯義、

也、下無法守也、朝不信

其惡於衆也。上無道揆

位、不仁而在高位、是播

乎。是以惟仁者宜在高

7. "Therefore only the benevolent ought to be in high stations. When a man destitute of benevolence is in a high station, he thereby disseminates his wickedness among all *below him*.

8. "When the prince has no principles by which he examines *his administration*, and his ministers have no laws by which they keep themselves *in the discharge of their duties*, then in the court obedience is not paid to principle, and in the office obedience is not paid to rule. Superiors violate the laws of righteousness, and inferiors violate the penal laws. It is only by a fortunate chance that a kingdom in such a case is preserved.

found in the Le-ke, X, ii, 10. 8. This par. is an expansion of the last clause of the prec , illustrating how the wickedness flows downwards, with its consequences. 上,—"the highest," i. e., the prince. 下, the next "below," his ministers. 朝,—*ch'aou*, low. 1st tone, "the court," and 工, as opposed to it, the various officers, as having their "work" to do. 君子 and 小人,—with reference to station. The 也 at the end of the two clauses shows that they are both equally assertive, though the prince, governed and governing by principles of righteousness, will be a law to his

幸也。故曰、城郭不完兵

甲不多、非國之災也、田

野不辟貨財不聚、非國

之害也、上無禮下無學、

賊民興、喪無日矣。詩曰、

天之方蹶、無然泄泄。

泄猶沓沓也。事君無義、

9. "Therefore it is said, 'It is not the exterior and interior walls being incomplete, and the supply of weapons offensive and defensive not being large, which constitutes the calamity of a kingdom. It is not the cultivable area not being extended, and stores and wealth not being accumulated, which occasions the ruin of a kingdom.' When superiors do not observe the rules of propriety, and inferiors do not learn, then seditious people spring up, and *that kingdom* will perish in no time.

10. "It is said in the 'Book of Poetry,'

'When such an overthrow *of Chow* is being
　　produced by Heaven,
　Be not ye so much at your ease!'

11. "'At your ease;'—that is, dilatory.

12. "And so dilatory may *those officers* be deemed,

ministers. 9. 城郭,—see II, Pt. II, i, 2. 辟＝闢, as in I, Pt. II, vii, 16. 田 野,—"fields and wilds." 喪,—up. 3rd tone. 10. See the She-king, III, ii, Ode X, 2. 蹶,—read *kwei*, up. 3rd tone. 泄,—*e*, low. 3rd tone.—From this par. it is the ministers of a prince who are contemplated by Mencius. They have their duty to perform, in order that the benevolent govt. may be realized. 11. 猶沓沓,—we are to understand

進退無禮言則非先王
之道者猶沓沓也故曰、
責難於君謂之恭陳善
閉邪謂之敬吾君不能
謂之賊。
孟子曰、規矩、方員之

who serve their prince without righteousness, who take office and retire from it without regard to propriety, and who in their words disown the ways of the ancient kings.

13. "Therefore it is said, 'To urge one's sovereign to difficult achievements may be called showing respect for him. To set before him what is good and repress his perversities, may be called showing reverence for him. *He who does not do these things, saying to himself*,—My sovereign is incompetent to this, may be said to play the thief with him.'"

CHAPTER II. 1. Mencius said, "The compass and square produce perfect circles and squares. By the

that this phrase was commonly used in Mencius's time with this acceptation. 12. 非,—used as a verb, "to slander," or "disown." 13. Comp. II, Pt. II, ii, 4. We are obliged to supply considerably in the translation, to bring out the meaning of the last sentence. 賊 may be taken as a verb—"to injure," or as I have taken it.

CH. 2. A CONTINUATION OF THE LAST CHAPTER;—THAT YAOU AND SHUN ARE THE PERFECT MODELS OF SOVEREIGNS AND MINISTERS, AND THE CONSEQUENCES OF NOT IMITATING THEM. 1. "The compass and square

民、賊其民者也孔子曰、道二、

者也、不以堯之所以治民治

之所以事堯事君、不敬其君

者、皆法堯舜而已矣、不以舜

君、盡君道、欲爲臣盡臣道二、

至也、聖人人倫之至也。欲爲

sages, the human relations are perfectly exhibited.

2.  "He who as a sovereign would perfectly discharge the duties of a sovereign, and he who as a minister would perfectly discharge the duties of a minister, have only to imitate—the one Yaou, and the other Shun.  He who does not serve his sovereign as Shun served Yaou, does not respect his sovereign, and he who does not rule his people as Yaou ruled his, injures his people.

3.  "Confucius said, 'There are but two courses,

are the perfection of squares and circles";—but we must understand the meaning as in the translation. So with the 2nd clause. 人倫,—see III, Pt. II, iv, 9.  2. 二者="these two" things, putting the above clauses abstractly, but we cannot do that so well in English.  The force of 而已, acc. to the 備旨, is "to show that there is no other way for the sovereign and minister to pursue."—Of "the human relations" only that of sovereign and minister is here adduced, because Mencius was speaking with reference to the rulers of his time.  3. If the remark were Mencius's own, we should translate 仁 by "benevolence."  The term in Confucius rather denotes "perfect virtue."  By the course of virtue is intended the imitation of Yaou and Shun; by its opposite, the neglect of

之世、此之謂也。

云、殷鑒不遠、在夏后

孫、百世不能改也。詩五郎

之曰幽厲、雖孝子慈

不甚、則身危國削、名

其民甚、則身弒國亡、

仁與不仁而已矣。暴西而

*which can be pursued,* that of virtue and its opposite.'

4. "*A sovereign who* carries the oppression of his· people to the highest pitch, will himself be slain, and his kingdom will perish. If one stop short of the highest pitch, his life will *notwithstanding* be in danger, and his kingdom will be weakened. He will be styled 'The dark,' or 'The cruel,' and though he may have filial sons and affectionate grandsons, they will not be able in a hundred generations to change *the designation.*

5. "·This is what is intended in the words of the 'Book of Poetry,'

> · The beacon of Yin was not remote,
> It was in the time of the sovereign of Hea.'"

them as models. 4. By sovereigns, who carry their oppression to the highest pitch, Mencius intends, as his examples, Keĕ and Chow, the last emperors of the Hea and Yin dynasties. By "The dark" and "The cruel," he intends the 12th (780 B. C.) and 10th (877 B. C.) emperors of the Chow dynasty, who received those posthumous indelible designations. 1 take 削 in the sense of "weakened" (dict. 弱), which it elsewhere has in Mencius. 5. See the She-king, III, iii, Ode J, st. 8, an ode of the time of the emperor Le (厲), intended for his warning. The sovereign of Hea is the tyrant Keĕ, and by Yin is intended the tyrant Chow, by whose fate, neglecting the lesson furnished him by that of Keĕ, it is suggested that Le should be admonished.

卿大夫不仁、不保宗
諸侯不仁、不保社稷、
天子不仁、不保四海、
以廢興存亡者、亦然。
下也以不仁國之所
天下也、以仁其失天
孟子曰、三代之得

CHAPTER III. I. Mencius said, "It was by benevolence that the three dynasties gained the empire, and by not being benevolent that they lost it.

2. "It is by the same means that the decaying and flourishing, the preservation and perishing, of states are determined.

3. "If the emperor be not benevolent, he cannot preserve the empire *from passing from him*. If the sovereign of a state be not benevolent, he cannot preserve his kingdom. If a high noble or great officer be not benevolent, he cannot preserve his ancestral

CH. 3. THE IMPORTANCE TO ALL, AND SPECIALLY, TO RULERS, OF EXERCISING BENEVOLENCE. 1. "The three dynasties" are the Hea, the Shang, and the Chow. It is a bold utterance, seeing the Chow dynasty was still existing in the time of Mencius, though he regarded it as old and ready to vanish away. He has a reference, acc. to Choo He, to the emperors Le and Yew, mentioned in the last ch. 2. 四海,—"the four seas," i. e., all with them, as subject to the emperor's jurisdiction. There is a special reference, however, to the emperor's right to offer all sacrifices:—those peculiar to himself, and those open to others. 社稷,—"the spirits of the land and the grain," i. e., the spirits securing the stability and prosperity of a particular state, which it was the prerogative of the

反其仁治人不治反　　孟子曰愛人不親、　酒。　不仁是猶惡醉而強　四體今惡死亡、而樂　廟、士庶人不仁、不保

temple. If a scholar or common man be not benevolent, he cannot preserve his four limbs.

4. "Now they hate death and ruin, and yet delight
in being not benevolent;—this is like hating to be
drunk, and yet being strong *to drink* wine."

CHAPTER IV. 1. Mencius said, "If a man love
others, and no *responsive* attachment is shown to
him, let him turn inward and examine his own
benevolence. If he *is trying to* rule others, and his
government is unsuccessful, let him turn inward and

ruler to sacrifice to. Hence the expression is here used figuratively.
See the Le-ke, Pt. II, iii, 6. 3. 惡,
—the verb, up. 3rd tone, "to hate,
dislike." 強 (up. 2nd tone) 酒,—like
the Hebrew idiom, Isa. 5:22. This is
spoken with reference to the princes
of Mencius's time.

CH. 4. WITH WHAT MEASURE A
MAN METES IT WILL BE MEASURED TO
HIM AGAIN, AND CONSEQUENTLY BE-
FORE A MAN DEALS WITH OTHERS,
EXPECTING THEM TO BE AFFECTED BY
HIM, HE SHOULD FIRST DEAL WITH
HIMSELF. The sentiment is expressed
quite generally, but a particular
reference is to be understood to the

princes of Mencius's time. 1. 反 is
used in a manner common in Mencius, = "to turn back from the course
being pursued, and then to turn
inward to the work of examination
and correction." In the next par.,
we have it followed by another verb,
求. In 治 人, 治 is low. 1st tone,
"to rule," "to try to rule"; in
不 治, 治 is low. 3rd tone, "to be
regulated," the government being
effective. The clauses—愛人不親,
etc., are very concise. The paraphrase in the 備旨 thus expands;—
爲治者體仁以愛人,宜乎人之我
親矣, 而顧有不親焉, 則必反其
仁,恐我之愛人有未至也, 云 云,

皆曰、天下國家、天下

孟子曰、人有恆言、

命、自求多福。

下歸之詩云、永言配

求諸己其身正、而天

敬。行有不得者皆反

其智、禮人不答、反其

examine his wisdom.　If he treats others politely, and they do not return his politeness, let him turn inward and examine his own *feeling of* respect.

2.　"When we do not, by what we do, realize *what we desire,* we must turn inward, and examine ourselves in every point.　When a man's person is correct, the whole empire will turn to him *with recognition and submission.*

3.　"It is said in the 'Book of Poetry,'

'Be always studious to be in harmony with the ordinances *of God,*
And you will obtain much happiness.'"

CHAPTER V.　Mencius said, "People have this common saying, — 'The empire, the state, the family.'

"He who administers government embodies benevolence to love men, and it may be expected men will love him.　Should he find, however, that they do not, he must turn in and examine his benevolence, lest it should be imperfect," etc., etc.　2. 不得＝不得其所欲, "does not get what he wishes."　皆,—"all," with reference to the general form of the preceding clause.　3. See II, Pt. I, iv. 6.

CH. 5.　PERSONAL CHARACTER IS NECESSARY TO ALL GOOD INFLUENCE. Comp. "The superior Learning," text of Conf., par. 4.　The common saying

慕、一國慕之、一

巨室巨室之所

不難不得罪於

■孟子曰爲政

在身。

本在家家之本

之本在國國之

The root of the empire is in the state. The root of
the state is in the family. The root of the family is
in the person *of its head.*"

CHAPTER VI. Mencius said, "The administration
of government is not difficult;—it lies in not offending the great families. He whom the great families
affect, will be affected by the whole state, and he

repeated by all probably means:—
the empire is made up of its component states, and of their component families;—i. e., the families
of the great officers. But Mencius
takes its meaning more generally,
and carries it out a step further.

CH. 6. THE IMPORTANCE TO A
RULER OF SECURING THE ESTEEM
AND SUBMISSION OF THE GREAT
HOUSES. The "not offending" is to
be taken in a moral sense;—the
ruler's doing nothing but what will
command the admiring approbation
of the old and great families in the
state. In illustration of the sentiment, Chow He refers to a story
related of Duke Hwan of Ts'e.
Lighting one day in hunting, on an
old man of 83, the duke sought his
blessing, that he might attain a like
longevity. The old man then prayed,
"May my sovereign enjoy great

longevity, despising gems and gold,
and making men his jewels." At the
duke's request he prayed a second
time, that he might not be ashamed
to learn even from his inferiors, and
a third time, "May my sovereign not
offend against his ministers and the
people!" This answer offended the
duke. "A son," he said, "may
offend against his father, and a
minister against his sovereign. But
how can a sovereign offend against
his ministers?" The old man replied,
"An offending son may get forgiveness through the intercessions of
aunts and uncles. An offending minister may be forgiven by the interces-
sion of the sovereign's favorites and
attendants. But when Këë offended
against T'ang, and Chow offended
against Woo;—those were cases in
point. There was no forgiveness for
them." 所慕,—"whom they affect,"

也順天者存逆天者

大弱役強斯二者天

大賢天下無道小役

小德役大德小賢役

圖孟子曰天下有道、

海。

故沛然德教溢乎四

國之所慕天下慕之、

whom *any* one state affects, will be affected by the whole empire. When this is the case, such a one's virtue and teachings will spread over all within the four seas like the rush of water.''

CHAPTER VII. 1. Mencius said, ''When right government prevails in the empire, *princes of* little virtue are submissive to *those of* great, and *those of* little worth, to those of great. When bad government prevails in the empire, *princes of* small power are submissive to those of great, and the weak to the strong. Both these cases are *the rule of* Heaven. They who accord with Heaven are preserved, and they who rebel against Heaven perish.

not what. Observe the force of 故.
CH. 7. HOW THE SUBJECTION OF ONE STATE TO ANOTHER IS DETERMINED AT DIFFERENT TIMES. A PRINCE'S ONLY SECURITY FOR SAFETY AND PROSPERITY IS IN BEING BENEVOLENT. 1. Many commen. say that by 大德 and 大賢 reference is made to the emperor, but the declarations may as well be taken generally. 斯二者天也,—''Heaven,'' it is said, ''embraces here the ideas of what must be in reason, and the different powers of the contrasted states'' (兼理勢言). This is true, but why sink the idea of a Providential government which is implied in ''Heaven''?

恥受命於先師也。如

受命焉、是猶弟子而

也、小國師大國而恥

也、涕出而女於吳今

令、又不受命、是絕物

亡。齊景公曰、既不能

2. "Duke King of Ts'e said, 'Not to be able to command others, and at the same time to refuse to receive their commands, is to cut one's self off from all intercourse with others.' His tears flowed forth while he gave his daughter to be married to *the prince of* Woo.

3. "Now the small states imitate the large, and yet are ashamed to receive their commands. This is like a scholar's being ashamed to receive the commands of his master.

2. 景公,—see Con. Ana., XII, xi. 絕物,—物 is taken as used for 人, "men," but the phrase is a contracted one, and＝與人喫絕, "separated from other men," or 絕 may be taken actively, which I prefer, and similarly supplemented. 女,—lower 3rd tone, "to give a daughter in marriage." Woo, corresponding to the northern part of the present Chekiang, and the south of Kiang-su, was in Confucius's time still reckoned a barbarous territory, and the princes of the Middle Kingdom were ashamed to enter into relations with it. Duke King, however, yielded to the force of circumstances and so saved himself. The daughter so married soon died. She pined away for her father and her native Ts'e, and was followed to the grave by her husband. The old king of Woo, barbarian as he was, showed much sympathy for his young daughter-in-law. 3. 師,—"to imitate," "to make a master of." Mencius's meaning is that the smaller states followed the example of the larger ones in what was evil, and yet did not like to submit to them. 弟子,—"a youth," here,＝a pupil. 4.

子曰仁不可爲衆也夫國

厥士膚敏裸將于京孔
、

于周服侯服于周天命靡

子其麗不億上帝既命侯

政於天下矣詩云商之孫
。五
　節

大國五年小國七年必爲

恥之莫若師文王師文王、

4. "For a prince who is ashamed of this, the best plan is to imitate King Wăn. Let one imitate King Wăn, and in five years, if his state be large, or in seven years, if it be small, he will be sure to give laws to the empire.

5. "It is said in the 'Book of Poetry,'

> 'The descendants of *the emperors of* the Shang dynasty
> Are in number more than hundreds of thousands;
> But, God having passed His decree,
> They are all submissive to Chow.
> They are submissive to Chow,
> Because the decree of Heaven is not unchanging.
> The officers of Yin, admirable and alert,
> Pour out the libations, and assist in the capital *of Chow.*'

Confucius said, '*As against so* benevolent *a sovereign,* they could not be deemed a multitude.' Thus, if the ·

為政.—"be exercising government," =giving law to. 5. See the She-king, III, i, Ode I, st. 4, 5. 不億＝不止 於億, "not hundreds of thousands only," 侯于周服 is an inversion for 侯服于周. 侯 is here an introduct. particle, ＝惟. 仁不可爲衆, is to be understood as a remark of Confucius on reading the portion of the She-king just quoted;—"against a

言哉、安其危而利其菑、

■孟子曰不仁者可與

以濯。

也、詩云、誰能執熱逝不

仁、是猶執熱而不以濯

欲無敵於天下、而不以

君好仁、天下無敵今也、六郎

prince of a state love benevolence, he will have no opponent in all the empire.

6. "Now they wish to have no opponent in all the empire, but they *do* not *seek to attain this* by being benevolent. This is like a man laying hold of a heated substance, and not having *first* wetted *his* hands. It is said in the 'Book of Poetry,'

'Who can take up a heated substance,
Without wetting *his hands?*'"

CHAPTER VIII. 1. Mencius said, "How is it possible to speak with those *princes* who are not benevolent? Their perils they count safety, their calamities they count profitable, and they have pleasure in

benevolent prince, like King Wăn, the myriads of the adherents of Shang ceased to be myriads. They would not act against him." 6. See the She-king, III, iii, Ode III, st. 5. The ode is referred to the time of the emperor Le, when the empire was hastening to ruin, and in the lines quoted, the author deplores

that there was no resort to proper measures. 逝 is taken as a mere particle of transition.

CH. 8. THAT A PRINCE IS THE AGENT OF HIS OWN RUIN BY HIS VICIOUS WAYS AND REFUSING TO BE COUNSELED. 1. Stress must be laid always on the 不 in 不仁. The expression does not denote the want of

斯濯纓濁斯濯足矣、自取之

濯我足孔子曰小子聽之清、

濯我纓滄浪之水濁兮、可以

子歌曰、滄浪之水清兮、可以

言、則何亡國敗家之有有孺

樂其所以亡者、不仁而可與

the things by which they perish.　If it were possible to talk with them who so violate benevolence, how could we have such destruction of kingdoms and ruin of families?

2.　"There was a boy singing,

 'When the water of the Ts'ang-lang is clear,<br>
 It does to wash the strings of my cap;<br>
 When the water of the Ts'ang-lang is muddy,<br>
 It does to wash my feet.'

3.　"Confucius said, 'Hear what he sings, my children.　When clear, then he will wash his cap strings, and when muddy, he will wash his feet with it.　This *different application* is brought *by the water* on itself.'

benevolence, but the opposite of it. 言＝忠言, "to give faithful advice to." 2. The name Ts'ang-lang (lower 1st tone) is found applied to difft. streams in difft. places.　That in the text was probably in Shantung.　3. 聽之,—之 referring to the words of the song.　斯,＝"this," intensive, or we may take it adverbially:—"*when clear, then* it serves to wash the cap

也夫人必自侮、然後人侮之、家

必自毀、而後人毀之、國必自伐、

而後人伐之太甲曰、天作孽、猶

可違、自作孽、不可活、此之謂也。

孟子曰、桀紂之失天下也、失

其民也失其民者失其心也、得

4. "A man must first despise himself, and then others will despise him. A family must first destroy itself, and then others will destroy it. A kingdom must first smite itself, and then others will smite it.

5. "This is illustrated in the passage of the T'ae Kёă, 'When Heaven sends down calamities, it is still possible to escape them. When we occasion the calamities ourselves, it is not possible any longer to live.'"

CHAPTER IX. 1. Mencius said, "Kёё and Chow's losing the empire, arose from their losing the people, and to lose the people means to lose their hearts.

strings," etc. 4. See II, Pt. I, iv, 6. | LENT CAN A PRINCE RAISE HIMSELF
CH, 9. ONLY BY BEING BENEVO- | TO BE EMPEROR, OR EVEN AVOID

壙也。故爲淵敺魚者獺
也、猶水之就下、獸之走
惡、勿施爾也民之歸仁
有道所欲、與之聚之所
其心、斯得民矣、得其心
天下矣、得其民有道、得
天下有道、得其民斯得

There is a way to get the empire:—get the people, and the empire is got. There is a way to get the people:—get their hearts, and the people are got. There is a way to get their hearts:—it is simply to collect for them what they like, and not to lay on them what they dislike.

2. "The people turn to a benevolent rule as water flows downward, and as wild beasts fly to the wilderness.

3. "Accordingly, *as* the otter aids the deep waters, driving the fish into them, and the hawk aids the

RUIN. 1. 與之聚之,—與 之=爲 民. Chaou K'e interprets it,—聚其 所欲而與之, takin 與 in the sense of "to give," hut this does not appear to be admissible here. To collect for the people what they like, is to govern in such a way that they shall enjoy their lives. Choo He illustrates the meaning from 錯 (Ch'aou) 錯, of the Han dynasty, who did service in the recovery of the ancient books, thus:—"Men like long life, and the founders of the three dynasties cherished men's lives and kept them from harm: Men love wealth, and those kings enriched them, and kept them from straits;" etc., etc. 2. It is best to take 仁 here in the concrete. 走, it is marked, is in the up. 2nd tone. The dict. gives it in the same in I, Pt. I, iii, 2. 3. 爲,—low. 3rd tone. 敺=驅, 爲淵敺魚者,—"he or that which drives the fish for the deep waters." The 獺 is the otter. For a curious particular about it, see the

猶七年之病、求三年之艾也、苟

欲無王、不可得已今之欲王者、

好仁者、則諸侯皆爲之敺矣、雖

民者、桀與紂也。今天下之君、有

也、爲叢敺爵者鸇也、爲湯武敺

thickets, driving the little birds to them, *so* Kĕĕ and Chow aided T'ang and Woo, driving the people to them.

4. "If among the present sovereigns of the empire, there were one who loved benevolence, all the *other* princes would aid him, by driving *the people to him.* Although he wished not to become emperor, he could not avoid becoming so.

5. "The case of *one of* the present princes wishing to become emperor, is like the having to seek mugwort of three years old, to cure a seven years' sickness.

Le-ke, IV (月令), i, 8. 爵 is given in the dictionary as 鳥名, "the name of a bird." Choo He takes it, how-ever, as＝雀, a general name for small birds. 4. 王,—low. 3rd tone,

不可與有言也、自
孟子曰、自暴者、
胥及溺、此之謂也。
詩云、其何能淑、載
憂辱、以陷於死亡。
苟不志於仁、終身
爲不畜、終身不得、

If it have not been kept in store, the patient may all his life not get it. If the princes do not set their wills on benevolence, all their days will be in sorrow and disgrace, and they will be involved in death and ruin.

6. "This is illustrated by what is said in the 'Book of Poetry,'

> 'How *otherwise* can you improve *the empire?*
> You will only with it go to ruin.'"

CHAPTER X. 1. Mencius said, "With those who do violence to themselves, it is impossible to speak.

and in next par. also. 5. 苟爲不畜, 終身不得 is by most commen. interpreted,—"If you now, feeling its want, begin to collect it, it may be available for the cure. You can hold on till it is so. If you do not at once set about it, your case is hopeless." Perhaps the 爲 and 不 should determine in favor of this view. Chaou K'e interprets as in the translation. The down of the mugwort, burnt on the skin, is used for purposes of cautery. The older the plant, the better. 6. The quotation from the She-king is of the two lines immediately following the last quotation in ch. vii. 載,—a particle, = 則.

CH. 10. A WARNING TO THE VIOLENTLY EVIL, AND THE WEAKLY EVIL. 1. 自暴者, "Those who are cruel to themselves," i. e., those who deny, and act contrary to their own nature. 非, a verb. "to disown," "to condemn." 與有言, 有爲.—"to have

棄者、不可與有爲也、言非
禮義謂之自暴也、吾身不
能居仁由義謂之自棄也。
仁、人之安宅也義、人之正
路也。曠安宅而弗居、舍正
路而弗由、哀哉。

With those who throw themselves away, it is impossible to do anything. To disown in his conversation propriety and righteousness, is what we mean by doing violence to one's self. *To say—'I* am not able to dwell in benevolence or pursue the path of righteousness,' is what we mean by throwing one's self away.

2. "Benevolence is the tranquil habitation of man, and righteousness is his straight path.

3. "Alas for them, who leave the tranquil dwelling empty, and do not reside in it, and who abandon the right path and do not pursue it!"

conversation (words), to have action (doing) with them." 3. 舍—for 捨, up. 2nd tone. The lamentation is to be understood as for the 自暴者 and the 自棄者.—It is observed that "this chapter shows that what is right and true (道) do really belong to man, but he extirpates them himself. Profound is the admonition, and learners should give most earnest heed to it."

友、弗獲於上矣、信於友

也、獲於上有道、不信於

獲於上民、不可得而治

圖孟子曰居下位而不

天下平。

人人親其親長其長、而

諸遠事在易、而求諸難、

圖孟子曰、道在爾而求

CHAPTER XI. Mencius said, "The path *of duty* lies in what is near and men seek for it in what is remote. The work *of duty* lies in what is easy, and men seek for it in what is difficult. If each man would love his parents and show the due respect to his elders, the whole empire would enjoy tranquillity."

CHAPTER XII. 1. Mencius said, "When those occupying inferior situations do not obtain the confidence of the sovereign, they cannot succeed in governing the people. There is a way to obtain the confidence of the sovereign:—if one is not trusted by his friends, he will not obtain the confidence of his sovereign. There is a way of being trusted by one's

CH. 11. THE TRANQUIL PROSPERITY OF THE EMPIRE DEPENDS ON THE DISCHARGE OF THE COMMON RELATIONS OF LIFE. 爾＝邇, with which it was anciently interchanged. 長,— up. 2nd tone. It comprehends elders

and superiors. 道,—as in the Chung Yung, i, 1.
CH. 12. THE GREAT WORK OF MEN SHOULD BE TO STRIVE TO ATTAIN PERFECT SINCERITY. See the Chung Yung, xx, 17, 18, which are here

有道、事親弗悅弗信於友
矣、悅親有道、反身不誠、不
悅於親矣、誠身有道、不明
乎善、不誠其身矣。是故誠
者、天之道也、思誠者、人之
道也。至誠而不動者、未之
有也、不誠、未有能動者也。

friends:—if one do not serve his parents so as to make them pleased, he will not be trusted by his friends. There is a way to make one's parents pleased:—if one, on turning his thoughts inward finds a want of sincerity, he will not give pleasure to his parents. There is a way to the attainment of sincerity in one's self:—if a man do not understand what is good, he will not attain sincerity in himself.

2. "Therefore, sincerity is the way of Heaven. To think *how* to be sincere is the way of man.

3. "Never has there been one possessed of complete sincerity, who did not move others. Never has there been one who had not sincerity who was able to move others."

substantially quoted. As the 20th chapter of the Chung Yung, however, is found also in the "Family Sayings," Mencius may have had that, or the fragmentary memorabilia of Confucius, from which it is compiled, before him, and not the Chung-yung.

曰、盍歸乎來、吾聞西伯

東海之濱聞文王作、與

善養老者、太公辟紂居

曰、盍歸乎來、吾聞西伯

北海之濱聞文王作、與

二
章孟子曰、伯夷辟紂、居

CHAPTER XIII. 1. Mencius said, "Pih-e, that he might avoid Chow, was dwelling on the coast of the northern sea. When he heard of the rise of King Wăn, he roused himself, and said, 'Why should I not go and follow him? I have heard that the chief of the west knows well how to nourish the old.' T'ae-kung, that he might avoid Chow, was dwelling on the coast of the eastern sea. When he heard of the rise of King Wăn, he roused himself, and said, 'Why should I not go and follow him? I have heard that

CH. 13. THE INFLUENCE OF GOV-ERNMENT LIKE THAT OF KING WĂN. 1. Pih-e,—see Con. Ana., V, xxii, et al. T'ae-kung was Leu Shang (呂尙), a great counselor of the kings, Wăn and Woo. He was descended from one of Yu's assistants in the regulation of the waters, and on his first rencontre with King Wăn, when he appeared to be only a fisherman, he said 吾太公望子久矣, "My grandfather looked for you long ago." This led to his being styled 太公望, or "Grandfather Hope." See the "Historical Records," Bk.

XXXII, 齊太公世家, at the beginning. Though Pih-e and T'ae-kung were led in the same way to follow King Wăn, their subsequent courses were very different. 辟＝避. Wăn was appointed by Chow chief or baron (伯), his viceroy in the west, to be leader of all the princes in that part of the empire. The comm. say this is referred to in 文王作. I should rather interpret 作 of Wăn's "move-ments," style of administration. With 善養老者, comp. the account of King Wăn's govt. in I, Pt. II, v, 3. 盍歸乎來＝盍歸來乎. Still

善養老者。二老者、天下之
大老也、而歸之、是天下之
父歸之也、天下之父歸之、
其子焉往諸侯有行文王
之政者、七年之內、必爲政
於天下矣。

the chief of the west knows well how to nourish the old.'

2. "Those two old men were the greatest old men of the empire. When they came to follow King Wăn, it was the fathers of the empire coming to follow him. When the fathers of the empire joined him, how could the sons go *to any others?*

3. "Were any of the princes to practice the government of King Wăn, within seven years, he would be sure to be giving laws to the empire."

the 來 is somewhat embarrassing. 2. I like the expansion of this par. in the 日講:—"Moreover, these two old men were not ordinary men. Distinguished alike by age and virtue, they were the greatest old men of the empire. Fit to be so named, the hopes of all looked to them, and the hearts of all were bound to them. All in the empire looked up to them as fathers, and felt as their children, so that when they were moved by the govt. of King Wăn, and came from the coasts of the sea to him, how could the children leave their fathers and go to any others?" 3. 爲政,—as in ch. vii, 4. Comp. Analects, XIII, v–vii. Confucius thought he could have accomplished a similar result in shorter time.

孔子者也、况於爲之強

行仁政、而富之皆棄於

之可也。由此觀之君不

我徒也、小子鳴鼓而攻

粟倍他日孔子曰求非

宰、無能改於其德、而賦

孟子曰、求也爲季氏

CHAPTER XIV. 1. Mencius said, "K'ew acted as chief officer to the head of the Ke family, whose *evil* ways he was unable to change, while he exacted from the people double the grain formerly paid. Confucius said, 'He is no disciple of mine. Little children, beat the drum and assail him.'

2. "Looking at the subject from this case, *we perceive that* when a prince was not practicing benevolent government, all *his ministers* who enriched him were rejected by Confucius: — how much more *would he have rejected* those who are vehement to fight

CH. 14. AGAINST THE MINISTERS OF HIS TIME WHO PURSUED THEIR WARLIKE AND OTHER SCHEMES, REGARDLESS OF THE HAPPINESS OF THE PEOPLE. 1. See Con. Ana., XI, xvi. Here is a plain instance of 德 used in a bad sense. 2. 爲之強戰,—爲, low. 3rd tone. 強 I take as in the up. 2nd tone, and the phrase 強戰 after the analogy of 強酒, ch. iii, 3. Choo He and others take 強, in the low. 1st tone, and make the phrase =

"who fight trusting in the powerfulness of weapons and strength (恃兵力之強而戰)." The proposed interpretation seems much preferable. With the whole phrase comp. 爲之聚斂, Ana., XI, xvi. The force of the 爲之, it seems to me, must be to make the whole equal to the rendering of Noel, which Julien condemus—"*qui suum principem ad arma adstimulant.*" To be strong to fight for his prince, is a minister's

任土地者次之。

諸侯者次之辟草萊、

故善戰者服上刑連

食人肉罪不容於死。

城此所謂率土地而

野爭城以戰殺人盈

戰爭地以戰殺人盈

for their *prince!* When contentions about territory are the ground on which they fight, they slaughter men till the fields are filled with them. When some struggle for a city is the ground on which they fight, they slaughter men till the city is filled with them. This is what is called ' leading on the land to devour human flesh.' Death is not enough for such a crime.

3. "Therefore, those who are skillful to fight should suffer the highest punishment. Next to them *should be punished* those who unite the princes in leagues; and next to them, those who take in grassy commons, imposing the cultivation of the ground *on the people.*"

duty. But to encourage a warlike spirit in him is injurious to the country. 罪 不 容 於 死=其 罪 大, 死 刑 不 足 以 容 之 "his crime is so great that even capital punishment is not sufficient to contain it." 3. Here we have three classes of adventurers who were rife in Mencius's times, and who recommended themselves to the princes in the ways described, pursuing their own ends, regardless of the people. Some advanced themselves by their skill in war; some by their talents for intrigue; and some by plans to make the most of the ground, turning every bit of it to account, but for the good of the ruler, not of the people. 辟=闢. 萊,—"a kind of creeper," "weeds," =fields lying fallow or uncultivated. 任 土 地,—the 土 地 is what had been occupied by the 草 萊. Choo He expands the phrase thus:—" 任 土 地 means,—to divide this land and give it to the people, making them undertake the charge of cultivating it."

儉者不奪人侮奪人之

鼉孟子曰、恭者不侮人、

人焉廋哉。

焉聽其言也、觀其眸子、

焉、胸中不正、則眸子眊

其惡胸中正、則眸子瞭

良於眸子、眸子不能掩

鼉孟子曰、存乎人者、莫

CHAPTER XV. 1. Mencius said, "Of all the parts of a man's body there is none more excellent than the pupil of the eye. The pupil cannot *be used to* hide a man's wickedness. If within the breast all be correct, the pupil is bright. If within the breast all be not correct, the pupil is dull.

2. "Listen to a man's words and look at the pupil of his eye. How can a man conceal his character?"

CHAPTER XVI. Mencius said, "The respectful do not despise others. The economical do not plunder others. The prince who treats men with despite and

CH. 15. THE PUPIL OF THE EYE THE INDEX OF THE HEART. 1. 存乎 人 者,一存＝在, "the things that are in man," i. e., in his body. The excellence of the pupil is from its truthfulness as an index of the heart. The whole is to be understood as spoken by Mencius for the use of those who thought they had only to hear men's words to judge of them. 2. Comp. Con. Ana., II, x.

CH. 16. DEEDS NOT WORDS OR MANNERS, NECESSARY TO PROVE MENTAL QUALITIES. 恭 者, 儉 者, though I have translated them generally, are yet spoken with a reference to the 君 that follows. The princes of Mencius's time made great pretensions, of which their actions proved the insincerity. 侮 and 不 奪 are to be understood of the disposition:— "not wish to contemn, etc." 奪,

君、惟恐不順焉、惡得

爲恭儉、恭儉豈可以

聲音笑貌爲哉、

臺淳于髠曰男女授

受不親禮與孟子曰、

禮也。曰嫂溺則援之

以手乎曰、嫂溺不援、

是豺狼也、男女授受

plunders them, is only afraid that they may not prove obedient to him:—how can he be regarded as respectful or economical? How can respectfulness and economy be made out of tones of the voice and a smiling manner?"

CHAPTER XVII. 1. Shun-yu K'wǎn said, "Is it the rule that males and females shall not allow their hands to touch in giving or receiving any thing?" Mencius replied, "It is the rule." K'wǎn asked, "If a man's sister-in-law be drowning, shall he rescue her with his hand?" Mencius said, "He who would not so rescue a drowning woman is a wolf. For males and females not to allow their hands to touch in

directly governing 人, is remarkable. 爲恭儉,—爲=以爲 or 名爲, "to be regarded," "to be styled." The final 爲=作爲, and in the passive, "to be made." 聲音, "tones" = words.

CH. 17. HELP—EFFECTUAL HELP —CAN BE GIVEN TO THE WORLD, ONLY IN HARMONY WITH RIGHT AND PROPRIETY. 1. Shun-yu K'wǎn was a native of Ts'e, a famous sophist, and otherwise a man of note in his day; see the "Historical Records," Bk. CXXVI, 列傳, lxvi. He here tries to entrap Mencius into a confession that he did not well in maintaining his dignity of reserve. For the rule of propriety referred to, see the Le Ke, I, ii, 31. 不親=不以手相視接. 權,—see Con. Ana., IX, xxix; XVIII, viii. 豺狼 may be

子之不教子、何
䲭公孫丑曰、君
手援天下乎。
援之以手、子欲
援之以道、嫂溺、
何也。曰、天下溺、
矣、夫子之不援、
也。曰、今天下溺
援之以手者、權
不親禮也、嫂溺

giving and receiving is the *general* rule; when a sister-in-law is drowning, to rescue her with the hand is a peculiar exigency."

2. *K'wăn* said, "The whole empire is drowning. How strange it is that you will not rescue it!"

3. *Mencius* answered, "A drowning empire must be rescued with right principles, as a drowning sister-in-law has to be rescued with the hand. Do you wish me to rescue the empire with my hand?"

CHAPTER XVIII. 1. Kung-sun Ch'ow said, "Why is it that the superior man does not *himself* teach his son?"

taken together as = "a wolf." The names belong to difft. animals of the same species. See on VI, Pt. I, xiv, 4. 2. 夫子 is complimentary, as K'wăn was not a disciple of Mencius. 3. Choo He expands here:—"The drowning empire can be rescued only by right principles;—the case is different from that of a drowning sister-in-law who can be rescued by the hand. Now, you, wishing to rescue the empire, would have me, in violation of right principles, seek alliance with the princes, and so begin by losing the means where-

with to rescue it. Do you wish to make me save the empire with my hand?" I do not see the point of the last question.

CH. 18. HOW A FATHER MAY NOT HIMSELF TEACH HIS SON. But this proposition is not to be taken in all its generality. Confucius taught his son, and so did other famous men their sons. We are to understand the first clause of the second par.,— 勢不行也, as referring to the case of a stupid or perverse child. As to what is said in the 3rd par. of the custom of the ancients, I have seen

也、父子相夷、則惡矣。

正也、則是父子相夷

我以正、夫子未出於

怒、則反夷矣、夫子教

行、繼之以怒繼之以

教者必以正以正不

也。孟子曰、勢不行也、

2.　Mencius replied, "The circumstances of the case forbid its being done.　The teacher must inculcate what is correct.　When he inculcates what is correct, and his lessons are not practiced he follows them up with being angry.　When he follows them up with being angry, then, contrary to what should be, he is offended with his son.　*At the same time, the pupil says,* 'My master inculcates on me what is correct, and he himself does not proceed in a correct path.'　The result of this is, that father and son are offended with· each other.　When father and son come to be offended with each other, the case is evil.

no other proof adduced of it.　2. 反, —"contrary," i. e., to the affection which should rule between father and son.　夷,—in the sense of 傷, which, however, we must take passively; not "to wound," but "to be wounded," that is, to be offended. We might take it actively in the first instance;—"contrary to what should be. he wounds—i. e,. beats—his son."　But below, in 父子相夷, we cannot give it such an active signification as to suppose that the son will proceed to beat his father.　傷 may well be taken passively, as in the comm. saying—眼見心傷. 夫子教我, 云云,—this is to be understood as the resentful murmuring of the son, whose feeling is strongly indicated by the use of 夫子, "my

不失其身、而能事其親者、

爲大守孰爲大守身爲大、

齊孟子曰事孰爲大事親

不祥莫大焉。

間不責善責善則離離則

古者、易子而教之父子之

3. "The ancients exchanged sons, and one taught the son of another.

4. "Between father and son, there should be no reproving admonitions to what is good. Such reproofs lead to alienation, and than alienation, there is nothing more inauspicious."

CHAPTER XIX. 1. Mencius said, "Of services which is the greatest? The service of parents is the greatest. Of charges which is the greatest? The charge of one's self is the greatest. That those who do not fail to keep themselves are able to serve their parents is

master," as applied to his father. 3. The comm. all say, that this only means that the ancients sent out their sons to be taught away from home by masters. But this is explaining away the 易. 4. 扡 善＝以 善責之使行, "laying what is good on them, and causing them to do it."

CH. 19. THE RIGHT MANNER OF SERVING PARENTS AND THE IMPORTANCE OF WATCHING OVER ONE'S SELF, IN ORDER TO DO SO. 1. 事孰爲大, —lit., "of services—i. e., duties of service which a man has to pay to others — which is great?" 守, — charges, what a man has to guard

吾聞之矣、失其身、而能事

其親者、吾未之聞也。孰不

爲事、事親事之本也、孰不

爲守、守身守之本也。曾子

養曾皙、必有酒肉將徹、必

請所與問有餘、必曰、有、曾

what I have heard. But I have never heard of any, who, having failed to keep themselves, were able *notwithstanding* to serve their parents.

2. "There are many services, but the service of parents is the root of all others. There are many charges, but the charge of one's self is the root of all others.

3. "The philosopher Tsăng, in nourishing Tsăng Seih, was always sure to have wine and flesh provided. And when they were being removed, he would ask respectfully to whom he should give *what was left*. If *his father* asked whether there was anything left, he was sure to say, 'There is.' After the death of Tsăng

and keep. The keeping one's self is from all that is contrary to righteousness. 2. 執不爲事,—"what is not a service?" i. e., the services a man has to perform are many. 本,—in the sense of "root" according to the Chinese way of developing all other services from filial piety; see the Heaou-king (孝 經), *passim*. There is more truth in the 2nd part of the par. 3. Seih was Tsăng Sin's father; see Con. Ana., XI, xxv. 養,—low. 3rd tone. "Nourishing the will," i.e., gratifying and carrying out the

晳死曾元養曾子、必有
酒肉、將徹不請所與、問
有餘、曰、亡矣、將以復進
也、此所謂養口體者也、
若曾子、則可謂養志也、
事親若曾子者、可也。

Seih, when Tsǎng Yuen came to nourish the philoso-pher Tsǎng, he was always sure to have wine and flesh provided. But when the things were being removed, he did not ask to whom he should give *what was left,* and if *his father* asked whether there was anything left, he would answer 'No';—intending to bring them in again. This was what is called—'nourishing the mouth and body.' We may call the philosopher Tsǎng's practice—'nourishing the will.'

4. "To serve one's parents as the philosopher Ts'ǎng served his may be accepted *as filial piety.*"

father's wishes. 4. The 可也 at the end occasions some difficulty. Choo He quotes from one of the brothers Ch'ing these words:—"To serve one's parents as Tsǎng Sin did his may be called the height of filial piety, yet Mencius only says that it might be accepted as such— 可 也: did he really think that there was something supererogatory in Tsǎng's service?" Possibly. Mencius may have been referring to Tsǎng's disclaimer of being deemed a model of filial piety. See the Le-ke, XXI (祭 義), ii, 14, where he says:— "What the superior man calls filial piety is to anticipate the wishes, and carry out the mind of his parents, always leading them on in what is right and true. I am only one who nourishes his parents. How can I be deemed filial?"

君、而國定矣。

君正莫不正。

不仁、君義莫不義、

君心之非、君仁、莫

也、惟大人爲能格

與適也、政不足閒

孟子曰、人不足

CHAPTER XX.   Mencius said, "It is not enough to remonstrate with a *sovereign* on account of *the malemployment of* ministers, nor to blame *errors of* government.   It is only the great man who can rectify what is wrong in the sovereign's mind.   Let the prince be benevolent, and all *his acts* will be benevolent.   Let the prince be righteous, and all *his acts* will be righteous.   Let the prince be correct, and everything will be correct.   Once rectify the prince, and the kingdom will be firmly settled."

CH. 20.  A TRULY GREAT MINISTER WILL BE SEEN IN HIS DIRECTING HIS EFFORTS, NOT TO THE CORRECTION OF MATTERS IN DETAIL, BUT OF THE SOVEREIGN'S CHARACTER.   1. 適,—read *chih,*=謫, "to reprehend." 閒, —*kien,* up. 3rd tone. 人 and 政 are to be taken as in the objective governed by 適 and 閒, and 不足 as used impersonally.  與=與君, "with the sovereign." Chaou K'e introduces 與 before 閒 as well. He seems to interpret differently from the transl., making 人 (= 小人, "little men") the subject of 不足:—"little men are not fit to remonstrate with their sovereign."   This is plainly wrong, because we cannot carry it on to the next clause.  格=正, "to correct."—The sent. of the ch. is illustrated by an incident related of Mencius by the philosopher 荀 (250 B.C.).—"As Mencius thrice visited Ts'e, without speaking to the king about the errors of his government, his disciples were surprised, but he simply said, '*I must first correct his evil heart.*'"

蘁樂正子從於子敖之齊。

人師。

蘁孟子曰、人之患、在好爲

無責耳矣。

蘁孟子曰、人之易其言也、

求全之毀。

蘁孟子曰、有不虞之譽、有

CHAPTER XXI. Mencius said, "There are cases of praise which could not be expected, and of reproach when the parties have been seeking to be perfect."

CHAPTER XXII. Mencius said, "Men's being ready with their tongues arises simply from their not having been reproved."

CHAPTER XXIII. Mencius said, "The evil of men is that they like to be teachers of others."

CHAPTER XXIV. 1. The disciple Yŏ-ching went in the train of Tsze-gaou to Ts'e.

CH. 21. PRAISE AND BLAME ARE NOT ALWAYS ACCORDING TO DESERT. 虞,—in the sense of 度, "to calculate," "to measure." For 毀 in the sense here, 譭 is often used in modern language.

CH. 22. THE BENEFIT OF REPROOF. 易,—read e, low. 3rd tone, "easy." Choo He supposes that this remark was spoken with some particular reference. This would account for the 耳 矣, "simply."

CH. 23. BE NOT MANY MASTERS. Comm. suppose that Mencius's lesson was that such a liking indicated a self-sufficiency which put an end to self-improvement.

CH. 24. HOW MENCIUS REPROVED YŎ-CHING FOR ASSOCIATING WITH AN UNWORTHY PERSON, AND BEING REMISS IN WAITING ON HIMSELF. 1. Yŏ-ching,—see I, Pt. II, xvi. 2.

長者乎曰克有罪。

之也、舍館定然後求見

乎曰舍館未定曰子聞

則我出此言也、不亦宜

幾日矣曰昔者曰昔者、

何爲出此言也曰子來

子亦來見我乎曰先生

樂正子見孟子孟子曰、

2. He came to see Mencius, who said to him, "Are you also come to see me?" Yŏ-ching replied, "Master, why do you speak such words?" "How many days have you been here?" asked Mencius. "I came yesterday." "Yesterday! Is it not with reason, then, that I thus speak?" "My lodging house was not arranged." "Have you heard that *a scholar's* lodging house must be arranged before he visit his elder?"

3. *Yŏ-ching* said, "I have done wrong."

Tsze-gaou was the designation of Wang Hwan, mentioned in II, Pt. II, vi. From that chapter we may understand that Mencius would not be pleased with one of his disciples associating with such a person. 之, —the verb,＝往. 2. The name is repeated at the beginning of this paragraph, the former being narrative, and introductory merely. 亦 來,— the 亦, "also" is directed against Tsze-gaou. Choo He explains 昔者 by 前日, which, in common parlance, means "the day before yesterday." But I do not see that it should have that meaning here. 昔 properly means "formerly," and may extend to the remotest antiquity. It is used also for yesterday, the time separated from the present by one rest— 息., as if the same sound of the two characters (昔 息) determined the meaning. 長 (up. 2nd tone) 者 is used by Mencius of himself before:— II, Pt. II, xi, 4.

告而娶爲無後也、

三、無後爲大舜不

<sup></sup>孟子曰不孝有

以餔啜也。

意子學古之道而

來、徒餔啜也我不

曰子之從於子敖

<sup></sup>孟子謂樂正子

CHAPTER XXV. Mencius, addressing the disciple Yŏ-ching, said to him, "Your coming here in the train of Tsze-gaou was only because of the food and the drink. I could not have thought that you, having learned the doctrine of the ancients, would have acted with a view to eating and drinking."

CHAPTER XXVI. 1. Mencius said, "There are three things which are unfilial, and to have no posterity is the greatest of them.

2. "Shun married, without informing his parents, because of this,— *lest he should have* no posterity.

CH. 25. A FURTHER AND MORE DIRECT REPROOF OF YŎ-CHING. 餔 啜 are both contemptuous terms, = our application of "the loaves and fishes." 而 以 餔 啜 = 而 以 餔 啜 爲 也。

CH. 26. SHUN'S EXTRAORDINARY WAY OF CONTRACTING MARRIAGE JUSTIFIED BY THE MOTIVE. 1. The other two things which are unfilial are, according to Chaou K'e, 1st, By a flattering assent to encourage parents in unrighteousness; and 2nd, Not to succor their poverty and old age by engaging in official service.

To be without posterity is greater than those faults, because it is an offense against the whole line of ancestors, and terminates the sacrifices to them.—In Pt. II, xxx, Mencius specifies five things which were commonly deemed unfilial, and not one of these three is among them. It is to be understood that here 不 孝 有 三 is spoken from the point of view of the superior man, and, moreover, that the first par. simply lays down the ground for the vindication of Shun. 2. 爲 無 後,— 爲, low. 3rd tone. 告 implies getting

君子以
為猶告
也。
矗 孟子
曰、仁之
實、事親
是也、義
之實、從
兄是也。

Superior men consider that his doing so was the same as if he had informed them."

CHAPTER XXVII. 1. Mencius said, "The richest fruit of benevolence is this,—the service of one's parents. The richest fruit of righteousness is this,— the obeying one's elder brothers.

the parents' permission, as well as informing them. But Shun's parents were so evil, and hated him so much, that they would have prevented his marriage had they been told of it.

CH. 27. FILIAL PIETY AND FRATERNAL OBEDIENCE IN THEIR RELATION TO BENEVOLENCE, RIGHTEOUSNESS, WISDOM, PROPRIETY, AND MUSIC. 1. 實 is sometimes opposed to 虛, "what is solid to what is empty, shadowy"; sometimes to 名, "what is real to what is nominal"; and sometimes to 華, "what is substantial to what is ornamental," "fruit to flower." In the text, it is used in the last way, and I cannot express it better than by the "richest fruit." 是 也 is emphatic;—"the fruit of benevolence is the service of parents;—*it is*." So in the other instances. Benevolence, righteousness, etc., are the principles of those, the capabilities of them in human nature, which may have endless manifestations, but are chiefly and primarily to be seen in the two virtues spoken of.—What strikes us as strange is the subject of music.

The difficulty has not escaped native commentators. The author of the 集 註 本 義 匯 叄 says, *in loc.*:— "Benevolence, righteousness, propriety, and knowledge are the four virtues, but this ch. proceeds to speak of music. For the principles of music are really a branch of propriety, and when the ordering and adorning, which belong to that, are perfect, then harmony and pleasure spring up as a matter of course. In this way we have propriety mentioned first, and then music. Moreover, the fervency of benevolence, the exactness of righteousness, the clearness of knowledge, and the firmness of maintenance must all have their depth manifested in music. If the ch. had not spoken of music, we should not have seen the whole amount of achievement.' The reader may try to conceive the exact meaning of this writer, who also points out another peculiarity in the chapter, which many have overlooked. Instead of 是 也 after 樂 斯 二 者, as at the end of the other clauses, we have 樂 則 生 矣, 云 云,

智之實知斯二者、弗去
是也、禮之實節文斯二
者是也、樂之實樂斯二
者、樂則生矣、生則惡可
已也、惡可已、則不知足
之蹈之、手之舞之。

2. "The richest fruit of wisdom is this,—the knowing those two things, and not departing from them. The richest fruit of propriety is this,—the ordering and adorning those two things. The richest fruit of music is this,—the rejoicing in those two things. When they are rejoiced in, they grow. Growing, how can they be repressed? When they come to this state that they cannot be repressed, then unconsciously the feet begin to dance and the hands to move."

"showing," says he, "most vividly how his admiration was stirred. It is as if from every sentence there floated up a 是 也 upon the paper, so true is it that perfect filial piety and frater. duty reach to spiritual beings, and shed a light over the world, and then do we know that in the greatest music there is a harmony with heaven and earth."

2. Julien translates 去 by *abjicere*. To have that meaning, it must have been in the up. 2nd tone, which it is not. The first 樂 is *yŏ*, "music"; the other two are *lŏh*, "to enjoy." 不 知 is used absolutely,—"unconsciously," though we might make 知 personal also,—"we do not know." 足 之 蹈 之,—"the feet's stamping it." So the next clause.

舜盡事親之道而瞽瞍

不順乎親不可以爲子、

不得乎親不可以爲人、

己猶草芥也、惟舜爲然、

將歸己、視天下悅而歸

孟子曰、天下大悅而

CHAPTER XXVIII. 1. Mencius said, "Suppose the case of the whole empire turning in great delight to an individual to submit to him. — To regard the whole empire *thus* turning to him in great delight but as a bundle of grass; — only Shun was capable of this. *He considered* that if one could not get *the hearts of* his parents he could not be considered *a man*, and that if he could not get to an entire accord with his parents, he could not be considered a son.

2. "By Shun's completely fulfilling everything by which a parent could be served, Koo-sow was brought

CH. 28. HOW SHUN VALUED AND EXEMPLIFIED FILIAL PIETY. 1. The first sentence is to be taken generally, and not with reference to Shun simply. It is incomplete. The conclusion would be something like — "this would be accounted the greatest happiness and glory." 芥 is properly "the mustard plant," but it is sometimes, as here, only synonymous with 草. 不 得, 云 云,—all this is the reasoning of Shun's mind. 不 得 乎,—like 不 獲 於, in ch. 16. 不 順, "not to obey," "not to accord with," but Choo He and others labor hard to make it out to mean,—"to bring the parents to accord with what is right, so as to be able then fully to accord with them." 2. Shun's father is known by the name of Koo-sow, but both the characters denote "blind," and he was so styled, it is

底豫、瞽瞍

底豫、而天

下化、瞽瞍

底豫、而天

下之爲父

子者定、此

之謂大孝。

to find delight *in what was good.* When Koo-sow was brought to find that delight, the whole empire was transformed. When Koo-sow was brought to find that delight, all fathers and sons in the empire were established *in their respective duties.* This is called great filial piety."

said, because of his mental blindness and opposition to all that was good, 豫, in the sense of "to be pleased," "joyful," understood here with a moral application. "All fathers and sons, etc.,"—i. e., all sons were made to see, that, whatever might be the characters of their parents, they had only to imitate Shun, and fathers, even though they might be like Koo-sow, were shamed to reformation.

## BOOK IV
### LE LOW. PART II

離婁章句下

孟子曰舜生

於諸馮、遷於負

夏、卒於鳴條、東

夷之人也。文王

生於岐周、卒於

畢郢、西夷之人

CHAPTER I. 1. Mencius said, "Shun was born in Choo-fung, removed to Foo-hea, and died in Ming-t'eaou;—a man near the wild tribes on the east.

2. "King Wăn was born in Chow by *Mount* K'e, and died in Peih-ying;—a man near the wild tribes on the west.

CH. 1. THE AGREEMENT OF SAGES NOT AFFECTED BY PLACE OR TIME. 1. The common view derived from the "Historical Records," Book I, is, that Shun was a native of K'echow, corresponding to the modern Shan-si, to which all the places in the text are accordingly referred. Some, however, and especially Tsăng Tsze-koo (曾子固), of the Sung dynasty, find his birthplace in Ts'inan in Shan tung, and this would seem to be supported by Mencius in this passage. There is considerable diffic. with Mingt'eaou, as we read in the "Historical Records," that in the 39th year of his reign, Shun died, while on a tour of inspection to the south, in the wilderness of Ts'angwoo (蒼梧), and was buried on the Kewe (九疑) hills in Keangnan, which are in Lingling (零陵). The discussions on the point are very numerous. See the 集證 and 四書摭餘說, *in loc.;* see also on the Shoo king, Pt. II. No doubt, Mencius was not speaking without book. 東夷之人, lit., "a man of the eastern *E*," or "barbarians," but the meaning can only be what I have given in the translation. So 四夷之人. Chow, the original seat of the house of Chow, was in the present department of Fungts'eang, in Shensi. Peihying is to be distinguished from Ying which was the capital of Ts'oo, and with which the paraphrast of Chaou K'e strangely confounds it.

也。　聖後聖其揆一　國若合符節先　歲得志行乎中　相後也千有餘　千有餘里世之　也地之相去也、

3. "Those regions were distant from one another more than a thousand li, and the age of the one *sage* was posterior to that of the other more than a thousand years. But when they got their wish, and carried their principles into practice throughout the Middle Kingdom, it was like uniting the two halves of a seal.

4. "*When we examine* the sages, — both the earlier and the later, — their principles are found to be the same."

Choo He says it was near to Fung (豐) and Kaou (鎬), the successive capitals of King Woo. The former was in Lingheen (郘 縣), and the latter in Heenyang (咸 陽), both in the dept. of Sengan; Peihying was in the dist. of Heenning (咸 寧) of the same dep., and there the grave of King Woo, or the place of it, is still pointed out. 得志行乎中國,— "when they got their wishes carried out in the Middle Kingdom." We are to understand that their aim was to carry out their principles, not to get the empire. 符 should be called a tally or token, perhaps, rather than "a seal." Anciently, the emperor delivered, as the token of investi-ture, one half of a tally of wood or some precious stone, reserving the other half in his own keeping. It was cut right through a line of characters, indicating the commission, and their halves fitting each other when occasion required, was the test of truth and identity. Originally, as we see from the formation of the character (符), the tally must have been of bamboo. 3. 先 聖 後 聖 is to be understood generally, and not of Shun and Wăn merely. 其 揆 一,—揆 is taken as a verb=度 "to reckon," "to estimate," and is under-stood of the mental exercises of the sages. 其 揆. —"their mindings," the principles which they cherished.

輿梁成、民未病　徒杠成、十二月　爲政。歲、十一月　子曰、惠而不知　濟人於溱洧。孟　之政以其乘輿　子產聽鄭國

CHAPTER II.　1. When Tsze-cn an was chief minister of the state of Ch'ing, he would convey people across the Tsin and Wei in his own carriage.

2.　Mencius said, "It was kind, but showed that he did not understand the practice of government.

3.　"When in the eleventh month of the year the footbridges are completed, and the carriage· bridges in the twelfth month, the people have not the trouble of wading.

CH. 2. GOOD GOVERNMENT LIES IN EQUAL MEASURES FOR THE GENERAL GOOD, NOT IN ACTS OF FAVOR TO INDIVIDUALS. 1. Tsze-ch'an,— see Con. Ana., V, xv. The Tsin and Wei were two rivers of Ch'ing, said to have their rise in the Maling (馬嶺) hills, and to meet at a certain point, after which the common stream seems to have borne the name of both the feeders. They are referred to the department of Honan in Honan province. 聽政,— "was hearing the govt.," i. e., was chief minister. 乘,—low. 3rd tone. Choo He explains 以其乘輿 by 以其所乘之輿, but 乘 so used is low 1st tone. He so expands, however, probably from remembering a conversation on Tsze-ch'an between Confucius and Tsze-yew, related in the Kea-yu, Bk. IV, iv, near the end, and to which Mencius has reference. The sage held that Tsze-ch'an was kind, but only as a mother, loving but not teaching the people, and, in illustration of his view, says that Tsze-ch'an, 以 所 乘 之 車 濟 冬 涉, "used the carriage in which he rode to convey over those who were wading through the water in the winter." 2. The subject here is the action, not the man. The practice of govt. is to be seen not in acts of individual kindness and small favors, but in the administration of just and beneficent laws. 3. The 11th and 12th months here correspond to the 9th and 10th of the present calendar, which follows the hea division of the year;—see Ana., XV x. Mencius refers to a rule for the repair of the bridges, on the termination of agricultural labors.

涉也君子平其政行辟

人可也焉得人人而濟

之故爲政者每人而悅

之日亦不足矣。

孟子告齊宣王曰君

之視臣如手足則臣視

君如腹心君之視臣如

犬馬則臣視君如國人、

4. "Let a governor conduct his rule on principles of equal justice, and when he goes abroad, he may cause people to be removed out of his path. But how can he convey everybody across the rivers?

5. "It follows that if a governor will *try to* please everybody, he will find the days not sufficient *for his work.*"

CHAPTER III. 1. Mencius said to the king Seuen of Ts'e, "When the prince regards his ministers as his hands and feet, his ministers regard their prince as their belly and heart; when he regards them as his dogs and horses, they regard him as any other man;

4. 君子＝爲政者, "a chief minister." 辟 read as 闢. Removing people from the way, when the prince went forth, was likewise a rule of the Chow dynasty; and not only did it extend to the prince, but to many officers and women. See the Chow-le, VII, ix. 5. "The days not sufficient,"—i. e., he will not have time for all he has to do.

CH. 3. WHAT TREATMENT SOVER- EIGNS GIVE TO THEIR MINISTERS WILL BE RETURNED TO THEM BY A CORRE- SPONDING BEHAVIOR. 1. "As his hands and feet,"—i. e., with kindness and attention. "As their belly and heart,"—i. e., with watchfulness and honor. "As his dogs and horses,"— i. e., without respect, but feeding them. "As any other man,"—lit., "as a man of the kingdom," i. e., without any distinction or reverence.

使人導之出疆、又先於

下於民、有故而去、則君

服矣。曰、諫行言聽、膏澤

舊君有服、何如斯可爲

視君如寇讐王曰、禮爲

君之視臣如土芥、則臣

when he regards them as the ground or as grass, they regard him as a robber and an enemy."

2. The king said, "According to the rules of propriety, a minister wears mourning when he has left the service of a prince. How must *a prince* behave that his *old ministers* may thus go into mourning?"

3. Mencius replied, "The admonitions *of a minister* having been followed, and his advice listened to, so that blessings have descended on the people, if for some cause he leaves *the country,* the prince sends an escort to conduct him beyond the boundaries. He also anticipates *with recommendatory intimations* his arrival in the country to which he is proceeding.

"As ground or as grass,"—i. e., trampling on them, cutting them off. 2. The Le here referred to is mentioned in the "Ritual Usages." See Bk. XI, about the middle. The passage, however, is obscure. 爲舊君,—"for an old prince," i. e., a prince whose service he has left.

The king falls back on this rule, thinking that Mencius had expressed himself too strongly. 3. 膏澤,—"fat and moistening influences,"= blessings. 先於其所往 must be supplemented by 稱道其賢欲其收用之, "mentions and commends his worth, wishing him to be received

則君搏執之又極之於其

膏澤不下於民有故而去、

爲臣諫則不行言則不聽、

焉、如此、則爲之服矣。今也

收其田里、此之謂三有禮

其所往去三年不反、然後

When he has been gone three years and does not
return, *only* then at length does he take back his
fields and residence.   This treatment is what is called
'a thrice-repeated display of consideration.'   When a
prince acts thus, mourning will be worn on leaving
his service.

4.   "Nowadays, the remonstrances of a minister
are not followed, and his advice is not listened to, so
that no blessings descend on the people.   When for
any cause he leaves the country, the prince tries to
seize him and hold him a prisoner.   He also pushes
him to extremity in the country to which he has

and used."   田,—"fields," = emoluments.   里,—used for an individual
residence.   We have not had the
character in this sense before.   The
"thrice-repeated display of consideration" refers, 1st, to the escort as
a protection from danger; 2nd, to
the anticipatory recommendations;
and 3rd, to the long continued emoluments, in expectation of the minister's return.   4. Here and above, 有
故 is not to be taken as 大故, in III,
Pt. I, ii, 1.   We must understand
"wishes to," or "tries to," before
搏 執 之, for if the minister were

所往去之日、逐收其田里、

此之謂寇讐、寇讐、何服之

有。

孟子曰、無罪而殺士、則

大夫可以去、無罪而戮民、

則士可以徙。

gone, and on the very day of his departure, he takes back his fields and residence. This treatment shows him to be what we call 'a robber and an enemy.' What mourning can be worn for a robber and an enemy?"

CHAPTER IV. Mencius said, "When scholars are put to death without any crime, the great officers may leave *the country*. When the people are slaughtered without any crime, the scholars may remove."

really imprisoned, he could not go to another kingdom.

CH. 4. PROMPT ACTION IS NECESSARY AT THE RIGHT TIME. 可 以, "may,"＝it is time to. If the opportunity be not taken, while the injustice of the ruler is exercised on those below them, it will soon come to themselves, and it will be too late to escape. The 日 講 concludes its paraphrase thus:—"We may see how the ruler should prize virtue, and be slow to punish; and how he should be cautious in execution of the laws, ever trying to practice benevolence. If he can indeed embody the mind of God, who loves all living things, and make the compassion of the ancient sages his rule, then both officers and people will be grateful to him as to Heaven, and long repose and protracted good order will be the result."

孟子曰君仁莫不仁、
君義莫不義。
孟子曰非禮之禮、非
義之義、大人弗爲。
孟子曰中也養不中、
才也養不才、故人樂有

CHAPTER V. Mencius said, "If the sovereign be benevolent, all will be benevolent. If the sovereign be righteous, all will be righteous."

CHAPTER VI. Mencius said, "Acts of propriety which are not *really* proper, and acts of righteousness which are not *really* righteous, the great man does not do."

CHAPTER VII. Mencius said, "Those who keep the mean, train up those who do not, and those who have abilities, train up those who have not, and hence men

CH. 5. THE INFLUENCE OF THE RULER'S EXAMPLE. See Pt. I, xx, where the same words are found, but their application is to stimulate ministers to do their duty in advising, or remonstrating with, their sovereign.

CH. 6. THE GREAT MAN MAKES NO MISTAKES IN MATTERS OF PROPRIETY AND RIGHTEOUSNESS. 非禮之禮、非義之義, expressions in themselves contradictory, must be taken with some latitude. "Respect," it is said, "belongs to propriety, but it may be carried so far as to degenerate into flattery," etc., etc.

CH. 7. WHAT DUTIES ARE DUE FROM, AND MUST BE RENDERED BY, THE VIRTUOUS AND TALENTED TO THE YOUNG AND IGNORANT. 中也、才也＝"given the mean," "given abilities." 中,—the mean, the rightly ordered course of conduct. Both it and 才 must be taken here in the

賢父兄也、如中也棄

不中才也棄不才、則

賢不肖之相去、其閒

不能以寸。

㊅孟子曰人有不爲

也、而後可以有爲。

㊆孟子曰言人之不

善、當如後患何。

rejoice in having fathers and elder brothers who are
possessed of virtue and talent. If they who keep the
mean spurn those who do not, and they who have
abilities spurn those who have not, then the space
between them—those so gifted and the ungifted—
will not admit àn inch."

CHAPTER VIII. Mencius said, "Men must be decided on what they will NOT do, and then they are
able to act with vigor *in what they ought to do*."

CHAPTER IX. Mencius said, "What future misery
have they and ought they to endure, who talk of
what is not good in others!"

concrete. 兄,—as in III, Pt. I, ii, 3.
如中也, 云云,—by neglecting their
duty, the one class bring themselves
to the level of the other. 賢 embraces both the 中 and the 才 above.
不肖,—see the Doctrine of the
Mean, iv. 以寸,—"with an inch,"
i. e., be measured with an inch.

CH. 8. CLEAR DISCRIMINATION OF
WHAT IS WRONG AND RIGHT MUST
PRECEDE VIGOROUS RIGHT-DOING.
Lit., "men have the not-do, and
afterwards they can have the do."
有爲 implies vigor in the action.

Chaou K'e's comm. is:—"If a man
will not descend to take in any
irregular way, he will be found able
to yield a thousand chariots."

CH. 9. EVIL SPEAKING IS SURE TO
BRING WITH IT EVIL CONSEQUENCES.
The 當 here, followed by 如何,
creates a difficulty. Choo He supposes the remark was made with
some peculiar reference. If we knew
that, the difficulty would vanish.
The original implies, I think, all that
I have expressed in the translation.

子孟

失其赤子之心者也。

孟子曰、大人者、不

義所在。

不必信、行不必果、惟

孟子曰、大人者言

已甚者。

孟子曰、仲尼不爲

CHAPTER X. Mencius said, "Chung-ne did not do extraordinary things."

CHAPTER XI. Mencius said, "The great man does not think beforehand of his words that they may be sincere, nor of his actions that they may be resolute;—he simply *speaks and does* what is right."

CHAPTER XII. Mencius said, "The great man is he who does not lose his child's-heart."

CH. 10. THAT CONFUCIUS KEPT THE MEAN. 已甚者,—i. e., "excessive things," but "extraordinary" rather approaches the meaning. It may strike the student that the meaning is—"Confucius's inaction (=slowness to act) was excessive," but in that case we should have had 矣, and not 者, at the end. We may comp. with the sentiment the Doct. of the Mean, xi, xiii; Ana., VIII, xx, *et al.*

CH. 11. WHAT IS RIGHT IS THE SUPREME PURSUIT OF THE GREAT MAN. Comp. Con. Ana., IV, x. 不必,—"does not *must*"; he is beyond the necessity of caring for that. 惟義所在,—"only that in which righteousness is"; that only is his concern. In fact, he can hardly be said to be *concerned* about this. It is natural to him to pursue the right.

CH. 12. A MAN IS GREAT BECAUSE HE IS CHILDLIKE. Chaou K'e makes "the great man" to be "a sovereign," 其赤子, "his children," i. e., his people, and the sentiment is that the true sovereign is he who does not lose his people's hearts. I mention this interpretation, as showing how learned men have varied and may vary in fixing the meaning of these books. It is sufficiently absurd, and has been entirely displaced by the interpretation which is given in the version. The sentiment may suggest the Savior's words,—"Except ye be converted, and become as little children, ye shall not enter into the kingdom of heaven." But Christ speaks of the child's-heart as a thing to be regained; Mencius speaks of it as a thing not to be lost. With Christ, to become as

其　深　章　當　事　者　章
自　造　孟　大　惟　不　孟
得　之　子　事　送　足　子
之　以　曰　。　死　以　曰
也　道　君　　　可　當　養
、　、　子　　　以　大　生
自　欲

CHAPTER XIII. Mencius said, "The nourishment of *parents when* living is not sufficient to be accounted the great thing. It is only in the performing their obsequies when dead, that we have what can be considered the great thing."

CHAPTER XIV. Mencius said, "The superior man makes his advances *in what he is learning* with deep earnestness and by the proper course, wishing to get hold of it as in himself. Having got hold of it in

children is to display certain characteristics of children. With Mencius, "the child's-heart" is the ideal moral condition of humanity. Choo He says:—"The mind of the great man comprehends all changes of phenomena, and the mind of the child is nothing but a pure simplicity, free from all hypocrisy. Yet the great man is the great man, just as he is not led astray by external things, but keeps his original simplicity and freedom from hypocrisy. Carrying this out, he becomes omniscient and omnipotent, great to the extremest degree." We need not suppose that Mencius would himself have expanded his thought in this way.

CH. 13. FILIAL PIETY SEEN IN THE OBSEQUIES OF PARENTS. 養生者,—者 字 指 養 生 之 事,—"the character 者 refers to the ways by which the living may be nourished." It belongs to the phrase 養 生, and not to 生 alone. 當=為,—"to be

considered," "to constitute." 送死, —lit., "to accompany the dead," but denoting all the last duties to them. It=慎 終, Ana., I, ix. The sentiment needs a good deal of explaining and guarding. The obsequies are done, it is said, once for all. If done wrong, the fault cannot be remedied. Probably the remark had a peculiar reference. The 日 講 supposes it was spoken against the Mihist practice of burying parents with a spare simplicity. See III, Pt. I, v.

CH. 14. THE VALUE OF LEARNING THOROUGHLY INWROUGHT INTO THE MIND. 深 造 之,—造, read *ts'aou*, up. 3rd tone, "to arrive at"; 之 must refer to the 理, or principles of the subject which is being learned. 以 道 is understood of the proper course or order, the successive steps of study,=依 着 次 序. 其 自 得 gives the key to the chapter;—"his self-getting," i. e., his getting hold of the subject so that the knowledge of it

說之、將以反說約也。

孟子曰、博學而詳

也。

故君子欲其自得之

則取之左右逢其原、

安、則資之深、資之深、

得之、則居之安、居之

himself, he abides in it calmly and firmly. Abiding in it calmly and firmly, he reposes a deep reliance on it. Reposing a deep reliance on it, he seizes it on the left and right, meeting everywhere with it as a fountain *from which things flow.* It is on this account that the superior man wishes to get hold of what he is learning as in himself."

CHAPTER XV. Mencius said, "In learning extensively and discussing minutely what is learned, the object *of the superior man* is that he may be able to go back and set forth in brief what is essential."

becomes a kind of intuition. 資=藉, "to rely on." The subject so apprehended in its principles is capable of indefinite application. "He seizes it on the right and left,"—i. e., he no longer needs his early efforts to apprehend it. It underlies numberless phenomena, in all which he at once detects it, just as water below the earth is found easily and anywhere, on digging the surface.—One may read scores of pages in the Chinese commentators, and yet not get a clear idea in his own mind of the teaching of Mencius in this ch. Chaou K'e gives 道 a more substantive meaning than in the translation; —"The reason why the superior man pursues with earnestness to arrive at the depth and mystery of 道, is from a wish to get hold for himself of its source and root, as something belonging to his own nature." Most comm. understand the subject studied to be man's own self, not things external to him. We must leave the subject in its own mist.

CH. 15. Choo He says, apparently with reason, that this is a continuation of the last chapter, showing that the object of the superior man in the extensive studies which he pursues, is not vainglory, but to get to the substance and essence of things. 約 conveys the two ideas of condensation and importance.

當之。祥、不祥之實蔽賢者🔲孟子曰言無實不王者、未之有也。天下、天下不心服而以善養人然後能服者、未有能服人者也、🔲孟子曰以善服人

CHAPTER XVI. Mencius said, "Never has he who would by his excellence subdue men been able to subdue them. Let *a prince* seek by his excellence to nourish men, and he will be able to. subdue the whole empire. It is impossible that any one should become ruler of the empire to whom it has not yielded the subjection of the heart."

CHAPTER XVII. Mencius said, "Words which are not true are inauspicious, and the words which are most truly obnoxious to the name of inauspicious, are those which throw into the shade men of talents and virtue."

CH. 16. The object of this chapter, say commentators, is to stimulate rulers to do good in sincerity, with a view, that is, to the good of others. I confess it is to me very enigmatical. Paul's sentiment,—"Scarcely for a righteous man will one die, yet peradventure for a good man some would even dare to die,"—occurs to the mind on reading it, but this is clashed with by its being insisted on that 養人以善 has no reference to the nourishing men's bodies, but is the bringing them to the nourisher's own moral excellence. Chaou K'e takes the first 善 as meaning 威力, "majesty and strength." But this is inadmissible. The point of the ch. is evidently to be found in the contrast of 服 and 養.

CH. 17. The translation takes 無實 as an adjective qualifying 言, and there is a play on the term in the use of 實 in the two parts. Choo He mentions another view making 無實 an adverb joined to 不詳,— "there are no words really inauspicious"; i. e., generally speaking, "only those are obnoxious to be regarded as really inauspicious which throw into." etc. He says he is unable to decide between the two interpretations, and thinks the text may be mutilated. 者 has reference to 言,

爲無本、七八月之閒雨集、

有本者如是、是之取爾苟

夜、盈科而後進放乎四海、

孟子曰、原泉混混、不舍晝

曰、水哉水哉何取於水也。

徐子曰仲尼亟稱於水

CHAPTER XVIII. 1. The disciple Seu said, "Chung-ne often praised water, saying, 'O water! O water!' What did he find in water *to praise?*"

2. Mencius replied, "There is a spring of water; how it gushes out! It rests not day nor night. It fills up every hole, and then advances, flowing on to the four seas. Such is water having a spring! It was this which he found in it to praise.

3. "But suppose that the water has no spring. —In the seventh and eighth months when the rain

not to 人, to "words," not to "men."

CH. 18. HOW MENCIUS EXPLAINED CONFUCIUS'S PRAISE OF WATER. 1. 亟,—read *k'e*, up. 3rd tone, "often." 稱 (in the sense of "to praise"), 於 水, —於 marking the objective case, or = found something to praise in water. See Con. Ana., IX, xvi, though we have not there the exact words—

水 哉 水 哉. 2. 科=坎, "a pit," i. e., every hollow in its course. 是 之 取 爾,—"*it was* just the seizing of this." One commen. brings out the 是 之 in this way—以 是 之 故 而 取 之 爾. 3. Here, again, the months are those of Chow, corresponding to the present 3rd and 6th. 雨 集,—"the

希、庶民去之、君子

以異於禽獸者、幾

鼍孟子曰、人之所

聞過情、君子恥之。

可立而待也、故聲

溝澮皆盈其涸也、

falls abundantly, the channels in the fields are all filled, but their being dried up again may be expected in a short time. So a superior man is ashamed of a reputation beyond his merits."

CHAPTER XIX. 1. Mencius said, "That whereby man differs from the lower animals is but small. The mass of people cast it away, while superior men preserve it.

rains are collected." 溝澮 were channels belonging to the irrigation of the lands divided on the nine-square system. 可立而待,—we might translate as="one may stand and wait till they are dry," but 立 is often used="quickly." 情=實, as in the Great Learning, Comm., ch. iv.

CH. 19. WHEREBY SAGES ARE DISTINGUISHED FROM OTHER MEN;--ILLUSTRATED IN SHUN. It is to be wished that Mencius had said distinctly what the small (幾, up. 1st tone, 希) point distinguishing men from birds and beasts was. According to Choo He, men and creatures have the 理 (intellectual and moral principle) of Heaven and earth to form their *nature*, and the 氣 (matter of Heaven and Earth to form their *bodies*, only men's 氣 is more correct than that of beasts, so that they are able to fill up the capacity

of their nature. This denies any essential difference between men and animals, and what difference it allows is corporeal or material. Chaou K'e says: 幾希, 無幾也知義與不知義之間耳, "幾希 means not much. It is simply the interval between the knowledge of righteousness, and the want of that knowledge." This is so far correct, but the difference which it indicates cannot be said to be "not great."—But is it not the object of Mencius to indicate the character of that which differences men and animals, and not its amount? 幾希=is something minute. A commen. Ch'in (陳) refers us to an expression in the Shoo-king,—人心為危,—as forming a key to the passage. In that, 人心 is the mind prone to err, in distinction from the 道心, "the mind of reason," which it is said

賢無方文王視民如
而好善言湯執中立
孟子曰禹惡旨酒、
行仁義也。
於人倫、由仁義行、非
存之舜明於庶物、察

2. "Shun clearly understood the multitude of things, and closely observed the relations of humanity. He walked along the path of benevolence and righteousness; he did not *need to* pursue benevolence and righteousness."

CHAPTER XX. 1. Mencius said, "Yu hated the pleasant wine, and loved good words.

2. "T'ăng held fast the mean, and employed men of talents and virtue without regard to where they came from.

3. "King Wăn looked on the people as *he would*

is minute. 2. Shun preserving and cultivating this distinctive endowment was led to the character and achievements which are here briefly described. The phrase 庶物, it is said, 該得廣, 凡天地間事物皆是, "covers a wide extent of meaning, embracing all matters and things between heaven and earth." The 日譯 refers to it all the governmental achievements of Shun related in the Shoo-king.

CH. 20 THE SAME SUBJECT;— ILLUSTRATED IN YU, T'ANG, WAN, WOO, AND CHOW-KUNG. 1. In "The Plans of the Warring States" (戰國策), a book continuing the Ch'un-Ts'ew on to the Han dynasty, it is said, "E-teih made wine which Yu tasted and liked, but he said, '*In after ages there will be those who through wine lose their kingdoms*';— so he degraded E-teih, and refused to drink pleasant wine." From the Shoo-king, III, iii, 6, we may infer that there was some foundation for this story. 好 (up. 3rd tone) 善言, —see II, Pt. I, viii, 2. 2. 無方, may be understood with reference to class or place. Comp. the Shoo-king, IV,

得之坐以待旦。

思之夜以繼日幸而

事其有不合者仰而

公思兼三王以施四

王不泄邇不忘遠周

傷望道而未之見武

on a man who was wounded, and he looked towards
the right path as if he could not see it.

4. "King Woo did not slight the near, and did not
forget the distant.

5. "The duke of Chow desired to unite in himself
*the virtues* of those kings, *those founders of the* three
*dynasties,* that he might display in his practice the
four things *which they did.* If he saw any thing in
them not suited *to his time,* he looked up and thought
about it, from daytime into the night, and when
he was fortunate enough to master the difficulty,
he sat waiting for the morning."

ii, 8, 5. 3. "As he would on one who
was wounded,"—i. e., he regarded
the people with compassionate ten-
derness. 而 is to be read as 如, with
which, according to Choo He, it was
anciently interchanged. See the
Shoo-king, V, xvi, 9, 10, for illustrations of Wan's care of the people,
and the She-king, III, i, Ode VI,
for illustration of the other characteristic. 4. 泄, read *sëě*=渫, "to
slight." The adjectives are to be
understood both of persons and
things. 5. 三王,—i. e., Yu, T'ang,
and the kings Wăn and Woo who are
often classed together as the founders
of the Chow dynasty. "The four
things" are what have been stated in
the prec. pars. 其 has 事 for its
antecedent. 得 之,—"apprehended
it," i. e., understood the matter in
its principles, so as to be able to bring
into his own practice the spirit of
those ancient sages.

齊桓晉文其文則

春秋、一也其事、則

乘、楚子檮杌、魯之

然後春秋作晉之

迹熄、而詩亡詩亡、

孟子曰、王者之

CHAPTER XXI. 1. Mencius said, "The traces of imperial rule were extinguished, and the *imperial* odes ceased to be made. When those odes ceased to be made, then the 'Ch'un Ts'ew' was produced.

2. "The 'Shing' of Tsin, the 'Taou Wuh' of Ts'oo, and the 'Ch'un Ts'ew' of Loo were books of the same character.

3. "The subject of *the* Ch'un Ts'ew was the affairs of Hwan of Ts'e and Wăn of Tsin, and its style was

CH. 21. THE SAME SUBJECT;— ILLUSTRATED IN CONFUCIUS. 1. The extinction of the true imperial rule of Chow dates from the transference of the capital from Fung-kaou to Loh, by the emperor P'ing, 769 B.C. From that time, the sovereigns of Chow had the name without the rule. By the 詩 is intended not the Book of Poems, but the Nga (雅) portion of them, descriptive of the imperial rule of Chow, and to be used on imperial occasions. 亡 does not mean that the Nga were lost, but that no additions were made to them, and they degenerated into mere records of the past, and were no longer descriptions of the present, Confucius edited the annals of Loo to supply the place of the Nga. See III, Pt. II, ix, 7. 2. Each state had its annals. Those of Tsin were compiled under the name of *Shing* (low. 3rd tone), "The Carriage"; those of Ts'oo under that of *Taou-wuh*, which is explained as the name of a ferocious animal, and more anciently as the denomination of a vile and lawless man. The annals of Loo had the name of "Spring and Autumn," two seasons for the whole. 3. 其 refers only to the annals of Loo. They did not contain only the affairs of Hwan and Wăn, but these

人也。孔子徒也予私淑諸五世而斬予未得爲五世而斬小人之澤、孟子曰君子之澤、竊取之矣。史、孔子曰、其義則丘

the historical. Confucius said, 'Its *righteous* decisions I ventured to make.'"

CHAPTER XXII. 1. Mencius said, "The influence of a sovereign sage terminates in the fifth generation. The influence of a mere sage does the same.

2. "Although I could not be a disciple of Confucius himself, I have endeavored to cultivate my virtue by means of others *who were*."

occupied an early and prominent place in them. 竊,—see II, Pt. I, ii, 20. 取 makes the expression still more humble, as if Confucius had "taken" the judgments from the historians, and not made them himself.

CH. 22. THE SAME SUBJECT;—ILLUSTRATED IN MENCIUS HIMSELF. 1. Here 君子＝聖賢有位者, "the sage and worthy, who has position," i. e., who occupies the throne, and 小人＝聖賢無立者, "the sage and worthy, who has no position." We might suppose that the influence of the former would be more permanent, but Mencius is pleased to say their influence lasts the same time. 澤 is to be taken as＝"influence," it being understood to be of a beneficial character. 2. From the death of Confucius to the birth of Mencius could hardly be 100 years, so that, though Mencius could not learn his doctrines from the sage himself, he did so from his grandson Tsze-sze, or some of his disciples. 私＝竊, in last ch. 淑＝善, taken actively. 諸人＝於人, the 人 referring to Tsze-sze and his school.— This and the three preceding chapters should be considered as one, whose purpose is much the same as III, Pt. II, ix, showing us that Mencius considered himself the successor of Confucius in the line of sages.

羿。
孟子曰、是亦羿有罪焉、公

思天下惟羿爲愈己、於是殺

逢蒙學射於羿、盡羿之道、

勇。

傷惠、可以死可以無死死傷

取傷廉可以與可以無與、與

孟子曰可以取可以無取、

CHAPTER XXIII. Mencius said, "When it appears proper to take a thing, and *afterwards* not proper, to take it is contrary to moderation. When it appears proper to give a thing and *afterwards* not proper, to give it is contrary to kindness. When it appears proper to sacrifice one's life, and *afterwards* not proper, to sacrifice it is contrary to bravery."

CHAPTER XXIV. 1. P'ang Mung learned archery of E. When he had acquired completely all the science of E, he thought that in all the empire only E was superior to himself, and so he slew him. Mencius said, "In this case E also was to blame. Kung-ming

CH. 23. FIRST JUDGMENTS ARE NOT ALWAYS CORRECT. IMPULSES MUST BE WEIGHED IN THE BALANCE OF REASON, AND WHAT REASON DICTATES MUST BE FOLLOWED. Such is the meaning of this chapter in translating the separate clauses of which, we must supplement them by introducing "afterwards."

CH. 24. THE IMPORTANCE OF BEING CAREFUL OF WHOM WE MAKE FRIENDS. The sentiment is good, but Mencius could surely have found better illustrations of it than the second one which he selected. 1. Of E, see Con. Ana., XIV, xiv. 逢蒙 (P'ang as formed with 夅, not 夆) is said both by Chaou K'e and Choo

射者也、夫子曰、吾生、何謂也。曰、

生矣。其僕曰、庚公之斯衞之善

誰也。其僕曰、庚公之斯也。曰、吾

弓、吾死矣夫、問其僕曰、追我者

孺子曰、今日我疾作、不可以執

侵衞、衞使庚公之斯追之、子濯

爾、惡得無罪。㆓鄭人使子濯孺子

明儀曰、宜若無罪焉、曰、薄乎云

E *indeed* said, 'It would appear as if he were not to be blamed,' but he thereby only meant that his blame was slight. How can he be held without *any* blame?"

2. "The people of Ch'ing sent Tsze-chŏ Yu to make a stealthy attack on Wei, which sent Yu-kung Sze to pursue him. Tsze-chŏ Yu said, 'To day I feel unwell, so that I cannot hold my bow. I am a dead man!' *At the same time* he asked his driver, 'Who is it that is pursuing me?' The driver said, 'It is Yu-kung Sze,' *on which* he exclaimed, 'I shall live.' The driver said, 'Yu-kung Sze is the best archer of Wei, what do you mean by saying—I shall live?'

He to refer to E's servants (家衆), but one man is evidently denoted by the name. E's servants did indeed make themselves parties to his murder, but P'ang Mung is the same, I suppose, with Han Tsuh, the principal in it. 云爾,—see II. Pt. II, ii, 4, and Con. Ana., VII, xviii.

曰薄乎云爾,—"saying (meaning to say), It was slighter than ... simply." 2. 侵,—"to attack stealthily." An incursion made with music, and the pomp of war, is called 伐, and one without these, 侵. The 之, in the names—庚公之斯

庾公之斯、學射於尹公之他、尹
公之他學射於我、夫尹公之他
端人也、其取友必端矣。庾公之
斯至曰、夫子何爲不執弓曰、今
曰我疾作、不可以執弓曰小人
學射於尹公之他、尹公之他學
射於夫子、我不忍以夫子之道、
反害夫子、雖然今日之事、君事

*Yu* replied, 'Yu-kung Sze learned archery from Yin-kung T'o, who again learned it from me. Now, Yin-kung T'o is an upright man, and the friends of his selection must be upright *also*.' When Yu-kung Sze came up, he said, 'Master, why are you not holding your bow?' *Yu* answered him, 'To-day I am feeling unwell, and cannot hold my bow.' *On this* Sze said, 'I learned archery from Yin-kung T'o, who again learned it from you. I cannot bear to injure you with your own science. The business of to-day, however, is the prince's business, which I dare not

and 尹公之佗 are mere vocal particles. 佗,—read *t'o*. The name is elsewhere found 尹公佗. In the 左傳, under the 14th year of Duke 襄, we have a narrative bearing some likeness to this account of Mencius, and in which 尹公佗 and 庾公差 figure as famous archers of Wei. It is hardly possible, however, to suppose that the two accounts are of

浴、則可以祀上帝。
之。雖有惡人、齊戒沐
潔、則人皆掩鼻而過
鼉孟子曰、西子蒙不
後反。
輪去其金發乘矢而
也、我不敢廢。抽矢扣

neglect.' He then took his arrows, knocked off their steel points against the carriage wheel, discharged four of them, and returned."

CHAPTER XXV. 1. Mencius said, "If the lady Se had been covered with a filthy *headdress*, all people would have stopped their noses in passing her.

2. "Though a man may be wicked, yet if he adjust his thoughts, fast, and bathe, he may sacrifice to God."

the same thing. 乘,—low. 3rd tone, "a team of four horses," here used for a set of four arrows.

CH. 25. IT IS ONLY MORAL BEAUTY THAT IS TRULY EXCELLENT AND ACCEPTABLE. 1. Se-tsze, or "western lady," was a poor girl of Yuĕ, named She E (施夷), of surpassing beauty, presented by the king of Yuĕ to his enemy the king of Woo, who became devotedly attached to her, and neglected all the duties of his government. She was contemporary with Confucius. The common account is that she was called "the western lady," because she lived on the western bank of a certain stream. If we may receive the works of 管子, however, as having really proceeded from that scholar and statesman, there had been a celebrated beauty named Se-tsze, two hundred years before the one of Yuĕ. In translating 蒙不潔, I have followed Chaou K'e. 2. 惡, both by Chaou K'e and Choo He, is taken in the sense of "ugly," in opposition to the beauty of the lady Se. I cannot but think Mencius intended it in the sense of "wicked," and that his object was to encourage men to repentance and well-doing. 齊,—read *chae*. See Con. Ana., VII, vii, *et al*. By the laws of China, it was competent for the emperor only to sacrifice to God. The language of Mencius, in connection with this fact, very strikingly shows the virtue he attached to penitent purification.

無惡於智矣、禹之行
者若禹之行水也、則
智者、爲其鑿也、如智
者以利爲本所惡於
性也、則故而已矣、故
孟子曰、天下之言

CHAPTER XXVI. 1. Mencius said, "All who speak about the natures *of things*, have in fact only their phenomena *to reason from*, and the value of a phenomenon is in its being natural.

2. "What I dislike in your wise men is their boring out *their conclusions*. If those wise men would only act as Yu did when he conveyed away the waters, there would be nothing to dislike in their wisdom. The manner in which Yu conveyed away

Сн. 26. How KNOWLEDGE OUCHT TO BE PURSUED BY THE CAREFUL STUDY OF PHENOMENA. Mencius here points out correctly the path to knowledge. The rule which he lays down is quite in harmony with that of Bacon. It is to be regretted that in China, more perhaps than in any other part of the world, has it been disregarded. 1. 性 is here to be taken quite generally. Julien finds fault with Noel for translating it by *rerum natura*, which appears to be quite correct. Choo He makes it—人物所得以生之理, than which nothing could be more general. Possibly Mencius may have had in view the disputes about the nature of man which were rife in his time, but the references to Yu's labors with the waters, and to the studies of astronomers, show that the term is used in its signification. 故 =our "phenomenon," the nature in its development. The character is often used as synonymous with 事, "facts." 則 is more than a simple conjunction, and is to be taken in close connection with the 而 已; Chaou K'e explains—則以故而已, "can only do so by the 故." And phenomena, to be valuable, must be natural, 利=順, "following easily," "unconstrained." 2. 智者 is the would-be wise ="your wise men." 其鑿, "their chiseling," or "boring,"

水也、行其所無事也、

如智者亦行其所無

事、則智亦大矣天之

高也、星辰之遠也、苟

求其故、千歲之日至、

可坐而致也。

公行子有子之喪、

the waters was by doing what gave him no trouble. If your wise men would also do that which gave them no trouble, their knowledge would also be great.

3. "There is heaven so high; there are the stars so distant. If we have investigated their phenomena, we may, while sitting *in our places*, go back to the solstice of a thousand years *ago*."

CHAPTER XXVII. 1. The officer Kung-hang having on hand the funeral of one of his sons, the Master

i. e., their forcing things, instead of "waiting" for them, which is a 行其 所事, "doing that in which they have *many* affairs, or much to do." Yu is said 行 水, rather than, according to the common phraseology about his labors, 治 水, because 行 more appropriately represents the mode of his dealing with the waters, according to their nature, and not by a system of force. 3. 千 歲 之 日 至, acc. to modern comm., refers to the winter solstice, from the midnight of which, it is supposed, the first calculation of time began;—致 是 推 致 而 得 之, "we may calculate up to and get it." Chaou K'e, however, makes the meaning to be simply:—

"We may sit and determine on what day the solstice occurred a thousand years ago." See the 四 書 撫 餘 說, where this view is approved.

CH. 27. HOW MENCIUS WOULD NOT IMITATE OTHERS IN PAYING COURT TO A FAVORITE. 1. Kunghang (low. 1st tone, "a rank," "a row." Various accounts are given of the way in which the term passed along with 公 into a double surname) was an officer of Ts'e, who "had the funeral of a son." Neither Chaou K'e nor Choo He offers any remark on the phrase, but some scholars of the Sung dynasty, subsequent to Choo He, explained it as meaning, 有 人 子 之 喪, "had the funeral duty

右師往弔、入門、有進而與右

師言者、有就右師之位、而與

右師言者孟子不與右師言、

右師不悅曰、諸君子皆與驩

言、孟子獨不與驩言是簡驩

也。孟子聞之曰、禮、朝廷不歷

of the Right went to condole with him. When *this noble* entered the door, some called him to them and spoke with him, and some went to his place and spoke with him.

2. Mencius did not speak with him, so that he was displeased, and said, "All the gentlemen have spoken with me. There is only Mencius who does not speak to me, thereby slighting me."

3. Mencius, having heard of this remark, said, "According to the prescribed rules, in the court,

that devolves on a son," i. e., was occupied with the funeral of one of his parents, and nearly all commentators have since followed that view. The author of the 四書擴餘說, in *loc.*, shows clearly, however, that it is incorrect, and that the true interpretation is the more natural one given in the translation. The Master of the Right here was Wang Hwan; see II, Pt. II, vi. At the imperial court, there were the high nobles, called 太師 and 少師,

"Grand Master," and "Junior Master." In the courts of the princes, the corresponding nobles were called 左師 and 右師, "Master of the Left," and "Master of the Right." 進,—as in Con. Ana., VII, xxx, 2. It is to be understood that all the condolers made their visit by the prince's order, and were consequently to observe the court rules. This is the explanation of Mencius's conduct. 3. 禮 refers to the established usages of the court; see the Chow Le, XXII,

禮存心。仁者愛人、有禮者敬人。

以其存心也、君子以仁存心、以

臺孟子曰、君子所以異於人者、

異乎。

我欲行禮子敖以我爲簡、不亦

位、而相與言、不踰階而相揖也、

individuals may not change their places to speak with one another, nor may they pass from their ranks to bow to one another. I was wishing to observe this rule, and Tsze-gaou understands it that I was slighting him:—is not this strange?"

CHAPTER XXVIII. 1. Mencius said, "That whereby the superior man is distinguished from other men is what he preserves in his heart;—namely, benevolence and propriety.

2. "The benevolent man loves others. The man of propriety shows respect to others.

iii, 1, *et al.* 階,—"steps," or "stairs," but here for the ranks of the officers arranged with reference to the steps leading up to the hall.

CH. 28. HOW THE SUPERIOR MAN IS DISTINGUISHED BY THE CULTIVA-TION OF MORAL EXCELLENCE, AND IS PLACED THEREBY BEYOND THE REACH OF CALAMITY. 1. 存心 must not be understood—"he preserves his heart." The first definition of 存 in K'ang-he's dictionary is 在, "to be

有禮矣、其橫逆由是也、君子

至哉其自反而仁矣、自反而

不仁也、必無禮也、此物奚宜

橫逆、則君子必自反也、我必

恆敬之。有人於此、其待我以

愛人者、人恆愛之、敬人者、人

3. "He who loves others is constantly loved by them. He who respects others is constantly respected by them.

4. "Here is a man, who treats me in a perverse and unreasonable manner. The superior man in such a case will turn round upon himself—'I must have been wanting in benevolence; I must have been wanting in propriety:—how should this have happened to me?'

5. "He examines himself, and is *specially* benevolent. He turns round upon himself, and is *specially* observant of propriety. The perversity and unreasonableness of the other, *however*, are still the same.

in." It is not so much an active verb, "to preserve," as = "to preserve in." 4. 橫 (low. 3rd tone) 逆 pre- suppose the exercise of love and respect, which are done despite to. 此 物 = 此 事. 5. 由 is used for 猶,

一朝之患也、乃若所憂、則有
焉。是故君子有終身之憂、無
禽獸奚擇哉、於禽獸又何難
此亦妄人也已矣、如此、則與
忠矣、其橫逆由是也、君子曰、
必自反也、我必不忠自反而

The superior man will *again* turn round on himself—
'I must have been failing to do my utmost.'

6. "He turns round upon himself, and proceeds
to do his utmost, but still the perversity and unreasonableness of the other are repeated. *On this*
the superior man says, 'This is a man utterly lost
indeed! Since he conducts himself so, what is there
to choose between him and a brute? Why should
I go to contend with a brute?'

7. "Thus it is that the superior man has a life-
long anxiety and not one morning's calamity. As
to what is matter of anxiety to him, that he has.—

as often elsewhere. 忠, in the sense
of 盡己, "doing one's utmost." 難,
—low. 3rd tone,＝校, "to compare
with." It is explained in the dict.
with reference to this passage, by 責,
"to charge," "to reprove." 6. 憂,—
proceeding from within; 患,—coming
from without. 一朝之患, must be
understood from the expressions
below. There may be calamity, but

如有一朝之患、則君子不患矣。

亡矣、非仁無爲也、非禮無行也、

如舜而已矣、若夫君子所患、則

鄉人也、是則可憂也、憂之如何、

天下、可傳於後世、我由未免爲

之舜人也、我亦人也、舜爲法於

*He says,* 'Shun was a man, and I also am a man. *But* Shun became an example to the empire, and *his conduct* was worthy to be handed down to after ages, while I am nothing better than a villager.' This indeed is proper matter of anxiety to him. And in what way is he anxious about it? Just that he may be like Shun:—then only will he stop. As to what the superior man would feel to be a calamity, there is no such thing. He does nothing which is not according to propriety. If there should befall him one morning's calamity, the superior man does not account it a calamity."

the superior man is superior to it. 乃, "but." We must supply,—"He should be without anxiety, *but* he has anxiety." 若夫,—夫, low. 1st tone. 亡＝無.

禹稷當平世、三過其門
而不入、孔子賢之顏子當
亂世、居於陋巷、一簞食、一
瓢飲、人不堪其憂顏子不
改其樂、孔子賢之孟子曰、
禹稷、顏回同道禹思天下

CHAPTER XXIX. 1. Yu and Tseih, in an age of tranquilizing government, thrice passed their doors without entering them. Confucius praised them.

2. The disciple Yen, in an age of confusion, dwelt in a mean narrow lane, having his single bamboo cup of rice, and his single gourd dish of water; other men could not have endured the distress, but he did not allow his joy to be affected by it. Confucius praised him.

3. Mencius said, "Yu, Tseih, and Yen Hwuy agreed in the principle of their conduct.

4. "Yu thought that if any one in the empire

CH. 29. A RECONCILING PRINCIPLE WILL BE FOUND TO UNDERLIE THE OUTWARDLY DIFFERENT CONDUCT OF GREAT AND GOOD MEN;—IN HONOR OF YEN HWUY, WITH A REFERENCE TO MENCIUS HIMSELF. 1. See III, Pt. I, iv, 6, 7, 8. The thrice passing his door without entering it was proper to Yu, though it is here attributed also to Tseih. 賢,—used as a verb, "to pronounce a worthy," ="to praise." 2. See Con. Ana., VI, ix. 平世 and 亂世 are contrasted, but a tranquil age was not a characteristic of Yu and Tseih's time. It was an age of tranquilization. 3. 同道,—道=理之當然, "what

髮纓冠而救之、可也。
之人鬪者、救之、雖被
地則皆然。六節 今有同室
其急也。五節 禹稷顏子、易
己飢之也、是以如是
稷思天下有飢者、由
有溺者、由己溺之也、

were drowned, it was as if he drowned him. Tseih thought that if any one in the empire suffered hunger, it was as if he famished him. It was on this account that they were so earnest.

5. "If Yu and Tseih, and the philosopher Yen had exchanged places, each would have done what the other did.

6. "Here now in the same apartment with you are people fighting:—*you ought to* part them. Though you part them with your cap simply tied over your unbound hair, your conduct will be allowable.

was proper in principle." 4. 由,— used for 猶. 5. 則 皆 然, lit., "then all so," the meaning being as in the translation. Yen Hwuy, in the circumstances of Yu and Tseih, would have been found laboring with as much energy and self-denial for the public good as they showed; and Yu and Tseih, in the circumstances of Hwuy, would have lived in obscurity contented as he was, and happy in the pursuit of the truth and in cultivation of themselves. 6. 被,—read

p'e, low. 1st tone. The rules anciently prescribed for dressing were very minute. Much had to be done with the hair before the final act of putting on the cap, with its strings (纓) tied under the chin, could be performed. In the case in the text, all this is neglected. The urgency of the case, and the intimacy of the individual with the parties quarreling, justify such neglect. 救 之.— lit., "to save them," i. e., to part them. This was the case of Yu and

遊、又從而禮貌之、敢問

皆稱不孝焉、夫子與之

公都子曰、匡章通國

戶、可也。

而往救之、則惑也、雖閉

鄉鄰有鬭者、被髮纓冠

7. "If the fighting be *only* in the village or neighborhood, if you go to put an end to it with your cap tied over your hair unbound, you will be in error. Although you should shut your door *in such a case,* your conduct would be allowable."

CHAPTER XXX. 1. The disciple Kung-too said, "Throughout the whole kingdom everybody pronounces K'wang unfilial. But you, Master, keep company with him, and moreover treat him with politeness. I venture to ask why you do so."

Tseih, in their relation to their times, while that in the next par. is supposed to illustrate the case of Yen Hwuy in relation to his. But Mencius's illustrations are generally happier than these.

CH. 30. HOW MENCIUS EXPLAINED HIS FRIENDLY INTERCOURSE WITH A MAN CHARGED WITH BEING UNFILIAL. 1. K'wang Chang was an officer of Ts'e. His name, acc. to 顧麟 士, was Chang, and designation Chang-tsze, so that Kung-too calls him by his name, and Mencius by his desig.

In opp. to this, 蔡虛齋 says that Kung-too merely drops a part of the designation, just as when Yen Hwuy is called Yen Yuen, instead of Yen Tsze-yuen. But both these explanations are to be rejected. Chang was the name, and the 子 in 章子 is simply equivalent to our Mr. 與之遊,—"ramble with him," i. e., as commonly understood, "allow him to come about your gate, your school." 又從,— "and moreover from that," i. e.,

何也。孟子曰、世俗所謂不孝者

五、惰其四支不顧父母之養、一

不孝也、博弈好飲酒不顧父母

之養、二不孝也、好貨財、私妻子、

不顧父母之養、三不孝也、從耳

目之欲以爲父母戮、四不孝也、

2. Mencius replied, "There are five things which are said in the common practice of the age to be unfilial. The first is laziness in the use of one's four limbs, without attending to the nourishment of his parents. The second is gambling and chess playing, and being fond of wine, without attending to the nourishment of his parents. The third is being fond of goods and money, and selfishly attached to his wife and children, without attending to the nourishment of his parents. The fourth is following the desires of one's ears and eyes, so as to bring his

in addition to that. 2. 博弈, may be taken together, simply = "chess playing," or separately, as in the translation; see Con. Analects, XVII, xxii. 私妻子,—"selfishly—i. e., partially putting them out of their

due place, above his parents,—loving wife and children." I cannot see why some should give a sensual meaning to 私 here. The advance of meaning from 戮 to 危 shows that the former is to be taken in the

妻子母之屬哉爲得罪於父、

之大者夫章子豈不欲有夫

朋友之道也父子責善賊恩

子父責善而不相遇也責善、

也章子有一於是乎夫章子、

好勇鬬狠以危父母五不孝

parents to disgrace. The fifth is being fond of bravery, fighting and quarreling so as to endanger his parents. Is Chang guilty of any one of these things?

3. "Now between Chang and his father there arose disagreement, he, the son, reproving his father, to urge him to what was good.

4. "To urge one another to what is good by re-proofs is the way of friends. But such urging between father and son is the greatest injury to the kindness *which should prevail between them.*

5. "Moreover, did not Chang wish to have *in his family* the relationships of husband and wife, child and mother? But because he had offended his father,

lighter sense of "disgrace." 3, 4. | precedes 父 here to show that
Comp. Pt. I, xviii. 子父責善,一子 | K'wang Chang had been the ag-

寇、或曰、寇至、盍去諸。

鬨曾子居武城、有越

大者、是則章子已矣、

爲不若是、是則罪之

身不養焉、其設心以

不得近、出妻屏子、終

and was not permitted to approach him, he sent away his wife, and drove forth his son, and all his life receives no cherishing attention from them. He settled it in his mind that if he did not act in this way, his would be one of the greatest of crimes.— Such and nothing more is the case of Chang."

CHAPTER XXXI. 1. When the philosopher Tsǎng dwelt in Wooshing, there came a band from Yuě to plunder it. Some one said *to him*, "The plunderers are coming:—why not leave this?" Tsǎng *on this left the city*, saying *to the man in charge of the house*,

gressor. 5. 屏,—upper 2nd tone. Readers not Chinese will think that Chang's treatment of his wife and son was more criminal than his conduct to his father. 是則罪之大者,—是, "this," embracing the two things, his giving offense to his father, and still continuing to enjoy the comforts of wife and son.

CH. 31. HOW MENCIUS EXPLAINED THE DIFFERENT CONDUCT OF THE PHILOSOPHER TSANG AND OF TSZE-SZE IN SIMILAR CIRCUMSTANCES. 1. Woo-shing,—see Con. Analects, VI, xii. It appears below that Tsǎng had opened a school or lecture room

in the place. Many understand that he had been invited to do so,—to be a 賓師, "guest and teacher,"—by the commandant. Woo-shing is probably to be referred to a place in the dis. of 嘉祥 in the dep. of Yenchow. It was thus in the south of Shantung. South from it, and covering the present Kiangsu and part of Chekiang, were the possessions of Woo (吳) and Yuě, all in Tsǎng-tsze's time subject to Yuě. See in the 集證, *in loc.*, a somewhat similar incident in Tsǎng's life (probably a different version of the same), in which the plunderers are from

行日是非汝所知也昔沈

寇退、則反殆於不可。沈猶

也、寇至、則先去、以爲民望、

曰、待先生如此、其忠且敬

我將反寇退、曾子反、左右

薪木。寇退、則曰、脩我牆屋、

曰、無寓人於我室、毀傷其

"Do not lodge any persons in my house, lest they break and injure the plants and trees." When the plunderers withdrew, he sent word to him, saying, "Repair the walls of my house. I am about to return." When the plunderers retired, the philosopher Tsăng returned *accordingly*. His disciples said, "Since our master was treated with so much sincerity and respect, for him to be the first to go away on the arrival of the plunderers, so as to be observed by the people, and then to return on their retiring, appears to us to be improper." Shin-yew Hing said, "You do not understand this matter. Formerly,

Loo. 曰, 無寓, 云 云,—the translation needs to be supplemented here considerably to bring out the meaning. 薪 is explained in K'ang-he's dictionary, with reference to this passage, by 草, "grass," or small plants generally. 寇退則曰,—this 曰 must = "sent word to." 牆屋.—we should rather expect 屋牆. If 待 be translated actively, we must supply as a nominative—"the governor of the city." Shin- (沈 is pronounced as 審. So, commonly. But the point is doubtful. See the 集證, *in loc.*) yew Hing is supposed to have been a disciple of Ts'ăng's, a native of Wooshing. The Shin-yew whom he mentions below was another person of the same surname with whom Tsăng and his disciples

也父兄也子思臣也微

曾子子思同道曾子師

伋去君誰與守孟子曰、

寇至盍去諸子思曰如

思居於衞有齊寇或曰、

者七十人未有與焉。

猶有負芻之禍從先生

when Shin-yew was exposed to the outbreak of the grass carriers, there were seventy disciples in our master's following, and none of them took part in the matter."

2. When Tsze-sze was living in Wei, there came a band from Ts'e to plunder. Some one said to him, "The plunderers are coming;—why not leave this?" Tsze-sze said, "If I go away, whom will the prince have to guard *the state* with?"

3. Mencius said, "The philosopher Tsăng and Tsze-sze agreed in the principle of their conduct. Tsăng was a teacher—in the place of a father or elder brother. Tsze-sze was a minister—in a meaner

(從 者＝左 右, above) were living. 與,—low. 3:d tone. Shin-yew Hing adduces this other case, as analogous to Tsăng's leaving Wooshing, intimating that he acted on a certain principle which justified his conduct. 2. 伋 was Tsze-sze's name. "Was living in Wei,"—i. e., was living and sustaining office. 3. Comp. ch. xxviii, 3, 5. The reader can judge how far

也、曾子子思易地則皆

然。

儲子曰、王使人瞷夫

子、果有以異於人乎。孟

子曰、何以異於人哉、堯

舜與人同耳。

齊人有一妻一妾、而

處室者、其良人出、則必

place. If the philosopers Tsăng and Tsze-sze had exchanged places, the one would have done what the other did."

CHAPTER XXXII. The officer Ch'oo said *to Mencius,* "Master, the king sent persons to spy out whether you were really different from other men." Mencius said, "How should I be different from other men! Yaou and Shun were just the same as other men."

CHAPTER XXXIII. 1. A man of Ts'e had a wife and a concubine, and lived together with them in his house. When their husband went out, he would

the defense of Tsăng's conduct is satisfactory.

CH. 32. SAGES ARE JUST LIKE OTHER MEN. This Ch'oo was a minister of Ts'e. We must suppose that it was the private manners and way of living of Mencius, which the king wanted to spy out, unless the thing occurred on Mencius's first arrival in Ts'e, and before he had any interview with the king.

CH. 33. THE DISGRACEFUL MEANS WHICH MEN TAKE TO SEEK FOR WEALTH AND HONORS. 1. As Choo He observes, there ought to be, at the beginning of the chapter, 孟子曰, "Mencius said." The phrase 而處 (up. 2nd tone) 室者 is not easily managed in translating. The subject of it is the "man of Ts'e," and not the wife and concubine. It is descriptive of him as living with

之徧國中、無與立談者、卒
之也、蚤起、施從良人之所
顯者來、吾將瞷良人之所
食者、盡富貴也、而未嘗有
饜酒肉而後反、問其與飲
妻告其妾曰、良人出、則必
與飲食者、則盡富貴也、其
饜酒肉而後反其妻問所

get himself well filled with wine and flesh, and then return, and, on his wife's asking him with whom he ate and drank, they were sure to be all wealthy and honorable people. The wife informed the concubine, saying, "When our good man goes out, he is sure to come back having partaken plentifully of wine and flesh. I asked with whom he ate and drank, and they are all, *it seems*, wealthy and honorable people. And yet no people of distinction ever come here. I will spy out where our good man goes." *Accordingly*, she got up early in the morning, and privately followed wherever her husband went. Throughout the whole city, there was no one who stood or talked with him. At last, he came to those

them, and being the head of a family,—有 刑 家 之 責, as is said in the 備 旨, "having the duty of setting an example to its members." 良 人,—corresponding to the Scottish term of "goodman" for husband.

所 與 飲 食 者,—not "who gave him to drink and eat," as Julien makes it. 所 之,—之, the verb, as also below, and in 之 東, 之 他. 施 從, —施, read *e*, i. e., either low. 1st, or low. 3rd tone. 圖,—plainly used

良人未之知也、施施從外來、驕

妾訕其良人、而相泣於中庭、而

所仰望而終身也、今若此、與其

道也。其妻歸告其妾曰良人者、

足、又顧而之他、此其爲饜足之

之東郭墦間之祭者、乞其餘、不

who were sacrificing among the tombs beyond the outer wall on the east, and begged what they had over. Not being satisfied, he looked about, and went to another party:—and this was the way in which he got himself satiated. His wife returned, and informed the concubine, saying, "It was to our husband that we looked up in hopeful contemplation with whom our lot is cast for life;—and now these are his ways!" On this, along with the concubine she reviled their husband, and they wept together in the middle hall. In the meantime the husband, knowing nothing of all this, came in with a jaunty air, carrying himself proudly to his wife and concubine.

for "city." 郭,—see II, Pt. II, i, 2. | 之他, "went to another place,"

其妻妾。二而
觀之、則人之所
以求富貴利達
者、其妻妾不羞
也、而不相泣者
幾希矣。

2. In the view of a superior man, as to the ways by which men seek for riches, honors, gain, and advancement, there are few of their wives and concubines who would not be ashamed and weep together *on account of them.*

"another party."　2. 幾 希, as in ch. xix, 1, but it is here an adjective, | "few."

## BOOK V

### WAN CHANG.　PART I

萬章章句

上

萬章問曰、

舜往于田、號<br>
泣于旻天、何<br>
爲其號泣也。

孟子曰、怨慕<br>
也萬章曰、父

母愛之、喜而<br>
不忘父母惡

CHAPTER I.　1. Wan Chang asked *Mencius*, saying, *When* "Shun went into the fields, he cried out and wept towards the pitying heavens.　Why did he cry out and weep?"　Mencius replied, "He was dissatisfied, and full of earnest desire."

2.　Wan Chang said, "When his parents love him, a son rejoices and forgets them not.　When his parents

This Book is named from the chief interlocutor in it, Wan Chang (see III, Pt. II, v).　The tradition is that it was in company with Wan Chang's disciples, that Mencius baffled in his hopes of doing public service, and having retired into privacy, composed the seven Books, which constitute his Works.　The first part of this Book is occupied with discussions about Shun, and other ancient worthies.

CH. 1. SHUN'S GREAT FILIAL PIETY:—HOW IT CARRIED HIM INTO THE FIELDS TO WEEP AND DEPLORE HIS INABILITY TO SECURE THE AFFECTION AND SYMPATHY OF HIS PARENTS. 1. 號,—low. 1st tone, "to cry out." It has another signification in the same tone, "to weep," which would answer equally well.　See the incident related in the Shoo-king, II, ii, 21, from which we learn that such

behavior was a characteristic of his earlier life, when he was "plowing" at the foot of the Leih hill. 旻天,— the name given to the autumnal sky or heavens. Two meanings have been assigned to 旻; "the variegated," with reference to the beautiful tints (文章) of matured nature; and "the compassionate," as if it were 愍, with reference to the decay of nature. This latter is generally acquiesced in.　I have translated 于 by "towards," but the paraph. in the 日講 is:—"He cried out and called upon pitying Heaven, that lovingly overshadows and compassionates this lower world, weeping at the same time."　怨慕,—simply, "he was murmuring and desiring."　The murmuring was at himself, but this is purposely kept in the background, and Chang supposed that he was murmuring at his parents.　2. 父母

之、勞而不怨、然則舜怨乎。

曰長息問於公明高曰、舜

往于田、則吾既得聞命矣、

號泣于旻天于父母、則吾

不知也、公明高曰、是非爾

所知也。夫公明高以孝子

之心爲不若是恝、我竭力

hate him, though they punish him, he does not murmur. Was Shun then murmuring *against his parents?*" Mencius answered, "Ch'ang Seih asked Kung-ming Kaou, saying, 'As to Shun's going into the fields, I have received your instructions, but I do not know about his weeping and crying out to the pitying heavens and to his parents.' Kung-ming Kaou answered him, 'You do not understand that matter.' Now, Kung-ming Kaou supposed that the heart of the filial son could not be so free of sorrow. *Shun would say*, 'I exert my strength to cultivate the fields,

. . . 不 怨,—see Con. Ana., IV, xviii. Kung-ming Kaou is generally understood to have been a disciple of Tsăng Sin, and Ch'ang Seih again to have been a disciple of Kaou. 吾既得聞命, "I have received your *commands*,"—"commands," said deferentially for "instructions," as in III, Pt. I, v, 5. 于父母 is also from the Shoo-king, though omitted above in par. 1. In translating we must reverse the order of 號 泣, "he wept and cried out,—to heaven, to his parents." 是非爾所知也,—see IV, Pt. II, xxxi, 1. 不若是恝, —"not so without sorrow," i. e., not so, as common people would have it, and as Ch'ang Seih thought would have been right, that he could refrain from weeping and crying out. 我竭, 云云, are the thoughts supposed to pass through Shun's mind.

遷之焉、爲不順於父

之者、帝將胥天下而

之中、天下之士多就

廩備以事舜於畎畝

男二女、百官牛羊倉

我何哉帝使其子九

矣、父母之不我愛於

耕田、共爲子職而已

but I am there by only discharging my office as a
son. What can there be in me that my parents do
not love me?'

3. "The emperor caused his own children, nine
sons and two daughters, the various officers,
oxen and sheep, storehouses and granaries, *all* to
be prepared, to serve Shun amid the channeled
fields. Of the scholars of the empire there were
multitudes who flocked to him. The emperor designed that *Shun* should superintend the empire along
with him, and then to transfer it to him entirely.
But because his parents were not in accord with

共=拱, up. 1st tone. 3. See the
Shoo-king, I, par. 12, but the various
incidents of the particular honors
conferred on Shun, and his influence,
are to be collected from the general
history of him and Yaou. There is,
however, an important discrepancy
between Mencius's account of Shun,
and that in the Shoo-king. There,
when he is first recommended to
Yaou by the high officers, they base
their recommendation on the fact

of his having overcome the evil that
was in his parents and brother, and
brought them to self-government.
The Shoo-king, moreover, mentions
only one son of Yaou, Tan Choo
(丹朱), and says nothing of the nine
who are here said to have been put
under the command of Yaou. They
are mentioned, however, in the "Historical Records," 虞史記. 帝將胥
天下＝將與之胥（＝相）視天下。而
遷之＝自移以與之. 不順於父母,

母、如窮人無所歸天下之士

悅之人之所欲也、而不足以

解憂好色人之所欲妻帝之

二女、而不足以解憂富人之

所欲富有天下、而不足以解

憂貴人之所欲貴爲天子、而

不足以解憂人悅之好色富

him, he felt like a poor man who has nowhere to turn to.

4. "To be delighted in by the scholars of the empire, is what men desire, but it was not sufficient to remove the sorrow *of Shun*. The possession of beauty is what men desire, and *Shun* had for his wives the two daughters of the emperor, but this was not sufficient to remove his sorrow. Riches are what men desire, and the empire was the rich property *of Shun*, but this was not sufficient to remove his sorrow. Honors are what men desire, and *Shun* had the dignity of being emperor, but this was not sufficient to remove his sorrow. The reason why the being the object of men's delight, the possession of beauty,

---

—see IV, Pt. 1, xxviii, 1.　4. 色，—色 is here=our "a beauty," "beauties." 妻—up. 2nd tone, here as a verb, "to

wive," "to have for wife." Observe the force of 者, leading on to what follows as the explanation of the

於大舜見之矣。

身慕父母、五十而慕者、予

不得於君、則熱中、大孝終

妻子、則慕妻子、仕則慕君、

父母、知好色、則慕少艾有

父母可以解憂人少、則慕

貴、無足以解憂者、惟順於

riches, and honors, were not sufficient to remove his sorrow, was that it could be removed only by his getting his parents to be in accord with him.

5. "The desire of the child is towards his father and mother. When he becomes conscious of the attractions of beauty, his desire is towards young and beautiful women. When he comes to have a wife and children, his desire is towards them. When he obtains office, his desire is towards his sovereign:— if he cannot get the regard of his sovereign, he burns within. *But* the man of great filial piety, to the end of his life, has his desire towards his parents. In the great Shun I see the case of one whose desire at fifty years was towards them."

preceding circumstances. 5. 少,— up. 3rd tone, "young," "little." 好色,—the term has a different acceptation from that in the prec. par., though I have translated it in the same way. 艾,—in the sense of 美, "beautiful."

倫以懟父母、是以不

也、如告則廢人之大

男女居室人之大倫

孟子曰告則不得娶、

舜之不告而娶何也。

信斯言也、宜莫如舜、

妻如之何、必告父母、

萬章問曰、詩云娶

CHAPTER II. 1. Wan Chang asked *Mencius*, saying, "It is said in the 'Book of Poetry,'

'In marrying a wife, how ought a man to proceed?
He must inform his parents.'

If the rule be indeed as here expressed, no man ought to have illustrated it so well as Shun. How was it that Shun's marriage took place without his informing *his parents?*" Mencius replied, "If he had informed them, he would not have been able to marry. That male and female should dwell together, is the greatest of human relations. If *Shun* had informed his parents, he must have made void this greatest of human relations, thereby incurring their resentment. On this account, he did not inform them."

CH. 2. DEFENSE OF SHUN AGAINST THE CHARGES OF VIOLATING THE PROPER RULE IN THE WAY OF HIS MARRYING, AND OF HYPOCRISY IN HIS CONDUCT TO HIS BROTHER. 1, 2. Comp. Pt. I, xxvi. 詩 云,—see the She-king, I, viii, Ode VI, st. 3. 告— low. 3rd tone, as in Ana., III, xvii. 信＝誠, "if indeed." 以懟父母,—if he had not married, then his parents would have had cause to be angry with him, for allowing the line of the family to terminate. This seems to be the meaning of

之象曰謨蓋都君咸我績、

瞍焚廩使浚井、出從而揜

曰父母使舜完廩捐階瞽

知告焉、則不得妻也。萬章

妻舜而不告何也。曰帝亦

娶、則吾既得聞命矣、帝之

告也。萬章曰、舜之不告而

2. Wan Chang said, "As to Shun's marrying with-out informing his parents, I have heard your instruc-tions; but how was it that the emperor gave him his daughters as wives without informing *Shun's parents?*" *Mencius* said, "The emperor also knew that if he informed them, he could not marry his daughters to him."

3. Wan Chang said, "His parents set Shun to repair a granary, to which, the ladder having been removed, Koo-sow set fire. They *also* made him dig a well. He got out, but they, *not knowing that,* proceeded to cover him up. Seang said, 'Of the scheme to cover up the city-forming prince the merit

the phrase. 聞命,—as in the last chap. 帝... 而不告,—告 here is understood as = "requiring Shun to inform his parents." 3. Shun's half brother is understood to have been the instigator in the attempts on his life here mentioned. The incidents, however, are taken from tradition, and not from the Shoo-king. Shun covered himself with two bamboo screens, and made his way through the fire. In the second case, he found a hole or passage in the side of the wall, and got away by means of it. 都君,—it is mentioned in the last chapter, how the scholars of the

牛羊父母、倉廩父母、干戈

朕、琴朕、弤朕、二嫂使治朕

棲、象往入舜宮、舜在牀琴、

象曰、鬱陶思君爾、忸怩、舜

曰、惟諸臣庶、汝其于予治、

不識舜不知象之將殺己

is all mine. Let my parents have his oxen and sheep. Let them have his storehouses and granaries. His shield and spear shall be mine. His lute shall be mine. His bow shall be mine. His two wives I shall make attend for me to my bed.' Seang then went away into Shun's palace, and there was Shun on his couch playing on his lute. Seang said, 'I am come simply because I was thinking anxiously about you.' *At the same time*, he blushed deeply. Shun said to him, 'There are all my officers:—do you undertake the government of them for me.' I do not know whether Shun was ignorant of Seang's wishing to kill him." *Mencius*

empire flocked to Shun. They say that if he lived in one place for a year, he formed a 聚, or "assemblage"; in two years, he formed a 邑, or "town," and in three, a 都, or "capital." With reference to this, Seang calls him 都君. 朕, now confined to the emperor, WE, was anciently used by high and low. 弤,—"a carved bow," said to have been given to Shun by Yaou, as a token of his associating him with him on the throne. 二嫂,—lit., "the two sisters-in-law." 棲＝牀, "a bed," or "couch." 鬱陶思君爾,—爾＝耳, as a final particle, "only."

與。曰奚而不知也、象憂亦憂、

象喜亦喜。曰、然則舜僞喜者

與。曰否昔者、有饋生魚於鄭

子產、子產使校人畜之池、校

人烹之反命曰、始舍之圉圉

焉、少、則洋洋焉、攸然而逝子

answered, "How could he be ignorant of that? But when Seang was sorrowful, he was also sorrowful; when Seang was joyful, he was also joyful."

4. *Chang* said, "In that case, then, did not Shun rejoice hypocritically?" Mencius replied, "No. Formerly, some one sent a present of a live fish to Tsze-ch'an of Ch'ing. Tsze-ch'an ordered his pond keeper to keep it in the pond, but that officer cooked it, and reported the execution of his commission, saying, 'When I first let it go, it appeared embarrassed. In a little, it seemed to be somewhat at ease, and then it swam away joyfully.' Tsze-ch'an

The expression literally is,—"with suppressed anxiety thinking of you only." 4. 校 (read *heaou*, low. 3rd tone) 人 is taken by all the commentators, as 主池沼小吏, "a small officer over the ponds," but I do not know that this meaning of the phrase is found elsewhere. 反命,一

之奚偽焉。

愛兄之道來、故誠信而喜

其方、難罔以非其道、彼以

得其所哉、故君子可欺以

既烹而食之曰、得其所哉、

校人出曰、孰謂子產智予

產曰、得其所哉得其所哉、

observed, 'It had got into its element! It had got into
its element!' The pond keeper then went out and
said, 'Who calls Tsze-ch'an a wise man? After I had
cooked and eaten the fish, he says, "It had got into
its element! it had got into its element!"' Thus a
superior man may be imposed on by what seems to be
as it ought to be, but he cannot be entrapped by
what is contrary to right principle. Seang came
in the way in which the love of his elder brother
would have made him come; therefore *Shun* sincerely
believed him, and rejoiced. What hypocrisy was
there?"

as in III, Pt. I, ii, 3. 故君子可欺.
云 云,—compare Con. Ana., VI,
xxiv. 以 其 方,—"by its class," the
meaning being as in the translation.
—Choo He says: "Mencius says
that Shun knew well that Seang
wished to kill him, but when he saw
him sorrowful, he was sorrowful, and
when he saw him joyful, he was

joyful. The case was that his
brotherly feeling could not be repressed. Whether the things mentioned by Wan Chang really occurred
or not, we do not know. But Mencius was able to know and describe
the mind of Shun, and that is the
only thing here worth discussing
about."

鯀于羽山、四罪而天下
崇山、殺三苗于三危、殛
共工于幽州、放驩兜于
或曰放焉萬章曰、舜流
之何也。孟子曰封之也、
舜爲事立爲天子、則放
萬章問曰、象日以殺

CHAPTER III. 1. Wan Chang said, "Seang made it
his daily business to slay Shun. When *Shun* was
made emperor, how was it that he *only* banished
him?" Mencius said, "He raised him to be a prince.
Some supposed that it was banishing him."

2. Wan Chang said, "Shun banished the superintendent of works to Yewchow; he sent away
Hwan-taou to the mountain Ts'ung; he slew *the prince
of* San Meaou in Sanwei; and he imprisoned K'wăn
on the mountain Yu. When the crimes of those four

CH. 3. EXPLANATION AND DEFENSE
OF SHUN'S CONDUCT IN THE CASE OF
HIS WICKED BROTHER SEANG;—HOW
HE BOTH DISTINGUISHED HIM, AND
KEPT HIM UNDER RESTRAINT. 1.
放＝寘, "to place," with the idea of
keeping in the place＝"to banish."
Chang's thought was that Seang
should have been put to death, and
not merely banished. 或曰,—it
seems best to understand 曰 as
meaning "supposed," and not "said."
2. The different individuals mentioned here are all spoken of in the
Shoo-king, Pt. II, i, 12, which see.
共工 is a name of office. The surname or name of the holder of it is
not found in the Shoo-king. Hwan-
taou was the name of the 司徒,

"minister of instruction." He appears in the Shoo-king, as the friend
of the 共工, recommending him to
Yaou; hence Choo He says that
these two were confederate in evil.
三苗 is to be understood, in the
text, as "*the prince of* San Meaou,"
which was the name of a state, near
the Tungt'ing lake, embracing the
present dep. of 岳州, and extending
towards Wuchang. K'wan was
the name of the father of Yu. The
places mentioned are difficult of
identification. Yewpe is referred to
the pres. 道州, and the dis. of
Lingling, in the dep. of 永州, in
Honan. 殛 is said by Choo He
to＝誅, "to cut off," but that is too
strong. 四罪＝治此四凶之罪,

也封之有庳富貴之也、身
之欲其貴也、愛之欲其富
宿怨焉、親愛之而已矣、親
人之於弟也不藏怒焉、不
則誅之在弟、則封之曰仁
焉、仁人固如是乎、在他人、
封之有庳有庳之人奚罪
成服、誅不仁也、象至不仁、

were thus punished, the whole empire acquiesced:—it was a cutting off of men who were destitute of benevolence. But Seang was *of all men* the most destitute of benevolence, and *Shun* raised him to be the prince of Yewpe;—of what crimes had the people of Yewpe been guilty? Does a benevolent man really act thus? In the case of other men, he cut them off; in the case of his brother, he raised him to be a prince." *Mencius* replied, "A benevolent man does not lay up anger, nor cherish resentment against his brother, but only regards him with affection and love. Regarding him with affection, he wishes him to be honorable: regarding him with love, he wishes him to be rich. The appointment *of Seang* to be the prince of Yewpe was to enrich and ennoble

taking 罪 as meaning "crimes." 服,—"submitted," i. e., acknowledge the justice of the punishments inflicted. 在他人 ... 誅之, appears to be incomplete, as if Mencius had not permitted his disciple to finish what he had to say. 宿怨.—"to lodge, as if for a night, resentment"; comp. 宿

然欲常常而見之故源源而

故謂之放豈得暴彼民哉雖

使吏治其國而納其貢稅焉、

曰、象不得有爲於其國天子

之乎敢問或曰放者、何謂也。

爲天子、弟爲匹夫、可謂親愛

him.　If while *Shun* himself was emperor, his brother had been a common man, could he have been said to regard him with affection and love?"

3.　*Wan Chang* said, "I venture to ask what you mean by saying that some supposed that it was a banishing of Seang?"　*Mencius* replied, "Seang could do nothing in his state.　The emperor appointed an officer to administer its government, and to pay over its revenues to him.　This treatment of him led to its being said that he was banished.　How *indeed* could he be allowed the means of oppressing the people?　Nevertheless, *Shun* wished to be continually seeing him, and, by this arrangement, he came incessantly *to*

諸, Ana., XII, xii, 2.　3. 不得有爲, —"did not get to have doing," i. e., was not allowed to act independ-

ently.　其貢稅＝其國所賦 (taking 貢 as a verb) 之稅.　源源,—"the uninterrupted flowing of a stream."

子、舜南面而立堯
得而臣父不得而
云、盛德之士、君不
咸丘蒙問曰、語
於有庫、此之謂也。
來、不及貢以政接

_court_, as is signified in that expression—'He did not wait for the rendering of tribute, or affairs of government, to receive the prince of Yewpe.'"

CHAPTER IV. 1. Hëen-k'ew Mung asked _Mencius_, saying, "There is the saying,—'A scholar of complete virtue may not be employed as a minister by his sovereign, nor treated as a son by his father. Shun stood with his face to the south, and Yaou, at the

不及貢 . . . 有庫, is a quotation by Mencius from some book that is now lost. There were regular seasons for the princes in general to repair to court, and emergencies of government which required their presence, but Shun did not wish his brother to wait for such occasions, but to be often with him. The 不 extends over the two clauses, which=不及貢期而見, 不以政事而見.

CH. 4. EXPLANATION OF SHUN'S CONDUCT WITH REFERENCE TO THE EMPEROR YAOU, AND HIS FATHER KOO-SOW. 1. Hëen-k'ew Mung was a disciple of Mencius. The surname Hëen-k'ew was derived from a place of that name where his progenitors had resided. The saying which Mung adduces extends to 岌岌乎. Two

entirely contrary interpretations of it have been given. One is that given in the translation. It is the view of Chaou K'e, and is found in the modern Pe-che (備旨), or "Complete Digest of Annotations on the Four Books." Most modern commentaries, however, take an opposite view:— "The scholar of complete virtue cannot employ his sovereign as a minister, or treat his father as a son." This view is preferred by Julien, who styles the other very bad. I am satisfied that the other is the correct one. If it were not, why should Mencius condemn the sentiment as that of an uninstructed man. 舜南面, 云云, follows as a direct example of the principle announced. Shun was the scholar of

帥諸侯北面而朝之瞽瞍
亦北面而朝之舜見瞽瞍、
其容有蹙孔子曰於斯時
也天下殆哉岌岌乎、不識
此語誠然乎哉孟子曰、否、
此非君子之言齊東野人
之語也堯老而舜攝也堯
典曰、二十有八載放勳乃

head of all the princes, appeared before him at court with his face to the north. Koo-sow also did the same. When Shun saw Koo-sow, his countenance became discomposed. Confucius said, *"At this time, in what a perilous condition was the empire! Its state was indeed unsettled."'*—I do not know whether what is here said really took place." Mencius replied, "No. These are not the words of a superior man. They are the sayings of an uncultivated person of the east of Ts'e. When Yaou was old, Shun was associated with him in the government. It is said· in the 'Canon of Yaou,' 'After twenty and eight years, the Highly Meritorious one deceased.

complete virtue, and therefore the emperor· Yaou, and his father Koo-sow, both appeared before him as subjects. 舜 見, 云 云, and the remarks of Confucius are to be taken as a protest against the arrangements described in the preceding pars. 南 面, 北 面,—see Con, Ana.,

VI, i. 野 is to be joined as an adj. with 人, and not as a noun with 東. The passage quoted from the Shoo-king is now found in the Canon of Shun, and not that of Yʻou;＝ see II, i, 13. 有,—lower 3rd tone. 載,—upper 2nd tone, "a year." 放 (upper 2nd tone; see III, Pt. I,

之不臣堯、則吾既得聞命矣、

喪是二天子矣。咸丘蒙曰、舜

又帥天下諸侯以爲堯三年

日民無二王、舜既爲天子矣、

海遏密八音孔子曰天無二

徂落、百姓如喪考妣、三年、四

The people acted as if they were mourning for a father or mother for three years, and up to *the borders of* the four seas every sound of music was hushed.' Confucius said, 'There are not two suns in the sky, nor two sovereigns over the people.' Shun having been emperor, and, moreover, leading on all the princes to observe the three years' mourning for Yaou, there would have been in this case two emperors."

2. Hëen-k'ew Mung said, "On the point of Shun's not treating Yaou as a minister, I have received your instructions. *But* it is said in the 'Book of Poetry,'

iv; 8) 勳 is not in the classic. 徂 (=殂) 落,—Choo He makes 殂=升, "to ascend." The *animus* ascends at death, and the *anima* 落, "descends": —hence the combination — "dissolution," "decease." The dict., however, makes 殂 simply =往, and the phrase = "vanish away." 百姓 is the people within the imperial domain; the 四海 denotes the rest of the empire, beyond that. Some, however, approved by the 日講, make 百姓=百官, "the officers," and 四海 = "all the

people." 考 妣,—the terms for a deceased father and mother. 三 年,— for 年 the classic has 載. The 八音, "eight sounds,"—are all instruments of music, formed of metal, stone, cord, bamboo, calabash, earthenware, leather, or wood.—The meaning is that up to the time of Yaou's decease, Shun was only vice emperor, and, therefore, Yaou never could have appeared before him in the position of a subject. 2. 舜之不臣 堯 is not to be taken with reference

我獨賢勞也、故說詩者不以文

不得養父母也、曰、此莫非王事、

詩也、非是之謂也、勞於王事而

矣、敢問瞽瞍之非臣如何曰、是

之濱莫非王臣、而舜既爲天子

詩云、普天之下、莫非王土率土

'Under the whole heaven,
Every spot is the sovereign's ground;
To the borders of the land,
Every individual is the sovereign's minister;'

—and Shun had become emperor.   I venture to ask
how it was that Koo-sow was not one of his ministers."
*Mencius* answered, "That ode is not to be understood
in that way:—it speaks of being laboriously engaged
in the sovereign's business, so as not to be able
to nourish one's parents, *as if the author* said, 'This
is all the sovereign's business, and *how is it that* I
alone am supposed to have ability, and am made
to toil in it?'   Therefore, those who explain the odes
may not insist on one term so as to do violence

to the phrase 君不得而臣, but to | and especially to Mencius's explana-
the general scope of the prec. par., | tion.   The  restricting  it  to  the

至莫大乎以天下養、
莫大乎尊親尊親之
無遺民也孝子之至、
子遺信斯言也是周
詩曰周餘黎民靡有
以辭而已矣雲漢之
意逆志是爲得之如
害辭不以辭害志以

to a sentence, nor on a sentence so as to do violence to the general scope. They must try with their thoughts to meet that scope, and then we shall apprehend it. If we simply take single sentences, there is that in the ode called 'The Milky Way,'—

> 'Of the black-haired people of the remnant of Chow,
> There is not half a one left.'

If it had been really as thus expressed, then not an individual of the people of Chow was left.

3. "Of all which a filial son can attain to, there is nothing greater than his honoring his parents. And of what can be attained to in the honoring one's parents, there is nothing greater than the nourishing

former, in opposition to the maxim 一不 以 辭 害 志, has led to the erroneous view of the whole passage animadverted on above. Mung is now convinced that it was only on Yaou's death that Shun became full emperor, but after that event there still remained the relation between him and Koo-sow, and how could he be at once sovereign and son to him? How was it that Koo-sow would be at once father and subject to him? 詩 云,—see the She-king, II, vi, Ode I, st. 2. 雲漢之詩,— see the She-king, III, iii, Ode IV, st. 3. 志,—"the scope," i. e., the

父不得而子也。
栗、瞽瞍亦允若、是爲
祇載見瞽瞍、夔夔齊
維則、此之謂也。書曰、
詩曰、永言孝思、孝思
以天下養養之至也、
爲天子父尊之至也、

them with the whole empire.   Koo-sow was the father of the emperor;—this was the height of honor.   *Shun* nourished him with the whole empire;—this was the height of nourishing.   In this was verified the sentiment in the 'Book of Poetry,'

> 'Ever cherishing filial thoughts,
> Those filial thoughts became an example *to after ages.*'

4.   "It is said in the 'Book of History,' 'Reverently performing his duties, he waited on Koo-sow, and was full of veneration and awe.   Koo-sow also believed him and conformed to virtue.'—This is the *true* case of *the scholar of complete virtue* not being treated as a son by his father."

mind or aim of the writer.  3. 詩曰, — see the She-king, III, i, Ode IX, st. 3, celebrating the praises of King Woo.—This par. shows that Shun, by his exaltation, honored his father only the more exceedingly.  He was the more "a son" to Koo-sow.  4. 書 曰,—see the Shoo-king, II, ii, 15. 齊 (read *chae*) 栗 (the classic has 慄),—this seems to be a supplement by Mencius, as if he said, "There is indeed a meaning in that saying that a scholar of complete virtue cannot be treated as a son by his father, for in the case of Shun and Koo-sow we see that the father was affected by the son, and not the son by the father."

萬章曰、堯以天
下與舜有諸孟子
曰、否天子不能以
天下與人然則舜
有天下也孰與之。
曰天與之天與之
者諄諄然命之乎。
曰、否天不言以行
與事、示之而已矣。

CHAPTER V. 1. Wan Chang said, "Was it the case that Yaou gave the empire to Shun?" Mencius said, "No. The emperor cannot give the empire to another."

2. "Yes;—but Shun had the empire. Who gave it to him?" "Heaven gave it to him," was the answer.

3. "'Heaven gave it to him':—did *Heaven* confer its appointment on him with specific injunctions?"

4. *Mencius* replied, "No. Heaven does not speak. It simply showed its will by his personal conduct, and his conduct of affairs."

CH. 5. HOW SHUN GOT THE EMPIRE BY THE GIFT OF HEAVEN. VOX POPULI, VOX DEI. 1. 有諸.—see I, Pt. II, ii,＝有之乎. 2. 天與之.—is it not plain that by "Heaven" in this chapter we are to understand God? Many commentators understand by it 理, "reason," or "the truth and fitness of things," saving in the expression—姑曰天 in par. 7, where they take it as＝數, "fate." On this the author of the 四書諸儒輯要, "A Collection of the Most Important Comments of the Learned on the Four Books," says—虞齋獨以此一天字指數言, 其餘天字指理言, 大謬. 此章天字以上帝之主宰言, 理與數皆在其中, 'Heu-chae supposes that in this one case (故曰天) the word Heaven means fate. But this is a great error. In this chapter 'Heaven' signifies the government of God, within which are included both reason and fate.' 3. 天與之者,一者,＝"as to what you say." 諄 (up. 2nd tone) 諄然,—"with repetitions."—The paraphrase in the 日講 is:—"As to what you say, *Heaven gave it to him*, did Heaven indeed express its instructions, and commands to him again and again? If it did not do so, where is the ground for what you say?" 4. 行,—low. 3rd tone, "conduct," as opposed to 事, "the conduct of affairs." 示之, "showed it," i. e., its will to give him the empire. The char. 示 takes here the place of 命, because to 命 would require the use of language, whereas 示 is the simple

受之故曰天不言以行與事示之

舜於天、而天受之暴之於民、而民

不能使諸侯與之大夫、昔者、堯薦

子與之諸侯、大夫能薦人於諸侯、

下、諸侯能薦人於天子、不能使天

子能薦人於天、不能使天與之天

曰、以行與事示之者、如之何、曰、天

5. "'It showed its will by his personal conduct and his conduct of affairs':—how was this?" Mencius's answer was, "The empire can present a man to Heaven, but he cannot make Heaven give that man the empire. A prince can present a man to the emperor, but he cannot cause the emperor to make that man a prince. A great officer can present a man to his prince, but he cannot cause the prince to make that man a great officer. Yaou presented Shun to Heaven, and the people accepted him. Therefore I say, 'Heaven does not speak. It simply indicated its will by his personal conduct and his conduct of affairs.'"

indication of the will. 5. 諸侯 is very plainly in the singular notwithstanding the. 諸, = "one of the princes." I leave the 昔者,—"formerly," out of the translation. 暴, —read *puh*, "to manifest," "to

而已矣。曰、敢問薦之於天、
而天受之、暴之於民、而民
受之、如何。曰、使之主祭、而
百神享之、是天受之、使之
主事、而事治、百姓安之、是
民受之也、天與之、人與之、
故曰、天子不能以天下與

6. *Chang* said, "I presume to ask how it was that *Yaou* presented *Shun* to Heaven, and Heaven accepted him; and that he exhibited him to the people, and the people accepted him." *Mencius* replied, "He caused him to preside over the sacrifices, and all the spirits were well pleased with them;—thus Heaven accepted him. He caused him to preside over the conduct of affairs, and affairs were well administered, so that the people reposed under him;—thus the people accepted him. Heaven gave *the empire* to him. The people gave it to him. Therefore I said, 'The emperor cannot give the empire to another.'

exhibit." 6. 百 神, "the hundred (=all the) spirits," is explained as 天 地 山 川 之 神, "the spirits of heaven, earth, the mountains, and the rivers," i. e., all spiritual beings, real or supposed. In the Shoo-king, II, i, 6, a distinction is made between the 羣 神, "host of spirits," and 上 帝, 六 宗, and 山 川, but the phrase here is to be taken as inclusive of all. The emperor is 百 神 之 主, and Shun entered into all the duties of Yaou, even while Yaou was alive. How the spirits signified their approbation of the sacrifices, we are not told.—Modern commen. take the 百 神 here as exclusive of Heaven and subordinate to it, being equivalent to the 鬼 神, "the energetic operations of Heaven."

者、不謳歌堯之子、而謳

之堯之子、而之舜謳歌

之子、而之舜訟獄者、不

下諸侯朝覲者不之堯

堯之子於南河之南、天

堯崩、三年之喪畢、舜避

非人之所能爲也、天也、

人舜相堯、二十有八載、

7. "Shun assisted Yaou *in the government* for twenty and eight years;—this was more than man could have done, and was from Heaven. After the death of Yaou, when the three years' mourning was completed, Shun withdrew from the son of Yaou to the south of South River. The princes of the empire, however, repairing to court, went not to the son of Yaou, but they went to Shun. Litigants went not to the son of Yaou, but they went to Shun. Singers sang not the son of Yaou, but they sang Shun. Therefore I said, 'Heaven *gave him the empire.*'

But such views were long subsequent to Mencius's time. 7. 相,—up. 3rd tone. 載,—up. 2nd tone. 有,—low. 3rd tone. In 天地, 天, it is said, 以 氣 數 言, "Heaven means destiny." But why suppose a different meaning of the term? Twenty-eight years were, indeed, a long time, for Shun to occupy the place of vice emperor as he did, and showed wonderful gifts. I consider that this is an additional illustration of the 行 above, by which Heaven intimated its will about Shun. The south of the South River (probably the most southern of the nine streams which Yu opened) would be in the present Honan. Thither Shun retired from K'echow, the present Shansi, where Yaou's capital was. For the difference between 朝 (ch'aou, low. 1st tone) and 覲, see the Leke, I, Pt. II, ii, 11, and notes thereon. 之 堯, 之 舜, 之 中 國,—之＝往, the verb. 訟 獄,—see Ana., XII, xiii, but Choo He makes no distinction between the terms here, and explains 訟 獄 謂 獄 不 決 而 訟 之. 謳 歌,—these two terms must be taken together. 歌 is the more general

萬章問曰、人有言、至於

謂也。

民視天聽、自我民聽、此之

天與也。泰誓曰、天視、自我

之宮、逼堯之子、是篡也、非

中國、踐天子位焉、而居堯

歌舜、故曰、天也、夫然後之

It was after these things that he went to the Middle Kingdom, and occupied the emperor's seat. If he had, *before these things,* taken up his residence in the palace of Yaou, and had applied pressure to the son of Yaou, it would have been an act of usurpation, and not the gift of Heaven.

8. "This sentiment is expressed in the words of The Great Declaration,—'Heaven sees according as my people see; Heaven hears according as my people hear.'"

CHAPTER VI. 1. Wan Chang asked *Mencius,* saying, "People say, 'When *the disposal of the empire* came to Yu, his virtue was inferior *to that of Yaou and Shun,*

name of the two. The 說 文 says that 謳 is 齊歌, "the singing of many together." The 正 字 通 makes 謳 to be the several tunes of the singers. 而＝若, or 使. 8. 泰誓曰,—see the Shoo-king, IV, i, Sect. II, 7.

CH. 6. HOW THE THRONE DESCENDED FROM YU TO HIS SON, AND NOT TO HIS MINISTER YIH; THAT YU WAS NOT TO BE CONSIDERED ON THAT ACCOUNT AS INFERIOR IN VIRTUE TO YAOU AND SHUN. 1. 至 於,—"coming to"; we must understand, "From Yaou and Shun," or translate somehow as I have done. Some say that

禹而德衰、不傳於賢、而傳
於子、有諸。孟子曰否、不然
也、天與賢則與賢天與子、
則與子、昔者、舜薦禹於天、
十有七年、舜崩三年之喪
畢、禹避舜之子於陽城、天
下之民從之若堯崩之後、
不從堯之子、而從舜也、禹

and he transmitted it not to the worthiest but to
his son.' Was it so?" Mencius replied, "No; it was
not so. When Heaven gave the empire to the worthiest, it was given to the worthiest. When Heaven
gave it to the son *of the preceding emperor*, it was
given to him. Shun presented Yu to Heaven. Seventeen years elapsed, and Shun died. When the three
years' mourning was expired, Yu withdrew from the
son of Shun to Yang-shing. The people of the empire
followed him just as after the death of Yaou, instead
of following his son, they had followed Shun. Yu

與賢, 與子, are not to be taken
with special reference to Shun and
Yu, and to K'e, but it seems best
to do so. A general inference may
be drawn as well from the special
cases. 有諸,—"was it so?" i. e., was
his virtue inferior, and his transmit-
ting the throne to his son a proof
that it was so? 昔者,—omitted in

translating, as before. Choo He
says, "Yang-shing and the north of
Mount Ke were both at the foot of
the Sung Mountains, places fit for
retirement, within deep valleys."
By many they are held to have been
the same place, and that 陰 is a
mistake for 陽. They were certainly
near each other, and are referred to

不肖、舜之子亦不肖、舜之

啓曰、吾君之子也丹朱之

謳歌者不謳歌益而謳歌

益而之啓曰吾君之子也、

山之陰、朝覲訟獄者不之

之喪畢、益避禹之子於箕

薦益於天、七年、禹崩、三年

presented Yih to Heaven. Seven years elapsed, and Yu died. When the three years' mourning was expired, Yih withdrew from the son of Yu to the north of Mount Ke. The *princes*, repairing to court, went not to Yih, but they went to K'e. Litigants did not go to Yih, but they went to K'e, saying, 'He is the son of our sovereign'; the singers did not sing Yih, but they sang K'e, saying, 'He is the son of our sovereign.'

2. "That Tan-choo was not equal *to his father*, and Shun's son not equal to him; that Shun assisted

the district of Tangfung (登封) in the department of Honan, in Honan. Yih was Yu's great minister, raised to that dignity, after the death of Kaou-yaou. His merit is attributed to the instructions of his mother. See the Shoo-king, II, iv. K'e was Yu's son, who succeeded him on the throne. 2. Tan Choo was

the son of Yaou; see the Shoo-king, I, 9. The son of Shun is not mentioned in the classic. His name was E Keun (義均), and often appears as Shang Keun, he having been appointed to the principality of Shang (商). In 之相 the 相 is up. 3rd tone. In this par., we have a longer sentence than is commonly

相堯、禹之相舜也、歷年多、施

澤於民久、啓賢能敬承繼禹

之道、益之相禹也、歷年少、施

澤於民未久、舜禹益相去久

遠、其子之賢不肖、皆天也、非

人之所能爲也莫之爲而爲

者、天也莫之致而至者、命也。

Yaou, and Yu assisted Shun, for many years conferring benefits on the people for a long time; that *thus*
the length of time during which Shun, Yu, and Yih,
*assisted in the government* was so different; and that
the sons of the emperors were—the one a man of
talents and virtue, and the other two inferior to
their fathers:—all this was from Heaven, and what
could not be produced by man. That which is done
without man's doing it is from Heaven. That which
happens without man's causing it to happen is from
the ordinance *of Heaven.*

found in Chinese composition, the 皆
in 皆天也, resuming all the previous
clauses, which are in apposition with
one another:—"Tan Choo's not being
like his father, Shun's son's not
being like him," etc. 相去久遠＝歷

年久遠之相去. 莫之爲而爲＝人
莫 (＝不) 爲 之 而 爲, the first 爲 is
active; implying the purpose of man,
the second is passive; so, as is indicated by the terms, with 致 and 至

二年、仲壬四年、太甲顛覆
天下、湯崩、太丁未立外丙
有天下。伊尹相湯以王於
紂者也、故益伊尹周公不
有天下、天之所廢、必若桀
故仲尼不有天下。繼世以
舜禹、而又有天子薦之者、
匹夫而有天下者、德必若

3. "In the case of a private individual obtaining the empire, there must be in him virtue equal to that of .Shu<sup>n</sup> or Yu, and moreover there must be the presenting of him *to Heaven* by the *preceding* emperor. It was on this account that Confucius did not obtain the empire.

4. "When the empire is possessed by *natural* succession, the emperor who is displaced by Heaven must be like Kĕĕ or Chow. It was on this account that Yih, E Yin, and Chow-kung did not obtain the empire.

5. "E Yin assisted T'ang so that he became sovereign over the empire. After the demise of T'ang, T'aé-ting having died before he could be appointed emperor, Wae-ping reigned two years, and Chung-jin four. T'ae-këă was then turning upside

in the next sentence. 4. E Yin was the chief minister of T'ang (see Con. Ana., XII, xxii, 6), and Chow-kung or the duke of Chow, the well-known assistant of his brother, King Woo. 5. 相,—up. 3rd tone. 王,—low. 3rd tone. 太 丁 . . . 四 年,—I have translated here according to Chaou

也、復歸于亳。

伊尹之訓已

義三年、以聽

於桐處仁遷

過、自怨自艾、

三年太甲悔

尹放之於桐、

湯之典刑、伊

down the statutes of T'ang, wnen E Yin placed him
in T'ung for three years. *There* T'ae-kĕă repented
of his errors, was contrite, and reformed himself.
In T'ung he came to dwell in benevolence and moved
towards righteousness, during those three years,
listening to the lessons given to him by E Yin. Then
*E Yin* again returned *with him* to Pŏ.

K'e. One of the Ch'ings gives a different view:—"On the death of T'ang, Wae-ping was only two years old, and Chung-yin was but four. T'ae-kĕă was somewhat older, and therefore was put on the throne"; and between this view and the other, Choo He professes himself unable to decide. The first view appears to me much the more natural, and is founded moreover on the account in the "Historical Records," though the histories have been arranged according to the other, and T'ae-kĕă appears as the successor of T'ang This arrangement of the chronology seems indeed required by the statements in the Shoo-king **IV,** iv, which do not admit of any reign or reigns being interposed between T'ang and T'ae-kĕă. The author of the 四書摭餘説 proposes the following solution: —"Chaou K'e's view is inadmissible,
being inconsistent with the Shoo-king. The scholar Ch'ing's view is also to be rejected. For how can we suppose that T'ang, dying over a hundred years old, would leave children of two and four years? And moreover, on this view Chung-yin was the elder brother, and Mencius would have mentioned him first. But there is a solution which meets all the difficulties of the case. First, we assume, with the old explanation, that Wae-ping and Chung-jin were both dead, when T'ae-kĕă succeeded to the throne. Then, with Ch'ing, we take 年 in the sense of 歲, years of life, and not of reign;— and the meaning thus comes out, that T'ae-ting died before his father, and his brothers Wae-ping and Chung-yin died also, the one at the age of two, and the other of four years." 刑,—in the sense of laws. "T'ung was the place where T'ang

六章
周公之不有

天下猶益之

於夏伊尹之

於殷也孔子

曰唐虞禪夏

后殷周繼其

義一也。

萬章問曰、

人有言伊尹

以割烹要湯、

6. "Chow-kung's not getting the empire was like the case of Yih and *the throne of* Hea, or like that of E Yin and *the throne of* Yin.

7. "Confucius said, 'T'ang and Yu resigned the throne *to their worthy ministers.* The sovereign of Hea and *those of* Yin and Chow transmitted it to their sons. The principle of righteousness was the same *in all the cases.*'"

CHAPTER VII. 1. Wan Chang asked *Mencius,* saying, "People say that E Yin sought an introduction to T'ang by his knowledge of cookery. Was it so?"

had been buried, and Pŏ the name of his capital. There is some controversy about the time of T'ae-kĕă's detention in T'ung, whether the three years are to be reckoned from his accession, or from the conclusion of the three years of mourning. The "Historical Records" sanction the latter view, but the former is generally received, as more in accordance with the Shoo-king　7. We must understand Confucius's saying—the second clause of it,—as referring to the first sovereigns of the dynasties mentioned, and 繼, opposed to 禪,= 傳, "to transmit to," i. e., their sons. 唐 and 虞 are Yaou and Shun: see the Shoo-king, I, II. 夏 后,—see Ana., III, xxxi, 1. Yu originally was the 伯, or baron, of Hea, a district in the pres. dep. of Kaifeng. The one principle of right-

eousness was accordance with the will of Heaven, as expressed in par. 1, 天 與 賢, 則 與 賢. 天 與 子, 則 與 子.

CH. 7. VINDICATION OF E YIN FROM THE CHARGE OF INTRODUCING HIMSELF TO THE SERVICE OF T'ANG BY AN UNWORTHY ARTIFICE. 1. 要, up. 1st tone, = 求, or 干, "to seek," i. e., an introduction to, or the favor of. E (伊 is the surname) Yin (尹, the "regulator," is the designation) was the chief minister of T'ang. The popular account (found also in the "Historical Records") in the times of Mencius was, that E Yin came to Pŏ, in the train of a daughter of the prince of Sin, whom T'ang was marrying, carrying his cooking instruments with him, that by 割 烹 "cutting and boiling," he might recommend himself to favor.

以幣聘之囂囂然曰、我何

一介不以取諸人湯使人

非其道也、一介不以與人、

馬千駟、弗視也、非其義也、繫

也、祿之以天下、弗顧也、

之道焉、非其義也、非其道

耕於有莘之野、而樂堯舜

有諸。孟子曰否、不然、伊尹

2. Mencius replied, "No, it was not so. E Yin was
a farmer in the lands of the prince of Sin, delighting
in the principles of Yaou and Shun. In any matter
contrary to the righteousness which they prescribed,
or contrary to their principles, though he had been
offered the empire, he would not have regarded it;
though there had been yoked for him a thousand
teams of horses, he would not have looked at them.
In any matter contrary to the righteousness which
they prescribed, or contrary to their principles, he
would neither have given nor taken a single straw.

3. "T'ang sent persons with presents of silk to
entreat him to enter his service. With an air of
indifference and self-satisfaction he said, 'What can

2. 有莘之野,—E Yin was a native
of Sin, the same territory which
under the Chow dynasty was called
Kih (虢), the present Shenchow
(陝州) of Honan. It was not far
distant from T'ang's original seat of
Pŏ, also in the present Honan. 有

莘=有莘氏, "the surname, i. e.,
the prince, holding Sin." 非其義也,
非其道也 are in apposition, the
one explanatory of the other. 祿
之,—lit., "emolument him." 駟,—
"a team of four horses." 介=芥. 3.
聘, "to ask," often used for "to ask

以湯之聘幣爲哉、我豈若處畎

畝之中、由是以樂堯舜之道哉。

湯三使往聘之、既而幡然改曰、

與我處畎畝之中、由是以樂堯

舜之道、吾豈若使是君爲堯舜

之君哉、吾豈若使是民爲堯舜

之民哉、吾豈若於吾身親見之

I do with those silks with which T'ang invites me? Is it not best for me to abide in the channeled fields, and so delight myself with the principles of Yaou and Shun?'

4. "T'ang thrice sent messengers to invite him. After this, with the change of resolution displayed in his countenance, he spoke in a different style,— 'Instead of abiding in the channeled fields and thereby delighting myself with the principles of Yaou and Shun, had I not better make this prince a prince like Yaou or Shun and this people like the people of Yaou or Shun? Had I not better in my own person see these things for myself?

in marriage"; here, "to ask to be minister." 4. 改 曰 may be 改 其 計 曰, "changed his plan, and said," or 改 其 言 曰, "changed his words, and said." 堯 舜 之 君, "a prince of,= like to, Yaou and Shun." I do not see exactly the force of 於 吾 身 in the last sentence, and have therefore simply translated the phrase literally.

推而內之溝中、其自任
不被堯舜之澤者若己
天下之民、匹夫匹婦、有
也、非予覺之而誰也。
也、予將以斯道覺斯民
覺也、予天民之先覺者
知覺後知使先覺覺後
哉。天之生此民也、使先

5.　"'Heaven's plan in the production of mankind is this:—that they who are first informed should instruct those who are later in being informed, and they who first apprehend principles should instruct those who are slower to do so. I am one of Heaven's people who have first apprehended;—I will take these principles and instruct this people in them. If I do not instruct them, who will do so?'

6.　"He thought that among all the people of the empire, even the private men and women, if there were any who did not enjoy such benefits as Yaou and Shun conferred, it was as if he himself pushed them into a ditch. He took upon himself the heavy charge

5. This par. is to be understood as spoken by E Yin. The meaning of 覺, "to apprehend," "to understand," is an advance on that of 知, simply "to know." The student will observe also that it is used actively three times, = "to instruct." In 生此民, the 此民, "this people," = "mankind." 6. 內,—read as, and = 納. 說,—read

以天下之重如此、故就湯
而說之以伐夏救民。吾未
聞枉己而正人者也、况辱
己以正天下者乎、聖人之
行、不同也、或遠或近、或去
或不去、歸潔其身而已矣。
吾聞其以堯舜之道要湯、
未聞以割烹也。伊訓曰、天

of the empire in this way, and therefore he went to
T'ang, and pressed upon him the subject of attacking
Hea and saving the people.

7. "I have not heard of one who bent himself, and
at the same time made others straight;—how much
less could one disgrace himself, and thereby rectify
the whole empire? The actions of the sages have been
different. Some have kept remote *from court,* and
some have drawn near *to them;* some have left their
offices, and some have not done so:—that to which
those different courses all turn is simply the keeping
of their persons pure.

8. "I have heard that E Yin sought an introduction
to T'ang by the doctrines of Yaou and Shun. I have
not heard that he did so by his knowledge of cookery.

9. "In the 'Instructions of E,' it is said, 'Heaven

*shwuy,* up. 2nd tone, "to advise," "to
persuade." 說 之 以, "advised him
about." 7. Comp. III, Pt. II, i, 1, 5.
歸=要 歸, "if we seek where they
came to, where they centered." 8.
要,—as in par. 1. 9. See the Shoo-
king, IV, iv, 2, but the classic and
this text are so different that many

誅造攻自牧宮朕

載自亳。

孔子於衛主癰疽、

[二]萬章問曰、或謂

於齊主侍人瘠環、

有諸乎孟子曰、否、

不然也、好事者爲

之也。於衛主顏讎

由、彌子之妻與子

destroying Kĕĕ commenced attacking him in the palace of Mŭh. I commenced in Pŏ.'"

CHAPTER VIII. 1. Wan Chang asked *Mencius*, saying, "Some say that Confucius, when he was in Wei, lived with the ulcer doctor, and when he was in Ts'e, with the attendant, Tseih Hwan;—was it so?" Mencius replied, "No; it was not so. Those are the inventions of men fond of strange things.

2. "When he was in Wei, he lived with Yen Ch'ow-yew. The wives of the officer Me and Tsze-loo

suppose Mencius to quote from some form of the book referred to which Confucius disallowed. The meaning is that Kĕĕ's atrocities in his palace in Muh led Heaven to destroy him, while E Yin, in accordance with the will of Heaven, advised T'ang in Pŏ to take action against him. 造 and 載, both＝始, "to begin."

CH. 8. VINDICATION OF CONFUCIUS FROM THE CHARGE OF LODGING WITH UNWORTHY CHARACTERS. 1. 癰,—"a swelling," "an ulcer," and 疽 (read *ts'eu*, upper 1st tone), "a deep-seated ulcer." Chow He, after Chaou K'e, takes the two terms, as in the translation. Some, however, take the characters as a man's name, called also 雍渠, 雍睢, and 雍雎. They are probably right. The "Historical Records" made 雍渠 to have been

the eunuch in attendance on the duke of Wei, when he rode through the market place, with the duchess, followed by the sage,—to his great disgust. 侍人＝奄人, "the eunuch." Eunuchs were employed during the Chow dynasty. Both the men referred to were unworthy favorites of their respective princes. 好 (up. 3rd tone) 事 者,—"one who is fond of raising trouble," and in a lighter sense, as here, "one who is fond of saying, and doing, strange things." 主＝舍 於 其 家, "lodged in his house," lit., "*hosted* him." In par. 4, 以 其 所 爲 主, "by those of whom they are hosts"; 以 其 所 主, "by those whom they host," i. e., make their hosts. 2. Yen Ch'ow-yew, called also 顏 濁 鄒, was a worthy officer of Wei. One account has it,

悅於魯衛遭宋桓司馬、
是無義無命也孔子不
而主癰疽與侍人瘠環、
以義得之不得、曰有命、
曰、有命孔子進以禮退
可得也子路以告孔子
子路曰、孔子主我衛卿
路之妻兄弟也、彌子謂

were sisters, and Me told Tsze-loo, 'If Confucius will lodge with me, he may attain to the dignity of a high noble of Wei.' Tsze-loo informed Confucius of this, and he said, 'That is as ordered *by Heaven.*' Confucius went into office according to propriety, and retired from it according to righteousness. In regard to his obtaining office or not obtaining it, he said, 'That is as ordered.' But if he had lodged with the attendant Tseih Hwan, that would neither have been according to righteousness, nor any ordering *of Heaven.*

3. "When Confucius, being dissatisfied in Loo and Wei, *had left those states,* he met with the attempt of Hwan, the Master of the Horse, of Sung, to intercept

that he was brother to Tsze-loo's wife, but this is probably incorrect. Me, with the name Hea (假), was an unworthy favorite of the duke Ling. 3. Comp. Con. Ana., VII, xxii; Hwan is the Hwan T'uy there. 要, upper

將要而殺之、微服而
過宋、是時、孔子當阨、
主司城貞子、爲陳侯
周臣吾聞觀近臣以
其所爲主、觀遠臣以
其所主若孔子主癰
疽、與侍人瘠環、何以
爲孔子。

萬章問曰、或曰、百
里奚自鬻於秦養牲

and kill him. At that time, though he was in circumstances of distress, he lodged with the city master Ching, who was *then* a minister of Chow, the prince of Ch'in.

4. "I have heard that *the characters of* ministers about court may be discerned from those whom they entertain, and those of stranger officers, from those with whom they lodge. If Confucius had lodged with the ulcer doctor, and with the attendant Tseih Hwan, how could he have been Confucius?"

CHAPTER IX. 1. Wan Chang asked *Mencius*, "Some say that Pih-le He sold himself to a cattle keeper

1st tone,＝攔 截, "to intercept." 微
服,—"small clothes," i. e., the dress of a common man. 貞, "the pure," is the honorary epithet of the officer who was Confucius's host, and 周 was the proper name of the prince of Ch'in with whom indeed the independence of the state terminated. Ching, it is said, afterwards became "city master" in Sung, and was known as such;—hence he is so styled here at an earlier period of his life. 4. 近 and 遠 here have a different application from what belongs to them in the last chapter, par. 7.

CH. 9. VINDICATION OF PIH-LE HE FROM THE CHARGE OF SELLING HIMSELF AS A STEP TO HIS ADVANCEMENT. 1. Pih-le He was chief minister to duke Muh (穆＝"the diffuser of virtue, and maintainer of integrity"), 659–620 B. C. His history will be found interestingly detailed in the 25th and some subsequent books of the "History of the Divided States"

諫、百里奚不諫。以伐虢宮之奇之乘、假道於虞棘之璧、與屈產人也、晉人以垂之也。百里奚虞不然、好事者爲信乎。孟子曰、否、牛、以要秦穆公、者、五羊之皮、食

of Ts'in, for the skins of five sheep, and fed his oxen, in order to find an introduction to the duke Muh of Ts'in;—is this the case?" Mencius said, "No; it was not so. This story was invented by men fond of strange things.

2. "Pih-le He was a man of Yu. The people of Tsin, by the inducement of a gem of Chuy-keih, and four horses of the Keŭĕ breed, borrowed a passage through Yu to attack Kih. *On that occasion,* Kung Chi-k'ĕ remonstrated *against granting their request,* and Pih-le He did not remonstrate.

(列國志), though the incidents there are, some of them different from Mencius's statements about him. With regard to that in this par., it is not easy to understand the popular account referred to. The account in the "Historical Records," 秦本記, is that, after the subversion of Yu, He followed its captive duke to Tsin, refusing to take service in that state, and was afterwards sent to Ts'in in a menial capacity, in the train of the eldest daughter of the house of Tsin, who was to become the wife of the duke Muh. Disgusted at being in such a position, He absconded on the road, and fleeing to Ts'oo, he became noted for his skill in rearing cattle. The duke Muh somehow heard of his great capacity, and sent to Ts'oo, to reclaim him as a runaway servant, offering also to pay for his ransom five ram's skins. He was afraid to offer a more valuable ransom, lest he should awaken suspicions in Ts'oo that he wanted to get He on account of his ability; and on obtaining him, he at once made him his chief minister. 食,—read *isze,* low. 3rd tone, = 飼, "to feed." 要,—as in ch. 7, up. 1st tone. 好事者,—as in last chapter. 2. Ch'uy-keih and Keŭĕ (so read) were the names of places in Tsin, the one famous for its gems, the other for its horses. 乘,—low. 3rd tone, "a team of four horses." Kih and Yu were small states, adjoining each other, and only safe against the attacks of their more powerful neighbor, Tsin, by their mutual union. Both the officers of Yu, Kung Che-k'o and Pih-le He saw this, but He saw also that no remonstrances would prevail with the duke of Yu against the bribes of

智乎、相秦而顯其君於天

與有行也、而相之可謂不

也、時舉於秦知穆公之可

亡、而先去之、不可謂不智

可謂不智乎、知虞公之將

可謂智乎、不可諫而不諫、

食牛干秦穆公之爲汙也、

秦年已七十矣曾不知以

知虞公之不可諫、而去之

3. "When he knew that the duke of Yu was not
to be remonstrated with, and, leaving that state,
went to Ts'in, he had reached the age of seventy.
If by that time he did not know that it would be
a mean thing to seek an introduction to the duke
Muh of Ts'in by feeding oxen, could he be called
wise? But not remonstrating where it was of no
use to remonstrate, could he be said not to be wise?
Knowing that the duke of Yu would be ruined, and
leaving him before that event, he cannot be said
not to have been wise. Being then advanced in Ts'in,
he knew that the duke Muh was one with whom he
would enjoy a field for action, and became minister
to him;—could he, *acting thus*, be said not to be
wise? Having become chief minister of Ts'in, he
made his prince distinguished throughout the empire,

Tsin. 3. 去 之 秦,—之＝往, the
verb. 而 先 去 之,—this may have
been prudent, but was not honorable. It is contrary to other accounts of He's conduct. He is said
to have urged Che-k'e to leave Yu
after his remonstrance, while ho

下、可傳於後

世、不賢而能

之乎、自鬻以

成其君、鄉黨

自好者不爲、

而謂賢者爲

之乎。

and worthy of being handed down to future ages;—
could he have done this, if he had not been a man
of talents and virtue?　As to selling himself in order
to accomplish all the aims of his prince, even a
villager who had a regard for himself would not do
such a thing, and shall we say that a man of talents
and virtue did it?"

remained himself to be with the
duke in the evil day which he saw

approaching. 鄉 黨 are to be taken
together.

## BOOK V

## WAN CHANG.　PART II

萬章章句下

孟子曰、伯夷、目不視
惡色耳不聽惡聲、非其
君不事、非其民不使、治
則進、亂則退、橫政之所
出、橫民之所止不忍居
也、思與鄉人處、如以朝
衣朝冠、坐於塗炭也、當

CHAPTER I. 1. Mencius said, "Pih-e would not allow his eyes to look on a bad sight, nor his ears to listen to a bad sound. He would not serve a prince whom he did not approve, nor command a people whom he did not esteem. In a time of good government he took office, and on the occurrence of confusion he retired. He could not bear to dwell either in *a court* from which a lawless government emanated, or among lawless people. He considered his being in the same place with a villager, as if he were to sit amid mud and coals with his court robes and court

CH. 1. How CONFUCIUS DIFFERED FROM AND WAS SUPERIOR TO ALL OTHER SAGES. 1. Comp. II, Pt. I, ii, 22, and ix; IV, Pt. I, xiii, 1. 橫 政 之 所 出,—"the place whence perverse government issues"; i. e., a court. 橫 民 之 所 止,—"the place

使先知覺後知、使先覺
亦進曰、天之生斯民也、
君、何使非民治亦進、
有立志。伊尹曰、何事非
夷之風者、頑夫廉懦夫
待天下之清也、故聞伯
紂之時、居北海之濱以

cap. In the time of Chow he dwelt on the shores of the North Sea, waiting the purification of the empire. Therefore when men *now* hear the character of Pih-e, the corrupt become pure, and the weak acquire determination.

2. "E Yin said, 'Whom may I not serve? My serving him makes him my sovereign. What people may I not command? My commanding them makes them my people.'. In a time of good government he took office, and when confusion prevailed, he also took office. He said, 'Heaven's plan in the production of mankind is this:—that they who are first informed should instruct those who are later in being informed, and they who first apprehend

where perverse people stop." 頑 is properly "stupid," "obstinate," but here as opposed to 廉, we must take it in the sense of "corrupt." Julien, indeed, takes 廉 in the sense of *"habere vim discernendi."* But it is better to retain its proper signif., and to alter that of 頑. with the gloss in the 備旨.—頑夫無知覺. 必貪昧嗜利. 故奧廉反. 2. Comp.

進不隱賢、必以其道、遺佚而

柳下惠不羞汙君不辭小官、

溝中、其自任以天下之重也。

堯舜之澤者、若己推而內之

下之民、匹夫匹婦、有不與被

予將以此道覺此民也、思天

覺後覺、予天民之先覺者也、

principles should instruct those who are slower in doing so. I am the one of Heaven's people who has first apprehended;—I will take these principles and instruct the people in them.' He thought that among all the people of the empire, even the common men and women, if there were any who did not share in the enjoyment of such benefits as Yaou and Shun conferred, it was as if he himself pushed them into a ditch;—for he took upon himself the heavy charge of the empire.

3. "Hwuy of Lew-hea was not ashamed to serve an impure prince, nor did he think it low to be an inferior officer. When advanced to employment, he did not conceal his virtue, *but* made it a point to

II, Pt. I, ii, 22; and V, Pt. I, vii, 5, 6. Obs. that here instead of 有不被...澤者, we have 有不與被... 澤者,="if there were any who did not have part in the enjoyment," etc. 3. Com. II, Pt. I, ix, 2. The

不怨阨窮而不憫、與鄉

人處、由由然不忍去也、

爾為爾、我為我、雖袒裼

裸裎於我側、爾焉能浼

我哉、故聞柳下惠之風

者、鄙夫寬薄夫敦孔子

之去齊、接淅而行、去魯、

carry out his principles. When dismissed and left without office, he yet did not murmur. When straitened by poverty, he yet did not grieve. When thrown into the company of village people, he was quite at ease and could not bear to leave them. *He had a saying*, 'You are you, and I am I. Although you stand by my side with breast and arms bare, or with your body naked, how can you defile me?' Therefore when men now hear the character of Hwuy of Lew-hea, the mean become generous, and the niggardly become liberal.

4. "When Confucius was leaving Ts'e, he strained off with his hand the water in which his rice was being rinsed, *took the rice*, and went away. When

clause 與 鄉 人, 云 云, which is wanting there, makes the 故 曰 of that place more plain. 袒 is "to have the arms bare," and 裼, "to put off all the upper garment." 裸 程, together, is "to have the body naked." Here and in par. 1, 風 is expressed more nearly by "character," than by any other English term. 4. 淅,—"to rinse or wash

者也孔子之謂集大成、集大

惠聖之和者也孔子、聖之時

者也、伊尹、聖之任者也、柳下

孔子也。孟子曰、伯夷、聖之清

久、可以處而處、可以仕而仕、

道也、可以速而速、可以久而

曰、遲遲吾行也、去父母國之

he left Loo, he said, 'I will set out by and by':—
it was right he should leave the country of his parents
in this way.   When it was proper to go away quickly,
he did so; when it was proper to delay, he did so;
when it was proper to keep in retirement, he did so;
when it was proper to go into office, he did so:—this
was Confucius."

5.   Mencius said, "Pih-e among the sages was the
pure one; E Yin was the one most inclined to take
office; Hwuy of Lew-hea was the accommodating one;
and Confucius was the timeous one.

6.   "In Confucius we have what is called a complete
concert.   A complete concert is when the *large* bell

rice," "the water in which rice is
washed."   The latter is the sense
here.   遲遲吾行, was the answer
given by Confucius to Tsze-loo, who
wished to hurry him away.   5.  I
have invented the adjective "timeous" to translate the 時 here, meaning that Confucius did at every
*time* what the circumstances of it
required, possessing the qualities of

all other sages, and displaying them
at the proper time and place.   6.
The illustration of Confucius here is
from a grand performance of music,
in which all the eight kinds of
musical instruments are united.   One
instrument would make a 小成,
"small performance."   Joined, they
make a 集大成, "a collected great

爾力也、其中、非爾力也。
射於百步之外也、其至、
則巧也、聖譬則力也、由
條理者聖之事也。智譬
始條理者、智之事也、終
玉振之也者、終條理也、
也、金聲也者、始條理也、
成也者、金聲而玉振之

proclaims the *commencement of the music*, and the ringing stone proclaims its close. The metal sound commences the blended harmony of all the instruments, and the winding up with the stone terminates that blended harmony. The commencing that harmony is the work of wisdom. The terminating it is the work of sageness.

7. "As a comparison for wisdom, we may liken it to skill, and as a comparison for sageness, we may liken it to strength;—as in the case of shooting at a mark a thousand paces distant. That you reach it is owing to your strength, but that you hit the mark is not owing to your strength."

performance," = "a concert." 聲, 始, and 終 are all used as verbs. 條理, "discriminated rules," indicates the separate music of the various instruments blended together. 金聲 and 振 之 are not parts of the concert, but the signals of its commencement and close, the 之 referring to 集大 聲. 7. Observe the comma after 智 and 聖. 由 = 猶. "The other three worthies," it is observed, "carried one point to an extreme, but Confucius was complete in every thing. We may compare each of them to one of the seasons, but Confucius was the grand harmonious air of heaven, flowing through all the seasons."

伯一位子男同一位、

一位公一位侯一位、

也嘗聞其略也天子

而皆去其籍然而軻

也諸侯惡其害已也、

子曰其詳不可得聞

班爵祿也如之何孟

📕北宮錡問曰、周室

CHAPTER II. 1. Pih-kung E asked *Mencius,* saying, "What was the arrangement of dignities and emoluments determined by the house of Chow?"

2. Mencius replied, "The particulars of that arrangement cannot be learned, for the princes, disliking them as injurious to themselves, have all made away with the records of them. Still I have learned the general outline of them.

3. "The EMPEROR constituted one dignity; the KUNG one; the HOW one; the PIH one; and the TSZE and the NAN each one of equal rank:—altogether

CH. 2. THE ARRANGEMENT OF DIGNITIES AND EMOLUMENTS ACCORDING TO THE DYNASTY OF CHOW. 1. Pih-kung E was an officer of the State of Wei. The double surname, "Northern-palace," had probably been given to the founder of the family from his residence. 2. Many passages might be quoted from the Le-ke, the Chow Le, and the Shoo-king, illustrating, more or less, the dignities of the empire and their emoluments, but it would serve little purpose to do so, after Mencius's declaration that only the general outline of them could be ascertained. It is an important fact which he mentions, that the princes had destroyed (生, up. 2ud tone) many of the records before his time. The founder of the Ts'in dynasty had had predecessors and patterns. 惡,—up. 3rd tone, "to hate." 3. 公, 侯, 伯, 子, 男, have been rendered "duke, marquis, earl, viscount, and baron," and also "duke, prince, count,

里、伯七十里、子　里、公侯皆方百　子之制、地方千　一位、凡六等。天　中士一位、下士　一位、上士一位、　位、卿一位、大夫　凡五等也、君一

making five degrees of dignity.   The SOVEREIGN *again* constituted one dignity; the CHIEF MINISTER one; the GREAT OFFICERS one; the SCHOLARS OF THE FIRST CLASS one; THOSE OF THE MIDDLE CLASS one; and THOSE OF THE LOWEST CLASS one:—altogether making six degrees of dignity.

4.   "To the emperor there was allotted a territory of a thousand li square.   A Kung and a How had each a hundred li square.   A Pih had seventy li, and

marquis, and baron," but they by no means severally correspond to those dignities.  It is better to retain the Chinese designations, which no doubt were originally meant to indicate certain qualities of those bearing them.  公＝ "just, correct, without selfishness."  侯, "taking care of," ＝ 侯, in the sense of "guarding the borders and important places against banditti; possessed of the power to govern."  伯, conveys the idea of "elder and intelligent," "one capable of presiding over others."  子＝孳, "to nourish," "one who genially cherishes the people."  男 (from 田, "field," and 力, "strength"), "one adequate to office and labor."  The name of 君, "ruler," "sovereign," is applicable to all the dignities enumerated, and under each of them are the secondary or ministerial dignities.  卿＝彰, "one who can illustrate what is good and right."  夫＝扶, "to support," "to sustain."  大夫,—"a great sustainer."  士,—"a scholar," "an officer," 任事之稱, "the designation of one intrusted with business."  4. 地方千里,—this means, acc. to the comm. 彭絲, 橫千里, 直千里, 共一百萬里也, "1,000 li in breadth, and 1,000 li in length, making an area of 1,000,000 li."  On this, however, the following judgment is given by the editors of the imperial edition of the five *king*, of the present dynasty:—"Where we find the word *square* (方), we are not to think of an exact square, but simply that, on a calculation, the amount of territory is equal to so many square li.  For

百里、君十卿祿、卿
視子男大國地方
地視伯、元士受地
受地視侯、大夫受
曰附庸天子之卿、
於天子、附於諸侯、
不能五十里、不達
男五十里、凡四等、

a Tsze and a Nan had each fifty li. The assignments altogether were of four amounts. Where the territory did not amount to fifty li, the chief could not have access himself to the emperor. His land was attached to some How-ship, and was called a FOO-YUNG.

5. "The chief ministers of the emperor received an amount of territory equal to that of a How; a great officer received as much as a Pih; and a scholar of the first class as much as a Tsze or a Nan.

6. In a great state, where the territory was a hundred li square, the sovereign had ten times as much income as the chief ministers; a chief

instance, we are told by the minister Tsan that, at the western capital of Chow, the territory was 800 li square. The meaning is that there were so many squares of 100 li. At the eastern capital again, the territory was 600 li square, or so many squares of 100 li. Putting these two together, we get the total of a square of 1,000 li square. So in regard to the various states of the princes, we are to understand that, however their form might be varied by the hills and rivers, their area, in round numbers, amounted to so much." See in the Le-ke, III, i, 2, where the text, however, is not at all perspicuous. 附,—"attached"; 庸,—"meritoriousness." These states were too small to bear the expenses of appearing before the emperor, and therefore the names and surnames of their chiefs were sent into court by the great princes to whom they were *attached*, or perhaps they appeared in their train. See on Ana., XVI, i, 1. 5. 元士, "head scholar," could only be applied to the scholars of the first class in the emperor's immediate government.

倍上士、上士倍中士、中

卿祿、卿祿三大夫、大夫

次國地方七十里、君十

同祿、祿足以代其耕也。

士、下士與庶人在官者

上士倍中士、中士倍下

祿四大夫、大夫倍上士、

minister four times as much as a great officer; a great
officer twice as much as a scholar of the first class;
a scholar of the first class twice as much as one
of the middle; a scholar of the middle class twice
as much as one of the lowest; the scholars of the
lowest class, and such of the common people as were
employed about the government offices, had the same
emolument;—as much, namely, as was equal to what
they would have made by tilling the fields.

7. "In a state of the next order, where the
territory was seventy li square, the sovereign had
ten times as much revenue as the chief minister;
a chief minister three times as much as a great
officer; a great officer twice as much as a scholar
of the first class; a scholar of the first class twice
as much as one of the middle; a scholar of the middle

6. 庶民在官 would be runners, │ appear in the Chow Le, as 府.
clerks, and other subordnates, which │ 史, 胥, and 徒. Choo Ho gives

士倍下士、下士與庶人在官
者同祿、祿足以代其耕也。小⁸⁷
國地方五十里、君十卿祿、卿
祿二大夫、大夫倍上士、上士
倍中士、中士倍下士、下士與
庶人在官者同祿、祿足以代

class twice as much as one of the lowest; the scholars
of the lowest class, and such of the common people
as were employed about the government offices,
had the same emolument;—as much, namely, as
was equal to what they would have made by tilling
the fields.

8. "In a small state, where the territory was fifty
li square, the sovereign had ten times as much
revenue as the chief minister; a chief minister had
twice as much as a great officer; a great officer twice
as much as a scholar of the highest class; a scholar
of the highest class twice as much as one of the
middle; a scholar of the middle class twice as much as
one of the lowest; scholars of the lowest class, and
such of the common people as were employed about
the government offices, had the same emolument;—
as much, namely, as was equal to what they would
have made by tilling the fields.

his opinion, that, from the sovereign | received their incomes from them, as
downwards, all who had lands ⌡ cultivated on the system of mutual

其耕也耕者之所獲、一夫百
畝百畝之糞、上農夫食九人、
上次食八人中食七人、中次
食六人下食五人庶人在官
者、其祿以是爲差。
萬章問曰敢問友孟子曰、

9. "As to those who tilled the fields, each husbandman received a hundred mow. When those mow were manured, the best husbandmen of the highest class supported nine individuals, and those ranking next to them supported eight. The best husbandmen of the second class supported seven individuals, and those ranking next to them supported six; while husbandmen of the lowest class only supported five. The salaries of the common people who were employed about the government offices were regulated according to these differences."

CHAPTER III. 1. Wan Chang asked *Mencius*, saying, "I venture to ask *the principles of* friendship." Mencius replied, "Friendship should be maintained

aid, while the landless scholars and other subordinates received according to the income from the land. ·9. 食, —read *tsze*. 差,—read *ts'ze*, "uneven," "different."

CH. 3. FRIENDSHIP MUST HAVE REFERENCE TO THE VIRTUE OF THE FRIEND. THERE MAY BE NO ASSUMPTION ON THE GROUND OF ONE'S OWN ADVANTAGES. 1. 問友＝問 交友之

不挾長、不挾貴、不挾兄弟而友、

友也者、友其德也、不可以有挾

也。二師獻子百乘之家也、有友五

人焉、樂正裘牧仲其三人、則予

忘之矣、獻子之與此五人者、友

也、無獻子之家者也、此五人者、

亦有獻子之家、則不與之友矣。

without any presumption on the ground of one's superior age, or station, or *the circumstances of his relatives.* Friendship *with a man* is friendship with his virtue, and does not admit of assumptions of superiority.

2. "There was Mang Hëen, *chief of* a family of a hundred chariots. He had five friends, namely Yŏ-ching K'ew, Muh Chung, and three others *whose names* I have forgotten. With those five men Heen maintained a friendship, because they thought nothing about his family. If they had thought about his family, he would not have maintained his friendship with them.

道. 長,—up. 2nd tone, having reference to age. 兄弟,—"one's brethren," in the widest acceptation of that term. Observe how 也者 takes up the preceding 友, and goes on to its explanation. 其 refers to the individual who is the object of the 友; friendship with him as virtuous will tend to help our virtue. 有挾,—"to have presumptions," with reference of course to the three points mentioned, but as of those the second most readily comes into collision with friendship, it alone is dwelt upon in the sequel. 2. Mang Heen,—see "Great Learning,"

非惟百乘之家爲然也、雖小國
之君亦有之、費惠公曰吾於子
思、則師之矣、吾於顏般、則友之
矣、王順長息、則事我者也。非惟
小國之君爲然也、雖大國之君
亦有之、晉平公之於亥唐也、入
云則入、坐云則坐、食云則食、雖

3. "Not only has the *chief of* a family of a hundred chariots acted thus. The same thing was exemplified by the sovereign of a small state. The duke Hwuy of Pe said, 'I treat Tsze-sze as my master, and Yen Pan as my friend. As to Wang Shun and Ch'ang Seih, they serve me.'

4. "Not only has the sovereign of a small state acted thus. The same thing has been exemplified by the sovereign of a large state. There was the duke P'ing of Tsin with Hae T'ang:—when *T'ang* told him to come into his house, he came; when he told him to be seated, he sat; when he told him to eat, he ate.

Comm. x, 22. 3. 般, read Pe,—see Con. Ana., VI, vii. We must suppose that, after the time of Confucius, some chief had held this place and district with the title of Kung. "The King (惠)" is the honorary epithet. Tsze-sze is Confucius's grand-son. 般,—read *pan*. Yen Pan appears to have been the son of the sage's favorite disciple. 4. P'ing ("The Pacificator") was the honorary epithet of the duke 彪, 556–531 B. C. Hae T'ang was a famous worthy of his state. 入 云,—"*enter* being said."

帝館甥于貳室、亦饗
之尊賢也。舜尚見帝、
之尊賢者也、非王公
也、弗與食天祿也、士
天位也、弗與治天職
於此而已矣、弗與共
蓋不敢不飽也、然終
疏食菜羹、未嘗不飽、

There might only be coarse rice and soup of vegetables, but he always ate his fill, not daring to do
otherwise. Here, however, he stopped, and went no
farther. He did not call him to share any of
Heaven's places, or to govern any of Heaven's offices,
or to partake of any of Heaven's emoluments. His
conduct was but a scholar's honoring virtue· and
talents, not the honoring them proper to a king
or a duke.

5. "Shun went up to *court* and saw the emperor,
who lodged him as his son-in-law in the second palace.
The emperor also enjoyed there Shun's hospitality.

疏 食,一 食, read *tsze*, low. 3rd tone.
The 之 after 平 公 and 王 公 is
wanting in many copies. 與 其 天
位, 云 云, would seem to be a complaint that the duke did not share
with the scholar his own rank, etc.,
but the meaning in the translation
which is that given by the commen.
is perhaps the correct one. Rank,
station, and revenue are said to
be Heaven's, as intrusted to the
sovereign to be conferred on individuals able to occupy them for
the public good. 5. In this par.,
Mencius advances another step, and
exemplifies the highest style of
friendship. Choo He, after Chaou
K'e, explains 尚 by 上, as if it were
"to go up to," i. e., to court. 貳室
＝副 宮, "attached or supplemental
palace." 饗是就舜宮而饗其食,
"饗 means that he went to Shun's
palace, and partook of his food."
The more common meaning of 饗,

心也孟子曰恭也曰郤之

萬章問曰敢問交際何

貴尊賢其義一也。

貴用上敬下謂之尊賢、

匹夫也。用下敬上謂之貴

舜迭爲賓主是天子而友

Alternately he was host and guest. Here was the emperor maintaining friendship with a private man.

6. "Respect shown by inferiors to superiors is called giving to the noble the observance due to rank. Respect shown by superiors to inferiors is called giving honor to talents and virtue. The rightness in each case is the same."

CHAPTER IV. 1. Wan Chang asked *Mencius*, saying, "I venture to ask what *feeling of the* mind is expressed in the presents of friendship." Mencius replied, "*The feeling of* respect."

2. "How is it," pursued *Chang*, "that the declining,

however, is "to entertain." 迭爲,—the subject is only Yaou. 賓,—"made a guest" of Shun, was the host. 主,—"made a host" of Shun, was the guest. 6. 用=以, "for." 義=事 之 宜, "the rightness or propriety of things."

CH. 4. HOW MENCIUS DEFENDED THE ACCEPTING PRESENTS FROM THE PRINCES, OPPRESSORS OF THE PEOPLE. 1. 際 is explained by 接, but that

term is not to be taken in the sense of "to receive," but as a synonym of 交. If we distinguish the two words, we may take 交 as=the 友 of the last chapter, and 際, the gift, expressive of the friendship. 2. Choo He says he does not understand the repetition of 郤之. It has probably crept into the text through the oversight of a transcriber, unless we suppose, with the 合 講, that the

可乎。曰、其交也以道、其

義也而以他辭無受、不

郤之、曰、其取諸民之不

曰請無以辭郤之、以心

以是爲不恭故弗郤也。

義乎、不義乎、而後受之、

者賜之。曰、其所取之者

郤之爲不恭何哉曰、尊

a present is accounted disrespectful?" The answer
was, "When one of honorable rank presents a gift,
to say *in the mind*, 'Was the way in which he got
this righteous or not? I must know this before I
can receive it';—this is deemed disrespectful, and
therefore presents are not declined."

3. *Wan Chang* asked *again*, "When one does not
take on him in so many express words to refuse the
gift, but having declined it in his heart, saying,
'It was taken by him unrighteously from the people,'
and then assigns some other reason for not receiving
it;—is not this a proper course?" *Mencius* said,
"When the donor offers it on a ground of reason, and

repetition indicates the firmness and
decision with which the gift is refused, but the introduction of that
element seems out of place. 曰, 其
(referring to 尊 者) 所 (所 以) 取 之,
—曰 is the reflection passing in the
mind, as in the next par. also. We

must suppose 人 as the nominative
in 以 是 爲 不 恭. 3. 請 is not to be
understood of Wan Chang, but as
indicating the hesitancy and delicacy
of the scholar to whom a gift is
offered. 其 交 也 以 道,—其 still
referring to 尊 者, and 道 to the

誅者也、殷受夏周受殷、
民罔不譈是不待教而
越人於貨閔不畏死凡
禦與。曰不可康誥曰殺
道、其餽也以禮斯可受
國門之外者其交也以
矣。萬章曰、今有禦人於
接也以禮斯孔子受之

his manner of doing so is according to propriety;—in such a case Confucius would have received it."

4. Wan Chang said, "Here now is one who stops and robs people outside the gates of the city. He offers his gift on a ground of reason, and does so in a manner according to propriety;—would the reception of it so acquired by robbery be proper?" Mencius replied, "It would not be proper. In 'The Announcement to K'ang' it is said, 'When men kill others, and roll over their bodies to take their property, being reckless and fearless of death, among all the people there are none but detest them':— thus, such characters are to be put to death, without waiting to give them warning. Yin received *this rule* from Hea, and Chow received it from Yin. It cannot

deservingness of the scholar, or something in his circumstances which renders the gift proper and seasonable. Comp. II, Pt. II, iii, 3, 4. The meaning of 接 is determined (contrary to Chaou K'e) by the 餽, which takes its place in the next par. 4. 國門之外,—國 as in IV,

Pt. II, xxxiii, 1. 斯可受之與,—斯, as in last par., adverbially,="in this case." 康誥曰,—see the Shoo-king, V, x, 15, though the text is somewhat altered in the quotation, and 閔 and 譈 take the place of 暋 and 懟. 于= "for the sake of," i. e., to take. 殷 ... 列 is a passage of which the

乎、夫謂非其有而取之者

乎、其教之不改、而後誅之

作、將比今之諸侯而誅之

何說也。曰子以爲有王者

禮際矣、斯君子受之、敢問

之於民也、猶禦也、苟善其

何其受之曰今之諸侯、取 五罪

所不辭也、於今爲烈、如之

be questioned, and to the present day is clearly acknowledged. How can the gift *of a robber* be received?"

5. *Chang* said, "The princes of the present day take from their people just as a robber despoils his victim. Yet if they put a good face of propriety on their gifts, then the superior man receives them. I venture to ask how you explain this." *Mencius* answered, "Do you think that, if there should arise a truly imperial sovereign, he would collect the princes of the present day, and put them all to death? Or would he admonish them, and then, on their not changing their ways, put them to death? Indeed, to call every one who takes what does not properly

meaning is much disputed. Choo He supposes it a gloss that has crept into the text. I have given it what seemed the most likely translation. 其受之—其 is the party to whom the gift is offered, and 之, the fruit of robbery. 5. 斯,—as above. By 君子 Chang alludes to Mencius himself. 比,—lower 3rd tone, "to take

事道也。事道奚獵較。

之仕也、非事道與。曰、

其賜乎。曰、然則孔子
六節

較、獵較猶可、而况受

魯人獵較、孔子亦獵

也、孔子之仕於魯也、

盜也、充類至義之盡

belong to him a robber, is pushing a point of resemblance to the utmost, and insisting on the most refined
idea of righteousness. When Confucius was in office
in Loo, the people struggled together for the game
taken in hunting, and he also did the same. If that
struggling for the captured game was proper, how
much more may the gifts of the princes be received!"

6. *Chang* urged, "Then, are we to suppose that
when Confucius held office, it was not with the view
to carry his doctrines into practice?" "It was with
that view," *Mencius* replied, and *Chang rejoined*, "If
the practice of his doctrines was his business, what
had he to do with that struggling for the captured

together." 充類至義之盡,—lit.,
"filling up a resemblance to the
extremity of righteousness"; the
meaning is as in the translation. 獵
較 (*koh*) is unintelligible to Choo He,
I have given the not unlikely explanation of Chaou K'e. But to get
rid of the declaration that Confucius
himself joined in the struggling, the
comm. all say it only means that he
allowed the custom —The introduction of this yielding on the part of
Confucius to a vulgar practice is an
adroit maneuver by Mencius. The
offense of the people against propriety in struggling for the game, and
the offense of the princes in robbing
their people, were things of a different class. Yet Mencius's defense
of himself in the preceding part of
the paragraph is ingenious. It shows
that he was eminently a practical
man, acting on the way of ex-
pediency. How far that way may
be pursued will always depend on circumstances. 6. 非事道與 (low. 1st
tone, interrog.)＝非以行道爲事與.
事道奚獵較 is evidently a question

可之仕、有公養之仕、於季

孔子有見行可之仕、有際

以未嘗有所終三年淹也。

以行矣、而不行、而後去、是

不去也。曰、爲之兆也、兆足

以四方之食供簿正。曰、奚

也。曰孔子先簿正祭器、不

game?'' *Mencius* said, ''Confucius first rectified his vessels of sacrifice according to the registers, and did not fill them so rectified with food gathered from every quarter.'' ''But why did he not go away?'' ''He wished to make a trial *of carrying his doctrines into practice.* When that trial was sufficient to show they could be practiced, and they were still not practiced, then he went away, and thus it was that he never completed in any state a residence of three years.

7. ''Confucius took office when he saw that the practice *of his doctrines* was likely; he took office when his reception was proper; he took office when he was supported by the state. In the case of his

of Chang. 先簿正祭器 is unintelligible to Choo He. The translation is after the commentator Seu (徐氏). ''Food gathered from every quarter,'' —i. e., gathered without discrimination. It would appear that the practice of 獵較 had some connection with the offering of sacrifices, and that Conf. thought that if he only rectified the rules for sacrifice, the practice would fall into disuse. But the whole passage and its bearing on the struggling for game is obscure. 兆.—''a prognostic,'' ''an omen,'' used figuratively. 7. See the ''Life of Confucius,'' though it is only here that we have mention of the sage's connection with the duke Heaou. Indeed, no duke appears in the annals of Wei with such

爲養也、而有時乎爲養。

而有時乎爲貧娶妻非

孟子曰、仕非爲貧也、

衞孝公公養之仕也。

衞靈公際可之仕也、於

桓子、見行可之仕也、於

relation to Ke Hwan, he took office, seeing that the practice of his doctrines was likely. With the duke Ling of Wei he took office, because his reception was proper. With the duke Heaou of Wei he took office, because he was maintained by the state."

CHAPTER V. 1. Mencius said, "Office is not *sought* on account of poverty, yet there are times when one seeks office on that account. Marriage is not entered into for the sake of being attended to by the wife, yet there are times when one marries on that account.

a posthumous title. Choo He supposes that the duke Ch'uh (see Ana., VII, xiv, note) is intended, in which the author of the 四書撫餘說 acquiesces. The text mentions Ke Hwan, and not Duke Ting, because the duke and his govt. were under the control of that nobleman.

CH. 5. HOW OFFICE MAY BE TAKEN ON ACCOUNT OF POVERTY, BUT ONLY ON CERTAIN CONDITIONS. 1. 仕 and 娶妻,—it is as well to translate here abstractly, "office," and "marriage."

爲,—low. 3rd tone, "for," "on account of." The proper motive for taking offices is supposed to be the carrying principles—the truth, and the right—into practice, and the proper motive for marriage is the begetting of children, or rather, of a son, to continue one's line. 乎,—not interrog., but serving as a pause for the voice. 養,—low. 3rd tone, "the being supported," but we may take it generally, as in the translation.

矣、嘗爲乘田矣、曰、牛

更矣、曰、會計當而已

關擊柝孔子嘗爲委

富居貧惡乎宜乎、抱

富居貧辭尊居卑、辭

爲貧者、辭尊居卑、辭

2. "He who *takes office* on account of his poverty must decline an honorable situation and occupy a low one; he must decline riches and prefer to be poor."

3. "What office will be in harmony with this declining an honorable situation, and occupying a low one, this declining riches and preferring to be poor? *Such an one as* that of guarding the gates, or beating the watchman's stick.

4. "Confucius was once keeper of stores, and he then said, 'My calculations must all be right. That is all I have to care about.' He was once in charge of the public fields, and he then said, 'The oxen and

2. 尊,—i. e., 尊位, "an honorable situation," and 富=富祿, "rich emolument." 3. 惡,—up. 1st tone, "how." The first 乎 as above, and helping the rhythm of the sentence. 抱關 (going round the barrier gates, "embracing" them, as it were) 擊柝 are to be taken together, and not as two things, or offices; see the Yih-king, App. I, Pt. II, ii, 8. 4. In Sze-ma Ts'een's History of Confucius, for 委 (upper 3rd tone) 吏 we have 季氏史, but in a case of this kind the authority of Mencius is to be followed. 會,—read *kwae*, upper 2nd tone, "entries in a book." Annual calculations of accounts are denominated 會, and monthly, 計, when a distinction is made between the terms. 當,—up. 3rd tone. 乘 (low. 3rd tone) 田=主苑囿芻牧之吏, but I don't understand the use of 乘 in this sense. Here again the history has 爲司職 (*yih*=橛) 吏. These

羊苗壯長而已
矣。位卑而言高、
罪也、立乎人之
本朝、而道不行、
恥也。
萬章曰、士之
不託諸侯、何也。
孟子曰、不敢也、

sheep must be fat and strong, and superior. That is all I have to care about.'

5. "When one is in a low situation, to speak of high matters is a crime. When a scholar stands in a prince's court, and his principles are not carried into practice, it is a shame to him."

CHAPTER VI. 1. Wan Chang said, "What is the reason that a scholar does not accept a stated support from a prince?" Mencius replied, "He does not

were the first offices Confucius took, before the death of his mother, and while they were yet struggling with poverty. 5. 立乎 (=于) 人 之 本 朝 (chaou, lower 1st tone),—it is difficult to express the force of the 本; "to stand in a man's proper court," i. e., the court of the prince who has called him to office, and where he *ought* to develop and carry out his principles. It is said that this par. gives the reasons why he who takes office for poverty must be content with a low situation and small emolument, but the connection is somewhat difficult to trace. The 四書味根錄 says: "Why did Conf. confine himself to having his calculations exact, and his cattle sleek and fat? Because in his humble position he had nothing to do with business of the state, and he would not incur the crime of usurping a higher office. If making a pretense of poverty, a man keep long clinging to high office, he stands, in his prince's court, but carries not principles into practice: —can he lay his hand on his heart, and not feel the shame of making his office of none effect? This is true, but it is not necessary that he who takes office because he is poor should continue to occupy it simply with the desire to get rich.

CH. 6. HOW A SCHOLAR MAY NOT BECOME A DEPENDENT BY ACCEPTING PAY WITHOUT OFFICE, AND HOW THE REPEATED PRESENTS OF A PRINCE TO A SCHOLAR MUST BE MADE. 1. 士 is here the scholar, the candidate for public office and use, still unemployed. 不 託,—"does not depend

則不受何也曰不敢

之曰周之則受賜之

曰君之於氓也固周

曰受之受之何義也

君餽之粟則受之乎

諸侯非禮也萬章曰

諸侯禮也士之託於

諸侯失國而後託於

presume to do so. When a prince loses his state, and then accepts a stated support from another prince, this is in accordance with propriety. But for a scholar to accept such support from any of the princes is not in accordance with propriety."

2. Wan Chang said, "If the prince send him a present of grain *for instance*, does he accept it?" "He accepts it," answered *Mencius*. "On what principle of rightness does he accept it?" "Why—the prince ought to assist the people in their necessities."

3. *Chang* pursued, "Why is it that the scholar will *thus* accept the prince's help, but will not accept his pay?" The answer was, "He does not presume to

on," i. e., assure himself of a regular support by receiving regular pay though not in office. On one prince, driven from his state, finding an assured and regular support with another, see the Le-ke, IX, i, 13. It is only stated there, however, that a prince did not employ another refugee prince as a minister. We know only from Mencius, so far as I am aware, that a prince driven from his own dominions would find maintenance in another state, according to a sort of law. 2. 何義,—"what is the principle of righteousness?" or simply—"what is the explanation of?" 周=賙, "to give alms," and generally to help the needy. 氓,—see II, Pt. I, vi, 4. A scholar not in office is only one of the people. 3. 賜之, "if he give him," i. e., 賜之祿, "give him pay." This

悅於卒也、摽使者出諸大門

思也、亟問、亟餽鼎肉子思不

識可常繼乎。曰、繆公之於子

不恭也。曰、君餽之、則受之、不

上、無常職而賜於上者以爲

關擊柝者皆有常職以食於

也。敢問其不敢、何也。曰、抱

do so." "I venture to ask why he does not presume to do so." "Even the keepers of the gates, with their watchmen's sticks, have their regular offices for which they can take their support from the prince. He who without a regular office should receive the pay of the prince must be deemed disrespectful."

4. Chang asked, "If the prince sends a scholar a present, he accepts it. I do not know whether this present may be constantly repeated." *Mencius* answered, "There was the conduct of the duke Muh to Tsze-sze—He made frequent inquiries after Tsze-sze's health, and sent him frequent presents of cooked meat. Tsze-sze was displeased, and at last having motioned to the messenger to go outside the great

brings out all the meaning that is in 託. 賜 於 上，—賜 is passive, or= "to receive pay." 不 恭. "disrespectful," is to be taken in its implication of a want of humility in the scholar, who is only one of the people having no office, and yet is content to take pay, as if he had.

4. 亟,—read *k'e*, up. 3rd tone (below, the same), "frequently." 鼎 肉, "caldron flesh," i. e., flesh cooked. 摽.—*peaou*, up. 1st tone, "to motion with the hand." 使 者,—使, up. 3rd

養君子、如何、斯可謂養矣。

謂悅賢乎。曰敢問國君欲

賢不能舉、又不能養也、可

畜伋、蓋自是臺無餽也、悅

受、曰今而後知君之犬馬

之外、北面稽首再拜而不

door, he bowed his head to the ground with his face to the north, did obeisance, twice, and declined the gift, saying, 'From this time forth I shall know that the prince supports me as a dog or a horse.' And from that time a servant was no more sent with the presents. When a prince professes to be pleased with a man of talents and virtue, and can neither promote him to office, nor support him *in the proper way*, can he be said to be pleased with him?"

5. Chang said, "I venture to ask how the sovereign of a state, when he wishes to support a superior man, must proceed, that he may be said to do so in the proper· way?" Mencius answered: "*At first,*

tone. 伋 was Tsze-sze's name. To bow, raising the hands to the bent forehead, was called 拜手; lowering the hands in the first place to the ground, and then raising them to the forehead, was called 拜; bowing the head to the earth was called 稽首· Tsze-sze appears on this occasion to have first performed the most profound expression of homage, as if in the prince's presence, and then to have bowed twice, with his hands to the ground, in addition. All this he did, outside the gate, which was the appropriate place in the case of declining the gifts. If they' were received, the party performed his obeisances inside. It is difficult to bring out the meaning of "for," that properly belongs to 蓋. 臺,—the designation of an officer or servant of a very

廩備以養舜於畎畝之中、
之二女女爲百官牛羊倉
之於舜也使其子九男事
拜也非養君子之道也。堯
以爲鼎肉使己僕僕爾亟
繼肉不以君命將之子思
而受其後廩人繼粟庖人
曰以君命將之、再拜稽首

the present must be offered with the prince's commission, and the scholar making obeisance twice with his head bowed to the ground will receive it. But after this the storekeeper will continue to send grain, and the master of the kitchen to send meat, presenting it as if without the prince's express commission. Tsze-sze considered that the meat from the prince's caldron, giving him the annoyance of constantly doing obeisance, was not the way to support a superior man.

6. "There was Yaou's conduct to Shun:—He caused his nine sons to serve him, and gave him his two daughters in marriage; he caused the various officers, oxen and sheep, storehouses and granaries, *all* to be prepared to support Shun amid the channeled

low class. 5. 以 君 命 將 之,—將＝ 奉. 君 命,—"a message from the prince," reminding of course the scholar of his obligation. 僕 僕 聞, —an adverb, "the appearance of being troubled." 6. See Pt. I, i, 3. 二 女 女 爲,—the second 女 is read *joo*, low. 3rd tone.

臣、不敢見於諸侯、禮
庶人、庶人不傳質爲
野曰、草莽之臣、皆謂
在國曰、市井之臣、在
諸侯、何義也。孟子曰、
■■萬章曰、敢問不見
曰、王公之尊賢者也。
後舉而加諸上位、故

fields, and then he raised him to the most exalted situation. From this we have the expression—'The honoring of virtue and talents proper to a king or a duke.'"

CHAPTER VII. 1. Wan Chang said, "I venture to ask what principle of righteousness is involved in *a scholar's* not going to see the princes." Mencius replied, "A scholar residing in the city, is called 'a minister of the market place and well,' and one residing in the country is called 'a minister of the grass and plants.' In both cases he is a common man, and it is the rule of propriety that common men, who have not presented the introductory present and become ministers, should not presume to have interviews with the prince."

CH. 7. WHY A SCHOLAR SHOULD DECLINE GOING TO SEE THE PRINCES, WHEN CALLED BY THEM. Comp. III, Pt. II, i, *et al.* 1. We supply 士 as the nominative to 見, and other verbs; Wan Chang evidently intends Mencius himself. 國,—"city," as in ch. iv, par. 4. 莽,—here as a synonym, in apposition with 草. 臣 in 市井, 草莽之臣 is difft. from

the 爲臣 below. Every individual may be called a 臣, as being a subject, and bound to serve the sovereign, and this is the meaning of the term in those two phrases. In the other case it denotes one who is officially "a minister." 傳,＝通 質,—*che*, up. 3rd tone; see III, Pt. II, iii, 1, and notes. There is a force in the 於, in 見於諸侯, which it is

天子不召師、而況諸侯

賢也。曰爲其多聞也、則

哉。曰爲其多聞也爲其

君之欲見之也何爲也

役義也、往見不義也。且<sup>三而</sup>

則不往見之、何也。曰往

則往役君欲見之召之、

也。<sup>三而</sup>萬章曰、庶人召之役、

2. Wan Chang said, "If a common man is called to perform any service, he goes and performs it;— how is it that a scholar, when the prince, wishing to see him, calls him to his presence, refuses to go?" Mencius replied, "It is right to go and perform the service; it would not be right to go and see the prince."

3. "And," *added Mencius,* "on what account is it that the prince wishes to see *the scholar?*" "Because of his extensive information, or because of his talents and virtue," was the reply. "If because of his extensive information," said Mencius, "such a person is a teacher, and the emperor would not call him;—how much less may any of the princes do

difficult to indicate in another language. 2. "It is right to go and perform the service," i. e., it is right in the common man, to perform service being his 賦, or office. And so with the scholar. He will go when called as a scholar should be called, but only then. 3. The 爲, are all low. 3rd tone. It must be borne in mind that the conversation

平、爲其賢也、則吾未聞欲
見賢而召之也。繆公亟見
於子思、曰古千乘之國以
友士、何如子思不悦、曰古
之人有言曰事之云乎、豈
曰友之云乎、子思之不悦
也豈不曰以位則子君也、
我臣也、何敢與君友也、以

so? If because of his talents and virtue, then I have not heard of any one wishing to see a 'person with those qualities, and calling him to his presence.

4. "During the frequent interviews of the duke Muh with Tsze-sze, he *one day* said to him, 'Anciently, princes of a thousand chariots have yet been on terms of friendship with scholars;—what do you think *of such an intercourse?*' Tsze-sze was displeased, and said, 'The ancients have said, "*The scholar should be served*, how should they have merely said that *he should be made a friend of?*"' When Tsze-sze was thus displeased, did he not say *within himself*,—'With regard to our stations, you are sovereign, and I am subject. How can I presume to be on terms of friendship with my sovereign?

is all about a scholar who is not in office; comp. par. 9. 4. 千乘 (low. 3rd tone) 之國=千乘之君, below, 以=with all his dignity, "yet." 云乎=云爾, IV, Pt. II, xxiv, 1, *et al*,

but the second 乎·also responds to 豈. The paraphrase in the 日講 is: 古之人有言, 人君於士當師事之, 豈但如君所言友之云乎.

德、則子事我者也奚可以與
我友、千乘之君、求與之友、而
不可得也、而況可召與。齊景
公田、招虞人以旌、不至、將殺
之志士不忘在溝壑勇士不
忘喪其元孔子奚取焉、取非
其招不往也。曰、敢問招虞人、

With regard to our virtue, you ought to make me your master. How may you be on terms of friendship with me?' *Thus,* when a prince of a thousand chariots sought to be on terms of friendship with a scholar, he could not obtain his wish:—how much less could he call him to his presence!

5. "The duke King of Ts'e, once, when he was hunting, called his forester to him by a flag. *The forester* would not come, *and the duke* was going to kill him. *With reference to this incident, Confucius said,* 'The determined officer never forgets that *his end may be* in a ditch or a stream; the brave officer never forgets that he may lose his head.' What was it *in the forester* that Confucius thus approved? He approved his not going *to the duke,* when summoned by the article which was not appropriate to him."

6. Chang said, "May I ask with what a forester

5. See III, Pt. II, i, 2. 6. The \ is from Choo He, after the Chow Le. explanation of the various flags here / The dict. may be consulted about

其道猶欲其入而閉之

人乎。<sub>入而</sub>欲見賢人、而不以

乎以不賢人之招招賢

庶人、庶人豈敢往哉、況

死不敢往以士之招招

大夫之招招虞人、虞人

旌、士以旂、大夫以旌。<sub>七編</sub>以

何以曰以皮冠、庶人以

should be summoned?" Mencius replied, "With a
skin cap. A common man *should be summoned* with
a plain banner; a scholar *who has taken office*, with
one having dragons embroidered on it; and a great
officer, with one having feathers suspended from the
top of the staff.

7. "When the forester was summoned with the
article appropriate to the summoning of a great
officer, he would have died rather than presume to
go. If a common man were summoned with the
article appropriate to the summoning of a scholar,
how could he presume to go? How much more may
we expect this refusal to go, when a man of talents
and virtue is summoned in a way which is inappropriate to his character!

8. "When a prince wishes to see a man of talents
and virtue, and does not take the proper course
*to get his wish*, it is as if he wished him to enter

them. 何 以=何 用. 7. A man of | called at all. The prince ought to
talents and virtue ought not to be | go to *him*. 8. 閉 之 門,—this is

也。　有官職而以其官召之　孔子非與。曰孔子當仕　命召不俟駕而行、然則　人所視。萬章曰孔子君　其直如矢君子所履小　是門也詩云周道如底、　惟君子能由是路出入　門也、夫義路也、禮門也、

*his palace*, and shut the door against him. Now, righteousness is the way, and propriety is the door, but it is only the superior man who can follow this way, and go out and in by this door. It is said in the 'Book of Poetry':

> 'The way to Chow is level like a whetstone,
> And straight as an arrow.
> The officers tread it,
> And the lower people see it.' "

9. Wan Chang said, "When Confucius received the prince's message calling him, he went without waiting for his carriage. And so—did Confucius do wrong?" Mencius replied, "Confucius was in office, and had its appropriate duties. And moreover, he was summoned on the business of his office."

another case of a verb followed by the pronoun and another objective; —lit., "shut him the door." 詩云, —see the She-king, II, v, Ode IX, st. 1. Julien condemns the translating 周道 "the way to Chow," but that is the meaning of the terms in the ode; and, as the imperial highway, it is used to indicate figuratively the great way of righteousness. 底,—in the ode 砥, *che*, upper 2nd tone. The ode is attributed to an officer of one of the eastern states, mourning over the oppressive and exhausting labors which were required from the people. The "royal highway" presents itself to him, formerly crowded by officers hastening to and from the capital, and the people hurrying to their labors, but now toiled slowly and painfully along. 9. See Con. Ana., X, xiii, 4.

善士爲未足又尙論

之善士以友天下之

下之善士斯友天下

斯友一國之善士天

之善士一國之善士、

鄉之善士斯友一鄉

孟子謂萬章曰一

CHAPTER VIII. 1. Mencius said to Wan Chang, "The scholar whose virtue is most distinguished in a village shall make friends of all the virtuous scholars in the village. The scholar whose virtue is most distinguished throughout a state shall make friends of all the virtuous scholars of that state. The scholar whose virtue is most distinguished throughout the empire shall make friends of all the virtuous scholars of the empire.

2. "When a scholar feels that his friendship with all the virtuous scholars of the empire is not sufficient *to satisfy him,* he proceeds to ascend to consider the

CH. 8. THE REALIZATION OF THE GREATEST ADVANTAGES OF FRIEND-SHIP, AND THAT IT IS DEPENDENT ON ONE'S SELF. 1. "The virtuous scholar of one village,—he shall make friends of the virtuous scholars of (that) one village":—the first 善 is in the superlative degree, and 友 is not only "to be friends with," but also "to realize the uses of friendship." The eminence attained by the individual attracts all the others to him, and he has thus the opportunity of learning from them, which no inflation because of his own general superiority prevents him from doing. 2. 尙=上. 又尙,—"he proceeds and ascends."

之卿。曰、君有大過、則

之卿。王曰、請問貴戚

有貴戚之卿、有異姓

曰、卿不同乎。曰不同、王

曰、王何卿之問也。王

齊宣王問卿孟子

也。

以論其世也、是尙友

書、不知其人可乎、是

古之人、頌其詩讀其

men of antiquity. He repeats their poems, and reads their books, and as he does not know what they were as men, to ascertain this, he considers their history. This is to ascend and make friends *of the men of antiquity*."

CHAPTER IX. 1. The king Seuen of Ts'e asked about *the office of* chief ministers. Mencius said, "Which chief ministers is your majesty asking about?" "Are there differences among them?" inquired the king. "There are," was the reply. "There are the chief ministers who are noble and relatives *of the prince*, and there are those who are of a different surname." The king said, "I beg to ask about the chief ministers who are noble and relatives of the prince." Mencius answered, "If the prince have great faults, they ought to remonstrate with him,

頌＝誦, "to repeat," "croon over." 可 乎＝可 否, "proper or not?" 其 世, "their age," i. e., what they were in their age.—We are hardly to understand the poetry and books here generally. Mencius seems to have had in his eye the Book of Poetry and the Book of History.

CH. 9. THE DUTIES OF THE DIFFERENT CLASSES OF CHIEF MINISTERS. 1. 君有大過.—such ministers will overlook small faults. To animadvert on them would be inconsistent with their consanguinity. No distinction is made of faults, as great or small, when the other class of

反覆之而不聽、則去。
之卿。曰、君有過則諫、
色定、然後請問異姓
臣不敢不以正對。王
曰、王勿異也、王問臣、
易位。王勃然變乎色。
諫、反覆之而不聽、則

and if he do not listen to them after they have done so again and again, they ought to dethrone him."

2. The king on this looked moved, and changed countenance.

3. Mencius said, "Let not Your Majesty be offended. You asked me, and I dare not answer but according to truth."

4. The king's countenance became composed, and he then begged to ask about chief ministers who were of a different surname *from the prince*. Mencius said, "When the prince has faults, they ought to remonstrate with him, and if he do not listen to them after they have done this again and again, they ought to leave *the state*."

ministers is spoken of. "Great faults," are such as endanger the safety of the state. 3. 勿異,— "don't think it strange," but = "don't be offended."—We may not wonder that Duke Seuen should have been moved and surprised by the doctrines of Mencius as announced in this chapter. It is true that the members of the family of which the ruler is the head have the nearest interest in his ruling well, but to teach them that it belongs to them, in case of his not taking their advice, to proceed to dethrone him, is likely to produce the most disastrous effects. Choo He notices that the able and virtuous relatives of the tyrant Chow (紂) were not able to do their duty as here laid down, while Hoh Kwang, a minister of another surname, was able to do it in the case of the king of Ch'ang-yih (昌邑王), whom he dethroned. This last event took place, 73 B. C.

## BOOK VI

### KAOU TSZE.　PART I

猶以杞柳爲　人性爲仁義、　猶桮棬也、以　猶杞柳也、義、　告子曰、性、　句上　告子章

CHAPTER I. 1. The philosopher Kaou said, "*Man's* nature is like the *ke* willow, and righteousness is like a cup or a bowl. The fashioning benevolence and righteousness out of man's nature is like the making cups and bowls from the *ke* willow."

Kaou, from whom this book is named, is the same who is referred to in II, Pt. I, ii. His name was Puh-hae (不 害), a speculatist of Mencius's day, who is said to have given himself equally to the study of the orthodox doctrines and those of the heresiarch Mih (III, Pt. I, v; Pt. II, ix). See the 四書撫餘說, on Mencius, Vol. I, art. xxix. He appears from this book to have been much perplexed respecting the real character of human nature in its relations to good and evil. This is the principal subject discussed in this Book. For his views of human nature as here developed, Mencius is mainly indebted for his place among the sages of his country. "In the first Part," says the 四書味根錄, "he treats first *of the nature;* then of *the heart;* and then of *instruction,* the whole being analogous to the lessons in the 'Doctrine of the Mean.' The second Part continues to treat of the same subject, and a resemblance will generally be found between the views of the parties there combated, and those of the scholar Kaou."

CH. 1. THAT BENEVOLENCE AND RIGHTEOUSNESS ARE NO UNNATURAL PRODUCT OF HUMAN NATURE. There underlies the words of Kaou here, says Choo He, the view of the philosopher Seun (荀) that human nature is evil (性 惡). This is putting the case too strongly. It is an induction from his words, which Kaou would probably have disallowed. Seun (see the *prolegomena,* and Morrison, under char. 子), accounted by many the most distinguished scholar of the Confucian school, appears to have maintained positively that all good was foreign to the nature of man;—人 之 性 惡, 其 善 者 僞 也, "Man's nature is bad; his good is artificial." 1. The 杞 and the 柳 are taken by some as two trees, but it is better to take them together, the first char. giving the species of the other. It is described as, "growing by the waterside, like a common willow, the leaf coarse and white, with the veins small and

柝棬。孟子曰子能順杞

柳之性、而以爲柝棬乎、

將戕賊杞柳、而後以爲

柝棬也、如將戕賊杞柳

而以爲柝棬、則亦將戕

賊人以爲仁義與率天

下之人、而禍仁義者、必

子之言夫。

2. Mencius replied, "Can you, leaving untouched the nature of the willow, make with it cups and bowls? You must do violence and injury to the willow, before you can make cups and bowls with it. If you must do violence and injury to the willow in order to make cups and bowls with it, *on your principles* you must in the same way do violence and injury to humanity in order to fashion from it benevolence and righteousness! Your words, alas! would certainly lead all men on to reckon benevolence and righteousness to be calamities."

reddish." 2. 順,—"according with," "following," i. e., "leaving un-touched," "doing no violence to." 戕賊人,—人＝人性, "man's nature," "humanity." Kaou had said that man's nature could be *made into* benevo. and right., and Mencius exposes the error by here substituting 戕賊 for 爲, in doing which he is justified by the nature of the action that has to be put forth on the wood of the willow. 禍仁義,—"calami-tize benevolence and righteousness," I take the meaning to be as in the translation. If their nature must be hacked and bent to bring those virtues from it, men would certainly account them to be calamities.

之善也猶水之就下也人
東西、無分於上下乎、人性
西也。孟子曰、水信無分於
不善也、猶水之無分於東
則西流、人性之無分於善
諸東方則東流決諸西方
告子曰、性猶湍水也、決

CHAPTER II. 1. The philosopher Kaou said, "*Man's nature is like water whirling round in a corner.* Open a passage for it to the east, and it will flow to the east; open a passage for it to the west, and it will flow to the west. Man's nature is indifferent to good and evil, just as the water is indifferent to the east and west."

2. Mencius replied, "Water indeed *will flow* indifferently to the east or west, but will it flow indifferently up or down? The tendency of man's nature to good is like the tendency of water to flow

CH. 2. MAN'S NATURE IS NOT INDIFFERENT TO GOOD AND EVIL. ITS PROPER TENDENCY IS TO GOOD. That man is indifferent to good and evil, or that the tendencies to these are both blended in his nature, was the doctrine of Yang Heung (揚 雄), a philosopher about the beginning of our era. We have the following sentence from him: "In the nature of man good and evil are mixed. The cultivation of the good in it makes a good man; the cultivation of the evil makes a bad man. The passion nature in its movements may be called the horse of good or evil" (十子全書, 揚子, 修身篇). 人 無 有 不 善 is the sum of the chapter on Mencius's part. His opponent's views were wrong, but neither did he have the whole truth. 1. 湍 水 is explained in the Dict. "water flowing rapidly," and "water rippling over the sand." Chaou K'e, followed by Choo Ho, explains it as in the translation, which is certainly better adapted to the passage. 2. 信,—as an adverb, "truly." 人性之 善,—lit., "the goodness of man's nature," but we must take 善 as =

告子曰、生之謂性、
亦猶是也。
之可使爲不善、其性
性哉、其勢則然也、人
可使在山、是豈水之
可使過顙激而行之、
下。今夫水搏而躍之、
無有不善、水無有不

downwards.　There are none but have this tendency to good, *just as* all water flows downwards.

3.　"Now by striking water and causing it to leap up, you may make it go over your forehead, and, by damming and leading it, you may force it up a hill;—but are such movements according to the nature of water?　It is the force applied which causes them.　When men are made to do what is not good, their nature is dealt with in this way."

CHAPTER III.　1.　The philosopher Kaou said, "Life is what is to be understood by nature."

"tendency to good."　3. 激, "to provoke," "to fret," the *consequence of a dam*. 激而行之,—"dam and walk it," i. e., by gradually leading it from dam to dam, Choo He says: "This chapter tells us that the nature is properly good, and if we accord with it, we shall do nothing which is not good; that it is properly without evil, and we must violate it, therefore, before we can do evil. It shows that the nature is not properly without a decided character, so that it may do good or evil indifferently."

CH. 3.　THE NATURE IS NOT TO BE CONFOUNDED WITH THE PHENOMENA OF LIFE.　1. "By 生," says Choo He, "is intended that whereby men and animals perceive and move," and the sentiment, he adds, is analogous to that of the Buddhists, who make 作用, "doing and using," to be the nature.　We must understand by the term, I think, the phenomena of life, and Kaou's idea led to the ridiculous conclusion that wherever there were the phenomena of life, the nature of the subjects must be the same.　At any rate, Mencius

與。之性牛之性猶人之性曰、然。然則犬之性、猶牛雪之白、猶白玉之白與。之白也、猶白雪之白、白白之謂白與。曰、然。白羽孟子曰、生之謂性也、猶

告子曰、食色、性也、仁、

2. Mencius asked him, "Do you say that by nature you mean life, just as you say that white is white?" "Yes, I do," was the reply. Mencius added, "Is the whiteness of a white feather like that of white snow, and the whiteness of white snow like that of a white gem?" *Kaou again* said "Yes."

3. "Very well," *pursued Mencius.* "Is the nature of a dog like the nature of an ox, and the nature of an ox like the nature of a man?"

CHAPTER IV. 1. The philosopher Kaou said, "*To enjoy* food and *delight in* colors is nature. Benevolence

here makes him allow this. '2' 3. The 與, low. 3rd tone, all interrogative, and="you allow this, I suppose."—We find it difficult to place ourselves in sympathy with Kaou in this conversation, or to follow Mencius in passing from the second par. to the third. His questions in par. 2 all refer to qualities, and then he jumps to others about the nature.

CH. 4. THAT THE BENEVOLENT AFFECTIONS AND THE DISCRIMINATIONS OF WHAT IS RIGHT AND EQUALLY INTERNAL. 1. 食色＝甘食悅色. We might suppose that 色 here denoted "the appetite of sex." But another view is preferred. Thus the commentator 熙周 observes: "The infant knows to drink the breast, and to look at fire, which illustrates the text 食色性." It is important

白馬之白也、無以異
故謂之外也曰、異於
白之從其白於外也。
於我也、猶彼白而我
長、而我長之、非有長
謂仁內義外也。曰彼
非內也。孟子曰、何以
內也、非外也義、外也、

is internal and not external; righteousness is external and not internal."

2. Mencius asked him, "What is the ground of your saying that benevolence is internal and righteousness external?" He replied, "There is a man older than I, and I give honor to his age. It is not that there is *first* in me a principle of such reverence to age. It is just as when there is a white man, and I consider him white;—according as he is so externally to me. On this account, I pronounce *of righteousness* that it is external."

3. Mencius said, "There is no difference between our pronouncing of a white horse to be white and our

to observe that by 義 is denoted 事物之宜, "the determining what conduct in reference to them is required by men and things external to us, and giving it to them." Kaou contends that as we are moved by our own internal impulse to food and colors, so we are also in the exercise of benevolence, but not in that of righteousness. 2. 長,—always up. 2nd tone. In 彼長, it is the adjective, but in the other cases it is the verb. 非有長於我=非先有長之之心在我. The second 白 is also a verb. 3. 異於, at the commencement, have crept by some oversight into the text. They must

故謂之內、長楚人之長、
愛也、是以我爲悅者也、
則愛之秦人之弟則不
乎、長之者義乎。曰吾弟
人之長與、且謂長者義
馬之長也、無以異於長
於白人之白也、不識長

pronouncing a white man to be white. But is there
no difference between the regard with which we acknowledge the age of an old horse and that with
which we acknowledge the age of an old man? And
what is it which is called righteousness?—the fact of
a man's being old? or the fact of our giving honor
to his age?"

4. *Kaou* said, "There is my younger brother;—
I love him. But the younger brother of a man of
Ts'in I do not love; that is, the feeling is determined
by myself, and therefore I say that benevolence is
internal. *On the other hand,* I give honor to an old

be disregarded. 白馬, 白人, 長馬,
長人,—白 and 長 are the verbs,=the
長之, below. 且謂, 云 云, "and do
you say? etc.," but the meaning
comes out better by expanding the
words a little. The 日 講 says:
"The recognition of the whiteness
of a horse is not different from the
recognition of the whiteness of a
man. So indeed it is. But when we
acknowledge the age of a horse, we
simply with the mouth pronounce
that it is old. In acknowledging,
however, the age of a man, there is at
the same time the feeling of respect
in the mind. The case is different
from our recognition of the age of
a horse." 4. 秦人, 楚人,=indifferent
people, strangers. 以 我 爲 悅, 以 長
爲 悅,—the meaning is no doubt. as

耆炙亦有外與。

則亦有然者也、然則

以異於耆吾炙、夫物、

也。曰、耆秦人之炙、無

爲悅者也、故謂之外

亦長吾之長、是以長

man of Ts'oo, and I also give honor to an old man of my own *people:* that is, the feeling is determined by the age, and therefore I say that righteousness is external."

5. *Mencius* answered him, "Our enjoyment of meat roasted by a man of Ts'in does not differ from our enjoyment of meat roasted by ourselves. Thus, *what you insist on* takes place also in the case of such things, and will you say likewise that our enjoyment of a roast is external?"

in the translation, but the use of 悅 in both cases occasions some difficulty. Here again I may translate from the 日 講, which attempts to bring out the meaning of 悅:—"I love my younger brother and do not love the younger brother of a man of Ts'in; that is, the love depends on me. Him with whom my heart is pleased, I love (悅乎我之心，則愛之), and him with whom my heart is not pleased, I do not love. But the reverence is in both cases determined by the age. Wherever we meet with age, there we have the feeling of complacency (凡遇長皆在所悅), and it does not necessarily proceed from our own mind." After reading all this, a perplexity is still felt to attach to the use of 悅. 5. 耆＝嗜.—Mencius silences his opponent by showing that the same difficulty would attach to the principle with which he himself started; namely, that the enjoyment of food was internal, sprang from the inner springs of our being.

此、所長在彼、果在外、非由
誰先。曰、先酌鄉人所敬在
一歲、則誰敬。曰、敬兄。酌則
謂之內也。鄉人長於伯兄
以謂義內也曰、行吾敬、故
孟季子問公都子曰、何

CHAPTER V. 1. The disciple Măng Ke asked Kung-too, saying, "On what ground is it said that righteousness is internal?"

2. Kung-too replied, "We *therein* act out our feeling of respect, and therefore it is said to be internal."

3. *The other objected,* "Suppose the case of a villager older than your elder brother by one year, to which of them would you show the *greater* respect?" "To my brother," was the reply. "But for which of them would you first pour out wine *at a feast?*" "For the villager." *Măng Ke argued,* "Now your feeling of reverence rests on the one, and *now* the honor due to age is rendered to the other;—this is certainly determined by what is without, and does not proceed from within."

CH. 5. THE SAME SUBJECT;—THE DISCRIMINATIONS OF WHAT IS RIGHT ARE FROM WITHIN. 1. Măng Ke was a younger brother of Măng Chung, mentioned II, Pt. II, ii. Their relation to each other in point of age is determined by the characters, 仲 and 季. Măng Ke had heard the previous conversation with Kaou, or heard of it, and feeling some doubts on the subject he applied to Kung-too (II, Pt. II, v) for their solution. "On what ground is it said?"—i. e., by our master, by Mencius. 3· The questions here are evidently by Măng Ke. 伯 is in the general sense of

庸敬在兄、斯須之敬在

故也子亦曰、在位故也。

敬叔父也。彼將曰、在位

將曰敬弟子曰惡在其

父。曰、弟爲尸、則誰敬。彼

乎、敬弟乎、彼將曰、敬叔

告孟子孟子曰、敬叔父

內也公都子不能答、以

4. Kung-too was unable to reply, and told the conversation to Mencius. Mencius said, "*You should ask him*, 'Which do you respect most,—your uncle, or your younger brother?' He will answer, 'My uncle.' Ask him *again*, 'If your younger brother be personating a dead ancestor, to which do you show the greater respect,—*to him or to your uncle?*' He will say, 'To my younger brother.' You can go on, 'But where is the respect due, as you said, to your uncle?' He will reply to this, '*I show the respect to my younger brother*, because of the position which he occupies,' and you can likewise say, '*So my respect to the villáger is* because of the position which he occupies. Ordinarily, my respect is rendered to my elder brother; for a brief season, *on occasion*, it is rendered to the villager.'"

昆, "elder." 4. The translation needs to be supplemented, to show that Mencius gives his decision in the form of a dialogue between the two disciples. 叔父,—"a father's younger brother," but used generally for "an uncle." 弟爲尸,—in sacrificing to the departed, some one— a certain one of the descendants, if possible,—was made the 尸, or "corpse," into whose body the spirit of the other was supposed to descend to receive the worship. 惡在其敬, —the 其 = "as you said." 斯須 = 暫時; comp. the "Doctrine of the

善、無不善也。或曰、性、可以

公都子曰告子曰、性無

食亦在外也。

飲湯夏日、則飲水然則飲

由內也。公都子曰　　則

則敬、敬弟則敬、果在外、非

鄉人季子聞之曰、敬叔父

'5' *Măng* Ke heard this and observed, "When respect is due to my uncle, I respect him, and when respect is due to my younger brother, I respect him; —the thing is certainly determined by what is without, and does not proceed from within." Kung-too replied, "In winter we drink things hot, in summer we drink things cold; and so, *on your principle,* eating and drinking also depend on what is external!"

CHAPTER VI. 1. The disciple Kung-too said, "The philosopher Kaou says, '*Man's* nature is neither good nor bad.'

2. "Some say, '*Man's* nature may be made to

Mean," i, 2. 5. 湯, 水,—"hot water," or "soup," and "water"; 水 must be taken as "cold" water. Kung-too answers after the example of his master in the last paragraph of the preceding chapter.

CH. 6. EXPLANATION OF MEN-CIUS'S OWN DOCTRINE THAT MAN'S NATURE IS GOOD. 1. Choo Ho says that the view of Kaou, as here affirmed, had been advocated by Soo Tung-po (東坡) and Hoo, styled Wǎn-ting Kung (胡文定公), near to his own times. 2. This is the view

且以爲君、而有微子啟、王子

爲父、而有舜以紂爲兄之子、

故以堯爲君、而有象、以瞽瞍

暴或曰、有性善、有性不善是

與、則民好善幽厲興、則民好

爲善、可以爲不善是故文武

practice good, and it may be made to practice evil,' and accordingly, under Wăn and Woo, the people loved what was good, *while* under Yew and Le, they loved what was cruel."

3. "Some say, 'The nature of some is good, and the nature of others is bad.' Hence it was that under such a sovereign as Yaou there yet appèared Seang; that with such a father as Koo-sow there yet appeared Shun; and that with Chow for their sovereign, and the son of their elder brother besides, there were found K'e, the viscount of Wei, and the prince Pe-kan.

propounded by Kaou in the 2nd chapter. 爲 is explained by 習, and 可以爲＝可以使爲. 3. 啟 was the name of the viscount of Wei; see Ana., XVIII, i. Both he and Pe-kan are here made to be uncles of Chow, while K'e, according to the Shoo-king, was his half brother. Choo-he supposes some error to have crept into the text. For convenience in translating, I have changed the order of 爲兄之子,且以爲君. 王子,— as the sons of the princes of states were callĕd 公 子.—This view of human nature found an advocate afterwards in the famous Han Wăn-kung (韓文公) of the T'ang dynasty.

比干今日性善、然則彼
皆非與。孟子曰、乃若其
情、則可以爲善矣、乃所
謂善也若夫爲不善、非
才之罪也。惻隱之心、人
皆有之、羞惡之心、人皆
有之、恭敬之心、人皆有
之、是非之心、人皆有之、

4. "And now you say, 'The nature is good.' Then are all those wrong?"

5. Mencius said, "From the feelings proper to it, it is constituted for the practice of what is good. This is what I mean in saying that *the nature* is good.

6. "If men do what is not good, the blame cannot be imputed to their natural powers."

7. "The feeling of commiseration belongs to all men; so does that of shame and dislike; and that of reverence and respect; and that of approving and

4, 5. 乃若,="as to," "looking at." Choo He calls them an initial particle. The 其, of course, refers to 性 or "nature," which is the subject of the next clause—可以爲善. This being the amount of Mencius's doctrine, that by the study of our nature we may see that it is formed for goodness, there seems nothing to object to in it. By 情 is denoted 性之動, "the movements of the nature," i. e., the inward feelings and tendencies, "stirred up."—Chaou K'e takes 若 here in the sense of 順, "to obey," "to accord with," on which the translation would be—"If

it act in accordance with its feelings, or emotional tendencies." The meaning, however, is the same on the whole. 可以爲善 is not so definite as we could wish. Choo He expands it;—人之情, 本但可以爲善, 而不可以爲惡, "the feelings of man may properly be used only to do good, and may not be used to do evil." This seems to be the meaning. 6. 才=材質, 人之能也, "man's ability," "his natural powers." 若夫 (low. 1st tone),—"as to," "in the case of." 7. Comp. II, Pt. I, iv, 4, 5. 恭敬之心, however takes the

倍蓰而無算者不能盡其才

曰求則得之舍則失之或相

也我固有之也弗思耳矣故

智也仁義禮智非由外鑠我

也恭敬之心禮也是非之心、

惻隱之心仁也羞惡之心義

disapproving. The feeling of commiseration *implies the principle of* benevolence; that of shame and dislike, the principle of righteousness; that of reverence and respect, the principle of propriety; and that of approving and disapproving, the principle of knowledge. Benevolence, righteousness, propriety, and knowledge are · not infused into us from without. We are certainly furnished with them. *And a different view* is simply from want of reflection. Hence it is said: 'Seek and you will find them. Neglect and you will lose them.' Men differ from one another in regard to them;—some as much again as others, some five times as much, and some to an incalculable amount: —it is because they cannot carry out fully their *natural* powers.

place of 辭讓之心 there. 弗思耳 is the *apodosis* of a sentence, and the *protasis* must be supplied as in the translation. 舍＝捨, up. 2nd tone.

或相倍云云,—與善相丟, 或一倍, 云 云. They lose them till they depart from what is good, some co

者也。詩曰天生蒸民、有物
有則、民之秉夷、好是懿德、
孔子曰、爲此詩者、其知道
乎。故有物必有則、民之秉
夷也、故好是懿德。
孟子曰富歲子弟多賴、

8. "It is said in the 'Book of Poetry':

'Heaven, in producing mankind,
Gave them their *various* faculties and relations with *their specific* laws.
These are the invariable rules of nature for all to hold,
And *all* love this admirable virtue.'

Confucius said, 'The marker of this ode knew indeed the principle *of our nature!*' We may thus see that every faculty and relation must have its law, and since there are invariable rules for all to hold, they consequently love this admirable virtue."

CHAPTER VII. 1. Mencius said, "In good years the children of the people are most of them good,

far again as others, etc." 8. 詩曰, —see the Shoo-king, III, Pt. III, Ode VI, st. i, where we have 烝 for 蒸, and 彛 for 夷. 有物有則.— "have things, have laws," but the things specially intended are our constitution with reference to the world of sense, and the various circles of relationship. The quotation is designed specially to illustrate par. 5, but the conclusion drawn is stronger than the statement there. It is said the people actually love (好, up. 3rd tone), and are not merely constituted to love, the admirable virtue.

CH. 7. ALL MEN ARE THE SAME IN MIND;—SAGES AND OTHERS. IT FOLLOWS THAT THE NATURE OF ALL MEN, LIKE THAT OF THE SAGES, IS GOOD. 1. 富歲.—"rich years,"=豐年, "plentiful years." 賴 is given

不同、則地有肥磽、雨
至之時皆熟矣、雖有
同、浡然而生至於日
之、其地同、樹之時又
今夫麰麥、播種而耰
以陷溺其心者然也。
之降才爾殊也、其所
凶歲子弟多暴、非天

while in bad years the most of them abandon themselves to evil. It is not owing to their natural powers conferred by Heaven that they are thus different. The abandonment is owing to the circumstances through which they allow their minds to be ensnared and drowned *in evil.*

2. "There now is barley.—Let it be sown and covered up; the ground being the same, and the time of sowing likewise the same, it grows rapidly up, and when the full time is come, it is all found to be ripe. Although there may be inequalities *of produce,* that is owing to the *difference of the* soil, as rich or poor, to the *unequal* nourishment afforded by the rains and

by Chaou K'e as＝善, "good," and 暴 ＝惡, "evil." But 暴＝the Mencian phrase—自暴, "self-abandonment," and there is the proper meaning of 恃, "to depend on," also in that term. "In rich years, 子弟 (sons and brothers, i. e., the young whose characters are plastic) *depend* on the plenty and are good." Temptations do not lead them from their natural bent. 爾殊也,—the use of 爾 here is peculiar. Most take it

as＝如此, "thus." Some take it in its proper pronominal meaning, as if Mencius in a lively manner turned to the young.—"It is not from the powers conferred by Heaven that you are different." 然, "so," referring specially to the self-abandonment. 2. 麰麥 go together＝"barley." 播種 (up. 2nd tone, the noun),—"sow the seeds." 耰,—prop. "a kind of harrow." 日至, not "the solstice," but "the days (i. e., the

露之養、人事之不齊也。故

凡同類者、舉相似也、何獨

至於人而疑之、聖人與我

同類者。故龍子曰、不知足

而爲屨、我知其不爲蕢也、

屨之相似、天下之足同也。

口之於味、有同耆也、易牙、

dews, and to the different ways in which man has performed his business *in reference to it.*

3. "Thus all things which are the same in kind are like to one another;—why should we doubt in regard to man, as if he were a solitary exception to this? The sage and we are the same in kind.

4. "In accordance with this the scholar Lung said, 'If a man make hempen sandals without knowing *the size of people's* feet, *yet* I know that he will not make *them like* baskets.' Sandals are all like one another, because all men's feet are like one another.

5. "*So* with the mouth and flavors;—all mouths have the same relishes. Yih-ya *only* apprehended

time, harvest time) are come." 3. 舉=皆, "all." 何獨, 云 云,—"why only come to man and doubt it?" 4. 故, illustrating, not inferring. So, below; except perhaps in the last instance of its use. Of the Lung who is quoted nothing seems to be known. 屨, see III, Pt. I, vi, 1. 5. 耆=嗜. 口之於味, 有 同耆 也,—lit., "The relation of

先得我口之所耆者也、如
使口之於味也、其性與人
殊、若犬馬之與我不同類
也、則天下何耆皆從易牙
之於味也、至於味、天下期
於易牙、是天下之口相似
也。惟耳亦然、至於聲、天下
期於師曠、是天下之耳相

before me what my mouth relishes. Suppose that
his mouth in its relish for flavors differed from that
of other men, as is the case with dogs or horses which
are not the same in kind with us, why should all men
be found following Yih-ya in their relishes? In the
matter of tastes the whole empire models itself after
Yih-ya; that is, the mouths of all men are like one
another.

6. "And so also it is with the ear. In the matter
of sounds, the whole empire models itself after the
music master K'wang; that is, the ears of all men are
like one another.

mouths to tastes is that they have the same relishes." Yih-ya was the cook of the famous duke Hwan of Ts'e (684–642 B. C.), a worthless man, but great in his art. 先得, 云云, is better translated "apprehended before me," than "was the first to apprehend," etc., and *only* is evidently to be supplied. 如使口之於味,—the 口 here is to be understood with reference to Yih-ya. 其性, "its nature," i. e., its likings and dislikings in the matter of tastes. 天下期於易牙,—期, "to fix a limit," or "to aim at." 6. 惟耳亦然,—惟 is here in the sense of our *but*, from *botan*, the connective particle, though it often corresponds to our other *but*, a disjunctive, or exceptive, = "only." 師曠, see IV, Pt.

同然者何也謂理也義也、
心獨無所同然乎心之所
之於色也有同美焉至於
耳之於聲也有同聽焉目
曰口之於味也有同耆焉、
子都之姣者無目者也故
天下莫不知其姣也不知
似也。惟目亦然、至於子都、

7. "And so also it is with the eye. In the case of Tsze-too, there is no man but would recognize that he was beautiful. Any one who would not recognize the beauty of Tsze-too must have no eyes.

8. "Therefore I say,—*Men's* mouths agree in having the same relishes; their ears agree in enjoying the same sounds; their eyes agree in recognizing the same beauty:—shall their minds alone be without that which they similarly approve? What is it, then, of which they similarly approve? It is, I say, the principles *of our nature,* and the determinations of righteousness. The sages only apprehended before me that of which my mind approves along with other men. Therefore the principles of our nature and the

I, i, 1. 7. Tsze-too was the designation of Kung-sun Ŏ (公孫閼), an officer of Chïng about 700 B. C., distinguished for his beauty. See his villainy and death in the 7th chapter of the "History of the Several States." 8. 無所同然乎,—然 is to be taken as a verb, "to approve," 謂 merely indicates the answers to the preceding question. It is not so much as "I say" in the translation. 理＝心之體, "the mental constitution," the moral nature, and 義＝心之用, "that constitution or nature,

之所潤、非無萌蘗之生
是其日夜之所息雨露
斧斤伐之、可以爲美乎、
美矣以其郊於大國也、
🀙孟子曰牛山之木嘗
猶芻豢之悅我口。
然耳、故理義之悅我心、
聖人先得我心之所同

determinations of righteousness agreeable to my mind,
just as the flesh of grass and grain-fed animals is
agreeable to my mouth."

CHAPTER VIII. 1. Mencius said, "The trees of the
New Mountain were once beautiful. Being situated,
however, in the borders of a large state, they were
hewn down with axes and bills;—and could they
retain their beauty? Still through the activity of the
vegetative life day and night, and the nourishing
influence of the rain and dew, they were not without
buds and sprouts springing forth, but then came the

acting outwardly." 芻, "hay," "fod-
der," used for "grass-fed animals,"
such as sheep and oxen. 豢="corn-
or rice-fed animals," such as dogs
and pigs.

CH. 8. HOW IT IS THAT THE NA-
TURE PROPERLY GOOD COMES TO AP-
PEAR AS IF IT WERE NOT SO;—FROM
NOT RECEIVING ITS PROPER NOURISH-
MENT. 1. The New Mountain was

in the southeast of Ts'e. It is
referred to the present district of
Lintsze (臨 淄) in the department
of Ts'ingchow. 以 其 郊 於 大 國=
以 其 所 生 之 郊 在 于 大 國. 可 以
爲 美 乎,—"could they be beautiful?" i. e., "could they retain their
beauty?" 是 其 日 夜 之 所 息,—
the 是 is difficult;—"there is what
they grow day and night," the 息

於木也、且旦而伐之、可以
放其良心者、亦猶斧斤之
豈無仁義之心哉、其所以
山之性也哉。雖存乎人者、
也、以爲未嘗有材焉、此豈
若彼濯濯也、人見其濯濯
爲、牛羊又從而牧之、是以

cattle and goats and browsed upon them. To these
things is owing the bare and stripped appearance *of the
mountain*, which when people see, they think it was
never finely wooded. But is this the nature of the
mountain?

2. "And so *also of* what properly belongs to man;
—shall it be said that the mind *of any man* was
without benevolence and righteousness? The way in
which a man loses his proper goodness of mind is
like the way in which the trees are denuded by
axes and bills. Hewn down day after day, can it—

referring to the 氣化生物, what we
may call "vegetative life." The use
of 濯濯 here is peculiar. 材＝材木,
"trees of materials," fine trees. 2.
The connection indicated by 雖,
"although," may be thus traced:
_-"Not only is such the case of the
New Mountain. Although we speak
of what properly belongs to man

(存＝在), we shall find that the same
thing obtains." The next clause is
to be translated in the past tense,
the question having reference to a
mind or nature, which has been
allowed to run to waste. 其, "he,"
＝"a man." 放＝失. 良心,—"the
good mental constitution or nature."

遠矣、人見其禽獸也、而以

不足以存、則其違禽獸不

則其夜氣不足以存、夜氣

爲、有梏亡之矣、梏之反覆、

也者、幾希、則其旦晝之所

旦之氣、其好惡與人相近

爲美乎、其日夜之所息、平

*the mind*—retain its beauty?　But there is a development of its life day and night, and in the *calm* air of the morning, just between night and day, the mind feels in a degree those desires and aversions which are proper to humanity, but the feeling is not strong, and it is fettered and destroyed by what takes place during the day. This fettering taking place again and again; the restorative influence of the night is not sufficient to preserve *the proper goodness of the mind;* and when this proves insufficient for that purpose, the nature becomes not much different from that of the irrational animals, which when people

平, "even," indicates the time that lies *evenly* between the night and day. It is difficult to catch the exact idea conveyed by 氣, in this clause, and where it occurs below, the calm of the air, the corresponding calm of the spirit, and the moral invigoration from the repose of the night, being blended in it. The next clause is difficult. Chaou K'e makes it:—"The mind is not far removed in its likings and dislikings (好, 惡, both upper 3rd tone) from those which are proper to humanity." The more common interpretation is that which I have given. 幾希,—see IV, Pt. II, xix, 1. 旦晝=日間.

惟心之謂與。

出入無時、莫知其鄉、

子曰、操則存、舍則亡、

失其養無物不消。孔

得其養、無物不長、苟

豈人之情也哉。故苟

爲未嘗有才焉者、是

see, they think that it never had those powers *which I assert*. But does this condition represent the feelings proper to humanity?

3. "Therefore, if it receive its proper nourishment, there is nothing which will not grow. If it lose its proper nourishment, there is nothing which will not decay away.

4. "Confucius said, 'Hold it fast, and it remains with you. Let it go, and you lose it. Its outgoing and incoming cannot be defined as to time or place.' It is the mind of which this is said!"

3. 無 物.—物 embraces both things in nature, and the nature of man. 4. This is a remark of Confucius for which we are indebted to Mencius. 舍=捨. 出 入, 云 云,—"its outgoings and incomings have no *set* time; no one knows its dissection." 與, low. 1st tone,="is it not?" or an exclamation. This paragraph is thus expanded by Choo He:—Confucius said of the mind, *If you hold it fast, it is here; if you let it go, it is lost and gone; so without determinate time is its outgoing and incoming and also without determinate place.* Mencius quoted his words to illustrate the unfathomableness of the spiritual and intelligent mind, how easy it is to have it or to lose it, and how difficult to preserve and keep it, and how it may not be left unnourished for an instant. Learners ought constantly to be exerting their strength to insure the pureness of its spirit, and the settledness of its passion nature, as in the calm of the morning, then will the mind always be preserved, and everywhere and in all circumstances its manifestations will be those of benevolence and righteousness."

夫弈之爲數、小數也、

吾如有萌焉、何哉。今

吾退而寒之者至矣、

生者也、吾見亦罕矣、

之十日寒之、未有能

易生之物也、一日暴

之不智也雖有天下

孟子曰、無或乎王

CHAPTER IX. 1. Mencius said, "It is not to be wondered at that the king is not wise!

2. "Suppose the case of the most easily growing thing in the world;—if you let it have one day's genial heat, and then expose it for ten days to cold, it will not be able to grow. It is but seldom that I have an audience of the king, and when I retire, there come *all* those who act upon him like the cold. Though I succeed in bringing out some buds *of goodness*, of what avail is it!

3. "Now chess playing is but a small art, but

CH. 9. ILLUSTRATING THE LAST CHAPTER.—HOW THE KING OF TS'E'S WANT OF WISDOM WAS OWING TO NEGLECT AND BAD ASSOCIATIONS. 1. 或 is used for 惑, "to be perplexed." 乎 is an exclamation. The king is understood to be the king Seuen of Ts'e; see I, ii. 2. 暴,—*puh*, often written 曝, "to dry in the sun," here =溫, "to warm genially." 未有, 云 云,—the 未, "not yet," "never," puts the general truth as an inference from the past. 見,—low. 3rd tone, *heen*. Choo He points the last clause

一吾如有萌焉, 何哉, "though there may be sprouts of goodness, what can I do?" In this way, 吾 and 何 哉 are connected, and there is the intermediate clause between them, which is an unusual thing in Chinese. Feeling this difficulty, Chaou K'e makes 吾 the nominative to 有萌 and interprets,—"Although I wish to encourage the sprouting of his goodness, how can I do so?" I have followed this construction, taking the force of the terms, however, differently. 3. 今夫 (low. 1st tone),

不專心致志、則不得也、弈

秋、通國之善弈者也、使弈

秋誨二人弈其一人專心

致志惟弈秋之爲聽一人

雖聽之、一心以爲有鴻鵠

將至思援弓繳而射之、雖

與之俱學、弗若之矣、爲是

其智弗若與、曰非然也。

without his whole mind being given, and his will
bent to it, a man cannot succeed at it. Chess Ts'ew
is the best chess player in all the kingdom. Suppose
that he is teaching two men to play.—The one gives
to the subject his whole mind and bends to it all
his will, doing nothing but listening to Chess Ts'ew.
The other, although *he seems to be* listening to him,
has his whole mind running on a swan which he
thinks is approaching, and wishes to bend his bow,
adjust the string to the arrow, and shoot it. Although
he is learning along with the other, he does not come
up to him. Why?—because his intelligence is not
equal? Not so."

云 云,—"now the character of chess
playing as an art, is that it is a
small art." 奕 秋,—Ts'ew was the
man's name and he was called *Chess
Ts'ew* from his skill·at the game.
鴻 鵠, "a great *kŭh*" which is also
called "the heavenly goose" = the
swan. 檄 (*chŏ*) 而 射 (*shih*) 之,—see
Ana., XII, xxvi. 爲 (low. 3rd tone)
是 其 智 弗 若 與 (low. 1st tone).—
"Is it because of this, the inferiority
of his (*natural*)· intelligence?" 是
and the following words being in
apposition.

者、故不爲苟得也死亦我所

生亦我所欲、所欲、有甚於生

不可得兼、舍生而取義者也。

所欲也、義亦我所欲也、二者、

舍魚而取熊掌者也、生亦我

亦我所欲也、二者、不可得兼、

孟子曰、魚、我所欲也、熊掌、

CHAPTER X.　1. Mencius said, "I like fish and I also like bear's paws.　If I cannot have the two together, I will let the fish go, and take the bear's paws.　So, I like life, and I also like righteousness.　If I cannot keep the two together, I will let life go and choose righteousness.

2.　"I like life indeed, but there is that which I like more than life, and therefore, I will not seek to possess it by any improper ways.　I dislike death

CH. 10.　THAT IT IS PROPER TO MAN'S NATURE TO LOVE RIGHTEOUSNESS MORE THAN LIFE, AND HOW IT IS THAT MANY ACT AS IF IT WERE NOT SO.　1. "Bear's palms" have been a delicacy in China from the earliest times.　They require a long time, it seems, to cook them thoroughly. The king Shing of Ts'oo, 625 B. C., being besieged in his palace, requested that he might have a dish of bear's palms before he was put

to death,—hoping that help would come while they were being cooked. 2. 生亦我所欲,—the 亦 is retained from the preceding par.　We may render it by "indeed."　所欲, 云云, is to be translated indicatively.　It is explanatory of the conclusion of the last par.,—舍生而取義. 不爲 (emphatic) 苟得, "I won't do improper getting," i. e., of life.　The paraphrasts mostly say—不爲苟 且 以 得 生, "I will not act improperly to get life."　患, "sorrow,"

爲也。由是則生、而有不用也、

死者、則凡可以辟患者、何不

不用也、使人之所惡莫甚於

甚於生、則凡可以得生者、何

所不辟也。如使人之所欲、莫

惡、所惡有甚於死者、故患有

indeed, but there is that which I dislike more than death, and therefore there are occasions when I will not avoid danger.

3. "If among the things which man likes there were nothing which he liked more than life, why should he not use every means by which he could preserve it? If among the things which man dislikes there were nothing which he disliked more than death, why should he not do everything by which he could avoid danger?

4. "There are cases when men by a certain course might preserve life, and they do not employ it; when

"calamity" = danger of death. 辟 = 避. It seems better to construe as I have done making 患 governed by 辟, than to make 患 = a clause by itself, and suppose 死 as the object of 辟. 4. I translate here differently both from Chaou K'e and Choo He. They take 由 是 to be = "From this righteousness-loving nature so dis-played," as if the par. were merely an inference from the two preceding. I understand the par. to be a repetition of the two preceding, and introductory to the one which follows. 由 是 則 生, "by this course (any particular course) there is life," 而 有 不 用, "and yet in cases it is not used." This gives a much easier

生、弗得則死、嘑爾而與之行

喪耳。六節一簞食、一豆羹得之則

是心也、人皆有之賢者能勿

惡有甚於死者、非獨賢者有

也。五節是故所欲有甚於生者、所

由是則可以辟患、而有不爲

by certain things they might avoid danger, and they
will not do them.

5. "Therefore, men have that which they like
more than life, and that which they dislike more than
death. They are not men of distinguished talents
and virtue only who have this mental nature. All
men have it; what belongs to such men is simply that
they do not lose it.

6. "Here are a small basket of rice and a platter
of soup, and the case is one in which the getting them
will preserve life, and the want of them will be death;
—if they are offered with an insulting voice, even

and more legitimate construction.
5. 能 勿 喪, (up. 3rd tone),—stress
must not be laid on the 能. 勿 is
simply negative, not prohibitive. 6.
嘑,—low. 3rd tone. 嘑 爾 is explained 咄啐 之 貌, "the appearance

識窮乏者得我與、

之美妻妾之奉所

我何加焉爲宮室

義而受之萬鍾於

也。萬鍾則不辨禮

而與之乞人不屑

道之人弗受蹴爾

a tramper will not receive them, or if you first tread
upon them, even a beggar will not stoop to take
them.

7. "*And yet* a man will accept of ten thousand
chung, without any consideration of propriety or
righteousness. What can the ten thousand chung
add to him? *When he takes them,* is it not that he
may obtain beautiful mansions, that he may secure
the services of wives and concubines, or that the poor
and needy of his acquaintance may be helped by him?

of reproachful clamor," but the 蹴
爾 shows that more than the idea of
"appearance," or demonstration is
intended. 行道之人＝乞人, below,
and not simply "any ordinary man
upon the way," as Choo He makes
it. 不屑, see II, Pt. I, ix, 1.—This
par. is intended to illustrate the 人
皆有之 of the preceding. Even
in the poorest and most distressed
of men, the 羞惡之心 will show
itself. 7. 萬鍾,—see II, Pt. II, x, 4.
萬鍾於我何加焉,—"what do they
add to me?" There is here a contrast with the case in the preced.
par., which was one of life or death.
The large emolument was not an
absolute necessity. But also there
is the lofty, and true, idea, that a
man's personality is something independent of, and higher than, all
external advantages. The meaning
is better brought out in English by
changing the person from the first
to the third. 爲妻妾之奉,—"be-
cause of the services of wives and
concubines." 妻 is plural as well as 妾,
though according to the law of China
there could be only one *wife*, however many concubines there might
be. 所識窮乏者得我＝所知識窮
乏者感我之惠, "that the poor of
his acquaintance may be grateful for
his kindness." A gloss in the 四書
味根錄 says: "The thinking of
the poor would seem to be a thought

其
本
心
。

亦
不
可
以
已
乎
、
此
之
謂
失

識
窮
乏
者
得
我
而
爲
之
、
是

鄉
爲
身
死
而
不
受
、
今
爲
所

不
受
、
今
爲
妻
妾
之
奉
爲
之
、

室
之
美
爲
之
、
鄉
爲
身
死
而

鄉
爲
身
死
而
不
受
、
今
爲
宮

8. "In the former case *the offered bounty* was not received, though it would have saved from death, and now *the emolument* is taken for the sake of beautiful mansions. *The bounty* that would have preserved from death was not received, and *the emolument* is taken to get the service of wives and concubines. *The bounty* that would have saved from death was not received, and *the emolument* is taken that one's poor and needy acquaintance may be helped by him. Was it then not possible likewise to decline this? This is a case of what is called—'Losing the proper nature of one's mind.'"

of kindly feeling, but the true nature of it is shown in the 得 我, *may get* ME. The idea is not of benevolence, but selfishness." 8. 鄉, up. 3rd tone, =向. 爲 (low. 3rd tone) 身 死,— "for the body dying," 1. e., to save from dying. 是 亦 不 可 以 已 乎,—是 is emphatic,=this large emolument, taken for such purposes.—For an example in point to illustrate par. 6, see the Le-ke, II, Pt. II, iii, 17.

已矣。
之道無他、求其放心而
有放心而不知求學問。
人有雞犬放、則知求之、
放其心而不知求、哀哉。
人路也。舍其路而弗由、
孟子曰、仁、人心也、義、

CHAPTER XI. 1. Mencius said, "Benevolence is man's mind, and righteousness is man's path.

2. "How lamentable is it to neglect the path and not pursue it, to lose this mind and not know to seek it again!

3. "When men's fowls and dogs are lost, they know to seek for them again, but they lose their mind, and do not know to seek for it.

4. "The great end of learning is nothing else but to seek for the lost mind."

CH. 11. HOW MEN HAVING LOST THE PROPER QUALITIES OF THEIR NATURE SHOULD SEEK TO RECOVER THEM. 1. "Benevolence is man's mind, or heart," i. e., it is the proper and universal characteristic of man's nature, as the 正義 on Chaou K'e says,—人人有之, "all men have it." "Benevolence" would seem to include here all the other moral qualities of humanity. Choo He says 仁者心之德; yet we have the usual Mencian specification of "righteousness" along with it. 4. 學問之道,—道=切要,

"that which is most important in." —The Chinese sages always end with the recovery of "the old heart"; the idea of "a new heart" is unknown to them. One of the Ch'ing says: "The thousand words and ten thousand sayings of the sages and worthies are simply designed to lead men to get hold of their lost minds, and make them again enter their bodies. This accomplished, "they can push their inquiries upwards, and from the lowest studies acquire the highest knowledge."

孟子曰、今有無名之指、

屈而不信、非疾痛害事也、

如有能信之者、則不遠秦

楚之路爲指之不若人也。

指不若人則知惡之心不

若人、則不知惡、此之謂不

知類也。

CHAPTER XII. 1. Mencius said, "Here is a *man* *whose* fourth finger is bent and cannot be stretched out straight. It is not painful, nor does it incommode his business, and yet if there be any one who can make it straight, he will not think the way from Ts'in to Ts'oo far *to go to him;*—because his finger is not like the finger of other people.

2. "When a man's finger is not like those of other people, he knows to feel dissatisfied, but if his mind be not like that of other people, he does not know to feel dissatisfaction. This is called—'Ignorance of the relative *importance of things.*'"

CH. 12. How MEN ARE SENSIBLE OF BODILY, AND NOT OF MENTAL OR MORAL, DEFECTS. 1. 無名之指, "the nameless finger," i. e., the fourth, reckoning from the thumb as the first. It is so styled, as of less use than the others, and less needing a name. 信,—read as, and with the meaning of, 伸, *shin*. 不遠秦楚之路=雖越秦楚相去之路, 不以爲遠, "though he should pass over all the way between Ts'in and Ts'oo, he will not think it far." 2. 不知類,—"not knowing kinds," or degrees. 類=等.

孟子曰、拱把之
桐梓、人苟欲生之、
皆知所以養之者、
至於身而不知所
以養之者豈愛身
不若桐梓哉、弗思
甚也。
孟子曰、人之於
身也、兼所愛、兼所

CHAPTER XIII. Mencius said, "Anybody who wishes to cultivate the *t'ung* or the *tsze*, which may be grasped with both hands, *perhaps* with one, knows by what means to nourish them. In the case of their own persons, men do not know by what means to nourish them. Is it to be supposed that their regard of their own persons is inferior to their regard for a *t'ung* or a *tsze?* Their want of reflection is extreme."

CHAPTER XIV. 1. Mencius said, "There is no part of himself which a man does not love, and as he

CH. 13. MEN'S EXTREME WANT OF THOUGHT IN REGARD TO THE CULTIVATION OF THEMSELVES. The *t'ung* and *tsze* resemble each other. The latter is called by the Chinese "the king of trees," and its wood is well adapted for their block engraving. Of the *t'ung* there are various arrangements, some making three kinds of it, some four, and some seven. The wood of the first kind, or white *t'ung* (白桐), is the best for making musical instruments like the lute. Both the *t'ung* and the *tsze* belong probably to the *euphorbiœ*. 至於身, —身, "the body," but here "the person," the whole human being. 豈 ... 哉 = "is it to be supposed?" A supplementary note in the 備旨 says that "by nourishing the 身 here is intended the ruling of the mind, to nourish our inner man, and paying careful attention to the body, to nourish our outer man."

CH. 14. THE ATTENTION GIVEN BY MEN TO THE NOURISHMENT OF THE DIFFERENT PARTS OF THEIR NATURE MUST BE REGULATED BY THE RELATIVE IMPORTANCE OF THOSE PARTS. 1. 身, —as in the last ch., but with more special reference to the body. 兼所愛, —"unites what he loves,"

愛、則兼所養也、無尺寸

之膚不愛焉、則無尺寸

之膚不養也、所以考其

善不善者豈有他哉、於

己取之而已矣。二體有貴

賤、有小大無以小害大、

無以賤害貴養其小者

爲小人養其大者爲大

loves all, so he must nourish all. There is not an inch of skin which he does not love, and so there is not an inch of skin which he will not nourish. For examining whether *his way of nourishing* be good or not, what other rule is there but this, that he determine by *reflecting on* himself where it should be applied?

2. "Some parts of the body are noble, and some ignoble; some great, and some small. The great must not be injured for the small, nor the noble for the ignoble. He who nourishes the little belonging to him is a little man, and he who nourishes the great is a great man.

i. e., loves all. 尺 寸,—"a cubit *or* an inch," but the meaning is—the least bit of,=our "an inch." 所 以 考, 云 云, requires to be supplemented a good deal in translating. The meaning is plain: A man is to determine for himself, by reflection on his constitution, what parts are more important and should have the greater attention paid to them. Compare the two last pars. of Con. Ana., vi, 28. 2. 體,—"the members of the body," but the character, like 身, is to be understood with a tacit reference to the mental part of our

寸之膚哉。

有失也、則口腹豈適爲尺

小以失大也。飲食之人、無

之人、則人賤之矣、爲其養

知也、則爲狼疾人也。飲食

其一指、而失其肩背、而不

其杙棘、則爲賤場師焉。

人今有場師、舍其梧檟養

3. "Here is a plantation keeper, who neglects his *woo* and *kea*, and cultivates his sour wild date trees;—he is a poor plantation keeper.

4. "He who nourishes one of his fingers, neglecting his shoulders or his back, without knowing *that he is doing so*, is a man *who resembles* a hurried wolf.

5. "A man who *only* eats and drinks is counted mean by others;—because he nourishes what is little to the neglect of what is great.

6. "If a man, *fond of his* eating and drinking, were not to neglect *what is of more importance*, how should his mouth and belly be considered as no more than an inch of skin?"

constitution as well. 3. The 場師 was an officer under the Chow dynasty, who had the superintendence of the sovereign's plantations and orchards. See the Chow Le, XVI, xx, 1. The *woo* and the *kea* are the *t'ung* and the *tsze* of the last chapter. 杙棘, go together, 杙 indicating the species. 棘 is generally used with the general meaning of thorns. But it here indicates a kind of small wild date tree. The date tree proper is 棗; this wild tree, 棘, the difft. forms indicating the *high* tree and the *low bushy* shrub respectively. See the 集證, *in loc.* 4. 失=遺. 狼疾,—"a wolf hurried," i. e., chased, and so unable to exercise the quick sight for which it is famous. 6. The meaning is that the parts considered small and ignoble may have their due share of attention, if the more important parts are first cared for, as they ought to be.

目之官不思、而蔽於
從其小體何也。曰、耳
人也、或從其大體、或
小體爲小人。曰、鈞是
其大體爲大人、從其
小人何也。孟子曰、從
人也、或爲大人、或爲
公都子問曰、鈞是

CHAPTER XV. 1. The disciple Kung-too said, "All
are equally men, not some are great men, and some
are little men;—how is this?" Mencius replied,
"Those who follow that part of themselves which
is great are great men; those who follow that part
which is little are little men."

2. Kung-too pursued, "All are equally men, but
some follow that part of themselves which is great,
and some follow that part which is little;—how is
this?" Mencius answered, "The senses of hearing
and seeing do not think, and are obscured by *external*

CH. 15. How SOME ARE GREAT
MEN, LORDS OF REASON, AND SOME
ARE LITTLE MEN, SLAVES OF SENSE.
1. 鈞＝均, "all equally." 體,—"the
members," but here, more evidently
than in the last chapter, it is spoken
of our whole constitution, mental as
well as physical. 2. 耳 目 之 官,—
"the offices of the ears and eyes."
We might suppose that the senses
are so styled, as being conceived to
be subject to the control of the
ruling mind. We have below, however, the expression 心 之 官, and 官
is to be taken in both cases, as＝
"prerogative," "business." Chaou
K'e and his glossarist do not take
耳 目 之 官 as the subject of 思 in 不
思, but interpret thus: "The senses,
if there be not the exercise of thought
by the mind, are obscured by external things." But the view of
Choo He, as in the translation, is
preferable. It is very evident how

物、物交物、則引之而

已矣、心之官則思、思

則得之、不思、則不得

也、此天之所與我者、

先立乎其大者、則其

小者不能奪也、此爲

大人而已矣。

things. When one thing comes into contact with another, as a matter of course it leads it away. To the mind belongs the office of thinking. By thinking, it gets *the right view of things;* by neglecting to think, it fails to do this. These—*the senses and the mind*—are what Heaven has given to us. Let a man first stand fast in *the supremacy of* the nobler part of his constitution, and the inferior part will not be able to take it from him. It is simply this which makes the great man."

心 indicates our whole mental constitution. 物交物,—the first 物 is the external objects, what is heard and seen; the second denotes the senses themselves, which are only things. 引之而已,—而已="as a matter of course." 得之,—之=事 物之理, "the mind apprehends the true nature of the objects of sense," and of course can guard against their deluding influence. 其大者,—"his what is great," the nobler part of his constitution, i. e., the mind.— Kung-tsoo might have gone on to inquire,—"All are equally men.

Some stand fast in the nobler part of their constitution, and some allow its supremacy to be snatched away by the inferior part. How is this?" and Mencius would have tried to carry the difficulty a step farther back, and after all have left it where it originally was. His saying that the nature of man is good may be reconciled with the doctrines of evangelical Christianity, but his views of human nature as a whole are open to the three objections stated in the note to the 21st ch. of the *Chung Yung.*

得人爵而棄其天爵、

其天爵以要人爵既

人爵從之今之人修

古之人修其天爵而

公卿大夫此人爵也。

樂善不倦此天爵也、

有人爵者仁義忠信、

孟子曰有天爵者、

CHAPTER XVI. 1. Mencius said, "There is a nobility of Heaven, and there is a nobility of man. Benevolence, righteousness, self-consecration, and fidelity, with unwearied joy in *these* virtues;—these constitute the nobility of Heaven. To be a *kung*, a *k'ing*, or a *ta-foo*;—this constitutes the nobility of man.

2. "The men of antiquity cultivated their nobility of Heaven, and the nobility of man came to them in its train.

3. "The men of the present day cultivate their nobility of Heaven in order to seek for the nobility of man, and when they have obtained that, they throw

CH. 16. THERE IS A NOBILITY THAT IS OF HEAVEN, AND A NOBILITY THAT IS OF MAN. THE NEGLECT OF THE FORMER LEADS TO THE LOSS OF THE LATTER. 1. 忠 is the *heart* true in itself, loyal to benevolence and righteousness, 信 is the *conduct* true to them. 公, 卿, 大 夫,—see V, Pt. II, ii, 3–7. 3. 要,—up. 1st tone, = 求. "Their delusion is extreme,"—this is well set forth in the 日 講:—夫 修 天 爵 以 要 人 爵, 是 修

之 之 曰, 原 先 有 棄 之 之 心, 已 不
免 於 惑 矣, 至 得 人 爵 而 棄 天 爵,
是 得 之 之 後, 並 不 及 要 之 之 時,
則 惑 之 甚 者 也, "Now when the nobility of Heaven is cultivated in order to seek for the nobility of man, at the very time it is cultivated, there is a previous mind to throw it away;—showing the existence of delusion. Then when the nobility of man has been got, to throw away the nobility of Heaven, exhibits

孟之所貴、趙孟能賤　所貴者、非良貴也、趙　於己者弗思耳人之二　之同心也、人人有貴　囗二孟子曰、欲貴者、人　必亡而已矣。　則惑之甚者也、終亦

away the other:—their delusion is extreme. The issue is simply this that they must lose *that nobility of man* as well."

CHAPTER XVII. 1. Mencius said, "To desire to be honored is the common mind of men. And all men have in themselves that which is *truly* honorable. Only they do not think of it.

2. "The honor which men confer is not good honor. Those whom Chaou the Great ennobles he can make mean *again*.

conduct after attainment not equal to that in the time of search, so that the delusion is extreme." 終亦必 亡而已矣,—亡 has reference to the nobility of man, and is best translated as an active verb, to which the 亦 also points.—Many commentators observe that facts may be referred to, apparently inconsistent with the assertions in this chapter, and then go on to say that such inconsistency is but a lucky accident; the issue *should* always be as Mencius says. Yes; but all moral teachings must be imperfect where the thoughts are bounded by what is seen and temporal.

CH. 17. THE TRUE HONOR WHICH MEN SHOULD DESIRE. 1. 爵 in the last ch. is the material dignity; 貴 in this is the honor, such as springs from such dignity. 2. 人之所貴,— 人 here and in the next par., refers to those who confer dignities. It is not to be understood—"what men consider honor." 趙孟, "Chaou the chief." This title was borne by four ministers of the family of Chaou, who at different times held the chief sway in Tsin. They were a sort of "king-making Warwicks." In the time of Mencius, the title had become associated with the name of

以一杯水、救一車薪之火

猶水勝火、今之爲仁者、猶

<ruby>嘗<rt>一節</rt></ruby>孟子曰仁之勝不仁也、

之文繡也。

廣譽施於身、所以不願人

願人之膏粱之味也、令聞

德、言飽乎仁義也、所以不

之詩云、既醉以酒、既飽以<ruby>〇<rt>三節</rt></ruby>

3. "It is said in the 'Book of Poetry,'

> 'He has filled us with his wine,
> He has satiated us with his goodness.'

'*Satiated us with his goodness*,' that is, satiated us with benevolence and righteousness, and he who is so, consequently, does not wish for the fat meat and fine millet of men. A good reputation and far-reaching praise fall to him, and he does not desire the elegant embroidered garments of men."

CHAPTER XVIII. 1. Mencius said, "Benevolence subdues its opposite just as water subdues fire. Those, however, who nowadays practice benevolence *do it* as if with one cup of water they could save a whole

the house. 3. 詩 云,—see the She-king, III, ii, Ode III, st. 1. The ode is one responsive from "his fathers and brethren" to the emperor who has entertained them. Mencius's application here is a mere accommodation.

CH. 18. IT IS NECESSARY TO PRACTICE BENEVOLENCE WITH ALL

而已矣。

黃稗夫仁亦在乎熟之

美者也苟爲不熟不如

孟子曰五穀者種之

者也亦終必亡而已矣。

火此又與於不仁之甚

也不熄則謂之水不勝

wagonload of fuel which was on fire, and when the flames were not extinguished, were to say that water cannot subdue fire. This conduct, moreover, greatly encourages those who are not benevolent.

2. "The final issue will simply be this—the loss *of that small amount of benevolence.*"

CHAPTER XIX. · Mencius said, "Of all seeds the best are the five kinds of grain, yet if they be not ripe, they are not equal to the *t'e* or the *pae*. So the value of benevolence depends entirely on its being brought to maturity."

ONE'S MIGHT. THIS ONLY WILL PRE-SERVE IT. 1. 不熄, 則謂之, 一謂之, "were to say of it." 與 is said by Choo He to = 助, "to aid." The 甚 is joined to 與, and not to 不 仁. Bad men seeing the ineffectiveness of feeble endeavors to do good are only encouraged in their own course. This meaning of 與 is found elsewhere. Chaou K'e interprets: "This also is worse than the case of those who practice what is not benevolent." But both the senti-ment and construction of this are more difficult than the other. 2. Comp. chapter xvi, 2.

CH. 19. BENEVOLENCE MUST BE MATURED. 1. "The five kinds of grain;"—see III, Pt. I, iv, 7. The *t'e* and *pae* are two plants closely resembling one another. They are a kind of spurious grain, *yielding a ricelike seed, but small. They are to be found at all times, in wet situations and dry, and when crushed and roasted, may satisfy the hunger in a time of famine." One kind of *pae* is called in the norm 鳥 禾, "bird paddy." Mencius's vivacity of mind and readiness at illustration lead him at times to broad un-guarded statements, of which this seems to be one.

亦必以規矩。

以規矩學者

大匠誨人必

亦必志於彀。

至於彀學者

之教人射、必

孟子曰、羿

CHAPTER XX. 1. Mencius said, "E, in teaching men to shoot, made it a rule to draw the bow to the full, and his pupils also did the same.

2. "A master workman, in teaching others, uses the compass and square, and his pupils do the same."

CH. 20. LEÁRNING MUST NOT BE BY HALVES. 1. E,—see IV, Pt. II, xxiv, 1. 志,—used as 期, in ch. vii, 5. 必志,—"found it necessary to," or simply the past tense emphatic. So, in the next par. 2. 大匠＝工師, "a master workman." Choo He says: "This ch. shows that affairs must be proceeded with according to their laws, and then they can be completed. But if a master neglect these, he cannot teach, and if a pupil neglect these, he cannot learn. In small arts it is so:—how much more with the principles of the sages!"

## BOOK VI

### KAOU TSZE. PART II

曰、以禮食、則　孰重。曰、禮重。　禮重色、與禮、　與食、孰重。曰、　屋盧子曰、禮、　任人有問　句下　告子章

CHAPTER I. A man of Jin asked the disciple Uh-loo, saying, "Is *an observance of* the rules of propriety *in regard to eating,* or the eating, the more important?" The answer was, "*The observance of* the rules of propriety is the more important."

2. "Is *the gratifying* the appetite of sex, or *the doing so only* according to the rules of propriety, the more important?" The answer *again* was, "*The observance of* the rules of propriety *in the matter* is the more important."

3. *The man* pursued, "If the result of eating only according to the rules of propriety will be death by

CH. 1. THE IMPORTANCE OF OB-SERVING THE RULES OF PROPRIETY, AND, WHEN THEY MAY BE DISRE-GARDED, THE EXCEPTION WILL BE FOUND TO PROVE THE RULE. EX-TREME CASES MAY NOT BE PRESSED TO INVALIDATE THE PRINCIPLE. 1. 任 (low. 1st tone) was a small state, referred to the present Tsening-chow (濟寧), of the department Yenchow, in Shantung. It was not far from Mencius's native state of Tsow, the distance being only be-tween twenty and thirty li. The disciple Uh-loo, who is said to have published books on the doctrines of Lao-tse, was a native of the state of Tsin. His name was Leen (連). His questions are not to be under-stood of propriety in the abstract, but of the rules of propriety under-stood to regulate the other things which he mentions. 2. 色 is to be understood as in the translation, and this is its common signif. in Men-cius. I include the 曰、禮重 in this par. 3. 以 禮 食,—see the Le-ke,

末、方寸之木可使高於岑

也何有不揣其本而齊其

以告孟子孟子曰、於答是

屋廬子不能對明日之鄒、

親迎則不得妻必親迎乎。

必以禮乎、親迎則得妻不

飢而死、不以禮食則得食、

starvation, while by disregarding those rules we may
get food, must they *still* be observed *in such a case?*
If according to the rule that he shall go in person
to meet his wife a man cannot get married, while
by disregarding that rule he may get married, must
he *still* observe the rule *in such a case?*"

4. Uh-loo was unable to reply to *these questions*,
and the next day he went to Tsow, and told them
to Mencius. Mencius said, "What difficulty is there
in answering these inquiries?

5. "If you do not adjust them at their lower
extremities, but only put their tops on a level, a piece
of wood an inch square may be made to be higher
than the pointed peak of a high building.

XXVII, 26; *et al.* 親迎 (lower 3rd
tone),—see the Le-ke, IX, iii, 8.
4. 之鄒,—之＝往. Chaou K'o reads

於 as 烏, *woo*, up. 1st tone, making
it an exclamation—"oh!" 5. 揣,—
"to measure, or feel with the hand."

色重往應之曰紾兄之臂、

與禮之輕者、而比之奚翅

之、奚翅食重取色之重者、

之重者與禮之輕者、而比

金、與一輿羽之謂哉。取食

樓。金重於羽者、豈謂一鈞

6. "Gold is heavier than feathers;—but does that saying have reference, on the one hand, to a single clasp of gold, and, on the other, to a wagonload of feathers?

7. "If you take a case where the eating is of the utmost importance and the observing the rules of propriety is of little importance, and compare the things together, why stop with saying merely that the eating is more important? *So*, taking the case where the gratifying the appetite of sex is of the utmost ·importance and the observing the rules of propriety is of little importance, why stop with merely saying that the gratifying the appetite is the more important?

8. "Go and answer him thus, 'If, by twisting

本 and 末 are used for 下 and 上 舉 (*ts'in*),— "a high and pointed small hill." Chaou K'e takes 舉 樓 together as meaning "a peaked ridge of a hill," and the dictionary gives this signification to the phrase. The view of Choo He, which I have followed, is better. 6. 金 ... 者,一

者 indicates the clause to be a common saying, and carries us on to some explanation of it. 豈 謂 ... 之 謂,—"How does it say (mean) the saying (meaning) of the gold of one hook, and the feathers of one wagon?" Comp. I, Pt. II, vii, l. 7. 奚 翅 (＝音)＝何 但. 8. 紾 (read

而奪之食則得食、不紾、

則不得食則將紾之乎、

踰東家牆、而摟其處子、

則得妻不摟、則不得妻、

則將摟之乎。

曹交問曰、人皆可以

your elder brother's arm, and snatching from him what he is eating, you can get food for yourself, while, if you do not do so, you will not get anything to eat, will you so twist his arm?  If by getting over your neighbor's wall, and dragging away his virgin daughter, you can get a wife, while if you do not do so, you will not be able to get a wife, will you so drag her away?'"

CHAPTER II.  1. Keaou of Tsaou asked *Mencius,* saying, *"It is said,* 'All men may be Yaous

*ch'in* or *t'een,* up. 2nd tone), both by Chaou K'e and Choo He, is explained by 戾, "to bend." I prefer the first meaning of the character given in the dictionary,—that of 紾, "to turn," here="to twist." 而奪之食,—here 奪 is followed by two objectives, 之 being="from him." Julien errs strangely in rendering—"*Si, rumpens fratris majoris brachium, xapias illud comedendum.*" 東家牆,—"the wall of the house on the east," i. e., a neighbor's wall. 東家 is a common designation for the master of a house, but the phrase

is not to be traced to Mencius's expression.  處 (up. 2nd tone) 子,—"a virgin daughter," one *dwelling* in the harem. 子, as sometimes elsewhere, is feminine.

CH. 2.  ALL MAY BECOME YAOUS AND SHUNS, AND TO BECOME SO, THEY HAVE ONLY SINCERELY, AND IN THEMSELVES, TO CULTIVATE YAOU AND SHUN'S PRINCIPLES AND WAYS. 1. Chaou K'e says that Keaou was a brother of the prince of Tsaou, but the principality of Tsaou had been extinguished before the time of Mencius. The descendants of the ruling

爲堯舜、有諸孟子曰、然。

交聞文王十尺、湯九尺、

今交九尺四寸以長食

粟而已、如何則可曰奚

有於是亦爲之而已矣、

有人於此、力不能勝一

匹雛、則爲無力人矣、今

and Shuns';—is it so?" Mencius replied, "It is."

2. *Keaou went on*, "I have heard that King Wăn was ten cubits *high*, and T'ang nine. Now I am nine cubits four inches in height. *But* I can do nothing but eat *my* millet. What am I to do to realize that saying?"

3. *Mencius* answered · him, "What has this—*the question of size*—to do with the matter? It all lies simply in acting as such. Here is a man, whose strength was not equal to lift a duckling:—he was *then* a man of no strength. But to-day he says,

---

house had probably taken their surname from their ancient patrimony. Tsaou is referred to the present district of Ting-t'aou (定陶) in the department of Tsaouchow, in Shantung. 有諸,—comp. I, Pt. II, ii, 1; *et al.* 2. On the heights mentioned here, see Con. Ana., VIII, vi. 以長,—"for my height." The 以, however, may be taken as simply euphonic. Keaou's idea is, that physically he was between Wăn and T'ang, who might be considered as having become Yaous or Shuns, and therefore he also might become such, if he were shown the right way. 3. 於是,—是 referring to the height, or body generally. 爲之,—之 referring to Yaou and Shun. 匹 is said to be an abbreviation for 鶩=鴄, "a wild duck." I do not see why it should not be taken simply as a numeral or classifier, and 一匹雛= "a chicken." Woo Hwŏ was a man

曰、舉百鈞、則爲有力人矣、然

則舉烏獲之任、是亦爲烏獲

而已矣、夫人豈以不勝爲患

哉、弗爲耳。徐行後長者謂之

弟、疾行先長者謂之不弟、夫

徐行者、豈人所不能哉、所不

'I can lift 3,000 catties' weight,' and-he is a man of strength. And so, he who can lift the weight which Woo Hwŏ lifted is just another Woo Hwŏ. Why should a man make a want of ability the subject of his grief? It is only that he will not do the thing.

4. "To walk slowly, keeping behind his elders, is to perform the part of a younger. To walk quickly and precede his elders, is to violate the duty of a younger brother. Now, is it what a man cannot do—to walk slowly? It is what he does not do.

noted for his strength. He is mentioned in connection with the king Woo of Ts'in (309–306 B. C.). Accounts go that he made light of 30,000 catties! 4. 後 and 先 (up. 3rd tone) are verbs. 弟=悌. Choo He here quotes from the commen. Ch'in (陳 氏): "Filial piety and fraternal duty are the natural outgoings of the nature, of which men have an intuitive knowledge, and for which they have an intuitive ability (良知良能). Yaou and Shun showed the perfection of the human relations, but yet they simply acted in accordance with this nature. How could they add a hair's point to it?" He also quotes another (陽 氏), who says: "The way of Yaou and Shun was great, but the pursuit of it lay

而受業於門。夫道若大
見於鄒君可以假館、願留
之行、是桀而已矣。曰交得
服桀之服、誦桀之言行桀
行堯之行、是堯而已矣、子
矣。子服堯之服、誦堯之言、
爲也、堯舜之道孝弟而已

The course of Yaou and Shun was simply that of filial piety and fraternal duty.

5. "Do you wear the clothes of Yaou, repeat the words of Yaou, and do the actions of Yaou, and you will just be a Yaou. And, if you wear the clothes of Kĕ̆, repeat the words of Kĕ̆, and do the actions of Kĕ̆, you will just be a Kĕ̆."

6. Keaou said, "I shall be having an interview with the prince of Tsow, and can ask him to let me have a house to lodge in. I wish to remain here, and receive instruction at your gate."

7. Mencius replied, "The way of truth is like

simply in the rapidity or slowness of their walking and stopping, and not in things that were very high and difficult. It is present to the common people in their daily usages, but they do not know it." 5. The meaning is simply—Imitate the men, do what they did, and you will be such as they were. 6. 交得見 (low. 3rd tone),—it is better not to translate this conditionally, as it shows how Keaou was presuming on his nobility. 7. 夫道,—"Now, the

孟子曰何以言之曰、

曰、小弁小人之詩也。

公孫丑問曰、高子

有餘師。

不求耳子歸而求之、

路然豈難知哉、人病

a great road. It is not difficult to know it. The evil is only that men will not seek it. Do you go home and search for it, and you will have abundance of teachers."

CHAPTER III. 1. Kung-sun Ch'ow asked *about an opinion of the scholar Kaou*, saying, "Kaou observed, 'The Seaou P'wan is the ode of a little man.'" Mencius asked, "Why did he say so?" "Because of the murmuring *which it expresses*," was the reply.

way"—i. e., the way of Yaou and Shun, or generally "of truth."

CH. 3. EXPLANATION OF THE ODES SEAOU P'WAN AND K'AE FUNG. DISSATISFACTION WITH A PARENT IS NOT NECESSARILY UNFILIAL. 1. Kaou appears to have been a disciple of Tsze-hea, and lived to Mencius's time. From the expression 高叟 in par. 2, it is plain, he is not to be confounded with Mencius's own disciple of the same surname, mentioned II, Pt. II, xii, 2. 小弁,—see the She-king, II, v, Ode III, 3. The ode is commonly understood to have been written by the master of E-k'ew (宜臼); the son and heir apparent of the emperor Yew (780-770 B. C.). Led away by the arts of a mistress, the emperor degraded E-k'ew and his mother, and the ode expresses the sorrow and dissatisfaction which the son could not but feel in such circumstances. Chaou K'e, however, assigns it another authorship, but on this and other questions, connected with it, see the

怨。
固哉、高叟之爲詩
也、有人於此越人關弓
而射之、則己談笑而道
之、無他、疏之也其兄關
弓而射之、則己垂涕泣
而道之、無他、戚之也、小
弁之怨、親親也、親親仁
也、固矣夫高叟之爲詩

2. *Mencius* answered, "How stupid was that old Kaou in dealing with the ode! There is a man here, and a native of Yuĕ bends his bow to shoot him. I will advise him *not to do so*, but speaking calmly and smilingly;—for no other reason but that he is not related to me. *But* if my own brother be bending his bow to shoot the man, then I will advise him not to do so, weeping and crying the while;—for no other reason than that he is related to me. The dissatisfaction expressed in the Seaou P'wan is the working of relative affection, and that affection shows benevolence. Stupid indeed was old Kaou's criticism on the ode."

She-king, *in loc.* 2. 固 is explained by Chaou K'e by 陋, "narrow," and by Choo He by 執滯不通, "bigoted and not penetrating." 爲詩＝治詩, 有人 ... 戚之,—here 己 is to be understood of the speaker or beholder, and 其兄 of his—the speaker's—brother. In 道 (＝言, the verb) 之, 疏之, 戚之, 之 refers to the shooter. 關, read *wan*,＝彎. The paraphrast of Chaou K'e point, however, and understands differently—"Here is a man of Yuĕ, who is about to be shot by another man. I see it and advise the man not to shoot, but coolly and smilingly, because I am not related to the man of Yuĕ. But if my brother is about to be shot, etc." This is ingenious, but not so apt to the subject of the Seaou P'wan. When native scholars can construe a passage so differently, we

不孝也不可磯、亦

是不可磯也、愈疏、

也、親之過小而怨、

大而不怨是愈疏

過大者也、親之過

小者也、小弁、親之

怨。曰、凱風、親之過

也。曰、凱風、何以不

3. *Ch'ow then said,* "How is it that there is no dissatisfaction expressed in the K'ae Fung?"

4. Mencius replied, "The parent's fault referred to in the K'ae Fung is small; that referred to in the Seaou P'wan is great. Where the parent's fault was great, not to have murmured on account of it would have increased the want of natural affection. Where the parent's fault was small, to have murmured on account of it would have been to act like water which frets and foams about a stone that interrupts its course. To increase the want of natural affection would have been unfilial, and to fret and foam in such a manner would also have been unfilial.

may be sure it is not very definitely expressed. 3. 凱風.—see the She-king, I, iii, Ode VII. The ode is supposed to be the production of seven sons, bewailing the conduct of their widowed mother, who could not live quietly and chastely at home, but they take all the blame to themselves, and express no dis-satisfaction with her. 4. We must think there was room enough for dissatisfaction in both cases. And indeed, many commentators say that the received account of the subject of the K'ae Fung must be wrong, or that Mencius's decision on it is ab-surd. But here again, see the She-king, *in loc.* 愈疏.—"mores [if we had such a verb] the distance." The father's act was unkind; if the son responded to it with indifference, that would increase the distance and alienation between them. 是不可磯也,—the three characters 不可磯 are to be taken together. The mother is compared to a rock or

不孝也。孔子曰、舜其至
孝矣、五十而慕。
宋牼將之楚、孟子遇
於石丘。先生將何之。
曰、吾聞秦楚搆兵我將
見楚王說而罷之、楚王
不悅、我將見秦王、說而

5. "Confucius said, 'Shun was indeed perfectly filial! *And yet*, when he was fifty, he was full of longing desire about his parents.'"

CHAPTER IV. 1. Sung K'ang being about to go to Ts'oo, Mencius met him in Shih-k'ew.

2. "Master, where are you going?" asked *Mencius*.

3. K'*ang* replied, "I have heard that Ts'in and Ts'oo are fighting together, and I am going to see the king of Ts'oo and persuade him to cease hostilities. If he shall not be pleased *with my advice*, I shall go to see the king of Ts'in, and persuade him in

stone in a stream, and the sons to the water fretting about it. But the case in the text is one where the children's affections should flow on undisturbed. 5. Comp. V, Pt. I, i.

CH. 4. MENCIUS'S WARNINGS TO SUNG K'ANG ON THE ERROR AND DANGER OF COUNSELING THE PRINCES FROM THE GROUND OF PROFIT, THE PROPER GROUND BEING THAT OF BENEVOLENCE AND RIGHTEOUSNESS. Comp. I, Pt. I, i; *et al.* 1. K'ang was one of the traveling scholars of the times, who went from state to state, making it their business to counsel (說, *shwuy*, up. 3rd tone) the princes, with a view for the most part, though not apparently with him, to exalt themselves. Shih-k'ew was in the state of Sung. Here, and also in the next par., 之 is the verb. 3. 搆 (=構) 兵,="crossing weapons." 罷之,—"make an end of it." 所

以罷三軍之師、是三軍之士、

秦楚之王、秦楚之王、悅於利、

生之號則不可。先生以利說

利也。曰、先生之志則大矣、先

說之將何如。曰、我將言其不

軻也、請無問其詳、願聞其指、

罷之二王、我將有所遇焉。曰、

the same way. Of the two kings I shall *surely* find that I can succeed with one of them."

4. *Mencius* said, "I will not venture to ask about the particulars, but I should like to hear the scope of your plan. What course will you take to try to persuade them?" *K'ang* answered, "I will tell them how unprofitable their course is to them." "Master," said Mencius, "your aim is great, but your argument is not good.

5. "If you, starting from the point of profit, offer your persuasive counsels to the kings of Ts'in and Ts'oo, and if those kings are pleased with the consideration of profit so as to stop the movements of their armies, then all belonging to those armies

遇,—see I, Pt. II, xv, 3. 4. 請＝our "if you'll allow me." Then follows —"not asking the particulars, I should like," etc. 其不利.—其 refers to the two states. 號,—I take the word "argument" from Julien. The gloss in the 備旨 is—號 是 不 利 之 名 號, "號 is the name and title of *unprofitable.*" 5. 三軍之師,

義說秦楚之王、秦楚之王、悅　不亡者未之有也。先生以仁　終去仁義懷利以相接、然而　以事其兄、是君臣父子兄弟、　利以事其父、爲人弟者、懷利　懷利以事其君、爲人子者、懷　樂罷而悅於利也、爲人臣者、

will rejoice in the cessation *of war*, and find their pleasure in *the pursuit of* profit. Ministers will serve their sovereign for the profit of which they cherish the thought; sons will serve their fathers, and younger brothers will serve their elder brothers, from the same consideration:—and the issue will be, that, abandoning benevolence and righteousness, sovereign and minister, father and son, younger brother and elder, will carry on all their intercourse with this thought of profit cherished in their breasts. But never has there been such a state *of society*, without ruin being the result of it.

6. "If you, starting from the ground of benevolence and righteousness, offer your counsels to the kings of Ts'in and Ts'oo, and if those kings are

—"the multitudes of the three | armies"; see Con. Ana., VII, x. 士

之有也、何必曰利。

義以相接也、然而不王者、未

是君臣父子、兄弟去利。懷仁

爲人弟者懷仁義以事其兄、

爲人子者懷仁義以事其父、

爲人臣者懷仁義以事其君、

軍之士、樂罷而悅於仁義也、

於仁義、而罷三軍之師、是三

pleased with the consideration of benevolence and righteousness so as to stop the operations of their armies, then all belonging to those armies will rejoice in the stopping *from war,* and find their pleasure in benevolence and righteousness. Ministers will serve their sovereign, cherishing the principles of benevolence and righteousness; sons will serve their fathers, and younger brothers will serve their elder brothers, in the same way:—and so, sovereign and minister, father and son, elder brother and younger, abandoning *the thought of* profit, will cherish the principles of benevolence and righteousness, and carry on all their intercourse upon them. But never has there been such a state *of society,* without the state where it prevailed rising to imperial sway. Why must you use that word 'profit'? "

embraces both "officers and soldiers."
6. 然 而 不 王 (low. 3rd tone) 者 未

之 有,—here the translation needs to be supplemented considerably.

喜曰、連得閒矣問曰、

齊、不見儲子、屋廬子

任見季子、由平陸之

而不報。他日、由鄒之

子爲相、以幣交受之

而不報、處於平陸、儲

任處守、以幣交受之

孟子居鄒、季任爲

CHAPTER V. 1. When Mencius was residing in Tsow, the younger brother of the chief of Jin, who was guardian of Jin at the time, paid his respects to him by *a present of* silks, which Mencius received, not *going* to acknowledge it. When he was sojourning in P'ing-luh, Ch'oo, who was prime minister of the state, sent him a similar present, which he received in the same way.

2. Subsequently, going from Tsow to Jin, he visited the guardian, but when he went from P'ing-luh to *the capital of* Ts'e, he did not visit the minister Ch'oo. The disciple Uh-loo was glad, and said, "I have got an opportunity *to obtain some instruction.*"

3. He asked *accordingly*, "Master, when you went

CH. 5. HOW MENCIUS REGULATED HIMSELF IN DIFFERENTLY ACKNOWLEDGING FAVORS WHICH HE RECEIVED. 1. 季任, and 季子, below, look much as if the former were the surname and name of the individual spoken of, yet Chaou K'e's explanation of the terms, which is that followed in the translation, is no doubt correct. 任,—see ch. i. 以 幣 交,—see V, Pt. II, iv. 不 報 = 不 往 報. 平 陸,—see II, Pt. II, vi, 1. 2. The two 之 here, and in next par. = 往. 之 齊, "went to Ts'e," i. e., to the capital of the state, as Ping-luh was in Ts'e. 閒,—k̆een, up. 3rd tone. 連 (Uh-loo's name) 得 閒 = 連 得 其 閒 隙 而 閒, "I have got

子得之平陸。

子曰、季子不得之鄒、儲

屋廬子悅或問之屋廬

志于享爲其不成享也。

不及物曰不享惟不役

曰、非也書曰、享多儀儀

不見儲子、爲其爲相與。

夫子之任見季子之齊、

to Jin, you visited the chief's brother, and when you went to Ts'e, you did not visit Ch'oo. Was it not because he is *only* the minister?"

4. *Mencius* replied, "No. It is said in the 'Book of History,' 'In presenting an offering to a superior, most depends on the demonstrations of respect. If those demonstrations are not equal to the things offered, we say there is no offering, that is, there is no act of the will in presenting the offering.'

5. "*This is* because the things so offered do not constitute an offering to a superior."

6. Uh-loo was pleased, and when some one asked him *what Mencius meant*, he said, "The younger of Jin could not go to Tsow, but the minister Ch'oo might have gone to P'ing-luh.

an opportunity (lit., crevice) to ask." 4. 書曰,—see the Shoo-king, V, xiv, 13, but in the classic the last clause 惟不役志于享, is not explanatory of the preceding, but is itself the first clause of a new sentence. See the Shoo-king, *in loc.* 5.

This is Mencius's explanation of the passage quoted. 6. The guardian of a state could not leave it to pay a visit in another. There was no reason, however, why Ch'oo should not have paid his respects to Mencius in person.

淳于髡曰、先名實
者爲人也、後名實者、
自爲也、夫子在三卿
之中、名實未加於上
下、而去之、仁者固如
此乎孟子曰、居下位、
不以賢事不肖者、伯

CHAPTER VI. 1. Shun-yu K'wăn said, "He who makes fame and meritorious services his first objects, acts with a regard to others. He who makes them only secondary objects, acts with a regard to himself. You, master, were ranked among the three chief ministers *of the state*, but before your fame and services had reached either to the prince or the people, you have left your place. Is this indeed the way of the benevolent?"

2. Mencius replied, "There was Pih-e;—he abode in an inferior situation, and would not, with his virtue,

CH. 6. HOW MENCIUS REPLIED TO THE INSINUATIONS OF SHUN-YU K'WĂN, CONDEMNING HIM FOR LEAVING OFFICE WITHOUT ACOMPLISHING ANYTHING. 1. Shun-yu K'wăn,—see IV, Pt. I, xvii. That chapter and the notes should be read along with this. 名 and 實 are not here opposed to each other, as often,—"name" and "reality." The "name" here is the fame of the "reality." 爲人、—"with a regard to others," i. e., such a man's motive in public life is to benefit others. 自 爲＝爲 己. "with a regard to himself," i. e., such a man's motive is to cultivate his own good and excellence, 上 refers to the prince; 下 refers to the people. 仁者、—it is assumed that the fact of Mencius being among the high ministers of the state took him out of the category of those who made themselves their aim in life, and the 仁者 therefore is a hit of the questioner. Throughout the ch., 仁 has perhaps more the idea of perfect virtue, free from all selfishness, than of benevolence. 2. Pih-e, etc., see V, Pt. II, i, with the other references there given. That

繆公之時、公儀子爲政、
仁而已矣、何必同曰、魯
者、何也、曰仁也、君子亦
者、不同道其趨一也、一
小官者、柳下惠也、三子
伊尹也、不惡汙君不辭
夷也、五就湯、五就桀者、

serve a degenerate prince. There was E Yin;—he five times went to T'ang, and five times went to Kĕĕ. There was Hwuy of Lew-hea;—he did not disdain to serve a vile prince, nor did he decline a small office. The courses pursued by those three worthies were different, but their aim was one. And what was their one aim? We must answer—'To be perfectly virtuous.' And so it is simply after this that superior men strive. Why must they all *pursue* the same *course?*"

3. *K'wăn* pursued, "In the time of the duke Mŭh of Loo, the government was in the hands of Kung-e,

E Yin went five times to T'ang, and five times to Kĕĕ is only mentioned here, however. He went to T'ang, it is said, in consequence of the pressing urgency of his solicitations, and then T'ang sent him to the tyrant to warn and advise him. Nothing could be farther at first from the wish of them both than to dethrone Kĕĕ. 趨,—"to run,"

used figuratively, up. 3rd tone. 3' In this par., K'wăn advances in his condemnation of Mencius. At first he charged him with having left his office before he had accomplished anything. Here he insinuates that though he had remained, he would not have served the state. Tsze-low is the Seĕ Lew of II, Pt. II, xi; comp. that ch. with this. Kung-e (named

子柳子思爲臣魯之削也、

滋甚若是乎賢者之無益

於國也曰、虞不用百里奚

而亡、秦穆公用之而霸、不

用賢則亡、削、何可得與。曰、

昔者、王豹處於淇、而河西

while Tsze-lew and Tsze-sze were ministers. *And yet,* the dismemberment of Loo then increased exceedingly. Such was the case, a specimen how your men of virtue are of no advantage to a kingdom!"

4. *Mencius* said, *"The prince of* Yu did not use Pih-le He, and thereby lost his state. The duke Muh of Ts'in used him, and became chief of all the princes. Ruin is the consequence of not employing men of virtue and talents;—how can it rest with dismemberment *merely?"*

5. *K'wăn* urged *again,* "Formerly, when Wang P'aou dwelt on the K'e, the people on the west of the

休) was prime minister of Loo, a man of merit and principle. Mencius might have denied the fact alleged by K'wăn, of the increased dismemberment of Loo under Duke Muh. 4. Pih-le He,—see V, Pt. I, ix. 用, 不 用,—the "using" means

following the minister's counsels and plans. 削, 何 可 得 與 (low. 1st tone),— before 削, we must understand 求,—"If you seek for dismemberment merely, as the consequence," etc. 5. The individuals named here all belonged to Ts'e, excepting the

無賢者也、有、則髠必識之。

功者、髠未嘗覩之也、是故

必形諸外、爲其事而無其

哭其夫、而變國俗、有諸內、

右善歌、華周杞梁之妻、善

善謳、緜駒處於高唐、而齊

*Yellow* River all became skilful at singing in *his* abrupt manner. When Mëen K'eu lived in Kaou-t'ang, the people in the parts of Ts'e on the west became skillful at singing in *his* prolonged manner. The wives of Hwa Chow and Ke Leang bewailed their husbands so skillfully, that they changed the manners of the state. When there is *the gift* within, it manifests itself without. I have never seen the man who could do the deeds *of a worthy*, and did not realize the work of one. Therefore there are *now* no men of talents and virtue. If there were, I should know them.''

first, who was of Wei. 歌 is the general name for singing, and 謳, a particular style, said to be 短壁, "short," "abrupt." 齊右, it is said 概指齊西鄙而言, i. e., "The right of Ts'e denotes all about the western borders of the state." How Hwa (up. 3rd tone) and Ke Leang were officers slain in battle, whose wives bewailed their loss in so pitiful a manner, as to affect the whole state. Their cries, it is said, even rent the wall of the capital of Ts'e. See the 集證 and the 四書摭餘說 *in loc.*—The object of K'wăn is simply to insinuate that Mencius was a pretender, for that wherever ability was, it was sure to come out. 6.

曰、孔子爲魯司寇、不用、
從而祭、燔肉不至、不稅
冕而行、不知者以爲爲
肉也、其知者、以爲爲無
禮也、乃孔子則欲以微
罪行、不欲爲苟去君子
之所爲、衆人固不識也。

6. *Mencius* answered, "When Confucius was chief
minister of justice in Loo, the prince came not to
follow *his counsels*. Soon after was the *solstitial
sacrifice*, and when a part of the flesh presented in
sacrifice was not sent to him, he went away even
without taking off his cap of ceremony. Those who
did not know him supposed it was on account of the
flesh. Those who knew him supposed that it was on
account *of the neglect* of the usual ceremony. The fact
was, that Confucius wanted to go away on occasion of
some small offense, not wishing to do so without some
apparent cause. All men may not be expected to
understand the conduct of a superior man."

Mencius shields himself behind Confucius, implying that he was beyond
the knowledge of K'wän.—The state
of Ts'e, afraid of the influence of
Confucius, who was acting as prime
minister of Loo, sent to the duke a
present of beautiful singing girls and
horses. The duke accepted them,
and abandoned himself to dissipation. Confucius determined to leave
the state, but not wishing to expose
the bad conduct of his prince, looked
about for some other reason which
he might assign for going away, and
found it in the matter mentioned.
The 祭 is the 郊祭. 稅,—used for
脫. 爲苟去,—"to do a disorderly
going away."

子、曰述職、春省耕而
曰巡狩、諸侯朝於天
罪人也。天子適諸侯、
之大夫今之諸侯之
侯、五霸之罪人也、今
王之罪人也、今之諸
孟子曰、五霸者三

CHAPTER VII. 1. Mencius said, "The five chiefs of the princes were sinners against the three kings. The princes of the present day are sinners against the five chiefs. The great officers of the present day are sinners against the princes.

2. "The emperor visited the princes, which was called 'a tour of inspection.' The princes attended at the court of the emperor, which was called 'giving a report of office.' It was a custom in the spring to

CH. 7. THE PROGRESS AND MANNER OF DEGENERACY FROM THE THREE KINGS TO THE FIVE CHIEFS OF THE PRINCES, AND FROM THE FIVE CHIEFS TO THE PRINCES AND OFFICERS OF MENCIUS'S TIME. 1. The "three kings" are the founders of the three dynasties of Hea, Shang, and Chow. The "five chiefs of the princes" were the duke Hwan of Ts'e (684–642 B.C.), the duke Wăn of Tsin (635–627), the duke Muh of Ts'in (659–620, the duke Seang of Sung (650–636), and the king Chwang of Ts'oo (613–590). There are two enumerations of the "five leading princes," one called 三代之五伯, or chiefs of the three dynasties, and the other 春秋之五伯, or chiefs of the

Ch'un-ts'ew. Only Hwan of Ts'e and Wăn of Tsin are common to the two. But Mencius is speaking only of those included in the second enumeration, and though there is some difference of opinion in regard to some of the individuals in it, the above list is probably that which he held. "Sinners against,"—i. e., violating their principles and ways. 2. 天子 . . . 不給,—see I, Pt. II, iv, 5. 辟=闢, see I, Pt. I, vii, 16. 俊傑在位,—see II, Pt. I, v, 1. 慶=賞, "to reward." 掊克=聚歛臣, "impost-collecting ministers"; literally, perhaps, "grasping and able men." Down to 讓 is explicatory of 巡狩. What follows belongs to 述職.

貶其爵再不朝則削其地三

掊克在位則有讓一不朝則

入其疆土地荒蕪遺老失賢

賢俊傑在位則有慶慶以地

其疆土地辟田野治養老尊

補不足秋省歛而助不給入

examine the plowing, and supply any deficiency *of seed*, and in autumn to examine the reaping, and assist where there was a deficiency of the crop. When *the emperor* entered the boundaries of a state, if the *new* ground was being reclaimed, and the *old* fields well cultivated; if the old were nourished and the worthy honored; and if men of distinguished talents were placed in office: then *the prince* was rewarded,—rewarded with an addition to his territory. *On the other hand*, if, on entering a state, the ground was found left wild or overrun with weeds; if the old were neglected and the worthy unhonored; and if the offices were filled with hard taxgatherers: then *the prince* was reprimanded. If *a prince* once omitted his attendance at court, he was punished by degradation of rank; if he did so a second time, he was deprived of a portion of his territory; if he did so a third

諸侯、束牲載書而不歃

霸桓公爲盛葵丘之會

霸者、三王之罪人也。

以伐諸侯者也、故曰、五

而不討、五霸者、摟諸侯

天子討而不伐、諸侯伐

不朝、則六師移之、是故

time, the imperial forces *were set in motion,* and he was removed *from his government.* Thus the emperor commanded the punishment, but did not himself inflict it, while the princes inflicted the punishment, but did not command it. The five chiefs, *however,* dragged the princes to punish other princes, and hence I say that they were sinners against the three kings.

3. "Of the five chiefs the most powerful was the duke Hwan. At the assembly of the princes in K'wei-k'ew, he bound the victim and placed the writing upon it, but did not *slay it to* smear their mouths with the

六師 (＝軍),—see Con. Ana., VII, x. 是故＝"in harmony with these things," all power being lodged with the emperor, and the princes being dependent on him. 討＝治, "to superintend, or order, punishment"; 伐, "to inflict the punishment." 3. The duke Hwan nine times brought together an assembly of the princes, the chief gathering being at K'wei-k'ew, 650 B. C. At those meetings, the usual custom was first to dig a square pit, over which the victim was slain. Its left ear was cut off, and its blood received in an ornamented vessel. The president then read the articles of agreement, with his face to the north, as in the presence of the spirits of the sun and moon, after which all the members of the meeting took the blood, and smeared the sides of their mouths with it. This was called 歃 (*shăh*) 血. The victim was then placed in the pit, the articles of agreement placed upon it, and the whole covered up. This was called 載書. See the 集證, *in loc.* On

血、初命曰、誅不孝、無易
樹子、無以妾爲妻、再命
曰、尊賢育才、以彰有德、
三命曰、敬老慈幼、無忘
賓旅四命曰士無世官、
官事無攝取士必得無
專殺大夫、五命曰、無曲
防、無遏糴、無有封而不

blood. The first injunction in their agreement was,—
'Slay the unfilial; change not the son who has been
appointed heir; exalt not a concubine to the rank of
wife.' The second was,—'Honor the worthy, and
maintain the talented, to give distinction to the virtuous.' The third was,—'Respect the old, and be kind
to the young. Be not forgetful of strangers and
travelers.' The fourth was,—'Let not offices be
hereditary, nor let officers be pluralists. In the selection of officers let the object be to get the proper men.
Let not a *ruler* take it on himself to put to death a
great officer.' The fifth was,—'Follow no crooked
policy in making embankments. Impose no restric-
tions on the sale of grain. Let there be no promotions

the occasion in the text, Hwan
dispensed with some of those ceremonies. 命 was the term appropriated to the articles of agreement
at such solemn assemblies, indicating
that they were enjoined by the
emperor. 樹子,—"the son who has
been tree-ed," i. e., set up. 賓,—
"guests," officers from other
countries. 士 無 世 官,—"officers
no hereditary offices"; see I, Pt. II,
v, 3. 取 士 必 得＝必 得 其 人. 無
曲 防,—"no crooked embankments."
曲 has a moral application. No embankments must be made selfishly
to take the water from others, or
to inundate them. 無 遏 糴,—"do
not repress the sale of grain," i. e.,

今之諸侯之罪人也。

皆逢君之惡故曰今之大夫、

逢君之惡其罪大今之大夫、

之罪人也。長君之惡其罪小、

此五禁故曰今之諸侯五霸

俊言歸于好今之諸侯皆犯

告曰凡我同盟之人旣盟之

without *first* announcing them *to the emperor*.' It was *then* said, 'All we who have united in this agreement shall hereafter maintain amicable relations.' The princes of the present day all violate these five prohibitions, and therefore I say that the princes of the present day are sinners against the five chiefs.

4. "The crime of him who connives at, and aids, the wickedness of his prince is small, but the crime of him who anticipates and excites that wickedness is great. The officers of the present day all go to meet their sovereigns' *wickedness*, and therefore I say that the great officers of the present day are sinners against the princes."

to other states in famine or distress. 封,—"appointments," to territory or to office. 4. 長君之惡,—"to lengthen the wickedness of the ruler," i. e., to connive at and to aid it. 逢君之惡,—"to meet the wickedness of the ruler," i. e., to anticipate and excite it.

魯欲使愼子爲

將軍孟子曰不教

民而用之謂之殃

民、殃民者、不容於

堯舜之世。一戰勝

齊、遂有南陽、然且

CHAPTER VIII. 1. *The prince of* Loo wanted to make the minister Shin commander of his army.

2. Mencius said, "To employ an uninstructed people *in war* may be said to be destroying the people. A destroyer of the people would not have been tolerated in the times of Yaou and Shun.

. 3. "Though by a single battle you should subdue Ts'e, and get possession of Nan-yang, the thing ought not to be done."

CH. 8. MENCIUS'S OPPOSITION TO THE WARLIKE AMBITION OF THE PRINCE OF LOO AND HIS MINISTER SHIN KŬH-LE. 1. At this time Loo wanted to take advantage of difficulties in Ts'e and get possession of Nan-yang. That was the name of the region on the south of Mount T'ae, which had originally belonged to Loo. On the north of the mountain was the territory of Ts'e. Between the two states there had been frequent struggles for the district, which the duke P'ing of Loo (平 公) now hoped to recover. Shin, below, calls himself Kŭh-le, but some say that that was the name of a Mihist under whom he had studied. His proper name was Taou (到). He was a native of 趙, and not of Loo, but having a reputation for military skill, the duke of Loo wished to employ his services. 將 軍, now the common term for general, appears to have come into vogue, about Mencius's time. In the text it = "commander in chief." 2. Comp. Con. Ana., XIII, xxx.—We may infer from this par. that Shin had himself been the adviser of the

不可。慎子勃然不悅、曰、此

則滑釐所不識也。曰、吾明

告子、天子之地方千里、不

千里、不足以待諸侯、諸侯

之地、方百里、不百里、不足

以守宗廟之典籍。周公之

封於魯爲方百里也、地非

不足、而儉於百里、太公之

4.　Shin changed countenance, and said in displeasure, "This is what I, Kŭh-le, do not understand."

5.　*Mencius* said, "I will lay the case plainly before you. The territory appropriated to the emperor is one thousand li square. Without a thousand li, he would not have sufficient for his entertainment of the princes. The territory appropriated to a How is one hundred li square. Without one hundred li, he would not have sufficient wherewith to observe the statutes kept in his ancestral temple.

6.　"When Chow-kung was invested with *the principality of* Loo, it was a hundred li square. The territory was indeed enough, but it was not more than one hundred li. When T'ae-kung was invested with the

projected enterprise. 5. 宗廟之典籍,—"the statute records of the ancestral temple." Those records prescribed every thing to be observed in the public sacrifices, interviews with other princes, etc., and were kept in the temple. 6. Comp. Con. Ana., VI, xxii. 儉,—"sparingly,"=

道、志於仁而已。

子之事君也、務引其君以當

不爲、況於殺人以求之乎君

徒取諸彼以與此、然且仁者

作、則魯在所損乎、在所益乎。

方百里者五、子以爲有王者

非不足也、而儉於百里今魯

封於齊也、亦爲方百里也、地

principality of Ts'e, it was one hundred li square. The
territory was indeed enough, but it was not more than
one hundred li.

7. "Now Loo is five times one hundred li square.
If a true imperial ruler were to arise, whether do you
think that Loo would be diminished or increased by
him?

8. "If it were merely taking the place from the one
*state* to give it to the other, a benevolent man would
not do it;—how much less will he do so, when the end
is to be sought by the slaughter of men!

9. "The way in which a superior man serves his
prince contemplates simply the leading him in the
right path, and directing his mind to benevolence."

only. 8. 徒,—"merely," i. e., if
there were no struggle and no
slaughter in the matter. 9. 當 道
here is quite difft. from the phrase
當 路, in II, Pt. I, i, 1.

能爲君約與國戰必克、今

仁、而求富之、是富桀也。我

民賊也、君不鄉道不志於

今之所謂良臣、古之所謂

我能爲君辟土地、充府庫、

孟子曰、今之事君者曰、

CHAPTER IX. 1. Mencius said, "Those who nowa-days serve their sovereigns say, 'We can for our sovereign enlarge the limits of the cultivated ground, and fill his treasuries and arsenals.' Such persons are nowadays called 'good ministers,' but anciently they were called 'robbers of the people.' If a sovereign follows not the right way, nor has his mind bent on benevolence, to seek to enrich him is to enrich a Kĕĕ.

2. *"Or, they will say*, 'We can for our sovereign form alliances with other states, so that our battles must be successful.' Such persons are nowadays

CH. 9. HOW THE MINISTERS OF MENCIUS'S TIME PANDERED TO THEIR SOVEREIGNS' THIRST FOR WEALTH AND POWER. 1. 辟 (=闢) 土 地.—it is to be understood that this was to be done; at the expense of the people, taking their commons from them, and making them labor. Otherwise, it does not seem objectionable.—Chaou K'e, however, gives the phrase another meaning' making it= 侵 小 國, "appropriate small states," but this is contrary to analogous passages, and confounds this par. with the next; compare IV, Pt. I, xv. 2. 約 與 國,—"ally with *other* states." Here Chaou K'e differs again, making 約=期, "to determine beforehand," "undertake," and joining 與 國 戰, "undertake in

之所謂良臣、古之所謂民賊

也、君不鄉道不志於仁、而求

爲之強戰是輔桀也。由今之

道、無變今之俗、雖與之天下、

不能一朝居也。

白圭曰吾欲二十而取一、

called 'good ministers,' but anciently they were called 'robbers of the people.' If a sovereign follows not the right way, nor has his mind directed to benevolence, to seek to enrich him is to enrich a Kĕĕ.

3. "Although a prince, pursuing the path of the present day, and not changing its practices, were to have the empire given to him, he could not retain it for a single morning."

CHAPTER X. 1. Pih Kwei said, "I want to take a twentieth *of the produce only as the tax.* What do you think of it?"

fighting with hostile countries to conquer." This also is an inferior construction. 3. 朝居=朝居其位, "occupy the position for a morning."
CH. 10. AN ORDERED STATE CAN ONLY SUBSIST WITH A PROPER SYSTEM OF TAXATION, AND THAT ORIGINATING WITH YAOU AND SHUN IS THE PROPER ONE FOR CHINA. 1. Pih Kwei, styled

Tan (see next ch.), was a man of Chow, ascetic in his own habits, and fond of innovations. Hence the suggestion in this chapter.—So, Chaou K'e, and Choo He has followed him. The author of the 四書拓餘說, however, contends that the Pih Kwei, described as above, on the authority of the "Historical Records," 列傳,

幣帛饔飱殮無百官有司、

宗廟祭祀之禮無諸侯

惟黍生之、無城郭宮室

用也。曰、夫貉五穀不生、

則可乎。曰不可、器不足

道也。萬室之國一人陶、

何如。孟子曰子之道、貉

2. Mencius said, "Your way would be that of the Mih.

3. "In a country of ten thousand families, would it do to have *only* one potter?" *Kwei* replied, "No. The vessels would not be enough to use."

4. *Mencius* went on, "In Mih *all* the five kinds of grain are not grown; it only produces the millet. There are no fortified cities, no edifices, no ancestral temples, no ceremonies of sacrifice; there are no princes requiring presents and entertainments; there is no system of officers with their various subordinates. On

lxix, was not the same here introduced. See that Work, *in loc.* 2. 貉 or 貊 was a common name for the barbarous tribes on the north. They were a pastoral people, and the climate of their country was cold. No doubt their civilization was inferior to that of China, but Mencius's account of them must be taken with allowance. 4. 城郭,—see II, Pt. II, i, 2. 宮室 go together as a general designation of edifices, called 宮, as "four-walled and roofed," and 室 (實) as furnished. So 祭 祀 go together as synonymous, and also 幣 帛, "pieces of silk, given as presents." 饔,—"the morning meal," 飱,—"the evening meal": together═

者、大桀小桀也。

貉也、欲重之於堯舜之道

之於堯舜之道者大貉小

以爲國況無君子乎。欲輕

何其可也。陶以寡且不可

中國、去人倫、無君子、如之

故二十取一而足也。今居

these accounts a tax of one twentieth of the produce is sufficient *there*.

5. "But now it is the Middle Kingdom that we live in. To banish the relationships of men, and have no superior men;—how can such a state of things be thought of?

6. "With but few potters a kingdom cannot subsist;—how much less can it subsist without men of a higher rank than others?

7. "If we wish to make the taxation lighter than the system of Yaou and Shun, we shall just have a great Mih and a small Mih. If we wish to make it heavier, we shall just have the great Këĕ and the small Këĕ."

"entertainments." 5, 6. 君子, 一 referring to the 百官, 有司. 7. The meaning is, that, under such systems China would become in the one case a copy of the Mih, and in the other of its state under the tyrant Këĕ.

也吾子過矣。

水者洪水也仁人之所惡

爲壑水逆行謂之洚水洚

四海爲壑今吾子以鄰國

治水水之道也是故禹以

於禹孟子曰子過矣禹之

白圭曰丹之治水也愈

CHAPTER XI. 1. Pih Kwei said, "My management of the waters is superior to that of Yu."

2. Mencius replied, "You are wrong, sir. Yu's regulation of the waters was according to the laws of water.

3. "He therefore made the four seas their receptacle, while you make the neighboring states their receptacle.

4. "Water flowing out of its channels is called an inundation. Inundating waters are a vast *waste* of water, and what a benevolent man detests. You are wrong, my good sir."

CH. 11. PIH KWEI'S PRESUMPTUOUS IDEA THAT HE COULD REGULATE THE WATERS BETTER THAN YU DID. 1. There had been some partial inundations, where the services of Pih Kwei were called in and he had reduced them by turning the waters into other states, saving one at the expense of injuring others. 2. 水之道 =順水之性. 4. See III, Pt. II, ix, 3, but 洪水 has there a particular application.

曰、否然則奚爲喜而不寐。

有知慮乎。曰否多聞識乎。

孫丑曰樂正子強乎。曰、否。

子曰、吾聞之喜而不寐。公

魯欲使樂正子爲政、孟

執。

孟子曰、君子不亮、惡乎

CHAPTER XII. Mencius said, "If a scholar have not faith, how shall he take a firm hold *of things?*"

CHAPTER XIII. 1. *The prince of* Loo wanting to commit the administration of his government to the disciple Yŏ-ching, Mencius said, "When I heard of it, I was so glad that I could not sleep."

2. Kung-sun Ch'ow asked, "Is Yŏ-ching a man of vigor?" and was answered, "No." "Is he wise in council?" "No." "Is he possessed of much information?" "No."

3. "What, then, made you so glad that you could not sleep?"

CH. 12. FAITH IN PRINCIPLES NECESSARY TO FIRMNESS IN ACTION. 亮 used as 諒. Choo He explains it by 信.

CH. 13. OF WHAT IMPORTANCE TO A MINISTER—TO GOVERNMENT—IT IS TO LOVE WHAT IS GOOD. 1. 爲政,— "to administer the government,"

as in ch. vi, 3. 2. 有知慮乎,—知 is in the low. 3rd tone;—"has he wisdom and deliberation?"—The three gifts mentioned here were those considered most important to government in that age, and Kung-sun Ch'ow knowing Yo-ching to be deficient in them, put his questions

千里之外、則讒諂面諛之人

色距人於千里之外、士止於

既已知之矣、訑訑之聲音顏

苟不好善、則人將曰訑訑予

將輕千里而來告之以善夫

乎。夫苟好善、則四海之内、皆

曰、好善優於天下、而况魯國

曰、其爲人也好善好善足乎。

4. "He is a man who loves what is good."

5. "Is the love of what is good sufficient?"

6. "The love of what is good is more than a sufficient qualification for the government of the empire;—how much more is it so for the state of Loo!

7. "If *a minister* love what is good, all within the four seas will count one thousand li but a small distance, and will come and lay their good thoughts before him.

8. "If he do not love what is good, men will say, 'How self-conceited he looks? *He is saying to himself*, I know it.' The language and looks of that self-conceit will keep men off at a distance of one thousand li. When good men stop one thousand li off, calumniators, flatterers, and sycophants will make their appearance.

accordingly. 4. On this par. it is said in the 日 講: "In the administration of govt., the most excellent quality is without prejudice and dispassionately (虛 中) to receive what is good. Now in regard to all good words and good actions, Yŏ-ching in his heart sincerely loves them." 5. 足 is what is simply sufficient. 優 is what is sufficient and more. 8. 訑 訑, as defined by Choo He, is—自 足 其 智, 不 嗜 善 言 之 貌, "the appearance of being satisfied with one's own knowledge, and having no relish for good words." 士＝善 人.

之禮貌未衰言弗行也、則去之。

敬以有禮言將行其言、也觀

孟子曰、所就三、所去三。迎之致

齏陳子曰、古之君子、何如則仕。

治、可得乎。

至矣、與讒諂面諛之人居、國欲

When a minister lives among calumniators, flatterers, and sycophants, though he may wish the state to be well governed, is it possible for it to be so?"

CHAPTER XIV. 1. The disciple Ch'in said, "What were the principles on which superior men of old took office?" Mencius replied, "There were three cases in which they accepted office, and three in which they left it.

2. "If received with the utmost respect and all polite observances, and they could say *to themselves* that the prince would carry their words into practice, then they took office with him. *Afterwards,* although there might be no remission in the polite demeanor of the prince, if their words were not carried into practice, they would leave him.

CH. 14. GROUNDS OF TAKING AND LEAVING OFFICE. Comp. V, Pt. II, iv. The three cases mentioned here are respectively the 行可之仕, the 際可, and the 公養, of that place. 1. The Ch'in is the Ch'in Tsin, II, Pt. II, iii. 2. 迎 is simply＝接待,

亦可受也免死而已矣。

餓於我土地吾恥之周之、

道又不能從其言也使饑

聞之曰吾大者不能行其

不食饑餓不能出門戶君

衰則去之其下朝不食夕

致敬以有禮則就之禮貌

其次雖未行其言也迎之

3. "The second case was that in which, though *the prince could not be expected* at once to carry their words into practice, yet being received by him with the utmost respect, they took office with him. But afterwards, if there was a remission in his polite demeanor, they would leave him.

4. "The last case was that of *the superior man* who had nothing to eat, either morning or evening, and was so famished that he could not move out of his door. If the prince, on hearing of his state, said, 'I must fail in the great point,—that of carrying his doctrines into practice, neither am I able to follow his words, but I am ashamed to allow him to die of want in my country.' The assistance offered in such a case might be received, but not beyond what was sufficient to avert death."

not "to go out to meet." 3. 雖未 行、其 言 is to be understood as thought in the scholar's mind, corresponding to 言 將 行 其 言 in the prec. par. In the 日 講, indeed, the 言 there is made to be the language of the ruler, but see the gloss of the 備旨, *in loc.* 4. The assistance is in the shape of employment offered. -If not, then 不 可 受 would not be a case of 就 仕. -

先苦其心志勞其筋
降大任於是人也、必
里奚舉於市故天將
士、孫叔敖舉於海、百
鹽之中、管夷吾舉於
築之間、膠鬲舉於魚
畝之中、傅說舉於版
孟子曰、舜發於畎

CHAPTER XV. 1. Mencius said, "Shun rose from among the channeled fields. Foo Yuĕ was called to office from the midst of his building frames; Kaou-kih, from his fish and salt; Kwan E-woo, 'from the hands of his jailer; Sun-shun Gaou, from *his hiding by* the seashore; and Pih-le He, from the market place.

2. "Thus, when Heaven is about to confer a great office on any man, it first exercises his mind with suffering, and his sinews and bones with toil. It

CH. 15. TRIALS AND HARDSHIPS THE WAY IN WHICH HEAVEN PREPARES MEN FOR GREAT SERVICES. 1. With Shun, Kwan E-woo, and Pih-le He, the student must be familiar. Foo Yŭe,—see the Shoo-king, Pt. IV, Bk. vii, where it is related that the emperor Kaou-tsung having "dreamt that God gave him a good assistant," caused a picture of the man he had seen in his dream to be made, and "search made for him through the empire, when he was found dwelling in the wilderness of Foo-yen (傅 巖 之 野)." In the "Historical Records," it is said the surname was given in the dream as 傅, and the name as 悅. Kaou-kih is mentioned, II, Pt. I, i, 8, where it is said in the notes that his worth, when living in retirement, was discovered by King Wan. He was then selling fish and salt, and on Wan's recommendation was raised to office by the last emperor of Yin, to whose fortunes he continued faithful. Sun-shuh Gaou was prime minister to Ch'wang of Ts'oo, the last of the five chiefs of the princes. So much is beyond dispute, but the circumstances of his elevation, and the family to which he belonged, are uncertain. See the 四 書 撮 餘 說, *in loc.* 版 築,—"planks and building." Most of the houses in China are built of earth and mortar beaten together within a movable frame, in which the walls are formed. 舉 士,—士 is the officer who was in

則無敵國外患者、國恆亡。

後喩入、則無法家拂士、出、

而後作、徵於色發於聲、而

然後能改困於心衡於慮、

性曾益其所不能人恆過、

拂亂其所爲所以動心忍

骨、餓其體膚、空乏其身行

exposes his body to hunger, and subjects him to extreme poverty. It confounds his undertakings. By all these methods it stimulates his mind, hardens his nature, and supplies his incompetencies.

3. "Men for the most part err, and are afterwards able to reform. They are distressed in mind and perplexed in their thoughts, and then they arise to vigorous reformation. When things have been evidenced in men's looks, and set forth in their words, then they understand them.

4. "If a prince have not about his court families attached to the laws and worthy counselors, and if abroad there are not hostile states or other external calamities, his kingdom will generally come to ruin.

charge of him. 2. 餓其體膚,—"hunger his members and skin." 空乏其身,—"empty his person." 行拂, 云云;—"as to his doings, confound what he is doing." 行 is taken as 行事, and 爲 as 心所謀爲. 曾, —used for 增. 3. The same thing holds true of ordinary men. They are improved by difficulties. 衡,—used for 橫. 徵於色,云云,—

the meaning is, that, though most men are not quick of apprehension, yet when things are clearly before them, they can lay hold of them. 4. The same thing is true of a state. 法家,—"law families," i. e., old families to whom the laws of the state are familiar and dear. 拂 is used for 弼. Such families and officers will stimulate the prince's

亦教誨之而已

之教誨也者、是

多術矣、予不屑

孟子曰、教亦

也。

患、而死於安樂

然後知生於憂

5. "From these things we see how life springs from sorrow and calamity, and death from ease and pleasure."

CHAPTER XVI. Mencius said, "There are many arts in teaching. I refuse, as inconsistent with my character, to teach a man, but I am only thereby still teaching him."

mind by their lessons and remonstrances, and foreign danger will rouse him to carefulness and exertion.

CH. 16. HOW A REFUSAL TO TEACH MAY BE TEACHING. The 亦 in 亦教 is not without its force, but we can hardly express it in a translation. 予不屑之教誨＝予不屑教誨之. The 者 carries us on to the next clause for an explanation of what has been said.

## BOOK VII

### TSIN SIN.　PART I

則　知　其　心　曰、　 　　盡
知　其　性　者、　盡　孟　句　心
天　性、　也、　知　其　子　上　章

CHAPTER I. 1. Mencius said, "He who has exhausted all his mental constitution knows his nature. Knowing his nature, he knows Heaven.

TITLE OF THIS BOOK.—Like the previous books, this is named from the commencing words—盡 心, "The exhausting of all the mental constitution." It contains many more chapters than any of them, being, for the most part, brief enigmatical sentences, conveying Mencius's views of human nature. It is more abstruse also, and the student will have much difficulty in satisfying himself that he has really hit the exact meaning of the philosopher. The author of the 四 書 味 根 錄 says: "This book was made by Mencius in his old age. Its style is terse, and its meaning deep, and we cannot discover an order of subjects in its chapters. He had completed the previous six Books, and this grew up under his pencil, as his mind was affected, and he was prompted to give expression to his thoughts. The first chapter may be regarded, however, as a compendium of the whole."

CH. 1. BY THE STUDY OF OURSELVES WE COME TO THE KNOWLEDGE OF HEAVEN, AND HEAVEN IS SERVED BY OUR OBEYING OUR NATURE. 1. 盡 其 心 is, I conceive, to make one's self acquainted with all his mind, to arrest his consciousness, and ascertain what he is. This of course gives a man the knowledge of his nature, and as he is the creature of Heaven, its attributes must be corresponding. It is much to be wished that instead of the term Heaven, vague and indefinite, Mencius had simply said, "God." I can get no other meaning from this par. Choo He, however, and all his school, say that there is no work or labor in 盡 其 心; that it is the 知 至 of the Confucian chapter in the "Superior Learning," according to their view of it; that all the labor is in 知 其 性, which is the 物 格 of that chapter. If this be correct, we should translate: "He who completely develops his mental constitution, has known (come to know) his nature," but I cannot construe

命　之　修　妖　以　養　矣。
也。　所　身　壽　事　其　存
　　以　以　不　天　性、　其
　　立　俟　貳　也。　所　心、

2. "To reserve one's mental constitution, and nourish one's nature, is the way to serve Heaven.

3. "When neither a premature death nor long life causes a man any double-mindedness, but he waits in the cultivation of his personal character *for whatever issue;*—this is the way in which he establishes his *Heaven*-ordained being."

the words so. 2. The "preservation" is the holding fast what we have from Heaven, and the "nourishing" is the acting in harmony therewith, so that the "serving Heaven" is just being and doing what it has intimated in our constitution to be its will concerning us. 3. 命 is our nature, according to the opening words of the *Chung Yung*,—天 命 之 謂 性. 立 is to be taken as an active verb. 不 貳＝不 疑, "causes no doubts," i. e., no doubts as to what is to be done. 俟 之,—之 referring to 妖 壽.—It may be well to give the views of Chaou K'e on this chapter. On the first paragraph he says: "To the nature there belong the principles of benevolence, righteousness, propriety, and knowledge. The mind is designed to regulate them (心 以 制 之), and having the distinction of being correct, a man can put forth all his mind to think of doing good, and then he may be said to know his nature. When he knows his nature, he knows that the way of Heaven considers what is good to be excellent." On the second par. he says: "When one is able to preserve his mind, and to nourish his correct nature, he may be called a man of perfect virtue (仁 人). The way of Heaven loves life, and the perfect man also loves life. The way of Heaven is without partiality, and only approves of the virtuous. Thus the acting *of the perfect man* agrees with Heaven, and hence it is said,—this is the way by which he serves Heaven." On the third par. he says: "The perfect man in his conduct is guided by one law. Although he sees that some who have gone before him have been short-lived, and some long-lived, he never has two minds, or changes his way. Let life be short as that of Yen Yuen, or long as that of the duke of Shaou, he refers either case equally to the appointment of Heaven, and cultivates and rectifies his own person to wait for that. It is in this way he establishes the root *of Heaven's* appointments" (此 所 以 立 命 之 本). These explanations do not throw light upon the text, but they show how that may be treated independently of the school of Choo He. And the equal unsatisfactoriness of his interpretation may well lead the student—the foreign student especially—to put forth his strength on the study of the text more than on the commentaries.

者、正命也。桎梏死　盡其道而死者、　立乎嚴牆之下。　是故知命者、不　命也、順受其正。　孟子曰、莫非

CHAPTER II. 1. Mencius said, "There is an appointment for everything. A man should receive submissively what may be correctly ascribed thereto.

2. "Therefore, he who has the true idea of what is *Heaven's* appointment will not stand beneath a precipitous wall.

3. "Death sustained in the discharge of one's duties may correctly be ascribed to the appointment *of Heaven.*

4. "Death under handcuffs and fetters cannot correctly be so ascribed."

CH. 2. MAN'S DUTY AS AFFECTED BY THE DECREES OR APPOINTMENTS OF HEAVENS. WHAT MAY BE CORRECTLY ASCRIBED THERETO AND WHAT NOT. Choo He says this is a continuation of the last chapter, developing the meaning of the last paragraph. There is a connection between the chapters, but 命 is here taken more widely, as extending not only to man's nature, but all the events that befall him. 正 命,— "the correct appointment," i. e., that which is directly the will of Heaven. No consequence flowing from evil or careless conduct is to be understood as being so. Choo He's definition is—莫 之 致 而 至 者 乃 爲 正 命, "that which comes without being brought on is the correct appointment."—Chaou K'e says there are three ways of speaking about the appointments or decrees of Heaven. Doing good and getting good is called 受 命, "receiving what is appointed." Doing good and getting evil is called 遭 命, "encountering what is appointed." Doing evil and getting evil is called 隨 命, "following after what is appointed." It is only the first of these cases that is spoken of in the text. It must be borne in mind, however, that by 命 here Ch'aou understands death, and that only, and we should acquiesce in this, if there did not seem to be a connection between this chapter and the preceding. 2. 知 命 者,—he who knows or has the true notion of, etc. 巖, "precipitous" and likely to fall. 4. The fetters are understood to be those of an evildoer. 桎 are fetters for the hands, and 梏 those for the feet.

孟子曰、求則得之舍、則
失之、是求有益於得也、求
在我者也。求之有道、得之
有命、是求無益於得也、求
在外者也。
孟子曰、萬物皆備於我

CHAPTER III. 1. Mencius said, "When we get by our seeking and lose by our neglecting;—in that case seeking is of use to getting, and the things sought for are those which are in ourselves.

2. "When the seeking is according to the proper course, and the getting is *only* as appointed;—in that case the seeking is of no use to getting, and the things sought are without ourselves."

CHAPTER IV. 1. Mencius said, "All things are already complete in us.

CH. 3. VIRTUE IS SURE TO BE GAINED BY SEEKING IT, BUT RICHES AND OTHER EXTERNAL THINGS NOT. This general sentiment is correct, but truth is sacrificed to the point of the antithesis, when it is said in the second case that seeking is of *no* use to getting. The things "in ourselves" are benevolence, righteousness, propriety, and knowledge, the endowments proper of our nature. The things "without ourselves" are riches and dignities. The proper course to seek these is that ascribed to Confucius, *advancing according to propriety, and retiring according to righteousness,* but yet they are not at our command and control.

CH. 4. MAN IS FITTED FOR, AND HAPPY IN, DOING GOOD, AND MAY PERFECT HIMSELF THEREIN. 1. This par. is quite mystical. The all things are taken only as the *principles* of all things, which all things moreover are only the relations of society. If we extend them farther, we only get

恥、無恥之恥、無恥矣。

也。

孟子曰人不可以無

由之而不知其道者衆

焉、習矣、而不察焉、終身

孟子曰行之而不著

彊恕而行、求仁莫近焉。

矣。反身而誠、樂莫大焉。

2. "There is no greater delight than to be conscious of sincerity on self-examination.

3. "If one acts with a vigorous effort at the law of reciprocity, when he seeks for *the realization of* perfect virtue, nothing can be closer than his approximation to it."

CHAPTER V. 1. Mencius said, "To act without understanding, and to do so habitually without examination, pursuing the proper path all the life without knowing its nature;—this is the way of multitudes."

CHAPTER VI. Mencius said, "A man may not be without shame. When one is ashamed of having been without shame, he will *afterwards* not have *occasion for* shame."

embarrassed. 2. The 誠 here is that so largely treated of in the Chung Yung. 3. 恕 is the judging of others by ourselves, and acting accordingly. Comp. the Doctrine of the Mean, xiii, 3.

CH. 5. HOW MANY ACT WITHOUT THOUGHT. Comp. Conf. Ana., VIII, ix. 行 之, 由 之,—之 is to be understood of 道, but 其 道="its nature," its propriety, which is the object of 著, and its grounds, which is the object of 察. Choo He defines 著 as 知之明, "knowing clearly," and 察 as 識之精, "knowing minutely and exactly." "There is much activity," says the 備 旨, "in the two verbs." This use of 著 is not common.

CH. 6. THE VALUE OF THE FEELING OF SHAME. The last 恥=shameful conduct.

獨不然、樂其道而忘人

善而忘勢、古之賢士、何

孟子曰、古之賢王好

若人有。

用恥焉。不恥不若人、何

矣。爲機變之巧者、無所

孟子曰、恥之於人大

CHAPTER VII. 1. Mencius said, "The sense of shame is to a man of great importance.

2. "Those who form contrivances and versatile schemes distinguished for their artfulness, do not allow their sense of shame to come into action.

3. "When one differs from other men in not having this sense of shame, what will he have in common with them?"

CHAPTER VIII. 1. Mencius said, "The able and virtuous monarchs of antiquity loved virtue and forgot power. And shall an exception be made of the able and virtuous scholars of antiquity, that they did not do the same? They delighted in their own principles, and were oblivious of the power of princes.

---

CH. 7. THE SAME SUBJECT. The former ch., it is said, was by way of exhortation (以 勸); this is by way of warning (以 戒). The sec. par. is aimed at the wandering scholars of Mencius's time, who were full of plots and schemes to unite and disunite the various princes. 機,— "springs of motion," "machinery." The third par. may also be trans-lated, "If a man be not ashamed at his being not like other men," etc.

CH. 8. HOW THE ANCIENT SCHOLARS MAINTAINED THE DIGNITY OF THEIR CHARACTER AND PRINCIPLES. 善 is not virtue in the abstract, but the good which they saw in others, in the scholars namely. 勢 is their own "power." As applied to the

之亦囂囂、人不知、亦囂

好遊乎、吾語子遊人知

㊀孟子謂宋句踐曰、子

之乎。

猶不得亟而況得而臣

禮、則不得亟見之見、且

之勢、故王公不致敬盡

Therefore, if kings and dukes did not show the utmost respect, and observe all forms of ceremony, they were not permitted to come frequently and visit them. If they thus found it not in their power to pay them frequent visits, how much less could they get to employ them as ministers?"

CHAPTER IX. 1. Mencius said to Sung Kow-ts'een, "Are you fond, sir, of traveling *to the different courts?* I will tell you about such traveling.

2. "If a prince acknowledge you and follow your counsels, be perfectly satisfied. If no one do so, be the same."

scholars, however, these things have to be reversed. They loved their own virtue (其 道), and forgot the power of men, i. e., of the princes.

CH. 9. HOW A PROFESSIONAL AD-VISER OF THE PRINCES MIGHT BE ALWAYS PERFECTLY SATISFIED. THE EXAMPLE OF ANTIQUITY. 1. Some make the party spoken to in this ch. to be Kow (句 read as 鉤)- ts'een

of Sung. Nothing is known of him, but that he was one of the adventurers, who traveled about tendering their advice to the different princes. 2. To translate 知之 as I have done here, can hardly be called a paraphrase. Choo He, after Chaou K'e, explains 囂囂 as "the appearance of self-possession and freedom from-desire." "Perfectly satisfied"

志澤加於民、不得志、修

民不失望焉。古之人、得

士得己焉、達不離道、故

達不離道。窮不失義、故

囂囂矣。故士窮不失義、

矣。曰、尊德樂義、則可以

囂。曰、何如斯可以囂囂

3. *Kow-ts'een* said, "What is to be done to secure this perfect satisfaction?" Mencius replied, "Honor virtue and delight in righteousness, and so you may *always* be perfectly satisfied.

4. "Therefore, a scholar, though poor, does not let go *his* righteousness; though prosperous, he does not leave *his own* path.

5. "Poor and not letting righteousness go;—it is thus that the scholar holds possession of himself. Prosperous and not leaving the *proper* path;—it is thus that the expectations of the people are not disappointed.

6. "When the men of antiquity realized their wishes, benefits were conferred by them on the people. If they did not realize their wishes, they cultivated

conveys the idea of the phrase. 3. It is to be understood that the "virtue" is that which the scholar has in himself, and the "righteousness" is the course which he pursues.

4. 窮＝人不知之; 達 is the reverse. 5. "Holds possession of himself,"— i. e., has what he chiefly loves and seeks. 6. 古之人,—人＝士,—Choo He observes: "This chapter shows

身見於世、窮、則獨善其身、

達、則兼善天下。

孟子曰、待文王而後興

者、凡民也、若夫豪傑之士、

雖無文王猶興。

孟子曰、附之以韓魏之

家、如其自視欿然、則過人

遠矣。

their personal character, and became illustrious in the world. If poor, they attended to their own virtue in solitude; if advanced to dignity, they made the whole empire virtuous as well."

CHAPTER X. Mencius said, "The mass of men wait for a king Wăn, and then they will receive a rousing impulse. Scholars distinguished *from the mass*, without a king Wăn, rouse themselves."

CHAPTER XI. Mencius said, "Add to a man the families of Han and Wei. If he then look upon himself without being elated, he is far beyond *the mass of* men."

how the scholar, attaching weight to what is internal, and holding what is external light will approve himself good in all places and circumstances."

CH. 10. How PEOPLE SHOULD GET THEIR INSPIRATION TO GOOD IN THEMSELVES. 凡 民,—"all the people," i. e., ordinary people. 豪 傑=俊 傑, in II, Pt. I, v, 1. When a distinction is made between the characters, he who in wisdom is the first of 10,000 men, is called 英; the first of 1,000 is called 俊; the first of 100 is called 豪; the first of 10 is called 傑.

CH. 11. NOT TO BE ELATED BY RICHES IS A PROOF OF SUPERIORITY. Han and Wei,—see I, Pt. I, i, 1, notes. "The families of Han and Wei,"—i. e., the wealth and power of those families. 附, used for 益, "to increase," indicates the externality of the additions. 欿 然 is defined—不 自 滿 足 意, "not being full of and satisfied with one's self."

王者之民、皞皞
之民、驩虞如也、
章孟子曰、霸者
雖死、不怨殺者。
怨、以生道殺民、
道使民雖勞、不
章孟子曰、以佚

CHAPTER XII. Mencius said, "Let the people be employed in the way which is intended to secure their ease, and though they be toiled, they will not murmur. Let them be put to death in the way which is intended to preserve their lives, and though they die, they will not murmur at him who puts them to death."

CHAPTER XIII. 1. Mencius said, "Under a chief, leading all the princes, the people look brisk and cheerful. Under a true sovereign, they have an air of deep contentment.

CH. 12. WHEN A RULER'S AIM IS EVIDENTLY THE PEOPLE'S GOOD, THEY WILL NOT MURMUR AT HIS HARSHEST MEASURES. The first part is explained rightly of toils in agriculture, road making, bridge making, etc., and the second of the administration of justice, where I should prefer thinking that Mencius had the idea of a just war before him Comp. Ana., XX, ii, 2. 佚道,—"a way of ease"; 生道,—"a way of life."

CH. 13. THE DIFFERENT INFLUENCE, EXERCISED BY A CHIEF AMONG THE PRINCES, AND BY A TRUE SOVEREIGN. 1. 虞 is explained in the dict., with reference to this passage, by 樂. It is the same as 娛 and 驩虞=歡娛. 皞皞 is 廣大自得之貌, "the appearance of enlargement and self-possession." In illustration of the condition of the people under a true sovereign, commentators generally quote a tradition of their state in the golden age of Yaou, when "entire harmony reigned under heaven, and the lives of the people passed easily away." Then the old men smote the clods, and sang,—日出而作, 日入而息, 鑿井而飲, 耕田而食, 帝力於我何有哉, "At sunrise we rise, and at sunset we rest. We dig our wells and drink; we cultivate our fields and eat.—What is the strength of the emperor

如也。殺之而不怨、

利之而不庸民日

遷善而不知爲之

者夫君子所過者

化、所存者神、上下

與天地同流豈曰、

小補之哉。

2. "Though he slay them, they do not murmur. When he benefits them, they do not think of his merit. From day to day they make progress towards what is good, without knowing who makes them do so.

3. "Wherever the superior man passes through, transformation follows; wherever he abides, his influence is of a spiritual nature. It flows abroad above and beneath, like that of Heaven and Earth. How can it be said that he mends society but in a small way!"

to us?" 2. 庸 is used in the sense of 功, "merit," or meritorious work, and the analogy of the other clauses determines the meaning of 不庸, as in the translation. 3. 君子 has reference to the 王者, par. 1. It is used here in its highest application, = "the sage." 所過, 所存,—the latter phrase is interpreted morally, being = "when he has fixed his mind to produce a result." This is unnecessary. 神,—"spiritual," "mysterious":—the effects are sure and visible, but the operation is hidden. In the influence of Shun in the time of his obscurity, when the plowmen yielded the furrow, and the potters made their vessels all sound, we have an example, it is said, of the 所過者化. In what it is presumed would have been the influence of Confucius, had he been in the position of a ruler, as described, Ana., XIX, xxv, we have an example of the 所存者神. 補之,—as an object for 之, I supply "society." It is understood that a leader of the princes only helps the people in a small way.

所不慮而知者、其良

學而能者、其良能也、

<sup>二</sup>孟子曰人之所不

善教得民心。

民愛之善政得民財、

也善政民畏之善教、

政不如善教之得民

<sup>二</sup>仁聲之入人深也。善

<sup>一</sup>孟子曰仁言不如

CHAPTER XIV. 1. Mencius said, "Kindly words do not enter so deeply into men as a reputation for kindness.

2. "Good government does not lay hold of the people so much as good instructions.

3. "Good government is feared by the people, while good instructions are loved by them. Good government gets the people's wealth, while good instructions get their hearts."

CHAPTER XV. 1. Mencius said, "The ability possessed by men without having been acquired by learning is intuitive ability, and the knowledge possessed by them without the exercise of thought is their intuitive knowledge.

CH. 14. THE VALUE TO A RULER F REPUTATION AND MORAL INFLU-ENCES. Kindly words are but brief, and on an occasion. A reputation for kindness must be the growth of time and of many evidences. With the whole chapter, compare Ana., II, iii.

CH. 15. BENEVOLENCE AND RIGHT-EOUSNESS ARE NATURAL TO MAN, PARTS OF HIS CONSTITUTION. 1. I translate 良 by "intuitive," but it serves also to denote the "good-ness" of the nature of man. Choo He so defines it: 良者本然之善

所以異於深山之野人者

中、與木石居、與鹿豕遊、其

𦥑孟子曰、舜之居深山之

義也、無他、達之天下也。

敬其兄也親親仁也、敬長、

其親也、及其長也無不知

知也。孩提之童、無不知愛

2. "Children carried in the arms all know to love their parents, and when they are grown *a little*, they all know to love their elder brothers.

3. "Filial affection for parents is *the working of* benevolence. Respect for elders is *the working of* righteousness. There is no other reason *for those feelings;*— they belong to all under heaven."

CHAPTER XVI. Mencius said, "When Shun was living amid the deep retired mountains, dwelling with the trees and rocks, and wandering among the deer and swine, the difference between him and the rude inhabitants of those remote hills appeared very small.

也. 2. 孩 is defined in the dict. by 小兒笑, "an infant smiling." When an infant has reached to this, then it is 人所提挈, "taken by people in their arms." 3. 達之天下 must be supplemented by 無不同, "extend them (carry the inquiry about them) to all under heaven, and they are the same." This is just laying down universality as a test that those feelings are intuitive to us. Chaou K'e, however, explains differently: "Those who wish to do good, have nothing else to do but to extend these ways of children to all under heaven."

CH. 16. HOW WHAT SHUN WAS DISCOVERED ITSELF IN HIS GREATEST

孟子曰、人之有德慧術

矣。

孟子曰、無爲其所不爲、
無欲其所不欲、如此而已

能禦也。

善行、若決江河、沛然莫之

幾希、及其聞一善言、見一

But when he heard a single good word, or saw a single good action, he was like a stream or a river bursting its banks, and flowing out in an irresistible flood."

CHAPTER XVII. Mencius said, "Let a man not do what *his own sense of righteousness tells him* not to do, and let him not desire what his *sense of righteousness tells him not* to desire;—to act thus is all he has to do."

CHAPTER XVIII. 1. Mencius said, "Men who are possessed of intelligent virtue and prudence in

OBSCURITY. 決江河,—the 決 is the water itself bursting its banks; the agency of man in the matter is not to be supposed. So in the 備旨— 決江河謂江之決也, 非人決之也. 江河 may be taken generally, or with special reference to the Yangtze and the Yellow River. I prefer the former.

CH. 17. A MAN HAS BUT TO OBEY THE LAW IN HIMSELF. The text is literally—"Not doing what he does not do," etc. Much must be supplied to make it intelligible in a translation. Chaou K'e interprets and supplies quite differently: "Let a man not make another do what he does not do himself," etc.

CH. 18. THE BENEFITS OF TROUBLE AND AFFLICTION. Comp. VI, Pt. II, xv. 德 and 慧, 術 and 知 (up. 3rd

知者、恆存乎疢

疾。獨孤臣孽子、

其操心也危、其

慮患也深、故達。

孟子曰、有事

君人者、事是君

則爲容悦者也。

affairs will generally be found to have been in sickness and troubles.

2. "They are the friendless minister and concubine's son, who keep their hearts under a sense of peril, and use deep precautions against calamity. On this account they become distinguished for their intelligence."

CHAPTER XIX. 1. Mencius said, "There are persons who serve the prince;—they serve the prince, that is, for the sake of his countenance and favor.

tone) go together,—"intelligence of virtue, and wisdom of arts." 存 retains its proper meaning of 在, "to be in" 疢 means properly "fever," "any feverish disease," but here 疢疾=distresses generally. 2. 惟,—not joined with 孤, but qualifying the whole sentence. 獨=孤, "fatherless," friendless, not having favor with the sovereign. 孽子 is not the child of one who is a concubine merely, but a concubine in disgrace, or one of a very low rank. 孽 is taken as if it were 蘖, the shooting forth of a tree after it has been cut down.

CH. 19. FOUR DIFFERENT CLASSES OF MINISTERS. 1. 有事君人者,= the 人 is joined with 有, and not to be taken with 君. Mencius speaks of 人, "persons," and not 臣 "ministers," to indicate his contempt. 爲容悦 is difficult. The common view is what I have given. 容是使君容我, 悦是使君悦我, "yung is to cause the prince to bear with—countenance—them; yuĕ is to cause the prince to be pleased with them." In this case, 爲 should be read in low. 3rd tone. It is said, however, to have 專務意, "the idea of aiming

樂、而王天下不與存　孟子曰君子有三　也。　人者、正己而物正者　而後行之者也。有大　民者、達可行於天下、　社稷爲悅者也。有天　有安社稷臣者、以安

2. "There are ministers who seek the tranquillity of the state, and find their pleasure in securing that tranquillity.

3. "There are those who are the people of Heaven. They, *judging that*, if they were in office, they could carry out *their principles*, throughout the empire, proceed *so* to carry them out.

4. "There are those who are great men. . They rectify themselves and others are rectified."

CHAPTER XX. 1. Mencius said, "The superior man has three things in which he delights, and to be ruler over the empire is not one of them.

exclusively." 2. 社稷臣, see Con. Ana., XVI, i, 2. 悅, it will be seen, is not used here, as in the last par. 3. 天民,—"Heaven's people," those who seem dearer to Heaven and more favored by it. Comp. V, I, Pt. I, vii, 5. 4. "The great men," are the sages, the highest style of men. 物 is to be understood of persons＝君 民, "the sovereign and the people."—The first class of ministers may be styled the mercenary; the second, the loyal; the third have no selfishness, and they embrace the whole empire in their regards but they have their defined aims to be attained by systematic effort, while the fourth, unconsciously but surely, produce the grandest results.

CH. 20. THE THINGS WHICH THE SUPERIOR MAN DELIGHTS IN. IMPERIAL SWAY IS NOT AMONG THEM. 1. 王天下 is to be taken as simply＝有 天下. The possession of the sovereign sway is indicated, and not the carrying out of the true imperial

君子欲之、所樂不存

孟子曰、廣土衆民、

存焉。

三樂、而王天下不與

育之三樂也君子有

也得天下英才而教

天、俯不怍於人二樂

故、一樂也仰不愧於

焉。父母俱存、兄弟無

2. "That his father and mother are both alive, and that the condition of his brothers affords no cause for anxiety;—this is one delight.

3. "That, when looking up, he has no occasion for shame before Heaven, and, below, he has no occasion to blush before men;—this is a second delight.

4. "That he can get from the whole empire the most talented individuals, and teach and nourish them;—this is the third delight.

5. "The superior man has three things in which he delights, and to be ruler over the empire is not one of them."

CHAPTER XXI. 1. Mencius said, "Wide territory and a numerous people are desired by the superior man, but what he delights in is not here.

principles. 2. 兄 弟 無 故 may be understood of every painful thing in the condition of his brothers, which would distress him. 3. We cannot but attach a personal meaning to "Heaven" here.

CH. 21. MAN'S OWN NATURE THE MOST IMPORTANT THING TO HIM, AND THE SOURCE OF HIS TRUE ENJOYMENT. 1. This describes the condition of the prince of a large state, who has thereby many opportunities

君子所性仁、義、禮、智、

居不損焉、分定故也。

雖大行不加焉、雖窮

性不存焉。君子所性、

海之民、君子樂之、所

焉。中天下而立定四

2. "To stand in the center of the empire, and tranquilize the people within the four seas;—the superior man delights in this, but the highest enjoyment of his nature is not here.

3. "What belongs by his nature to the superior man cannot be increased by the largeness of his sphere of action, nor diminished by his dwelling in poverty and retirement;—for this reason that it is determinately apportioned to him *by Heaven.*

4. "What belongs by his nature to the superior man are benevolence, righteousness, propriety, and

of doing good. 2. This advances on the meaning of the first par. The individual indicated is the emperor, who by his position can benefit the myriads of the people, and therein he feels delight. 所性—what belongs to him by nature. 3. 君子 is not to be interpreted only of the prince of a state or the emperor. Indeed, in the two preceding paragraphs, though the individuals indicated are in those positions, the phrase, as well as here, has its moral significancy. 分 (low. 3rd tone) 定故也,—the nature is complete as given by Heaven. It can only be developed from within. Nothing can be added to it from without. This seems to be the idea.

歸乎來、吾聞西伯善養老

海之濱、聞文王作、與曰、盍

᷑孟子曰伯夷辟紂、居北

體不言而喻。

於面、盎於背、施於四體、四

根於心、其生色也、睟然見

knowledge.　These are rooted in his heart; their growth and manifestation are a mild harmony ˎappearing in the countenance, a rich fullness in the back, and the character imparted to the four limbs. Those limbs understand *to arrange themselves*, without being told."

CHAPTER XXII.　Mencius said, "Pih-e, that he might avoid Chow, was dwelling on the coast of the northern sea when he heard of the rise of King Wăn.　He roused himself and said, "Why should I not go and follow him?　I have heard that the chief of the West knows well how to nourish the old.'

4. 其 生 色 也, extend over all the rest of the par.　生 and 色 are in apposition; 色 is not to be taken as under the government of 生.　The meaning is simply that moral and intellectual qualities indicate themselves in the general appearance and bearing.　睟 然 is explained as 清 和 潤澤之 貌, "the appearance of what is pure, harmonious, moistening, and rich," and 盎 as 豐 厚 盈 溢 之 意, "meaning what is affluent, generous, full, and overflowing."—The whole description is rather strained.

CH. 22.　THE GOVERNMENT OF KING WĂN BY WHICH THE AGED WERE NOURISHED.　1. Comp.　IV, Pt. 1,

五母雞、二母彘、無失其
之、則老者足以衣帛矣、
宅、樹牆下以桑匹婦蠶
人以爲己歸矣五畝之
者、天下有善養老、則仁
乎來、吾聞西伯善養老
濱、聞文王作興曰、盍歸
者、太公辟紂居東海之

T'ae-kung, to avoid Chow, was dwelling on the coast of the eastern sea. When he heard of the rise of King Wăn, he said, 'Why should I not go and follow him? I have heard that the chief of the West knows well how to nourish the old.' If there were a prince in the empire, who knew well how to nourish the old, all men of virtue would feel that he was the proper object for them to gather to.

2. "Around the homestead with its five mow, the space beneath the walls was planted with mulberry trees, with which the women nourished silkworms, and thus the old were able to have silk to wear. *Each family* had five brood hens and two brood sows, which were kept to their *breeding* seasons, and thus

viii, 1. 2. This is to be translated historically, as it describes King Wăn's government. Comp. I, Pt. I, iii, 4. 匹婦, corresponding to 匹夫, below;—"the private woman," "the private man." 蠶之,—"silkwormed them," i. e., nourished silkworms with them. It is observed by 淮南子:"The silkworm eats and does not drink, going through its transformations in twenty-seven days. The wife of the Yellow Emperor (2607–2597 B.C.), whose surname was Se-ling (四陵氏), first taught the people to keep silkworms, and to manage their silk, in order to provide clothes. Future ages sacrifice to her as the 先 蠶." Mencius has not mentioned before

時、老者足以無失肉矣、百
畝之田、匹夫耕之八口之
家、可以無飢矣。所爲西伯
善養老者、制其田里、教之
樹畜導其妻子、使養其老、
五十非帛不煖七十、非肉
不飽、不煖不飽爲之凍餒、
文王之民、無凍餒之老者、
此之謂也。

the old were able to have flesh to eat. The husbandmen cultivated their farms of one hundred mow, and
thus their families of eight mouths were secured
against want.

3. "The expression, 'The chief of the West knows
well how to nourish the old,' refers to his regulation
of the fields and dwellings, his teaching them to
plant *the mulberry* and nourish those animals, and his
instructing the wives and children, so as to make
them nourish their aged. At fifty, warmth cannot be
maintained without silks, and at seventy flesh is
necessary to satisfy the appetite. Persons not kept
warm nor supplied with food are said to be starved
and famished, but among the people of King Wăn,
there were no aged who were starved or famished.
This is the meaning of the expression in question."

the number of brood sows and hens
apportioned to a family. 3. 此之謂
responds to 所謂 . . . 者, at the
beginning. The whole paragraph is

the explanation of that expression,
田里,—里 is the dwelling place, tho
five mow allotted for buildings.

孟子曰、易其田疇薄其
稅斂、民可使富也。食之以
時、用之以禮、財不可勝用
也。民非水火不生活、昏暮
叩人之門戶、求水火、無弗
與者、至足矣、聖人治天下、

CHAPTER XXIII. 1. Mencius said, "Let it be seen to that their fields of grain and hemp are well cultivated, and make the taxes on them light;—so the people may be made rich.

2. "Let it be seen to that the people use their resources of food seasonably, and expend their wealth only on the prescribed ceremonies:—so their wealth will be more than can be consumed.

3. "The people cannot live without water and fire, yet if you knock at a man's door in the dusk of the evening, and ask for water and fire, there is no man who will not give them, such is the abundance of these things. A sage governs the empire so

CH. 23. TO PROMOTE THE VIRTUE OF THE PEOPLE, THE FIRST CARE OF A GOVERNMENT SHOULD BE TO CONSULT FOR THEIR BEING WELL OFF. 1. 易, e,—low. 3rd tone, as 1, Pt. I, v, 3, et al. 田,—"grain fields." 疇,—"flax fields." 易 and 薄 are both in the imper., indicating the work of the ruler or government. So 食 and 用 in par. 2, where 之 may be referred to 財, or the resources arising from the government just indicated. 以 時 may be best explained from I, Pt. I, iu, 3, 4. 以 禮,—the 禮 are the festive occasions of capping, marriage, etc., excepting on which a strict economy should be enforced. 3. Comp. I, Pt. I, vii, 19. 昏 properly denotes half an hour after sunset, or thereabouts. 暮 is 日 晚, "the evening of the day." The time of the request is inopportune, and the manner of it not

遊於聖人之門者、難爲

下、故觀於海者難爲水、

而小魯、登太山而小天

醬孟子曰、孔子登東山

者乎。

如水火、而民焉有不仁

使有菽粟如水火菽粟

as to cause pulse and grain to be as abundant as water and fire. When pulse and grain are as abundant as water and fire, how shall the people be other than virtuous?"

CHAPTER XXIV. 1. Mencius said, "Confucius ascended the eastern hill, and Loo appeared to him small. He ascended the T'ae Mountain, and all beneath the heavens appeared to him small. So, he who has contemplated the sea, finds it difficult to think anything of *other* waters, and he who has wandered in the gate of the sage, finds it difficult to think anything of the words of *others*.

according to propriety;—and yet it is granted. 菽 is the general name for all kinds of peas and beans. 粟,— as in Ana., XII, xi, 3.

CH. 24. HOW THE GREAT DOCTRINES OF THE SAGES ARE TO BE ADVANCED TO BY SUCCESSIVE STEPS. 1. This par. illustrates the greatness of the sage's doctrines. The eastern hill was on the east of the capital of Loo. Some identify it with a small hill, called Fang (防), in the district of K'euhfow (曲阜), at the foot of which Confucius's parents were buried; others with a hill named Mung (蒙), in the district of Pe in the department of Echow. The T'ae Mountain is the chief of the five great

孳孳爲善者舜之徒

蓋孟子曰、鷄鳴而起、

達。

志於道也不成章不

不盈科不行君子之

照焉流水之爲物也、

瀾、日月有明、容光必

言觀水有術、必觀其

2. "There is an art in the contemplation of water. —It is necessary to look at it as foaming in waves. The sun and moon being possessed of brilliancy, their light admitted *even* through an orifice illuminates.

3. "Flowing water is a thing which does not proceed till it has filled the hollows *in its course.* The student who has set his mind on the doctrines *of the sage,* does not advance to them but by completing one lesson after another."

CHAPTER XXV. 1. Mencius said, "He who rises at cockcrowing, and addresses himself earnestly to the practice of virtue, is a disciple of Shun.

mountains of China. It lay on the extreme east of Ta'e, in the present district of T'aengan, in the department of the same name. In 雞 爲 水, 爲 衆, is used as in IV, Pt. I, vii, 5. 2. This illustrates how the very greatness of the sages' doctrines leads to the thought of their elementary principles. Who can look at the foaming waves and suppose they are fortuitous and sourceless? So light penetrating every cranny assures us of its source in the great luminaries. 3. 君 子 is here the aspiring student 章,—"an elegant piece," here for "one lesson," "one truth."

CH. 25. THE DIFFERENT RESULTS TO WHICH THE LOVE OF GOOD AND THE LOVE OF GAIN LEAD. 1. "A disciple of Shun,"—i. e., although such a man may not himself attain to be

也。鷄鳴而起、孳

孳爲利者、蹠之

蹠之分、無他、利

徒也。欲知舜與

與善之閒也。

孟子曰楊子

取爲我、拔一毛

而利天下不爲

2. "He who rises at cockcrowing, and addresses himself earnestly to the pursuit of gain, is a disciple of Chih.

3. "If you want to know what separates Shun from Chih, it is simply this,—the interval between *the thought of* gain and *the thought of* virtue."

CHAPTER XXVI. 1. Mencius said, "The principle of the philosopher Yang was—'Each one for himself.' Though he might have benefited the whole empire by plucking out a single hair, he would not have done it.

a sage, he is treading in the steps of one. 2. Chih (蹠 being used for 跖) is the robber Chih; see III, Pt. II, x, 3. 爲利,—爲 is used here as in ch. xix, 1. I should prefer myself to read it in the low. 3rd tone. It is observed by the scholar Ch'ing that "by *good* and *gain*" are intended the public mind and the selfish mind (公私而已). 3. 利與善之間 is intended to represent the slightness of the separation between them, in its initial principles, and I therefore supply "the thought of."

CH. 26. THE ERRORS OF YANG, MIH, AND TSZE-MOH. OBSTINATE ADHERENCE TO A COURSE WHICH WE MAY DEEM ABSTRACTLY RIGHT IS PERILOUS. 1. "The philosopher Yang,"—see III, Pt. II, ix, 9, 10, 14. Choo He says: 取者僅足之意, "取 conveys the idea of what is barely sufficient." This is not correct, 楊子取＝楊子所取, "that which the philosopher Yang chose, was . . . . In the writings of the scholar Lĕĕ (列子), Bk. VII, we find Yang Choo speaking of Pih-shing Tsze-kaou (伯成子高) that "he would not pull out one of his hairs to benefit others," and when questioned himself "if he would pull out

一而廢百也。

爲其賊道也、舉

也。所惡執一者、

中無權、猶執一

執中爲近之、執

爲之。子莫執中、

頂放踵、利天下

也。墨子兼愛、摩

2. "The philosopher Mih loves all equally. If by rubbing *smooth* his whole body from the crown to the heel. he could have benefited the empire, he would have done it.

3. "Tsze-mŏh holds a medium *between these*. By holding that medium, he is nearer the right. But by holding it without leaving room for the exigency of circumstances, it becomes like their holding their one point.

4. "The reason why I hate that holding to one point is the injury it does to the way *of right principle*. It takes up one point and disregards a hundred others.'"

a hair to hel, an age," declining to reply. 2. The philosopher Mih,—see III, Pt. I, v, 1; Pt. II, ix, 9, 10, 14. We are not to understand the rubbing the body smooth as an isolated act which somehow would benefit the empire. The smoothness would arise from labors undergone for the empire, like those of the great Yu, who wrought and waded till he had worn away all the hair on his legs. See the 集證, *in loc.* 3. Of Tsze-moh nothing seems to be known, but that he belonged to Loo. 執中, must be clearly understood as referring to a mean between the selfishness of Yang Choo and the transcendentalism of Mih Teih. 近之 = 近道, the 道 mentioned in par. 4. The necessity of attending to the exigency of circumstances is illustrated by saying that a case may be conceived when it would be duty to deny a single hair to save the empire, and a case when it would be duty to rub the whole body smooth to do so. The orthodox way (道) of China is to do what is right with reference to the whole circumstances of every case and time.

人不爲憂矣。

渴之害爲心害、則不及

亦皆有害人能無以飢

口腹有飢渴之害、人心

正也飢渴害之也豈惟

者甘飲、是未得飲食之

孟子曰、飢者甘食、渴

CHAPTER XXVII. 1. Mencius said, "The hungry think any food sweet, and the thirsty think the same of any drink, and thus they do not get the right taste of what they eat and drink. The hunger and thirst, in fact, injure *their palate*. And is it only the mouth and belly which are injured by hunger and thirst? Men's minds are also injured by them.

2. "If a man can prevent the evils of hunger and thirst from being any evils to his mind, he need not have any sorrow about not being up with other men."

CH. 27. THE IMPORTANCE OF NOT ALLOWING THE MIND TO BE INJURED BY POVERTY AND A MEAN CONDITION. 1. 甘 perhaps is used adverbially,= "readily"; comp. II, Pt. I, i, 11. The two clauses 是未 and 飢渴 run parallel to each other, the latter being explanatory of the former. 害之,一之＝口腹. With reference to the mind, hunger and thirst stand for poverty and a mean condition. 2. 能無以 ... 爲="can prevent being," 無 being emphatic. 不及人.一人 refers to great men, sages, and worthies. Such a man has himself really advanced far in the path of greatness.

孟子曰、柳下惠、不以三
公易其介。

孟子曰、有爲者辟若掘
井、掘井九軔、而不及泉、猶
爲棄井也。

孟子曰、堯舜性之也、湯

CHAPTER XXVIII. Mencius said, "Hwuy of Lew-hea would not for the three highest offices of state have changed his firm purpose of life."

CHAPTER XXIX. Mencius said, "A man with definite aims to be accomplished may be compared to one digging a well. To dig the well to a depth of seventy-two cubits, *and stop* without reaching the spring, is after all throwing away the well."

CHAPTER XXX. 1. Mencius said, "*Benevolence and righteousness* were natural to Yaou and Shun. T'ang

CH. 28. HWUY OF LEW-HEA'S FIRM-NESS. 1. "Hwuy of Lew-hea,—see II, Pt. I, ix, 2, 3; IV, Pt. II, i, 3, 5; VI, Pt. II, vi. 2. 和, "mildness," "friendly impressibleness," was a characteristic of Hwuy, and Mencius, therefore, notices how it was associated with firmness of mind. The "three *kung*," are the three highest officers about the imperial court, each equal in dignity to the highest rank of nobility.

CH. 29. THAT LABOR ONLY IS TO BE PRIZED WHICH ACCOMPLISHES ITS OBJECT. 辟,—used for 譬. 軔 = 仞,

"eight cubits." In the Ana., XIX, xxiii, 3, it is said, in the note, that the 仞 was seven cubits, while here its length is given as eight. Its exact length is a moot point. See the 集註, *in loc.* 有爲者,—"one who has that which he is doing." The application may be very wide.

CH. 30. THE DIFFERENCE BETWEEN YAOU, SHUN, T'ANG, AND WOO, ON THE ONE HAND, AND THE FIVE CHIEFS, ON THE OTHER, IN RELATION TO BENEVOLENCE AND RIGHTEOUSNESS. 1. 之 no doubt refers to 仁 義, "benevolence and righteousness,"

不賢、則固可放與孟子曰、
悅。賢者之爲人臣也、其君
大悅、太甲賢又反之民大
狎于不順放太甲于桐、民
公孫丑曰、伊尹曰予不
假而不歸惡知其非有也。
武身之也、五霸、假之也久

and Woo made them their own. The five chiefs of the princes feigned them.

2. "Having borrowed them long and not returned them how could it be known they did not own them?"

CHAPTER XXXI. 1. Kung-sun Ch'ow said, "E Yin said, 'I cannot be near *and see him so* disobedient *to reason*,' and therewith he banished T'ae-kĕă to T'ung. The people were much pleased. When T'ae-kĕă became virtuous, he brought him back, and the people were *again* much pleased.

2. "When worthies are ministers, may they indeed banish their sovereigns *in this way*, when they are not virtuous?"

3· Mencius replied, "If they have the same·

and . a translation can hardly be made without supplying those terms. Though Yaou and Shun stood on a higher platform than T'ang and Woo, they agreed in sincerity, which is the common point of contrast between . them and the chiefs. 身之.—"incorporated them"=made them their own. 2. Choo He explains 歸 by 還, "returned." Admitting this, the meaning of 假 passes from "feign-

ing" to "borrowing." He seems to prefer viewing 惡知, as="how could they themselves know?" but I much prefer the view in the translation.

CH. 31. THE END MAY JUSTIFY THE MEANS, BUT THE PRINCIPLE MAY NOT BE EASILY APPLIED. Comp. V, Pt. I, vi, 5. 伊尹曰,—see the Shooking, Pt. IV, v, Bk. I, 9. The words are taken somewhat differently in the comm. on the *king*, but I have

有伊尹之志、則可、無伊
尹之志、則簒也。
盍公孫丑曰、詩曰不素
餐兮、君子之不耕而食、
何也。孟子曰君子居是
國也、其君用之、則安富、
尊榮、其子弟從之、則孝、
悌忠信不素餐兮、孰大
於是。

purpose as E Yin, they may.  If they have not the same purpose, it would be usurpation.''

CHAPTER XXXII.  1. Kung-sun Ch'ow said, "It is said, in the 'Book of Poetry,'

'He will not eat the bread of idleness!'

How is it that *we see* superior men eating without laboring?''  Mencius replied, "When a superior man resides in a country, if its sovereign employ his counsels, he comes to tranquillity, wealth, honor, and glory.  If the young in it follow his instructions, they become filial, obedient to their elders, true-hearted, and faithful.—What greater example can there be than this of not eating the bread of idleness?''

followed what seems the most likely meaning of them.  志 is the purpose, not suddenly formed on an emergency, but the determination and object of the whole life.  It is said— 志 以 其 素 定 者 言.

CH. 32.  THE SERVICES WHICH A SUPERIOR MAN RENDERS TO A COUNTRY ENTITLE HIM, WITHOUT HIS DOING OFFICIAL DUTY, TO SUPPORT.  This is an instance of the oft-repeated insinuation against Mencius, that he was content to be supported by the princes, while he would not take office; comp. III, Pt. I, iv; Pt. II, iv.  詩 曰,—see the She-king, I, ix, Ode VIII.  素=空, "empty," without doing service.  The old comm. and the new differs somewhat in their interpretations of the ode, but they agree in understanding its great lesson to be that people should not be receiving emolument, who do not actively serve their country.  耕.— "plowing," laboring.  This term is suggested from the ode, where it occurs.  用 之,—"use him," i. e., his counsels, not as a minister.

義大人之事備矣。

惡在義是也居仁由

也居惡在仁是也路

非其有而取之非義

矣殺一無罪非仁也、

謂尚志曰仁義而已

事孟子曰尚志曰何

鹽王子墊問曰士何

CHAPTER XXXIII. 1. The king's son, Teen, asked *Mencius*, saying, "What is the business of the *un-employed* scholar?"

2. Mencius replied, "To exalt his aim."

3. *Teen* asked *again*, "What do you mean by exalting the aim?" The answer was, "*Setting it* simply on benevolence and righteousness. *He thinks* how to put a single innocent person to death' is contrary to benevolence; how to take what one has not *a right to* is contrary to righteousness; that one's dwelling should be benevolence; and one's path should be righteousness. When benevolence is the dwelling place *of the heart*, and righteousness the path *of the life*, the business of a great man is complete."

CH. 33. HOW A SCHOLAR PREPARES HIMSELF FOR THE DUTIES TO WHICH HE ASPIRES. 1. Teen was the son of the king of Ts'e. His question probably had reference to the wandering scholars of the time, whose ways he disliked. They were no favorites with Mencius, but he prefers to reply to the prince according to his ideal of the scholar. 3. 仁 . . . 義是也 represent the scholar's thoughts, his nursing his aim. 居惡在,—"the dwelling—what is it?" but in translating we are obliged to drop the direct interrogation. We can hardly take 大人 as in ch. xxx, 4, where it denotes the sages, the very highest style of men. Here it denotes rather the individuals in the various grades of official employment, to which "the scholar" may attain.

可哉。

其小者信其大者奚

亡親戚君臣上下以

羮之義也人莫大焉、

皆信之、是舍簞食豆

與之齊國而弗受人

曰孟子曰、仲子不義、

CHAPTER XXXIV. Mencius said, "Supposing that the kingdom of Ts'e were offered contrary to righteousness, to *Ch'in* Chung, he would not receive it, and all people believe in him, *as a man of the highest worth*. But this is *only* the righteousness which declines a dish of rice or a platter of soup. A man can have no greater *crimes* than to disown his parents and relatives, and the relations of sovereign and minister, superiors and inferiors. How can it be allowed to give a man credit for the great *excellencies* because he possesses a small one?"

CH. 34. HOW MEN JUDGE WRONGLY OF CHARACTER, OVERLOOKING, IN THEIR ADMIRATION OF ONE STRIKING EXCELLENCE, GREAT FAILURES AND DEFICIENCIES. 1. 仲子 is the Ch'in Chung of III, Pt. II, x, which see. I substitute the surname to avoid translating 子. In the translation of 人莫大焉, 焉 is taken as used for 乎, and what follows is under the regimen of 大, as if we were to complete the construction in this way: 人之罪莫大乎亡親，云云. Chaou K'e interprets quite differently: "But what a man should exalt is the greatest virtues, the propriety and righteousness in the great relations of life. He, however, denies them, etc." Perhaps the solecism of taking 焉 for 乎 is better than this. 亡,—used for 無, but as a verb.

所受之也。然則舜如之
夫舜惡得而禁之、夫有
已矣。然則舜不禁與。曰、
如之何。孟子曰、執之而
皐陶爲士瞽瞍殺人、則
豐桃應問曰、舜爲天子、

CHAPTER XXXV. 1. T'aou Ying asked, saying, "Shun being emperor, and Kaou-yaou chief minister of justice, if Koo-sow had murdered a man, what would have been done in the case?"

2. Mencius said, "*Kaou-yaou* would simply have apprehended him."

3. "But would not Shun have forbidden such a thing?"

4. "Indeed, how could Shun have forbidden it? *Kaou-yaow* had received *the law* from *a proper* source."

5. "In that case what would Shun have done?"

CH. 35. WHAT SHUN AND HIS MINISTER OF CRIME WOULD HAVE DONE, IF SHUN'S FATHER HAD COMMITTED A MURDER. 1. T'aou Ying was a disciple of Mencius. This is all that is known of him. 士 is not to be understood here as merely = 士師, Ana., XVIII, ii; XIX. xix. The 士 of Shun's time was the same as the 大司寇 of the Chow dynasty, the officer of crime, under whom were the 士師, and other subordinates. See the 集證, *in loc.* 2. We must understand Kaou-yaou as the nominative to 執. 之 must refer to Koo-sow though common, now understand 法 as the antecedent. No doubt the meaning is, "He would simply have observed the law, and dealt with Koo-sow accordingly." 3. 有所受之,—comp. III, Pt. I, ii, 3. It is here implied that the law of death for murder was the will of Heaven, that being the source to which a reference is made. Kaou-yaou again must be understood as the nominative to 有. He, as minister of crime, had to maintain its authority superior to the imperial will.

何。日舜視棄天下、猶
棄敝蹝也、竊負而逃、
遵海濱而處、終身訴
然樂而忘天下。
𥁕孟子自范之齊、望
見齊王之子、喟然歎
曰居移氣養移體、大
哉居乎、夫非盡人之

6. "Shun would have regarded abandoning the empire as throwing away a worn-out sandal. He would privately have taken *his father* on his back, and retired into concealment, living somewhere along the seacoast. There he would have been all his life, cheerful and happy, forgetting the empire."

CHAPTER XXXVI. 1. Mencius, going from Fan to Ts'e, saw the king of Ts'e's son at a distance, and said with a sigh: "One's position alters the air, *just as* the nurture affects the body. Great is the influence of position! Are not *we* all men's sons?"

CH. 36. HOW ONE'S MATERIAL POSITION AFFECTS HIS AIR, AND MUCH MORE MAY MORAL CHARACTER BE EXPECTED TO DO SO. 1. Fan was a city of Ts'e, a considerable distance from the capital, to which we must understand Mencius was proceeding. It still gives its name to a district of Puhchow (濮州), in the department of Tungch'ang (東昌). Chaou K'e says that Fan was a city of Ts'e, the appanage of the king's sons by his concubines. On this view we should translate 王子 in the plural, but it proceeds from supposing that it was in Fan that Mencius saw the 王子, which the text does not at all necessitate. In 之齊 and 之宋 (p. 3), 之=往. 養=奉養, "revenues." 夫非盡人之子與,—some understand 王子 in the phrase between 夫 and 非, "now, are not king's sons all," etc. But I prefer to understand with Chaou K'e, 凡人與王子, and in

子與孟子曰王子宮室車馬衣服、

多與人同、而王子若彼者其居使

之然也、況居天下之廣居者乎魯

君之宋、呼於垤澤之門、守者曰、此

非吾君也、何其聲之似我君也、此

無他、居相似也。

2. Mencius said, "The residence, the carriages and horses, and the dress of the king's son, are mostly the same as those of other men. That he looks so is occasioned by his position. How much more *should* a *peculiar air distinguish* him whose position is in the wide house of the world!

3. "When the prince of Loo went to Sung, he called out at the T'ĕĕ-chih gate, and the keeper said, 'This is not our prince. How is it that his voice is so like that of our prince?' This was occasioned by nothing but the correspondence of their positions."

English to supply *we* rather than *they.*. 2. 孟子曰 seem here to be superfluous. 天下之廣居,—see III, | Pt. II, iii, 3. 垤澤, "ant-hill marsh," was simply the name of a gate in the capital of Sung.

醫孟子曰、形色天性

無實君子不可虛拘。

之未將者也恭敬而

獸畜之也。恭敬者、幣

豕交之也、愛而不敬、

醫孟子曰、食而弗愛、

CHAPTER XXXVII. 1. Mencius said, "To feed *a scholar* and not love him, is to treat him as a pig. To love him and not respect him, is to keep him as a domestic animal.

2. "Honoring and respecting are what exist before any offering of gifts.

3. "If there be honoring and respecting without the reality of them, a superior man may not be retained by such empty *demonstrations.*'"

CHAPTER XXXVIII. Mencius said, "The bodily organs with their functions belong to our Heaven-

CH. 37. THAT HE BE RESPECTED IS ESSENTIAL TO A SCHOLAR'S ENGAG-ING IN THE SERVICE OF A PRINCE. 1. 豕 交 之,—"having pig intercourse with him." 交＝接 or 待. 獸, as dis-tinguished from 豕, leads us to think of dogs or horses, animals to which we entertain a sentiment higher than to those which we keep and fatten merely for our eating. 2. 恭敬者＝所謂恭敬者. The paragraph is an explanation of what is meant by those terms. 將＝奉, "presented," "offered." 3. 拘＝留.

CH. 38. ONLY WITH A SAGE DOES THE BODY ACT ACCORDING TO ITS DESIGN. This is translated according to the consenting view of the modern commentators, but perhaps not cor-rectly. 形 is taken for the bodily organs,—the ears, eyes, hands feet, etc.; and 色 for their manifested

徐云爾、亦教之孝弟而

其兄之臂子謂之姑徐

已乎。孟子曰是猶或紾

丑曰、爲朞之喪、猶愈於

齊宣王欲短喪、公孫

形。

也、惟聖人、然後可以踐

conferred nature. But a man must oe a sage before he can satisfy the design of his bodily organinzation."

CHAPTER XXXIX. 1. The King Seuen of Ts'e wanted to shorten the period of mourning. Kung-sun Ch'ow said, "To have one whole year's mourning is better than doing away with it altogether."

2. Mencius said, "That is just as if there were one twisting the arm of his elder brother, and you were merely to say to him—'Gently, gently, if you please.' Your only course should be to teach such a one filial piety and fraternal duty."

operations,—hearing, seeing, handling, etc. 踐 is used as in the phrase 踐 言, "to tread upon the words," that is, to fulfill them, to walk, act, according to them. The use of 色 in ch. xxi, 4, is analogous to this use of it here. One critic says: 形 色 天 性, 言 形 色 皆 天 性 所 在, 非 指 形 色 爲 天 性 也, "The bodily organs with their operations belong to our

Heaven-conferred nature; the meaning is that in these is our Heavenly nature, not that they are that nature."

CH. 39. REPROOF OF KUNG-SUN CH'OW FOR ASSENTING TO THE PRO POSAL TO SHORTEN THE PERIOD OF MOURNING. Comp. Con. Ana., XVII, xxi. 1. The mourning is to be understood as that of three years for a

也。

謂夫莫之禁而弗爲者

得也雖加一日愈於已

也曰是欲終之而不可

公孫丑曰若此者何如

其傅爲之請數月之喪

已矣王子有其母死者

3. *At that time*, the mother of one of the king's sons had died, and his tutor asked for him that he might be allowed to observe a few months' mourning. Kung-sun Ch'ow asked, "What do you say of this?"

4. *Mencius* replied, "This is a case where the party wishes to complete the whole period, but finds it impossible to do so. The addition of even a single day is better than not mourning at all. I spoke of the case where there was no hindrance, and the party neglected the thing himself."

parent. 3. The king's son here must have been a son by a concubine. Choo He, after Chaou K'e, supposes that he was not permitted to mourn the three years, through the jealous or other opposition of the full queen. In this case the son was anxious to prolong his mourning as much as he could. This explanation, bringing in the opposition of the full queen or wife, seems to be incorrect. See the 集證, *in loc.* While the father was alive, a son shortened the period of mourning for his mother. 4. 謂夫,—夫 has a pronominal force.

孟子曰、君子之所
以教者五有如時雨
化之者有成德者、有
達財者有答問者有
私淑艾者此五者君
子之所以教也。

CHAPTER XL. 1. Mencius said, "There are five ways in which the superior man effects his teaching.

2. "There are some on whom his influence descends like seasonable rain.

3. "There are some whose virtue he perfects, and some of whose talents he assists the development.

4. "There are some whose inquiries he answers.

5. "There are some who privately cultivate and correct themselves.

6. "These five ways are the methods in which the superior man effects his teaching."

CH. 40. HOW THE LESSONS OF THE SAGE REACH TO ALL DIFFERENT CLASSES. 1. The wish of the superior man is in all cases one and the same,—to teach. His methods are modified, however, by the different characters of men. 2. This class only want his influence, like plants which only need the dew of heaven. So was it, it is said, with Confucius and his disciples Yen Yuen and Tsăng Sin. 3. 成德者＝成其德者. ` So a 其 is to be understood before 財 (＝村) and 問. So was it with Confucius and the disciples Yen and Min. 4. So was it with Mencius and Wan Chang. 5. This is a class, who never come into actual contact with their teacher, but hear of his doctrines, and learn them. His teachings, though not delivered by himself in person, do notwithstanding reach to them.

君子引而不發躍如

不爲拙射變其彀率。

爲拙工改廢繩墨羿

孽也孟子曰大匠不

彼爲可幾及、而日孳

似不可及也、何不使

矣、美矣宜若登天然、

公孫丑曰、道則高

CHAPTER XLI. 1. Kung-sun Ch'ow said, "Lofty are your principles and admirable, but *to learn them* may well be likened to ascending the heavens, something which cannot be reached. Why not *adapt your teaching so as to* cause learners to consider them attainable, and so daily exert themselves."

2. Mencius said, "A great artificer does not, for the sake of a stupid workman, alter or do away with the marking line. E did not, for the sake of a stupid archer, change his rule for drawing the bow.

3. "The superior man draws the bow, but does not discharge the arrow. *The whole thing* seems to leap *before the learner.* Such is his standing exactly in the

CH. 41. THE TEACHER OF TRUTH MAY NOT LOWER HIS LESSONS TO SUIT HIS LEARNERS. 1. 何 不 使 彼,—彼, "those" refers to learners, which antecedent has been implied in the words 宜 若, 云 云, "it is right they should be considered," etc. 爲 可 幾 及,—爲＝以 爲, "to consider,"

"regard." 2. 繩 墨,—"string and ink," a carpenters' marking line. 彀 率 (road *leüh*),—"the limit to which a bow should be drawn." 3. The difficulty here is with the words 躍 如 也, lit., "leaping-like." They belong, I think, to the superior man in all the action which is represented.

門也、若在所禮而不答、

圖公都子曰滕更之在

者也。

殉道未聞以道殉乎人

道殉身、天下無道、以身

圖孟子曰、天下有道、以

也、中道而立、能者從之。

middle of the right path. Those who are able, follow him."

CHAPTER XLII. 1. Mencius said, "When right principles prevail throughout the empire, one's principles must appear along with one's person. When right principles disappear from the empire, one's person must vanish along with one's principles.

2. "I have not heard of one's principles being dependent for their manifestation on other men."

CHAPTER XLIII. 1. The disciple Kung-too said, "When Kăng of T'ăng made his appearance in your school, it seemed proper that a polite consideration should be paid to him, and yet you did not answer him. Why was that?"

No man can be taught how to hit. That is his own act. He is taught to shoot, and that in so lively a manner that the hitting also is, as it were, set forth before him. So with the teacher and learner of truth. As the learner tries to do as he is taught, he will be found laying hold of what he thought unapproachable.
CH. 42. ONE MUST LIVE OR DIE WITH HIS PRINCIPLES, ACTING FROM HIMSELF, NOT WITH REGARD TO OTHER MEN. 殉 means "to bury along with

the dead," to associate with in death as in life. Another meaning is 以身 從物, "with the person to follow after things," = to pursue. The first 道 is right principles in general. The other 道 are those principles as held by individual men.
CH. 43. HOW MENCIUS REQUIRED THE SIMPLE PURSUIT OF TRUTH IN THOSE WHOM HE TAUGHT. Kăng was a younger brother of the prince of T'ang. His rank made Kung-tao think that more than ordinary

退速。

無所不薄也。其進銳者其

者無所不已、於所厚者薄、

孟子曰、於不可已而已

答也、滕更有二焉。

勞而問、挾故而問、皆所不

賢而問、挾長而問、挾有勲

何也。孟子曰、挾貴而問、挾

2. Mencius replied, "I do not answer him who questions me presuming on his nobility, nor him who presumes on his talents, nor him who presumes on his age, nor him who pesumes on services performed to me, nor him who presumes on old acquaintance. Two of those things were chargeable on Kăng of T'ăng."

CHAPTER XLIV. 1. Mencius said, "He who stops short where stopping is not allowable, will stop short in everything. He who behaves shabbily to those whom he ought to treat well, will behave shabbily to all.

2. "He who advances with precipitation will retire with speed."

respect should have been shown to him, and yet it was no doubt one of the things which made Mencius jealously watch his spirit. Comp. VI, Pt. II, ii, 6, 7.

CH. 44. WHERE VIRTUES ARE WANTING, DECENCIES MAY NOT BE EXPECTED. PRECIPITATE ADVANCES ARE FOLLOWED BY SPEEDY RETREATS. The first par., it is said, has reference to errors of defect (不 及 者 之 弊), and the second to. those of excess (有 過).

堯舜之知、而不徧物、急

不愛也、急親賢之爲務、

也當務之爲急仁者無

䷿孟子曰知者無不知

民、仁民而愛物。

仁之而弗親、親親而仁

也、愛之而弗仁、於民也、

䷿孟子曰君子之於物

CHAPTER XLV. Mencius said, "In regard to *inferior* creatures, the superior man is kind to them, but not loving. In regard to people generally, he is loving to them, but not affectionate. He is affectionate to his parents, and lovingly disposed to people *generally*. He is lovingly disposed to people *generally*, and kind to creatures."

CHAPTER XLVI. 1. Mencius said, "The wise embrace all knowledge, but they are most earnest about what is of the greatest importance. The benevolent embrace all in their love, but what they consider of the greatest importance is to cultivate an earnest affection for the virtuous. Even the wisdom of Yaou Shun did not extend to everything, but they attended

CH. 45. THE SUPERIOR MAN IS KIND TO CREATURES, LOVING TO OTHER MEN, AND AFFECTIONATE TO HIS RELATIVES. This was intended, no doubt, against the Mihist doctrine of loving all equally. 物=animals. The second 親 is not to be understood only of parents. Compare 親親, D. M., xx, 12.

CH. 46. AGAINST THE PRINCES OF HIS TIME WHO OCCUPIED THEMSELVES WITH THE KNOWLEDGE OF, AND REGARD FOR, WHAT WAS OF LITTLE

IMPORTANCE. 1. 無不知, 無不愛 are not our "omniscient," and "all-loving," but show the tendency and adaptation of the wise and the benevolent. The clauses that follow,— 當務之爲急, 急親賢之爲務, show in what way truly great rulers come to an administration which appears to possess those characters. The use of the 之 in those clauses is idiomatic. To reduce it to the ordinary usages of the particle, we must take the first as=惟當務之事爲急, "but

是之謂不知務。

歡、而問無齒決、

功之察放飯流

年之喪、而緦小

親賢也不能三

仁、不徧愛人急

先務也、堯舜之

earnestly to what was important.　Their benevolence did not show itself in acts of kindness to every man, but they earnestly cultivated an affection for the virtuous.

2.　"Not to be able to keep the three years' mourning, and to be very particular about that of three months, or that of five months; to eat immoderately and swill down the soup, and at the same time to .inquire about *the precept* not to tear the meat with the teeth;—such things show what I call an ignorance of what is most important."

only are they earnest about the things which it is most important *to know*," and 惟急于親賢之當務, "but only are they earnest about what is most important, the cultivating affection for the virtuous." The teaching of the chapter is substantially the same as that of Confucius, Ana., XII, xxii.　2. 緦,—"coarse, unbleached, hempen cloth," worn in mourning the period of three months for distant relatives. 小功 is the name applied in the case of mourning which extends for five months. 放飯云云,—see the Book of Rites, I, Pt. I, iii, 54, 55.—These are cases adduced in illustration of what is insisted on in the previous paragraph;—the folly of attending to what is comparatively trivial, while overlooking what is important.

## BOOK VII

### TSIN SIN.  PART II

土地之故、糜爛其民而

丑曰、何謂也梁惠王以

所不愛、及其所愛公孫

其所不愛、不仁者以其

王也、仁者以其所愛、及

孟子曰不仁哉、梁惠

盡心章句下

CHAPTER I.  1. Mencius said, "The opposite indeed of benevolent was the king Hwuy of Leang! The benevolent, beginning with what they care for, proceed to what they do not care for. Those who are the opposite of benevolent, beginning with what they do not care for, proceed to what they care for."

2.  Kung-sun Ch'ow said, "What do you mean?" *Mencius answered*, "The king Hwuy of Leang, for the matter of territory, tore and destroyed his people,

CH. 1.  A STRONG CONDEMNATION OF KING HWUY OF LEANG, FOR SACRIFICING TO HIS AMBITION HIS PEOPLE AND EVEN HIS SON. Comp. I, Pt. I, v, and other conversations with King Hwuy.  1. 不 仁 is more than "unbenevolent" would mean, if we had such a term.  It is nearly = "cruel," "oppressive."  仁 者, 云 云,—comp. Pt. I, 45.  Only 愛, being there opposed to 仁, is used with reference to animals, while here it expresses the feeling towards children and people and animals, and I have rendered it by "to care for."  In the first case in the text, the progress is from one degree of love to another; in the second, from one degree of infliction to another.  2. 糜, "to boil rice till it is 糜爛, reduced to a pulpy mass."  So did Hwuy seem to deal

國不相征也。
矣。征者、上伐下也、敵
戰、彼善於此則有之
孟子曰、春秋無義
愛也。
以其所不愛及其所
子弟以殉之是之謂
不能勝故驅其所愛
戰之大敗將復之恐

leading them to battle. Sustaining a great defeat, he would engage again, and afraid lest they should not be able to secure the victory, urged his son whom he loved till he sacrificed him with them. This is what I call—'beginning with what they do not care for, and proceeding to what they care for.'"

CHAPTER II. 1. Mencius said, "In the 'Spring and Autumn' there are no righteous wars. Instances indeed there are of one war better than another.

2. "'Correction' is when the supreme authority punishes its subjects by force of arms. Hostile states do not correct one another."

with the bodies of his subjects. 所 愛子弟 refers to Hwuy's eldest son (I, Pt. I, v, 1). He is called a 子弟, as being one of the youth of the kingdom. 殉之,—comp. Pt. I, 45.

CH. 2. HOW ALL THE FIGHTINGS RECORDED IN THE CH'UN TS'EW WERE UNRIGHTEOUS:—A WARNING TO THE CONTENDING STATES OF MENCIUS' TIME. 1. 無義戰,—"no righteous battles." Both Chaou K'e and Choo He make 戰=戰伐之事, "the affairs of fighting and smiting," i. e., all the operations of war detailed in the Ch'un Ts'ew. And rightly; for Mencius himself uses the term 伐 in the 3rd par. In the Ch'un Ts'ew itself there are mentioned of "fightings"

(戰) only 23, while the "smitings" (伐) amount to 213. There are specified in it also "invasions" (侵); "sieges" (圍); "carryings away" (遷); "extinguishings" (滅); "defeats" (敗); "takings" (取); "surprises" (襲); "pursuits" (追); and "defenses" (戍); all of which may likewise be comprehended under the term 戰. 3. Explains the assertion in the first. In the wars recorded by Confucius, one state or chief was said to 征 another, which could not be according to the meaning of the term. By 上 is intended the emperor; by 下 the princes. Comp. VI, Pt. II, vii, 2.

流杵也。

不仁而何其血之

天下以至仁伐至

已矣。三都仁人無敵於

武城取二三策而

則不如無書吾於

孟子曰盡信書、

CHAPTER III. 1. Mencius said, "It would be better to be without the 'Book of History' than to give entire credit to it.

2. "In the 'Completion of the War,' I select two or three passages only, which I believe.

3. "The benevolent man has no enemy under heaven. When *the prince*, the most benevolent, was engaged against him who was the most the opposite, how could the blood *of the people* have flowed till it floated the pestles of the mortars?"

CH. 3. WITH WHAT RESERVATION MENCIUS READ THE SHOO-KING. This is a difficult chapter for Chinese commentators. Chaou K'e takes 書 of the Shoo-king, which is the only fair interpretation. Others understand it of books in general. Thus Julien translates—"*Si omnino fidem adhibeas libris.*" Many say that Mencius had in view only the portion of the Shoo-king to which he refers in the next par., but such a restriction of his language is entirely arbitrary. The strangest view is that of the author of the 四書撫餘說, whose judgments generally are sound and sensible. But he says here that Mencius is anticipating the attempts that would be made in after ages to corrupt the classics, and testifying against them. We can see how the remarks were directed against the propensity to warfare which characterized his contemporaries. 2. 武成 is the title of the third book in the 5th part of the Shoo-king, professing to be an accoun' by King Woo of his enterprise against the tyrant, Chow. The words quoted in the next par. are found in par. 8. For 杵 there are diff. readings; see the 集證, *in loc.* Doubtless there is much exaggeration in the language, but Mencius misinterprets the whole passage. The bloodshed was not done by the troops of King Woo, but by the forces of the tyrant turning against one another.

殷也革車三百兩虎賁三

怨曰、奚爲後我武王之伐

征、北狄怨東面而征、西夷

好仁、天下無敵焉。南面而

陳、我善爲戰大罪也。國君

孟子曰、有人曰、我善爲

CHAPTER IV. 1. Mencius said, "There are men who say—'I am skillful at marshaling troops, I am skillful at conducting a battle!'—They are great criminals.

2. "If the sovereign of a state love benevolence, he will have no enemy in the empire.

3. "When *T'ang* was executing his work of correction in the south, the rude tribes on the north murmured. When he was executing it in the east, the rude tribes on the west murmured. Their cry was —'Why does he make us last?'

4. "When King Woo punished Yin, he had *only* three hundred chariots of war, and three thousand life guards.

CH. 4. COUNSEL TO PRINCES NOT TO ALLOW THEMSELVES TO BE DECEIVED BY MEN WHO WOULD ADVISE THEM TO WAR. 1. Comp. IV, Pt. I, xiv, 3. 2. Comp. I, Pt. II, xi, 2. It is spoken of T'ang. 3. 革 車,— "leathern carriages, or chariots," said by some to be baggage wagons, but, more probably by others, chariots of war, each one of which had 72 foot soldiers attached to it, so that Woo's army would number 21,600, few as compared with the forces of his opponent. 兩 used for 輛, low. 2nd tone, a numeral for carriages. 虎 賁 (*pun*)—these appear to have

千人。〔五節〕王曰、無畏寧爾也、非

敵百姓也、若崩厥角稽首。

征之爲言正也、各欲正己〔六節〕

也、焉用戰。

〔五章〕孟子曰梓匠輪輿、能與

人規矩、不能使人巧。

5. "The king said, "Do not fear. Let me give you repose. I am no enemy to the people! *On this*, they bowed their heads to the earth, like the horns of animals falling off.'

6. ""Imperial correction' is but another word for rectifying. Each state wishing itself to be corrected, what need is there for fighting?"

CHAPTER V. Mencius said, "A carpenter or a carriage maker may give a man the circle and square, but cannot make him skillful *in the use of them*."

been of the character of life guards, named from their tigerlike courage and bearing. 4. See the Shoo-king, Pt. V, i, Sect. II, 9. But the text of the classic is hardly recognizable in Mencius's version of it. The original is: "Rouse ye, my heroes. Do not think that he is not to be feared, but rather hold that he cannot be withstood. The people are full of awe, as if their horns were falling from their heads." 5. Perhaps it would be well to retain the sound of 征 in the translation, and say—"Now *ching* means to rectify." 各 欲 正 己, "each people wishes the *ching-er* to correct itself."

CH. 5. REAL ATTAINMENT MUST BE MADE BY THE LEARNER FOR HIM-SELF. Comp. Pt. I, iv, 41. 梓匠輪輿, see III, Pt. II, 3.

二孟子曰舜之飯糗茹

草也若將終身焉及其

爲天子也被袗衣鼓琴

二女果若固有之。

二孟子曰吾今而後知

殺人親之重也殺人之

父人亦殺其父殺人之

CHAPTER VI. Mencius said, "Shun's manner of eating *his* parched grain and herbs was as if he were to be doing so all his life. When he became emperor, and had the embroidered robes to wear, the lute to play, and the two daughters *of Yaou* to wait on him, he was as if those things belonged to him as a matter of course."

CHAPTER VII. Mencius said, "From this time forth I know the heavy consequences of killing a man's near relations. When a man kills another's father, that other will kill his father; when a man kills

CH. 6. THE EQUANIMITY OF SHUN IN POVERTY AND AS EMPEROR. 草 must be taken as＝茅. 茹 is a word used for 食, applied to eating herbs. 飯＝食, "to eat." The "embroidered robes" are the imperial dress. On Shun's lute, see V, Pt. I, ii, 3. 果 used for 婐, *wo*, "a female attendant."
CH. 7. HOW THE THOUGHT OF ITS

CONSEQUENCES SHOULD MAKE MEN CAREFUL OF THEIR CONDUCT. Choo He observes that this.remark must have been made with some special reference,—吾 今 而 後. It is a maxim of Chinese society, that "a man may not live under the same heaven with the slayer of his father, nor in the same state with the slayer

兄、人亦殺其兄、然則
非自殺之也、一閒耳。
孟子曰、古之爲關
也、將以禦暴今之爲
關也、將以爲暴。
孟子曰、身不行道、
不　疢妻子、使人不

another's elder brother, that other will kill his elder brother. So he does not himself indeed do the act, but there is only an interval *between him and it*."

CHAPTER VIII. 1. Mencius said, "Anciently, the establishment of the frontier gates was to guard against violence.

2. "Nowadays, it is to exercise violence."

CHAPTER IX. Mencius said, "If a man himself do not walk in the *right* path, it will not be walked in *even* by his wife and children. If he do not order

of his elder brother," but the remark does not seem to regard that so much as to take occasion from it to warn rulers to make their government firm in the attachment of their subjects, and not provoke their animosity by oppressive acts. 一 閒 耳,—"there is only one interval;" that is, the death of a man's father or brother is the consequence of his previous conduct, the slayer only intervening.

CH. 8. THE BENEVOLENCE AND SELFISHNESS OF ANCIENT AND

MODERN RULE CONTRASTED. Comp. I, Pt. II, v, 3; II, Pt. I, v, 3. But one does not see exactly how the ancient rule of examining the person, and not taking the goods, guarded against violence. Here, as elsewhere. Mencius is led away by his fondness for antithesis.

CH. 9. A MAN'S INFLUENCE DEPENDS ON HIS PERSONAL EXAMPLE AND CONDUCT. To the second 行 we are to suppose 道 as the nominative, while the third is like a verb in the

色。

其人簞食豆羹見於

能讓千乘之國苟非

孟子曰好名之人、

者、邪世不能亂。

凶年不能殺周于德

孟子曰、周于利者、

以道、不能行於妻子。

men according to the *right* way, he will not be able to get the obedience of *even* his wife and children."

CHAPTER X. Mencius said, "A bad year cannot prove the cause of death to him, whose stores of gain are large; an age of corruption cannot confound him whose equipment of virtue is complete."

CHAPTER XI. Mencius said, "A man who loves fame may be able to decline a kingdom of a thousand chariots, but if he be not *really* the man *to do such a thing*, it will appear in his countenance, in the matter of a dish of rice or a platter of soup."

*hiphil* conjugation. The 人 is not so much 他人, "other men." The whole 使人不以道 simply＝出令不當理, "if his orders are not according to reason."

CH. 10. CORRUPT TIMES ARE PROVIDED AGAINST BY ESTABLISHED VIRTUE. 不能殺, 不能亂, may be taken either actively or passively. 周于利者,—"he who is complete in gain," i. e., he who has gained much, and laid much by.

CH. 11. A MAN'S TRUE DISPOSITION WILL OFTEN APPEAR IN SMALL MATTERS, WHEN A LOVE OF FAME MAY HAVE CARRIED HIM OVER GREAT DIFFICULTIES. Choo He here expounds well: 觀人不於其所勉、而於其所忽、然後可以見其所安之實, "A man is seen not so much in things which require an effort, as in things which he might easily despise. By bearing this in mind when we observe him, we can see what he really rests in."

有也。 仁而得天下、未之 得國者、有之矣、不 孟子曰不仁而 事、則財用不足。 義、則上下亂無政 賢、則國空虛無禮 孟子曰、不信仁

CHAPTER XII. 1. Mencius said, "If men of virtue and ability be not confided in, a state will become empty and void.

2. "Without the rules of propriety and distinctions of right, the high and the low will be thrown into confusion.

3. "Without *the great principles of* government and their various business, there will not be wealth sufficient for the expenditure."

CHAPTER XIII. Mencius said, "There are instances of individuals without benevolence, who have got possession of a *single* state, but there has been no instance of the whole empire's being got possession of by one without benevolence."

CH. 12. THREE THINGS IMPORTANT IN THE ADMINISTRATION OF A STATE. 1. 不信, "be not confided *to*"; perhaps rather "confided *in*." "Will become empty and void,"—Chaou K'e supplements thus, "If the prince do not consort with and confide in the virtuous and able, then they will go away, and a country without such persons is said to be empty and void." 2. "The high and the low,"—that is, the distinction of ranks. 禮 義 may be considered a hendiadys, and so 政事 in the next paragraph. 義 is the right, or *rightness*, on which the rules of propriety are founded, and 事 is the various business that flows from the right principles of government.

CH. 13. ONLY BY BENEVOLENCE CAN THE EMPIRE BE GOT. Many comm. put 有之 in the potential mood, as if it were 或有之. This is not allowable. Facts may be alleged that seem to be in opposition to the concluding statement. The commentator Tsow (鄒) says "From the dynasty of Ts'in downwards, there have been cases, when the empire was got by men without benevolence, but in such cases, it has been lost again after one or two reigns."

侯、得乎諸侯、爲

得乎天子、爲諸

丘民而爲天子、

爲輕是故得乎

貴社稷次之君

靈孟子曰、民爲

CHAPTER XIV. 1. Mencius said, "The people are the most important element *in a nation;* the spirits of the land and grain are the next; the sovereign is the lightest.

2. "Therefore to gain the peasantry is the way to become emperor; to gain the emperor is the way to become a prince of a state; to gain the prince of a state is the way to become a great officer.

CH. 14. THE DIFFERENT ELEMENTS OF A NATION—THE PEOPLE, TUTELARY SPIRITS, AND SOVEREIGN, IN RESPECT OF THEIR IMPORTANCE. 1. 社 is properly the altar, or resting place of the spirit or spirits of the ground, and then used for the sacrifice to that spirit or those spirits. 稷,—"pannicled millet," and then generally the spirit or spirits presiding over grain. Together, the characters, 社稷 denote the "tutelary spirits of a country," on whom its prosperity depends, and to sacrifice to whom was the prerogative of its sovereign.—It is often said that the 社 was "to sacrifice to the spirits of the five kinds of ground, and the 稷 to sacrifice to those of the five kinds of grain." But this is merely one of the numerical fancies of which Chinese writers are fond. The five kinds of ground are mountains and forests (山 林), rivers and marshes (川 澤), mounds (丘 陵), places of tombs (墳 衍), and plains (原 濕). But it would be easy to make another division, just as we have six, eight, and other ways of speaking about the kinds of grain. The regular sacrifices to these tutelary spirits were three: one in spring to pray for a good harvest; one in autumn, to give thanks for the harvest; and a third in the first month of winter. On occasions of calamity there were special services. 2. 丘 民＝回野之民, "the people of the fields and wilds," the peasantry. According to the Chow Le, nine husbandmen, heads of families, formed a *tsing* (井); four *tsing* formed a *yih* (邑); and four *yih* formed a *k'ew* (丘), which would thus contain 144 families. But the phrase 丘人, signifying the peasantry, is yet equivalent to "the people." Mencius uses it, his discourse being of the spirits of the land and grain.

夷之風者頑夫廉、

下惠是也、故聞伯

世之師也、伯夷、柳

蠹孟子曰聖人、百

則變置社稷。

時、然而旱乾水溢、

粢盛既潔祭祀以

則變置犠牲既成、

大夫。諸侯危社稷、

3. "When a prince endangers the altars of the spirits of the land and grain, he is changed, and another appointed in his place.

4. "When the sacrificial victims have been perfect, the millet in its vessels all pure, and the sacrifices offered at their proper seasons, if yet there ensue drought, or the waters overflow, the spirits of the land and grain are changed, and others appointed in their place."

CHAPTER XV. Mencius said, "A sage is the teacher of a hundred generations:—this is true of Pih-e and Hwuy of Lew-hea. Therefore when men now hear the character of Pih-e, the corrupt become pure,

4. The change of the 社稷 is taken by most commentators as merely a destroying of the altars and building others. This is Choo He's interpretation: 土穀之神,不能爲民禦災捍患,則毀其壇壝而更置之, "when the spirits of the ground and grain cannot ward off calamities and evils from the people, then their altars and fences are thrown down and others in different places erected." Chaou K'e is more brief. He simply says that in such a case 毀社稷而更置之, which may mean that

they destroyed the altars or displaced the spirits themselves. A changing of the altars merely does not supply a parallel to the removal of the princes in the preceding paragraph. And there are traces of deposing the spirits in such a case, and appointing others in their places. See the 四書 摭餘說, in loc.

CH. 15. THAT PIH-E AND HWUY OF LEW-HEA WERE-SAGES PROVED BY THE PERMANENCE OF THEIR INFLU-ENCE. Comp. V, Pt. II, 1; et al. "A

懦夫有立志、聞柳下惠
之風者、薄夫敦鄙夫寬、
奮乎百世之上百世之
下、聞者莫不興起也、非
聖人而能若是乎、而况
於親炙之者乎。
○孟子曰仁也者、人也、
合而言之、道也。

and the weak acquire determination. When they hear the character of Hwuy of Lew-hea, the mean become generous, and the niggardly become liberal. *Those two* made themselves distinguished a hundred generations ago, and after a hundred generations, 'those who hear of them, are all aroused *in this manner.* Could such effects be produced by them, if they had not been sages? And how much more did they affect those who were in contiguity with them, and were warmed by them!"

CHAPTER XVI. Mencius said, "Benevolence is *the distinguishing characteristic of* man. As embodied in man's conduct, it is called the path *of duty.*"

hundred generations" is spoken generally. Between the two worthies themselves several hundred years intervened.

CH. 16. THE RELATION OF BENEVOLENCE TO MAN. This chapter is quite enigmatic. 合 is taken as＝合 仁于人身, "unite benevolence with man's person," and 道 as the 率性 之道 of the Chung-yung. The glossarist of Chaou K'e refers to Con.

Ana., XV, xxviii, which is very good. Choo He, however, mentions that in an edition of Mencius found in Korea. after 人也, there follow accounts of "righteousness," "propriety," and "wisdom";—義也者宜也. 云云. If that was the original reading, the final clause would be: "These, all united and named, are the path of reason."

之交也。

於陳蔡之間、無上下

蠢孟子曰君子之戹

道也。

接淅而行、去他國之

父母國之道也、去齊、

魯、曰、遲遲吾行也、去

壨孟子曰、孔子之去

CHAPTER XVII. Mencius said, "When Confucius was leaving Loo, he said, 'I will set out by and by';—this was the way for him to leave the state of his parents. When he was leaving Ts'e, he strained off with his hand the water in which his rice was being rinsed, *took the rice,* and went away;—this was the way for him to leave a strange state."

CHAPTER XVIII. Mencius said, "The reason why the superior man was reduced to straits between Ch'in and Ts'ae was because neither the princes *of the time* nor their ministers communicated with him."

CH. 17. HOW CONFUCIUS'S LEAV-ING LOO AND TS'E WAS DIFFERENT. Comp. V, Pt. II, i, 4.

CH. 18. THE REASON OR CON-FUCIUS'S BEING IN STRAITS BETWEEN CH'IN AND TS'AE. See Con. Ana., XI, ii. The speaking of Confucius simply by the term 君子 is to be noted; comp. Ana., X, vi, 1, *et al.* Cnaou K'e observes that Confucius, in his exceeding modesty, said that he was not equal to the threefold way of the superior man (Ana., XIV, xxx), and therefore he might be spoken of as a superior man. It is difficult to see the point of this observation, nor does it meet the difficulty which arises from the use of the designation in the text. 上= 君, "the sovereigns," and 下=臣, "their ministers." The princes did not honor him and seek his services. Their ministers did not honor him, and recommend him to employment. This is the meaning of 無上下之交. The commentators, in their quest for profound meanings, make out the lesson to be that though a sage may be reduced to straits, the way of truth cannot be so reduced.

厥問、文王也。　不殄厥慍、亦不隕　于羣小、孔子也、肆　詩云、憂心悄悄、慍　傷也、士憎茲多口。　理於口孟子曰、無　貉稽曰、稽大不

CHAPTER XIX. 1. Mih K'e said, "Greatly am I from anything to depend upon from the mouths *of* men."

2. Mencius observed, "There is no harm in that. Scholars are more exposed than others to suffer from the mouths *of men*.

3. "It is said, in the 'Book of Poetry,'

> 'My heart is disquieted and grieved,
> I am hated by the crowd of mean creatures.'

*This might have been said by* Confucius. And again,

> 'Though he did not remove their wrath,
> He did not let fall his own fame.'

*This might be said of* King Wăn."

CH. 19. MENCIUS COMFORTS MIH K'E UNDER CALUMNY BY THE REFLECTION THAT IT WAS THE ORDINARY LOT OF DISTINGUISHED MEN. 1. Of Mih K'e, nothing is known beyond what is here intimated. 理 is used in the sense of 賴, "to depend on." This is given to it in the dict., with a reference to this passage. The meaning is that not only did he not have a good word from men, but was spoken ill of by them. 2. 憎, it is concluded, from the comment of Chaou K'e, is a mistake for 增, "to increase," and 茲 has substantially the same meaning. Retaining 憎, however, and taking 茲 in its sense of *this* or *these*, we get a tolerable meaning:—"The scholar hates those many mouths." 3. For the first quotation, see the She-king, I. iii, Ode I, st. 4, a description of her condition by the ill-used wife of one of the dukes of Wei (according to Choo He), and which Mencius somewhat strangely would apply to Confucius. For the second, see III. i, Ode III, st. 8, descriptive of the king T'ae, though applied to Wăn. 問 is in the sense of 聞, "report," "reputation."

矣今茅塞子之心矣。

路為間不用則茅塞之

之蹊閒介然用之而成

蠶孟子謂高子曰山徑

昏使人昭昭。

昭、使人昭昭今以其昏

蠶孟子曰賢者以其昭

CHAPTER XX. Mencius said, "*Anciently*, men of virtue and talents by means of their own enlightenment made others enlightened. Nowadays, it is tried, *while they are themselves in darkness*, and by means of that darkness, to make others enlightened."

CHAPTER XXI. Mencius said to the disciple Kaou, "There are the footpaths along the hills;—if suddenly they be used, they become roads; and if, as suddenly they are not used, the wild grass fills them up. Now, the wild grass fills up your mind."

CH. 20. HOW THE ANCIENTS LED ON MEN BY THEIR EXAMPLE, WHILE THE RULERS OF MENCIUS'S TIME TRIED TO URGE MEN CONTRARY TO THEIR EXAMPLE. In translating, I supply 古之 before 賢者, in contrast with the 今 below. To the two 使 a very different force is given. The former is the constraining influence of example; the latter is the application of pains and penalties.

CH. 21. THAT THE CULTIVATION OF THE MIND MAY NOT BE INTERMITTED. 蹊間,—"spaces for the foot,"=footpaths; 山徑之蹊間,—the "footpaths of the hill ways." 介 (read *hĕā*, according to Choo He, though the dict. does not give such a sound to the character, nor do we find in it the meaning which suits this passage) 然,—"suddenly"; nearly = 為間. The Kaou here must have been a disciple of Mencius, different from the old Kaou, VI, Pt. II, iii. Chaou K'e says that after studying with Mencius for some time, and before he fully understood his principles, he went off and addicted himself to some other teacher, and that the remark was made with reference to this course, and its consequences.

與。

之軌、兩馬之力

是奚足哉、城門

之曰、以追蠡曰、三

孟子曰、何以言二

聲、尙文王之聲。

蠶高子曰、禹之一

CHAPTER XXII. 1. The disciple Kaou said, "The music of Yu was better than that of King Wăn."

2. Mencius observed, "On what ground do you say so?" and the other replied, "Because at the pivot the knob of Yu's bells is nearly worn through."

3. *Mencius* said, "How can that be a sufficient proof? Are the ruts at the gate of a city made by a single two-horsed chariot?"

CH. 22. AN ABSURD REMARK OF THE DISCIPLE KAOU ABOUT THE MUSIC OF YU AND KING WĂN. 2. 追,—read *tuy*, "the knob, or loop, of a bell," the part by which it is suspended. 蠡,—low. 2nd tone, "an insect that bores through wood"; hence, metaphorically, anything having the appearance of being eaten or worn away. 3. The meaning is that what Kaou noticed was only the effect of time or long use, Yu being anterior to King Wăn, and did not necessarily imply any superiority of the music of the one over that of the other. The street contracts at the gate, and all the carriages that have been running over its breadth are obliged to run in the same ruts, which hence are deeper here than elsewhere.—There is much controversy about the phrase 兩馬之力. Chaou K'e understands 兩馬 as meaning "two kinds of horses";—the 國馬, levied from the state, and employed on what we may call the postal service, and the 公馬, or "public horses," principally used in military service. On this view the meaning would be that the ruts in question were not made by these two kinds of carriages only. Choo He, after the commentator Fung (豐 氏), takes the meaning as I have given it in the translation. Another view takes 兩 in the sense of 車, taking it in the low. 3rd tone, as in ch. iv, 4. See the 四書摭餘 說, *in loc.*

望見馮婦趨而迎之、

虎虎負嵎莫之敢攖、

善士則之野有衆逐

馮婦者善博虎卒爲

是爲馮婦也晉人有

棠殆不可復孟子曰、

皆以夫子將復爲發

齊饑陳臻曰國人

CHAPTER XXIII. 1. When Ts'e was suffering from famine, Ch'in Tsin said *to Mencius,* "The people are all thinking that you, Master, will again ask that the granary of T'ang be opened for them. I apprehend you will not do so a second time."

2. *Mencius* said, "To do it would be to act like Fung Foo. There was a man of that name in Tsin, famous for his skill in seizing tigers. Afterwards, he became a scholar of reputation, and going once out to the wild country, he found the people all in pursuit of a tiger. The tiger took refuge in a corner of a hill, where no one dared to attack him, but when they saw Fung Foo, they ran and met him. Fung Foo

CH. 23. HOW MENCIUS KNEW WHERE TO STOP AND MAINTAIN HIS OWN DIGNITY IN HIS INTERCOURSE WITH THE PRINCES. 1. At T'ang, whose name is still preserved in the village of Kant'ang, in the district of Tseihmih (郇 鼆), in the department of Laechow, the princes of Ts'e, it would appear, kept grain in store, and on some previous occurrence of famine, Mencius had advised

the king to open the granary. In the meantime, however, some difference had occurred between him and the prince. He intended leaving Ts'e, and would not expose himself to a repulse by making an application which might be rejected. 2. 善士,—"a good scholar," or "officer," but 善 is not to be taken at all emphatically. 之 野,—之=往. It did not belong to Fung Foo, now an

馮婦攘臂下車、眾皆悅之、

其爲士者笑之。

孟子曰、口之於味也、目

之於色也、耳之於聲也、鼻

之於臭也、四肢之於安佚

也、性也、有命焉、君子不謂

性也、仁之於父子也、義之

*immediately* bared his arms, and descended from the carriage. The multitude were pleased with him, but those who were scholars laughed at him."

CHAPTER XXIV. 1. Mencius said, "For the mouth to desire *sweet* tastes, the eye to desire *beautiful* colors, the ear to desire *pleasant* sounds, the nose to desire *fragrant* odors, and the four limbs to desire ease and rest;—these things are natural. But there is the appointment *of Heaven in connection with them,* and the superior man does not say *of his pursuit of them,* 'It is my nature.'

2. *"The exercise of* love between father and son, *the observance of* righteousness between sovereign and

officer, to be fighting with tigers, playing the part of a bravo.

CH. 24. HOW THE SUPERIOR MAN SUBJECTS THE GRATIFICATION OF HIS NATURAL APPETITES TO THE WILL OF HEAVEN, AND PURSUES THE DOING OF GOOD WITHOUT THINKING THAT THE AMOUNT WHICH HE CAN DO MAY BE LIMITED BY THAT WILL. 1. 口之於味,—"the mouth's to tastes"; that is, its constitution so as to be pleased with certain tastes. So, all the other clauses. 有命焉,—"there is the appointment *of Heaven,*" i. e., every appetite naturally desires its unlimited gratification, but a limited

於君臣也、禮之於
賓主也、智之於賢
者也、聖人之於天
道也、命也、有性焉、
君子不謂命也。
蓋浩生不害問曰、
樂正子、何人也孟
子曰善人也、信人

minister, the rules of ceremony between guest and host, *the display* of knowledge *in* recognizing the talented, and *the fulfilling* the heavenly course by the sage;—these are the appointment *of Heaven.* But there is *an adaptation of our* nature *for them.* The superior man does not say, *in reference to them,* 'It is the appointment of Heaven.'"

CHAPTER XXV. 1. Haou-sang Puh-hae asked, saying, "What sort of man is Yŏ-ching?" Mencius replied, "He is a good man, a real man."

amount or an entire denial may be the will of Heaven. 2. 智之於賢者 is not "the possession of knowledge by the talented," but the exercise of wisdom in reference to them, recognizing and appreciating their excellence. The sentiment is well illustrated by the case of An Ying, the minister of Ts'e, able and wise, and yet insensible to the superior excellence of Confucius and his principles.—Choo He says well upon this chapter: "I have heard it observed by my master that the things mentioned in both of these paragraphs are in the constitution of our nature, and likewise ordained by Heaven. Mankind, however, consider that the first five are more especially natural, and, though they may be prevented from obtaining them, still desire them; and that the last five are more especially appointed by Heaven, so that if they do not come to them readily, they do not go on to put forth their strength to reach them. On this account, Mencius shows what is most important in each case, that he may induce a broader way of thinking in regard to the second class, and repress the way of thinking in regard to the first."

CH. 25. THE CHARACTER OF THE DISCIPLE YOH-CHING. DIFFERENT DEGREES OF ATTAINMENT IN CHARACTER, WHICH ARE TO BE AIMED AT. 1. Chaou K'e tells us that Haou-sang is the surname and Puh-hae the name and that the individual was a man of Ts'e. This is all we know of him.

聖而不可知之之謂

大大而化之之謂聖。

充實而有光輝之謂

之謂信充實之爲美。

可欲之謂善有諸己

也何爲善何爲信曰、

2. "What do you mean by 'A good man,' 'A real man'?"

3. The reply was, "A man who commands our liking is what is called a good man.

4. "He whose *goodness* is part of himself is what is called a real man.

5. "He whose *goodness* has been filled up is what is called a beautiful man.

6. "He whose completed goodness is brightly displayed is what is called a great man.

7. "When this great man exercises a transforming influence, he is what is called a sage.

8. "When the sage is beyond our knowledge, he is what is called a spirit man.

3. It is assumed here that the general verdict of mankind will be on the side of goodness. Hence when a man is *desirable,* and commands universal liking, he must be a *good* man. 4. 有諸己,—"having in himself"; i. e , when a man has the goodness, without hypocrisy or pretense. Comp. VI, ii, 13. Goodness is an attribute entering into all the others, and I have therefore thrice expressed it in the translation. 8. 聖而不可知之之謂神,—with this we may compare what is said in the Doctrine of the Mean, 至誠如神, "the individual possessed of the most complete sincerity is like a spirit " In the critical remarks in the 四書合講, it is said,

神樂正子、二之中、四

之下也。

䯅孟子曰、逃墨必歸

於楊逃楊必歸於儒、

歸斯受之而已矣。今

之與楊墨辯者、如追

放豚、既入其苙、又從

而招之。

9. "Yŏ-ching is between the two *first* characters, and below the four last."

CHAPTER XXVI. 1. Mencius said, "Those who are fleeing from *the errors of* Mih naturally turn to Yang, and those who are fleeing from *the errors of* Yang naturally turn to orthodoxy. When they so turn, they should at once and simply be received.

2. "Those who nowadays dispute with the followers of Yang and Mih, do so as if they were pursuing a stray pig, the leg of which after they have got it to enter the pen, they proceed to tie."

indeed, that the expression in the text is stronger than that there, but the two are substantially to the same effect. Some would translate 神 by "divine," a rendering which it never can admit of, and yet, in applying to man the term appropriate to the actings and influence of Him whose way is in the sea, and his judgments a great deep, Chinese writers are guilty of blasphemy, in the sense of derogating from the prerogatives of God.

ÇH, 26. RECOVERED HERETICS SHOULD BE RECEIVED WITHOUT CASTING THEIR OLD ERRORS IN THEIR TEETH. 1. 歸於儒,—"they turn to the learned." "The learned" in Chinese phrase is equivalent to our "the orthodox." The name is still claimed in China by the followers of Confucius and other sages, in opposition to the Taoists and Buddhists. 2. The disputations are with those who *had been* Yangists and Mihists. This sense of 招, "to tie the legs," is found in the dict. with reference to this passage.

者殃必及身。

土地人民政事寶珠玉

釁孟子曰諸侯之寶三、

父子離。

二而民有殍用其三而

子用其一緩其二用其

粟米之征力役之征君

釁孟子曰有布縷之征、

CHAPTER XXVII. Mencius said, "There are the exactions of hempen cloth and silk, of grain, and of personal service. The prince requires but one of these *at once*, deferring the other two. If he require two of them *at once*, then the people die of hunger. If he require the three *at once*, then fathers and sons are separated."

CHAPTER XXVIII. Mencius said, "The precious things of a prince are three—the territory, the people, the government and its business. If one value as most precious pearls and stones, calamity is sure to befall him."

CH. 27. THE ·JUST EXACTIONS OF THE GOVERNMENT ARE TO BE MADE DISCRIMINATINGLY AND CONSIDERATELY. 布 is cloth, made from flax. 縷,—"silken fibers not spun," but here, probably, silk, spun or unspun. 粟,—"grain unthreshed"; 米,—the same threshed:—here together, grain generally. The tax of cloth and silk was due in summer, that of grain after harvest, and personal service was for the leisure of winter. 君 子＝君. The prince might only require them, one at a time, and in their proper seasons.

CH. 28. THE PRECIOUS THINGS OF A PRINCE, AND THE DANGER OF OVERLOOKING THEM FOR OTHER THINGS. 土,—"the productive ground," and 地,—"land generally." 人 as distinguished from 民＝"officers," but the terms are not to be taken separately. So of 政事; see ch. xii.

孟子之滕、館於上宮、有

足以殺其軀而已矣。

才、未聞君子之大道也、則

將見殺曰、其爲人也、小有

門人問曰、夫子何以知其

死矣、盆成括。盆成括見殺、

盆成括仕於齊、孟子曰、

CHAPTER XXIX. P'wan-shing Kwoh having obtained an official situation in Ts'e, Mencius said, "He is a dead man,—P'wan-shing Kwoh!" P'wan-shing Kwoh being put to death, the disciples asked, saying, "How did you know, Master, that he would meet with death?" Mencius replied, "He was a man who had a little ability, but had not learned the great doctrines of the superior man.—He was just qualified to bring death upon himself, but for nothing more."

CHAPTER XXX. 1. When Mencius went to T'ăng, he was lodged in the upper palace. A sandal in the

CH. 29. How MENCIUS PREDICTED BEFOREHAND THE DEATH OF P'WANSHING KWOH. Comp. Conf. prediction of Tsze-loo's death, Con. Ana., XI, xi. Little is known of this Kwoh. He is said to have begun learning with Mencius, but to have soon gone away, disappointed by what he heard.

CH. 30. THE GENEROUS SPIRIT OF MENCIUS IN DISPENSING HIS INSTRUCTIONS. This, which is the lesson of the chapter, only comes out at the end, and has been commemorated, as being the remark of an individual, not of extraordinary character, and at first disposed to find fault with Mencius's disciples. 1. 之滕,—之＝往. 宮,—comp. 雪宮, I, Pt. II, iv. This was evidently a palace appropriated by the duke of T'ăng for the lodging of honorable visitors. The first 館 is a verb, "was lodged." The second makes a compound noun

業屨於牖上、館人求之
弗得。或問之曰、若是乎、
從者之廋也曰、子以是
為竊屨來與曰、殆非也、
夫子之設科也、往者不
追、來者不拒、苟以是心
至、斯受之而已矣。

process of making had been placed there in a window,
and when the keeper of the place *came to* look for it,
he could not find it.

2. *On this,* some one asked *Mencius,* saying, "Is it
thus that your followers pilfer?" Mencius replied,
"Do you think that they came here to pilfer the
sandal?" The man said, "I apprehend not. But
you, Master, having arranged to give lessons, do not
go back to inquire into the past, and you do not
reject those who come to you. If they come with the
mind to learn, you receive them without any more
ado."

with 人. 業屨,—the dict. has, with
reference to this passage, 事物已爲
而未成曰業, "things being done,
but not completed, are said to be
業." 2. 廋,—*sow,* up. 1st tone, "to
hide,"＝to steal and hide. 曰, 子 以
是,—是, "these," referring to "followers." 夫子之設科, 云 云,—
according to Choo He, this is the
observation of Mencius's questioner,
suddenly awaking to an understanding of the philosopher. Anciently,
夫子 was read 夫子, "now, I," and
Mencius was supposed to be himself
the speaker. Choo He is probably
correct. 設科 is better than 設教,
科 convoying the idea of "exercises"
suited to different capacities. 是
心＝向道之心.

之心、而義不可勝用也。

勝用也、人能充無穿窬

欲害人之心、而仁不可

其所爲義也。人能充無

人皆有所不爲達之於

忍、達之於其所忍仁也、

孟子曰、人皆有所不

CHAPTER XXXI. Mencius said, "All men have some things which they cannot bear;—extend that feeling to what they can bear, and benevolence will be the result. All men have some things which they will not do;—extend that feeling to the things which they do, and righteousness will be the result."

2. "If a man can give full development to the feeling which makes him shrink from injuring others, his benevolence will be more than can be called into practice. If he can give full development to the feeling which refuses to break through, or jump over, *a wall*, his righteousness will be more than can be called into practice.

CH. 31. A MAN HAS ONLY TO GIVE DEVELOPMENT TO THE PRINCIPLES OF GOOD WHICH ARE IN HIM, AND SHOW THEMSELVES IN SOME THINGS, TO BE ENTIRELY GOOD AND CORRECT. This is a sentiment which we have found continually occurring in these analects. It supposes that man has much more power over himself than he really has. 2. 穿＝穿穴, "to make a hole through." 窬＝窬墻, "to jump over a wall." The two

闔孟子曰言近而指遠

穿窬之類也。

是以不言話之也、是皆

話之也、可以言而不言、

未可以言而言、是以言

無所往而不爲義也。士

人能充無受爾汝之實、

3. "If he can give full development to the real feeling of dislike with which he receives the salutation, 'Thou,' 'Thou,' he will act righteously in all places and circumstances.

4. "When a scholar speaks what he ought not to speak, by *guile of* speech seeking to gain some end; and when he does not speak what he ought to speak, by *guile of* silence seeking to gain some end;—both these cases are of a piece with breaking through *a neighbour's wall*."

CHAPTER XXXII. 1. Mencius said, "Words which are simple, while their meaning is far-reaching, are

together are equivalent to "to play the thief." 3. "Thou," is a style of address greatly at variance with Chinese notions of propriety. It can only be used to the very young and the very mean. A man will revolt from it as used to himself, and "if he be careful to act so that men will not dare to speak to him in this style, he will go nowhere where he will not do righteousness."—This is rather far-fetched. 4. 話,—"to lick with the tongue." To find an antecedent to the 之, we must understand the per-

son, who is spoken to; or before whom silence is kept; or, perhaps, 之 merely gives effect to the verb in the general sense of "to gain some end."

CH. 32. AGAINST AIMING AT WHAT IS REMOTE, AND NEGLECTING WHAT IS NEAR. WHAT ARE GOOD WORDS AND GOOD PRINCIPLES. 1. 不下帶.—see the Book of Rites, I, Pt. II, iii. 14. The ancients did not look at a person below the girdle, so that all above that might be considered as near, beneath the eyes. The phrase = 近言, "words which are near," i. e.,

以自任者輕。

田所求於人者重而所

人病舍其田而芸人之

之守、修其身、而天下平。

不下帶、而道存焉。君子

者、善道也、君子之言也、

者善言也守約、而施博

good words.　Principles which, as held, are compendious, while their application is extensive, are good
principles.　The words of the superior man do not
go below the girdle, but *great* principles are contained
in them.

2.　"The principle which the superior man holds is
that of personal cultivation, but the empire is thereby
tranquilized."

3.　"The disease of men is this: that they neglect
their own fields, and go to weed the fields of others,
and that what they require from others is great, while
what they lay upon themselves is light."

on common subjects, simple, plain.
So, Choo He; but the passage in the
Le-ke is not so general as his commentary.　It gives the rule for looking at the emperor.　A minister is
not to raise his eyes above the emperor's collar, nor lower them below
the girdle.　Chaou K'e tries to explain
the expression without reference to
the ancient rule for regulating the
looking at men.　Acc. to him, "words
not below the girdle are all from near
the heart."　2. This is the explanation of 守約而施博.　The paragraph
is a good summary of the teaching of
the Great Learning.

子行法以俟命而已矣。

語必信、非以正行也。君

德不囘、非以干祿也、言

死而哀、非爲生者也、經

中禮者、盛德之至也、哭

湯武、反之也。動容周旋

孟子曰、堯舜、性者也、

CHAPTER XXXIII. 1. Mencius said, "Yaou and Shun were what they were by nature; T'ang and Woo were so by returning *to natural virtue*.

2. "When all the movements, in the countenance and every turn of *the body*, are exactly what is proper, that shows the extreme degree of the complete virtue. Weeping for the dead should be from *real* sorrow, and not because of the living. The regular path of virtue is to be pursued without any bend, and from no view to emolument. The words should all be necessarily sincere, not with any desire to do what is right.

3. "The superior man performs the law *of right*, in order that he may wait simply for what has been appointed."

CH. 33. THE PERFECT VIRTUE OF THE HIGHEST SAGES, AND HOW OTHERS FOLLOW AFTER IT. 1. Comp. Pt. I, xxx, but 之 has not here a special reference to certain virtues as there. 2. This is an exhibition of the highest style of virtue—that of Yaou and Shun, which does everything right, with no motive beyond the doing so.

"Weeping is from real sorrow, and not because of the living,"—i. e., there is nothing of show in it, and no wish to make an impression on others. 3. Describes the virtue that is next in degree, equally observant of right, but by an intellectual constraint. 法＝天理之當然, "the proper course indicated by Heavenly principles."

騁田獵、後車千乘、我得志、

得志弗爲也、般樂飲酒、驅

食前方丈、侍妾數百人、我

榱題數尺、我得志弗爲也、

勿視其巍巍然堂高數仞、

㆓而孟子曰、說大人則藐之、

CHAPTER XXXIV. 1. Mencius said, "Those who give counsel to the great should despise them, and not look at their pomp and display.

2. "Halls several times eight cubits high, with beams projecting several cubits;—these, if my wishes were to be realized, I would not have. Food spread before me over ten cubits square, and attendant girls to the amount of hundreds;—these, though my wishes were realized, I would not have. Pleasure and wine, and the dash of hunting, with thousands of chariots following after me;—these, though my wishes were

CH. 34. HE WHO UNDERTAKES TO COUNSEL THE GREAT, SHOULD BE MORALLY ABOVE THEM. 1. 大人.— "great men." The phrase is to be understood not of the truly great, as in ch. xxv, 6, et al., but of the socially great, with an especial reference to the princes of the time, dignified by their position, but without corresponding moral qualities. 2. 堂高,

云云, all the corresponding clauses, are under the government of some words like 彼大人有,—"those great men have," to which 我弗爲,—"I would not do," respond. 榱題,— these may be seen in the more important temples and public buildings throughout China, projecting all round, beneath the eaves. 般樂,— see II, Pt. I, iv. 4. 驅騁田獵,—

弗爲也、在彼者、皆我所不爲
也、在我者、皆古之制也吾何
畏彼哉。

■孟子曰養心莫善於寡欲、
其爲人也寡欲、雖有不存焉
者寡矣其爲人也多欲、雖有
存焉者寡矣。

realized, I would not have. What they esteem are what I would have nothing to do with; what I esteem are the rules of the ancients.—Why should I stand in awe of them?"

CHAPTER XXXV. Mencius said, "To nourish the heart there is nothing better than to make the desires few. Here is a man whose desires are few: in some things he may not be able to keep his heart, but they will be few. Here is a man whose desires are many: in some things he may be able to keep his heart, but they will be few."

"spurring and galloping in hunting." 在彼者,—"what are in them," the things which they esteem so. 在我者＝the things which I esteem.

CH. 35. THE REGULATION OF THE DESIRES IS ESSENTIAL TO THE NOUR-ISHMENT OF THE HEART. 欲 must be taken in a bad, or, at least an inferior sense, ＝the appetites, while 心 is the heart naturally disposed to all virtue. 雖有不存焉,—"although there are" —virtues of the heart, that is,— "which are not preserved."

獨也。
不諱姓、姓所同也、名所
同也、羊棗所獨也、諱名
而不食羊棗。曰、膾炙所
然則曾子何爲食膾炙、
子曰、膾炙哉。公孫丑曰、
曰、膾炙與羊棗孰美。孟
不忍食羊棗。公孫丑問
曾皙嗜羊棗、而曾子

CHAPTER XXXVI. 1. Mencius said, "Tsăng Seih was fond of sheep dates, and *his son*, the philosopher Tsăng, could not bear to eat sheep dates."

2. Kung-sun Ch'ow asked, saying, "Which is best, —minced meat and roasted meat, or sheep dates?" Mencius said, "Minced and roasted meat, to be sure." Kung-sun Ch'ow went on, "Then why did the philosopher Tsăng eat minced and roasted meat, while he would not eat sheep dates?" Mencius answered, "For minced and roasted meat there is a common liking, while that for sheep dates was peculiar. We avoid the name, but do not avoid the surname. The surname is common; the name is peculiar."

CH. 36. THE FILIAL FEELING OF TSĂNG-TSZE SEEN IN HIS NOT EATING DATES. 1. 羊棗,—"sheep dates," the small black northern date, so called from its resembling sheep's dirt. Such is Choo He's account of the fruit. The writer of the 四書撫餘說, *in loc.*, however, seems to make out a case for 羊棗 being a kind of persimmon. Still, why call it *a date?*

2. Shih's liking for the small dates was peculiar, and therefore the sight of them brought him vividly up to his son, and he could not bear to eat such dates. There are many rules for 諱名,—"avoiding the name," of parents, ancestors, emperors, etc.; see the Le-ke, I, Pt. I, v, 15-20; *et al.*

也、孔子豈不欲中道哉、

者進取獲者有所不爲

而與之必也狂獲乎、狂

孟子曰、孔子不得中道

子在陳、何思魯之狂士。孔

狂簡進取、不忘其初、孔

曰、盍歸乎來、吾黨之士、

萬章問曰孔子在陳

CHAPTER XXXVII. 1. Wan Chang asked, saying,
"Confucius, when he was in Ch'in, said, 'Let me
return. The scholars of my school are ambitious but
hasty. They are for advancing and seizing their object, but cannot forget their early ways.' Why did
Confucius, when he was in Ch'in, think of the ambitious scholars of Loo?"

2. Mencius replied, "Confucius not getting men
pursuing the true medium, to whom he might communicate *his instructions*, determined to take the
ardent and the cautiously-decided. The ardent would
advance to seize their object; the cautiously-decided
would keep themselves from certain things. It is not
to be thought that Confucius did not wish to get men
pursuing the true medium, but being unable to assure

CH. 37. To call to the pursuit of the right medium was the object of Confucius and Mencius. Various characters who fail to pursue this, or are opposed to it. 1. See Con. Ana., V, xxxi. The dif-ferences between that text and what we have here will be noted. Perhaps

考其行而不掩焉者也。

然、曰古之人、古之人、夷

謂之狂也。曰其志嘐嘐

孔子之所爲狂矣。何以

曰、如琴張、曾晳、牧皮者、

敢問何如斯可謂狂矣。

不可必得、故思其次也。

himself of finding such, he therefore thought of the next class."

3.   "I venture to ask what sort of men they were who could be styled 'The ambitious'?"

4.   "Such," replied Mencius, "as K'in Chang, Tsang Seih, and Muh P'ei, were those whom Confucius styled 'ambitious.'"

5.   "Why were they styled 'ambitious'?"

6.   The reply was, "Their aim led them to talk magniloquently, saying, 'The ancients!' 'The ancients!' But their actions, compared with *their words*, did not come up to them."

Wan Chang was quoting from memory.  2. See Con. Ana., XIII, xxi. As Mencius quotes that chapter, some think that there should be a 曰 in the text after 孔子.  4. K'in Chang is the Laou mentioned in Con. Ana., IX, vi.  6. So acc. to Choo He, who quotes an instance from the Taoist philosopher Chwang, of the waywardness of Laou, but Chwang's accounts of Confucius and his disciples are not much to be trusted.  The identification of the individual in the text with Laou, however, is no doubt correct, though Chaou K'e makes him to be the Sze of the Analects, referring to XI, xvii, 3, "Sze is specious," and adding that he played well on the *k'in*, and was therefore styled K'in.  See the 四書撫餘説 *in loc.*  Of Muh P'ei nothing is known.  夷,—in the sense of 平, "even."  夷考,—"evenly examining."  掩,—"to cover,"=to make

狂者、又不可得、欲得不屑不
潔之士而與之、是獳也、是又
其次也。孔子曰、過我門、而不
入我室、我不憾焉者、其惟鄉
原乎、鄉原德之賊也、曰、何如
斯可謂之鄉原矣。曰、何以是
嘐嘐也、言不顧行、行不顧言、

7. "When he found also that he could not get such as were *thus* ambitious, he wanted to get scholars who would consider anything impure as beneath them. Those were the cautiously-decided, — a class next to the former."

8. *Chang pursued his questioning*, "Confucius said, 'They are only your good careful people of the villages at whom I feel no indignation, when they pass my door without entering my house. Your good careful people of the villages are the thieves of virtue.' What sort of people were they who could be styled 'Your good careful people of the villages'?"

9. *Mencius replied*, "They are those who say, 'Why are they so magniloquent? Their words have not respect to their actions, and their actions have

good. 8. The first part of the saying here attributed to Confucius is not found in the Analects. For the sec- ond, see XVII, xiii. 9. Before this par. we must understand 孟子曰. The 曰 in the text has for its subject

也、刺之、無刺也、同乎流俗、
德之賊、何哉曰非之、無舉
往而不爲原人孔子以爲
曰、一鄉皆稱原人焉、無所
於世也者、是鄉原也。萬章
斯世也、善斯可矣、閹然媚
爲踽踽涼涼、生斯世也、爲
則曰、古之人古之人、行何

not respect to their words, but they say,— *The ancients! The ancients!* Why do they act so peculiarly, and are so cold and distant? Born in this age, we should be of this age, to be good is all that is needed.' Eunuchlike, flattering their generation;— such are your good careful men of the villages."

10. Wan Chang said, "Their whole village styles those men good and careful. In all their conduct they are so. How was it that Confucius considered them the thieves of virtue?"

11. Mencius replied, "If you would blame them, you find nothing to allege. If you would criticize them, you have nothing to criticize. They agree with the current customs. They consent with an

鄉原, or we may take it in the infinitive, making the whole par. down to 也者 the nominative to the 是 that follows. 善斯可矣,—"to be good is enough," i. e., to be accounted good by the age in which they live is enough for them. 踽踽,—"the appearance of walking alone," i. e., acting peculiarly. 11. 流俗 is literally our "current customs," but 流,

其亂信也惡鄭聲恐其

恐其亂義也惡利口恐

惡莠恐其亂苗也惡佞

也孔子曰惡似而非者、

堯舜之道故曰德之賊

自以爲是而不可與入

行之似廉潔衆皆悅之、

合乎汙世居之似忠信、

○十二節

impure age. Their principles have a semblance of
right-heartedness and truth. Their conduct has a
semblance of disinterestedness and purity. All men
are pleased with them, and they think themselves
right, so that it is impossible to proceed with them
to the principles of Yaou and Shun. On this account
they are called 'The thieves of virtue.'

12. "Confucius said, 'I hate a semblance which is
not the reality. I hate the darnel, lest it be confounded with the corn. I hate glib-tonguedness, lest
it be confounded with righteousness. I hate sharpness of tongue, lest it be confounded with sincerity.
I hate the music of Ch'ing, lest it be confounded with

at the same time, stigmatizes the customs, as bad. 居之＝居之於心者; 行之＝行之於身者. 12. These are sayings of Confucius which are only found here. Such a string of them is not in the sage's style. 恐其亂苗,—"lest it confound the corn," ＝be confounded with it. So in the other phrases. 鄭聲,—see Con. Ana.

亂樂也、惡紫恐其亂朱也、惡

鄉原恐其亂德也君子反經
十三

而已矣、經正、則庶民與、庶民

與、斯無邪慝矣。

孟子曰、由堯舜至於湯、五

百有餘歲若禹、皐陶、則見而

*the true* music. I hate the reddish blue, lest it be confounded with vermilion. I hate your good careful men of the villages, lest they bè confounded with the *truly* virtuous.'

13. "The superior man seeks simply to bring back the unchanging standard, and that being rectified, the masses are roused to virtue. When they are so aroused, forthwith perversities and glossed wickedness disappear."

CHAPTER XXXVIII. 1. Mencius said, "From Yaou and Shun down to T'ang were five hundred years and more. As to Yu and Kaou-yaou, they saw *those earliest*

---

XV, x. 紫,—see Con. Ana., X, vi, 2.
13. This par. explains the rest of the chap. The 經 or "unchanging standard," is the 中道, "the right medium," which the sage himself pursues, and to which he seeks to recall others.
CH. 38. ON THE TRANSMISSION OF THE LINE OF DOCTRINE FROM YAOU

TO MENCIUS'S OWN TIME. Compare II, Pt. II, xiii; III, Pt. II, x, *et al.* 1. From the commencement of Shun's reign to that of T'ang's were 489 years, while from T'ang to the rise of the Chow dynasty were 644 years. Here, as before, II, Pt. II, xiii, Mencius uses 500 as a round

聞而知之。由孔子而來、至於
宜生、則見而知之、若孔子、則
子、五百有餘歲若太公望散
則聞而知之、由文王至於孔
尹、萊朱、則見而知之、若文王、
至於文王、五百有餘歲、若伊
知之、若湯、則聞而知之。由湯

*sages,* and *so* knew their doctrines, while T‘ang heard their doctrines *as transmitted,* and *so* knew them.

2. "From T‘ang to King Wăn were five hundred years and more. As to E Yin and Lae Choo, they saw *T‘ang* and knew his doctrines, while King Wăn heard them *as transmitted,* and so knew them.

3. "From King Wăn to Confucius were five hundred years and more. As to T‘ae-kung Wang and San E-sang, they saw *Wăn,* and so knew his doctrines, while Confucius heard them *as transmitted,* and so knew them.

4. "From Confucius downwards until now, there

number. In 知之, the 之 refers to the doctrines of the sages. 2. Lae Choo is not exactly identified. Most make him the same with T‘ang's minister, Chung-hwuy; see the Shoo-king, IV, ii. 3. T‘ae-kung Wang,—see IV, Pt. I, xiii. Of San E-sang more can hardly be said to be known than that he was an able minister of King Wăn. Choo He seems to be wrong, however, in making San, instead of San-e, to be the surname. See the 四書撦餘說, *in loc.* 4. The concluding sentences here wonderfully vex commentators. In the "Supplemental Commentary" (翼註) are found five different interpretations of them. But all agree

今、百有餘歲、去

聖人之世、若此

其未遠也、近聖

人之居、若此其

甚也、然而無有

乎爾、則亦無有

乎爾。

are *only* one hundred years and *somewhat* more. The distance in time from the sage is so far from being remote, and so very near at hand was the sage's residence. In these circumstances, is there no one *to transmit his doctrines?* Yea, is there no one *to do so?*"

that Mencius somehow takes upon himself the duty and responsibility of handing down the doctrines of the sage.

**University of California**
**SOUTHERN REGIONAL LIBRARY FACILITY**
Return this material to the library
from which it was borrowed.

REC'D LD-URL BIOMED MAY 0 9 1989

OCT 3 0 1989

10/7/91

NOV 29 97

RECEIVED URL
OCT 17 URI
JUN 2 8 1994

WS - #0029 - 190825 - C0 - 229/152/54 [56] - CB - 9780331818529 - Gloss Lamination